ELDEST SON

ELDEST SON

Zhou Enlai and the
Making of Modern China,
1898–1976

HAN SUYIN

KODANSHA INTERNATIONAL
New York • Tokyo • London

Kodansha America, Inc.
114 Fifth Avenue, New York, New York 10011, U.S.A.

Kodansha International Ltd.
17-14 Otowa 1-chome, Bunkyo-ku, Tokyo 112, Japan

Published in 1995 by Kodansha America, Inc. by arrangement with
Hill and Wang, a division of Farrar, Straus and Giroux.

First published in hardcover in 1994 by Hill and Wang,
a division of Farrar, Straus and Giroux.

This is a Kodansha Globe book.

Library of Congress Cataloging-in-Publication Data

Han, Suyin, pseud.
Eldest son : Zhou Enlai and the making of modern China, 1898-1976
/ Han Suyin.
p.   cm. — (Kodansha globe)
Originally published: 1st ed. New York : Hill and Wang, 1994.
Includes bibliographical references and index.
ISBN 1-56836-084-3
1. Chou, En-lai, 1898-1976. 2. Statesmen—China—Biography.
3. China—History—1949-1976. I. Title. II. Series.
DS778.C593H36 1995
951.05′092—dc20
[B]   94-48630

Book design by Bernard Klein

Printed in the United States of America
95 96 97 98 99 RRD/H 10 9 8 7 6 5 4 3 2 1

Foreword

Nearly two decades after the death of Zhou Enlai, Premier of China, statesman of recognized world stature, an avalanche of articles, poems, and books continues to pour out about him, the personal memories of hundreds of Chinese who met him, worked with him, and felt the magic of the man's personality enhance their own lives. Millions of young students who have never known him yet talk of him as the most honest, the most dedicated and selfless personality in China's history. This enduring love, admiration, and respect for the man still known as "the beloved" makes writing a book about him a difficult task. I have tried to find faults, defects, in the man, and have written them down. But in China these foibles are regarded as only more evidence of his regard for others, of his willingness to see someone else's point of view, of trust and faith in others.

My thanks are due to hundreds of Chinese scholars, students, schoolteachers, working-class men and women, as well as to the dozens of men, many of them ambassadors or ministers, whom Zhou Enlai trained over the decades. I want above all to thank the Association for Friendship with Foreign Countries and its successive presidents, Chu Tunan, the late Wang Bingnan, the late Zhang Wenjing, and Han Xu, its present president, together with the staff of the Association. They all helped me through the years to gather manuscripts, to conduct interviews, to travel up and down China. I also thank many English, Indian, American, and French friends, among them Dick Wilson, Ambassador P. K. Bannerjee, James Reston, the late Ambassador Etienne Manoel Manach, for their contribution.

I also want to thank all those, both Chinese and from outside China, who so generously sent me their own memoirs concerning their meetings with Zhou Enlai. All these will be carefully stored in the author's archives, deposited in Special Collections, Mugar Memorial Library, Boston University.

Last, but not least, I want to thank Upton Birnie Brady, who plodded patiently through a thousand pages of the original manuscript and cut it down to manageable size for a Western audience. This has meant leaving out many of the Chinese whom I interviewed, but they will not feel chagrined, because the original version in Chinese contains their names. But in the West, Chinese names still confuse a great many readers, and Upton and I trimmed down what we felt might make the book too academic for the reader with only slight knowledge of China.

H.S.

Contents

III
1935–1949

*The Second United Front · Yenan · World War II
The Rectification · The Chinese Communist Revolution
Zhou Enlai becomes "China's housekeeper"*
145

IV
1949–1966

*Building the New China · The Korean War · The Hundred
Flowers Movement · The Great Leap Forward · China explodes
an atom bomb and reenters the world stage*
213

V
1966–1978

*The Cultural Revolution · The treachery, flight, and death of Lin
Biao · The Nixon opening · The Gang of Four ·
Zhou's death · Epilogue*
311

ELDEST SON

Note on Genealogical Table

Every Chinese family—even peasant families, as soon as they lift themselves out of illiteracy—keeps a genealogy book, which is patrilineal, based only on the male offspring in any family.

The book of the Zhou clan in Shaoxing, Zhejiang province, goes back several centuries.

In this abridged table, only that part of the family descended from Zhou Panlong, who left Shaoxing and settled in Huai An, Jiangsu province, is recorded.

An exception is made for Zhou Yiqian, because Zhou Enlai had a good deal of connection with him, although Yiqian was a descendant of another grandfather, one of Zhou Panlong's brothers.

In China the family name comes first, and then the personal name.

In each generation, the same ideogram in a two-ideogram combination makes up an individual's personal name. This is a kind of coding, which enables the families—extended families sometimes number up to seven hundred or eight hundred individuals in two or three generations—to know immediately which *generation* a family member belongs to. This is very important in the hierarchy of families, which is governed by a strict Confucian code.

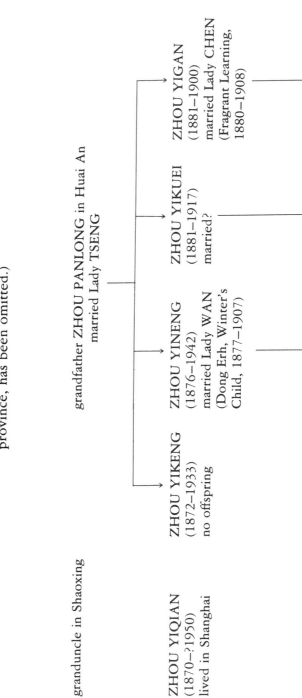

ABRIDGED GENEALOGICAL TABLE OF THE
ZHOU FAMILY IN HUAI AN, JIANGSU PROVINCE
(The original family genealogy tree in Shaoxing, Zhejiang
province, has been omitted.)

granduncle in Shaoxing

grandfather ZHOU PANLONG in Huai An
married Lady TSENG

ZHOU YIQIAN
(1870–?1950)
lived in Shanghai

ZHOU YIKENG
(1872–1933)
no offspring

ZHOU YINENG
(1876–1942)
married Lady WAN
(Dong Erh, Winter's
Child, 1877–1907)

ZHOU YIKUEI
(1881–1917)
married?

ZHOU YIGAN
(1881–1900)
married Lady CHEN
(Fragrant Learning,
1880–1908)

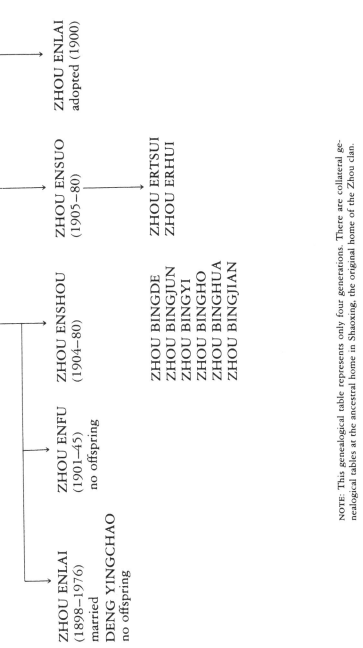

ZHOU ENLAI
(1898–1976)
married
DENG YINGCHAO
no offspring

ZHOU ENFU
(1901–45)
no offspring

ZHOU ENSHOU
(1904–80)

ZHOU BINGDE
ZHOU BINGJUN
ZHOU BINGYI
ZHOU BINGHO
ZHOU BINGHUA
ZHOU BINGJIAN

ZHOU ENSUO
(1905–80)

ZHOU ERTSUI
ZHOU ERHUI

ZHOU ENLAI
adopted (1900)

NOTE: This genealogical table represents only four generations. There are collateral genealogical tables at the ancestral home in Shaoxing, the original home of the Zhou clan.

I

1898–1924

Youth, adolescence, and education
The Russian Revolution
The May 4, 1919, Movement
Travel to Europe
The founding of the
Chinese Communist Party

1

March 5, 1988

A cold wind bit our faces, swept across the stubble fields and the drained marsh. We stood on a leveled square marked by chalk strips. Half a mile away the pink brick villages began, their inhabitants, standing in front of the houses, watching the small gathering we made. At one end of the square was a large bamboo screen covered with white flowers, the flowers of mourning. But it was topped by a bright red silk banner proclaiming: COMMEMORATION OF THE NINETIETH BIRTHDAY ANNIVERSARY OF THE LATE BELOVED PRIME MINISTER ZHOU ENLAI.

Beloved Premier Zhou. Automatically, so many of my generation spoke of him thus, running the words together. But perhaps our grandchildren would no longer understand why so many millions had loved him. The world was changing, China was changing. How much would be left of the memory, and the work, of Zhou Enlai in, say, another ten years?

From the flowered screen his portrait looked down upon our neat ranks. A glossy enlarged photograph, retouched. Only the eyes seemed real; they held both quizzical watchfulness and challenging mirth. The mouth was recognizable, with that half smile which seemed so spontaneous, and efficiently masked so much private agony.

Had Zhou Enlai been alive, he would not have smiled. He would have been angry, with that cold anger when his voice was lowered, not raised. He would have forbidden our gathering, for he had wanted no monument, no tomb, no grave, no stela, nothing to remember him by. "Let my ashes be scattered on the mountains and rivers of my country," he had said, and this had been done, so that not even a handful of dust remained to be enthroned anywhere.

But he had been mourned, in millions of homes, without any official prodding. Statues and paintings and photographs were found throughout the land, and people talked of him and wrote about him. Endlessly reminiscences appeared, stories of his kindness and wit, his skill and achievements. Almost, for some, he had become an immortal, a saint. Those of us, like myself, who had known him, talked with him, and elected to serve him, because one could not do otherwise when one knew him, still wept, many years later, when we remembered some phrase, a gesture, the echo of his laugh in our ears. He had changed our lives, we said. Because of him we had done things and felt the passion of entering history. He had had that power to kindle in others a fury for endeavor. He had enlarged and ennobled our days on earth, and now we continued to believe, even when assailed by defeat and despair.

Before us, between us and the screen, stood, collared by loose earth, a small white stone, the foundation stone for a memorial building that would be erected to him. It was surrounded by red-beribboned shovels. The provincial governor, accompanied by the mayor of Huai An, Zhou Enlai's native town, stood up to speak. No great leader, no minister of state, had come from the capital to attend this ceremony. His widow, too frail, had not been allowed to travel. A small gathering, then, no more than a thousand of us. Yet his name had been known throughout the world. He had been admired, praised, and genuinely liked by statesmen and kings and politicians but also by scholars and artists and peasants and workers. But this was a local ceremony, only a few of his relatives and old friends, and I, with two American newsmen, the only people "from abroad," from outside China.

The speeches were the briefest I have ever heard in a China where prolixity is synonymous with respect. "Beloved Premier Zhou liked brief speeches, he detested verbiage," the governor says to me. "So we kept them short, in memory of him. He would not have wanted even this very small ceremony, but the people of Huai An want something to remember him by. He was born here, so we had to give in." Apologetically, he glances at the portrait.

All of us bow three times toward the screen, as is the custom. "Beloved Premier Zhou, you live in our hearts forever." Then his nephews and nieces, and I—a great honor—take up the shovels and heap some of the loose soil around the foundation stone, partly embedding it in the ground.

We return to the town of Huai An along the dirt road. I visit the house where Zhou Enlai was born. He had never wanted it repainted or turned into a shrine, but the people did not see it that way. So many millions had quietly come, in the past years, to stand in silence outside the house, to bow, perhaps to say, "Beloved Premier Zhou."

"Why, why did people love him?" one of the two American newsmen asks me that evening. "After all, he made a lot of mistakes. Why is it that people often weep when they speak of him?"

It is difficult to say why. Except that, somehow, because of him, we all felt life was worth living. Even when everything went wrong. "Perhaps because he never forgot to care. Even his mistakes were because he cared. He couldn't help caring. It was bred in him. He was the eldest son."

Eldest son, eldest grandson. In the Confucian scholar families of China, the eldest son was marked out for uncommon responsibilities and duties. The eldest son, or, failing him, the eldest grandson, must provide care and education for all the younger male children in the same generation as himself and for their offspring. He must also provide comfort, food, and lodging to the two generations above him, parents and grandparents. He must be a model. A model of filial piety, of traditional virtue, upholding family honor and status, sacrificing himself always so that the family will thrive. He is the embodiment of the Confucian tradition, the magic bond with the past, his life one of unending care, responsibility, and abnegation. Tsunghuai, a young man of forty, says to me, "I think that Zhou Enlai, throughout his life, was unconsciously marked by the fact that he was eldest son, eldest grandson."

The twin townships of Huai An and Huai Ying lie close to each other, watered by the Huai River. In 352 A.D. both became prefectural sites when the Grand Canal was dug. That man-made waterway, 1,350 kilometers in length, linked the Yangtse River of Central China to the Yellow or Huangho River of North China. It was the great highway of internal commerce, bringing the wealth of the fertile southern China plains to the more arid north. Grain and silk and salt, goods of all kinds, went up in an endless procession of barges northward to the Capital of the Empire. It was imperative that the political center should be in the north, where strong garrisons were maintained to repel invasions of nomads swooping down from Siberia and Central Asia upon the prosperous plains. Huai An and Huai Ying flourished, both as inland ports on the Grand Canal and as garrisoned towns to keep the waterway safe. They acquired repute as sites of learning, breeding scholars and sustaining a famous Buddhist monastery, one of the earliest in China, dating back to the Tang dynasty in the seventh century A.D.

In a quiet part of Huai An, near a small willow-lined canal, runs Fuma Lane. Fuma means "imperial son-in-law." But no one remembers such an august personage ever living here, or even passing through in a carriage or on horseback. It is not even a wealthy residential district. The Zhou family house is graceful, the eaves of its gray roofs upturned, its entrance gate, lacquered brown, flanked by two small lion-dogs of stone. It is not a large house, only six courtyards and some eighteen rooms, most of them very small—the house of a scholar, certainly not of a wealthy high official. Past the entrance gate is a narrow brick-paved path, screened by a wall. It turns sharp left to prevent demons (who always travel in straight lines and never turn corners) from invading the inner courtyards.

The courtyards are fairly small, angling away from each other, each one marked off by a small brick archway with delicate carving. This creates within a small area an illusion of space and privacy. It is the technique used in the famous gardens of Suzhou, with their diminutive pools and rocks and pavilions, conveying a sensation of ampleness within the cramped compass of a few yards.

In each courtyard dwelt a son of the family with his wife and children. Family etiquette made it discourteous to intrude into other courtyards. This maintained harmony among the numerous members of the extended family, where casualness infringes upon good manners. "The house was always filled with kinsmen, relatives who came from the ancestral clan or other places," Zhou Erhui, the nephew of Zhou Enlai, says to me as we amble through the house. He shows me where the bedrooms were, and the inner apartments of his great-grandfather, and the small classroom where the children of the family were tutored. "Sometimes these relatives stayed for months, for years. . . . Our Zhou family was a typical scholar-official family, very conscious of face, of status. We could never refuse a room, or money, to anyone of the family, even if we had to borrow or pawn."

The Zhou family was not native to Huai An. Its ancestral site, for the past three centuries, was the famous city of Shaoxing, in Zhejiang province. There stands the ancestral hall, whose carved and lacquered tables held the soul tablets of the ancestors, generation after generation. Shaoxing was, still is, a lovely city, with a crisscross of canals, and charming old houses. It was a great center of trade and learning until the nineteenth century, with an Arab quarter, where Muslim merchants had lived since the twelfth century. Shaoxing was famous for its wine, and its scholar-officials. It provided the Empire with its best civil servants, cultured and competent. "Everywhere one went, one found an official from Zhejiang," Zhou Enlai himself would laughingly say, when describing his ancestry. As for its golden wine, drunk warm, it was given to male children to quaff by the bowlful from the age of six.

From Shaoxing, Zhou Enlai's grandfather, Zhou Panlong, was appointed in the late 1870s to the prefecture of Huai An on the Grand Canal, in Jiangsu province. But on arrival he was prevented from taking office, because the functionary he was to replace refused to hand over to him the seals of office. Without the seals, he could not stamp documents, or attend any ceremony, or render valid any directives. "The emperor is far away in the Northern Capital, the local magistrate is all-powerful," was the Chinese equivalent of "Possession is nine tenths of the law." Panlong, knowing his rival to be powerful, bided his time while protesting through the proper channels, which seems to have taken some years.

What befell Panlong was typical of the times, of the tragic disarray of China. By the end of the nineteenth century the Empire was deliquescent. China had been subject to invasion, pillage, and destruction since the first Opium War in 1840, a war Western countries waged to force China to take opium as payment for silk, tea, and other goods. War had followed war, each one of them waged by the Western powers either separately or together, extorting huge indemnities and levies, and imposing "treaties" upon the helpless land. The culmination had been the total destruction of the Imperial Summer Palace in 1870 by the combined armies of France and Great Britain. As a result of the merciless plunder and despoliation, China was reduced to massive misery. The Manchu court lost control of its vast bureaucracy, and the officials in turn extorted money from the people they ruled. "There are no longer father and mother officials, only wolves feeding on the flesh of men," went a song of those times. Huge peasant revolts were common, but they only compounded China's chaos.

Zhou Panlong was one of the many scholar-officials whose income was severely affected. With his elder brother he had bought the small house in Fuma Lane to lodge his family, and there was no money left to purchase fields and become a landlord with an assured income from tenant farmers, as many mandarins did. Besides his house, he could afford only a small piece of land for a graveyard outside Huai An town. A private graveyard was important, for the dead must be lodged properly as well as the living. Panlong finally did occupy a post, although it is not clear whether it was the one originally meant for him. There were more expenses as he now arranged the marriages of his sons into families of suitable status and rank. The second of his four sons, Yineng, was married in 1896 to the daughter of an official of renowned academic achievement, Wan Tsingxian, from the next town, Huai Ying. Their family house was very large, with more than ninety rooms and many courtyards. A noble house, with a high threshold gate, indicating rank, and imposing walls surrounding the property. Wan Tsingxian had eighteen sons and daughters. It was his twelfth daughter, called Dong Erh, or Winter's Child, who became Yineng's wife.

I stare at the family portraits hanging on the walls of a room in the Zhou house. Here is Yineng, with a vague expression and a pendulous mustache. A timid, ineffectual man, who repeatedly failed the official examinations, and his whole life through would be employed in low-paid minor clerkships. Next to him is the portrait of Winter's Child, his wife. She is strikingly beautiful, with large eyes, a small straight nose, a gentle mouth. A very lovely woman. The third picture is that of another woman, not beautiful, but with a strong chin and a direct gaze. That is Lady Chen. She too came from a family of noted scholars, and was married to Panlong's youngest son, Yigan. But her picture hangs next to that of Winter's Child because of what happened between them.

On March 5, 1898, Winter's Child was delivered of a son, Panlong's first grandson. A first grandson is a great event. It confirms and assures another generation in the patrilineal system of the family. It is a cause for great rejoicing. But the child was born on a day of grief, for precisely on that day Wan Tsingxian, the father of Winter's Child, lay dying. Round the huge canopied redwood bed where Wan Tsingxian lay were all his sons and daughters, the wives of his sons, his grandchildren . . . but not Dong Erh, who had given birth that afternoon. She sent the eight astrological signs, the conjunction presiding over the exact time of birth of her infant son, to her dying father, and this consoled him. He predicted a great career for the newborn.

Yineng and his wife went about choosing names for the infant with sedulous care. Of course he must have the formal "generation" or official name, and since it had been determined that the generation name would begin with the ideogram En, meaning grace or favor, he was named Enlai, the Coming of Grace. But he must also have a "child" name, and a *hao*, or public name. He received the child name of Da Luan, or Great Argus, a bird akin to the phoenix. To it was added the *hao* of Xiang Yu, Soaring in Space, so that his mind should take wing, untrammeled in its capacity to acquire knowledge and wisdom.

Yineng's younger brother, Yigan, scarcely twenty and married to Lady Chen, was gravely ill with tuberculosis. He lay in bed, sweating and coughing blood, and his young bride, she of the strong chin and resolute gaze, sought doctor after doctor, who vainly prescribed potions including ground pearls and cinnabar. A wise relative with a reputation for pious deeds suggested a remedy. "If Great Argus becomes son to you and to your husband, joy will fill your abode, bad luck will be banished, and your husband will recover."

The family held council. Winter's Child, imbued with Confucian tradition, put her duty as daughter-in-law above her own feelings. She must save the life of her husband's brother. She brought her firstborn son, scarcely a year old, across the courtyard, to Lady Chen. With due ceremony, he was adopted as son to the childless and dying Yigan.

And that is why the two portraits hang together. Enlai now had two mothers, but would have to call Lady Chen "mother," and not his own mother.

Yigan died, and Lady Chen remained a widow all her life. But now she had a son. The dead man was saved from committing the horrendous crime of leaving no male posterity behind him, the most unfilial misdeed of all. Now, with a son, Yigan would have his soul tablet placed on the ancestors' altar, dotted with a drop of blood from the left index finger of the child that had come "across the courtyard." Without the dotting, he would have no soul tablet, no place in the family lineage. Lady Chen was saved from being a childless widow, than which there is no more contemptible state of being. She engaged a wet nurse, Jiang, for the baby.

When talking in later life of his childhood, Zhou Enlai would often say that he had "three mothers." "My own mother was gentle and tender, but she was not well educated, for the Wan family did not believe in education for women. But from her I learned kindness, forbearance. I have some of her character . . . ambition has been left out of me. My adoptive mother was well educated, her parents were enlightened. She taught me to love knowledge and to use my mind. My nurse took me to her home by the Grand Canal, and from her I learned how the working people lived. She taught me unselfishness."

As soon as the child could toddle, Lady Chen began to teach him the ideograms, and by four he could read and write several hundred words. He recited the basic classics at six. Lady Chen, well versed in the histories and the poets, read poems and classic tales to the child. She was a skillful storyteller, even at times playacting, with appropriate gestures, the events she recounted. She told the young boy the stories of Huai An's heroes. One of them was Han Hsin, a brilliant strategist and loyal minister, who defended the Han dynasty and made it possible for the first Han emperor to rule, in 206 B.C. "Han Hsin was brave and bold, he never bragged. He always spoke quietly. He listened much. Once a bully and his ruffians came to the town. Han Hsin was helpless, he had no soldiers. The bully, to shame him, ordered him to crawl between his legs. Han Hsin knew that he would be killed unless he complied. He crawled."

Enlai listened, his large eyes, so like his mother's, fixed upon Lady Chen. "People who say Han Hsin was a coward only see the skin of things. Han Hsin knew he had great things to do. He must keep alive to do them. And so it was. He saved the dynasty. In later years he met the bully, and instead of killing him, he rewarded him. 'Thank you, bully, you taught me a good lesson.'"

"But did he not want revenge?" asked Enlai.

"Only mean, small people seek vengeance for personal offenses. The superior man rises above resentment."

Lady Chen told Enlai how ill rewarded Han Hsin had been by the very emperor whose throne he had safeguarded. The emperor listened to his wicked wife, the cruel Lady Lu, and killed Han Hsin.

Enlai's father, Yineng, obtained a lowly clerkship in another province, Hubei, and was away most of the time. It was Winter's Child who had to care for the family, cook, clean, wash the clothes. She gave birth to two more sons, and her health deteriorated. Penurious relatives descended upon the house like hungry locusts. There was not enough money to hire a good tutor for Enlai, and a distant relative came occasionally to give lessons. After the death of Grandfather Panlong and the costly funeral—to gain face—money was scant, and Winter's Child spent sleepless nights thinking of ways of getting money. In desperation, she one day bought a lottery ticket—and won a fairly large sum. But her joy and relief were short-lived, for creditors came pounding at the gate, and a new influx of kinsmen to congratulate her . . . and stay to be fed and housed.

One day, Dong Erh, Winter's Child, made up her mind to escape, at least for a short while, the pressures upon her, by paying a visit to her own family in Huai Ying. Enlai was five years old. She took with her her three sons, Nurse Jiang, and Lady Chen. All six at first were made welcome by the Wans, and by the Kung and Li families, allies by marriage of the Wan. Enlai was delighted. He studied under the same tutor as the Wan boys, and discovered his maternal grandfather's library. Shelves upon shelves of books. Enchantment. Paradise. He now had many playmates, and joined in kite flying and boating, and was astonished that the Kung girls were being tutored as well as the boys. Many years later, he still wrote letters to a female "cousin" in the Kung clan.

As the weeks went by, the welcome chilled. "Six mouths to feed," said dowager Lady Wan aloud. Despite a show of wealth, the Wan family was also in straitened circumstances, selling fields to maintain its status. Lady Chen now suggested a visit to her own Chen family. Its mansion of many rooms and courtyards was not too far from the Wan mansion. Thither the six proceeded. But now Dong Erh was very ill. She had been infected with tuberculosis. In the spring of 1907 she died swiftly, husband Yineng arriving too late. There were only a hundred silver dollars left. But Lady Wan insisted on a costly funeral as befitting the status of the family. Yineng obeyed, and all was spent.

Help came from another quarter. Lady Chen had a relative, Chen Shizhou, a scholar, who took them to his home fifty kilometers from Huai Ying. He too had an extensive library. More, he had many "foreign" books—that is, translations of foreign works. There was a difference of thirteen years between Chen Shizhou and Enlai, but the two would become very good friends, and many years later, from London, from Paris, Zhou Enlai would write long letters to Chen, pouring out his impressions of the outside world, his doubts, and his hopes.

Tragedy struck again. Lady Chen died in the summer of 1908. Clad in coarse white cloth, Enlai followed the coffin, taken by boat to Huai An, and by pallbearers to the Zhou family graveyard, to be buried next to her husband. He had, the year before, followed his natural mother's coffin to the graveyard. Now with his two brothers he returned to the house in Fuma Lane. Nurse Jiang stayed on, even though she was not paid. She belonged to that breed of devoted servants who, right up to the revolution of 1949, would sell their own belongings, even their pitiable jewelry, to provide for their masters and mistresses. Now she would look after Enlai, and often took him to her own home, so that he might eat his fill.

Enlai was now not only an impoverished orphan; he was also cast into his destined role of "eldest son," keeper of the family, provider for its needs. He was barely ten years old.

His father's younger surviving brother, Yikuei, and the latter's wife rummaged through the family chests, selecting garments, porcelain, books, paintings, calligraphy scrolls, which Enlai took to the pawnbroker in Huai An. The pawnshop had an imposing counter, raised on a platform to inspire awe and humility in the needy. Enlai was small for his age. He had to lift his arms high above his head to deposit the objects he brought upon the counter, where the pawnbroker would finger them disdainfully. "Yours must be a family with much treasure to spare, since you come so often," he sneered. Impassive, the little boy stood, controlling his face. He thus learned never to show emotion, never to weep. He took the money flung at him and went home with it. Everyone waited to see how much he brought back. Neighbors who had once been polite and hospitable now ignored the Zhou family. Only Nurse Jiang, unshakable, unpaid, went on caring for the boy and his two brothers.

This went on for about two years. Then Uncle Yiqian, the son of Panlong's elder brother, turned up. Yiqian would later obtain a good position in Shanghai and become fairly prosperous. But at the time he was encumbered with a young family. He suggested, however, that Uncle Yikeng, Yineng's elder brother, take the young Enlai and put him through school. Yikeng lived in Manchuria; he had a wife and a concubine, but no children. It was his duty to raise his brother's children, especially since Yineng, at the time, appears to have had difficulties in keeping his clerkship. And so it was arranged. Enlai would leave Huai An to stay with Uncle Yikeng in Manchuria. It was the spring of 1910. New clothes were made for Enlai and he took leave, formally, of his family. "You are now really soaring into the wide sky," wept Nurse Jiang, who felt Manchuria was the end of the earth. A photograph was taken of Enlai before departure. A silk jacket. A round cap. He is twelve. He does not smile. There is a stunned look in his eyes.

Manchuria. Exaltation of immense, seemingly limitless plains. A long, harsh winter, only 120 frost-free days a year. This was the original land of the Manchus, who had conquered China in 1644. But now there were few Manchus left in China. A life of ease—each Manchu was pensioned at birth—had decimated them more swiftly than any plague. The race had melted into the vast Han multitude, and now Manchuria was peopled by millions of Chinese, chiefly from the northern provinces, notably Shandong. The city of Shenyang—previously known as Mukden—was thriving. It had a budding industry, because local deposits of coal and iron had led to the establishment of factories by early Chinese businessmen. Uncle Yikeng had a post in the provincial government service and, though not wealthy, was able to make ends meet. Enlai quickly adapted to the cold and to the food. His love for roughage, for eating coarse millet buns, or *wotou*, rather than fine-milled rice, dates back to those years in Manchuria. "I grew strong in the north. I was tempered by the climate, the food. It made me healthy and it stood me in good stead later in life." Yikeng kept up the Shaoxing tradition, imbibing the warm golden Shaoxing wine, and he gave it to Enlai to drink.

Enlai first attended an old-fashioned school because, when his uncle had decided he must be enrolled, the "new learning" establishment was not yet ready. Uncle Yikeng wanted the best education available. Persistent unemployment was now the lot of the scholars trained in the old way. A flood of "new learning" was sweeping through China, and the old classical education was no longer needed.

The story of the schools of "new learning" is intimately linked to the development of China's Long Revolution, and to the formation of a generation of radicals, among them Zhou Enlai. By 1898, the year in which he was born, China was beaten to her knees and the Western powers were ready to parcel her out among themselves as they had done with Africa. A reformist movement among the Chinese scholars had been drowned in blood that year by the conservative Dowager Empress Tsu Hsi. But the ravages of the Western powers in China had aroused deep hatred and fury, which led to the insurrection of 1900, quaintly called the "Boxer Rebellion" in the West and "the uprising of the righteous fists" in China. The Boxers slaughtered Chinese Christians and foreign missionaries. But even greater slaughter was perpetrated when the combined forces of the Western powers and Japan walked into the capital, Beijing—then known as Peking—and for eight days killed, raped, looted at will.

Nevertheless, all plans for "cutting up the Chinese cake" were abandoned and instead an open door policy was adopted. China's unity would be ostensibly maintained, but all the powers would now cooperate in its continued exploitation. This was called "safeguarding legitimate Western interests in China." But it was now obvious that there must be reforms, and in 1902 the imperial system of public examinations for the civil service dating back 1,600 years was abolished while schools of "new learning," teaching science and mathematics, replaced the old classical curriculum. With enormous enthusiasm young Chinese crowded the new schools, for science was a magic word. Science would provide the wisdom and the power to save China and bring her out of medievalism. The schools of "new learning" were the product of a staggering ambivalence. They were encouraged by the Western powers for two contradictory reasons. The missionaries wanted to Christianize China through education. The governments thought the schools would breed compliant Westernized Chinese to serve their interests, a colonialization of the mind. The British had successfully brought into being a class of Indian civil servants to service their empire in India; why not repeat the performance in China? But the young Chinese who went to those schools were, at the time, imbued with fierce resentment. They wanted to acquire the knowledge, the strength of the West so that China might become powerful and throw off the shackles imposed upon her. They had to learn from those who had destroyed not only their country's pride and dignity but also their faith in its traditional values.

Uncle Yikeng wanted Enlai to succeed, to acquire "new learning," even if the school was three times as expensive as a traditional school. In the autumn the Tung Guan model school opened, and Enlai was admitted into its sixth year. The children were to learn mathematics, elements of natural science, English, singing, and gymnastics, as well as Chinese, history, geography, and literature. Paradoxically, because the children also read translations of Western books, they learned about freedom, about democracy, they learned about the French and the American revolutions. Hence the institutions designed to produce a submissive Westernized elite would become the training ground of China's revolutionaries.

The geography teacher, named Mao, owned a small replica of the globe, which he showed to the students, explaining why people did not fall off the round earth. Enlai learned about physics, about Newton. He stared at the globe, memorized the names of countries and cities. "I found out how small Europe was, so small compared to China. I made up my mind to travel to many places."

Tung Guan school had a uniform, modeled after the Japanese uniform, and there is a school photograph of Enlai with his schoolmates. His short stature is still evident, but he does not look unhappy. In fact, he did well, made friends, was popular. Tung Guan school held oratorical contests, to develop in the students the ability to think cogently and systematically. Enlai's first speech was against opium. "How can our country prosper, our people become strong, unless this poison is prohibited?"

Enlai describes how his education in revolt began with his history teacher, Gao Yuwen. "My going to Manchuria was a turning point. Had I not left home, I would not have achieved anything. Gao spoke of what had happened to China during the nineteenth century at the hands of the Western powers. He greatly influenced me. He was already a revolutionary." Teacher Gao led his students through every episode since the 1840 Opium War, described the unequal treaties, the burning of the Imperial Summer Palace. He gave his young students books to read, and spoke of a strange man, Sun Yatsen, who wanted to overthrow the Manchu dynasty and turn China into a republic.

Enlai listened. Twelve is a threshold age, the age when the mind shuffles off the coils of childhood and starts to roam, to wonder. In that same year, 1910, Japan, with its well-trained army and navy, had occupied Korea and turned it into its own colony, with the assent of the Western powers. And Korea was next door to Manchuria.

Gao Yuwen loaned Enlai the works of two famous Chinese reformers, Kang Yuwei and Liang Qichao. Enlai found Kang Yuwei's prose difficult to assimilate, but was very taken by Liang, whom he found "very clear, very easy to understand." Liang's lyrical style, his mellifluous sentences, influenced Enlai, who would for a few years model his own writing style upon Liang's.

In October 1911, the first volcanic eruption in China's Long Revolution took place as a result of the actions over the previous two decades of that mild-mannered, gentle-looking Cantonese, trained in medicine in Japan, Sun Yatsen. Despite his appearance, Sun was an extraordinarily tenacious man, totally unconcerned with his own welfare. He held stubbornly to the opinion that the Manchu dynasty must be removed and China must become a republic, on the French or American model. To this he dedicated his life, despite a price on his head and the hostility of the Western powers, who considered him a dangerous bandit and connived with the Manchu rulers against him. He founded a United League to overthrow the dynasty. He infused overseas Chinese communities with enthusiasm for a Chinese republic and repeatedly launched armed insurrections in China itself. All of them ended in failure and in the slaughter of the insurgents. In the spring of 1911, another attempt had ended in disaster, when suddenly a spontaneous mutiny in a military garrison in the city of Wuhan, on the Yangtse River, took place. Within days, everything changed. The Manchu dynasty was overthrown, or rather melted away like ice cream in the sun. A republic was proclaimed on October 10, and Sun Yatsen's adherents clamored for his return, and for him to become President.   . The instigator of it all meanwhile was in Denver,

Colorado, and learned of the event from his morning newspaper. Sun made his way back to China via Paris and London, where he was treated with hostility. On his arrival in China, he appealed to the Western powers for their help. China, he said, wanted parliamentary democracy. Sun went in a formal ceremony to the imperial tombs of the Ming dynasty, the dynasty that had been overthrown by the Manchus, to inform the imperial souls of the change.

In Tung Guan school there was great joy. The students blew off firecrackers, pulled down the Manchu flag, and hoisted the five-color flag of the new republic. Gao Yuwen had long ago cut off his pigtail, the badge of servitude imposed by the Manchus. Zhou Enlai was the first boy in the school to cut off his, despite the fact that he had been told, "Cut your pigtail, cut your life." Patriotism was now all-pervasive, the very air the young breathed, an emotional torrent rushing through all the magazines and newspapers, as well as the essays and speeches of professors and students in many of the schools of "new learning." Zhou Enlai's essay, on the second anniversary of his school, embodies the emotions of that time and of that generation. It was reproduced in the local press, and reprinted in 1915 in an anthology published in Shanghai of the best student essays of the year.

Zhou Enlai was pretty before he became handsome, and because of his small size and apparent delicacy, he was bullied and sometimes beaten by older boys. He devised his own protection by acquiring friends, many friends, who would walk with him out of school, so that he would not be alone. These friends he kept throughout life. Even when he was a man with a price upon his head he went to see them, and not one of them ever betrayed him.

One friend, named Ho, took him to his home. Ho's grandfather, an old soldier, brought the boys to a large plain outside Shenyang. Here, said the old man, the Japanese and the Russians, in 1904, had fought their own war, borrowing China's earth to do so. Of course, the Japanese had now learned strength from the West, ever since the Meiji reforms of 1860, and now they despised the Chinese. "We did nothing, nothing to stop them from using our land," shouted the old man. "Now our hopes rest with you, the young, for revenge." Enlai echoed this thought in his speeches. "The future of China is our responsibility. Let us not evade it."

He read avidly, newspapers, magazines. He read Darwin, and Rousseau, and John Stuart Mill. He read of the slave trade, and made a speech: "The black slaves will be liberated one day." When asked in class "Why do you study?" his schoolmates would give various reasons—"To please my father" or "To earn a living"— but Zhou Enlai proudly said, "I study so that China may rise again." His passion for knowledge now blended with a fierce, total dedication to his country. It was something which happened, and could not be undone, a fusion within his spirit, so that there would be no other life for him but a life given to restoring, not the fortunes of the Zhou family, but the fortunes of that much bigger family, the land of the ancestors, China.

Zhou Enlai graduated in 1913 from Tung Guan. Uncle Yikeng and Uncle Yiqian were determined that he should continue his studies. Father Yineng does not seem to have had any say in the matter. For a while he too was living with his brother Yikeng, possibly because he was temporarily jobless.

Zhou Enlai applied to enter Tsinghua school, established in Beijing with American funds, and reputed for its excellence. He did not pass the English-language test. Tsinghua's entrance examinations were stringent. Worse, there was a quota imposed against too many students from South China. They tended to excel, and northern students felt aggrieved. Uncle Yikeng was not discouraged. Enlai would now try to enter Nankai school in Tianjin. It also had high standards and an excellent reputation.

Uncle Yikeng, by great good luck, managed to get himself posted to Tianjin for a year. He, his concubine, and Enlai stayed in a small house on Yuan Wei Road, Yuan Jieli No. 4. During the three months of the summer Enlai was given private tuition in English, so as to be sure to pass the entrance examination. He did, and was enrolled as a student at Nankai school in September 1913. He was fifteen.

2

The Victorian colonial building which was the original Nankai school is now a museum, housing the memorabilia of Zhou Enlai's four years at Nankai. Nothing has been changed, not even the color of the walls and the woodwork. The empty classrooms, with their brown pulpits, their blackboards, are dusted every day as if, at any time, the souls of those youths who sat here might return.

Nankai was founded in 1906 by two dedicated men, the scholar-academician Yen Fangsun, a reformist who felt it urgent to combine the best of both Chinese and Western education to prepare the young generations for the future; and a Christian Chinese, Zhang Boling, educated in the United States. Funds from missionary sources in the United States and professors of English and mathematics from Great Britain were available in its first years. The curriculum comprised chemistry, biology, algebra, and geometry, as well as Chinese and English literature. Every student was required to be of sound mind, sound morals, in a sound body. The school was an elite establishment, expensive by Chinese standards. The uniform was a long robe, pale blue or gray, over long trousers.

Tianjin, a word meaning the Heavenly Ford, was opened to Western trade after the Opium Wars of the nineteenth century. Here were foreign concessions, extraterritorial enclaves where only foreign law was recognized and no Chinese jurisdiction could be exercised. British, French, German, Italian, and, later, Japanese concessions ran next to each other along the muddy brown river from which the city derived its name. Turbaned Sikhs and Corsican gendarmes, Italian and Japanese guards, patrolled their respective territories. In the factories of Tianjin gaunt women and children from the age of eight toiled fourteen hours a day, 362 days a year. When floods or drought hit the northern farmlands of China, starving peasants seeped into Tianjin, to beg, to sell their children. Every winter the river streamed its corpses to the sea, and this was regarded as normal in a China where plague, cholera, and starvation killed possibly a million people a year.

In the bookshops of Tianjin there were many translations of Western books, journals, and magazines, an ample trove of new ideas for the fifteen-year-old Zhou Enlai. His heart hungered for the knowledge contained within these volumes, spread out for anyone with money to buy them. But Uncle Yikeng and his concubine lived meagerly. Enlai cost them a good deal, for he was a boarder at Nankai, returning only on weekends to the cramped rooms on Yuan Wei Road. The concubine, whose name is not recorded, was devoted to Enlai. She knitted socks and scarves for him, sometimes in bright colors, for she was a peasant woman. But the other boys made fun of Enlai's red socks, and she stopped. She embroidered tablecloths and napkins, and sold her work, because money was scarce, and every weekend she would press money into his hands, for food. Enlai bought books instead.

Yen Fangsun became interested in this shy and diligent student from Shaoxing, who excelled in every subject. Yen and Zhang Boling discovered that Enlai could not always afford the canteen meals; he would walk out of the school to buy, at the stalls in the street, a few coppers' worth of bean curd soup or a bowl of millet gruel. Both men decided to help Enlai. He was given jobs to do, such as stencil work or cataloguing the books in the library. In his second year, because of his high grades, he became the only student in Nankai exempt from paying tuition fees.

After a year in Tianjin, Uncle Yikeng returned to Manchuria and Enlai was left alone. New Year was particularly trying for him, for then all his schoolmates went home, and he was alone in the empty school. "I detest solitude, loneliness," Enlai wrote in his diary. "I like to make friends. I shall never forget my friends."

He was teased, of course, because of his looks and an apparent shyness. He held back, examining the person in front of him, waiting for a word, a gesture, before committing himself. This was a habit he would retain throughout his life. Because he was smaller than the tall, big-boned northerners around him, he might have been bullied at first, but soon he was popular. His friendships went across all barriers of province and even of religion. This was remarkable, for many students had a tendency to make friends only with those who came from the same region as themselves. Enlai became a good friend of Wu Dagen, a brawny, tall Manchu, who was something of a wrestler. Another close friend, Ma Jun, was a Hui, or Muslim Chinese. "I am sure that in my own family we have blood from national minorities," Zhou Enlai told me one day in the 1960s. An affinity of mind made him seek out bold spirits such as Zhang Pengxian and Zhang Hungjie, both to become revolutionaries. "Enlai's mind was always busy with great affairs, with the state of the country. He considered China's destiny to be the responsibility of each one of us," says his classmate Zhang Lungyuan. But Zhou Enlai would never be a pure intellectual, content with the play of ideas, deploring cruelty, injustice, oppression, but skirting away from action. To think was also to act, and throughout his life he would serve what he believed in. Because of this linkage between thought and action he became a leader among his schoolmates.

"Zhou Enlai always got his way. He was so persuasive. And so sincere. Somehow, people rushed to do what he wanted. But he always gave an example. He never gave orders, but when he said, 'Think about it,' somehow one was convinced," continues Lungyuan.

Nankai school encouraged extracurricular activities, notably sports, and Zhou Enlai went running every morning. He once won at the high jump. He sang in the choir. He developed an ear and a liking for Western music, and his retentive memory served him well. Once he heard it, he would remember a tune, a melody, a musical phrase. In the early 1970s, on a tour of the Yangtse gorges with Prince Norodom Sihanouk of Cambodia, who not only played the saxophone but composed catchy songs, Zhou Enlai would delight the prince by singing one of his recent creations right back to him.

He bought books. He went without meals to buy a book. To this habit he would later ascribe his extraordinary stamina. "It is not necessary to eat or to sleep at regular hours. Regularity ossifies the mind."

Abstemiousness, imposed by financial straits, became for him a source of energy. He did not eat meat for days on end, eating bean curd instead, for it was the cheapest food. He had few clothes, and washed and mended them with care. That extraordinary parsimony toward himself which marked his life began at Nankai.

Nankai school shaped Zhou Enlai into the man he would become. Its high educational standards, its mixture of Chinese and Western culture, engendered in him a lack of inhibition toward acquiring Western habits, acknowledging ways of thought different from his own. Here he first came across *New Youth*, a magazine begun in 1915, founded by two Chinese scholars who would become China's first Communists, Chen Duxiu, French-educated, and Li Dazhao, educated in Japan.

Li Dazhao was then librarian at Peking University, a pivotal post, enabling him to fill the bookshelves with radical literature. For a while, he employed a tall, gangling, and dreamy-looking youth with a great shock of unruly hair, who spoke with a strong Hunan accent. His name was Mao Dzedong. Li Dazhao promptly forgot him.

New Youth was eclectic, brimful of new concepts, answering the yearning for new ideas among the young. It was a rallying publication for the radicals who, in 1915–16, were discovering with anger and despair that the buoyant hopes of 1911, when Sun Yatsen had proclaimed China a republic, were unfulfilled, and that China was now in a far greater turmoil, heaped with more disasters than during the last wretched days of her empire. Hundreds of militarists, known as warlords, sprang into being in every province. Like the medieval barons of Europe, they plundered and pillaged, levied taxes at will, fought each other for territory and power, formed and disrupted coalitions, and found backing, and weaponry, by granting one or another Western power further benefits at the expense of their unfortunate people.

In 1914–18, World War I removed, for a short while, the threat of direct European intervention in China. Japan took advantage of her geographical proximity, and the absence of other predators, to push her own domination. To the coalition of warlords in Beijing, known as the Northern Coalition and recognized as "the Chinese government," Japan addressed peremptory demands for concessions of territory and rights which jeopardized Chinese sovereignty. The paper on which the outrageous demands were written was decorated, in its margins, with guns and dreadnoughts.

New Youth magazine denounced the Japanese demands, but though Enlai shared the general indignation, he was not particularly attracted by the political content of the articles he read. "Study, study well, then you will be able to serve your country,"

Zhang Boling exhorted his students. He believed that, somehow, all would be well if every man fulfilled his task, and he was apprehensive of "extremism." But even he could see that China was being ruined at a frightening pace. In the province of Sichuan taxes were paid on every piece of cloth, every cup and teapot, the length and breadth of windows, the heights of gates and thresholds. This money went to the warlords. Some of these enterprising militarists even collected a happiness tax, to be paid spontaneously, expressing the joy one felt at paying taxes.

Zhou Enlai shared in the wrath, the protests, the indignation. He penned essays, made fiery speeches, and won top place with a lyrical, emotional piece in a contest among the 800 students of Nankai in 1914. But he appeared less "political" than some of his friends. Nevertheless, with six other students, he set up the Jingye Society. Jingye means "respect work and rejoice in companionship."

It was a debating club, and Enlai became editor of its journal, writing articles and poems. He used the pseudonym Fei Fei, Flying, an echo of his *hao*, Soaring in Space. During his life he would use sixteen pseudonyms, including a Russian one, Strelitzoff, when he contributed articles for some Comintern publications in Moscow.

Enlai's first poems were published in the Jingye journal. They are written in the classical style. One of them, addressed to a classmate who left Nankai in 1916 to study in England, is charmingly wistful.

> Affinity, duckweed chance,
> Brought us together,
> Swinging our satchels, sharing our thoughts.
>
> Now
>
> As a brood of ravens under foliage
> We linger here
> While you, lone crane, scour the heavens.

Through the Jingye Society, Zhou Enlai asserted his patriotic feelings in a speech against the warlords, "who care not a whit for the country." Delivered on October 3, 1916, it was an impassioned and eloquent performance. But he always insisted that the responsibility for China's future "lies upon each one of us. . . . Let us not forget it, no, not for a moment." This ardent love of country brought Zhou the friendship of Ma Qianli, one of Nankai's young teachers of literature. The name means the Thousand-Mile Horse, and Ma would indeed prove fiery and bold. Ma wrote poems against the warlords, which Enlai capped with one of his own:

> The whirlwind pounds our heart-torn land,
> The nation sinks, and no one cares.
> Compounding grief, autumn is back,
> Its insect choirs deafen our ears.

Since Nankai was a prestigious establishment, the Jingye Society, which had earned a good reputation for the quality of its journal, was able to invite noted scholars to address its members. To it came the famed Liang Qichao, whose elegance of style Zhou had admired and emulated, Tsai Yuanpei, and Wu Yuzheng, all noted for their erudition, all ardent patriots and reformists. A New Theater Society was formed, and this was indeed astonishingly modern. But Zhang Boling was not afraid of modernism, and even wrote the scenario for a play. Zhou Enlai joined the New Theater Society and became an actor, or rather an actress. In China in those years female roles were always assumed by men, as in eighteenth-century Europe. Zhou acted the part of a girl in at least two plays. One of them, *A Dollar Coin*, proved very popular and was performed several times for a public audience in the city, after being shown at the school auditorium.

At his graduation in 1917—with an average of 87.2 out of 100—Zhou Enlai received a major encomium from Zhang Boling. "He is mellow and rich in feeling, attentive to friendship. Whatever has to do with the public good, or with a friend's need, that he will attend to with all his might."

Rich in feeling. Passionate, at times exuberant, but also capable of great self-control, of long silences. Zhou acquired the reputation for being a totally reliable friend, and this reputation he would keep throughout his life. "He will do anything to help a friend in distress." In China, where friendship is highly valued, this was the greatest compliment that could be paid to anyone.

There were high expectations for his future. Yen Fangsun, the co-founder of Nankai, was so fond of him that he wanted the nineteen-year-old to become his son-in-law, and a suggestion to that effect was made to Enlai through one of his friends. This proposal was in the Chinese classical tradition. Brilliant scholars were often selected by wealthy men for their daughters, to enlarge family influence. And despite his progressive ideas, Yen was a traditionalist in family matters.

Enlai told the friend who had transmitted the message, "I am a poor student. Should I accept this alliance with the influential Yen family, I shall also have to submit to their guidance in all matters." He politely declined. Far from being angry, Yen admired him all the more for rejecting security and wealth and wanting to strike out on his own.

Zhang Boling recommended that the young man go abroad, preferably to the United States. But this was beyond Zhou Enlai's means. Then what about Japan? There were many Nankai graduates in Japan. Wu Dagen, Enlai's brawny friend, had left for Kyoto, endowed with a "government" scholarship. But was not Japan threatening China? Zhou asked, his eyes steady upon Zhang Boling's smooth and kindly face. "Yes . . . but we still have to learn from Japan, just as Japan learned from the West," Zhang Boling replied.

Uncle Yikeng could not pay for the trip. Enlai sold many of his books, and his friends contributed money, here a silver dollar, there two or three. Thousand-Mile Horse gave him five dollars. But it was Yen Fangsun who gave him enough for his boat passage to Japan.

Zhou Enlai went back to Shenyang to take his leave of good Uncle Yikeng and the concubine who had been so caring and affectionate. He visited old friends and classmates and teachers from Tung Guan school. In typical Chinese fashion, he wrote grandiloquent poems before his departure, and sent them to his friends.

> In vain have I searched all schools of thought
> For clues to a better world . . .
> Ten years, staring at a wall . . .
> Now I shall break through
> Or, treading the sea, die a hero.

To say that at the age of nineteen he had been searching for the truth like the Boddhidharma, who sat for ten years staring at

a rock face before receiving Illumination, is poetic license indeed.
But it does show Zhou's omnivorous capacity for absorbing knowledge. He must have been reading books on Zen Buddhism, whose
founder, an Indian monk, had come to China from India in the
sixth century. There are, throughout Zhou's poems and the writings in his diary, traces of the influence of Buddhism, a search for
truth. But truth for Enlai was a way of salvation for his country,
not a metaphysical concept. In Confucian fashion, he was looking
for a set of guiding principles, an ideology, which would bring
regeneration to China. Defiantly, as he left his friends, his goodbye
would be: "Let us hope to meet again when China soars high in
the world." China. His country. Would he now truly soar into
space, like the Great Argus, and bring back with him the key to
China's future? Would he find the answer to his search in Japan?

In less than sixty years since the Meiji reforms of the 1860s Japan
had modernized, become a power on the Western model, and
joined with the West in exploiting and warring upon China. Toward the scimitar-shaped archipelago hugging their coast the
Chinese felt both superior and inferior. They admired, but also
resented, those "yellow dwarfs" who had borrowed their culture
from China and now humiliated her. Despite this ambivalence,
more than four thousand Chinese students were in Japan, many
more than in Europe and the United States.

Zhou Enlai arrived by boat, crossing from Korea, which had
become a Japanese colony. In Tokyo he was met by Nankai schoolmates, and helped to find lodgings with two other students in the
upper story of a small house belonging to a Japanese carpenter.
It was in the Ushigome district, close to the East Asian Preparatory
High School, where he now enrolled to learn Japanese and to
prepare himself for the entrance examinations to the Teachers
College of Tokyo. Because Enlai had very little money, Wu Dagen
and several other Nankai students, more affluent than Zhou,
agreed to pool together the sum of ten dollars a month to help
him.

Tokyo was a bustling city, though in many ways it remained a
conglomerate of villages. Enlai did not find it difficult to accom-
modate to Japanese life, and the food delighted him. Once again
he fed mostly on cheap bean curd. "You make bean curd far better-
tasting than we do," he would reminisce, many years later, to a
Japanese delegation he received in Beijing.

He planned to become a teacher. Not only was this a way of making a living but it would allow him to remain involved in "national affairs" and to influence many students. Schools were breeding grounds for patriotism, and Enlai remembered how Gao Yuwen had influenced him in Tung Guan school.

But something went wrong.

He could not study. He could not concentrate He suffered from intellectual and emotional block.

In vain did he try to reason with himself, bestir himself to attend classes. In vain did friends encourage him. It was, they said, the strangeness of a different country. It would pass. After all, Japan was less strange than Europe. It was in Japan that Sun Yatsen had organized his United League and found many sympathizers. It was in Japan that Lu Xun, China's radical writer, and others had discovered Western literature. Many works of science had become accessible to the Chinese through Japan. . . . Enlai nodded, and agreed. Yes, there was some good in Japan. He would also remark that Lu Xun was a distant relative. But his mind wandered. He wrote in his diary: "Learning can be acquired anywhere . . . why only through perusing books?" He prowled the streets, and felt another kind of knowledge seep into him. Perhaps he was conscious of a certain arrogance in his teachers. "Language is also a means of colonization. I realize this in Japan." He could not blot out of his consciousness Japanese attitudes, Japanese threats against China.

In Nankai, he had written and spoken against Japan's military and political pressures upon China. The failure of Sun Yatsen's republic, China's slide into anarchy. . . . What, he asked his friends in Japan, what could his generation do to save China? "Study," replied Wu Dagen, nodding wisely, well settled at Kyoto University, happily married. Wu Dagen believed that a "strong man" would emerge and would save China. Meanwhile China needed an elite, knowledgeable doctors, engineers, and teachers. . . .

In October 1917 the Russian Revolution took place. The event was widely reported in Japan, but it did not sweep Zhou Enlai off his feet. He went to the newsstands, for he maintained the habit of assiduously reading the newspapers, but he remained in an opacity of mind, a sluggishness of spirit, which he could not shake off. He discovered the journal *Studies of Social Problems*, whose editor was the well-known Japanese economist Kawakami Hajime, professor at the Imperial University of Waseda and one of Japan's first socialists. This was Zhou Enlai's introduction to socialism, but he was not immediately entranced, nor did he feel the earth move under his feet. He took the journal home to read carefully.

In January 1918 he received a letter telling him that Uncle Yikuei had died in the house in Fuma Lane. Now only his father, Yineng, and Uncle Yikeng were left. The Zhou family in Huai An was in great financial distress. Uncle Yikeng of Manchuria cared for both of Zhou Enlai's brothers. "There is nothing left to pawn or to sell . . . no one will lend any more money," Zhou wrote in his diary. And he was abroad, almost penniless, dependent on the charity of friends. Briefly, he turned to Buddhism for solace, recording it in his diary as well: "Everything in the world . . . is but appearance. . . . It is a bitter sea . . . best to cast away all material care, and go the way of total detachment. . . ." But, he continues, "I am unable to sever all links. . . . I cannot, like the Boddhidharma, face the rock wall."

The crisis passed. Spring came, and the beauty of Japan lifted his spirits. "I must forever try to think new thoughts, perform new actions, acquire the newest knowledge." He penned resolutions for the guidance of his own spirit. "Think freely, act realistically, study thoroughly." And as if in answer to his striving, as a reward for the long agony in which he had wrestled with the dark night of his soul, he fell once again upon *New Youth*, the magazine he had already glanced through at Nankai.

This time, he was caught.

The color of the sky changed for him. The streets became enchanted daubs of color. "I have suddenly awakened. . . . I am very, very happy."

At last, he had a clue. Science, learning alone, would not save China. Nor would the ancient virtues, nor a strong man. There must be a political theory underpinning, guiding the actions taken to change, to revitalize his beloved land. There must be a body of people dedicated to carrying out this enterprise.

He made his own rules of work. Thirteen and a half hours a day studying, reading books and newspapers. Three and a half hours attending to his bodily needs. He would sleep seven hours.

In the spring of 1918, Japan's pressures on the Northern Coalition of warlords which ruled in Beijing increased. Many Chinese students found Japanese imperiousness and arrogance unbearable and they began to return home. Enlai had now joined a student organization in Tokyo named the New China Society, which organized protests against the Chinese warlords "shamefully selling our country to Japan." Enlai, with about a hundred of the three hundred fifty student members of the society, marched on the Chinese consulate in Tokyo. They were stopped by the police. Zhou Enlai told the chief of police that this was not agitation; they merely wanted to hand in a petition. He was both polite and persuasive, so that the Japanese not only withdrew his men but praised the students . . . or so it is said. (This episode seems slightly exaggerated, and may only be part of the legend which has grown up around Zhou's activities in Japan and which tends to make him appear to have been an early Marxist. He was not.) That evening a fiery Zhou made an impassioned speech to the students. "The reason for China's weakness is that the country can neither plan for the new nor preserve the old, nor can it undertake reforms." A remarkably acute observation. He went on to say that in the past China had always been able to absorb her conquerors, but this would not happen now. It was up to the Chinese people to conquer themselves, to abandon their weaknesses. A thorough spiritual renewal was necessary before there could be any political progress. Zhou Enlai was stating what would remain, for him, a lifelong conviction: that man must change himself before society can be changed.

In April 1918 the two founders of Nankai, Yen Fangsun and Zhang Boling, arrived in Tokyo on their way to the United States. Nankai was to become a full-fledged university, and much of the funding had to come from America.

The Nankai students in Tokyo gave a banquet in honor of the two visitors, which Enlai attended. He later went to see Yen Fangsun and appears, from a terse note in the latter's diary, to have had a long talk with him. Obviously Yen was a little disappointed with Zhou Enlai's scholastic nonperformance. Perhaps he again helped him with money. But Enlai failed in the examinations for Teachers College. His knowledge of Japanese proved inadequate. "I am very despondent," he confided to his diary.

In that July, he briefly returned to China and met his father, Yineng, in Beijing. Yineng and the family in Huai An were finding it very difficult to make ends meet, which added to Enlai's dejection. There was no prospect for his father but to sink into deeper poverty, or rely upon more fortunate members of the family. . . . In September, Enlai was back in Japan, determined to make another attempt.

Wu Dagen worried about Enlai, and invited him to come to Kyoto and stay with him. "Please come. . . . The social science faculty in Kyoto University is very good . . . you may like it. . . . We are all foreigners in this country. Should we not help each other?" Greatly moved, Enlai packed his suitcase, took the train to Kyoto, and burst into tears when he saw Wu Dagen waiting for him at the station. He remained with Wu and his wife almost five months.

Though Enlai did enroll at Kyoto University as a part-time student and sporadically attended courses, he still could not study. He became aware of the plight of the Japanese workers and peasants. He witnessed a vast protest movement arising from the distress of the farmers and a march to aid the impoverished peasantry, called the March for Rice. His ideas matured. He had condemned Chinese warlordism, but Japan was a militarist government too. He asked Wu Dagen whether he could arrange for him a meeting with Kawakami Hajime, the editor of *Studies of Social Problems*, who was in Kyoto. But Wu let the matter drop. Enlai would never meet the professor. In April 1918, Zhou had penned his first remarks on socialism: "Socialism's first field of experiment . . . appears to be in Russia."

In the Wu home Zhou helped Mrs. Wu by cooking and cleaning, getting up early in the morning to sweep the rooms and put away the futons, light wadded covers serving as mattress and blankets.

The plenitude of mothers that Zhou enjoyed as a boy is probably the reason for his easy, happy relationships with women throughout his life. He would always look upon women as equals, enjoy their company, appreciate their conversation, without any need of exhibiting "manliness" or virility. In a culture where the division between the sexes is so strong, he saw no disgrace in doing "woman's work"—cooking, sweeping, tidying a room. He did, in fact, ascribe to the climate of feminine love and care bestowed on him by his three very dissimilar mothers the reason for this non-Confucian attitude.

Mrs. Wu not only had a full study schedule, but on returning from her classes she would do the housework as well. Now she came home to find that Zhou Enlai had cooked dinner. Mindful of Enlai's liking for wine, Wu Dagen would sometimes bring home a bottle of sake. The two friends would sit and talk. But increasingly, differences surfaced. Enlai was now obsessed with the socialist journals he read and could talk of little else. Only a revolution, carried out by the Chinese people, could save China. "One strong man . . . what can one man do? There should be many, united in the same endeavor, organized . . . then great things are possible." The arguments grew more heated as Zhou talked and drank, drank and talked. "There must be a revolution, otherwise there will be no change . . . this is our task." Wu could not bear it any longer. "You won't save China if you go on drinking as you do," he exclaimed, and knocked the wine bottle to the floor, where it broke.

Enlai fell silent, stared at the floor, rose to get a small broom and mop, swept up the shards, and wiped the floor clean. Wu's wife, rather distressed, expostulated, "You do drink a lot, Enlai. Even at school you were too fond of wine."

Spring came again to Japan. The lovely, enchanted spring. Zhou Enlai wandered in Arashiyama Park, where each corner was a vision of breathtaking beauty. "I want to know, to learn from the four ends of the world . . . the scholar wishes to know all things under heaven. . . . Should he lack knowledge in one thing, he feels ashamed."

Not only knowledge but also the sensuous enjoyment of beauty captured him, for a while.

> Arashiyama in the rain,
> Blue pines on either bank
> And cherry trees between.
> A peak springs high at road's end
> Water, jade green, winds among rocks,
>
> Soft rain and mist,
> And suddenly
> A beam of sunlight through the clouds.
> All the more shaking my heart . . .

Walking about, with spring decking itself in the glory of cherry blossoms, he fingered in his pocket the letter he had received from

Ma Jun, his classmate at Nankai. "If our country is to disappear, what is the use of studying?"

He walked and was enchanted, but within him another being moved, who would not allow him to drown in beauty. His poems show this dichotomy. Here is celebration of beauty, but also taking leave of beauty. Each verse is acknowledgment, but also dissociation.

> Has there ever been
> All flower, eternal spring,
> Perfect loveliness
> Without
> A mind unflawed
> To enjoy it all?

The mind unflawed, untouched, unconstrained, was not his.

> Dusk falls, yet on the wide green
> Lo, the nimbus of cherry blossom . . .

Beauty could not trammel him. Contemplation, intellectual detachment, was not possible. He had to become involved. So leave he must, and write leave-taking poems to the land and the people he both loved and resented. Here in Japan he had lost himself, had groped to find himself. Here his attempt to forge a personal career had failed. But possibly, he had been vouchsafed a glimpse, a premonition of the future.

He left by train for Tokyo. On the train he met Shoto Motogi, a Japanese professor at the Hakodate Commercial School. They conversed. "He spoke with such affection, such concern, of both our peoples, and with so much fire," Shoto Motogi recalled. Zhou gave the professor his card, on which he had inscribed, besides his official name of Enlai, his *hao*, Xiang Yu, Soaring in Space.

On May 5, 1919, Enlai left Japan and was met by his brother Enshou at the landing quay in Korea. Both proceeded to Shenyang, where Enshou lived with Uncle Yikeng. Two days later Zhou Enlai left for Tianjin, reaching the city on May 9, in time to take part in the most momentous event in his country's contemporary history, the May 4, 1919, Movement, China's first cultural revolution.

3

May 4, 1919. A date to remember, remembered today, for it was the first day of a massive, China-wide arousal, when two generations—or more—of scholars of the old learning and students of the new exploded in bitterness, frustration, and anger. Then was born a leap of consciousness, a radicalization, which would determine the course of history for the next half century. The repercussions of May 4, 1919, seventy years later, in May 1989, were still felt. And who knows but that another historical change for the country might not be brought about by memories of that date, to remember as the French Revolution is remembered by a single event, the taking of the Bastille, on July 14, 1789?

For those unacquainted with Chinese history, an explanation is needed. In World War I, China had been an ally of Great Britain and France. By China is meant the coalition of warlords in North China who had established a government in Beijing and were recognized as the Chinese government by the Western democracies, including the United States. This coalition government had sent more than 300,000 Chinese workers to man the labor-depleted factories of France and England. In return, the democracies—as they were known then in China—had promised that China's just claims against the unequal treaties imposed upon her since the iniquitous Opium Wars of the nineteenth century, the monopoly of salt, the customs, in the hands of Western powers, the extraterritorial rights in the concessions—all this would be reconsidered after victory, and in China's favor.

But this did not happen. Despite the well-meaning speeches of a fumbling Woodrow Wilson at the newly set-up League of Nations, with its exalted promises of a "new world order," the European powers ignored or rebuffed China's demands at the Peace Conference in Versailles. They reasserted their colonial rights in

Asia and their semicolonial domination in China. Through secret pledges made in 1917, France and Great Britain had guaranteed to Japan the previous German "sphere of influence" in China, the province of Shandong.

In China, a whole generation of literates, educated in the schools of "new learning," enamored of the words "democracy" and "freedom," learned that these words were only for the Western, white races, not for the colonized, and not for China.

The Chinese delegation in Paris, sent by the coalition government to sign the treaty, could not do so because the Hotel Lutetia, where they stayed, was surrounded by Chinese laborers and students. They were prevented from going to Versailles, and so China never signed the Treaty of Versailles concluding the war against Germany.

"Throughout the world, like the voice of a prophet, have gone the words of Woodrow Wilson, strengthening the weak. . . . The Chinese . . . have heard. They have been told that . . . nations like China would have an opportunity to develop unhampered. . . . They looked for the dawn of this new era . . . but no sun rose for China in the west." This was the May 4 declaration of China's youth. Enormous demonstrations took place all over the country. They were the outcome of the ambivalence that existed since the beginning of the century. The very democracies which were teaching democracy, and which Sun Yatsen had sought to emulate in 1911, were now preventing democracy in China and arrogating to themselves once again the right to parcel China at their will.

Sun Yatsen had already known this double-crossing of democracies. He had wanted democracy on the Western model, but the Western democracies had backed a military dictator instead of him, and civil war had followed, tearing the country apart. The coalition of warlords ruling in Beijing was recognized as "the government" while Sun was driven into exile. Sun tried to establish himself, precariously, in one city in the south, and was constantly imperiled by the actions of the democracies to overthrow him.

Within the next two years, thousands of China's newly educated youth would turn toward the country, and the system, which held out a promise of justice and equality. This was the new-fledged Soviet Union, which had had its revolution in 1917. The saving truth, destroying all oppression, appeared to be the doctrine of

Communism, and already agents of the Communist International, later known as the Comintern, were making contact with prominent scholars such as Li Dazhao and Chen Duxiu.

Zhou appeared at a meeting of Nankai students on the evening of May 10. "We've waited for your return. We need people like you to organize the students," said Thousand-Mile Horse to him. The first skirmish was in Nankai University itself, where a pro-Japanese militarist was to become a member of the board. Zhou was deputized to speak to Zhang Boling and express the objections of his fellow students. But Zhang angrily told him that "students must study, not indulge in extremist politics." Zhou wrote to the Nankai students in Japan to denounce Zhang and the board, "which admits national betrayers." Zhang Boling was incensed, and wanted to efface the laudatory inscription in the school records which graced Zhou Enlai's graduation in 1917. But in the end this was not done.

Through Thousand-Mile Horse, Zhou enrolled in the literature department of Nankai University. This enabled him to visit the campus, although he never attended classes. "I never studied in a university, not for a single day," he told university students in 1950, when as Prime Minister of China he launched a new education program. He rented a small room in a crowded house on Hebei Street, and became, without realizing it, a professional agitator, organizing protest marches, meetings, picketing pro-Japanese shops.

The magazine *New Youth* was now the bible of the radicalized students. The editors, Li Dazhao and Chen Duxiu, were now committed to Marxism. They were engaged in recruiting, among the young, suitable material to found Marxist cells, and later a Chinese Communist Party. Despite reading *New Youth* and actively engaging in protests, Zhou remained uncommitted. He became one of the organizers of the Tianjin Students' Union, which gathered support from many educational institutions in the city. The union had a wide, all-embracing platform, and its avowed aim was "to struggle against the warlords and against imperialism, and to save China from extinction."

Zhou's work with the union took him several times to Beijing, since Peking University, where Li Dazhao and Chen Duxiu had their base, was the spearhead of the May 4, 1919, Movement. Again he was involved in producing a paper, *Tianjin Student*, whose masthead bore, in English, the motto: DEMOCRACY: OF THE PEOPLE, FOR THE PEOPLE, BY THE PEOPLE.

Enlai was the paper's editor, and the choice of motto shows that he was a believer in democracy, in Abraham Lincoln. His first editorial, on July 21, once again insists on self-change. "To bring about the new, one must first change one's own heart."

Success came swiftly. From a paper appearing every third day, *Tianjin Student* turned into a four-page daily, selling 20,000 copies, a very large number then. It was read in Beijing and in Shanghai. Under various pseudonyms, editor Zhou Enlai wrote the art column, the news column, and a "new thought" column. He received articles and letters from all over China, and read and answered each one. He never left the paper without having finished all the day's correspondence. He now wrote in *baihua*, or the vernacular, abandoning the classic style. "All of us must be interested in affairs of state, for upon our generation lies the responsibility of saving our country." These words epitomize Zhou Enlai's profound conviction, that "sense of responsibility" inherent in the tradition of the Chinese scholar. Newspapers such as the Christian-backed *Shen Bao* commented favorably on the tone and style of *Tianjin Student*.

Those who worked with him found him untiring, never pushing himself forward "nor seeking power for himself, or to dominate others." "He dealt with everything immediately . . . he tried to turn out the most perfect work possible." The printing press was small, the workers few, the machines old. Thousands of ideograms had to be set up manually before the paper could be printed. Zhou Enlai watched the workers operate, learned how to set the type, and moved his lodgings to be nearer the press, where he often went at night to do the layout himself. He breakfasted on soybean milk and long fried doughnuts costing two cents. Since there was no toilet in his lodgings, he patronized, as so many did, one of the public lavatories. It was there, in communal fashion, that he would read the newspapers and plan his own editorial. Throughout his life he maintained the habit of taking batches of documents with him to read in the privy.

Because of his mild ways, his lack of personal pushiness, he maintained a good esprit de corps among the volatile young men he worked with.

In August several students were killed in Shandong province by the pro-Japanese militarist there. Enlai wrote a passionate editorial: "Oh, my people, my people, the forces of darkness are now ready to flatten mountains and empty the seas. . . ." He denounced Japan. "They do not treat China as a nation on its own . . . we must be ready . . . there must be preparation, there must be method, there must be sacrifice."

On August 22, the police seized the printing press and closed down *Tianjin Student*. Zhou Enlai organized a march of several hundred students to go to Beijing, where there had been many arrests, and such was the agitation—for the hundreds were joined by thousands of middle school adolescents—that the jailed students were released. It was on this journey that Zhou first had the idea of forming a society that would be a "hard core" of knowledgeable, dedicated individuals. "Demonstration fatigue" had begun. Enthusiasm can only keep up for a certain time; after that, there is a falling-off.

Societies were being formed throughout China. In Changsha, Hunan province, a gangling, dreamy, tall peasant named Mao Dzedong had organized a New People's Study Society. Through these bodies recruitment for the formation of Marxist groups took place. Zhou Enlai, however, had no intention of forming a Marxist group when, on September 6, he founded the Awareness Society with twelve men and eight women. "We discussed all kinds of philosophies. We did not, at the time, concentrate only on Marxism." But in one respect the society broke new ground. Women members must be admitted and treated as equal with the men. "All feudal ideas must be cast away . . . reform starts with the self," wrote Zhou Enlai. A merger between the all-male Tianjin Students' Union and the all-female Women's Patriotic Association of Tianjin was the first step. It drew a good deal of criticism from conservative scholars. In order to avoid being considered immoral, the students strictly eschewed romantic attachments. "You have all been inspired by twentieth-century thinking, you are aware that Chinese society must be radically altered. This is our aim . . . we must change the thinking of students, of intellectuals. We must awaken the consciousness of laboring people. Together we must transform society." Zhou Enlai's speech was well received, and he laid down the society's rules. "We discussed and we studied everything, every current of modern thought . . . Marxism, anarchism . . . we were not yet Marxists," said Deng Yingchao, one of the eight women members of the Awareness Society.

Two women would affect Enlai's life irrevocably. One of them,

Liu Qingyang, tall and graceful, was already a Marxist, a friend of Li Dazhao. She was engaged to a Nankai student, Zhang Shenfu, who helped Zhou Enlai with *Tianjin Student*. It was through this couple that, two years later, Zhou Enlai would be inducted into the Communist Party.

The other was the diminutive, five-foot-one, round-faced, fifteen-year-old Deng Yingchao. She was the youngest of all the participants, but so competent, so blazing with energy, that she had become the head of the publicity section in the directing committee of the Women's Patriotic Association of Tianjin. Her name originally was Deng Wenshu, but finding it too tame, she changed it to the ringing one of Deng Yingchao, Surpassing Brightness.

Deng Yingchao's mother, Yang Zhende, had been married to an officer of the imperial army and was rejected by her husband's family when he was killed in 1908. A widow with a small daughter—Yingchao was born in 1904—she earned a living partly as a teacher and partly as an herbalist, having acquired some notions of herbal medicines from an uncle who kept a medicine shop. She did not bind the feet of her daughter, and sent her to one of the best schools of "new learning," the First Teachers Middle School for Women.

With such a mother, no wonder Yingchao had been a leader in patriotic activities since the age of thirteen. She read *Tianjin Student*, and had written to Enlai: "I am a faithful reader. . . . Do not give in to the forces of evil, stand firm." She signed herself Little Chao, and Enlai was puzzled, for he could not tell whether the name belonged to a boy or to a girl.

Now she came up to him. "I am the Little Chao that wrote to you." He was delighted. From the loftiness of his twenty-one years and his five feet seven, he gazed at the pugnacious fifteen-year-old and thought her a charming younger sister. "We did not think of love. Anyway, love between members of the Awareness Society was forbidden." When, years later, they did fall in love and marry, Enlai, who would always call her Little Chao, would say, "She was the youngest of us all, but even then she was better at making speeches and organizing people than I was."

Even if not a Marxist group, Awareness expected reprisals from the warlord government, so the members decided to use secret pseudonyms for the articles they wrote. Numerals were placed in a cup and drawn, and pseudonyms allotted according to the sound of the number picked. Enlai drew Number Five, and took the pseudonym Wu Hao.

Deng Yingchao proved to be fearless. A mass demonstration was organized on October 10. The police started clubbing the students. Deng Yingchao led a number of girls to hurl themselves at the police, shouting, "Policemen must love their country . . . do not beat up the young people who love China." "It was a fine battle," Deng Yingchao would reminisce. "We were so young then, and somewhat reckless."

Awareness issued its first pamphlet in December, another article by Zhou Enlai on knowledge of the self: "Necessary for continuous advance . . . which is endless." This unrelenting emphasis on man's individual conscience, on self-realization, shows that he is still far from being a Marxist. It is also reflected in his poems of that period, which are compassionate, not political.

> The west wind howls
> Winter is here
> I hail a rickshaw
> The puller's padded coat is like mine
> Even with it on I feel a chill
> But he removes his
> Says it is too heavy
> Places it round my feet
> I thank him for his care
> He thanks me for helping him
>
> Is this coexistence?
> Are we linked together?
> Do we share the same life?
>
> No No
>
> The labor of the living
> The inertia of the dead

In January 1920, several members of Awareness were arrested at the printing press, including Ma Jun. Arrests continued the following days. Thousand-Mile Horse was also detained. On January 29, Zhou Enlai led a group of students to the mansion of the governor to demand the release of the prisoners. A large police force guarded the walled premises, and the four delegates—among them Zhou Enlai and a Hui Muslim girl, Guo Lungzhen—were kept outside the barred main gate. Darkness fell, the temperature dropped well below freezing, and the students wanted to go home. But when the gate was closed the police forgot to put back the heavy log acting as a sill, so that a foot-high space below the two leaves of the gate enabled a nimble, slim Zhou Enlai to crawl into the mansion's front courtyard. The other three delegates followed him. In the courtyard Enlai found a ladder the police had used to watch the demonstrators from the wall tops. But now the police had retired into the warm rooms, and the courtyard was empty. Zhou climbed the ladder and addressed the shivering students outside. "Please wait and keep order. If we're not back in an hour, think of another way." And he proceeded to walk toward the mansion. The police emerged from the rooms and arrested the four, then streamed outside the gate to club and kick the waiting youths.

Altogether twenty-eight students, including the four delegates, were arrested and put in maximum-security cells, reserved for criminals condemned to death. Agitation for their release began. Deng Yingchao led teams to call on prominent citizens, organized "comfort the wounded" groups to visit the hospitals, launched a leaflet campaign. In March, Zhou and his companions went on hunger strike, and the news leaked out immediately, through sympathetic jailers. Deng Yingchao took two dozen girls to call on the chief of police. "Release the men students. It is our turn to go to jail, we too are student representatives."

The hunger strike made banner headlines throughout China. Protests poured in. On April 7 a dozen of the detainees were released because of ill health. Three of them were under fifteen years old.

Enlai and the remaining prisoners were moved to more comfortable quarters, allowed books, letters, and visits. Enlai asked for books on history, law, English, economics, and psychology, to organize a "prison university." Books on Marxism found their way in and Enlai would lecture on Marxism five times weekly. "We must keep our morale," he wrote in his diary. So the prisoners put together a variety show with singing and music on the anniversary of the May 4 Movement. A theater night was also held, and the same play Enlai had appeared in at Nankai, *A Dollar Coin*, was performed, much to the enjoyment of the jailers.

Li Yuju, a woman friend of Yingchao and Enlai, went to the jail to see Zhou and to say goodbye, for she was leaving for Europe. Did Zhou for a while fall in love with her? Did he change his mind? The answer is obscure. Deng, in one of her numerous interviews with me, did say that "Enlai was for a short while in love with someone else, but nothing came of it." "I am happy for you, do go on studying, and keep your innocence," Enlai wrote to Yuju, meaning not sexual innocence, but unsullied dedication. He wrote a long poem to her, a somewhat tedious one. In it he writes that they may meet "in Marseilles . . . or Paris." He was in jail, and though they all talked about going abroad, how could he know that he would be going to France? Enlai seems very pleased with this rather pedestrian poem. "I wrote it from 4 p.m. to 6:30. . . . I believe that, among my poems, this one can rate as 'upper middling.' "

The trial of the detained youths took place from July 6 to July 17. Zhou Enlai wrote to his lawyer, Liu Chungyu, who had offered his services free, crisply making four points for the defense. In court he rose to speak. While in the criminal section of the jail his head had been shaved, but the hair had now grown back. "All we wanted was to see the governor and present a petition. . . . How can this be accounted a crime?" Lawyer Liu was impassioned and eloquent; the judges, afraid of being accused of selling out to the imperialists, set the prisoners free after nominal charges for breaking and entering.

Now they were heroes. Offers of marriage came for Zhou Enlai, including a hint from lawyer Liu, who had a beautiful niece. "The country requires of us all our energy," was Zhou's reply. A grand procession of nine hired cars took the released youths to Taoranting Park, a lovely garden with its willows, its red-pillared pavilions and shaded footpaths. Opera singers performed, asking no fee. Firecrackers added to the "hot and noisy" happiness. Li Dazhao, squat, brisk, and beaming, made an impassioned speech. Zhou Enlai replied with one so stilted, so steeped in political phraseology, that reading it makes one ache for the awkwardness of his youthful enthusiasm. Possibly he was carried away by the Marxist literature he had read while in prison. "The road to saving our nation is . . . to immerse ourselves in the working people, rely on the working class, integrate all organizations in a common aim. . . . Only thus can China be saved."

Surely, among these tested and heroic youths, excellent material for the projected Communist Party could be found. Li Dazhao seems to have solicited the advice of Comintern agents on this matter of recruitment. Zhou Enlai and other potential recruits were taken to meet a Russian teacher at Peking University. The Russian was not particularly impressed by Enlai, possibly because Zhou, as usual, appeared "shy," examining and appraising the man who talked to him. The pomposity of his speech at Taoranting Park had disappeared. Other youths were chosen to go to Moscow for training, but not Zhou Enlai.

It was decided that Zhou would go to Europe, and first to France. Obviously, the decision was not his alone, since he had no money. Li Dazhao must have had a good deal to do with the choice. Even then, Zhou had made no definite commitment to Marxism, though he was studying it. Li Dazhao saw in him an organizer, an excellent communicator, as well as a young man of good looks and considerable charm, one whose persuasive talent and charisma would be of great value to the future Party.

Zhou Enlai was now twenty-two years old. His childhood had been marked by loss, poverty, and upheaval, yet he had managed to obtain a solid education in both the classics and the "new learning."

He had made a virtue of the strictures imposed upon him and learned to prefer an ascetic—and healthy—diet, though he could and did enjoy his drink, for which he had developed a very good head. He had perhaps lapsed into too great a love of sake during his period of depression in Tokyo (as Wu Dagen pointed out forcefully), but only twice in his future life was he known to overindulge again.

The Confucian code required of him that he take care of his family, but both the code and the family had fallen apart along with the Chinese Empire, and he himself had not so much abandoned Confucianism as begun to look for an ideology that could deal with the realities of his life. He had toyed with Zen Buddhism, and now, with his usual carefulness, he was feeling his way into Communism. But he never lost the feeling of responsibility as eldest son that Confucianism laid on him. As he was forced to wander farther and farther from his own family, the object of that responsibility became the whole of China.

Deng Yingchao was left in charge of the Awareness Society. She would be the indispensable link between Zhou and the other group members. Newspapers in Tianjin asked Zhou to write articles for them from Europe. They would pay him for these pieces. Zhou agreed. Deng Yingchao was perhaps already in love with Enlai, for she knitted a sweater for him and sewed at the back a small tape with the words "Take good care of your health" embroidered in minute stitches. On November 7, 1920, Enlai boarded the Messageries Maritimes ship *Porthos*, sailing from Shanghai.

To pay for the ticket to Marseilles, Yen Fangsun gave Zhou Enlai five hundred dollars, and so did lawyer Liu. This would enable Zhou to live for a few months on arrival in Europe. He traveled steerage, carrying in his luggage a Chinese-French dictionary. One hundred and ninety-six students were on the same ship bound for France.

4

In the four years that he was away in Europe, Zhou must have written hundreds of letters, sent hundreds of postcards, to all his friends. Deng Yingchao alone received more than 250 letters. He wrote at every stopover of the *Porthos*, from Saigon, Singapore, Colombo. At each of these ports, in countries then colonies of France or Great Britain, the Chinese students on board were humiliated. They needed passes to leave the ship for a stroll, while the Europeans on board came and went at will. "Now we realized that we were looked upon as inferior beings," commented Enlai. But in Saigon the large Chinese community turned out with flags and firecrackers to welcome the Chinese students. Enlai describes the scene to his brother Enshou in a long letter dated November 16. "They treat us as if we were of their own family. Saigon is much like Tianjin. . . . The river has many bends, and large boats sail up to dock." In Colombo he noted the flies which swarmed around the emaciated bodies of road laborers. "They are regarded as beasts, not men." But to his indignant fellow students, irked by the arrogance displayed toward the Chinese by the Westerners on board, he would remark, "Is not the fault also in ourselves? There are internal as well as external causes for a country's downfall." They were going abroad to learn how to change this. "We must never forget that the responsibility lies upon our generation." One of his pastimes on board ship was to try to learn French from the sailors, a dictionary in his hand.

The *Porthos* docked at Marseilles on December 13. The students were met by a member of the Sino-French Education Committee and boarded a train to Paris. In Paris, Enlai stayed with a former Nankai schoolmate, Li Fujing, who had taken the male lead when Enlai took the female lead in *A Dollar Coin*. He met again Liu Tsingyang and her husband, Zhang Shenfu. Liu Tsingyang had been jailed at the same time as Zhou Enlai, and with her husband had sailed on the *Cordillère* two weeks before Enlai left on the *Porthos* from Shanghai. Almost as soon as he arrived, Enlai became involved in the wrangle between the students and the education authorities running the "work and study" program.

The students were supposed to work in factories part of the time and study as well, their attendance at universities subsidized by the Boxer Indemnity Fund, an indemnity imposed on China for the "rebellion" of 1900–1. The funds were administered by the Sino-French Education Committee, and seemed to find their way into the pockets of officials rather than getting to the students. The net result was that the students simply provided a pool of cheap labor for the French, but did not receive the education for which they had come.

Enlai wrote to Yen Fangsun denouncing the committee. He penned articles for the *Yi Shibao* newspaper in Tianjin and for the *Awareness Bulletin*, describing how the students milled for hours in the crowded committee office, waiting for their stipends. "After eight hours of labor, most of them are exhausted. . . . They do not have enough energy left to study." He also noted that many of the youths arriving in France were ill prepared, their knowledge of the language inadequate. Quite a few were in poor health, and some went hungry. Their very low wages made it difficult to save enough to pay for their studies. "It takes five years of labor to save enough for three years of study." Zhou Enlai also noted that "French workers do not welcome the Chinese . . . they are resentful. The Chinese work for lower pay and take away jobs."

Perhaps because of this situation, Enlai and Li Fujing left for London on January 5. They stayed for a while at 35 Bernard Street, a student boardinghouse near Russell Square. Both applied for entrance to Manchester University, and Enlai also applied to Edinburgh. While waiting for the replies, he walked through London, wrote numerous letters and postcards, and collected material for more articles for *Yi Shibao*. He bought the English newspapers every morning and studied their contents. He visited the docks of the East End. He noticed the handicapped, the wounded of World War I, studied unemployment figures, commented on English institutions, on parliamentary democracy, and was very interested in the formation of the Labour Party. To his cousin Chen Shizhou he wrote: "My ideas are not yet coherent. I dare not draw any conclusions." He then speculates on revolution. If, in the U.S.S.R., revolution had been achieved through the violent overthrow of the ruling regime, perhaps in other countries it might be achieved "by other means." Quite obviously, the social revolution which was happening in England, and which he witnessed, seemed to him a nonviolent way of change. But could it apply to China? "My main aim is to study . . . to understand foreign countries and the character of their citizens . . . for the benefit of our people."

Of the fifty-seven articles he wrote for *Yi Shibao* during 1921 and 1922, many are on British foreign policy, on the coal miners' strikes in England, on the Labour Party, on British police brutality in Ireland and in the Middle East.

Edinburgh University accepted him; he need not take an entrance examination, only a test in English. But the university term started in October, and it was February. How would Zhou Enlai live while waiting until the autumn? He wrote again to his benefactor Yen Fangsun. He had decided to study, and could Yen help him to obtain a scholarship by using his influence with the education authorities? Possibly a provincial scholarship, from Zhejiang province, since his family originated from there? A scholarship was not forthcoming, but in February, Yen Fangsun sent more money to Enlai, as well as to Li Fujing. However, by March, Enlai was back in France. Life was too expensive in England, he wrote to cousin Chen Shizhou.

Back in France, he moved from suburb to suburb of Paris, finally settling at Montargis, where there was a school with many Chinese students. He moved in with Zhang Shenfu and Liu Tsingyang, who had begun to set up a Communist cell, which included a fiery, disputatious, and irascible young man named Tsai (now Cai) Hosen, his sister Tsai (now Cai) Chang, and his wife, Xiang Jingyu. All three had been members of Mao Dzedong's New People's Study Society. Enlai became part of the group, and in May 1921 Liu and Zhang sponsored him to become a Communist Party member. His Party membership was reconfirmed in the summer of 1922.

Did he join the Communist Party out of unquestioning conviction? He had hesitated for a long time. His was not, even when he joined, a blind faith in the tenets of Marxism, though it seemed to him the most likely way of changing China. "It is scientific, like the laws of Einstein," he said, somewhat naively. But he would never be an ideologue.

Ideas without practice, without action, seemed to him worthless, the question of whether they were correct or not a mere intellectual exercise. "Our country's great handicap is low productivity and undeveloped education. We need both industrial and agricultural techniques, but education is basic. . . . Productivity and education must go hand in hand." Certainly, dogma alone would never save China, but a political framework was needed to guide and to change Chinese society. Zhou Enlai would try Marxism.

He was immediately entrusted with "political and organizational work," in which he was seconded by another student, Zhao Shiyen. He organized Marxist talks and meetings for the students, interviewed prospective recruits for the Communist Party, arranged debates with non-Marxist groups, kept records, and last, but not least, ensured confidentiality, secrecy. Within two years the need for secrecy among Party members became obvious, as the French police, alerted to the activities of the foreign students, began a hunt for "extremists."

He enrolled for two months in a school to study French. He also received some private tutoring from a French Communist named Rappoport. But the demands of Party work made his attendances fitful. Since he had no money of his own, and his work was unpaid, he supported himself by writing articles, not only for *Yi Shibao* but for other newspapers as well.

During his first year in France, Zhou was involved in two major confrontations. One against the representatives of China's "government"—i.e., the Northern Coalition of warlords—and one against the Sino-French educational authorities.

The first was the affair of the so-called loan to China for flood relief. There had been catastrophic floods in North China, and a loan was floated, ostensibly to help the afflicted millions. But Zhou, as he carefully scrutinized the newspapers, realized that it was a fraud. One third of the 300 million francs granted went as commission to the Chinese warlords and to the arms companies of France. The remaining two thirds were earmarked to buy weaponry from these same armaments businesses. How could this be called a loan for flood relief? Zhou prepared a protest meeting, wrote a fiery denunciation which would be printed in *Yi Shibao* and other newspapers, and called a meeting, to which he also invited French newsmen. He denounced the loan, as well as the fact that, as collateral, China was to grant major concessions on her railways and on inland levies. *Yi Shibao* published the report, and the protests in China were so clamorous that the agreement had to be canceled. Zhou had discovered the power of the press.

The second incident in which Zhou was partly involved was the scheme to set up a new Sino-French university at Lyons. It sounded excellent, and the work-and-study students looked forward to such a university. But it soon became clear that only selected students from the French-Chinese university in Beijing and the Catholic university Aurore in Shanghai would be admitted, and not the work-and-study students. In fact, the Sino-French authorities, when the students protested, canceled the stipends they were giving. "If you cannot provide for yourself, then go back to China."

Fiery Tsai Hosen called a mass meeting in Paris. At this meeting an immediate march on Lyons, and the occupation of the university building by the students, was proposed, and seconded by Li Lisan, a student as forceful as Tsai Hosen. Zhou Enlai at first said not a word, then he rose to counsel prudence. "The enemy is trying to provoke us. If we take any action, there must be good preparation and planning." The marchers should divide into two teams. An "advance guard" would proceed to Lyons and occupy the buildings, but a "rear guard" should remain behind "and prepare for any emergency that might occur." Obviously, Zhou felt that a head-on confrontation with the French "forces of order" was risky. Together with Nie Rongzhen, he chose to be in the rear. Led by Tsai Hosen, 105 students went to Lyons, and entered the premises of the new university on September 21, 1921. On the twenty-second they were surrounded by 200 French policemen and arrested. They were imprisoned in deserted army barracks, and promptly went on a hunger strike.

In Paris, Enlai now mobilized public opinion, receiving the help of some French Communist Party members and members of the Chinese community. He arrived in Lyons at the head of a "comfort" delegation, carrying provisions and a black bag full of books. He demanded visiting rights, the distribution of blankets, the right to legal representation. "Why have you brought all these books?" asked a curious friend. "They will be useful to them should they have to stay in jail for a while," replied an utterly serious Zhou Enlai.

The 105 captives were released on October 13, only to be immediately expelled from France. Tsai Hosen, his wife, and his

Zhou Enlai at age ten with Manchu pigtail (1908)

Zhou Enlai as a student in Tianjin at age thirteen or fourteen (1912)

Zhou Enlai just before leaving
for Japan (1915)

一九一八年の七月二九日、当時函館商業学校の
国漢教師をしていた元木省吾（現在、北海道史編集
審議会委員）が、香川県丸亀に行く途中、東京発下
関行き急行列車の車中で周恩来と乗り合わせ、名
刺を交換している。周恩来はこのとき、浙江省の
ものだが休暇で天津に帰ることになった、などと
語っている。周恩来が元木氏に渡した名刺は石版

東京神田区高等予備学校
周恩来
翔宇

⑭周恩来の詩碑「雨中の嵐山」の除幕をする鄧穎超女史（一
九七九年四月一六日、京都・嵐山で）⑮元木省吾氏に渡され
た周恩来の名刺

Zhou's name card which he gave to Professor Shoto
Motogi on July 29, 1918

Zhou Enlai on his way to
France (1921–22)

Zhou Enlai with his wife,
Deng Yingchao, taken just
before or at their marriage in
August 1925

The main courtyard of the Zhou home in Huai An. Photo taken by the author on her visit in March 1988

Feng Yuxiang (Fong Yuxiang) with his son; Chou Yentong with his daughter, Han Suyin, and her nurse, Liu Ma (c. 1920)

sister Tsai Chang were shipped back to China, as was a burly, dashing student from Sichuan named Chen Yi. Besides washing dishes in restaurants and loading barges along the Seine quays, Chen Yi had also worked at Michelin and then at Le Creusot, and attended occasional courses at an art academy. He played football, recited classical poetry, and had a feisty sense of humor that Zhou relished. Zhou missed his boisterousness, his love of fun. Perhaps he missed Tsai's virtuous admonitions as well.

There were two thousand Chinese students in France, about two hundred in Belgium, the same number in England. The exact number in Germany is not known, possibly three to four hundred. For the next four years, not only in France but also in Belgium and Germany, Zhou Enlai was the chief recruiter, organizer, and coordinator of the activities of the Socialist Youth League. This put an end to any hope of his ever attending university courses, or taking a degree, or, as a nominal work-and-study Chinese student, holding a steady job in any factory.

His success with the students was immediate, and very satisfying. By 1922 no fewer than forty had been recruited, and more were being considered. Among this "French contingent" would be some of China's most prestigious, talented, and influential leaders in the revolution to come. All remained linked, not only by the particular loyalty of having been together in France but also by an enlarged vision of the world that they shared.

Enlai moved to the Billancourt area. At 19, rue Godefroy, a small boardinghouse, he rented a room on the second floor, a very small room, with a narrow bed, a table and a chair, the washbasin on the stairwell. A photograph taken outside the house shows him gaunt, wearing ill-fitting clothes, the sleeves of the jacket too short, the trousers riding well above his ankles. He was at the time short of money, and carried with him a small stove to warm up bread slices dipped in cabbage soup, his main meal.

In November 1921, Yen Fangsun again sent him money, and for this unquestioning liberality Zhou Enlai was always grateful. "Old and patriotic gentlemen helped us, with no personal political aims in view." When friends queried Yen Fangsun about helping a Communist, Yen replied, "Every able person must fulfill his own destiny."

Zhou's commitment to Marxism was not complete until the personal shock of a friend's death. Huang Ai, a member of Awareness, was killed in March 1922 while leading a strike among textile workers in Hunan province. He was the first Communist martyr of China. Deng Yingchao wrote two letters to Enlai telling him of Huang Ai's death. Zhou was grieved, and composed a poem to mourn his friend. "Huang Ai's sacrifice has greatly strengthened my commitment. I believe that I shall prove worthy of my friend." Not ideological conviction, then, but a surge of the heart. Zhou was aware that passion, emotion, play a role in political choice. "But once I had made up my mind, I never wavered."

"We all depended on Enlai to prepare our public statements, to handle all matters. . . . Once he arranged a meeting and read out a statement, one could be sure that, somehow, all the groups involved would agree," said one of his recruits. Unanimously, all those who worked with Zhou agreed that he was the best choice in the complex work of organizing Party branches.

And now the work became more demanding. There were still 40,000 Chinese workers in France, the remainder of the 200,000 sent in 1917. The small Communist Party vied for their allegiance against the "boss" system, against other parties, such as the anarchists. Night classes in Marxism were organized for the workers and of course this was also part of Zhou's responsibility. This meant a good deal of "verbal struggle," chiefly against the anarchists, who were strong in France at the time. There were clashes, and in one of these violence erupted and a few students were hurt. Zhou Enlai insisted on visiting not only the sympathizers but all those who had been wounded, including his opponents.

The work became more complex, secrecy imperative. He now traveled constantly, though unremarked, between Belgium, Germany, and France. He went in 1922, and again in 1923, to the Socialist University (Université de Travail) of Charleroi, where he spoke and organized seminars on Marxism for the Chinese students. There he cemented his lifelong close friendship with Nie Rongzhen, a Sichuanese. Nie studied engineering. He possessed a shrewd mind, grasping essentials swiftly. He remembered that even then Zhou discussed the need to study military science. "The Party cannot remain a debating club. . . . An army will be needed." Decades later, Nie would become known in China as the father of China's nuclear bomb.

He learned how to dress well. No longer was he an unkempt young man, but a smiling, quiet, and handsome Asian, who behaved admirably and wore well-cut clothes. Since he had no money, it is certain that the financing for these and for his travels came through the Comintern, now interested in Chinese recruits. A certain Suzanne Girault, a French Communist Party member, regularly brought money for the use of the Chinese Party cells.

Zhou Enlai was the man who safely conveyed future Party members from France and Belgium, through Berlin, to entrain for Moscow, there to be taught the art of revolution. He personally saw to the safety of each and every one of them. Zhou spent the greater part of the winter 1921–22 in Berlin and was there again in the spring and autumn of 1922. He stayed in lodgings on Kant Avenue, for which he paid twelve dollars a month. He also had the use of a room on the Wilhelmstrasse, possibly an accommodation provided by the Comintern. In Germany, as in France, he was popular, being polite, well-mannered, charming. He became a favorite of his landlady, and, it is said, of her young daughter, although there is no record of any romantic entanglement. Here, as in Paris, he mixed with the students, watching them play Ping-Pong, sometimes going with them to beer cellars. The nucleus of a Party cell was formed in Berlin, and he returned to Paris in June 1922 to represent the German branch of the Young Communist League of the Chinese students in Europe. The French and Belgian branches were represented by Zhao Shiyen and Nie Rongzhen. The League was formally inaugurated that June at a three-day meeting in the Bois de Boulogne. A publication called *Youth* was decided upon. Enlai was to be its editor and editorial writer. *Youth* was mimeographed in Paris, and Enlai was ably assisted by a stocky, square-faced youth, scarcely five feet four in height, whose name was Deng Xiaoping. Also from Sichuan province, Deng Xiaoping worked for five years in a rubber shoe factory in Garenne-Colombes by day. At night he wielded the mimeograph to print *Youth* magazine, as well as pamphlets, circulars, and papers for the workers' night classes. He thus acquired the nickname of King of the Printing Press. His friendship with Zhou began over this work and continued to the end of Zhou's life.

Zhou made a friend of the most unlikely recruit to Communism that one could imagine. Scarlet Virtue, Zhu De, was also from Sichuan province. Born in 1886, he had become a small warlord, with five concubines and an addiction to opium. But in May 1919 he became fired with patriotism, gave up opium, dismissed his concubines, and set out to search for Truth, by which he meant China's salvation. Through friends he managed, in late 1921, to meet with scholarly Chen Duxiu, prestigious editor of *New Youth* magazine and now the head of the newborn Chinese Communist Party, which had been inaugurated July 1, 1921, in Shanghai. "I would like to join the Communist Party," said Scarlet Virtue, who was already a member of some other parties as well as of the Gelao, or Brothers of the Robe, Sichuan's major secret society. Put off by Scarlet Virtue's past, his lack of finesse, and his piratical looks, Chen Duxiu gave him some Marxist literature to read and saw him out. Miffed but still hopeful, this strange would-be disciple of Marx took ship for Europe and landed in Paris. There, through some Sichuan traders and restaurant owners, he heard of Zhou Enlai, "the man who really decides." It was October 1922. Zhou Enlai was in Berlin. Zhu De managed to find him at the Kant Avenue address, where he saw, as the door opened, "a slender man, with a face so striking that it bordered on the beautiful." As usual, Zhou Enlai let his guest talk, while he watched, scanned him, and listened, head slightly cocked. Scarlet Virtue told his life story. Enlai was silent for a while, then asked, "Elder Brother, have you eaten?" It was dinnertime.

Enlai spent the next five or six days speaking with Zhu De. He then sponsored him to become a Party member, but enjoined upon Scarlet Virtue strict secrecy. "It is better not to be too open about such things now . . . the Party cannot remain merely a debating club." Both men discovered affinities. Zhu De loved orchids and music, and they shared a liking for Beethoven.

In beautiful Paris, handsome Enlai led an exemplary life, and there is no trace of any sexual relations in his years there. This was often commented on by his comrades. "I am too busy," he would reply, grinning. "It's better to stay single." He wrote to Deng Yingchao. Wrote and wrote. "We fell in love . . . writing to each other," Deng Yingchao said later.

Li Yuju, the girl who had come to see Enlai when he was in jail, arrived from London, and she and Enlai are photographed with a group of friends, on a walk through the Bois de Boulogne. Guo Lungzhen, the Muslim girl, also arrived in Paris in 1922. But it was to Deng Yingchao that he wrote of his delight in the beauty of France. He had gone with friends to the top of Notre Dame, and after climbing hundreds of steps, they had reached the roof, where "weird creatures, like the evil demons in our legends, crouched. . . . We looked at Paris in the deepening dusk. The waters of the Seine flowed, pale blue. The woods . . . were aglow with the rays of the setting sun. . . . We shouted *très bien*."

Before he was deported, hot-tempered Tsai Hosen viewed rather severely that streak of enjoyment in all things beautiful so apparent in Enlai. Zhou would exclaim, "What a pretty girl," or write to a friend, "Paris is beautiful . . . the girls are so pretty," and Tsai Hosen would protest. "You should not be intoxicated by beauty. The eyes of a true revolutionary must forever be fixed upon the suffering and exploitation of the working people." Zhou Enlai contritely wrote to Yingchao: "The company of Hosen is enough for me. . . . I have not made a single female friend . . . nor do I intend to do so."

Before being swallowed up by the need for utter secrecy, Zhou Enlai had had a photograph of himself, amiably colored, turned into a postcard, which he sent to all his friends in China. His friends told him that this was dangerous. The police might get hold of the postcards—he had ordered three dozen. There was also the dancing. He loved dancing. He learned to dance by going to popular ballrooms, where he never lacked partners. "I found the French people extremely friendly. . . . There seems to be no race distinction among you . . . and people of various races can intermarry," Zhou Enlai said decades later to French minister Alain Peyrefitte.

But not all Chinese students found it so. Wang Rofei, a friend of Enlai, wrote in his journal: "The people of this country treat us with a certain amount of contempt. . . . If one is trying to exchange courteous remarks, they will pretend that they do not hear."

In 1923 a major change in the policy of the young CCP—the Chinese Communist Party—was to take place. It was a change intimately linked to the directives of the Comintern.

Established in July 1921 by twelve delegates, among them the tall, dreamy-looking peasant from Hunan, Mao Dzedong, the CCP had rejected at its First Congress the suggestions made by Comintern agents of establishing a "united front" with Sun Yatsen and his newly founded Nationalist Party, or Guomindang.

The idea of a united front originated with Lenin, and it had been effective in countering the invasion of the U.S.S.R. by Western powers. Similarly, it could work in China, said Lenin. But of the twelve men who founded the CCP only two voted for the motion, and at first Sun Yatsen too was hostile when approached by Comintern agent Sneevliet, alias Maring. "I don't believe the leopard can change his spots. Russia's expansionist policies have not changed," Sun Yatsen said to Sneevliet-Maring.

The mild but incredibly tenacious Sun Yatsen, driven out by Western-sponsored militarists, had returned and clung with undiminished optimism to his aim of establishing a democratic republic in China. His stronghold was Guangzhou, and he had formed a party, the Guomindang—or Nationalist—Party. He had proclaimed a republican government, although controlling only one city. By 1922, he was changing in favor of a united front, which his Finance Minister, Liao Zhungkai, considered essential, as did his young and brilliant wife, Wellesley-educated Soong Chingling. They envisaged an anti-imperialist alliance of workers and peasants and the bourgeoisie. Nationalism and Communism together would drive out both the warlords and the imperialists.

The idea also made headway in the CCP, and at the Second Party Congress in 1922 "support" for "a democratic united front" was tabled and approved. Finally, in June 1923, at the Third Congress, a united front was adopted as the platform of the CCP, and Sun Yatsen had also become eager to have such an alliance in working order.

Zhou Enlai, the coordinator of Europe's Party branches, was now informed that the policy had changed and that confrontation with the Guomindang must now be replaced by cooperation with the Guomindang and its representatives in Europe. Zhou accordingly met with Sun Yatsen's Guomindang Party representative in Paris, Wang Jingqi, and suggested organizing a joint committee. He mentioned the Hui Muslim girl, Guo Lungzhen, as a person who could organize united front activities among the women students. Wang Jingqi was impressed by Zhou's practical suggestions and by the fact that he could produce eighty individuals to help the Guomindang reorganize itself. For indeed the Guomindang was badly run and needed the disciplined spirit which animated Communist Party cells. A united front with the Socialist Youth League was mooted. The magazine *Youth* now had to change its tone and the tenor of its articles. It also changed its name to *Purple Light* and became a united front publication.

In November, the Guomindang held its own party meeting in Lyons, and Zhou Enlai, invited to it, was co-opted as the director of its Executive Committee. He wrote to Wang Jingqi: "We wish at this time to exert every effort to make the Democratic Revolution, to perform the tasks required by it . . . We offer to help in all organizational work for the Guomindang." By January 1924, Zhou Enlai, his friend Nie Rongzhen, and the husband of Tsai Chang, Li Fuchun, were running the press and publicity sector of the Guomindang in Europe.

If intelligence is the capacity to hold two utterly different concepts at once in one's mind, then Zhou certainly qualified. He had to reconcile two very different political parties, find ground for agreement in the midst of discord. He had to remain a staunch Marxist yet adapt his actions, speeches, and writings to reassure, to sustain, to expand a patently non-Communist party. He had to manifest sweet reasonableness, mollify hostility, and lull suspicion. Here began his apprenticeship as statesman, as diplomat. He remained throughout his life, in fact, far more an artist of the united front proposition, with a genius for reconciling the irreconcilable, than a pure Marxist.

In the spring of 1924, Zhou took another group of Chinese students from France and Belgium to Berlin, and waved them off as they boarded the train for Moscow. Among them was Nie Rongzhen. Oddly enough, Zhou himself was not asked to go to Moscow. Perhaps his work—which was highly valued—was considered too important.

After attending the Guomindang Party Congress in July in Paris, Zhou received an order from the CCP Central Committee to return immediately, and to take charge of united front work between the CCP and the Guomindang in China itself. Evidently his European success in promoting cohesion, handling heterogeneous groups of disputatious youths with patience and skill, bringing about a united front despite much opposition—had been noted. Besides these achievements, he was known for a blameless life.

He was precisely the kind of person that was most needed to build the Party, cool, shrewd, and painstaking. He was gifted with the power of persuasion, and would exhort, discuss, convince the hesitant, reassure the confused. He never lost his temper and had great patience in arguing with choleric and excitable individuals. The brief upsurge of doctrinaire pomposity he had shown after being in prison had evaporated, and was replaced by shrewd practicality. That he was not a theoretician, that he was "ideologically weak," he would freely acknowledge. Unlike him, Tsai Hosen and another student from Hunan, Li Lisan, were addicted to much hairsplitting, especially Li Lisan, who was a brilliant speaker, and knew it. But whenever there was any work to do, his comrades always thought of Zhou Enlai.

His talent for acting stood him in good stead. In one of his personae, he was a handsome, diffident young student, much liked by the French because of his excellent manners, his courtesy, his way of saying "Madame" or "Mademoiselle" with a winning smile. His landladies at Colombey, where he stayed briefly, and in Berlin, were taken with the good looks and excellent manners of "Monsieur Knight." (His name had been Anglicized to John Knight on his passport, and this was the name by which he was sometimes known.) Well dressed and well behaved, above suspicion, he met with Chinese traders and restaurateurs who contributed money to help poor students. He was patriotic, eloquent, grateful. When he presented petitions of protest to the diplomats of the Chinese legation—representing the warlord coalition in Beijing—he became the authentic heir to the classical tradition, exuding righteousness. His dexterity in conciliating quarreling factions was even then remarkable. Unlike some of his colleagues, who developed at times a certain paranoia, he never broke down, never assumed an attitude of superiority. He continued to appear the most overt of men, even while practicing seamless concealment. Gone was the struggling, undirected, ambivalent student of Tokyo. Now he was many-faced, but consistent unto himself, like a rainbow which displays a many-colored arc by refracting colorless light.

Zhou Enlai left Marseilles in the beginning of August and arrived in Hong Kong on September 1, 1924.

Three months after his departure from France, the French security police discovered that he had been the main organizer of Communist cells in Europe. John Knight, alias Zhou Enlai, whose name they could not even spell properly, that handsome, smiling, suave student, who always sent flowers and remember-me cards to his landladies . . .

II

1924–1935

The First United Front
Wooing and winning Deng Yingchao
Chiang Kaishek takes over and
massacres Communists
The Long March
Mao Dzedong triumphs

5

Zhou Enlai was undoubtedly deeply in love with Deng Yingchao, yet when he returned from France and reached Hong Kong that September, he did not go to see her in Beijing. He was a responsible Party man, he had to set an example of selflessness and discipline, and so he went directly to Canton—now known as Guangzhou—arriving there on September 10. But he continued to write to Yingchao, and it seems he asked her several times to marry him. Yingchao was then a teacher and bookkeeper at the Tajen school for girls in Beijing, a school established and run by Thousand-Mile Horse, Ma Qianli. Zhou sent a good many letters to her in care of him as school director, but Ma was afflicted with absentmindedness and shoved the letters into a drawer until a friend of Enlai came to inquire. Enlai was worried when he received no reply. "I think they're here," Ma said, opening the drawer. Out from it spilled a dozen unopened letters.

The headquarters of the regional committee in Guangzhou were on the second floor of a building on Wen De Road. It was the only Communist office which operated openly in China. Zhou was appointed secretary of the United Front Regional Committee for the two provinces of Guangdong and Guangxi. Guangdong was the province over which Sun Yatsen exercised precarious control, and in adjacent Guangxi, the warlords, for the time being, supported Sun's "government."

Guangzhou was a vital and boisterous city, with a fertile hinterland and abundant water from the Pearl River. It was a major port, its existence dating back to two centuries before Christ, when, legend said, a genie leading five rams settled here. Hence it was also called the City of Rams. Its people are energetic, quarrelsome, and even today cling fiercely to their own dialect, Cantonese. One wonders how Zhou managed, since he did not speak

Cantonese. Yet he is reported to have made a major speech in October to a crowd of 5,000.

In that year the people of Guangzhou were filled with hope. They had a long history of opposition to the *fankui*, the foreign devils. Whole villages had gone to war against the British during the nineteenth century armed with nothing but spears. For the last two centuries the province had supplied immigrants to many countries, since the colonial powers required labor for their plantations in Southeast Asia. Immigration had accelerated in the nineteenth century, and thousands had flocked abroad, bought at eight dollars a head, to build the railways of the New World and to dig the Panama Canal. Half of the Overseas Chinese communities came from this one province.

Sun Yatsen was partly an Overseas—though born in China— having been educated in Hawaii and having stayed many years abroad. He had strong connections with communities outside China. His Foreign Minister, Eugene Chen, was an Overseas, born in Trinidad. His Finance Minister, Liao Zhungkai, came from a distinguished Overseas family, as did his wife, Soong Chingling.

Zhou Enlai's four years in Europe, enlarging his horizons, made it easy for him to mix and communicate with the Overseas. In the CCP office at Wen De Road, he met a motley crowd, workers and students, the latter from all over China, peasants from the surrounding villages, officials of the Guomindang, merchants, bankers, and traders. Everyone seemed dedicated to the United Front. In January 1924, Sun Yatsen had officially proclaimed an alliance between the Guomindang and Communist parties and a plan for a military expedition to unify China and destroy the warlords. Now Russian ships unloaded crates of weaponry at the docks of Guangzhou. Comintern advisers from Moscow came and went in Sun's entourage. The Huangpu Military Academy was set up in March to train officers for the armies that would march against the warlords. In October, little more than a month after his return, Zhou became director of its political department.

But though the United Front was acclaimed, it remained, for many, more figment than fact. The Guomindang government of Sun Yatsen was riddled with intrigue, "as a sponge with holes," as his own wife said. Hostility to the alliance with the Communists ran deep among the bankers and businessmen of the Guild of Merchants, fearful of change. The Western powers too regarded this alliance with much distaste. From Hong Kong, money and weapons went to the Guild to foment trouble, and Zhou was aware of the danger. "The Guild has the help of the British imperialists. They are mustering their own armed forces, and their weaponry is better than ours," he told Sun Yatsen when he called upon him to pay his respects in October. The Guild also had the support of several local warlords.

The CCP regional committee had organized a workers' militia and a peasant militia. When the Guild declared a general strike, it failed to rouse the populace. The planned coup petered out, but it convinced Zhou that the CCP, in order to survive, must have "an army of its own." "The Guomindang is a coalition of treacherous warlords," he told his friend Nie Rongzhen, who came from Moscow to join him in the City of Rams.

The army to be formed was supposed to be under the direction of the "revolutionary Guomindang," as Sun's party was then known. To create a separate, Communist-led army, to organize nuclei of officer-cadets who were CCP members—and this in the Huangpu Military Academy—was this not going against the principles of the United Front? Not at all, Zhou would argue, since one could be *both* Guomindang and Communist. Mao Dzedong and Zhou himself were members of both parties, as were many others. If in France he had worn two hats, as a Communist promoting Guomindang organizations, he now wore several more, since he was in charge of both civil and military affairs in two provinces, and giving courses in politics at the Huangpu Military Academy, reconciling the thousand and one incompatibilities between the Guomindang and its variegated groups of landlords, warlords, opportunists of all kinds, and the austere, high-caliber intellectuals who formed the core of the CCP leadership at the time. But how could he make the Guomindang accept that the peasantry and the workers must no longer be exploited, when the income of so many of its members was founded upon this exploitation? "We need a society of Great Harmony . . . these have been the ideals of our civilization for many centuries. When the Great Way comes into being, the world belongs to the public, and all benefits the people." Paraphrasing the classics, and also Sun Yatsen, Zhou sounded reverently traditional, while actually speaking of Communism.

He dutifully called on Chen Duxiu, secretary-general of the CCP, then in Guangzhou. Chen told the younger man that the urgent need was to preserve "unity." There must be no violent discord, no overt provocation. Zhou went to see Liao Zhungkai, then Sun Yatsen's Finance Minister. The Liao family were world-traveled, multilingual, and dedicated patriots. Liao Zhungkai's son, Liao Chengzhi, then a youth of eighteen, describes his meeting with Zhou. "He was neatly dressed. He walked quietly. He had keen eyes, thick eyebrows . . . he never missed anything . . . he seemed to photograph the room, the people in it."

The Liao home became one of Zhou's favorite haunts. Here he met Soong Chingling, Sun Yatsen's wife. Somewhat frustrated by the devious characters milling around her husband, Chingling often came to see her friend Madame Liao, a well-known painter. Soong Chingling found Enlai very courteous. "He spoke with women as he did with men. . . . One felt at ease with him."

In the winter of 1924–25, everyone in the city knew that Sun Yatsen was ill, was dying of liver cancer. What would happen when he died?

Comintern chief adviser Michael Grusenberg, better known as Borodin, and Vasili Blucher, known as Galen, were the top advisers of Sun's government. Blucher was the military expert, Borodin the political expert. Borodin was an imposing six-footer, with a handlebar mustache, a booming voice, and an American wife. "No friction, no ruction," he warned Zhou Enlai. Moscow's directives were to keep the United Front in smoothly running order. To Zhou's argument that "without an army there cannot be a strong party, and therefore no revolution," Borodin replied that Zhou was "too much in a hurry." Obediently, Zhou praised the doctrine of Sun Yatsen, the democratic revolution, the Guomindang Party; at the same time, he covertly exerted himself to create, within the Huangpu Military Academy, a cadet corps that would follow the principles of Marx.

Nie Rongzhen was now appointed vice-director at the Huangpu Military Academy. Chen Yi arrived and became an instructor. Zhou discovered tall, handsome Ye Jianying, Heroic Sword. Ye was a Hakka, from a district in the province that had produced more heroes and martyrs for Sun Yatsen's ill-fated insurrections than any other group in China. Heroic Sword was Enlai's age, fond of well-cut clothes, in appearance almost a dandy, and from a family of merchant traders. Another discovery was Ye Ting, a Cantonese, from a well-to-do family with relatives in Hong Kong. The two men were to become Zhou's intimate friends and loyal supporters. With them he began to organize a special corps of cadets for a future Red Army. He held seminars for these prospective Party members. His spirits rose. Perhaps, in the end, he would succeed. . . .

The Huangpu Military Academy was as much a hotbed of intrigue as any other arm of Sun's government. Zhou discovered with dismay that of the first batch of 800 cadets, enrolled in May 1924, two thirds were affiliated with the Shanghai secret societies. This was not altogether surprising. Secret societies have a long history in China, and Sun Yatsen himself had relied on their help. Here was a dilemma, one with which Zhou would have to live for many years. Could membership in a secret society be reconciled with Party membership? In the end, which loyalty would prevail?

With the second and third batches of cadets admitted to Huangpu, Zhou had more luck. In the fourth term, among 460 cadets attending his lectures, 90 would become Party members. Ye Ting also succeeded in organizing an armored regiment, later to be known as the Ironsides, and Ye Jianying formed two pro-Communist companies of cadets.

For a while it all seemed very easy. Zhou Enlai and his band of young Marxists met no hindrance to their activities, even from the director of the Huangpu Military Academy, Chiang Kaishek, who at the time appeared fiercely revolutionary.

Chiang Kaishek was forty years old. He had been trained in Baoding at China's first military academy, and then in Japan. He was trusted by Sun Yatsen for several reasons: He had rescued the ever-trustful Sun from a warlord who had kidnapped him, and he was well connected with the secret societies. Chiang's adoptive "father" was the right-hand man of China's most notorious Godfather, head of the Shanghai Green Gang, Du Yuesheng, known as Big-Eared Du.

The two nephews of Chiang's adoptive "father," Chen Lifu and Chen Guofu, known as the CC clique, were very active in the Huangpu Military Academy, organizing the cadets against the CCP. The creation of the Blueshirts in the 1930s, a pro-fascist organization modeled on Hitler's Brownshirts, is attributed to the Chen brothers. The Blueshirts took an oath of loyalty to the Leader—i.e., Chiang Kaishek. *Mein Kampf* later became compulsory reading for them.

"I have full trust in you," Chiang Kaishek said, smiling broadly, exhibiting the flash of his false teeth—he wore dentures very early—to Zhou Enlai. They came from the same province. They vied in an exchange of compliments. Chiang had been to the U.S.S.R. He had left his son there to study at the Moscow Far East University. "I would kill my own brother should he turn against the revolution," asserted Chiang Kaishek. "Do not cross Chiang in any way. We must work with him. I am sure he is fundamentally sympathetic to us," Borodin told Zhou Enlai.

As political director, Zhou emphasized in his lectures that a revolutionary army protected the people, cared for them. It did not loot or rape. "Our army is not a tool of oppression, it is to liberate the people and overthrow their oppressors." There must be iron discipline, at all times. To help the cadets grasp these new concepts—new in China, where the peasantry was considered hardly more than an expendable pool of cheap labor—Zhou wrote some textbooks and a small booklet on imperialism, a brief history of the invasions of China by the Western powers. It was used in the classes for adult literacy set up by the Party Regional Committee, as well as by the cadets of Huangpu.

Sickly pale, his emaciated frame wrapped in a padded robe, Sun Yatsen set off in December 1924 for Beijing. The warlord coalition there had gone through some changes, and they had made tentative approaches to Sun Yatsen. Within his Guomindang Party, the powerful right wing was bitterly opposed to the Communist alliance. They sensed that the projected military expedition to oust the warlords might turn out to the advantage of the Communists. Far better to negotiate with the Beijing coalition. "Making deals with one or another warlord is doomed to failure," Zhou warned. "It is a betrayal of the revolution." But Sun was an eternal optimist. With his wife, Sun first went to Japan, where he received a most enthusiastic welcome from the Chinese community and his many Japanese friends. He arrived in Beijing in January, and it was very clear that he was much worse. He could not keep up with the grinding round of banquets and talks, banquets and countertalks, proposals and counterproposals. In February he was carried to the hospital, where he was attended by the best doctors and nurses. He died on March 12. A crowd of 100,000 followed his coffin to the railway station, from where a train would take it to South China.

Sun was not only a physician, a politician, a revolutionary, and a secret society man; he was also a Christian, and his wife insisted that a Christian hymn be played by the band that accompanied the coffin. Sun was fifty-eight years old, his wife thirty-two. She was expected to remain secluded, a model widow, but her alert mind, her unyielding integrity, her love for her country, dictated otherwise. Soong Chingling would play an important role in the next decades of China's revolution. Her friendship with Zhou Enlai may also have influenced the choices she made.

No sooner was Sun dead than trouble broke out in Guangzhou. A warlord named Chen Chiungming, who had never forgiven Sun because the latter, after seeking his help, had ignored him, now made a bid to reconquer the city and the province.

The East Expedition, as the military offensive against Chen Chiungming was called, was Zhou Enlai's first opportunity to test the quality of his cadets. Some three hundred of them made up the political core of the forces, maintained discipline, assured liaison with superior officers. The expedition started in late March. The troops were backed by young pioneers of the Communist Youth League and the workers' militia. It was a new kind of army that went against warlord Chen, and the first battles were crowned with success. Zhou Enlai and Ye Jianying personally led the battalions in combat. The response of the peasantry was remarkable. The villagers lined the roads to welcome the troops, brought water and food, carried the wounded on improvised litters—the wooden doors of their own houses. "Never has this been seen in China before," wrote the newspapers. Zhou personally investigated any lapse of discipline. He collected the names of the dead, to give them honorable burial. He condoled with the families. He delegated men from the Regional Committee to the villages to organize peasant militia and self-protection units in the conquered territory.

Zhou returned to Guangzhou in a blaze of glory. Chiang Kai-shek, apparently very pleased, promoted him to head Huangpu's martial law bureau. He also became director of the political department of the recently organized First Army. He swiftly crushed an attempted coup by another warlord in the city itself, and became even more well regarded.

In October 1925, Chen, the warlord, beaten but obstinate, once again took the field, and again Zhou led the cadets of the First Army in battle against him. He had with him 160 trained political cadres, who proselytized the population. Zhou did not preach

Communism; he praised the doctrines of Sun Yatsen, called the Three Principles. But the manner of doing things, the fraternization with the populace, the slogans against imperialism and the warlords, were certainly Communist-inspired. In November he captured the important city of Shantou—also known as Swatow —on the South China coast. This was a major victory. He was immediately promoted special commissioner of Shantou and of the surrounding region.

The British, hostile to Sun Yatsen's government, were enforcing a blockade of the port of Guangzhou. Shantou could become a substitute port, where Russian ships could land their equipment and weapons without interference. Zhou started to build up a Party branch in Shantou itself. Membership was kept secret, and this would prove to be lifesaving.

These military exploits, achieved by novices in the art of war, were not so much due to technique as to the enthusiasm, the discipline, the political motivation of the army units. They were also the result of support by the people. In the history of the CCP, Zhou is recognized as the man who first applied the precepts of a "revolutionary army" to China, although this does not negate the fact that Mao would do the same, and under far more difficult circumstances, some years later. The contributions of Nie Rongzhen, of Ye Jianying, of Ye Ting, all three trained at the military academy in Moscow, were essential. Among the Party leadership, the concept of an independent "Red Army," still embryonic, was strengthened by the success of the East Expedition carried out by Zhou Enlai.

A congress of the CCP was held in Shanghai in January 1925. There were then 995 registered Party members. Two years later there would be 58,000. Divergences arose as to the way the United Front should be managed. The more militant members, among them Mao, stated that the CCP would lose credibility if it did not carry out its promises of land reform and stop the inhuman exploitation of workers in the factories. But Chen Duxiu, with Borodin's backing, insisted that this would bring unbearable pressures on the Guomindang. The delegates were to "restrain"—which in effect meant almost to punish, at least to suppress—the spontaneous uprisings among peasants dispossessing their landlords.

Mao Dzedong was very dissatisfied. He mentioned the daily clashes in Guangzhou itself. He pointed out, "We are very vulnerable to a coup from the right wing of the Guomindang." Zhou shared his view and argued that "too much compromise . . . will end in failure," but did not sound as extreme as Mao. He described the creation of Party nuclei among the officer-cadets in Huangpu. Mao was impressed, and ten years later he would mention in an interview to foreign newsmen Zhou's early contribution to building the Red Army.

Borodin overrode the objections made by Party members such as Mao. All precipitancy must be avoided, and the congress contented itself with repeating that "a worker-peasant alliance is fundamental to the prosecution of the projected expedition against the warlords," but did not actively take any steps. However, Mao did open a Peasant Training Institute in Guangzhou, and a year later Zhou Enlai was asked by Mao to deliver a lecture to the classes. There is no clue as to what Mao's and Zhou's first impressions of each other were, nor is it clear when, and how, and where, they first met. But Zhou did not appear to despise or to disregard Mao Dzedong, as did some other Party leaders. Zhou printed Mao's first essay on the peasantry in a journal used by his classes in Huangpu, whereas Chen Duxiu had refused to publish it in the official Communist newspaper. Mao was not reelected to the Central Committee, however, and returned to his province of Hunan. It was there, in the midst of his own peasantry, that he was to produce his pathbreaking major works, asserting the strength of China's peasantry and its potential for revolution. This view was for many years regarded by Russian-trained Communists as unorthodox, as "peasant mentality," un-Marxist.

Zhou had another opportunity at a congress meeting to send a letter proposing marriage to Yingchao. By then, the latter had also entered the Party (in 1924) and was in charge of the Party's women's section for the province of Hebei, in North China. At the congress Zhou had met a Party member named Gao, who suffered from unrequited love. Zhou confessed to him his own feelings, and Gao offered to take yet another letter and deliver it directly into Yingchao's hands. "Thank you for being our matchmaker," Yingchao said demurely to Gao when she received the letter. And that meant yes. Party approval was swiftly obtained. By the summer Yingchao had been transferred to work in Guangzhou, as director in charge of the women's section of the Regional Committee headed by Enlai. At last, the two were together.

They married on August 8, 1925, in such simple fashion that

the occasion went almost unperceived. They gave a small reception for a few friends at the White Cloud Hotel, sited in a beautiful cluster of low hills some kilometers away from the city. Perhaps they spent a few days there, on honeymoon, but even today Yingchao almost blushes when talking of those blissful days. For undoubtedly they loved each other, and the photographs show it. Palpably, there is fulfillment, tenderness radiates from these black-and-white prints. They would occasionally—seldom, for Zhou was a busy man—lie late in bed, talking and laughing, surrounded by newspapers and books. They would also have loud arguments, for Yingchao had a mind of her own. They quarreled violently, as the young do, then fell sobbing into each other's arms.

A triumvirate to run the Guomindang government was established in Guangzhou after Sun Yatsen's death in March 1925. It was formed by Liao Zhungkai, who represented what was called the "left wing" Guomindang—i.e., those in favor of the alliance with the Communists. The right wing was represented by a man named Hu Hanmin. The third man was Wang Jingwei, a remarkable personage, who began his career as an ardent patriot and ended as a stooge of Japan.

In May 1925, British soldiers killed fifty-six workers in front of Shameen Island, an enclave reserved for European commercial firms and houses. In Shanghai, a dozen Chinese workers were shot dead by British police. Throughout China, uprisings against foreigners took place. This was called the May 30 Movement.

A strike was declared by the workers' unions in Hong Kong, and 100,000 workers left the colony to come to Guangzhou. The strike was to last eighteen months. It seriously crippled Hong Kong's commerce, but it proved a heavy financial burden upon Guangzhou. The CCP organized a Strike Committee to care for the workers, but the finances of the city suffered, daily necessities became scarce, and inflation set in.

On August 20, 1925, twelve days after Zhou Enlai's marriage to Deng Yingchao, Liao Zhungkai was murdered by two hired thugs. "It is a sinister plan," said an apprehensive Zhou. Chiang Kaishek clamped military rule upon the city, "to prevent a counterrevolutionary coup." He took over the police, organized a security corps, sent his own trusted men into every trade union, and thus assumed control of Guangzhou.

Borodin, who seems to have been totally unaware of Chiang's disguised takeover, lauded Chiang's action "to protect the revolution." And to compound the double-crossing comedy, the right-wing member of the triumvirate, Hu Hanmin, was forced to resign, as apparently one of his relatives was implicated in the hiring of the thugs who murdered Liao Zhungkai. Now in charge of the Guomindang government of the city and the province were only two men: Wang Jingwei, accounted "left" and favorable to the Communists, a man both unpredictable and treacherous, and Chiang Kaishek, commander in chief of the Guomindang armies. The second would prove far more dangerous in the end.

"High did our spirits soar, higher than heaven," wrote a poet. It was good to believe in those young days, when revolution seemed the answer to all the ills of mankind. Communists from other countries now came to the City of Rams. André Malraux from France, Anna Louise Strong from America . . . In the autumn of 1925 came a wispy, fragile-looking Vietnamese who at the time called himself Nguan Ai Guoc—Love of Country. He would be known, some years later, throughout the world, as Ho Chi Minh. He and Zhou had met in Paris in 1921, but it was with Tsai Chang, sister of the impetuous Tsai Hosen, that Ho had formed an easy friendship. And now Tsai Chang and her husband, Li Fuchun, were both in Guangzhou, and took Ho Chi Minh under their care. In a small house on Wenmin Road lived some thirty Vietnamese revolutionaries who had escaped the French colonial police by slipping across the border into China. The Regional Committee looked after them, and Tsai Chang and Deng Yingchao were delegated to give them lessons in Chinese. Zhou Enlai enrolled Ho Chi Minh in the Huangpu Military Academy under a pseudonym. News from inside Vietnam came more or less regularly through a courier system in Guangxi province, which has a common border with Vietnam. In a very short time, Ho Chi Minh could speak the dialect, and he also acted as "secretary"—interpreter—to Borodin. "He was my teacher . . . my elder brother," said Zhou Enlai of him. "He was more mature, politically, than I was."

The euphoria was broken in January 1926 when Zhou Enlai's secretary was arrested for sending a report on the Marxist cells in Huangpu to the Communist headquarters in Shanghai. Chiang Kaishek summoned Zhou. Zhou was cheating, he was two-timing the United Front by establishing clandestine groups. Zhou denied any double-dealing. The CCP was trying to make the United Front work successfully. Of course it had the right to recruit members, as the Guomindang did. The issue was shelved, but Zhou warned Borodin that "some of the leaders may not be as friendly as you think they are." He suggested an indirect threat, such as temporarily cutting off supplies to the Guomindang. "All friction must be avoided," repeated Borodin. The incident was trivial. "There are too many incidents, large and small ones," countered Zhou. He had noticed a falling-off in adherents to the CCP among the Huangpu cadets. Many were giving up their membership, claiming that peasant turmoil in several provinces was the result of Communist influence. Patriotic the cadets might be, but they came from landlord or merchant families and did not want a change in the feudal system. "You are asking me to renounce my ancestors," one of them said to Zhou, who in vain tried, for some hours, to bring him around.

On March 18, while Borodin was in Shanghai enrolling his children in the American School there, the commander of a gunboat belonging to the Guomindang received a telephone message to proceed to the Huangpu docks, with full equipment, there to be inspected by Commander in Chief Chiang. The naval man did so, arriving in battle array, to find troops and police platoons mustered in large numbers at the docks. He was arrested, along with his crew. A swoop upon the First Army headquarters followed. Forty Communists were arrested. Another twenty-five, including Nie Rongzhen, were arrested at the Huangpu Military Academy. The Strike Committee, the trade union headquarters, were raided. A state of emergency was declared, with curfew and street patrols.

Zhou Enlai had just returned from Shantou. He was detained for forty-eight hours, then released. He immediately went to see Chiang Kaishek and accused the latter of breaking the United Front. "No, it is a plot by your party," Chiang replied. Why had a gunboat, armed for battle, suddenly appeared at the docks? The naval officers involved were students in Zhou Enlai's classes at Huangpu. . . .

There followed some confused exchanges, and then Borodin returned from Shanghai.

Chiang, it is said, fell sobbing upon his neck, and spoke of plots to kidnap him. Borodin reassured Chiang, swore there was no plot, rebuked Zhou Enlai, whose trainees "have indulged in excesses." Chen Duxiu came in person to apologize to Commander in Chief Chiang. The Guomindang Executive Committee ratified Chiang's decision to withdraw all Communist officers from the First Army. "In view of the events, the comrades of the left . . . should retire for a while." Wang Jingwei, at the time reckoned "left wing," was persuaded to leave for Europe on a study tour. Chiang asked for lists of names of all the members of the CCP who were also members of the Guomindang. Chen Duxiu, on Borodin's advice, supplied the lists, though Zhou withheld the names of those he had inducted secretly.

On April 11, Zhou Enlai was dismissed from the directorship of the Huangpu political department. On the fifteenth he was relieved of his assignment as head of the Regional Committee for Shantou.

The evidence, so far as one can tell, points to a manufactured crisis, possibly engineered by Chiang, an exercise in psychological warfare, to test Communist strength and willingness to react to a challenge, its preparedness for a showdown. Had the CCP reacted energetically, had Borodin threatened to cut off supplies, history might have been different.

Chen Duxiu wrote in the Party paper, *The Guide*: "Anyone who criticizes or attacks Mr. Chiang . . . is a counterrevolutionary."

Zhou's reputation shredded like cloud in a buffeting breeze. Discredited, he refused to discuss, to comment, or to complain. He continued to give political training classes, but now at the Tafosze, the Big Buddha temple in the city. He went to see Ye Ting, in charge of the armored battalion, the Ironsides. "This corps is now the only formation directly under Party leadership, and it must remain so." He told Ye Ting that he would no longer visit him in his house, in order not to compromise him. "We shall meet again, perhaps in Wuhan."

Wuhan, the large metropolis on the Yangtse River, was the first target of the planned Northern Expedition to be launched against the Beijing government and the warlords in July. And because it could not be carried out without the help of the Communists, a compromise was worked out. The expelled Communist cadres and officers were reintegrated into the First Army.

In *Random Notes on China*, Edgar Snow reports a conversation with Zhou which throws light on his thinking during the years 1924–26 in Guangzhou.

"Our first mistake, unquestionably, was in not deepening the revolution among the peasantry, especially in Guandong and Guangxi provinces, where peasants were already armed. Secondly, we failed to develop the necessary leadership among cadres of the Guomindang army. We let slip out of our grasp many good officers. . . . In 1926 it would still have been possible for us to enlist and equip ten divisions . . . had we energetically sought to do so. We threw away our chance." But that was hindsight.

Zhou Enlai continued to teach and to train political cadres for the several army corps of the Northern Expedition. He also fulminated against the Guomindang "right-wingers" who objected to the mobilization of peasants and workers. They must be involved, wrote Zhou, for the success of the expedition depended on it. He stressed the need for unity. However, he did not accompany the armies marching to Wuhan, though his friends Nie and Ye Ting went off with the troops on July 9.

The expeditionary forces were cheered by exultant crowds. People lined the streets, waved banners, beat drums, and clashed cymbals. Success was astonishingly swift, not so much due to military prowess as to the eager cooperation of the population. A good many astute warlords, instead of fighting the oncoming armies, joined with their troops, thus swelling the numbers of the expeditionary forces, but also bringing a dilution of idealism and discipline. In October, the Northern Expedition reached its goal, the metropolis of Wuhan.

Zhou Enlai was given two assignments in December, which appear bafflingly contradictory, the result of the crisis taking place in Moscow, the conflict between Stalin and Trotsky. One of the major subjects of this dispute was Comintern policy in China. Trotsky asserted that the CCP must break off with the Guomindang, because the latter would inevitably betray the revolution and ally itself with the imperialists. Stalin maintained the opposite. *Theses on the China Problem*, published by the Comintern, insisted that the United Front must be maintained, the Communists must stay with the Guomindang and support its "left wing," against its "right wing."

Dutifully, Zhou passed on the directives. Comrades must join the Guomindang-led army under Chiang Kaishek. They must strengthen it, "and not carry out independent work." This was quite contrary to what he had been doing in Huangpu. But together with these directives came others. Zhou Enlai must now go to Shanghai, there to prepare a workers' uprising, to confirm Stalin's correctness. For the revolution was to be made by "the proletariat," the workers.

Leaving Deng Yingchao in Guangzhou, Zhou Enlai went to Shanghai in December. Yingchao had become pregnant three months after her marriage in August 1925. Owing to the uncertainty prevailing at the time, the couple had decided on an abortion. "We felt a child would interfere with our work for the revolution." But by July 1926 she was pregnant again, and since the Northern Expedition had started and the future looked promising, they decided to keep the baby.

6

Shanghai, the most glamorous city of the Far East, was known throughout the world as the paradise of adventurers. Here merchant princes dealing in opium and weapons lived in fabulous luxury. Here lived 80,000 prostitutes and 800,000 workers. The workers endured nightmarish lives, toiling under inhuman conditions, huddled in festering slums. Dead bodies were picked off the streets in winter and dumped casually on garbage heaps. The women workers in the textile factories who gave birth kept their babies under their machines. Shanghai was the domain of secret societies, such as the Green Gang of Big-Eared Du, and of Chiang's adoptive father, or its rival the Crimson Gang. The gangs owned houses and hotels, banks and brothels, even in the foreign concessions; their favorite haunts were in the French Concession with its dance halls, luxury hotels, and accommodating police. Paradoxically, it was also in the French Concession that the Chinese Communist Party had been founded, at 21, rue Beyle, in July 1921. It was in the French Concession that Zhou Enlai now had his headquarters, at 25, rue Lafayette.

Zhou had two jobs, one running the Front for Military Affairs, the other as head of the Regional Committee for the province of Zhejiang. He lived, and had an office, in the Shanghai Commercial Press Building. With him were several of the men who had been in Paris: Zhao Shiyen; dour Wang Rofei, who had not found the French as amiable as Zhou did; Li Lisan, expelled after the Lyons incident. But the key man, with seven years' experience of Shanghai and its working class, was an agile southerner named Lo Yinung. The first thing that Lo did was to set up a bodyguard for Zhou Enlai. "In this city it only costs twenty dollars to kill a man." Lo Yinung was versatile, zealous, and had many connections. Though not a secret society man, he knew a good many of them and so could easily arrange for safe houses.

Revolution permeated the air the Shanghai workers breathed. There had been a strike in May 1926, another one in October. Lo Yinung and Zhao Shiyen, who worked with the trade unions, were planning a third strike for February 1927. Zhou did not take part in it, though he observed what his comrades did. The time seemed propitious. The forces of the Northern Expeditionary armies had reached Hangzhou, the beautiful city of temples and lakes not far from Shanghai, on February 18, 1927. A good augury, thought Lo Yinung. The strike started with 150,000 workers on the nineteenth, and 350,000 were on strike by the twenty-second. But the local warlord, Sun Chuanfang, sent in his troops and executioners; the Northern Expeditionary armies in Hangzhou did not move. On the twenty-second Zhou decided the strike should be wound up. "This is only a rehearsal," he told the puzzled workers. "The next strike will have to be well prepared." With satisfaction he pointed to the "panic among the imperialists in the concessions caused by the February strike."

In March, the Northern Expeditionary forces took control of the two provinces of Jiangsu and Zhejiang. Shanghai was isolated, and warlord Sun Chuanfang fled. Only a petty militarist with 3,000 men still hung on in the vicinity of the city. Zhou decided that the time was ripe. He sent messages to the CCP in Wuhan. All the "left" Guomindang government had moved from Guangzhou to Wuhan, including Wang Jingwei, who had returned from his European tour. The CCP leaders were also there. But Chiang Kaishek was not. He had set up separate headquarters in Nanjing, farther down the Yangtse River. To Nanjing, Zhou learned, flocked Shanghai businessmen and bankers, and representatives of Western companies. They crowded the antechambers of Chiang's mansion. . . . What was he up to? On March 6, 1927, Chiang had executed a trade unionist in the province of Jiangsu. "This is a signal," said Lo Yinung to Zhou. "Chiang Kaishek may turn against us." But Zhou, Zhao Shiyen, and Lo Yinung received Comintern orders to carry on. Five thousand guns and the sum of 30,000 silver dollars arrived to help the planned uprising.

Zhou organized some three hundred crack shots and armed other workers. They drilled and marched, attended classes at night. Zhou mapped out the city—the Chinese section of Shanghai, not including the International Settlement or the foreign concessions—into seven sectors. Each one had its designated targets.

On March 20, the insurrection began. The insurgents seized the police stations, the post office, the railway station, and the arsenal. There was little violence and practically no bloodshed. Elated by this easy victory, the Workers' Committee, with Zhou Enlai and Lo Yinung, proclaimed a "provisional people's government" of Shanghai. "After this victory, won with the blood of the Shanghai working class, it is indeed proven that the working class is the most revolutionary and that it can take the leadership of the expedition against the warlords. . . . A new revolutionary democratic power can be established," said an exalted Zhou.

The great stir in Shanghai was not unique in China. In Wuhan, 600,000 workers in the factories had also organized themselves and taken over the British Concession. In Tianjin too there were strikes.

On March 21, some of Chiang Kaishek's forces reached Lunghua, ten miles from Shanghai's city center. On March 26, Chiang Kaishek himself arrived. Banners were unfurled, welcoming the commander in chief. The soldiers fraternized with the workers; army bands gave concerts to delight the crowds.

Chiang sent word to the Front for Military Affairs—i.e., Zhou Enlai—that the workers' squads must lay down their weapons and be placed under the control of Chiang's officers. The "provisional workers' government" refused, and so did Zhou. "These are mass organizations. They belong to the people and cannot be handed over to the army."

The Western companies in China were alarmed. They were mustering gunboats, threatening to send soldiers to safeguard their interests. Chiang Kaishek moved more troops to surround Shanghai, some of them belonging to warlords who had come to an entente with him. He held meetings, attended by some of the higher members of the Green Gang. Was not Chiang himself the "son" of a top gangster?

On April 5, Chen Duxiu and Wang Jingwei issued a joint statement praising Chiang Kaishek for his "cooperation." On the same day, in Moscow, Stalin told 3,000 Party members that Chiang could not turn against the Communists. "He may have no sympathy for the revolution, but he directs the army and cannot do anything else but direct it against the imperialists." On April 6, Zhou and Lo Yinung received a cable from Chen Duxiu. "The delegate of the Comintern has ordered us to hide or to bury all the weapons, to avoid clashes between the workers and Chiang's army. . . ." Lo Yinung, it is said, tore up the telegram. On April 7, Zhou held a meeting of the Workers' Committee. The weapons would not be surrendered. "The armed workers must exercise more vigilance, by day and by night."

On the night of April 11, the massacre began. Toward midnight the troops from warlord armies affiliated with Chiang, and some of Chiang's own, entered the working-class suburbs. With them were squads of armed secret society gangsters, conveyed in dozens of trucks supplied by the British police of Shanghai. The workers, lulled by the previous ambiance of trust, welcomed these squads as friends. They were machine-gunned. Methodically, the thugs of Big-Eared Du drove to the trade union headquarters, to other nerve centers of workers' resistance, and killed the sentries and any other workers they found. The massacres lasted five days. Appalling cruelties were committed, including boiling railwaymen alive in the steam engines of their own locomotives. "Heads rolled in the gutters of the narrow lanes like ripe plums. . . . Heads hung in cages from telegraph poles," I was told by Rewi Alley, a New Zealander then in Shanghai. The death toll is not known, though estimates put it at 5,000. Zhou Enlai was arrested at the Commercial Press Building around 3 a.m. on April 12. A commander of the Twenty-sixth Army, Su Lie, took him to his headquarters at the Catholic church on Baoshan Road. Lo Yinung, alerted to the killing taking place, rushed to tell Zhou, only to discover that he had been taken away. What would be Zhou Enlai's fate?

This is, possibly, one of the most obscure points in Zhou's life. Did Chiang Kaishek want him killed? Probably not. This would have been very unpopular, for among his officers were many Huangpu cadets, "students" of Zhou Enlai. They might not mind killing hundreds of peasants or workers, but would hesitate to kill a "teacher." In Confucian tradition, parricide is the only crime greater than killing one's teacher.

Lo Yinung reached a secret Communist, Huang Yifeng, a Huangpu cadet. With a platoon of his soldiers, Huang went to Paoshan Road and found Zhou there, in a small room, with Su Lie standing guard over him. There were signs of struggle, overturned chairs, broken teacups. Zhou was shouting at Su Lie, "You have betrayed the people, betrayed the teachings of Sun Yatsen." Since Su Lie's orders were to hold Zhou until someone came for him, he let Huang take Zhou away. Huang took Zhou to Lo

Yinung, who rushed him to a safe house, that of an antique dealer, also a Party member. Huang himself disappeared. "He was taken care of by the Communist underground. He could not, of course, return to his unit for fear of being executed."

On the next day, April 13, Zhou Enlai and Zhao Shiyen marched with 50,000 workers to the Twenty-sixth Army headquarters on Paoshan Road. The workers were mowed down by the troops. Dozens were killed. The others fled. Zhao Shiyen and Enlai escaped. On April 14, Nie Rongzhen and Li Lisan came from Wuhan, bringing with them the new Comintern adviser, Voitinsky. Also present that day was the poet Guo Moro, erudite and ardently revolutionary. Guo was dean of the faculty of literature at the university in Guangzhou, where he met Zhou. He had chosen to join the Northern Expedition. In the last ten days, he had seen a great deal of butchering of workers and peasants, done by the very armies he had so eagerly wanted to laud in his poems.

Zhou was haggard, in a state of shock from grief and rage. He had not eaten since April 11. Guo Moro remembers well that Zhou told Voitinsky, very bitterly, "The Comintern must also bear responsibility for what has happened."

With Lo Yinung and Li Lisan, Zhao Shiyen, Nie Rongzhen, and other Party men, Zhou composed a telegram to the Politburo in Wuhan. "You must go straightway to Wuhan and denounce Chiang Kaishek," Guo remembers telling Zhou. But Zhou said there was unfinished work in Shanghai, and sent a telegram instead: "An opportunity to control events was already lost in the south. Now a gross error has been committed in Shanghai . . . If we again fail to go forward, political leadership will fall entirely into the hands of the right-wing Guomindang, and lead to the total failure of the revolution." He accused Chiang Kaishek of being the main mover in the killings. "If despite all these acts of betrayal which he has committed we continue to be indecisive, Chiang will consolidate his counterrevolutionary regime . . . will form closer ties with the imperialists. Chiang must be attacked in Nanjing, where only five divisions are directly under him. . . . We must no longer hesitate."

But in Wuhan, indecision prevailed. Chen Duxiu and Wang Jingwei did not agree to a military offensive against Chiang, although they denounced Chiang and "expelled" him from the Guomindang, as if they controlled it. Chiang was unaffected.

On April 24, the CCP held its Fifth Plenum. Only 80 members

were present, so many were in hiding. Zhou was not at the gathering. Still in Shanghai with Nie, he was trying to find trade unionists still alive and in hiding, to help them to get out of the city. It was then that he began to plan an underground network, with codes and passwords and routes, which would prove important for the survival of the Party in later years. At the end of April or in early May, clad in a silk robe with a fedora hat and a cane, the usual garb of a prosperous merchant, he boarded a British company boat to sail upriver to Wuhan.

In Wuhan he found the CCP Politburo in disarray. There was no firm policy. He was reappointed to the Central Committee and to the Military Affairs Commission. No one could blame him for having obeyed the orders he had been given, even though Chen Duxiu accused him of needless provocation. He continued to press for a military showdown against Chiang, but Wang Jingwei, Chen Duxiu, and Borodin rejected the idea.

The killings now spread all over China, and they continued for the next four years. "Rather slay a thousand innocent men than let one Communist escape," ordered Chiang Kaishek. Zhou's colleague Zhao Shiyen was captured, tortured, and executed in June. Lo Yinung, who had remained in Shanghai, was betrayed, tortured, and executed in April 1928. Li Dazhao, the editor of *New Youth*, the man who had first promoted Marxism in China, was captured and strangled, along with twenty other Communists, although they had taken refuge in the Soviet embassy in Beijing. The British Dean of the Diplomatic Corps waived diplomatic immunity and allowed Chinese troops to break into the Soviet embassy and take Li Dazhao and his colleagues. The Muslim girl Guo Lungzhen was captured and executed. So was Zhou's Muslim classmate, Ma Jun, and Ma Qianli (Thousand-Mile Horse) and many others.

On April 15, 1927, the day the massacres had begun in Guangzhou, Deng Yingchao went into labor. "There were shootings and beheadings in the streets. . . . My mother was with me. She knew a Christian nun who ran a small maternity clinic in the suburbs and we went there. My labor was very difficult, the child was large. A doctor came, he applied forceps, and the baby was born dead. His skull was deformed by the instrument . . . it was a boy." Terse, apparently without emotion, Deng Yingchao tells me the story. "I have not told this to anyone else."

"We had arranged a code between us, Enlai and I. He would put a coded message in the *Shen Bao* and I would do the same. In case anything happened to either of us. I put a message in the newspaper. . . . The Party underground sent someone to fetch us and to bring us to Wuhan." Yingchao asserts that "Enlai had all along been suspicious of Chiang Kaishek, but he could not go against the Party, against the Comintern. We were very immature; we did not know what a master plotter Chiang Kaishek was."

The triple metropolis of Wuhan consisted of Hankow, where lay the foreign concessions, Henyang, an industrial area with 600,000 workers, and Wuchang. In that May the city was going bankrupt; food was scarce, and refugees flocked in from the killings that were going on elsewhere. The hospitals were crowded with the wounded from the Northern Expeditionary forces, since sporadic battles against warlords still took place. Meanwhile Chiang thrived in Nanjing. His coffers were filled with money, showered upon him by grateful Western companies. A number of "left Guomindang" members were quietly leaving Wuhan to join Chiang in Nanjing.

Borodin sat in the living room of his apartment in Hankow, where both electric light and running water were available, explaining the revolution to tall, buxom Anna Louise Strong, an American journalist, and a Communist. In a house not far from Borodin's lived Sun Yatsen's widow, Soong Chingling. She had come to Wuhan and was organizing care for the wounded in the hospitals. She was scathing about Chiang Kaishek. He had betrayed her husband, Sun Yatsen, he was a murderer. . . . Alas, the rest of Soong Chingling's family were not as single-minded as she. Her younger sister, Meiling, would marry the "murderer" in 1928, even though Chingling sent a telegram: "Don't marry that Bluebeard." Her older sister, Ailing, married Chiang's Finance Minister. Her brother joined Chiang's government. "Expect the worst," Soong Chingling said to Anna Louise Strong.

Zhou also expected the worst. He had few illusions left. He pinned all his hopes on a single solution: military action. There were fierce disputes within the Party. Chen Duxiu was violently taken to task by Li Lisan and also by a garrulous young poet named Chu Chiubai. Enlai did not rant, but insisted that there *must* be a military offensive. He drew up a plan to march on Nanjing, but Borodin, Chen, and Wang again turned it down. Mao Dzedong was also in Wuhan; he too attacked Chen Duxiu. But he was deprived of the right to vote when he suggested intensifying the peasant struggle. "You have provoked the killings of peasants in Hunan," Chen Duxiu told him. Zhou and Mao both were demanding armed struggle, but there was a major difference. Zhou still thought in classic Marxist terms of city insurrections. Mao, however, was working toward the idea of rural, peasant uprisings. "Enlai did not talk much about politics. . . . He concentrated on military affairs," observed another Party leader who was there, Zhang Guotao. Zhang Guotao was one of the twelve men who had founded the Party in 1921. He had spent some years in the U.S.S.R., was proficient in Russian, and was highly thought of by the Comintern because he had met Lenin. Because of his knowledge of Russian, Zhang Guotao translated the cryptic telegrams from Moscow, telegrams that now poured in on the CCP leaders, "each one saying exactly the opposite of the previous one," Mao remarked.

Zhou continued planning a military program for the United Front. "There must be a plan for military work in Southeast China. Designations for army units, persons to take charge, arrangements for confidential communications." He went again to Shanghai, despite the danger, to bring out more Party men, to organize routes and couriers. He asked Borodin for weapons. "We must have guns, and better guns." He set up caches of weapons. Wang Jingwei, who now headed the left wing of the Guomindang, was very disquieted. He did not mind Communism as parlor entertainment, confined to intellectual discussion. But worker and peasant militancy were abominable to him. Borodin, to placate Wang, told Zhou he must disarm the workers in Wuhan. Zhou turned in one thousand rifles. "What's the use of keeping them? There are no bullets. Most of the guns don't function properly."

Zhou's plans crystallized. A major city must be captured by the CCP. This would restore confidence, regain the badly shaken trust of officer-cadets and their men who had remained loyal to the revolution. A plan to take Nanchang, the capital of Jiangsi province, was formulated in June. Nanchang was strategically important, a communications center, with abundant water and fertile countryside. The armies around Nanchang were accounted "more friendly" because they were not killing too many Communists. And the man in charge of public security in Nanchang, the deputy

commander of its garrison, was none other than Zhu De, Scarlet
Virtue, whom Zhou had enrolled as a secret Party member in
Berlin.

One hundred Communists were publicly beheaded in Changsha,
Hunan province, by the Guomindang commander running the
city. Appalled, his political commissar rushed to see Zhou in
Wuhan to denounce this monstrous action. But the slaughter-
happy commander was a friend of Wang Jingwei, and though the
pretense of the United Front was wearing extremely thin, it was
still to be supported. Orders of the Comintern. "We have to keep
quiet, we cannot protest," said Enlai. "Why? Are we concubines,
prostitutes, to accept being beaten, killed, without speaking up?"
"Yes, comrade," Zhou replied. "For the sake of the revolution we
must play the concubine, even the prostitute." Did he then remember the story of Han Hsin, who crawled before the bully?

It was not yet possible for the CCP to have an army of its own.
The capture of Nanchang would have to be done under the flag
of the Guomindang. "I still thought of Wuhan as revolutionary,
not knowing how far the swing toward the right had carried it,"
Anna Louise Strong reminisced. "Ever see a rabbit before an an-
aconda, trembling, knowing it is going to be devoured, yet fascinated? That is the civil power before the military," a now
embittered, and wiser, Borodin had told her.

Wang Jingwei now sought the help of a new warlord who appeared on China's warlord-encumbered stage. Feng Yuxiang, Auspicious Jade, was six feet four, with a round head and a mellow
baritone voice. He cultivated an air of earthy peasant simplicity,
ate and dressed like a soldier, and was also a Christian, reputedly
baptizing his troops with a fire hose. Through the luck of war he
had wrested from his rivals control of Northwest China, and to
gain his support both Chiang in Nanjing and Wang in Wuhan
began to court him. "At that time, we were even more mistaken
in our judgment of Feng Yuxiang than of Chiang Kaishek," Zhou
would remark sardonically some years later. "The Comintern did
not know his background. They thought he was the leader of a
peasant army." Auspicious Jade agreed to talk with Wang Jingwei
at Zhengzhou, a city on the Yellow River. Thither Wang and his
ministers proceeded in a luxury train loaded with canned aspar-
agus, iced soda pop, Sunkist oranges, and Caillers chocolate. The
meeting was true Chinese opera. Amid adulatory phrases, Aus-

picious Jade advised Wang to send Borodin and his colleagues back to Moscow, as they were "fatigued by their arduous labors." Wang Jingwei was also looking tired, observed Feng. He had exerted himself greatly and probably needed a long trip abroad.

Auspicious Jade had chosen Chiang Kaishek, who had sent him a wagonful of money. Another Comintern adviser arrived, a garrulous Bengali from Calcutta, M. N. Roy, who knew nothing about China—that was the main characteristic of all Comintern advisers—but could talk everyone around him into a stupor. Unconscionably maladroit, he showed Wang Jingwei a telegram dated June 1 from Stalin ordering the CCP to infiltrate the army, accelerate peasant confiscation of land, organize workers' battalions. "Everyone is very nervous about Communist intentions," said Wang to Roy. And that was the end of the United Front, though Zhou did not know it. Wang now spoke only of maintaining law and order. No one knows how much Chiang paid him to leave Wuhan before the suffocating summer dropped its leaden heat upon the triple metropolis, and the killing began. Wang went to Europe; he would not return for some years.

July 1927 and massacres on the streets of Wuhan. Zhou and his wife fled from their house. They stayed for three days in the home of American bishop Logan Herbert Roots on Tungting Road, Hankow. Soong Chingling had arranged this temporary haven. Bishop Roots found Zhou open-minded, willing to discuss all beliefs. "I thought he would be a good Christian—he believed so deeply in the spiritual value of man."

On July 18 the CCP held an emergency session, and at last Chen Duxiu, the perpetual vacillator, was suspended. A temporary Politburo was organized consisting of Zhou, Zhang Guotao, Li Lisan, Li Weihan, and Zhang Tailei. The decision to start a military offensive on Nanchang was confirmed. A peasant insurrection, to be led by Mao Dzedong, was considered, but Comintern approval was delayed until August 7. On July 25, Enlai left Wuhan to proceed to Nanchang. "In July, when the killing began in Wuhan, Enlai left me. Of course, he did not tell me where he was going or what he would do. Enlai knew how to keep secrets. He never told me anything about the Party that I should not know. 'I am going,' he said to me one morning. 'You are going,' I replied, and that was all. Every time he left me, I thought: Perhaps I shall never see him again," Deng Yingchao told me. She too left Wuhan. "The Party underground took care of me. My mother and I went into hiding. And later we went to Shanghai."

On July 27, Borodin, with Anna Louise Strong, left Wuhan by train to return to the U.S.S.R. He was given a most courteous send-off, while on the streets of Wuhan workers, trade unionists, and members of the Youth League were being shot, or beheaded, by order of the smiling Guomindang officials who waved him goodbye.

Zhou Enlai's decision to take Nanchang was not guided merely by cold reason. A streak of passionate anger carried him onward. "The blood of the dead clamors for revenge. Shall we fold our arms?" He estimated that with the small nucleus of former Huangpu cadets, now officers in the armies around Nanchang, perhaps 10,000 men could be mustered. His excellent memory, which unfailingly reproduced for him the names and faces of every one of the students he had met at Huangpu, served him in good stead. Even forty years later, he would remember exactly not only the name but what every Chinese student he had met in France had done.

Zhang Guotao gave him a batch of Comintern telegrams. They recommended caution. "If we fail, all is lost," said Guotao. "But to wait to be killed is certainly to lose," replied Zhou Enlai. "I shall decide in Nanchang what the situation is like." He arrived on July 27, the same day Borodin left Wuhan for Russia, and stayed in the house of Zhu De in the Flower Garden Compound. There they came, by ones and twos, Zhou Enlai's friends, fired by the same passion as he. Nie Rongzhen and Chen Yi, Li Lisan and Ye Jianying, Heroic Sword, and Ye Ting. Guo Moro the poet, with a parcel of books, among them his translation of Walt Whitman. Liu Bocheng and Lin Boju, both from Sichuan province, old friends of the late Sun Yatsen. To Nanchang came an extraordinary middle school teacher turned warrior, Hsu Teli (Xu Deli), once Mao's tutor in Hunan, and a young, sallow-faced Huangpu cadet, already going bald, named Lin Biao. Companions in an undoubtedly reckless adventure, held together by ideals, but also by Zhou's personality. "If we do not fight, we surely die. If we fight, we may die, but we may win," said Zhou Enlai.

Zhou established a working headquarters at the Jiangxi Grand Hotel, registering himself as a banker. On July 28, an anguished

Zhang Guotao sent a coded cable. Moscow urged a postponement. Guotao was on his way to talk to Zhou about it. Meanwhile, Zhu De had told Zhou of a non-Communist military commander, called Ho Lung (now spelt He Lung), commander of the Twentieth Army. "He is trustworthy and he detests Chiang Kaishek."

Ho Lung was already a legend, having, at the age of twelve, killed with a kitchen knife a brute who threatened his mother. He had been a Robin Hood, taking from the wealthy, giving to the poor. "Isn't that Communism?" asked Zhu De. Ho Lung had joined the Guomindang, and was also a member of the Gelao, or Elder Brother secret society, one of the most powerful in West China. To the Gelao also belonged Scarlet Virtue, and Liu Bocheng and Lin Boju. Ho Lung was a "double-head dragon" in the society, high in the hierarchy. He was very handsome, with excellent features, and that rakish attractiveness which Zhou seemed to like in his friends. "Elder Brother, I put my life in your hands," said Enlai to the Dragon, and told him the plan to capture Nanchang. "I've been waiting for something like this. I'll do anything you tell me," Ho replied.

Zhang Guotao arrived the next day with a telegram from verbose Bengali Roy. "Postpone the insurrection. The equilibrium of forces is not satisfactory." "The Comintern recommends that you contact commander Zhang Fakuei, who is in charge of all the armies at Nanchang," said Guotao. Zhou had avoided meeting Zhang Fakuei. He felt that the overall commander might turn against the revolutionaries. A one-day postponement—till August 1—was agreed upon. When, some hours later, Zhang Guotao advocated another delay, Zhou lost his temper. "I was sent to perform a task and I'll do it. Let the responsibility be on me. Enough vacillation." He named Ho Lung commander in chief of the insurrection, seconded by Ye Ting and Lin Boju.

On the night of July 31, Scarlet Virtue hosted a banquet for the Nanchang officials and local commanders. In the midst of the revelry, a junior officer rushed into the banquet room to report that "unexpected" troop movements were taking place. Zhu De reassured his guests, and Ho Lung left to "inquire"—actually to reach Zhou. "Someone has alerted the enemy." Zhou advanced the timetable by six hours. Instead of starting at dawn, the rising would start at once. It was near midnight. Ho Lung slipped away from the feast and led the troops to occupy the city's railway station, the mayor's mansion, the stadium, and the government offices. Zhou had done the usual mapping out of the city into five sectors. Some firing took place, but by 7 a.m. on August 1, Nanchang was in the hands of Zhou and his followers. A proclamation announced to the provincial government officials, now hastily assembled, that a committee representing the Revolutionary Guomindang Party was formed, comprised of Soong Chingling, widow of Sun Yatsen, Ho Lung, Ye Ting, Zhu De, the widow of Liao Zhungkai—and Zhou Enlai. The reason for including the two absent widows was to give the committee respectability by invoking the memory of Sun Yatsen. But there was a hitch. All this was being done under the flag of the Guomindang, a flag under which workers and peasants had been butchered everywhere. "What do we say to the people? They are confused." "Say that this is a New Revolutionary Guomindang," replied Zhou, for once sounding very unconvincing. A victory parade was held at the sports stadium, and 50,000 of Nanchang's inhabitants dutifully waved flags and shouted slogans. But that very night, a commander named Tsai Tingkai, in charge of the 10th Army Division, killed thirty Communist officers among his own forces. "Only one has escaped, our assets in the 10th Division have been destroyed," Zhou said somberly. "It is my fault. I was not vigilant enough."

On August 3, Chiang dispatched forces against Nanchang and on August 4 the city was evacuated. The revolutionary forces "withdrew according to plan." Zhou had prepared for a retreat. "But I lacked experience. My revolutionary career had started abroad with limited knowledge, all from books. . . . We still did not know either how to exploit our success or the tactics of retreat." The decision to leave Nanchang remained a controversial subject, brought up later in Party caucuses, when every phrase, every action, every lapse of Zhou Enlai was scrutinized, sometimes with excessive animosity. "I feel the main mistake was not to remain on the spot. The army should not have pulled out. If we had stayed and started an agrarian revolution, it would have been possible to expand our forces. But after the Nanchang uprising, we went all the way to Shantou."

On August 7, at a stormy party meeting in Wuhan, Chen Duxiu was finally toppled. Only eleven members had turned up, among them Mao Dzedong. Mao expressed himself pleased with the fact that he had contributed to discarding Chen Duxiu. But Zhou, when he read the report of the meeting, was unhappy. "It was a vindictive meeting. It set a bad precedent for inner-Party struggle." Chen had not been allowed to defend himself. Throughout his life Zhou would strive to conduct these battles in a dignified, reasoned, nonemotional manner, but few seem to have followed his example. Chen Duxiu was the scapegoat for the Comintern's deplorable ineptness, for Stalin's grotesque mistakes of judgment. He therefore could not be given a chance.

Mao was given permission to start a peasant insurrection in Hunan. Known as the Autumn Harvest uprising, it was a heroic failure. Mao, with remnant forces, fled into the Jingang Mountains, on the border of Jiangsi and Hunan provinces. There, in the fashion of peasant rebels in China's past, he established a mountain stronghold. What was a failed attempt turned out to be a breakthrough of genius, for thus did the Communist Party's first rural guerrilla base come into being. And from this small beginning evolved the grand strategy which, twenty years later, would bring victory to the CCP.

The forces leaving Nanchang divided into two groups. Zhu De, with Chen Yi and Lin Biao, went southwest, roving for months, until in April 1928 they joined Mao Dzedong at the Jingang mountain base. Zhou, with Ye Ting and Ye Jianying, Li Lisan, Nie Rongzhen, Ho Lung, Zhang Guotao, and poet Guo Moro, struck southward toward the port of Shantou. To reach it, they had to battle their way through hordes of warlord forces. The peasants were hostile, and malaria decimated the soldiers. Nevertheless, they reached Shantou on September 20 and captured it on September 24. Zhou knew the area well, having taken the city in 1925, and established there a Communist underground. For a week the fewer than 2,000 men with him bivouacked here. He even attended a welcome meeting and made a speech, with He Lung and Ye Ting by his side. On September 29, foreign gunboats appeared, British ships, carrying Chiang Kaishek's troops. A massed attack by four warlord armies was launched against Zhou's forces at the same time. Shantou had to be abandoned, and the depleted battalions retreated westward. They would try, said Zhou, to reorganize at the peasant base of Hailufeng, created upon a matrix of villages with solid communal traditions by a young revolutionary named Peng Bai.

Zhou assembled his colleagues at the village of Flowing Sands, where a temple to the Queen of Heaven, Mistress of the Seas, sheltered them. There were fewer than 800 men left. "From now on we no longer fight under the Guomindang flag. If any of you have misgivings, it is time to part." Ho Lung said, "I stay." Guo Moro said, "I stay." Enlai was running a fever of 40 degrees centigrade. He had had bouts of malaria for the past two weeks. Shaking with emotion and physical weakness, Enlai now inducted Ho Lung and Guo Moro as Party members, administering the oath of loyalty in front of the enthroned statue of the Queen of Heaven. A solemn moment, unwavering commitment at a time when all seemed lost.

After the ceremony, Zhou told Li Lisan and Zhang Guotao that they should return to Shanghai to report to the Central Committee. Once again, it was in Shanghai, fortress of capitalism, that the Communist Party had found shelter. He and the others would stay with the soldiers. "I don't know how many of us will survive. But I shall stay." During the retreat from Shantou, they had lost all the money and gold they had collected in two baskets. In small fishing boats, Liu Bocheng, Lin Boju, and Guo Moro managed to reach Hong Kong, and made their way to Shanghai. Zhou continued toward Hailufeng with the two Ye's and Nie Rongzhen. He was half dead, so weak he had to be carried on a stretcher. When the stretcher bearers abandoned him and fled, Nie and Ho Lung carried him. In his memoirs, and in a talk with me, Nie would recount the whole episode.

"Ye Ting and I stuck to Zhou Enlai. There was a total mess, and at the end only a handful of us. We could not speak the local dialect, we had no protection, no armed guards . . . everyone had fled. Fortunately I found a comrade, named Yang. I told him, 'You have to look after us.' He did. He found us a boat. The boat was extremely small. Standing room only for the four of us, Enlai, Ye Ting, Yang, and myself. . . . We had to give Enlai more space, he could not stand. We stood, and the waves tossed us, the boat rocked. I found a rope and tied myself to a plank. It took us two days and two nights to reach Hong Kong."

Ye Ting had relatives in Hong Kong, and they managed to book Zhou, under an assumed name, in the Empress Lodge in Kowloon. They called a doctor, who administered quinine. Zhou recovered. Separately, they made their way to Shanghai. Zhou, traveling alone, reached the city in early November.

7

They were quarreling as usual, their infatuation with theoretical constructs undiminished despite the disasters that had almost destroyed their Party. The intellectuals of the Politburo and the Central Committee poured torrents of words upon each other, and tried to rationalize their failures, or rather those of the all-dominant Comintern. Despite their useless loquacity, many of these young men would show much courage, and some would die heroically for their beliefs.

The temporary acting secretary, in lieu of Chen Duxiu, was now the fiery poet Chu Chiubai (now spelt Qiubai). Zhou faced some criticism for the Nanchang uprising's failure. But once again, when the time came to do something, it was Zhou who was called upon. The task of pulling together the demoralized, exsanguinated Party fell upon him.

"War is a matter of vital importance to the state, the province of life and death, the road to survival or to ruin. It is mandatory that it should be thoroughly studied." These had been the precepts of Sun Tzu the strategist, in his book *The Art of War*. "Power grows out of the barrel of a gun," would be Mao Dzedong's succinct way of paraphrasing Sun Tzu. Without an army, the Party could not survive, and Zhou was placed in charge of both civil and military work. He would hold a position in the Organization Department of the Party and in the Military Affairs Commission. The Party-army was now a unitary structure, fused by the terror unleashed against it.

The years 1928–31 are confusing because the Party went into hiding, and camouflage does not yield easily to clear depiction. A soupy mélange of fact and fable existed for a long while over Zhou's activities during those years. Some facts have come to light, though many events are still shrouded in obscurity.

One thing at least is well known: The Comintern held stubbornly that there was a "high tide of revolution" throughout China, though nothing could be further from reality. Uprisings must therefore be fomented, said Lominadze, the new Comintern adviser. Zhou did not demur. He too appeared for a while to accept this perception of the situation. Hence the next tragedy, in December 1927.

The City of Rams, Guangzhou, had been lost. Moscow, through Lominadze, declared that it must be recaptured and a "commune" established. Perhaps Stalin wanted to prove that he was not capitulating to "imperialists and the reactionaries," as Trotsky was accusing him of doing, and decided that once again the Chinese comrades had to be sacrificed. . . . Heinz Neumann, a twenty-seven-year-old German, with a record of total ignorance of China, led the debacle.

Ye Jianying had organized several groups of officer-cadets while he had been an instructor at the Huangpu Military Academy. He had moved them away from Wuhan in July 1927, to save them from being killed. They were comparatively safe in Guangzhou, provided their membership in the Party remained unknown. Ye felt that these cadets should now make their way out of Guangzhou to build a new Red Army in other, less exposed areas. He thought that the simulacrum of an uprising would cover their escape. But Neumann did not see it that way. The city must be taken, it must be turned into a "Soviet commune." Ye Ting, who was also involved in this messy operation, clashed with Neumann when he suggested a "lightning recuperation" attack. "But Neumann cursed Ye Ting . . . screaming: attack, attack, and again attack," Zhou Enlai recalled, when he told the story, in 1943, to the young cadres who were learning Party history.

What could the two Ye's do against Neumann? Nothing. And so, valiantly, they fought, and Guangzhou was a "commune" for three days, when the warlord in charge was absent in another part of the province. "If we had then made an orderly retreat, there would not have been such panic . . . more cadres could have been saved," Zhou Enlai recalled. But the warlord returned. Many were caught within the city and could not escape.

In this rout several dozen Vietnamese revolutionaries who fought alongside their Chinese comrades were killed. In later years Zhou Enlai and Ho Chi Minh would together visit their graves to pay their respects to the dead.

Ye Ting was held responsible for the failure, and when he went to Moscow in early 1928 "no one would have anything to do with him," narrated Zhou. Ye Ting was a man who had given up wealth and comfort for his ideals. He withdrew from the Party and went to Germany, where he lived for some years, until in 1936 Zhou Enlai sent for him, and once again he took up arms to fight for the revolution.

As if there had not been enough blood spilled, Li Lisan was sent to Guangzhou to investigate what had happened. There were survivors, and Li Lisan wanted to prepare a case and "severely punish" them for the failure of the uprising. Zhou Enlai opposed him. "You were not there . . . you did not know what took place. There must be no condemnations of good comrades."

On a "suggestion" of the Comintern, the CCP held its Sixth Congress in the spring of 1928 in Moscow, and not in China. The reasons given sound plausible. Safety. Secrecy. But it was also because Moscow, after the catastrophes of 1927, wanted to reassume control of the CCP. Disguised as a couple of dealers in antiques, Zhou Enlai and Deng Yingchao went by ship from Shanghai to Dalien (Dairen). There, Zhou encountered suspicious police inspectors who thought they recognized him. His picture had been widely circulated and there was a price on his head. He managed to talk his way out and went on to Manchuria to see his uncle Yikeng and brother Enshou in Shenyang, proceeding to Harbin to visit his youngest brother, Enfu. (Enshou had, for a while, been in Guangzhou with him. But neither brother had become a Party member.) Then on to Moscow.

In Moscow, Stalin received the CCP leaders Li Lisan, Zhou Enlai, Chu Qiubai, and lectured them. There was no high tide of revolution at the moment. Qiubai had the audacity to argue that there were spontaneous revolts. Stalin cut him short. "Comrade, ebb tides also produce ripples." Stalin had emerged victorious from his struggle with Trotsky, but now was concerned over Japanese encroachment in Manchuria, particularly on the Manchurian railways jointly held by the U.S.S.R. and the Chinese, an arrangement dating back to Czarist days. The CCP could be useful in Manchuria, so it must not dissipate its strength, and Trotskyism must be eliminated among the Chinese comrades. The CCP's North China bureau particularly interested the U.S.S.R. It was controlled by a tall, big-nosed man from Hunan named Liu Shaoqi.

Liu had already proven himself adept in organizing workers, for Moscow an important quality.

The usual bickering and name calling took place at the Sixth Congress. Chu Qiubai was criticized for military adventurism, putschism, commandism, and left opportunism. Zhou was upbraided by Bukharin. "You should have been better able to estimate the strength of your men at Nanchang." Zhou accepted the remarks, then raised the subject of the Guangzhou commune fiasco. The Russian agreed that Neumann had erred. . . .

In Moscow were some forty orphans, the children of revolutionaries killed in the massacres. Deng Yingchao and Tsai Chang cared for them, and spent a good deal of time seeing to their comfort in the schools where they boarded. Zhou gave lectures, and attended lectures. He probably took some lessons from the NKVD on organizing secret police. He did not argue, justify, exculpate, as did Li Lisan and other leaders. He could laugh, and dance, and toss down vodka with creditable stamina. He settled a quarrel between Russian teachers and their Chinese students at the University in Moscow. Among the youths enrolled there was Chiang Chingkuo, son of his enemy Chiang Kaishek; his father had brought him to Moscow in 1924. Chingkuo fierily denounced his father. "That is good, but don't forget to write to him from time to time," advised Zhou Enlai.

From Moscow, Zhou proceeded to Germany and to France. There is no documentation about his activities, except an article by him in a German Communist newspaper. He was back in China in October, based in Shanghai. Chu Qiubai, shorn of his post, remained in the U.S.S.R. to "study"—a euphemism for being shelved—and to work on a Chinese-Cyrillic dictionary. Li Lisan, Zhou Enlai, and a trade unionist boatman, Xiang Zhungfa, were designated to head the Party, Xiang because of being working class. The Comintern had noticed that there were no working-class representatives among the CCP leaders. "But our workers don't know how to read or write," protested the ever frank Qiubai. The Comintern paid no heed. There must be a proletarian among the leaders. "At the time there was hostility in the Party toward the intellectuals," remarks a Chinese historian to me as he points to Zhou's speeches deploring this tendency. Xiang Zhungfa's tenure was brief. He was caught by Chiang's secret police, and, to save his life, abjured the Party. But this did not help. He was not an intellectual, therefore he could be liquidated at will. He was executed in 1931.

Strengthened by the authority of the Sixth Congress, Zhou could now deal with refractory factions within the CCP. The Party was almost destroyed. From around 58,000 members in January 1927, there remained fewer than 10,000 in December. The remnants of the Party were torn by betrayals and desertions. "Instances of Party members giving themselves up and informing against comrades have spread," Zhou Enlai remarked drily. Chiang Kaishek had organized an efficient secret police, which hunted down ruthlessly anyone suspected of Communism. Renegades and informers were handsomely rewarded and given good jobs. Abominable tortures awaited captured suspects. On top of all this, factionalism based on personal relationships, pervasive throughout Chinese society, was rampant among the Party intellectuals as well, and the talkfests they indulged in destroyed discipline and the secrecy required of a group threatened every day by a ruthless and powerful police.

Only implacable discipline could stop runaway defeatism and betrayals. Zhou Enlai was, of course, the person designated to restore the Party, for he built no cliques, had no factions, was trusted because he was impartial, unflappable, "a man of steel." He was now to create a tightly knit organization, the "special department," or Te Ke.

The Te Ke kept Party files on each member, collected information, punished betrayals, operated radio stations, and instituted protection teams and justice squads, which administered swift death to those suspected of betraying Party affairs, leaking secrets, or causing the arrest and death of comrades.

Secrecy, a habit which Zhou had cultivated since his days in Paris, now became an essential part of the Communist organization. Information was confined to a small elite; the rank and file were asked only to trust and to obey. The methods used were akin to those employed by the secret societies for some centuries, even though the similarity was possibly ignored at the time.

So thorough, so competent was the work of the Te Ke that it was known as Wu Hao's Dagger. Wu Hao was the pseudonym Zhou had acquired when running the Awareness Society in his former years, years now very remote to him. Wu Hao and his dagger were known throughout the Shanghai underworld and inspired awe even among the gangs. No one seems at first to have identified Zhou with Wu Hao. This part of Zhou's life, the establishment of the Te Ke, reveals a man very different from the warm, humane person he undeniably was. But if we think of the continual atrocities perpetrated by Chiang Kaishek's police, the manhunts which went on day and night, perhaps we can understand that Zhou should have responded in kind. A student, a girl, was tortured and executed because she had a bright pink handkerchief in her pocket . . . anything red was suspect. "Someone had to do this work, or the Party would have been destroyed," Chinese Party historians say. Not only the Party member who betrayed but also his family, anyone who protected him, were hit by the Te Ke squads. The tight-knit family group in China has always been held responsible for the delinquency of any one member.

Te Ke information gathering was excellent. Zhou spun a spiderweb, tenuous and loose, fast-holding, working on a one-to-one basis. No one involved would contact more than one Party member. Connections, affiliations, entwinings, associations, moles, buried deep within Chiang Kaishek's apparatus of government, his ministries, armies, and those of his allied warlords, in all the services, the post and telegraph and telephone offices . . . all shades and nuances of informers, some not even knowing they were informing. A widespread, ramifying network, recruited through schoolmate ties, family relationships, provincial associations. The planning of safe routes for dispersal and flight: a small army of passers and couriers. "Our most efficient cells were within Chiang Kaishek's own police . . . they were badly paid, so they talked," my friend Xiung Xianghui, a Zhou mole for more than a decade, told me.

Many innocuous associations became places of concealment and information gathering. History-study associations, musical associations, athletic clubs, even Bible-reading societies. Zhou had agents in barbers' clubs, their shops being places where messages could easily be transmitted. There are many reminiscences of those years, including those of my friend the playwright and film director Xia Yan, and also writer Zhou Yang, both at the time involved with the left-wing association of writers. "But writers are not so good at this kind of thing. Five of them were buried alive by Chiang Kaishek's police in 1933," Xia Yan said to me.

The Te Ke expanded, divided into several departments. There were such men as Li Kenung, later to be nicknamed the Smiling Buddha, because of his round-faced affability; and Kang Sheng, later to become the most feared and detested man in China, and Zhou Enlai's bête noire. Kang Sheng had been a labor organizer in Shanghai and had escaped the massacres of April 1927 by disguising himself as a public tramcar ticket collector.

Discipline. Coordination. Professionalism in revolution. From his ancestors the imperial officials, Zhou Enlai inherited that talent for administration. Now, both in the open activities of the Party and its far more important underground life, he would lay down rules, check behavior, install an efficient machine for control, decry amateurism.

Zhou also took in hand the military buildup of the Party. In this respect, he was still thinking in terms of city taking rather than of the formidable strength in the countryside. An understanding of what really moved that ocean of humanity which was China would only come to him several years later.

The military buildup undertaken in those years reflects the wildly fluctuating policies inflicted upon the CCP by the Comintern. In early 1928, when the "high tide" theory held sway, Zhou sent Ho Lung, the Winsome Dragon, to establish a military base near Wuhan. There were very few men with Ho Lung, and most of them were Gelao members.

The acceptance—tacit, never openly recognized—of secret society men into the Party was thus confirmed. The base under Ho Lung expanded, and sat astride the borders of Hunan and Hubei provinces. Marginal areas were often unpatrolled, since the various warlords running the provinces were chary of coming into conflict with one another on border territory. At the time Mao was in the Jingang mountain stronghold, reinforced in April 1928 by the forces under Zhu De, Chen Yi, and Lin Biao. Rural bases, areas of refuge, survived; there would be altogether a dozen by the end of 1930.

Zhou's main concern was to bring these disparate settlements under a central, unified command. From 1928 well into 1929, Zhou's detailed letters and directives concerned with army organization stick to professionalism. No rhetoric, no prophetic utterances, no doctrinal preachments. During those years he also battled, within the Party caucuses, for more and more free discussion of political issues. "Every effort should be made to discuss all the Party's political questions and to encourage all comrades to express their views freely." He obviously felt constrained, hampered, by the fact that he could not summon enough comrades to freely discuss, and occasionally go against, the imposed Comintern line. But at the time Moscow was not only the fount of all wisdom, it was also the only source of money and equipment for the battered CCP. Using both his own powers of persuasion and the Te Ke, Zhou brought rebellious groups in North China in line with the Party leadership in Shanghai. He set up training schools for cadres, ten to twenty of these at a time, no more. Instruction lasted a month or two, then the cadres were sent to teach in the provinces. "In general the level of knowledge of Marxism is rather low," remarked Zhou, euphemistically. The illiteracy rate among the rank and file—the new recruits of the Party—was high. How could people scarcely able to write their own names be taught the intricacies of the doctrine? Add to this difficulty the fact that a gathering of more than two people, in those Chiang Kaishek days, was forbidden . . . and punishable by death. How could classes be safely held under such conditions? Zhou managed, somehow.

But now he came in conflict with Mao Dzedong. The Military Affairs Commission, of which he was the head, believed that there should not be large bases functioning in rural areas. The whole point of building an army was to take cities, therefore the bases must be mobile, and small enough not to attract the attention of the enemy. This view had been elaborated at the Sixth Congress. It was, of course, totally contradictory with what Mao was now doing. Perhaps Mao himself at the time was not aware of his own discovery, but very soon he would be the first—and for a while the only—man in the Party who abandoned the city orientation and devised a major strategy born from China's reality. The masses were not the very few workers—no more than 3 million in a population of some 350 million—but the peasantry, 85 percent of China's people. Mao saw that setting up rural bases, dedicated to the liberation of the peasantry from the oppression of landlordism, was the only way in which revolution would succeed. But the intellectuals in Shanghai feared that such rural bases would lead to the growth of separate strongholds of power. Lenin had pronounced: "All power to the center." Zhou Enlai issued an order that the army, under Zhu De and Mao, should "disperse" into separate units to attack cities. Mao had the habit of not answering missives, directives, injunctions he did not like. "They are often totally contradictory. . . . One asks me to do this, for it is the most correct policy, the next, a month later, tells me the exact opposite."

In the winter of 1928–29 the Jingang mountain base suffered from a dearth of food and supplies, and from warlord attacks. Mao and Zhu De then smashed their way out, and after some battles, established themselves in what would become the Party's most important base, straddling the borders of Fujian and Jiangxi provinces. They ignored the order from Zhou to disperse.

A further order then asked Mao, Zhu De, and Chen Yi to come to Shanghai for "study." "You are far too pessimistic about the situation," Mao wrote back. Zhou was angry, but controlled his temper. He insisted that a "reliable representative" of Mao's Fourth Army should come to Shanghai to explain matters. Li Lisan, who never liked Mao, pushed through an order to demote him and Zhu De. "Let us first listen," Zhou expostulated. Chen Yi, the poet-footballer, arrived in August, and Zhou was very pleased to see his old friend. "Have you got a football field in your base?" he asked. Chen Yi gave Zhou a glowing account of the base, of how it was being run, and Zhou incorporated the information into a circular sent to all the Red Army units in other bases. "Many valuable experiences can be found here . . . unique to China, never seen nor heard of before. . . . All Party branches and Red Army units ought to learn from them." At an enlarged meeting of the Politburo and Military Affairs Commission, Zhou admitted that the criticism of Zhu De and Mao Dzedong had been inapposite. Their downgrading was annulled. "Please tell Comrade Dzedong to keep his position," he told Chen Yi when the latter made ready to return to the base. "There must first be a Red Army in the rural areas; only afterward can power be wrested in the cities." Ever flexible, Zhou was beginning to realize that what was best for China was not necessarily what the Comintern advisers dictated.

Unceasingly, Zhou Enlai and Deng Yingchao changed houses, changed appearance. "We never stayed longer than a month in the same place," says Yingchao to me. Zhou was the most wanted man on Chiang's secret police list. His face was well known to many of Chiang's officers, former Huangpu cadets. He grew a beard, or shaved, added mustaches, altered eyebrows, gait, and

voice. His brief training as an actor (actress) was useful. He only
went out on the streets around 4:30 a.m. and was back by 7 a.m.
He knew every narrow lane, called *nilung*, in Shanghai. And he
was formidably lucky. When he went to Tianjin to settle the Party
dissension there, he called on Nankai University president Zhang
Boling. Zhang did not denounce Zhou Enlai.

In 1929 the couple stayed for three weeks with Uncle Yiqian,
the only fairly well-off member of the family, who lived on Sey-
mour Road in Shanghai. For a short while, they relaxed. Zhou
indulged his hobby of cooking dumplings and dishes from Shaoxing. "He cooks better than you girls do," Yiqian's wife said to
her daughters-in-law. He involved himself in family affairs, trying
to reconcile his cousin Enzhu with his wife, who was aggrieved
because Enzhu was overfond of a certain opera star. "You should
go to the theater with your husband," advised Zhou Enlai. "But
I hate these shows." Enlai sighed. He loved the theater, but could
never go to see an opera or a play, for fear of being recognized.
On the hundredth birthday anniversary of the late grandfather
Zhou Panlong, it was Zhou, the eldest grandson, who conducted
the ceremonies. "You should really have a better job," Uncle
Yiqian told his likable nephew, who, he thought, was an employee
in a commercial concern. "You have many talents." Zhou smiled
modestly. "Better prospects might turn up someday."

Clandestinity is corrosive. It was on Deng Yingchao that the
stress told. Perpetually moving, "never knowing in the morning
whether we would see each other again that night." Her health
deteriorated. She had already been afflicted with a bout of tuberculosis when in Beijing. The disease had appeared dormant for a
while but it now again affected her. Her mother lived in one of
the safe houses of the French Concession, registered in her name,
but actually used by the Party. She was supposed to be a well-to-
do widow, knowledgeable in herbal remedies. She became an
excellent courier for the Party, as did other elderly, respectable-
looking women, such as the mother of Tsai Hosen and Tsai Chang.

Soong Chingling was also in Shanghai, living in a house on the
rue Molière in the French Concession. The house was watched
by the Guomindang's secret police. Zhou never went to see her.
But he had links with some Europeans and Americans, and sympathizers such as Rewi Alley. The rue Molière house was the
rendezvous of the liberal intelligentsia, both Chinese and Western.
Here Bernard Shaw met Lu Xun; Harold Isaacs, Vincent Sheean,

and Agnes Smedley called on the famous widow of Sun Yatsen, and stayed to tea. A few of these visitors were helping the Party, buying radio transmitters and apparatus, receiving letters and money, transmitting messages. At least one businessman I know well helped the Party in gold and silver transactions, but still wishes to remain anonymous, even sixty years later.

In 1930 the ever restless Li Lisan announced that a new "high tide" was beginning. Chiang Kaishek was struggling with a rebellion of warlords, among them Feng Yuxiang, Auspicious Jade. The time had come to set up Communist power "in one or more provinces," argued Li Lisan. The writer Xia Yen remembers how Li then organized "flying demonstrations" in the streets of Shanghai. Of course, they only led to more executions. Li Lisan had ordered Mao to seize Changsha, the capital of Hunan province. Mao protested, tried to obey, and failed. Undeterred, Li Lisan conceived of a plan to take Wuhan. "Our horses shall drink the water of the Great River," he quoted from an ancient poem. "The total number of Party Youth League members and trade unionists in Wuhan is less than 300 . . . the situation is not sufficiently ripe," replied long-suffering Zhou Enlai. In the summer of 1930, Li Lisan conceived of another major offensive. No less than to take Nanjing, the capital of Chiang Kaishek. By then, Zhou was in Moscow, where he had gone in April, sailing for France on a fake passport. "Li Lisan must have gone mad," Zhou said to the Russians in Moscow.

Zhou went to Moscow to discuss Moscow's growing restlessness regarding the conduct of affairs in the CCP. The Japanese had now attacked the Chinese railways in Manchuria, as augured in 1928. The U.S.S.R., as always, was deeply apprehensive of a war on two fronts. Threatened by the West, they wanted to be sure that Chiang Kaishek would not join with the Japanese in a thrust into Siberia. Chiang's strange reluctance to do anything against Japan, even when the latter invaded China, was already obvious. Liu Shaoqi organized strikes among the railway workers in Manchuria, drew up plans for sabotage in case of a Japanese attack. But the Comintern still felt insecure. The CCP must be brought under total control. Zhou was well received in Moscow, but obviously he failed to become the ideal choice. A group of Russian-trained students were on tap, ready to return to China and to take over from the current leaders.

Zhou Enlai pleaded for Li Lisan. "We accept the criticism of the

Comintern. Comrade Lisan should shoulder more responsibility in ideological interpretation . . . merely repeating the Comintern line is not going to solve . . . the concrete problems." Zhou was trying to save Li Lisan, but also to give an accurate account of what was happening. He praised Mao's "rich peasant" policies. "Should we ill-treat the rich peasant [by confiscation or physical extermination] the middle peasant will vacillate even more . . . we cannot afford to alienate him at this time." This did not endear him to the young and ambitious trainees of the Comintern. "Zhou Enlai is a compromiser," was their verdict. It is not merely coincidental that just then Stalin was eliminating the kulaks in the U.S.S.R.

Zhou returned to Shanghai to make a major report, known as the Shaoshan Report—Shaoshan being one of the pseudonyms he used at the time. It was a cogent analysis of the Chinese Party and the Chinese revolution. "The revolution will have to go through a great many preparatory stages—so as to gradually transform . . . into a socialist revolution."

The analysis of the situation, the notion of gradualism, was sound and realistic. Surprisingly, he would abandon this notion of gradualism eighteen months later.

Zhou brought back with him Chu Qiubai, probably with the idea of strengthening his hand in the Politburo. But the Comintern would wait no longer. In October 1930, a letter reached the Politburo accusing Li Lisan of being against the Comintern. Li had committed errors of *line*, a serious accusation. Zhou was accused of "compromising" and of petty-bourgeois mentality. In November, Comintern man Pavel Mif arrived. Ill-mannered, uncouth, shockingly rude, he insisted on a plenum, at which he sat in the presidential chair.

It was mid-December, bitterly cold. No fires were lit. The assembled men huddled in their overcoats. Zhou sat between the Li Lisan faction and the new favorites of the Comintern, known as the Twenty-eight Bolsheviks. Discussions lasted seven days, and a resolution was rammed through. Some of Li Lisan's supporters, sensing the Comintern as too powerful to resist, abandoned him. Right deviationism was Li Lisan's crime, and he was out. Zhou was blamed for having tried to defend him. Self-criticism sessions took place, some of Li Lisan's erstwhile friends distinguishing themselves by obsequiousness toward the new leaders. Among these was Kang Sheng. Zhou Enlai refused to condemn

Li Lisan. "I am releasing my original document, without any revision."

The leader of the Twenty-eight Bolsheviks, known by his Party name of Wang Ming, was twenty-five years old in 1931. His second-in-command, Po Ku (Bo Gu), was twenty-four. They loftily considered "international solidarity" to be their goal, which meant doing what Moscow demanded. China's real situation was beneath their notice. They wanted to "bolshevize" the Party. There must be a "reorganization at every level." Party members were demoted and shifted, or purged at will. Political commissars with enforcement squads were sent to secure "bolshevization," to purge "right deviationists" in every base and every Party branch. The real power of the Te Ke passed into the hands of Kang Sheng, who had shifted over to Wang Ming's side. He had written an article in a Comintern publication, published in the same issue as one by Wang Ming.

Discontent in the Party was plain. A faction formed against the Twenty-eight. Surprisingly, all thirty-six of the rebels were betrayed to the Guomindang, and twenty-five were executed. Who had informed so efficiently? "Kang Sheng," it was whispered among the frightened Party members.

In later years, Mao Dzedong would call the putsch by Pavel Mif an "ambush," and he would always term the Politburo of that period the "provisional" Politburo. Zhou Enlai now volunteered to be sent to Mao Dzedong's base, but permission was withheld that spring of 1931. He might have lost his seat in the Military Affairs Commission and the Politburo, but only six out of the thirteen members wanted to remove him. So he stayed, hanging on. No discussion was possible . . . all important matters were in the hands of Pavel Mif. "I have to be patient, for the sake of the Party," Zhou is reputed to have said to Nie Rongzhen. But later he would remark: "These were destructive years, which needlessly made victims out of good comrades."

Back in 1927 a handsome young man named Gu Shunchang had joined the Party. He had worked courageously during the massacres in Shanghai, had become a Politburo member. Like Ho Lung, Zhu De, and others, Gu Shunchang was a member of a secret society, the Shanghai Red Gang. Gu was talented. He could sing, do conjurer tricks, and kill so efficiently with his bare hands that no trace of injury could be found on the body of his victim. Now he was dismayed, discontented with the changes in the Party. It was the arrival of the Twenty-eight which, probably, catalyzed his decision to betray.

Zhang Guotao, well regarded by the Comintern, was sent to one of the main bases, called the Oyuwan base. It straddled Hubei, Hunan, and Anhui provinces. Gu Shunchang was detailed to carry out arrangements for Zhang Guotao's safety during his journey. He did so, and on his return, passing through Wuhan disguised as a juggler, was arrested by the Guomindang police. He forthwith offered to tell all he knew but only to a "high authority" in Nanjing. It was Friday evening. The Wuhan chief of police sent an urgent cable to Nanjing. His superior was away, and it was one of Zhou Enlai's moles, planted in police headquarters, who received the message.

The mole, Tsian (Qian) Juangfei, was the son-in-law of Li Kenung, the smiling Buddha, Zhou's right-hand man in the Te Ke. Li was then operating in Nanjing, and when told by the mole of Gu's defection immediately took the train to Shanghai to warn Zhou Enlai.

Gu Shunchang knew everything. The safe houses. The hideouts of Party leaders. The liaison and supply routes. Zhou Enlai had to act immediately, and with him were Nie Rongzhen and Li Kenung. Every Party leader moved at once and went into hiding. All the routes had to be altered, the couriers warned. All the safe houses evacuated. "These were really some very frightening days," says Nie Rongzhen, recalling the events. "Zhou Enlai and we did not close our eyes in sleep for several days." A good many Party members were caught, despite Zhou's efforts, but not one of the Twenty-eight Bolsheviks. "Many good friends were killed," Deng Yingchao confirms, "including Tsai Hosen." She, Tsai Chang, and other women took up the work of warning families. "But the Party did not want us to run too many risks. My mother and I left Shanghai." For a while they hid as nuns in a Buddhist temple in Hangzhou.

According to Guomindang sources, Gu Shunchang tried to assassinate Chiang Kaishek, who was in Wuhan at the time. Then he had a change of heart, and confessed. But the Communist version is that Gu "had already decided to betray. He had written a letter. His family were all in the plot. They had been told to

give the letter to Chiang's secret police in case Gu did not succeed."

Zhou Enlai gave the orders. Gu's whole family, seventeen of
them, were executed, save for a young boy of twelve. They were
buried in their own courtyard. Despite his going over to the
Guomindang, Gu did not fare well. He was executed by Chiang's
secret police some years later.

For a few more months, the Party leaders lingered in a Shanghai
increasingly unsafe. Summer went and autumn came. The Japanese
army carried out massive maneuvers in North China, and occupied
Manchuria in September 1931. Manchuria was proclaimed the
independent state of Manchukuo a year later. Puyi, last emperor
of China's Manchu dynasty, was crowned its emperor by the
Japanese.

As head of the Military Affairs Commission of the Party, Zhou
drafted an appeal to be circulated to all the armies of China,
including those of Chiang Kaishek. "We propose to Guomindang
armies throughout the country an armistice . . . so as to unite to
fight Japan." But Zhou's proposal was not supported by Pavel Mif
and the internationalists. "Compromising again! No compromise
is possible with Chiang Kaishek!" The Twenty-eight Bolsheviks
regarded the occupation of Manchuria as a threat to the Soviet
Union. Instead, they announced in the summer that the time had
come to found a "Soviet Chinese Republic." The idea was that
this would prevent Chiang Kaishek from entering into an alliance
with Japan against the U.S.S.R.

In November 1931, the Soviet Republic was duly proclaimed;
its site was to be Mao Dzedong's base. Zhou, as representative of
the new "Soviet central government," was to leave Shanghai and
go to Mao's base to prepare for the arrival of the central
government—i.e., the CP leaders.

In that November the newspapers in Shanghai carried notices
of munificent rewards—up to 100,000 silver dollars—for any information leading to the capture of Zhou Enlai. He had at last
been identified as Wu Hao, whose dagger was so lethal. Chiang
Kaishek told Dai Lee, the head of his secret police: "If we capture
Zhou Enlai, the whole party will collapse."

Zhou Enlai spent his last weeks in Shanghai making sure that
the secret wireless network functioned properly. For a while the
receiving station would be set on the roof of a house belonging

to a British engineer, a friend of Rewi Alley, the New Zealander.

Disguised, some say as a Catholic priest, others say as a Muslim imam with a thick black beard, Zhou Enlai left Shanghai and, using small coastal boats, landed at Shantou, the city port for which he had fought in 1925 and in 1927.

He arrived at the guerrilla base founded by Mao Dzedong in December 1931.

8

The base that Mao established after leaving the Jingang Mountains covered 19,000 square miles in a fertile, well-watered region astride the borders of Fujian and Jiangxi provinces. It had a population of 3 million and some pleasant towns, of which the largest was Ruijin, with about 20,000 inhabitants. It possessed tin mines, and this brought traders and merchants to the area. Chiang Kaishek had mounted no fewer than three "annihilation campaigns" against the Ruijin base since early 1930. In the first one, his 100,000 men encountered the elusive guerrilla tactics which Mao favored. "Lure the enemy deep into the territory, cut him up in small groups, harass him, attack from unexpected quarters, and at night." Chiang's forces were defeated. A second campaign in May 1931 with 200,000 men led by Chiang's Defense Minister also failed. A third began in July 1931, but in September, Japan seized Manchuria, and some of Chiang's allied warlords refused to go on fighting a civil conflict. In fact, one warlord army, with around 10,000 men, went to join the base, bringing field guns, ammunition, and precious radio equipment.

In January 1932, the Japanese attacked Shanghai. The city was defended by Tsai Tingkai, the very man who, at Nanchang in August 1927, had executed thirty Communist cadets in his division. But he was a patriot, and the show his Nineteenth Route Army put up to defend Shanghai electrified millions of people in China. Suddenly Chiang was confronted with a wave of protests, thousands of petitions from the intelligentsia, demanding resistance to Japan. "Internal pacification first, before external resistance," was his stubborn stance. He negotiated a truce—the Tangku truce—with Japan in April. He cut off supplies to the Nineteenth Route Army, and sent Tsai Tingkai to fight the Ruijin Communist base.

For the next two and a half years, Zhou Enlai's behavior, his actions, his published speeches, contradict much of what one would expect from a coolheaded, fair-minded leader. Only in his continuing efforts to moderate the inquisitional methods applied in the "thorough bolshevization" purges do we still find the person we know. But he seems to have enthusiastically adopted some of the foolhardy policies of the Wang Ming–Bo Gu clique. Yet these policies brought the loss of almost all the bases, the destruction of nearly 90 percent of the Communist Party and its armies. There is no trace of the gradualism which Zhou had so clearly enunciated in 1930.

The Ruijin base was to be a "Soviet" seeding ground of what would one day—so went the grandiose verbiage of Wang Ming—become the Soviet Republic of China. But here, as elsewhere, bolshevization produced local conflicts. On his arrival in December, Zhou had reproved the purge of the "AB group," dubbed counterrevolutionaries and Guomindang infiltrators, carried out in the spring of 1931 with implacable severity. "I have been here only three days . . . but the pernicious effects . . . are obvious. . . . Even poor peasants are afraid to approach us now."

Zhou's observation made no difference. The policies of bolshevization went on. Mao Dzedong, who enjoyed popular support among his men, had been voted chairman of the local "soviet." He was inferior in the Party hierarchy to Zhou, who represented the "central government" of the Soviet Republic, and who was a member of the Central Committee, of the Politburo, of the Military Affairs Commission. Mao was only an alternate member of the Central Committee. Mao was not shorn of prestige or power by Zhou, quite the contrary. In March, Zhou wrote to the Politburo, still in Shanghai, recommending that Mao should be made political commissar of the First Front Army in Ruijin. "Comrade Mao Dzedong has rich experience . . . he should be given an opportunity to deploy his talents." Zhu De and Chen Yi countersigned Zhou's suggestion. The Politburo assented at first, but within two months Wang Ming and Bo Gu had changed their minds and Mao was deprived of any army command. Meanwhile Zhou and the military commanders received directives from the Twenty-eight Bolsheviks regarding army building. The Soviet Republic must have a strong, aggressive, and *professional* army. The base must be enlarged, with conquest of more territory and more cities. There must be an end to "passivity" and "conservatism." In the civil sector, the "right opportunist, deviationist, rich peasant policy" practiced by Mao must be thoroughly eradicated and bolshevization carried out. "Peasant localism" was thoroughly condemned. Though Mao objected, he was in a minority. Though chairman of the local government of the base, he had no high rank at the center, and his chairmanship was circumscribed by two vicechairmen, one of whom, Xiang Ying, was hostile to him, a hostility that continued to the end of his life.

Zhou Enlai dithered, hesitated. He was possibly unsure, for Mao's ideas were certainly unorthodox. Zhou did not want to split the Party, which was just emerging from total disarray. Hence he supported the Party line. But one must ask: Was he afraid of being purged? Or was he truly convinced that Wang Ming's line, bolshevization, was the correct policy? Zhou was a courageous man, but he was a member of the Politburo, bound to preserve unity. Hence, for a while, he persuaded himself. He wrote enthusiastic articles and made speeches lauding "thorough bolshevization."

For a brief five weeks in 1932, Wang Ming appeared at the base, but soon departed for Moscow, leaving his second-in-command, Bo Gu, in overall charge. From Moscow, Wang Ming directed everything in the base through long, coded telegrams.

This "revolution by telegram," as Mao dubbed it, was relayed through the wireless transmitters in Shanghai. Only in 1934, when the transmitters were captured by Chiang's secret police, was contact broken off.

In Ruijin, Zhou took charge of the radio transmission apparatus. Trained radio operators, valuable anonymous heroes, manned the stations. Their general name was "Ninety-nine," much as Americans call all radio operators "Sparks." "The wireless was our most important means of communication. Without it no other bases could be reached, we would have had no news." The living conditions and training of the operators was a priority with Zhou, as was the security and secrecy of the codes. He had his office and living quarters next to the largest radio station of the base and brooked "not the slightest neglect or mistake." "Not once did the Guomindang ever break our codes," Zhou Enlai told Edgar Snow in 1936.

"Conflict," what would later be called in Communist parlance "a struggle between two lines," began in 1932 between the "internationalists" and Mao Dzedong.

Mao Dzedong maintained that the base should not, could not, support a large professional army. Guerrillas cost far less and were far more effective. Armed peasants required no special encampments and no uniforms. They could work in the fields, sharing in agricultural labor. They were "like fish in water," among their own families, their own village communities.

Mao also objected to drastic land reform. He had carried out some attenuated kind of reform, only against the most hated, most tyrannous "big tigers" among the landlords, and left the rich peasant and the middle peasant in peace and in control of their land. This was now condemned as "opportunism." A campaign against moderately well-to-do peasants was to take place and Mao predicted disaster. "They criticized me for not doing enough burning and killing," Mao told Edgar Snow some years later. Traders, merchants, who came to the base and brought needed goods, were now dubbed capitalists, their belongings confiscated and they themselves shot as spies. "Some people really do not wish to be contaminated by reality," Mao remarked sarcastically to Bo Gu when the latter fulminated against "peasant mentality."

Mao was not alone in his objections. There were others, among them Lo Min and Deng Xiaoping. Deng Xiaoping had returned from France in 1926. After serving some three months with the troops of warlord Feng, Auspicious Jade, he was sent by Zhou Enlai to establish a base in Guangxi province. This base provided sanctuary to three hundred Vietnamese revolutionaries, since it is next to North Vietnam, and Ho Chi Minh also went there frequently. In 1929, it boasted two training camps for Vietnamese revolutionaries, but it was overrun in 1931, and Deng Xiaoping had then joined Mao in Ruijin. He now edited the Red Army newspaper at the base and sided with Mao and Lo Min. Mao was very popular, so he was not always directly attacked. Instead, Lo Min and Deng Xiaoping were "struggled against," dragged from village to village to be exhibited as shameful examples of "liquidationism." Deng's wife was encouraged to divorce him, and did.

Zhou Enlai, the conciliator, the eternal compromiser, did his best. He tried to protect Lo Min, and he also brought Deng Xiaoping, who had helped him so loyally in Paris, back to his job as editor of the paper. But in speeches he fulminated against "those rightist opportunists who regard the seizure of one or several provinces as not an immediate but a distant goal, who are hesitant about outward expansion, who prefer to tie the hands of our armed comrades with assignments such as propaganda in the villages and raising funds for the army, who are unwilling to move directly to deal a fatal blow to the enemy in non-Communist areas." This was a most exact description of precisely how Mao Dzedong was feeling and what he was doing at the time. Perhaps Zhou was evolving the technique he would use throughout the Cultural Revolution: an apparent enthusiastic cooperation while at the same time trying to limit the extent of physical liquidation . . . but it did not add up to a consistent policy, based on China's reality, to counter the fatal directives of the Comintern and of Wang Ming. Perhaps, used to pursuing two contradictory courses at once, as he had done during the United Front period, Zhou gave lip service to the Wang Ming line, meanwhile striving to preserve the lives of its opponents.

On February 16, 1932, an article appeared in a Shanghai newspaper with the banner headline: WU HAO AND 242 OTHERS RENOUNCE COMMUNISM. Wu Hao was Zhou Enlai. A legend, a James Bond dealing mercilessly with renegades and traitors. If Wu Hao had abjured, then the whole edifice of faith and loyalty that sustained so many Party members in these agonizing times was shaken. Dismay was intense, and Zhou, at the Ruijin base, could not appear in person to refute the so-called news. Roundabout and obscure messages were printed in the newspapers that indirectly refuted the article. In March, a French lawyer in Shanghai, Louis Barreau, who had defended Chen Duxiu when Chiang Kaishek had arrested him, was approached, and a statement in the name of Zhou Shaoshan (another pseudonym of Zhou Enlai) was issued to deny the story.

Deng Yingchao and her mother arrived. Yingchao was in very poor health. She had broken down under the stress, the privations, and Enlai was horrified when he watched her coughing up blood. It brought back to mind his mothers, Winter's Child and Lady Chen, both of whom had died coughing blood. Medical care at the base was very limited because of lack of medicines. Fortunately it could boast an admirable physician, Nelson Fu, the son of a Christian stevedore who admired the hero of Trafalgar. He had been trained at the Gospel Hospital in Changting, Fujian province, and as its assistant director had attended to the wounded soldiers of Ho Lung and Ye Ting when they passed through the city on their way to Shantou in late 1927, on the retreat from Nanchang. He found the soldiers very different from the ruffians of the warlord armies, and this began his conversion from Christianity to Communism. Nelson reached Mao's Jingang mountain base in 1929, followed Mao to Ruijin, and here ran hospitals, clinics, and a nursing school. There were twenty doctors and three hundred nurses in the base. "I've had tuberculosis myself. I know how to deal with it," he said to Zhou Enlai. Deng Yingchao was put on bed rest and remained partly inactive for the next eighteen months. Her mother enrolled in the medical service and was an asset with older patients, who preferred herbal remedies to newfangled Western pills and treatments.

Chiang Kaishek began his fourth annihilation campaign with 400,000 men in July 1932, three months after signing a truce with Japan. Instead of inveigling the enemy into the base and chopping up his units, in true guerrilla style, the Red Army pursued tactics of mobile as well as fixed positional warfare, even while Zhou still praised guerrillas as "efficient help." Offensives against cities followed, successful at first. Zhou Enlai wrote detailed accounts of the military operations and of the triumphs achieved. But as the months went by, the cost in manpower and equipment began to tell. Zhou's enthusiasm turned to worry. He balked at "attacking cities with no possibility of success due to an unequal balance of forces." He discovered that the peasantry was no longer cooperative. Of a particular encounter he would write that "the bloodshed was considerable . . . this is a lesson we must ponder." However, orders were orders, and they poured across the wireless, and Ninety-nine decoded them. Zhou still paid lip service to the line, even when he was assailed by growing doubt. "The main task of revolution is to use revolutionary war to liquidate imperialist war . . . to turn the imperialist war, which seeks to morsel China, into an anti-imperialist, anti-Guomindang, people's war."

The Guomindang now attacked every Communist base in China. Many were overrun. The commanders and their troops retreated to Ruijin, which still seemed solid and successful. The dour, competent organizer Liu Shaoqi was compelled to flee from North China. Yet in Ruijin all was not well. Mao Dzedong went on a survey, and reported that agricultural output had fallen. There was trouble obtaining daily necessities, since traders were no longer coming.

In October 1932, a major meeting was held at Ningdu, a town fifty kilometers from Ruijin. At the meeting, Bo Gu led the Politburo in an attack against the "liquidationists"—i.e., Mao Dzedong. He called violently for a purge against those "who sabotage our revolutionary effort."

For a while things looked pretty serious for Mao. He was to be demoted, expelled from the Party. After expulsion, of course, more charges were to be laid against him. It was Zhou Enlai who refused to approve any more drastic measures against Mao Dzedong. Yet it was he who was ordered to "criticize" Mao very severely. This was a custom in the Party, one which is found again and again through the years. Anyone condemned for deviation is criticized not only by his revilers but also by those suspected of being not entirely against the culprit. Zhou's criticism of Mao was considered to be far too measured, and again he was called a "compromiser." "I did not compromise, I only spoke somewhat benignly," said Zhou. "You harbor nonrevolutionary ideas," accused Bo Gu. In the end, Mao was not expelled, but temporarily suspended from any activity, though he remained chairman of the base. He became conveniently ill with malaria.

In June 1933, as the fourth annihilation campaign wound to an end—and to apparent victory for the Communists—a very long telegram from Wang Ming in Moscow was received, concerning the conduct of military affairs and the expansion of the base.

Zhou Enlai, Zhu De, Peng Dehuai, and Nie Rongzhen protested against the extravagant orders given. In his memoirs Nie recalls that "all of us at the front were against the plan in the 'long telegram,' but the *provisional* leadership of the center [he means Bo Gu] would not accept the advice of the front-line comrades." Moscow brooked no dissent. Total obedience was required. Zhou cabled back: "We shall obey, and implement," but nevertheless added objections. "There are certain details which one cannot enter into in a telegraphic message." He urged a meeting to discuss the feasibility of the proposed plans.

Recruitment at the base had been intensified since early 1933. Two hundred thousand conscripts that year, twice as many for 1934. Rallies for volunteers took place. Under the pretext of assessing the size of fields, the Communists took peasants off the land and sent them to the front. Because of the damaging loss of revenue by mid-1933 and the scarcity of meat and grain, arbitrary confiscations, compulsory levies of money, and searches in homes for caches of gold were carried out.

In September 1933, another expert, Otto Braun, arrived at the base from Moscow. For many years, he was to be described as sent by the Comintern. Only recently has it been proved that he was an agent of the KGB; the latter did not trust the "recalcitrant" Chinese comrades.

Otto Braun's Chinese name was Li De. He became the de facto head of the Military Affairs Commission. Zhou Enlai, Zhu De, Ye Jianying, Peng Dehuai . . . everyone had to obey Comrade Li De, who thought that the armies needed German discipline and set out to enforce it. He antagonized the younger officers, used to at least a minimum of discussion with their superiors.

Meanwhile, an opportunity had been missed. In that summer of 1933, Tsai Tingkai, who resented the obscure role assigned to him of fighting the Communists when he wanted to fight the Japanese, sent an emissary to Zhou Enlai. "It is Japan, not each other . . . that we must fight." Zhou was overjoyed. He immediately sent Ye Jianying and Liu Bocheng, senior veterans in the army, to hold a meeting with Tsai Tingkai's delegates. This was an opportunity to be seized, and though the disgraced Mao Dzedong was not officially contacted, Zhou sent him copies of the telegrams between himself and Tsai. The meetings took place in Fujian province, and further good news came when the provincial government announced that it wanted to break away from Chiang Kaishek in Nanjing. Could a United Front against Japan be created? Would not this encourage other warlords, restive because of Chiang's singular passivity toward the invading Japanese?

Zhou selected one of his most subtle, sophisticated underground men, Pan Hannien, to handle the negotiations. Pan was well educated, had a wealthy wife from Hong Kong, and was a friend of Green Gang godfather Big-Eared Du. Pan went back and forth, projecting an image of suave reasonableness, until the wireless began to chatter: another long telegram from Wang Ming, shattering the project. There must be no alliance of any kind with "reactionaries." There could be no "middle ground." Zhou sent an unhappy message to Tsai Tingkai, asking him to persevere, not to lose courage. But Chiang's armies swept into Fujian province and Tsai lapsed into sullen compliance, to emerge again only in 1949 when he joined the Communist regime.

If the Communist base had its German expert, so had Chiang. Adolf Hitler had sent him von Falkenhausen and von Seeckt. The latter was an excellent strategist. "We choke off the base. All I need is three hundred thousand laborers." He erected four lines of blockhouses around the base, a Maginot Line in reverse. The blockade entailed a total denial of provisions, and especially of salt and iron. Without salt man cannot live. Any villager found with salt in his house was butchered, along with his family. All iron implements were confiscated from tens of thousands of households around the base, including cooking *kwoks* and the tips of plowshares.

To obtain salt, the inhabitants of the base now boiled the bricks of old privies. The grain allowance fell to four ounces per adult per day. In Nelson Fu's overcrowded hospitals, rows of corpses were carted out. Under these conditions the Communist armies now had to engage the well-fed forces of the Guomindang, who had new German guns. The Guomindang troops advanced, consolidating their gains by building more blockhouses at each advance. Otto Braun evolved a plan to build counterfortifications. "Not an inch of territory must be given up." Another bright idea of his was "swift, sharp thrusts" from Communist-held positions.

Not only did building counterblockhouses fail, but it drained whatever able-bodied manpower remained available. The base shrank, from twenty counties to seven, to six, to five. . . . Chiang's secret police captured the few remaining Communists in Shanghai, and the wireless link with Moscow was sundered.

Perhaps this was a blessing. In June 1934, Zhou called a meeting of all the military commanders, the Central Committee members and alternates at the base. He also asked Mao to attend the meeting. It was necessary to unite, the danger of total defeat was present, said Zhou. What were the suggestions? Mao came up with several. Make a feint toward Nanjing, to force the half-million-strong army of Chiang to withdraw. Attack the blockhouses from the rear. But these schemes had no chance of success. There was not enough ammunition left. Zhou had a different plan. Evacuate the armies and move westward to join Ho Lung at his base, on the border of Hunan-Hubei provinces.

To leave the base, however, the armies would have to break

across four lines of blockhouses. "Westward is the line of least resistance," said Zhou. The warlord whose troops were stationed along the west flank, Chen Jitang, happened to be a disgruntled man. Unsurprisingly, Zhou Enlai had his mole in the warlord's entourage; negotiations took place. Chen agreed to withdraw his troops twenty kilometers from the route the Communists would take westward when they broke out of the base.

Otto Braun opposed Zhou's plan, but by September he realized the situation was untenable. On October 2, Zhou's suggestion was adopted. Only two weeks were allotted to carry out the massive exodus.

Bo Gu, Otto Braun, and Zhou were placed in command of the withdrawal, with Zhou—of course—in charge of the logistics, the real work to be done. It was an awesome task to organize nearly 100,000 men for this breakaway. Meticulously, Zhou drew up plans for each corps, each unit. Not all the Communists would leave. Some 20,000 men were to remain, to fight rearguard actions, to disperse later into guerrilla bands and await better days.

Chen Yi, now very thin, though still cracking jokes, was to remain, entrusted with converting the base into a "fluid guerrilla area." Only fit men were to be left behind, but Bo Gu did not agree to take Chu Qiubai, who was ill with asthma. "He is superfluous . . . his time is past," said Bo Gu. Poet Qiubai was left behind, to be captured and executed when the base was overrun. Some thirty women, including Deng Yingchao, Tsai Chang, and the wives of Politburo or Central Committee members, were selected to leave. Yingchao was on a stretcher, still very ill. Her mother was left behind. She was jailed when the Guomindang secret police found out who she was.

Dr. Nelson Fu placed the sick and wounded in peasant families, hoping they would be cared for and survive. Most were killed. Children under twelve, young babies, were left behind. Mao Dzedong abandoned two of his children by his wife, Ho Dzejen. Sturdy boys over twelve went with the soldiers. They would grow up into Red Army men, officers, commanders. Day and night the air was black with smoke as stacks of documents and files, the archives of the "Soviet Republic," were burned.

On October 16, as the first winter fog crept over Ruijin, the exodus began.

Zhou Enlai stood by the roadside, watching the armies file by. He was responsible for what had happened. He had decided on the exodus. The soldiers marched out singing. Red banners headed every regiment. This was not defeat, oh no. A defiant manifesto had been issued. The Red Army was marching northward to fight Japan! Once again, it offered alliance with any army in China that would do the same.

Had the Moscow wireless been on, this might not have happened. But the manifesto had been drafted by Mao Dzedong, along with Zhu De, Zhou Enlai, and the military commanders. Two of the Twenty-eight Bolsheviks, who were at the base and who soon would dissent from the policies of Wang Ming and Bo Gu, also signed the manifesto.

Otto Braun was not asked to comment.

Eighty-seven thousand soldiers. Ten thousand political cadres. Ten thousand Youth Corps members. Five thousand porters, one hundred twenty mules, one hundred twenty-five stretcher bearers . . . a procession ten kilometers long, making up what Zhu De called the Scorpion. The right pincer was formed by the First Front Army with sallow-faced Lin Biao as commander and Nie Rongzhen as political commissar; the left was commanded by Peng Dehuai, also named Boring Through Rock, burly, plain-speaking, adored by his men. The Eighth and Ninth armies brought up the rear.

The body was made up of the leaders, the cadres, the Youth Corps, the stretcher bearers, the porters with the equipment. This included printing presses—one for printing bank notes; tools for gun making, which required six men to carry a casing; a drill and a gear; and Nelson Fu's treasure, his bulky X-ray machine, which needed twenty men in three relays. Here in the body were also the radio operators, the Ninety-nines, the radio transmitters, the security guards with gold and silver bullion, and Chairman Mao, riding his horse, an oilpaper umbrella on his back, his nine-pouch bag stuffed with maps slung across his shoulder. There followed the army cooks, carrying their big iron *kwoks*, weight fifteen kilos, plus the regulation three kilos of rice in sausagelike bandoliers crossing their chests. And last, the army tailors carrying their Singer sewing machines.

Thus began on a cold October afternoon the exodus, later to be known as the Long March.

They broke through the blockhouses. The warlord had kept his word, and was away when the Scorpion crawled through his territory. But very soon German-piloted planes strafed and machine-gunned the marching columns. Many died. The decision to walk by night was taken, but now the marching multitude stretched over ten, then twenty, thirty kilometers. Fragmented, units lost contact; porters, dumping their loads, slipped away. Many of the soldiers were new recruits—many veterans had died in the last campaign. They deserted. On November 24, the first two armies reached the Hsiang River, a deep and broad stream barring the way to Ho Lung's base. Ninety-nine tried to reach Ho Lung by radio, but there was no answer. Ho Lung was being attacked and was on the run at the time.

The River crossing was frightful, the battles so deadly, so bloody, that for a long time no one among the leaders wanted to talk about it. Later accounts would vary, memory effacing unbearable episodes. But half of the vanguard First Army became casualties, and one third of the Youth Corps died. Here began Nelson Fu's agony. After each battle he had to select those he would save, those he must let die. For many years he remembered the wails of those left to die.

The women pitched in. Sturdy Kang Keqing, the wife of Zhu De, carried the guns of three wounded soldiers. Tsai Chang would walk, walk almost all the way, giving up her mule to Dr. Nelson Fu.

Zhou Enlai quarreled. With Bo Gu. With Otto Braun, alias Li De. The army was going to pieces. Deserters. Disappearing equipment. Arson and sabotage. At a village called Long Ping, the thatched hut in which Zhou slept was suddenly a blazing inferno. He was saved by his bodyguard. It was said that Guomindang infiltrators had set the fire. Here in Long Ping the Scorpion paused, waiting for its dismembered parts to reassemble. In the bare, deserted village school hall the leaders met. Where now would they head? Where would they go? Zhu De suggested his own Sichuan province. In North Sichuan, Zhang Guotao had formed a new base because the Oyuwan base, to which he had been sent in 1931, had been overrun in 1932. Zhang and the military commander, Xu Xiangqian—which means Going Forward—had settled in North Sichuan. But Otto Braun thought they should try to reach Ho Lung in the north of Hunan province. Zhou remarked that 300,000 of Chiang's troops were positioned between the Red Army and Ho Lung's base. He asked Mao Dzedong to speak. "The Red Army cannot possibly fight another battle now," said Mao. It had not recovered from the frightful losses at the Hsiang River. He suggested going west, into Guizhou province. Three warlords held sway over it, and Chiang's rule was weak. These warlords' troops were well known as "two gun" soldiers. They carried a gun and an opium pipe. They detested bloodshed, preferring the solace of the drug. Zhu De and Liu Bocheng—the latter nicknamed the one-eyed dragon because he had lost an eye in battle—agreed with Mao. The Guizhou warlords were members of the Kelao, the Brothers of the Robe. "It is always easy to talk with a brother," said Scarlet Virtue. Otto Braun was angry. "Comrade Zhou Enlai, you have called an illegal meeting. No plenum of the Politburo was convened, and you have asked liquidationists to give their views." Zhou looked at the German impassively.

"This was a spontaneous decision of the military commanders, Comrade Li De. They wanted to hear other views. Anyway, there were not enough chairs in Long Ping village for a plenum."

Onward and westward, through the Miao minority country. "That's it—we've walked ourselves out of China," said the soldiers, who had no idea that the Miao were one of China's fifty-odd national minorities. The Miao ran away before the Red Army, left no food, and broke their millstones. Some of the soldiers in Zhou's column found unhusked paddy lying in a field. Zhou set to with them, using fragments of stone to rub the husk off the rice grains. The story ran through the army.

December, and not a twitter on the wireless from Moscow. Ninety-nine persisted in trying to reach Ho Lung, and also Zhang Guotao, but in vain. At the halts, military commanders went to talk with Mao Dzedong. He cracked a joke, and everyone laughed uproariously. Nie Rongzhen strolled to where Zhou Enlai sat. "Enlai, we have to draw certain conclusions from the events that have taken place."

They reached the small town of Li Bing, on the edge of fabulous Guizhou province. The name of its capital city, Guiyang, means Precious Sun, because the sun so seldom shines in this land of mist. At the end of December plum trees were beginning to blossom on the hill slopes. At Li Bing, Zhou Enlai called an enlarged meeting of the Military Affairs Commission and the Central Committee. Chen Yun, a thin man with an aquiline nose, had said to him, "It is time to do some accounting." Chen Yun—the name means Cloud—was one of the very few Party leaders from a working-class family. He was to become one of China's major economists.

Each commander gave a report on the state of his unit. Fewer than 30,000 remained of the 87,000 that had set out. Once more Zhou turned to Mao. "What is your opinion, Comrade Mao Dzedong?"

Mao suggested pressing on to take Tsunyi (Zunyi), a city three hundred kilometers to the northwest, and creating a new base there. But a major task was to restore political motivation and confidence to the exhausted remnants of the Red Army. Suddenly Mao was lashing out at Otto Braun, at Bo Gu. The army had been cut off from the people . . . it was no longer what a revolutionary army ought to be. It had become a rootless mob. "Our army has not been informed . . . their views were not taken into account." . . . Zhou listened impassively, though each word was also a condemnation of him. He had been as guilty as anyone else of trying to create a professional army, cut off from the people. The decision to press on to Tsunyi was passed by a majority vote.

Otto Braun now realized that the Chinese comrades had decided to drop him. A new constellation of power was in the heavens. They were gathering around Mao, the new sun. And he was silently, but relentlessly, being pushed out.

The political commissars told their battalions that they were going to Tsunyi, where a new base would be created. No more suicidal pitched battles. On they marched, and Nelson Fu became a happy physician because they hit the town producing the famous *mao-tai* wine, that fiery liquor, distilled seventeen times, burning at the touch of a match. "I can now disinfect the wounds and sterilize my instruments." The soldiers, and Zhou Enlai, also discovered *mao-tai*, and from that time Zhou Enlai came to love *mao-tai* better than any other drink. That is why it became famous all over China when Zhou became Prime Minister.

The Wu River, which barred the way to Tsunyi, was a stampede of water roaring between banks of sheer rock. There was only a tiny beach from which rafts could be launched. Red Army ensign Geng Biao, a former coal miner, plunged into the river to lead a party of swimmers across and to capture the garrison on the opposite shore. "I did not really know how to swim. . . . I had two inflated bicycle tires wrapped around me," Geng Biao told me in Geneva in 1984. Enough boats were seized to make passage possible, and the Tsunyi garrison surrendered without fighting. The soldiers entered the lovely sleepy city, bedecked with magnolia, wintersweet, and forsythia amid the two-storied houses with carved brick portals.

Tsunyi was wealthy. Its population was part Han Chinese and part Miao. There was plenty of food, and the opium trade flourished. The soldiers entered, and behaved well, for discipline had been restored. On January 5, all was made ready to welcome the leaders, waiting outside the city. Flags of red cloth hung from upper windows. Walls were painted with slogans. The schoolchildren waved paper flowers. The army bands made music. The spruced-up soldiers of the First Front Army under Nie Rongzhen and Lin Biao lined the main street, the inhabitants crowding behind them. Tactfully, the warlords and the wealthier merchants had run away.

They came in on their horses, Bo Gu, and Zhu De, and then Mao Dzedong. At the sight of Mao a massive ovation rose from the army ranks. "Chairman Mao, Chairman Mao." On and on they roared his name. The army had chosen its leader.

Impassive, Zhou Enlai rode on. He had taken good care to be a little behind the others, behind everyone else. He let Mao ride ahead, and followed behind.

.

9

Accounts of the Long March have been published in many books, beginning with Edgar Snow's *Red Star over China* and ending with Harrison Salisbury's *The Long March: The Untold Story*. Each one of these records contributes something new, for there are as many Long Marches as there are Long Marchers. Here I mention only the episodes related to Zhou Enlai himself.

January was spring in Tsunyi, and as the regiments marched into the town, one by one, there was new hope, a sense of ease. The army rested, and fed well. The rules laid down for the soldiers were repeated at sunrise, at sunset, and before the noon meal. "No raping. No looting. Not a thread or a needle to be taken from the people. Everything to be paid for. And speak politely."

The political commissars cultivated the inhabitants. They held friendship meetings with the shopkeepers along the picturesque paved streets. The art and propaganda teams put on shows free of charge almost every night. The Communists demanded contributions, but were less exacting than the warlords. The empty houses of wealthy merchants were requisitioned for lodging the leaders, the sick and the wounded. One fifth of the money and clothes found in them were distributed to the poor of Tsunyi. The troops kept their encampments clean.

Zhou Enlai announced that an enlarged meeting would now be held. Otto Braun was outraged. He told his interpreter, Wu Xiuquan: "Zhou should have come in person to tell me."

"He is somewhat busy," replied Wu.

They gathered in the elegant upper room of an absent warlord's mansion: Ten members of the Politburo; another five were in other bases, and Wang Ming was in Moscow. Seven Red Army commanders and commissars. Sitting in a corner was Deng Xiaoping, editor of *Red Star*, newly named secretary to the Central Committee. In another corner sat Otto Braun and his interpreter, Wu Xiuquan. Also taking notes was aquiline-nosed Chen Yun the Cloud. Wang Jiaxiang, one of the Twenty-eight Bolsheviks, wounded in both legs and propped up on cushions, presided. The meeting would last six days, from the evening of January 8 to January 15.

It began with deceptive tranquillity. Mao inquired solicitously about Otto Braun's health. He had found some excellent tobacco in Tsunyi . . . would comrade Li De like some? Braun showed annoyance. What was Deng Xiaoping doing here? "Taking notes," said Wu. Braun was ill at ease. This meeting, which would decide the future of the Party, its army, was being held without any "guidance" from the Comintern. He, Otto Braun, was *not* conducting it, nor had his permission to hold it been asked. Wireless man Ninety-nine had been totally unable to get even a faint sound from Moscow on his apparatus, or so he said. "Too many mountains." He and his fellow operators were scouring the city for equipment, wiring, spare parts, batteries.

Bo Gu spoke first. The military strategy had been absolutely right, since so many victories had been won during the Fourth Annihilation Campaign. But later the odds against the Red Army had been overwhelming. However, the international context must be kept in mind. "We tied down a considerable number of Chiang's forces, and for a long time. To see matters merely from a localist viewpoint is incorrect." Zhou Enlai spoke after Bo Gu. All eyes were upon him. Everyone knew that his attitude, his words, would be decisive. The decision was in his hands. Would he side with Bo Gu?

Zhou began by recognizing his own responsibilities in the debacle. "To take the initiative in recognizing one's own mistakes and taking responsibility for them is the duty of a Communist." He had made mistakes, both politically and militarily. Particularly in the last few months, in the matter of fighting fortifications with fortifications. At no time did he blame anyone else, or attempt to throw the blame on Otto Braun. "I am to blame," he said. When he sat down, there was an audible murmur of sympathy, a stir of admiration toward the man who never shirked his responsibility, never threw the onus of failure on others. Wang Jiaxiang then called upon Mao to speak.

Mao talked for over an hour. He was scathing, sarcastic, unsparing, and scatologically colorful. He demolished Bo Gu's arguments. He criticized Braun by name. He railed against the recruitment policy in the base; all the men from eighteen to forty had been hauled away into the Red Army. Agriculture had suffered. There had been a dearth of food, which had forced the evacuation. The military direction had been all wrong. The armies had been forced to march, without caring for their safety, without planning for their needs. There had been no real study of the actual terrain and geography before undertaking any military action, leading to enormous losses. Not only were the military tactics wrong, but political motivation had been ignored, resulting in a loss of spirit. Yet spirit, motivation, was the very raison d'être of a Red Army. To levy an army of raw, untutored recruits in such haste, in such numbers, then fling it into a hasty, ill-thought-out retreat, was utter foolishness. . . . Braun became very angry and upset as Wu translated, especially when Mao was approved by the commanders present. Mao then brought up the failure to make a "united front against Japan" with the Nineteenth Army of Tsai Tingkai in 1933. "We did not take advantage of this to get behind the blockhouse lines and attack the enemy from the rear." He, Zhou Enlai, and others had been in favor of an alliance with Tsai Tingkai, but this had been turned down. Otto Braun tried to argue, to bring in the "international perspective," but Zhou Enlai stopped him. "We are in a life-and-death situation. . . . We must attend to immediate problems." No political questions would be discussed.

Commander after commander, commissar after commissar, now rose in support of Mao in meeting after meeting every night. Zhou Enlai spoke again at the end. He had to bear "the greater part of the blame." Military planning had been erroneous from the start. "Comrade Mao Dzedong time and again has pointed out our errors." But Mao had been ignored, and since "a Communist should never try to evade responsibility, or lay the fault upon others," he, Zhou, should now step down from his rank as commissar of the Red Armies, withdraw from command and from the Military Affairs Commission. "Comrade Mao Dzedong is best qualified to lead us in military matters, and he should now do so." Not only the Red Army but also the Party should be under a unified authority. This was necessary to assure the survival of both in the grave situation confronting them.

The reaction to Zhou's speeches was extraordinary. "Everyone was moved . . . everyone's heart burned with a feeling of great hope—for here was a man who did not fight for himself, but for the Party," Wu Xiuquan told me in 1984. By so doing, Zhou Enlai put himself at the mercy of Mao, made it impossible for anyone to rescue him from criticism, should they have wanted to do so. But by his relinquishment of authority, his lack of personal rancor, his refusal to exculpate himself, he had raised the minds of those present to a higher level, away from fault-finding and recrimination, onto a plane where each man felt his worth enhanced, his dedication meaningful.

"If Zhou had a fault, it was too great an attachment to Party rules, to Party discipline. But he applied these rules rigorously to himself. He had rescued the Party from near-collapse in 1928. He knew how easily factions arose, bickering and ambition led to cliques. He strove to preserve unity. He would wait a long time before dissenting from a majority resolution. Perhaps sometimes too long," said Wu.

Mao, however, had a bellyful of rancor to work out of his system. He railed against the hasty "house moving" from the base: precipitate, ill thought out, involving tons of cumbersome equipment, so that the soldiers turned into squads of furniture movers who could not even fire their guns before putting their loads down. "We defended what? Sewing machines, printing presses. . . . Men were sacrificed for that." This was a direct attack upon Zhou. Mao wound up another attack on Braun by saying Comrade Li De "cut off toes to fit a shoe." Exasperated, Braun appealed to Liu Bocheng. "You studied in the Soviet Union, you were in favor of a professional army." Liu Bocheng replied: "If there is no skin, how can one grow hairs?"

The resolutions passed at the Tsunyi meeting contained many of these criticisms by Mao, even if personal names were replaced by pseudonyms such as Hua Fu for Otto Braun. The three-man military directorate of Bo Gu, Otto Braun, and Zhou Enlai was dissolved. Zhang Wentian, one of the Twenty-eight Bolsheviks, who now sided with Mao, was made Party secretary in place of Bo Gu. Mao became chairman of the Politburo and chairman of the Military Affairs Commission in place of Zhou. Zhou became vice-chairman, but was renominated overall army political commissar. Zhu De retained his post as commander in chief.

Tsunyi was the watershed, the great divide. Here began Mao Dzedong's supremacy. Here too began the bond between Zhou Enlai and Mao Dzedong, an indissoluble linkage, until their deaths. Not an easy alliance. Deep entente, and profound discord. Devotion and loyalty, but also resentment. The two men exercised upon each other a mutual fascination, because they were so utterly different, in character, mentality, physical build. It was a coupling understandable only if one keeps in mind the tradition of Chinese history. The founder of every dynasty is brought to power, and rules well, because of a staunch, wise, and loyal Grand Vizier. Greatness, in China, not only lies in personal achievement but is also organically linked to the discovery of talent and genius in others.

Zhou had discovered Mao Dzedong. Discovered genius, an amplitude, a breadth of vision, in which his own passion for China could recognize itself. The tragedy of this bond would come later, much later. When Mao, betrayed by the power lust of all around him, feared and envied Zhou Enlai, the only man who had never betrayed him, who had never wanted to wrest power from him, because he had never needed power to assert himself. Robert Frost has a line of poetry: "The heart knows no devotion, greater than the shore for the ocean." Zhou was the shore to Mao's ocean, forever stemming the transcending waves, yet inseparable from them. A Chinese scholar has another view. "Zhou Enlai knew Mao was a tiger. He, Zhou, thought he could ride that tiger."

What had started as an ill-planned flight, threatened with inner disintegration as well as outer destruction, now became an epic. The Long March. Much of the continuing unpleasantness after Tsunyi has been effaced, rubbed out by the accomplished deception of man's memory, which prefers to remember the glory, not the price paid for it.

The days at Tsunyi had been well spent resting, feeding, reorganizing the fewer than 20,000 men who had reached it. Four thousand more were recruited, and at a meeting held in the Roman Catholic cathedral the plans for continuing the march were announced. Chiang Kaishek was mobilizing to attack Tsunyi. It was impossible to fashion a base here. To the several hundred military and political cadres gathered in the church nave, Mao, Bo Gu, Zhang Wentian, Zhou Enlai, spoke in turn. Total unity, smiles on their faces, reassurance. Mao explained the decision. They would go northward, and establish a safe base there. Meanwhile, no more pitched battles. Instead, "fluidity," "ferreting out the enemy's weakness," "leading Chiang Kaishek by the nose," making him pursue an enemy who was elsewhere. "The enemy must not know where I intend to give battle. If he does not know, he must prepare in a great many places," said Mao, quoting Sun Tzu's *The Art of War*, and all present, who knew their Sun Tzu, laughed appreciatively. They were back with what they knew . . . no more outlandish, incomprehensible orders from Otto Braun.

Ninety-nine at last got in touch with Zhang Guotao. Zhang was informed of the meeting at Tsunyi and of the plans to reach his base. The head having changed, the metamorphosis of the body followed. Leaving behind the printing presses, Singer sewing machines—except two—and even Nelson Fu's treasured X-ray apparatus, the army was light on its feet, and swift. Marching out of Tsunyi, they sang the famous formula coined by Mao: "The enemy advances, we withdraw. The enemy halts, we harass. The enemy avoids fighting, we attack. The enemy retreats, we pursue."

Zhou Enlai took care of the logistics, the minutiae of battle preparation, the care of men and weapons. Every night he, Mao, and Zhang Wentian held a consultation, read the dispatches, decided the next move. Chiang Kaishek was aware of the Red Army plans to march northward and threw massive forces to block it. "Make a noise in the east when you attack west," said Mao. Instead of going north the armies were now ordered into the most bewildering marches and countermarches, backwards and forwards, crossing and recrossing rivers, going south, south into Yunnan province as if to capture its capital, Kunming, and then suddenly veering away from it. "The Red bandit remnants are in their death throes," gloated Chiang, seeing the erratic course the marchers took. The vanguard First Front Army suffered the worst losses. Lin Biao, the commander, on his fourth crossing of the same river, lost his temper, called Mao's orders nonsense, and asked blunt Peng Dehuai, Boring Through Rock, to join him in a protest. The pace was killing, the men were tired to death, the whole affair was pointless. Zhou, who went over every aspect of the deceptive feints and thrusts concocted by Mao, sent Lin Biao a stern reprimand. "Every time, we tire the enemy out a little more—but *we* shall never get tired," said Zhou Enlai.

Mao's authority was not yet well established. When the commanders voted to attack a force composed of some local warlords, Mao demurred and, turning to Zhou, said, "You talk to them, Comrade Enlai. They will listen to you." Zhou spent some hours patiently dissuading stubborn Boring Through Rock. Mao got into the habit of letting Zhou do all the convincing. He would sketch out his vision, his plans, maps spread before him. And Zhou would discuss, refine, sometimes add an item of importance. In the end he always knew exactly how things should be done.

Chiang Kaishek had now blocked any attempted crossing of the Yangtse River and its main tributaries. Mao, poring over the maps, decided to go westward, as if retreating to Tibet. Westward, *away* from the route the army should have taken. Westward lay wild unknown territory, but here ran the River of Golden Sands, a tributary of the Yangtse. There was no army here to stop the marchers. It took nine days to cross the river, to reach a paradisal land, the foothills of Tibet, covered with azalea and rhododendron and oleander. The inhabitants, Miao girls clad in twenty necklaces of silver and embroidered dresses, greeted the soldiers with baskets of apricots and cherries.

They had now bypassed Chiang's waiting cohorts, and they could walk north again. But not all regions were friendly. More marching and they were among the Yis, who believed themselves heaven-born, dressed in black mantles with black turbans twisted in a horn, and savagely attacked the marchers. Zhou Enlai ordered the commanders: "Do not retaliate." He sent Liu Bocheng, who had had some acquaintance with Yi aristocrats in his young days, to parley a peace, and by drinking the blood of a fine purple-and-gold cock with the Yi princeling, and swearing an oath of brotherhood, Liu procured assurance of safe passage.

There are hundreds of anecdotes about this extraordinary trek, unique in the history of the world. Some are verifiable, others pure legend. Zhou personally led one attack, rushing forward in the thick of battle. In another encounter, he ordered that the two old mountain guns, acquired in Ruijin way back in 1931, be tossed in a stream. Many of the personal stories told about him make him out an insufferable Boy Scout, such as when he refused to eat a pear because it could not be paid for—no one knew the owner of the pear tree. The soldiers' feet would walk them to victory. Feet became an obsession for Zhou. They must be cared for. Up and down the lines he went, looking at feet. He had grown a beard, his hair was long, and he got the nickname "the Beard."

One more river to cross, the torrential Dadu. A legendary stream, evil water. The Dadu was embedded in the collective memory of the peasant-soldiers as carrying the sobbing, desperate ghosts of the last Taiping rebels who had died here. The enormous revolt of the Taiping, which had shaken the Empire in the nineteenth century, was still vivid in the minds of these Red Army men engaged in a similar rebellion. Zhou Enlai walked along the banks of the feared river. The rain pelted down, and the black muscular water, its pace that of a galloping steed, indeed seemed to scream with the voices of the thousands of restless specters it had swallowed. Over the river went a single bridge, a span of iron chains, with narrow wooden planks threaded through. Only one person at a time could walk it. But the planks had been removed, and on the other bank a garrison waited for the Red Army.

Zhu De tried to cheer the soldiers. "No ghost can scare me!" But this was not enough. Huddled under a makeshift tent, Zhou, Mao, and Zhu De sat for many hours, devising a plan. A small number of Red Army men would leave and walk further upstream, where there was another crossing, no bridge but boats of yak and goat skin laid over wicker, such as are still used in China's far west. They would cross the river by night in these boats, and attack the garrison from behind, timing it to coincide with an attempt on the bridge itself. Here forty volunteers would crawl, hand over hand, dangling from the chains, with planks tied to their backs, to repair the bridge. This was done. The garrison opened fire on the volunteers and seventeen were hit, their bodies dropping into the Dadu. But the diversionary forces had reached the garrison, and they rushed it and overpowered it. Zhou himself carried planks to repair the bridge. "When you walk it, don't look down, keep your eyes on the opposite bank." He was one of the first to cross. It took a week for the soldiers to cross, one by one. It was now May 29, 1935. In front of them rose the Snow Mountains, a massive clutter of peaks, with passes at 15,000 feet. The air was thin, there was no shelter in the freezing nights. Many of the underfed, exhausted soldiers fainted, some died of heart failure due to oxygen lack. A baby, born to one of the women, fell out of its basket tied on a mule's back into a deep snow crater, and no one could clamber down to rescue it. "The mother never quite recovered from seeing that happen. She began trembling, her hands shook. They still shake." This I was told in 1958, twenty-three years later. Those who had the worst of it were the carriers and the cooks. The heavy *kwoks* were too much for heart and lung. Half the cooks died.

Ever since crossing the Dadu River, Zhou Enlai had suffered from intermittent attacks of fever, nausea, abdominal pain. Nelson Fu thought it was appendicitis, then pneumonia, and dosed Enlai with hot pepper and ginger water. Zhou's body swelled, but he helped to carry the stretchers, for there were not enough stretcher bearers. Those who survived crossing the mountains stopped at Maogung, at the northern end of the range, where Ninety-nine's radio finally captured a message from Zhang Guotao, who had been strangely silent after being told that the Red Army was on its way to his base. Now he agreed to meet Zhou, who woke Mao to tell him the news. "Good," Mao said, and went back to sleep.

Mao, Zhou, Zhu De, and Zhang Wentian had collectively sent a long message by radio to Zhang Guotao, to suggest that a base straddling Sichuan, Gansu, and Shaanxi provinces be established. The First and Fourth armies, joined at last, should strive for a strategic position "for the planned offensive against Japan." The base could expand into Xinjiang province as well, which would give access to the U.S.S.R. In his reply Zhang Guotao objected to an eastward and northward expansion, suggesting going westward instead. Mao said, "He is keen on safety." More diplomatic, Zhou had cabled back: "Our aim is to fight Japan. There are no Japanese to fight by going westward. The Japanese have invaded North China. . . . We hope you will come to discuss the matter with us."

Through intercepted radio messages, and the newspapers, which Mao and Zhou procured as soon as they reached any town, Zhou was informed of the discontent among the Chinese population at Japan's continuing advance and at Chiang's passivity. Conditions were ripe, Mao said, and Zhou concurred, for the establishment of a common patriotic front. This was the Party's mission: To lead the people of China in their own liberation, and this began with resistance to the Japanese invasion. On this hinged the Party's future survival, its destiny. Zhang Guotao had to be convinced that this was not a wild dream.

At a place called Two-River Mouth, Liang He Kou, some forty kilometers north of Maogung, Zhou Enlai waited for Zhang Guotao. The latter appeared, riding a glossy horse, with thirty body-guards, and Zhou went forward, exhibiting great cordiality. Zhang showed concern at Zhou's thinness, his evident ill health. That evening, Zhou explained what had happened at Tsunyi. He explained the strategy of a common patriotic front. As usual, he ticked off, on his fingers, the various items. "The course of events is now favorable to our Party. The time has come for our Party to lead the people in resistance. . . . Chiang Kaishek is increasingly isolated." . . . He explained that even within Chiang's own entourage there was anger, protests at Chiang's refusal to fight Japan. The Japanese could only hold cities and railway lines. They could not dominate the rural areas. Zhang Guotao almost laughed outright. He knew of the Red Army's losses, its sorry physical plight. "How many soldiers do you have?" Inflating a little, Zhou with careless assurance said, "Oh, some thirty thousand." It was less than half that number. Zhang Guotao thought that the retreat from Ruijin had been proof of failure, and here was Zhou calmly talking of going north to fight the colossal military power of Japan! "There will be insurmountable difficulties," said Zhang. Zhang controlled 80,000 troops in his Fourth Front Army, had 80,000 noncombatant followers, in an area of 90,000 square kilometers, with a population of 300,000—this was a good, solid base, which could expand westward, obtain supplies from the U.S.S.R. . . .

What Zhang Guotao did not say was that a good deal of the revenue of his base came from dealing in opium, opium coming from the south and going north, which had to pass through North Sichuan. "Your base is insecure. As soon as he can, Chiang Kaishek will attack it," warned Zhou Enlai.

The next day a ceremony was held. A platform had been erected with bunting and slogans: "Let us enlarge the *Northwest* Sichuan base." Mao exhibited great friendliness toward Zhang, and Zhang showed Mao a newspaper item dated June 14 asserting that Mao had been killed by the "Lolos," a pejorative epithet for Tibetans. This was the third time that Mao was reported dead. "You are very hard to kill," said Zhang, and everyone laughed heartily, including Zhou, who watched the two men, aware of the hostility between them. Zhang Guotao had never liked gawky, long-haired Mao, with that visionary look in his eyes, his scalding wit. He liked Zhou Enlai, and he could not understand why Zhou was now so deferential, so respectful to Mao, always turning to him and letting him speak first. "That peasant . . . who is he?" Zhang would mutter, loud enough for his entourage to hear. Mao almost gave up talking with Zhang. "Enlai, you deal with him," he said to Zhou.

They now heard that, on June 10, Chiang had accepted, in an agreement with the Japanese commander in North China, all of Japan's demands, and restated that Japan was helping in "joint suppression of Communism" in China. "Very soon Chiang will launch an attack against your base," warned Zhou. He was now shivering with bouts of recurrent high fever. Deng Yingchao, who, surprisingly, was much better, became very worried. But Zhou could not rest, for Zhang Guotao now argued that the Tsunyi meeting was illegal. He, not Mao, should wield Party authority. Zhou offered to sacrifice himself. Zhang Guotao could have his post of vice-chairman of the Party and the Military Affairs Commission. But Zhang wanted Mao's office. "That is not possible. You can replace me, but Mao is not replaceable," said Zhou Enlai.

Zhou's resignation from the vice-chairmanship was accepted, and a resolution nominated Zhang Guotao in his place. "Our next move is to take the city of Songpan, because it controls the major roads," Mao told Zhang, showing him his maps, clear and accurate. These had been seized when a convoy of Guomindang trucks full of supplies, food, and weapons had fallen into the army's hands in March. "Chiang Kaishek is sending one of his best generals, Hu Tsungnan, to Songpan. But Hu Tsungnan's main body of troops has not yet arrived. The city can be taken now."

Zhang Guotao, with two army battalions, marched toward Songpan, but his heart was not in the enterprise. He made a simulated assault, fired some guns, and then withdrew. Hu Tsungnan himself would tell the story. "I was in Songpan, but with very few troops. The Reds could easily have taken me prisoner. Had they done so, I would have thrown myself on the mercy of Zhou Enlai, since we knew each other at the Huangpu Military Academy. With him my life would be spared."

Chiang Kaishek, accompanied by von Falkenhausen, flew into Sichuan to direct operations against the Communists. Zhou was proved correct: Zhang Guotao's base was the next target.

The Red armies shifted northward to Maoerkai, a large Tibetan town. Here, at a place called Shawo, Sandy Burrow, another meeting was held. Beyond Maoerkai, barring their way northward, were the Great Marshes, 10,000 square kilometers of grass and thickets and bulrushes growing on bogs of slime, traversed by streams, where clouds of insects hummed and fed on travelers, and Tibetan marauders swooped upon the unwary or the unarmed. The marshes had to be crossed to go northward. No other way was possible. Every other road was blocked by Chiang's armies.

Zhou collapsed. He could not attend the meeting at Sandy Burrow, for he was delirious, with high fever. "He has a hepatic abscess," said Nelson Fu, who thought he would die. Because of Zhou's absence, the talks between Mao and Zhang were at an impasse. Zhang thought Mao a man "who knows no heaven above him, nor any of the rules of mankind." Mao thought Zhang wanted to become a warlord, waxing rich on the opium trade.

Here the armies stuck for eighteen days, while Zhou hovered between life and death. Somehow, his fever subsided. The abscess resorbed. He improved. He was up, though still weak. He had been moved to Zhang's headquarters, a built encampment where there were beds and blankets. One morning, through the window, he saw a file of manacled prisoners being led across the drilling ground. Among them, a familiar face: Liao Chengzhi, son of the late Liao Zhungkai, Sun Yatsen's erstwhile Finance Minister, murdered in Guangzhou in August 1925! Why was his son here? "These are counterrevolutionaries and spies," the bodyguard told Zhou. When the armies moved, they would probably be shot.

Young Liao, Liao the Sailor, was an adventurous spirit. He had shipped himself on boats to Belgium, to Holland, to Africa. He had studied at Hamburg University in 1928, returned to work in Shanghai. He was often seen at Soong Chingling's house on the rue Molière, with his sister Grace, Chingling's secretary. He was an able liaison man, with connections in Hong Kong, in Japan, and among the Overseas Chinese. Chiang's secret police arrested him in 1932. He was spared because of Soong Chingling, who pleaded for his life with her detested brother-in-law. He had followed Zhang Guotao to the base at Oyuwan. The "bolshevization" purges had caught up with him there, and he was accused of spying for the Guomindang. Zhou asked Zhang Guotao to let him see Liao. When the young man appeared, Zhou interrogated him with seeming harshness. "Do you now realize what mistakes you have committed?" Zhou played this comedy to save Zhang Guotao's face. Zhang had been carrying out the orders of the Twenty-eight

Bolsheviks. Zhou had to appear to concur with Zhang Guotao's verdict, and at the same time find extenuating circumstances for Liao. In later years, many times, Zhou would do the same, saving many people in this peculiar manner, particularly during the Cultural Revolution.

Zhang Guotao took the hint. If Zhou knew young Liao, then of course this meant that Liao was not altogether bad. Liao was freed, to accompany Zhou northward. Zhou managed to send young Liao to Hong Kong, where he would do most useful intelligence work until 1941.

Zhou, well again, worked out a compromise between Mao and Zhang. Much of the First Front Army, under Lin Biao, and a portion of Zhang Guotao's Fourth Army, under Xu Xiangqian—Going Forward—were to make up one column, moving through the Great Marshes by the eastern route, a series of treacherous pathways through bogs and shifting streams. Mao, Zhou Enlai, and Ye Jianying would be with this eastern column. Zhang Guotao, with most of the Fourth Army, but also elements of the First, including Zhu De, would pick his way across the western route through the marshes. Both columns would join after the perilous crossings and go northward to found a base. This bizarre arrangement amounted to Zhang and Mao giving hostages to each other.

Before leaving, the Party, proclaiming itself "united as never before," broadcast a solemn appeal to "all our fellow countrymen" to form a united front for resistance to Japan and for national salvation. Loudspeakers broadcast the message to the collected armies, and everyone sang the Internationale.

Crossing the marshes. "This was the darkest time of all . . . the darkest period in our history. . . . Our condition was desperate. We not only had nothing to eat, but nothing to drink. The water was foul . . . yet we survived," says Wu. The agony was not only physical. Both Mao and Zhou also endured mental stress, not knowing whether Zhang Guotao would cooperate. Zhou was carried, part of the time, on a stretcher. The bearers, slipping in the putrid slime underfoot, tipped him into the water. Deng Xiaoping came to his rescue. He insisted that Zhou, who wanted to walk, could not do so "with water up to the chest," so back he went on a stretcher. The men were wet all the time. It rained. They suffered from diarrhea. "Everything we ate seemed to come out exactly the same." Tibetan marauders shot at them. The corpses could not be buried. They were laid away from the path, among the tall bulrushes. Five hundred men died in the crossing. Zhou got up, insisted on walking. He suggested that the soldiers undo their leggings and tie them into a rope, tying themselves into a chain, so that if one fell when crossing the many streams, he could be pulled up by the others, the stronger helping the weaker. He would have tied himself with them, but he was not allowed. The soldiers took off their leather belts and boiled them in water, adding wild herbs. "The three delicacies soup," Zhou called the concoction, and tasted it. "It is excellent."

The marshes took eight days to cross. Beyond was Bashi town, and Hu Tsungnan's 49th Division waiting for them. But nothing could stop the Red Army now. They fought like demons, desperate, fierce, and routed the enemy. Then they waited for Zhang Guotao. Elements of his Fourth Army arrived, to be greeted with joy, but on September 4 Zhang sent a message. He could not come because of floods. And, furthermore, he had changed his mind. Going north was suicidal. The land was arid, almost desert, the people were Hui Muslims, renowned for their cruelty. They fought and killed Han Chinese whenever they could. Zhang Guotao ordered the Fourth Army battalions who were with Mao's column to return to him. In code, he sent another message to a trusted commander of his in the eastern column. He hoped Mao and Zhou would give up their mad ideas. . . . "If they do not, we might have to have a struggle." The coded message, coming to Ninety-nine, was intercepted by Ye Jianying, who brought it to Zhou Enlai. Zhou was very upset. "This is worse, worse than the Great Marshes or the Snow Mountains." This augured a split in the Party, and a split meant the ruin of all their hopes, of expectations for the creation of a united front against Japan. Zhou then went to see Commander Xu Going Forward. "What kind of a struggle does Comrade Guotao have in mind?" he asked, showing him the telegram. Going Forward was dumbfounded. "Have you ever heard or seen the Red Army attack the Red Army?" he asked.

Mao decided to leave immediately, giving no warning, with his First Army. They were no more than 6,000, perhaps fewer. They walked away, and Zhang Guotao's loyal officer sent troops in pursuit. Zhou Enlai, who had placed himself in the rear guard, faced the pursuers. "What are you trying to do? If you want to shoot, shoot me. Are you Chinese? Are you Communists? Chinese do not fight Chinese. . . . We turn our weapons against the Japanese." The pursuers wavered. Zhou went on talking, trying to get them to join him, but they were in loyalty bound, and so they went back.

There were now too few of them to establish a large new base as projected. Mao and Zhou had no other choice except to join an obscure, small, and poor Red base which had been founded years ago by a man named Liu Jidan.

The base was in the north of Shaanxi province. Liu Jidan had been a Huangpu cadet, had become a Communist, and in 1929 Zhou Enlai had sent him to found a base, at the same time as he had sent Ho Lung. Strategically, it was well placed. It gave access eastward to the Yellow River plains, northward to Ninxia province, southward to the capital city of Shaanxi province, Xian. Though poor, in the "yellow earth" loess region of North China, it had survived. Ninety-nine sent a radio message and received a warm reply. Yes, the marchers were welcome.

North they marched, in September, the cold winds of Siberia beginning to blow. Another fierce battle at the pass of Ladzukou, with a grievous loss of men, and on to climb the Six-Detour Mountain, Liupan Shan, and again a battle. In front of them now the yellow desolation of the loess, a lunar landscape, gullies and cliffs carved by rain, changing with the wind. But also, here, were the remains of the Great Wall, and it made their hearts beat faster, for they were back in the cradle of their culture and their people. This is where the Hans had begun, where the entity called China had been born, and not far was the grave of the Yellow Emperor, that semimythical ruler-founder of the race. It was October 19, 1935.

A dust storm hit them as they arrived at a bare huddle of cave dwellings scooped out of the malleable cliffs, the town of Wuzhichen, where they were met by a welcoming party of Red Army soldiers from the base. But Liu Jidan was not with them. He was chained in a hovel that served as a jail. "Bolshevization" had taken place. Liu and his supporters, dubbed counterrevolutionaries, were due for execution. In March 1989, the vice-president of the National Assembly, Xi Jungxun, told me the story, with gusts of laughter. "I was a poor peasant boy of fourteen when I ran away from home to join the Party. But the Twenty-eight Bolsheviks did not spare me. I too was due for execution, or rather for burying alive, because there were not enough bullets. I was saved by the arrival of Mao and Zhou."

Zhou explained that "bolshevization" was no longer the line. Everything had changed since Tsunyi. Liu Jidan was released.

The Long Marchers were now no more than 4,000. Every man was issued a padded jacket, but Zhou would not accept his. He had an old leather coat, bought in France, which he wore, and he gave the jacket to his bodyguard, young Wei, who had almost gone blind on the way with infection and lack of vitamins. Zhou had cared for him, put Wei on his horse to ride, while he walked.

The newcomers settled in the district of Bao An, and scooped caves out of the loess, as everyone else did. Zhou Enlai and Deng Yingchao now had a home, a womblike burrow of yellow earth in which they would live. On a rough-hewn table Zhou placed his inkwell, ornate and rather heavy, which he had bought in France and which bodyguard Wei, knowing Zhou liked it, had carried throughout the Long March. In this wasteland of sand and wind, the most unfavorable territory one could imagine, the Grand Design took shape.

That October, Zhang Guotao, back in North Sichuan, declared his own Central Committee, proclaimed that the Tsunyi meeting was illegal, and expelled Zhou Enlai from the Communist Party. Zhou was the culprit. He had raised Mao to the Party chairmanship at Tsunyi.

Zhou used conciliatory language. Another offer to Zhang Guotao to become vice-chairman of a united Party. This did not work. He sent other messages. Only Zhang Guotao would be blamed, no one else, if anyone from Zhang's army came over and joined the base.

In April 1936, Ho Lung arrived with his remnant battalions, and Zhou was overjoyed to see his old friend. The two men hugged each other, and Ho Lung scooped a cave for himself not far from the Zhous.

In October 1936, Zhang Guotao, totally defeated, at last came to join Mao Dzedong and Zhou Enlai. He was received with effusive joy. Zhu De was with him, "thin as a ghost," and told Zhou that he had been held against his will. Zhou was not going to rake up the past. Let oblivion bury it, as the sand buries graveyards. There was so much work to do, so much. Zhou was already, with Mao, preparing the future.

III

1935–1949

The Second United Front
Yenan
World War II
The Rectification
The Chinese Communist Revolution
Zhou Enlai becomes "China's
housekeeper"

10

"Even during the Long March the Party never lost touch alto-gether. Zhou Enlai kept his underground working." Rewi Alley, a pivotal figure during those years of duress, told me the story, a story he has not published in full. "Couriers, quiet young men, were arriving in my house in Shanghai. I was above suspicion, as inspector of factories. I kept in touch with Agnes Smedley, who never read Marx, but was all for action. It was Agnes who brought the couriers. 'This is Charlie,' she'd say, or 'Call him Bill.' They would say to me: 'We need this . . . can you try?' We tried. . . . Soong Chingling was in it too. She was an excellent smuggler. And we smuggled, how we smuggled. . . . Soong Chingling sent casefuls of pistols and ammunition to the new base. A Dr. Herbert Wunsch, a refugee from Hitler's Germany, established a dentist business in Xian, the capital of Shaanxi province. Since a foreigner enjoyed extraterritorial rights, no police ever looked into any of the cases sent to him. . . ."

The new troglodytes of the loess cliffs, 4,000 of them, had to survive. They planted their own millet, spun their own cloth. Enough land reform was carried out to win support from the villages, but not so much as to antagonize the better-off farmers. Traders and merchants with their mule packs were welcome. Ab-olition of usury—which ran to 60 percent per month—was a pop-ular measure. The Red Army survived its first winter. . . .

Zhou and Ye Jianying personally monitored the messages sent and received. Zhou lived next to the radio station set up at Bai-jiaping, until December 1936. In mid-1936 Zhou created what is today known as the Xinhua, or New China, News Agency. "My friend Camplin, a British engineer, received the messages from Xinhua, and from Shanghai they were transmitted to Hong Kong, where Liao the Sailor operated a distributing agency," said Rewi.

Zhou also tackled local community relations. He directed his agents to enter the powerful Gelao secret society. On this entente depended the unimpeded passage of goods, of kerosene, of weaponry.

But Zhou's greatest success, the task for which he was now preparing himself, was the "capture" of Chiang Kaishek, one of the most fascinating episodes of the Chinese revolution's tortuous history.

In January 1936, the Red Army commanders at the new base sent out an all-China appeal, offering cessation of internal warfare, urging unity to save the country, and proclaiming the Communist Party's intention to wage an anti-Japanese war of resistance. The message was well timed. In December and January, massive student demonstrations against Japan had taken place in Beijing and Nanjing. Chiang crushed the student protests, but the agitation continued. An All-China Federation for National Salvation was created, and among its supporters was Soong Chingling.

Suddenly, the small base, smothered in yellow earth, became important, a focus for the patriotism aroused by Japan's invasion.

Xian was the headquarters of two armies: one under General Yang Hucheng—Yang Tiger City—and the other under Zhang Xueliang—Learning Excellence—also known as the Young Marshal. Chiang Kaishek ordered them to "annihilate the Red bandit remnants." In December, soon after the Long Marchers had reached the area, Zhang made a sortie against the Reds. But his troops were defeated. The captured officers and men were treated as guests. Zhou went to see them and talk with them. The Great Charmer, with a voice full of emotion, spoke of Manchuria, where they came from and where he had been to school, and recalled learning patriotism there. When the prisoners had been returned to Xian, even their uniforms had been washed clean. They were now the best ambassadors of the Communists. The Communist radio broadcast every night a repertoire of songs recalling the beauty of the Manchurian rivers. The armies in Xian listened. The Young Marshal's aide-de-camp suggested shooting the "traitors," but Zhang Xueliang's father had been killed by the Japanese, and he had been driven from Manchuria by the invaders when Chiang failed to help him fight them. Gazing at the bleak winter-wrapped land, he said, "No, let them be."

Zhou had also dug from his encyclopedic memory the name of a student in Berlin, Wang Bingnan. Wang was a relative of Yang Tiger City. Zhou sent for him, and he returned in February 1936 with his German wife, Anna. It was totally natural that he should be frequently in Xian, talking with his relative General Yang. The latter was even less happy than the Young Marshal about Chiang's strange reluctance to fight Japan. "How shall I face my ancestors?" he asked.

The CCP now sent an open letter to both army commanders in Xian, welcoming anyone who would come to discuss an anti-Japanese alliance. So well did these deft approaches succeed that on April 9 Zhou and the Young Marshal met in the abandoned Catholic church of Yenan, a town on the Yen River, surrounded by loess cliffs riddled with troglodytic caves and distinguished by a tall Song dynasty pagoda. At the time Yenan was not within the Red base, but by the end of 1936 Yang graciously ceded it to the Communists. The word Yenan would soon denote the entire base, and would become a talismanic word, symbol of hope and love of country, a new Jerusalem for many thousands of young Chinese students and intellectuals who began in 1936 to walk, to ride, toward Yenan, despite the fact that prison, torture, and sometimes death, was their fate if they were caught.

In the nave, facing the dusty altar, Young Marshal Zhang and Zhou talked. At a discreet distance stood the bodyguards, among them Li Kenung and "Charlie." Zhang wore an impeccable uniform and the black wool cape which Chiang Kaishek had made fashionable. Zhou wore an uncouth gray cotton padded jacket and trousers. An anti-louse campaign was on in the base, and his head and beard were shaved. The talk lasted five hours, and several times, according to the bodyguards, one or the other was seen to weep.

At the next meeting Zhou had the postulates of an agreement ready. "Should Chiang be willing to head a *Government of National Defense* against Japan, we shall gladly cooperate and recognize him as our leader." Of course, such a government would comprise "representatives from *all* parties, groups, sectors of society, whatever their political beliefs or religion. . . ." And this was the heart of the matter. Through this preamble to any agreement, the CCP would get legal recognition as a party. Zhang conveyed this proposal to "Generalissimo Chiang." His letter elicited no reply, only an order to launch an assault on the Red base. In June, with a heavy heart, Zhang Xueliang complied with the order "to prove my loyalty," and failed. Zhou wrote to him, "Inhuman is he who slays his own brother to feed the wolf." Upon which, it is said, Zhang burst into tears.

A tripartite agreement between the Communists, Yang Hucheng, and Zhang Xueliang was now worked out, declaring unity of purpose in resistance against Japan. By the middle of summer, training sessions for Yang's and Zhang's staff were taking place under the able direction of Ye Jianying, Heroic Sword. Supplies to the base were now assured.

Zhou wrote a stream of letters to well-known intellectuals, to eminent personages in the Nanjing government, to professors, to Guomindang officials, describing the Long March as "preserving our vital forces to fight Japan," insisting that its purpose was to resist the invader: "We cannot endure that five of our provinces should have been surrendered to Japan," he wrote. "To lose North China is to lose all of China. . . . Without distinction of party or belief or religion, let us unite to create a government of national defense." In August he drafted, for the Central Committee, an "open letter to the Guomindang Party," reiterating the proposal for a united front. Again the timing was excellent. For in June, Chen Jitang, the southern warlord who had so obligingly pulled back twenty kilometers to allow the Red Army free passage out of Ruijin, joined with two other warlords to rebel against Chiang Kaishek. They proclaimed their intention to march northward to fight Japan. Obviously, patriotic fever was catching. Chiang defeated the attempt, but its shock waves rippled through the land. On September 22, Zhou wrote to Chiang Kaishek himself. Addressing Chiang as "elder born," Zhou recollects that it is a decade since they became adversaries. "Meanwhile the Japanese have wrested half of our mountains and rivers. Their further objective is the control of China." Sun Yatsen had proclaimed a united front in 1924, and all successes were due to what Chiang had then accomplished, the Huangpu Military Academy, the Guomindang army, the Northern Expedition to Wuhan. "But as soon as elder born . . . had split the united front, there were revolts among the people, disagreement with near ones." (This not only refers to Soong Chingling but hints that Chiang is encountering protests even from his brother-in-law, T. V. Soong, and his own wife, Soong

Meiling.) The loss of Manchuria and five years of external invasion and internal turmoil had followed. "Elder born . . . should not become a pawn to traitors and pro-Japanese elements." The Red Army was ready to send representatives to discuss the great plan of resistance to Japan.

Chiang never answered the letter.

Stalin was not happy with the Chinese Communists. The Tsunyi meeting was not recognized or validated by the Comintern, and Otto Braun possibly made quite sure that it would not be.

Stalin was worried about war on two fronts, west and east. The rise of fascism in Germany and Italy, the victories of a powerful, militaristic Japan, confronted the U.S.S.R. with a situation in which, once again, she needed the CCP. The U.S.S.R. now promoted vigorously a united front with Chiang Kaishek, just as it was pushing, in Europe, for "united fronts" in every country. But Stalin could not see the difference between winning over Chiang Kaishek and handing over the power and the gun to him. Mao exploded with scatologically expressed outrage. "Our Russian comrades have not clearly analyzed the situation," was Zhou Enlai's acceptable interpretation of Mao's outburst. Zhou sent meticulous analyses to Moscow, including a detailed study of the composition of the Guomindang government in Nanjing and of its various factions: pro-Japan, pro-American. He concluded that Chiang Kaishek was already on the horns of a dilemma, and that this was the time for the CCP to assert itself. He also suggested that it was time Moscow sent some supplies to the Yenan guerrilla base.

In September, Chiang flew to Xian to upbraid Young Marshal Zhang and Yang Tiger City for their laxity toward the Reds. He lectured their assembled officers. His remarks were ill received. "You are undisciplined," he fumed to the Young Marshal. With this warning, he flew to Loyang on the Yellow River, where he kept a massive number of troops in the province, controlled by pro-Japanese warlord Yen Xishan. Yang Tiger City and the Young Marshal realized that Chiang planned to move them away and replace them with troops from Loyang. On October 1, Chiang awarded medals to all his commanders, except to Yang Hucheng and Zhang Xueliang.

Zhou continued his dexterous operation: conciliation, explanation, seduction, at all levels. He told Red Army commanders and the political commissars to "use political sense, not weapons," in their sporadic clashes with the local troops. He became quite worried when brash, battle-loving Peng Dehuai wanted to gain a military victory on the battlefield. "Give in a little bit, let them get away. . . . Win friends." Now he geared the Xinhua News Agency, and the newspaper printed at the base, to "speak softly." He went over the articles, frowning at inflammatory phrases, crossing out provocative sentences. "Not so much fire . . . it smells of gunpowder here . . . use a reasonable tone."

Chiang prepared for a final annihilation campaign against the base. He returned to Xian, flying in on December 4.

Zhang Xueliang had now worked himself up into a mood of ancient, classical tragedy. In China's tradition, a loyal official tries to expostulate with the emperor "by words"; if this is ignored, "with tears"; if this does not succeed, then expostulation "by force" is permissible. The Young Marshal began the three expostulations. On December 7 he had reached the "tears" stage. Chiang, staying at the Palace of Glorious Purity, originally built in the Tang dynasty, sternly watched his subordinate weep. "You've been influenced by the Reds, no doubt Zhou Enlai, the man of a thousand different tunes. . . . I tell you that even if I were to die tomorrow, I would first suppress the Communists."

Now the subtle machinery Zhou had set in place began to work. On December 9, 15,000 students paraded in the streets of Xian demanding to fight Japan. Many of them were from Manchuria. Crowds of ordinary citizens came out in support. Zhang Xueliang went to meet them. "My heart is with you. . . . I promise you that we shall fight. . . . Within a week, events will prove it." "You should have shot them," Chiang shouted at him.

Now only expostulation "by force" was left.

It is difficult to believe that what happened next was not known to Zhou Enlai before it took place. Yet, even today, the official version is that the Communists were "completely surprised."

On December 12, around 4 a.m., detachments of army men immobilized Chiang Kaishek's retinue at their residences, occupied the airport and Chiang Kaishek's headquarters in the city. A special posse was detailed to the Palace of Glorious Purity and arrived at 5 a.m. Some of Chiang's bodyguards in the vast mansion were alerted, and a skirmish, lasting twenty minutes, took place, which gave Chiang Kaishek—up at 5 a.m. to do his physical

Zhou Enlai and Karl Marx; his "haircut" after the delousing campaign at the Communist Base (*c.* 1937)

With Bishop Logan Roots
in Wuhan in April 1938

Zhou Enlai with Edgar
Snow (c. 1938)

Zhou Enlai making a speech in Yenan during the "Rectification" campaign. On his right, Mao Dzedong (1942)

Zhou Enlai with Mao in Yenan. Photo probably taken by an American of the Dixie Mission (c. 1944)

Zhou Enlai with American Special Envoy (later Ambassador) Patrick Hurley on November 7, 1944. At extreme right is Colonel David Barrett

Zhou Enlai thankin American pilots for ferrying his staff. T young woman is author's friend, Gu Peng, who was in charge of Zhou's public relations (c. 1945)

Zhou Enlai at pres conference in Shanghai with journalists and staf members, lecturing on the situation in China (1946)

exercises in front of an open window despite the freezing weather —time to flee, leaving his dentures behind. He climbed the ring wall round the palace, but fell in a ditch, then managed to hide in a rock crevice on the hill behind the palace. He was only found there at 9 a.m., and taken to a comfortable apartment in the headquarters of General Yang.

The Young Marshal and Yang Tiger City then sent telegrams to every province in China, and to the Nanjing government, explaining their action, proposing an eight-point program, including the release of political prisoners and a national salvation conference to comprise all parties. This program was in substance what Zhou Enlai had suggested. A telegram was sent to the Red base, inviting Communist representatives to come to Xian and discuss saving the country. Moscow thundered. This was a *Japanese-inspired coup!* In Nanjing, the people seemed dazed. Throughout the world there was stupefaction, apprehension. . . .

"Chiang Kaishek owes us a blood debt high as a mountain. . . . Now is the time to settle the debt," said Mao Dzedong.

Zhou Enlai went into action immediately, to *prevent* any "nationwide" demand to try Chiang or to execute him. Through the radio station, through private messages, went the orders. "Tim," a friend of mine, told me the story. "I had taken part in the student demonstrations in Beijing. On December 12, 1936, Saturday morning, we heard on the radio that Chiang Kaishek had been nabbed. We were very excited; we fully expected him to be tried and executed. That afternoon I had lunch with retired General Gung Chengzhou, whose two daughters were my great friends. They were both Communists, although their father was Guomindang. But he did not go against his daughters' political leanings. He said to me, 'Tim, this is a turning point. But it is dangerous. Should anything happen to Chiang, China will fall apart, and the pro-Japanese in the government will win.' I was no sooner home than the Party man in charge of our student committee came to see me. 'Tim, you must call a students' meeting at the university. We *must* pass a resolution to release Chiang Kaishek, on condition that he agrees to stop the civil war and to fight Japan.' " "Tim" did this. "We found that other universities and groups of liberal intellectuals had been alerted and had received the same message. On Sunday afternoon, December 13, we passed the resolution. But it was only on Monday morning, December 14, that we heard that the CCP Central Committee in Yenan had passed the same resolution, so that it looked as if the CCP had followed national demand, and not the other way round."

A head-on clash in the Party with those who wanted to kill Chiang Kaishek was avoided, as well as a clash with Moscow. The Comintern (Stalin) asked that Chiang be released "immediately."

On December 14, taking with him Ye Jianying, Li Kenung, Bo Gu, and a staff of twenty, Zhou left for Xian. On the fifteenth a telegram in the name of Mao, Zhou, and Zhu De announced that the CCP stood for a "peaceful solution of the Xian incident." It warned that "any hasty or inconsiderate move . . . would only delight the Japanese."

Defense Minister Ho Yingching, portly and treacherous, promptly ordered air squadrons to "bomb Xian flat," and troops from the Loyang army camps to march upon the city. But he also sent a cable to none other than Wang Jingwei, erstwhile "left Guomindang" President, now an admirer of Hitler and of Mussolini, and residing in Italy. "Come back," cabled Ho. Chiang's pro-Japanese Defense Minister was certain that Chiang would be executed. He wanted to set up a government with Wang Jingwei as President. Then peace would be made with Japan and he, Ho Yingching, would be splendidly rewarded. . . .

But there were other ideas among the pro-American group, headed by Chiang's wife, Soong Meiling, and her brother, T. V. Soong. Meiling had seen her sister Soong Chingling in Shanghai. The latter had already received word from Zhou Enlai. . . .

"Do you want my husband murdered?" Meiling brusquely asked the Defense Minister. He had to rescind the orders to bomb Xian, though the army continued to march from Loyang. On Monday the fourteenth she and T. V. Soong sent the Australian W. H. Donald to Xian. Donald had, in the past, been the Young Marshal's teacher and adviser, and was now friend and adviser to Soong Meiling and her husband.

Donald arrived in Xian before Zhou Enlai did. Zhou had had to ride horseback for a full day and a half before catching the plane sent for him by the Young Marshal at Yenan's small airport. Donald pleaded with Learning Excellence to release Chiang Kaishek. But the Young Marshal appeared stunned by his own bold action and could only repeat, "All he's got to do is to say yes, he'll fight Japan. Then all will be well."

Zhou Enlai now turned up. Smoothly courteous, giving an impression of great calm, he told Donald, "We do not want the death of Generalissimo Chiang. We want to save him from himself, from following erroneous policies, from being used by the wrong people around him."

Chiang Kaishek had his pride, a Confucian concern for dignity, for face. He could not appear to lose face. Zhou Enlai had told the Politburo: "We must be very cautious. We must not begin to accuse him of crimes. We must talk quietly, carefully . . . try to convince him. We want his own good and the good of the country. If he agrees, then we must release him, for he still controls the largest armies in China." I doubt that many of Zhou's colleagues were convinced. To transform Chiang from an enemy into an ally, from a killer of Communists to a partner with them . . . could it be done?

Riots had broken out in the city of Xian. Vandals, shouting, "The Reds are coming," were raiding houses and stores. Upon Zhou, upon his talent for persuasion, hung the fate of China. He had to cope with the military commanders of both armies who now broke out in open brawls, for or against Chiang. Zhou received dozens of officers, officials, all wanting something from him: reassurance, explanation, reward or promotion. . . . He had to deal with the envoys who now arrived from Nanjing. . . .

Yang Hucheng was irate. "Have you forgotten how many people Chiang killed?" he shouted at Zhou. Zhou spent hours "reasoning" with Tiger City. The Young Marshal began to have delusions of grandeur. He had a wild idea of setting up an independent government in the northwest, under Stalin's protection, and reconquering Manchuria. Zhou had to bring him back to reality. "Zhou was getting quite hoarse," Wang Bingnan tells me. Some angry Manchurian officers wanted to murder Chiang. "Not a hair of his head must be touched," Zhou said. He represented the "temporary detention" of Chiang as "an expression of the will of patriotic people, like yourselves, to fight Japan." Chiang was not the main enemy. He was, in fact, being *protected* against the maneuvers of a pro-Japanese clique in his Nanjing government. . . . So said Zhou Enlai. He stopped excited young students who came out with red flags and slogans to proclaim the "revolution" in the city of Xian. "That is not our intention, not at all."

Donald, who had brought a letter from Soong Meiling to her

husband—warning him of the Ho–Wang Jingwei maneuver—saw
Chiang, and was reassured. Chiang was over his initial panic.
Through Donald he ordered his Defense Minister to stop troop
movements for three days. Donald returned to Nanjing to confer
with the Soong clan, and was back on December 20 with T. V.
Soong, the intelligent, powerful brother of Chingling and Meiling.
T. V. now conferred with Zhou Enlai. The talk lasted six to seven
hours, and on December 21 T.V. flew back to Nanjing with Zhou's
proposals. He returned with his sister Meiling on the twenty-
second, her presence in itself evidence of a breakthrough. "I have
come to live or die with you," she had cabled her husband, but
when she saw him her talk was tartly practical. "You've now got
a great opportunity. . . ." On Christmas Eve, the twenty-fourth,
at 8 p.m., Zhou Enlai called on Chiang Kaishek.

"Zhou saluted him with great seriousness," relates Wang Bingnan. He brought to this occasion not only the right word style but
also the right body gestures. He was calm, courteous, but not
obsequious. It is a scene that has not been recorded, alas, in its
entirety. Only Wang Bingnan, who stood behind the door, would
hear part of it.

Zhou recapitulated the offer of the CCP. "All this you already
know, and you know there is no other road," he said to Chiang.
He only once referred to "erroneous policies . . . which have been
very costly, especially to the country." "Chiang was moved by
Zhou's frankness," says Wang Bingnan, and after a silence, "invited
Zhou to come to Nanjing to pursue negotiations." Zhou then
spoke to the captive about his son Chiang Chingkuo, still in Moscow. "He assured Chiang that his son would return, that he was
patriotic, and undoubtedly wished his father to resist the invaders."

The only problem left was when and how to release Chiang
Kaishek. "All of us wanted him to sign the agreement, which meant
keeping him a few more days. . . . We did not trust his word."
"All of us" means the Politburo, Mao, the military commanders
of the Red Army.

But on the next day, Christmas Day, in the afternoon, as Zhou
was busy in his office, an aide rushed in. "They're leaving." Zhou
hastened to the airport. The plane was a speck in the sky, carrying
away Chiang Kaishek, his wife, T. V. Soong, and also the Young
Marshal. Their departure had been so hurried that Chiang had left
the whole of his retinue behind.

Zhou gazed sadly at the empty sky, then turned away. "Learning Excellence has read too many old tales of loyalty, seen too many old operas. . . . He held in his hand domination over events, now he will be treated as a criminal, and called upon to expiate. . . ." He sent a telegram to Mao and to the Politburo. "T. V. Soong insisted that we trust Chiang. He requested that we allow Chiang and Soong Meiling to leave today. Zhang Xueliang had agreed, and was ready to accompany Chiang personally to Nanjing . . . but we thought that there should be a political document drawn up before their departure. We did not agree to Chiang leaving today, nor to Zhang going with him. . . ."

Should Chiang go back on his word, all would be lost. Zhou Enlai sat in his office in Xian. He was grim. He could—almost—hear Mao say, in that dangerously mild way, "You were always *too* trustful, Enlai." But Wang Bingnan, telling me the story, says, "Zhou knew well that signing would hurt Chiang's feelings. A gentleman's word needs no bond. We had to trust his word. . . . If he wanted to break it, a piece of paper would certainly not have stopped him."

Chiang's return to Nanjing was a triumph. Besides rewriting the incident in a manner that restored his face, he made the Young Marshal stand trial for insubordination. Learning Excellence was sentenced to ten years imprisonment. But he was to remain a virtual prisoner for four decades.

Xian was in turmoil. Friends of the Young Marshal came to abuse and threaten Zhou. Forty officers erupted into Zhou's office and threatened to kill him unless Zhang Xueliang was freed. "Killing me will greatly please Chiang Kaishek, but it will not release the Young Marshal," Zhou replied. Others came to weep and to kneel, begging Zhou to find a way to release Zhang. They could not believe that Zhou was powerless. There were sporadic mutinies among the soldiers. Fighting broke out between some officers, and one of them was killed. Zhou waited, waited, weathering all the vagaries of the situation, persuading, exhorting, explaining. . . . Visitors from all over China came, among them the indestructible Agnes Smedley, who witnessed the death of her friend, dentist Herbert Wunsch, hit by a stray bullet as he came out of his clinic.

Zhou wrote, cabled, both to Zhang Xueliang, on January 10, and to Chiang Kaishek, on January 11. He pleaded with the latter to release the Young Marshal. But in mid-January the sentries of the Northeast Manchurian Army who manned the customs entry post into Xian arrested Zhou's intelligence agent, Pan Hannien, on his way back from Nanjing to report to Zhou. "We found on him documents concerning *direct* Guomindang-Communist negotiations. . . . The Red base was to be recognized as a special area. . . . There would be payment to the Red armies by the Nanjing government." This was selling them and the Young Marshal out, clamored the infuriated officers of the Northeast (Manchurian) Army. Zhou Enlai then showed them the cable he had sent to Chiang Kaishek asking for the release of Learning Excellence. He could do no more. Guomindang armies now entered Xian, and with them was Dai Lee, the head of Chiang's secret police. Immediately posters were put up: INTERNAL PACIFICATION FIRST. "We could hear the knives being sharpened against us," says Wang Bingnan. "We were walking on the edge of a precipice . . . but we had to keep calm."

Chiang's representatives arrived in Xian in February. But no agreement was reached. In early March the Northeast Army was ordered by Chiang out of Xian, to move eastward. Zhou sent members of his staff to see the officers, to console the families. He arranged that a number of his own cadres should join the Northeast Army. Some years later, a good many soldiers of that army would join the Communist armies in the final sweep to victory. Then he called on the Young Marshal's family, his wife and concubine, and consoled the children. He would keep in touch with them through the next decades.

In mid-March, Chiang Kaishek sent another representative, a high-ranking general, to meet Zhou in Xian. Negotiations were now to take place. In April, and in Hangzhou. Chiang had not broken his word.

Zhou Enlai could now leave Xian. He returned to Yenan to report on the whole situation. The plane he flew in was loaned by a Guomindang general. He was gaunt, bone-tired, and had again grown a beard. At the airport was the whole Politburo, and Mao, to greet him.

Zhou had brought it off. The Second United Front. A photograph shows him leaning against the plane's body. He seems strangely detached from the smiling men around him. For a short ten days, he was in Yenan, with his wife. The couple had been allotted a two-room cave, fairly comfortable. Yingchao had begun a vegetable garden on a diminutive plot of land. She had also planted a rosebush in a pot. For a few days, in between long talks with Mao and his colleagues on how the negotiations should be conducted, he rested. . . .

He went to Hangzhou in April. Chiang Kaishek set many conditions, most of them unacceptable. Through all the words, the innuendos, the demands, one thing was clear. Chiang wanted control of the Red Army. In June, on one of his trips by jeep from Yenan to Xian, Zhou was ambushed by armed bandits and one of his aides was killed. At first it was thought that he was the victim. Zhou never raised the issue, although convinced that it was secret police head, Dai Lee, who had arranged the ambuscade.

Had the Japanese realized the very difficult game being played between Zhou and Chiang at the time, had they not moved for some months, negotiations for the United Front might have broken down. But they were heady with success. "We can take all of China in three months," one of their generals gloated.

In July 1937, at a place known as the Marco Polo Bridge, outside Beijing, a clash occurred between Japanese and Chinese patrols, and the Chinese had the audacity to fire back. By then the Japanese troops in North China had grown to 160,000 men, and they moved, heavily, drastically. On July 17, Chiang, who could no longer stall, announced that his government would resist. On the twenty-sixth the Japanese sent an ultimatum, then bombed military camps around Beijing. On the twenty-eighth they bombed Nankai University in Tianjin. In August they attacked Shanghai.

Chiang Kaishek had no alternative but "to walk with Zhou Enlai." Zhou had won. He had captured Chiang Kaishek. But for how long? And how would he keep Chiang bound to his promise?

11

Zhou was no longer the bearded revolutionary, the shaven-headed guerrilla of the caves. He now appeared at receptions in Nanjing, elegant in a foreign suit, the de facto Foreign Minister of the CCP. He became popular with Chinese officials, scholars, with foreign diplomats and journalists. Everything he said seemed reasonable, totally acceptable. "Zhou was that rarest of all creatures, a pure intellectual in whom action was perfectly coordinated with knowledge and conviction," raved Edgar Snow. Agnes Smedley enthused: "The most realistic, able, efficient . . . a man of broad knowledge and culture . . . his judgment free from sectarianism."

Zhou had brought Chiang Kaishek into the alliance against Japan. But it was now difficult to make Chiang accept what Mao insisted on, total control over the Red Army, the bases, by the Communists themselves. "Political and military agreement does not mean . . . to merge with other regimes and armed forces . . . though placed under the unified command of a government of national defense," said Mao. The independence of the Red Army and the bases must be preserved. There must be no interference by Guomindang officials in the Red Army command, in the organization and administration of the base areas.

The Japanese attacked Shanghai in August 1937. Zhou came and went, between Yenan and Nanjing, between Mao and Chiang. In that August a Politburo and Military Affairs Commission meeting was held at Lochuan, a town halfway between Xian and Yenan. Zhou brought to the meeting a package deal from Chiang, who wanted the Red Army to engage in military operations to defend Taiyuan, the capital of Shanxi province, which was threatened by the Japanese. Mao said Chiang would use the Red Army for suicidal assaults against the Japanese while he simply "folds his arms and waits." Mao wanted no fixed warfare, no professional campaigns, no defense of cities. Only fluid, elusive guerrilla war. "Our work should be based uniquely on guerrilla warfare," he stressed, and found that Peng Dehuai, Boring Through Rock, was at odds with him. Surely, to establish credibility, to gain Chiang's trust, the Red Army must engage in some fixed battles, "otherwise Chiang won't give us any subsidies or any guns." The dispute became very bitter. Mao spat out at Peng: "All you want is honors and medals and a beautiful uniform." This was totally undeserved, and finally Mao had to give in partly, and "some mobile and positional operations" were agreed upon. Zhou again acted as a conciliator, and penned some stirring and lyrical statements. "The task of turning bright promise into reality and creating a new China will demand dauntless struggle," he wrote. The Communist Party would give up its policies, discontinue confiscation of landlord land; the Red Army would be reorganized as part of the National Revolutionary Army. "*Un chef est un marchand d'espérances*," Napoleon had said. Zhou Enlai was selling hope with great skill. He thus obtained the recognition of the Yenan base as a provincial government, which also meant legal acceptance of the CCP. The Red Army was redesignated the Eighth Route Army. But it would still operate as a separate force, even if under overall orders from Chiang's Military Council.

In September, Zhou went to the front with the Eighth Route Army to defend Taiyuan, and this compliance with Chiang's wishes brought money and supplies to the army and to the base.

The Eighth Route Army fought what at the time was considered a "side battle" against Japanese forces at a pass called Ping Xing. Though involving a small number of troops, it did rout a Japanese division, and was the first victory in the field of any Chinese army against the Japanese. It made the "BALU," as the Eighth Route Army is called in Chinese, and the commander, Lin Biao, famous throughout the country. "Months later Lieutenant General Joseph W. Stilwell spent half a day with me analyzing the battle," wrote Agnes Smedley. But Taiyuan could not be held. The Japanese brought massive reinforcements. Zhou, covering the retreat, nearly lost his life, crossing the last bridge from the city minutes before it was bombed.

Mao's strategy was proven right, but Zhou had succeeded in making a tactical point. He returned to propose a training program. "If guerrilla warfare is to be carried out successfully, then the

Eighth Route Army must have well-trained political cadres . . . trained in the Japanese language, in Japanese military organization and methods." At Linfeng, in Shanxi province, he and Nie Rong-zhen established the nucleus of what would become a major guer-rilla base straddling three provinces. This was the first extension of Communist power in North China after the Yenan base, and it would become the fulcrum for subsequent Red Army victories in the war against Chiang Kaishek which took place after the defeat of Japan in 1945.

In that hectic 1937, Deng Yingchao's health again worsened. She was sent to a sanatorium near Beijing in the spring. There she made herself popular, and constantly extolled the bliss of the married state, talking endlessly about her husband, "so handsome . . . so kind." When in July the Japanese took Beijing she fled in disguise, and Edgar Snow relates how he helped her to get away. In the autumn she accompanied her husband to Nanjing. Both of them became members of a new organization grouping all parties and all tendencies, named the People's Political Council (PPC). Seven seats in the council were allotted to the Communists. The PPC would have a very long history, and continues to exist today under a modified name. Through the decades Zhou and his wife remained members, and it is the nearest thing to a form of dem-ocratic representation that exists.

Zhou was instrumental in creating a second Communist army composed of the commanders and troops left behind at the Ruijin base when the Long March began in 1934. Reluctantly, Chiang agreed to an army of 12,000 men, but insisted that the top com-mander must be a non-Communist. Like a magician pulling a rabbit out of a hat, Zhou Enlai produced his old friend Ye Ting, who had lived some years in Germany and was now in Hong Kong. The news was relayed to footballer Chen Yi, who had remained at the Ruijin base. At first the guerrillas could not believe their ears. Chiang Kaishek now an ally? When Chen Yi tried to convince them, he was almost shot at by angry comrades. The New Fourth Army, as this nucleus of fighters would now be called, was limited to 12,000 men, but it soon expanded . . . to 20,000, 30,000, 40,000. Its territory was to be north of the Yangtse River, but it acquired units south of the river very soon.

Zhou Enlai's greatest success, however, is one scarcely men-tioned or even well documented. He created, for the Communist government of the future, a "second front" amid the intelligentsia. Students, intellectuals, streaming away from the coastal cities, trekked to the hinterland, and he would strive to reach them. He insisted on starting training courses in all fields in Yenan: in language (Japanese, English) but also in techniques. There was an extensive middle ground, he told his colleagues. This was the intelligentsia from the coast, now crowding into China's west. Some of them had studied in America, in Europe. They were valuable. Engineers, translators, doctors, newsmen, writers, artists, technical personnel. No government could be run without them. His work as head of the Liaison Office favored access to the hinterland universities, which suddenly saw this influx of knowledge and talent. There are any number of stories of how he and his wife took a personal interest, recruited potential talent, in this far-reaching enterprise. Deng Yingchao believed that woman is as able as man, and most of the women who worked in her husband's offices were recruited by her. One of these women, Kang Daisha, told me her story. "My father was a very wealthy banker and businessman. I ran away to Yenan, and there I was visited by a small woman, dressed in baggy blue trousers and jacket. 'I don't want to have anything to do with my parents, they are capitalists,' I told her. 'It is not class origin which is important, it is one's own attitude and actions. Your mother is ill, she has sent us a message, you must return to see her,' the woman said. It was Zhou's wife. She told me that, with my background, I would be far more useful remaining in my environment, going to a university, talking to people who were hesitant, or hostile, convincing them."

Neither Zhou Enlai nor Deng Yingchao subscribed to the "class origin" dogma, and this became increasingly clear through the following decades. Over 85 percent of China's ambassadors and diplomats in the past forty years have, at one time or another, been "with Zhou Enlai." So have uncounted numbers of news editors, members of the Academy of Sciences, and many others. Zhou's "second front," that middle ground he conquered, was a decisive factor in the war against Chiang Kaishek which would begin as soon as the Japanese war had ended.

Late November 1937. Zhou was back in Yenan for consultations with Mao. A dull roar in the sky broke the winter silence. An airplane was landing: a Tupolev. In the small ambulance car which served as a vehicle for important guests—a gift from the Chinese Laundrymen's Association of New York—Mao and Zhou went to the airport. Out of the plane stepped Wang Ming, once head of the Twenty-eight Bolsheviks. He had been elected to the prestigious steering committee of the Comintern. Back with him was Kang Sheng, the chain-smoking myopic man who had run the Te Ke in Shanghai after Zhou left. Wang Ming and Kang Sheng had gone to Moscow together in 1932.

At dinner that evening Mao exuded caustic irony. "It is happiness that has dropped upon us from the skies. Here at last is Comrade Wang Ming, whose immense services to the revolution, whose inspiration and guidance, have proved invaluable in the past. . . . He now again puts himself out to guide us . . . at this historical moment."

Zhou drank, and drank again, tossing off the strong 64-proof local liquor. Wang Ming's presence meant renewed attempts at Comintern influence. At this moment of crisis, when Shanghai had fallen to the Japanese, when Nanjing was threatened, obviously the U.S.S.R. wanted the CCP to make sure Chiang Kaishek would not capitulate. The Politburo met a few days later and Wang Ming spoke on "how to win the war." "*Everything* must go through the United Front. . . . Chiang *must* be the leader." "How can we do this? You want us to give lists of our members to Chiang once again?" said Zhou. Wang Ming's motion was defeated.

Cave living, cabbage and millet, washing once a week, and other non-amenities of Yenan life did not appeal to Wang Ming. He chose to become a member of the United Front Liaison Office, going with Zhou Enlai to Nanjing. Until 1942, he and Bo Gu would work with Zhou, and though there is little on record of a conspicuous entente, Zhou appears to have tolerated them well.

The Communist Party had mapped out sectors of work and influence throughout China, calling them bureaus. Thus the able, blunt Liu Shaoqi had run the Northern Bureau for some years. Wang Ming now was put in charge of the Yangtse River Bureau, covering three provinces in the middle section of the river. This, and Comintern backing, made him a potential rival to Mao. The territory of his bureau coincided with the area where the New Fourth Army was active.

Nanjing fell to the Japanese on December 13, 1937 Zhou,

Wang Ming, and others had to leave, but Zhou remained until the last day, and helped Major Evans Carlson, the American naval attaché, to get away. The Japanese perpetrated horrifying massacres—300,000 people were killed in ten days—and expected China to sue for peace. But confronted with such barbarity, it was impossible for Chiang Kaishek to give in without losing face totally. The Japanese would have to make do with only Wang Jingwei on their side.

Zhou and his wife moved to Wuhan, where they lived in a small but pleasant house on a hill slope, Gejiashan. The area was surrounded by peach trees, and was accessible because of good roads. The intelligentsia in Wuhan welcomed Zhou Enlai, who had already paid some visits in the previous year and given a speech at Wuhan University. He now reached out for them, helped by Guo Moro the poet, who had returned from Japan in 1937. He lectured widely at universities, in schools. He and Yingchao were seen everywhere, Yingchao in pretty, well-fitting Chinese dresses. As in Moscow, the childless Zhous went to the homes where orphans of revolutionaries killed in battle were being reared. Deng Yingchao intensified a search for more war orphans, and they became the proxy parents of some forty such waifs. When well-meaning friends commiserated with Zhou for having no posterity, he would throw back his head and roar with laughter. "No children? Little Chao and I have so many children . . . every child in China is our child." Zhou delighted in playing with children, and his friends would bring their offspring to him on a Sunday. Zhu De, with twelve of his own, offered Zhou four of them. Zhou thanked him for these "children by affection." To Zhou's office in Wuhan came one afternoon a girl of fourteen, Sun Weishi. Her father had been a Huangpu cadet, executed by Chiang in 1931. With the consent of her mother, an actress in Shanghai, the Zhous "adopted" her. This is the only child recorded as formally adopted by the Zhous.

The Zhou house became a focal point for many visitors, Chinese intellectuals, and Westerners, including General Stilwell, John Gunther the author, Bob Hart, Eugene Burckhardt, S. T. Steele of *The Christian Science Monitor*, Tillman Durdin of *The New York Times*, and his wife. Zhou looked aristocratic, elegant, never sounded vehement. He spent an agreeable two hours chatting with W. H. Auden and Christopher Isherwood.

Zhou would smile when asked whether he truly believed in Communism. "We do believe in revolution, but after the war we shall need help from Western countries," he said to Western visitors. He spoke as if the Party already had a foreign policy of its own. "We want to encourage foreign investments in China. Any outstanding problems, such as unequal treaties, extraterritoriality, can be settled by negotiation and peaceful agreement." He gave due praise to Chiang Kaishek. "The generalissimo is the right person to lead the nation to victory, due to his experience and dedication."

But he had a disagreeable shock in April when the disgruntled Zhang Guotao decided to defect, fled from Yenan, and arrived in Wuhan to offer his services to Chiang. Zhou met him twice and tried to make him change his mind. In vain. He then solemnly read an announcement expelling Zhang Guotao from the Party.

"A rupture between Mao and Zhou is inevitable." This was the consensus of experts. Zhou merely smiled. Did Wang Ming influence him? He certainly sounded very conciliatory, but that was, after all, his job as head of the Liaison Office. The floating rumors of his possible defection probably made his task easier, though he would say with a twinkle, "But what good would I be to the Guomindang? There is so much talent at every level in that party."

His main target, all through, was the "middle ground," scholars, writers, artists, non-Communists, vaguely liberal, patriotic. He renewed old friendships, meeting again with Bishop Logan Roots, who still hoped that Zhou would become a Christian one day. "Zhou and my father's ideas seemed to mesh so beautifully," Bishop Roots's daughter would say to me in 1987. Dutch moviemaker Joris Ivens, who had come to make a film at the invitation of Chiang Kaishek's wife, Soong Meiling, met Zhou at a reception. "When he came in it was like an electric shock. Suddenly we all felt more alive." Ivens told Zhou he had made a film on the Spanish Civil War. "Ah now, be careful how you talk to people here about *that*," said Zhou. They met again the next day. "Zhou was another man, terse, meticulous, asking about the Spanish war, its military aspects." Zhou tried to get Joris Ivens to Yenan, but Joris was stopped at Xian, where Chiang had stationed his commander Hu Tsungnan, with around 200,000 of his best troops, to blockade the Yenan base and stop intellectuals and students from reaching it. Soong Meiling cabled Ivens that the film project was canceled.

"We have young filmmakers, actors, writers in Yenan, but no equipment, not even a camera, no film," Zhou said to Ivens when they met again in Wuhan. "I gave my camera and all the film I had to Zhou Enlai," Ivens told me. The few pictures of Yenan in those years are due to his generosity.

A melodrama was being enacted in Yenan. Among the actresses from Shanghai was Blue Apple, Lan Ping. Mao fell in love with her, and she moved into his cave. Romantic accidents happened in Yenan, where there were thirty men to every woman. Some of the leaders were divorcing their old wives and replacing them with younger ones. Sex, though prudishly frowned upon in public, was a constant topic in the warm burrows through the long winter nights. But Blue Apple's behavior was a shock. Mao was Party chairman, his wife, Ho Dzejen, one of the thirty heroines of the Long March; badly wounded by shrapnel, she had given birth on that terrible trek. Lan Ping was no virgin, she had had lovers, she did not behave demurely. "Whenever she visits a couple one can be sure husband and wife will quarrel after she has left," my friend Szeto Huimin, a film director who knew her, told me.

The outraged Politburo met. Zhou Enlai was asked to cable to Sailor Liao in Hong Kong, who was in touch with the Shanghai underground, and ask him to investigate Lan Ping's political background. Liao did. The report he sent back was not favorable. Kang Sheng stepped in. He was now the head of "social affairs," that branch of intelligence which concerns Party members. He came from the same province as Lan Ping, and gave her a clean bill of political health. Mao divorced Ho Dzejen and married Blue Apple. The Politburo ruled that she could "care for and comfort the Chairman" but could never hold any official position. Mao changed her name to Jiang Qing, Limpid Stream. Limpid Stream would never forget, nor forgive, what had happened in 1938 in the cave city of Yenan.

The United Front was falling apart. There were harassments and wanton arrests, in proportion to the successes reaped by the Communists, both in expanding their armies and in extending their bases. The covert winning over of the intelligentsia—Zhou's particular domain—was also being monitored with growing anger by Dai Lee of the secret police. In August 1938, Zhou went back to

Yenan from Wuhan. "As matters stand, we cannot expect that no conflict will arise between Chiang and ourselves . . . especially since there will be, as Comrade Mao stated, a situation of protracted war for some years." Communist mass organizations were closed down, internment camps, called thought-reform centers, were opened by the Guomindang for left-inclined intellectuals.

Wuhan was now threatened by a Japanese offensive. Wang Ming thought that Wuhan must be defended and that Communist armies *must* join in the defense. Mao objected. It is said that Zhou signed, with Wang Ming, a proclamation to defend Wuhan. But this is not proven. Mao entrusted Zhou with a letter for Chiang. "Your leadership has inspired the nation," he wrote, and asked Chiang to confer with Zhou to prepare for a long-term protracted war of resistance, and long-term cooperation between the two parties. "With total deceitfulness," writes Otto Braun, "Mao tried to represent both lines [the Comintern line of everything through the United Front and his own line of autonomy and independent strategy] in his one person."

The Yangtse Bureau, previously run by Wang Ming, was dissolved and two others created, the Southern Bureau and the Central China Bureau. The Southern Bureau was placed under Zhou Enlai. It covered a vast area, the provinces of Sichuan, Yunnan, Guangdong and Guangxi and also Hong Kong.

It was pretty obvious that, despite the calls to "defend Wuhan to the last man," Chiang would not fight against the Japanese onslaught upon the city. He prepared his retreat, to Sichuan province. His new capital was to be Chongqing. On October 22, 1938, the Japanese captured Guangzhou. Wuhan was taken on the twenty-sixth. "They are now overstretched," Mao commented. "The time has come for further expansion of our own bases . . . the Japanese only control the cities, the vast countryside is ours."

Chiang Kaishek's move to Chongqing entailed the ponderous displacement of a whole government, and this was done by stages. Zhou Enlai and his staff also took part in the trek, a circuitous meander from Wuhan to Changsha, and from thence to Guilin and onward and northward to Chongqing.

Changsha city was chaotic, with hundreds of thousands arriving from Wuhan, and as many attempting to leave. Suddenly, the city was set on fire. The decision had been taken to deny Changsha to the Japanese. It was "an order from the government," but no warning was given, and many inhabitants were caught in the fires which destroyed their houses. Zhou and Ye Jianying suddenly found their house being doused with gasoline.

Zhou was indignant. He stayed four days in the city to organize rescue teams. Chiang Kaishek denied having given the order to burn down Changsha, and its unfortunate mayor was shot.

Zhou was in Chongqing by mid-December 1938, and found Deng Yingchao waiting for him there. "Now we are in the land of warriors and poets," said Zhou. So many of his friends were from Sichuan, the rice basket of China, the paradise enclosed, a most fertile province, feeding five other provinces. "Ah, so much heart blood, so much pain, for a poem to come to birth, and so much more for a handful of rice," recited Guo Moro. And now the people of Sichuan would have to feed twenty, thirty million extra mouths, those who flocked in from the Japanese-conquered provinces.

Chongqing is a promontory of rock, jutting between the Yangtse and its beautiful tributary the Chialing. It is an engine boiler in the summer and a fog-swathed ghost in winter. Precipitous crags fall to the two rivers 400 feet below. The lichen-clinging hovels of a million refugees huddled on the steep declines. There were few horizontal roads; most of the streets were ladderlike paths going up and down. With the arrival of the Guomindang government a few tarred roads were built, more motorcars came, buildings were erected on the heights, and bomb shelters were blasted out of the rock. Zhou's office/home was at No. 50 Tseng Family Cliff. The Eighth Route Army Liaison Office was at Red Cliff No. 52, and the Xinhua News Agency occupied a house at Tiger Head Cliff.

No. 50 was a three-storied house; the first floor and the houses to right and left were occupied by Dai Lee's plainclothes police. All the rooms faced toward the inner courtyard, and there were no windows streetward. The attic was windowless, but that is where Ye Jianying stayed. One suffocating summer he picked a hole through the roof, removing the tiles, for air. A thunderstorm poured sheets of water through the hole, through the disjointed planks of the attic floor, and onto Zhou's bedroom-cum-office. Zhou sat under an umbrella to receive his guests that day.

In 1939, Zhou Enlai's main worry was the growing harassment by the Guomindang. The chief problem was the expansion not only of the Red armies but of the territory they controlled. In 1937, the Eighth Route Army had had 30,000 men in three divisions. By the end of 1939, it had 150,000 and a peasant militia of 200,000. The New Fourth Army, in 1939, was 40,000 strong instead of the agreed-upon 12,000. Xiang Ying, its political commissar, a good man but rough and headstrong, had sent many troops into the southern part of Anhui province in the hope of engaging the Japanese. This was dangerously provocative, since the Guomindang forces were strong in that area. In addition, the New Fourth Army had begun to infiltrate Jiangsu and Hunan provinces, south of the Yangtse, despite Chiang's formal interdiction. It had units in Zhejiang, Chiang's—and Zhou's—native province. Zhou conferred with Mao in Yenan, then went to Anhui and spent a good deal of time urging Xiang Ying to expand to the north—the Guomindang general in northern Anhui, Ku Tsutung, was "friendly," said Zhou—and to the east, toward Japanese-held coastal territory. "The Red Army is never merely a military force. It is an instrument of land reform, of propaganda and education." That meant guerrilla units, not professional army troops. But Xiang Ying, who disliked Mao, does not seem to have heeded Zhou's advice.

Zhou visited his native province, Zhejiang, his real motive fact-finding, but ostensibly to meet the Zhou family clan in Shaoxing. He was warmly welcomed, swept his ancestors' graves, accomplished the required ceremonies in the Hall of Longevity, where rested the ancestral soul tablets, correctly inscribed the names of himself and his brothers born in Huai An in the family book of genealogies. He gave speeches, paid his respects to the stela in honor of Great Yu the Flood Tamer, who three millennia before had saved the land from floods. That he, a Communist, was so knowledgeable of ancient rites made an excellent impression.

He returned to Chongqing with a nagging sense that something might happen. The New Fourth Army was too visible, too obvious . . . and in a sensitive area, one that Chiang Kaishek considered his own particular domain.

Zhou's father, Yineng, arrived in Chongqing, to be cared for by a respectful, but distant son. There was no real meeting of minds, but Zhou gave him a comfortable room in the house allotted to families of party members, and paid his father's keep out of his own meager allowance. Yineng was surprised at his son's frugality. He died in 1942, a death as quiet, as unassuming, as his life had been. Deng Yingchao's mother also reached Chongqing. Released after five years in prison, she had been sent to Wuhan through the Communist underground in 1938. She refused to leave with her daughter when the city fell, saying she could manage on her own. She trudged out on foot with other refugees. It took her a year to get to Chongqing in 1939. She died in 1940.

During those years of the Second United Front, Zhou laid down the foundation of his future Foreign Affairs Ministry. He developed good relations with Western diplomats, with United States Ambassador Clarence Edward Gauss, a scholar of high caliber, and the military attaché, David D. Barrett; with British Ambassador Archibald Clark Kerr and his staff. He had around him Wang Bingnan, Huang Hua, Zhang Hanfu, Zhang Wenjing, Gung Pusheng, Qiao Guanhua, Gung Peng, and others—all brilliant, dedicated men and women.

He sent Gung Pusheng to the United States, where she became a friend of Eleanor Roosevelt. He enrolled the German wife of Wang Bingnan, Anna Wang, who was multilingual, to write articles for the foreign press. He spent two hours each night at Tiger Head Cliff correcting Xinhua News Agency articles and editorials. He found a talented editor, Pan Hannien's brother, Pan Dzenien. "Ask Dzenien, he knows," he said to the newsmen who crowded round him. Seldom did he give anyone total trust, but he seems to have trusted Pan Dzenien. Zhou even corrected the plays of his friend Guo Moro, "for the public." He had a NO SMOKING sign on his table, because he detested the smell, and it made his nose bleed —his nosebleeds were frequent and aggravated as he grew older. Gung Peng told him that Westerners might feel unhappy without a cigarette. Zhou had the sign removed.

Zhou became a friend of the late Theodore White, who represented Time-Life Inc. in Chongqing. Zhou invited White to dinner, and a roasted piglet with burnished crackling skin was served. "I am a Jew, I don't eat pork," said Teddy, greatly embarrassing Zhou's entourage. Zhou pointed his chopsticks at the piglet. "Teddy, you think this is pig. Anywhere else it would be pig. But we are in China. This is not pig, but duck." Teddy ate a morsel of the "duck," and everyone's face was saved.

Clashes between Guomindang troops and the New Fourth Army escalated. A major conflict occurred in the summer of 1939. Zhou wrote lengthy protests, denunciations. Defense Minister Ho

Yingching—the one who had recalled Wang Jingwei from Italy
when Chiang was kidnapped in 1936—told Zhou that "this is
because the New Fourth Army is sheltering deserters from our
armies." Which was probably true. The Guomindang soldiers,
peasants hauled off the fields and manacled in long chains to be
brought to army camps, were not only badly paid but often beaten
by the officers. Many starved to death on the way to the recruiting
stations.

In July 1939, Zhou returned to Yenan to confer with Mao
regarding the new developments, including the prewar situation
in Europe. Mao asked him to give a lecture at the Central Committee school for cadres. "You explain these things better than I
do." Zhou got on his horse, since the school was some ten kilometers away. On the road the saddle girth broke and he fell,
fracturing his right arm above the elbow. A story repeated in many
books relates that Zhou's fall was due to Mao's wife, Limpid
Stream, who, riding a white horse, swerved and caused Zhou's
mount to rear. "She was not there," Dr. George Hatem, an American doctor many years in China, where he is known as Ma Haide,
told me. "I was called to attend to Zhou. We had an Indian medical
team at Yenan, but none of us were experts on fractures." It was
decided that Zhou should go to the Soviet Union for treatment.
In a gesture of concern, Chiang Kaishek sent his private plane to
take Zhou, Deng Yingchao, their adopted daughter Sun Weishi,
and Tsai Chang to Urumchi, whence a Russian plane flew them
to Moscow. Zhou was lodged in the Kremlin hospital, reserved
for the highest Russian leaders. The surgeons discussed several
methods of dealing with his complicated fracture. "I have a lot of
work to do, and very little time. Do what you think will take the
least amount of time for me to heal." His right arm was restored
to use, but remained bent at the elbow.

He had come to Moscow not merely for medical treatment but
also to thrash out the whole context of relations between China
and the U.S.S.R., including a review of Comintern activities in
China. At the time, the idea of *equality* between the nations of
the world was still extremely frail. Even if France talked a great
deal about liberty and fraternity, she would be the last country to
give up—and only after sanguinary wars—her colonies. In the
same way, the Soviet Union, though loudly anticolonialist, still
behaved like a Czarist autocracy. Moscow had not officially ac-

knowledged the Tsunyi meeting at which Mao had been made chairman, and Wang Ming was still the Comintern spokesman in China, still in the Politburo.

Zhou Enlai began to explain Mao's strategy, Mao's views. With clearness but tact, he let it be known that the CCP was an *independent Communist Party*, with a right to fashion its own policies, hold its own views. He delivered a letter from Mao, a blistering attack on Otto Braun, as a prelude to questioning *every* directive that had ever been given by the Comintern. The Steering Committee was presented with a hundred-page report by Zhou on the situation in China. He lectured, four to six hours at a stretch. With maps, sketches, diagrams, descriptions of military moves, descriptions of bases. He gave an account of Mao's military strategy, the "countryside surrounding the cities" concept of guerrilla war and its importance. He outlined the program for expansion of rural Red bases. "He often prefaced his comments with 'Comrade Mao's view on the subject is,'" writes his interpreter, Shi Ji.

What was the reaction? "His hearers were dazed . . . they could not follow." This was a way of thinking, of doing, of reasoning, totally alien to them. The Chinese names, the geography, the intricacy of events . . . everything was too much. Zhou was talking to the pseudo-knowledgeable, to individuals imbued with a fatuous sense of their own superiority but with no practical experience. The only one who understood was the Japanese Comintern representative, who went back to China with Zhou. Among his audience were Dimitrov, Kosygin, André Marty, Antonescu of Romania, Gottwald of Germany. "It's like a huge novel with far too many characters in it," said André Marty the Frenchman. "I lose the thread." "They were not accustomed to the concrete situation in China," Shi Ji remarks, with admirable understatement.

There was no debate. No one could debate such an avalanche of facts. "Only the Chinese themselves can deal with such complicated matters wisely," said Antonescu of Romania. Dimitrov "warmly shook hands with Zhou," writes Shi Ji. A resolution was passed by the Comintern and read out to Zhou, who took it down by hand as it was being translated by Shi Ji. "It was an important resolution, because it gave the CCP Central Committee scope for making its own decisions. . . . Previously some of the Comintern resolutions had been inappropriate, and had led to inner-Party

controversy." If nothing else, Zhou had demonstrated that the
Steering Committee was out of its depth. The resolution "made
it possible for Comrade Mao, at the Party congress in 1945, to
proclaim the congress one of victory, one of unity." Divested of
foggy verbiage, it means that the resolution was vague enough to
allow Mao Dzedong, at last, to begin eliminating Wang Ming and
his supporters.

Another incident in favor of Mao occurred. Pavel Mif was in
trouble. He now became a "counterrevolutionary." This assured
the downfall of his devoted followers. The resolution recommended "unity," meaning unity with Chiang Kaishek, but with
gentle skill Zhou pointed out that Mao's "unity and independent
initiative" formula allowed unity with forces outside the Party but
it did not mean merging or obedience.

Mao had wanted Otto Braun expelled from the Comintern. But
the steering committee decided that even if Braun had given the
wrong advice, "the Chinese comrades were not bound to follow
it." This was rather hypocritical. Li Lisan had been overthrown for
differing with the Comintern's advice.

Zhou obtained the release of Chen Yao, a member of the Central Committee who had run afoul of Wang Ming in 1928, and
for twelve years had been employed as a low-grade laborer at the
Stalingrad tractor factory. Zhou took him back to China.

Zhou and his wife settled their adopted daughter Sun Weishi
at the Stanislavsky School, and left the U.S.S.R. in March 1940.
Landing in Urumchi, Zhou was banqueted by the local warlord,
Shen Shitsai, who would kill Mao Dzedong's brother some years
later. The party traveled to Yenan by lorry; at each stop Zhou was
greeted by Guomindang officers and officials. In Yenan, Zhou was
closeted for weeks in long discussions with Mao. Deng Yingchao
went back alone to Chongqing, and replaced him in writing articles
for the Xinhua News Agency and a Communist daily.

That Mao now felt liberated from Comintern diktats is evident
in his May 1940 proclamation. "Freely expand the anti-Japanese
forces and resist the onslaughts of anti-Communist diehards." The
time had come to push onward. More bases. Bigger Communist
armies. This would further strain the fragile edifice of the United
Front, but Mao no longer cared about the United Front.

Zhou did care, however, or continued to appear to, carrying on
in Chongqing, where he returned in June, the same policies of

protest, but conciliation, as in the past. Now, however, there was another problem.

The unexpected fall of France in May 1940 had again shifted tactical prospects. The German ambassador in Chongqing, Trautmann, approached Chiang to urge him to reach a settlement with Japan. Moscow countered this with an offer of additional aid to Chiang. Zhou, in unison with the British and American press, thundered against the "capitulationists," against collaborationists. On July 7, the anniversary of the Marco Polo Bridge incident, he held a large meeting. "Our country must strive to achieve in external relations a clear and determined line, as well as achieving progress, cooperation, and improvement in internal relations." However, to avoid clashes with the Guomindang, Zhou, as vice-chairman of the Military Affairs Commission, ordered guerrilla units to operate "only in their own territory," but indicated that this did not apply to North China, which since 1937 had been an uncontested area of operations for the Red Army. It was South and Middle China which made Chiang and his commanders apprehensive. It was the New Fourth Army which was again enjoined to be careful.

In August 1940, the Red Army commanders and the Politburo decided to start a major guerrilla offensive against Japanese forces in North China. The idea was to disrupt the railways, to cut the roads which convoys used, to harass garrisons, and to kill collaborationists. Nie Rongzhen, whose base was involved in these operations, tells the story. The offensive was to be led by Peng Dehuai, as usual eager for "some real fighting." But what in Mao Dzedong's original plan was to be a well-coordinated guerrilla offensive, carried out by small units to ambush, disrupt, and paralyze the Japanese forces and convoys, now turned into something quite different. "Heads got overheated with success," writes Nie Rongzhen. Peng launched 200,000 men in an operation later named the Hundred Regiments Offensive. Pitched battles. Major assaults. Frontal attacks. It was costly in manpower, and brought as a result massive retaliation from the Japanese, in a scorched-earth campaign, which lay waste large areas of Communist territory, making food scarce and new recruits even scarcer. Mao was enraged. He cursed Peng Dehuai for days. Zhou did not curse. He warned that "a high tide of anti-Communist action is in the offing." Chiang had now realized the strength of the Eighth Route Army.

On October 19, Chiang's deputy sent an ultimatum to the Communists. All troops of the New Fourth Army must withdraw north of the Yellow River by the end of the month. Zhou transmitted the ultimatum to Yenan. "Even if we protest, we cannot ignore this ultimatum. We must answer it." He suggested two solutions. Either the bulk of the New Fourth Army would move north, but keep some forces battle-ready in the present territory, or the forces south of the Yangtse would disperse in small guerrilla units and continue the struggle. He again began his agitation among the "middle ground," in preparation for a public opinion offensive. He urged that Zhu De, Peng Dehuai, along with the New Fourth Army commander, Ye Ting, and political commissar Xiang Ying, jointly answer the ultimatum, stating they were ready to move but "on condition they would not be ambushed during the move." On November 11 the Party in Yenan replied, agreeing to a partial withdrawal. Through multiple demarches and approaches, Zhou, to avoid a showdown, had obtained from Chiang an extension of the removal period to December 31.

On Christmas Day, Chiang invited Zhou to dinner and thanked him for saving his life four years previously. He repeated that no action would be taken against the New Fourth Army "until the end of January." At the close of dinner the two had an argument regarding the meaning of democracy. "Me not a democrat? You think I'm undemocratic?" Chiang said, astonished, to Zhou.

Mao continued to be strangely provocative. "We must stress struggle, not unity. . . . We must expand the Eighth Route Army *and the New Fourth Army* in every possible way." By the end of December some 60,000 New Fourth Army troops had crossed northward, but 10,000 remained south of the river, with Ye Ting the commander, Xiang Ying the political commissar, the school for cadres, and the medical staff. In January, Ye Ting discovered that the road mapped out for their withdrawal was blocked by a Japanese garrison and went to the local Guomindang headquarters to discuss the matter. He was held a prisoner, and his remaining troops massacred. Almost 9,000 were butchered, and Xiang Ying was killed. This happened on January 7.

Zhou learned of it on January 11. He appeared at the Xinhua News Agency building. He was pale, his voice shaking with grief and anger. He sent Wang Bingnan and Ye Jianying to inform the members of the People's Political Council. He sent his press officer, Gung Peng, to inform the foreign correspondents, and Anna Wong to tell the British and other Western diplomats. The *Xinhua Daily* printed the news, but this was censored, and the newspaper came out with large blanks. However, a poem written by Zhou, a sixteen-word classic, was published:

> No greater wrong was done
> than south of the river
> a lonely leaf
>
> In the same room brothers clash swords
> the burning stalk ignores
> its own beans are on fire

International opinion was against the massacre. "This is deplorable," said the British ambassador to me. So did David Barrett, the U.S. military attaché. Roosevelt sent a private warning to Chiang Kaishek. The United States was sending aid to China for its war against Japan, but this aid would not be forthcoming should such distressing incidents occur.

Chiang Kaishek was surprised by the strength of the reaction, both in China and abroad. On January 28 he stated that this had been a matter of military discipline. "Disobedience, insubordination, cannot be tolerated." He ordered the dissolution of the New Fourth Army. Zhou gave a major press conference. "As long as there is no peace between Guomindang and Communist, American aid to China cannot be well used." But to someone who hinted that Chiang had lied by promising safe passage to the New Fourth Army, he replied, "No, someone lied to the generalissimo." He then spelled out conditions for the settlement of the incident, among them the immediate liberation of Ye Ting. In February 1941, he gave a public speech in Chongqing, attended by thousands, denouncing "those who have slain true patriots" but also insisting that "we must look ahead and continue our efforts to achieve victory." Far from being dissolved, the New Fourth Army was reorganized. Mao Dzedong made Liu Shaoqi its political commissar, and Chen Yi its commander.

Zhou moved to prevent more Guomindang arrests and possible

murders. He dispersed the staff of the Xinhua News Agency and other Communist organizations in Chongqing. He did the same in Guilin, writing to the governor, Li Tsishen, a sympathetic non-Communist, asking him to care for the artists there and provide for their safety. He scattered the cadres of his Southern Bureau, some to Yenan, some overseas, others posted in different regions of China. "We must now practice long-term clandestinity and total secrecy . . . until the time is ripe. Not only Party members but many non-Party sympathizers are vulnerable," said Zhou.

Meanwhile he continued to extend his influence in the "middle ground." He attended the sixtieth birthday celebration of Feng Yuxiang, Auspicious Jade, the Christian warlord who baptized his troops with a fire hose. Auspicious Jade was now accounted a patriot, because he had not gone over to the Japanese. Zhou cultivated Feng, made a friend of him, asked him to plead for the release of Ye Ting. When British ambassador Archibald Clark Kerr left Chongqing in February 1942 on another assignment, Zhou presented him with a Japanese sword "which was captured from the enemy by valorous Commander Ye Ting." Deng Yingchao cared for Ye Ting's wife and daughter for the next five years.

In April 1941, Japan and the U.S.S.R. signed a neutrality pact, the equivalent of the pact signed between the U.S.S.R. and Nazi Germany two years previously, which seemed to guarantee Moscow from attack. "Japan will now direct itself toward South Asia," predicted Zhou Enlai. Stalin, relieved of the fear of war on two fronts, could move his Far East divisions westward, though not in time to meet the onslaught of Nazi Germany that summer.

On December 7, 1941, Japan bombed the United States fleet at Pearl Harbor. This brought the United States into the war. President Roosevelt now focused his attention on the China theater. Chiang Kaishek was overjoyed, assured of generous amounts of money and weaponry from the United States. But the Americans would not countenance fighting between the Guomindang and the Communists at this time. Hence the fiction of the United Front had to be preserved, the yawning rifts papered over. But beneath the apparent harmony, below the smiles, both parties now readied themselves for the inevitable "after the war" confrontation.

Mao took action. Now that Moscow had its hands full fighting Germany, he could start a shake-up of the Party, a massive *rectification*, to unify, consolidate, under himself as unchallenged head, this instrument for power. The documents—Mao's theoretical writings, and also those of Liu Shaoqi, now promoted to theoretician—for the study of "rectification" were sent to Zhou in May 1942. He and Deng Yingchao held study sessions with the Xinhua News Agency staff and the Southern bureau leaders. "I need to study, to study a great deal," said Zhou gravely, and wrote down for himself a program of behavior, of rectitude in thinking and in doing. He and his wife should have gone to Yenan, but Zhou became very ill, and was admitted to the central hospital in Geleshan near Chongqing, where he was operated on. The hepatic abscess he had suffered from in 1935 seems to have recurred.

The capture of Hong Kong by Japan in early 1942 presented Zhou with some problems. His men there had returned to China but had promptly been jailed by Chiang Kaishek, among them Liao Chengzhi (Liao the Sailor), who would only be released in 1945. Zhou had a great deal to do to leave his Liaison Office in good order before, in June 1943, he, his wife, and 150 members of the Liaison Office left for Yenan in a convoy of trucks, arriving on July 16. All of them would have to undergo scrutiny, criticism . . . rectification in their thinking. And Zhou Enlai was not spared.

12

Mao Dzedong's aim in launching the Party shake-up, called the Rectification, was not merely personal ambition, nor only to eliminate opponents such as Wang Ming. Mao held a messianic view of China's future role, of the Party's conquest of China. He was convinced that theory alone, imported from another culture, could not possibly work. China needed her own brand of Communism, and to this he had applied himself, writing theoretical texts since his arrival at the base in 1935. "No political party can possibly lead a great revolutionary movement until it possesses revolutionary theory *and a knowledge of history and has a profound grasp of the practical movement.* In China, Marxism-Leninism must be practiced *with the specific characteristics of China* . . . acquiring a definite *national form.*" He was the first man to realize that revolution must fit different cultures, for any theory, however excellent, was bound to fail otherwise. He was lucky in his timing, for in 1942 the U.S.S.R. was involved in war with Germany and in mid-1943 the Comintern was dissolved.

It was to be expected that Zhou Enlai, who had already intimated to the Comintern that China's Communist Party would make its own decisions, would be immediately included in the group which supported Mao's ascent to power. Such was not the case. Zhou, though agreeing with Mao's grand design, had refused to break off with Wang Ming, Bo Gu, and other "Bolsheviks." "They are also comrades," he said. He had also diverged with Mao on ways of handling the United Front with Chiang Kaishek and on the matter of sending the Eighth Route Army to Taiyuan in 1937.

Zhou was attacked by Mao's chief supporter, Liu Shaoqi. This humorless but capable organizer, head of the Northern Bureau, and now head of the New Fourth Army, had been acknowledged as a Marxist theoretician; his writings, as well as Mao's, were being studied throughout the Party. It was Liu who coined the expression "Mao Dzedong Thought." And it is one of history's paradoxes that, in the Cultural Revolution twenty-two years later, what Liu had written at the time of Rectification, which helped Mao to power, was to cause his downfall.

Another man who contributed to Mao's apotheosis was Kang Sheng. He had flown back with Wang Ming from Moscow, but now abandoned him. He had helped Mao to marry Blue Apple —Limpid Stream—and also was in charge of internal security, the files concerning the background, words, and actions of every Party member.

Zhou had no faction in the Party. The Southern Bureau he headed was in the regions where Chiang Kaishek held sway, and most of his recruits were intellectuals, nonproletarian. The Yenan newspaper, *Liberation Daily*, ran diatribes against "the *very many* Party members whose origin is nonproletarian and who must be closely investigated." Zhou, and Deng Yingchao, had both plainly said that for them "class origin" was secondary. But in the Rectification it would be used as a criterion. "What Liu Shaoqi said against Zhou at the time was as bad as anything one heard during the Cultural Revolution," a member of a Zhou study group tells me. The first point made by Liu against Zhou was that Wang Ming and Bo Gu had been with Zhou in the Liaison Office in Wuhan and then in Chongqing; that in Wuhan, Wang Ming had tried to establish a new "center," against Mao, and had even sent messages to the Central Committee members as if he had authority to do so. "Wang Ming could only do so because he was with Zhou Enlai. He utilized Zhou's position and prestige," say the historians who made a close study of this particular period. Zhou was accused of having been an "empiricist . . . helping dogmatism."

The second point raised was the Taiyuan military offensive of late 1937. Zhou had tried to use the armies of Shanxi province warlord Yen Xishan, and even to train some of them, with the help of a Communist, Bo Yibo. He had done this because he did not want to use the Eighth Route Army in frontal attacks against Japan. But Liu Shaoqi strongly disagreed. He had wanted to "go it alone" with the Eighth Route Army. Zhou Enlai, apparently, had sent a telegram to the Military Affairs Commission complaining of Liu's attitude. . . .

The third item against Zhou was the "defend Wuhan to the last man" proclamation, launched by Wang Ming. "Zhou Enlai did not sign the proclamation; he was not there when it was issued. He had returned to Yenan to consult with Mao. Wang Ming at one time even faked Mao's signature, and it seems he simply added Zhou's signature to his proclamation."

The mishaps of the New Fourth Army were also queried. By failing to establish a strong guerrilla base, it did not adhere to Mao's prescriptions. But was this Zhou's fault? "The New Fourth Army failures were also brought up as part of Liu's criticism against Zhou," the scholars in charge of research on Zhou Enlai tell me.

The probe delved further, into Zhou's activities at the Sixth Congress of the CCP, held in 1928 in Moscow. Zhou had played a prominent part at the congress. "We have indeed had many disputes, and heated ones, over how to evaluate the Sixth Congress," Zhou told a large assembly of cadres. "I took part in its work and was one of those bearing major responsibility. There are nine other comrades here in Yenan who also took part." One of the nine was Liu Shaoqi.

"I went to Soviet Russia to tell them of the errors of the Wang Ming line," Zhou stated. He had, indeed, done so, in the recent past, and presented the case in such a way that the Comintern had to "trust" the CCP. The attempt to associate him with the Wang Ming line thus failed.

Zhou's ordeal lasted six weeks. He had to explain everything he had ever said or done. He was accused of "subjectivism and empiricism." Zhou bore through the sessions with such fortitude and unruffled calm, in such a civilized manner, and with such apposite replies that all criticisms had, in the end, little impact.

Kang Sheng took part in the purge and of course was now against Wang Ming. As head of the social affairs department, the files of all Party members were in his hands. He began a witch-hunt which, though it lasted only ten months, was traumatic. It was Kang Sheng who first used the *Bigungsin* method: extract a confession, believe the confession, a method resurrected during the Cultural Revolution twenty years later and under the same Kang Sheng. "I know how many of you here are spies," he shrieked at terrified intellectuals. "Why do you want to kill us? Here you have enough to eat, everything you need, yet you complain and plot." Some critical essays on conditions in Yenan had indeed been written by a few writers who had come there driven by their own idealism. But they had not reckoned on the primitiveness of peasant China. Now they were dubbed enemies and infiltrators. Every organization must ferret them out, and up to 30 percent in every unit are suspect, declared Kang Sheng. "Some people then confessed to things they had never done. They believed they had committed crimes . . . it was quite strange," a woman writer, Ge Cuiling, told me in 1988.

Both Zhou and Chen Yi intervened to save the intellectuals, Chen Yi going directly to Mao to express his outrage. Zhou successfully saved a woman, Chen Muhua, who was accused of spying because one of her relatives was a general in Chiang Kaishek's army. Finally Kang Sheng was stopped, and had to do a selfcriticism, in which he blamed his subordinates for excessive zeal. He was now superseded by Li Kenung, the smiling Buddha. Many cadres were reinstated. Mao personally apologized for the excesses at two public meetings.

Zhou Enlai, lecturing at the cadres' school on Party history, summed up Mao Thought. "The views of Comrade Mao . . . have developed into a *sinicized* Marxist-Leninist line. The Chinese Communist Party will solve the problems of the Chinese revolution still more independently, and with an even greater sense of responsibility." He refused to join the almost hysterical praise of Mao that now began. "Even Comrade Mao had to learn through experience. . . . It also took Comrade Mao some time to understand these problems. . . . I think that Comrade Mao still believed that our work should be centered on cities at the time of the Sixth Congress." And he quoted a letter from Mao to support this contention. "Comrade Mao's development is representative of the development of our party."

He criticized Wang Ming, but in measured terms. It is probably due to Zhou that Wang Ming and Bo Gu, and the other Bolsheviks, were not liquidated. Wang Ming remained a member of the Central Committee until 1956.

Yenan resounded with praise of Mao, hymns to Mao. Poems and articles about Mao appeared daily. One example, penned by a famous poet, gives the drift: "Whenever Mao Dzedong appears, there the sound of clapping seethes. . . . He thinks incessantly, one hand pushing aside the enemy, the other gathering more friends."

Zhou continued to argue with Mao regarding the policies of the

United Front with Chiang Kaishek. He left maneuvering for power within the Party to others, but was adamant that the handling of relations with the Guomindang be linked to the war situation and also to a possible relationship which might be forged between the CCP and the United States government. There were signs that America was interested in establishing contact with Yenan. Reports from American diplomats and correspondents in China were uniformly favorable to the Communists, asserting that they fought Japan while Chiang pocketed American money but avoided any conflict with Japan. However, Zhou did not believe that the Americans were going to abandon Chiang Kaishek. Therefore, it was necessary not to assume a hostile stance toward the latter; the United Front must remain a platform, demonstrating the CCP's goodwill and forbearance, despite all harassments. "The people hope for peace and for democratic reforms. The Americans are also urging Chiang to make some democratic reforms. We must therefore continue consultations with the Guomindang, such to be held on equal footing, on the basis of mutual concession . . . though let no one conceive of cooperation as integration."

Did Zhou truly believe that a coalition government, with Chiang Kaishek and the Communists as equal partners, was possible? He certainly appeared to try very hard to bring such a scheme into existence. This seemed to be the burden of his work and that of his wife while in Chongqing. And now, with a deepening involvement by the United States in the war in China, there was added need for keeping all options open. Zhou knew, through his contacts, that American military experts at that time considered China's vast manpower to be "the ultimate weapon" to use against Japan. Would the Americans consider some form of cooperation with the Communists, who were fighting so unrelentingly against Japan?

On March 12, 1944, Zhou presided over a ceremony in honor of Sun Yatsen, who had died on March 12, 1925. This was to create goodwill among the Guomindang officials, who claimed to follow Sun Yatsen's precepts. In June, he invited Chinese and Western correspondents from Chongqing to visit Yenan. Few managed to come, because of Chiang Kaishek's interdiction, but the newspapers wrote up the invitation. On the Fourth of July, Zhou presided over a meeting celebrating American Independence Day.

During Zhou's fifteen-month absence in Yenan, the Liaison Office in Chongqing was being managed by Lin Biao, who had returned from a four-year stay in the U.S.S.R., where he had been treated for health problems (so it was said). He was unfitted for the job, but Wang Bingnan, Dung Biwu, and Lin Tsuhan, long associated with Zhou, carried on well. Chiang Kaishek continued to harass the Communists in the city, with arbitrary arrests and newspaper closures. Wang Bingnan kept Zhou informed. Zhou wrote to Wang, telling him never to forget to answer letters "from American friends." He asked for penicillin to be sent through these friends if possible, for Wang Jiaxiang, wounded during the Long March, suffered from a deep bone infection. "I know how few you are," writes Zhou to Wang, "thank you for valuable information." A charming aside in a letter: "Did you receive the melons and tomatoes Little Chao sent to your wife?" Yingchao's vegetable garden seemed to continue to thrive in Yenan, purge or not.

The arrival of U.S. Vice-President Henry Wallace in June 1944 appeared to the Communists as a shift in their favor. The reports of American newsmen and diplomats on Chiang were far from flattering, and Lieutenant General Stilwell, sent by Roosevelt as military adviser to the generalissimo, simply could not bear the latter, an aversion which was heartily reciprocated. Chiang at the time felt aggrieved, because the promises made to him by Roosevelt at Cairo in 1943 had been nullified at the Teheran meeting later that year. Wallace brought a personal message from Roosevelt, asking Chiang Kaishek to allow an American observer mission to visit Yenan.

Grudgingly, Chiang gave permission. The Dixie mission—as it was to be known—was led by State Department diplomat John Service and military attaché David Barrett, both many years in China, fluent in Chinese. The mission flew to Yenan on July 17, 1944, accomplishing the unexpected by being the only airplane ever to smash its propeller on a hitherto undiscovered gravestone at the makeshift small airport of Yenan. The accident broke any ice—had there been ice—around. The Americans emerged laughing heartily, and Ye Jianying, who was at the airport heading the welcome group, was utterly charmed. "I like you Americans. We Chinese felt that we would have lost face."

"A hero was wounded," Zhou would say that night at the banquet for the mission. "We consider your plane a hero."

Yenan's spartan virtues, honesty, egalitarianism, the good health and discipline of the Eighth Route Army, the efficiency of the radio stations . . . the living in caves . . . everything impressed the Americans. It was so utterly different from Chongqing with its corrupt officials, its heartless way of treating the poor. "No, not everything is perfect, but we are trying hard," Zhou said. He spoke honestly. He was convincing. Soberly, he would describe Chiang Kaishek as "not a bad man," but one who "drifts between factions . . . surrounded by stupid men who do not give him good advice." But he predicted no imminent collapse of Chiang's government. John Service, Barrett, and others of the Dixie Mission filed favorable comments on their visit, and as a result would become victims of McCarthyism in the following years. "The mistake I made in 1944 was in not considering the Chinese Communists as enemies of the United States . . . I thought of them primarily as allied with us in fighting the Japanese," wrote David Barrett.

Zhou said he hoped that a coalition government could come into being if Chiang admitted the CCP as an equal partner. "The United States will find us more cooperative than the Guomindang. China must industrialize. This can only be done by free enterprise and with the aid of foreign capital. Chinese and American interests are correlated. The two countries fit well together."

Mao went further, hinting that, although dedicated to socialism, the CCP would delay drastic social reforms for "twenty years or more . . . should American help be forthcoming." He and Zhou envisaged for China something akin to the Marshall Plan that later put Western Europe back on its feet. "The U.S.S.R. has suffered greatly from the war. . . . It will be far too busy with its own reconstruction. We are quite willing to make concessions." "Revolution is a very gradual process, and we shall have to go through a comparatively long new-democratic stage," asserted Zhou Enlai. This long-term policy, advocating a mixed economy, would be the one that Zhou would endeavor to pursue through the following decades. And even though at times contrary winds blew, and schemes utterly different took hold for a while, the "opening of China," attributed to Deng Xiaoping in the 1980s, goes right back to those concepts forged by Zhou Enlai and Mao in 1944 in Yenan.

However, while the Dixie mission was still in Yenan, the politics of Washington were changing. The unpredictability of the aging, ailing President manifested itself. Roosevelt was now captivated with the idea of a dialogue with Stalin, and regarded the stability of the postwar world as a matter to be decided between himself and the master of Moscow. He now appeared to have given himself the right to allocate pieces of other nations' territories according to his own ideas of how the world should be run. De Gaulle found the American President's suggestions for the partition of France obnoxious. Stalin was pleased when Roosevelt concurred with the idea of an all-weather port for the U.S.S.R., ice-free in winter; none other than the Chinese port of Dalien (Dairen) in Manchuria, which could be placed "under international supervision," meaning control by the United States and the U.S.S.R. Roosevelt agreed to Russian rights on Manchurian railways and recognized Outer Mongolia as an "independent" state (Stalin's suggestion). Edgar Snow, in Washington to meet Roosevelt for a talk, was puzzled by Roosevelt's attitude. "I distinctly got the impression that he was thinking in terms of two Chinas. One North China under the Communists, one South China under Chiang Kaishek." The partition of several countries was accomplished by Stalin and Roosevelt at the Yalta meeting in January 1945. Thus was Europe divided and Korea in Asia. Secret clauses placed Stalin in the enviable position of sending his troops into Manchuria. Five years later, it would be up to Mao and to Zhou to make Stalin disgorge some of these "gifts" so generously handed to him by President Roosevelt . . . at China's expense.

The Dixie mission had raised many hopes in Zhou . . . Perhaps too many. Now disillusion crept in. In November 1944, Roosevelt sent his special envoy, Patrick Hurley, to China. Hurley would soon be appointed the U.S. ambassador in Chongqing. His brief was to see what could be done about setting up a postwar democratic government in China. His picturesque arrival in Yenan is described by Barrett: "On the afternoon of November 7, Zhou and I were among a large crowd to greet the arrival of the plane from Chongqing. Out stepped a tall, gray-haired, soldierly, extremely handsome man . . . Major General Patrick Hurley. No one had thought to inform us of his intention to visit Yenan. 'Who is he?' asked Zhou." Barrett told him. Zhou gasped. "Please hold him here until I can bring Chairman Mao." Zhou disappeared in a cloud of dust to reappear in another dust cloud with Mao, in the small ambulance car. "Hurley drew himself up to his full height and let out an Indian war whoop. I shall never forget the expression on the faces of Mao and Zhou," wrote Barrett.

Hurley produced a draft agreement in five points for a "coalition" government, written after consultation with Chiang. There was a decidedly American ring to it, including the phrase "government of the people, by the people, for the people." Did Zhou, at this point, remember his own student magazine with these words at its masthead?

Mao was angered by the draft. He accused the Guomindang of not fighting Japan. "Chiang uses 779,000 of his 1,965,000 troops to block us." Hurley and Mao and Zhou agreed on redrafting the document. The main point was that the Red armies should *not* be under Chiang's control. Other clauses were a repetition of the demands tabled since 1937.

Zhou returned to Chongqing with Hurley and Barrett, and now it was Chiang's turn to be angry. A counterdraft was handed to Hurley, the main feature being the incorporation of the Communist armies into a National Army and relinquishment of control by the CCP. "This means handing the knife to Chiang to slaughter us," said Zhou to Barrett, with an expressive gesture at his own throat. A fourth draft was prepared, containing the offer to appoint one high-ranking Communist commander as a member of a National Military Council. Zhou said he would have to fly back to Yenan to consult with Mao.

Barrett and Zhou flew off some days later, and on the way the pilot lost his bearings. Zhou realized it. "I think we are off course. The terrain outside looks unfamiliar to me. We are flying west rather than north. Have the pilot make a 180-degree turn and fly till he comes to a river, and then head north." This was done, and two hours later Yenan's slim pagoda came in sight.

Mao flew into another one of his rages at the new draft and called Chiang Kaishek the son of a turtle. "To place our troops under his control puts us at his mercy," Zhou repeated. Back went a saddened Barrett to Hurley, who also exploded. "The motherfucker tricked me," he said of Mao. Yet Mao and Hurley had together signed the first altered draft in Yenan.

At the end of December, Zhou wrote to the American military attaché, suggesting that Mao and he should travel to Washington, to meet President Roosevelt and present their case. For such a cautious man, he seems to have misunderstood American officialdom, for he penned a remark somewhat derogatory to Hurley: "I do not trust him." Unfortunately, Hurley was shown the letter.

He treated the urgent request as a casual suggestion, at the end of a very long report to Roosevelt, and certainly did not back it.

Hurley himself then wrote to Mao, asking for further talks, for which he was prepared to go to Yenan. Mao refused to receive him. For Mao, war, and only war, would settle the issue. Zhou could go on believing in the possibility of a coalition government, not Mao. In April, Roosevelt died, and his successor, Truman, lost little time finding out how much the U.S.S.R. had gained territorially, both in Europe and in Asia. The Cold War, a product of post-Yalta panic, had begun, and would swiftly breed McCarthyism in America. Meanwhile, in China, in that April, the Seventh Congress of the CCP confirmed Mao's supremacy as chairman of the Central Committee, the Politburo, the Military Council. Liu Shaoqi became No. 2, and Zhou Enlai came fourth after Zhu De, who was reconfirmed as commander in chief. Liu's Northern Bureau had sustained few casualties during the Rectification at the hands of Kang Sheng, but Zhou's Southern Bureau had suffered a good deal since so many members were intellectuals whom Kang Sheng dubbed "spies of the Guomindang."

Despite this, Zhou Enlai continued to organize the "second front" of the intelligentsia. He was well aware of the scholars' passionate desire for peace and for democratic reforms. He was aware that no weapons, no help, would come to the CCP from the United States: Hurley had recommended that no American weapons should be supplied except to Chiang Kaishek. "Does not Hurley realize that Chiang will use these weapons against us?" asked Zhou of the American attaché. Only at the negotiating table could he perhaps, perhaps, win. At least, he could buy time, time during which the Communist armies could be readied for the inevitable war to come. "It was like restraining a bully by holding his small finger," said Wang Bingnan. "The Communists are winning the mainland . . . with Zhou sitting at the negotiating table," remarked a Guomindang official. Zhou succeeded in convincing all the small parties, now united in a Democratic League, to sign an agreement with the CCP in the spring, pledging themselves not to submit to Guomindang one-party domination, or to negotiate with it, without prior consultation with the CCP.

August 1945, and the atom bombs dropped on Japan. The U.S.S.R. declared war on Japan on August 9, and on August 14 World War II ended.

On that very day a peace treaty was signed between Chiang Kaishek and Stalin, ratifying the secret clauses agreed to at Yalta concerning Dalian (then known as Dairen) and the Manchurian railways. "This is only to be expected," said Zhou, bitter at Stalin's treachery.

Hurley, who blamed State Department officials and American newsmen for exaggerating the importance of the Communists, was now certain that with the treaty between Chiang and Stalin, the CCP would have to come to terms with Chiang. He was jubilant. And he was wrong.

Within six hours of the news of the Japanese surrender, Mao and Zhou had given their marching orders to the Red armies, now renamed the People's Liberation Armies (PLA). Mao, Zhu De, and Zhou had prepared plans of the campaigns to be waged against Chiang Kaishek. But it was Zhou who dealt with the minutiae of what would now be dubbed a "counteroffensive" against Japan. Directive No. 1, drafted by Zhou, ordered the march into formerly Japanese-held territory, to capture the guns and the arsenals and take prisoners. Directives 2 to 7 laid down regulations on how to behave toward captured enemy personnel, toward collaborationists. Zhou also laid down behavior toward the Soviet troops who had now entered Manchuria and occupied some cities.

Manchuria was, of course, the Red armies' first target. The PLA men marched on foot, their pace swift, and everywhere there were partisans, peasant militia alerted to feed and lodge them, through the dozens of Red bases, large and small, which now honeycombed North China. Chiang sent an order to Zhu De to halt all advance, but Zhu De ignored it, of course. On August 14, the very day he had signed the peace treaty with Moscow, Chiang sent a telegram to Mao Dzedong asking him to come to Chongqing for talks.

Mao refused.

The news leaked out. There was an immediate reaction of alarm. "No more war, no more war . . . since 1913, thirty-two years of war . . . warlord wars, civil wars, Japanese war . . . we can bear it no longer . . . we want peace." Zhou told Mao that the people were pinning their hopes on a meeting, that perhaps Mao should reconsider. Chiang sent a longer cable on August 20, and Mao replied that Zhou was available for talks. A frenzy seized the scholars, the intellectuals. They wrote, they called on Zhou Enlai at No. 50 Tseng Family Cliff. A Mao-Chiang summit might effect the expected miracle: a coalition government, and democracy. "It is the hope of every Chinese," the newspaper *Takungpao* editorialized. Zhou flew back to Yenan to persuade the recalcitrant Mao. "We *must* respond. Otherwise the people will not understand. Chiang will use this against us, say that we want war," he told Mao.

Chiang Kaishek sent a third telegram on August 23. Since everything goes by threes in China, this was the finale. And Mao agreed, replying that Zhou was arriving immediately and that he would follow. But Ambassador Hurley now entered this Chinese scene, eager to show that the United States had a major role to play in this historic meeting. He flew to Yenan and brought Mao and Zhou to Chongqing in his own plane.

The airport was crowded on the afternoon of August 28 when Mao walked down the ladder, a tropical hat—called a topee—on his head. The hat may have come from Ye Jianying, Heroic Sword, who had relatives overseas. With the hat Mao looked a little like the late Sun Yatsen, who often wore such headgear. Was this image building due to Zhou? Zhou's collaborators were all there, Wang Bingnan, and Liao the Sailor, whom Chiang had jailed in 1942 and released a few weeks previous to the meeting.

Throughout the visit Zhou stuck close to Mao, personally inspecting Mao's room every night. The sofas and the chairs and the bed were examined by him, in case a bomb had been placed. He watched over Mao's food and drink. He would seize the cup from Mao's hand and drink it himself if he had not first vetted the bottle. He thus gave Mao immense prestige, knowing that Mao needed it, needed ego bolstering, for he was in a condition of suppressed fury every time he looked at Chiang. The latter, after all, had killed his first wife. It was also a signal to the secret police not to try any tricks. "No personal initiative, Dai Lee," Chiang had warned the police head, but Zhou took no chances. Chiang put at Mao's disposal the Lin Garden mansion, cool and tree-surrounded. There he could hold meetings, receive the numerous people who called. But Mao decided to sleep at the Eighth Army Liaison Office at Red Cliff, and would climb up and walk down the slope every day. Zhou organized meetings, a publicity campaign. Western correspondents, Chinese newsmen, scholars. Chiang brought his son, Chingkuo, to call on Mao. Chingkuo had returned to China from Moscow in 1937.

The talks. They seemed so important for China's future. But Mao and Chiang knew too well that "the same sky cannot cover us both." Both played the required game. Zhou sat at the negotiating table, talking. The Guomindang had discovered hundreds of thousands of peasant militia. "You don't seem to know much about the countryside," said Zhou with a hint of malice. "They support us, not because of Communism, but because of what we have done for them." He disarmed his opponents by occasionally agreeing with them. "Yes, perhaps we are, at times, illogical. But with sincerity we can correct our mistakes." The word "sincerity" was very much overworked by both sides during those weeks of total deception. Mao left Chongqing on October 12, saying that the talks were constructive but that "difficulties remained, which could be overcome."

In November, three weeks after the "summit" had ended, the United States landed troops at ports in North China, marines who would hold these ports for Chiang Kaishek until his armies reached them. Chiang asked Stalin not to remove Soviet forces from the cities in Manchuria they occupied until his own troops were ready. By arrangement, many of Chiang's battalions were flown into the cities of coastal China courtesy of the American Air Force.

Thus ended 1945, with encounters brewing, clashes breaking out. Hurley resigned, and was replaced by the former chancellor of Yenjing University, Leighton Stuart. President Truman now planned to send General George Marshall to China as his special representative to arrange a truce, and once again take up with Chiang the idea of a "democratic" government. Unlike Hurley, Leighton Stuart knew many Chinese intellectuals. A good number of his students, even those Christian students who sang the *Messiah* in the Yenjing University choir, had opted for Yenan and now were Communists or pro-Communist. Christianity also carries the seed of revolutionary ferment.

To prepare the right ambiance for the Marshall mission, Zhou made an impassioned appeal for a "coalition government" at the session of the People's Political Council on January 10, 1946. "Mutual recognition, mutual consultation, mutual concessions . . . We acknowledge Mr. Chiang Kaishek's leadership . . . we recognize the Guomindang as the largest party . . . but there must be recognition of all other parties as well." Zhou did not forget to call for the release of Young Marshal Zhang Xueliang and of Yang

Tiger City and his family, all of them imprisoned by Chiang Kaishek. "We still hope for peace," said Zhou. But while he spoke the Communist armies were hotfooting to Manchuria, and the Guomindang armies were attacking "Red bandit groups" wherever they found them.

The first meeting between Zhou Enlai and George Marshall was "delightful." Both men were impressed with each other, and Zhou again expressed hope for a peaceful settlement. Perhaps, Zhou said, the United States would stop *talking* of democratic reforms while at the same time pouring lavish amounts of money and weaponry on Chiang Kaishek, the military dictator?

Zhou did all he could during Marshall's tour to impress him with the moderation and reasonableness of the Communists. One of his interpreters, Ms. Zhu Qing, told me of those days with Marshall. "Zhou always wanted to get the exact meaning of every statement. He had everything that was translated into English pored over by all of us, querying every word. The same was done for the Chinese translation of what Marshall said. He had begun to train a lot of us young people in Chongqing, and he continued this in Nanjing. Almost all of us of the Southern Bureau had been underground. We knew that if there was any danger, he would contrive to move us to safety. I was then twenty-two years old, and with me in Nanjing were Zhang Wenjing, Huang Hua, and Wang Bingnan. We worked about sixteen hours a day. At first I was quite taken aback. Zhou, the others, were in smart Western clothes. I had been told that anyone who wore Western clothes was decadent, was bourgeois, but Zhou laughed at me. 'It is not clothes that matter, little Zhu. If we dress like soldiers, we'll smell of gunpowder.' Every night he instructed us, after a full day of discussion. He went over every one of the complicated points in the negotiations. He was never tired, and he could be called at any time by any of us. He spent a great deal of time perfecting my English, telling me not only to look at a dictionary but to listen to *how* words were being used. We got into the habit of always being ready, always alert, because if Zhou knew anything before his staff did, he would criticize the staff for slackness. He was always asking for new ideas, for fresh perceptions. 'Read the Western magazines, the newspapers. . . . If there is anything new, tell me,' he said to us.

"Our greatest problem was to persuade Marshall and the others that our party was independent and did not listen to the U.S.S.R. But somehow the Americans persistently thought of us as Moscow's satellites."

Marshall was legal-minded. He thought in terms of an organized government, with an apparatus to enforce the law. It was not possible to make him understand that in China no law, no government, could prevail against the gun.

Marshall had six meetings with Zhou between February and April 1946. Truce teams, supervised by a three-man cease-fire committee, composed of Marshall, Zhou, and Guomindang general Chang Chichung, were empowered to enforce cease-fires. The truce teams were sent to embattled cities, flew here and there to try to stop the clashes. In vain.

The Guomindang agreed to a military subcommittee to work out the reorganization of armed forces. "Now there is hope, perhaps," said Zhou. Marshall went to Yenan to see Mao, was greeted by dancing and singing crowds, and a special song was composed in his honor: "Let us extol you, great spirit. You use your might to extinguish the fires of war. . . . Oh, General Marshall . . . we honor you."

Marshall was moved by the candor, the puritan aspect of Yenan. He asked Mao whether he would go to Nanjing. Chiang had now returned to his former capital, and Zhou, with Deng Yingchao, had also moved to Nanjing. "Whenever Generalissimo Chiang calls me, I shall go," replied Mao, with his best "simple peasant" look. Marshall was optimistic. "I can assure you, China will enter into an unprecedentedly great era." He left for the United States, and three days after his departure, on March 10, fighting in Manchuria erupted on a large scale. He returned on April 18 to find a grim-faced Zhou Enlai and an unmanageable situation.

Chiang's military hardware had grown impressively. He was raising his armies to 5 million men, U.S.-equipped. But they lacked that potent mix of motivation, dedication, social and political propaganda which the Communists used so well. Chiang sent—or rather flew—his armies into cities, thus cloistering his own forces, while around them the ocean-countryside rose to submerge these strongholds of his might. Marshall talked, arranged truces and cease-fires, and Ambassador Leighton Stuart appealed to Chiang to institute reforms. Marshall loaned his plane to Chiang for an "inspection tour," but Chiang used it to fly to Changchun City

(Enduring Spring) in Manchuria. His armies took the city. An angry Zhou accused Marshall of collusion with Chiang and of partiality. Chiang took Harbin, despite Marshall's protest that it was against the recent truce agreements. "It can't go on like this. ... We've been fighting for twenty years, now it looks like another twenty," cried an anguished Zhou to Marshall. There was discontent, turbulence among the people in Chiang's territories, due to inflation and gross corruption. The intelligentsia in the universities, led by the Democratic League, held protest meetings, demonstrations. Chiang and police head Dai Lee decided on "suppression." Two professors at Kunming University, both members of the Democratic League, and the son of one of them were shot at and died on the steps of the university. The killing, said Zhou, was part of "a nationwide plan for the massacre of Communists and their sympathizers." Zhou wrote to Yenan, asking for protection teams for important non-Communists, members of the Democratic League and other small parties. In August, Marshall instituted a seven-month blockade of weapons to the Guomindang, to stop the growing number of attacks by the latter. But he could not stop the ships already on the way. He was a good man in an untenable position, mediating between two embattled armies while his country was supplying money, weapons, planes, and other equipment to one of them only.

Zhou Enlai was to lose a friend that summer. Ye Ting, jailed in 1941, was released in the spring of 1946. Zhou personally brought Ye's daughter back from Yenan, by plane, and the family was reunited in Nanjing. A grand welcome celebration for Ye was planned in Yenan for July. Together with Bo Gu and Wang Jofei, Zhou's old friend from France, Ye Ting and his wife and child took the plane to Yenan. The weather was good, the American pilots experienced, but the plane blew up and there were no survivors. "Zhou wept for a long time," Gung Peng, his press officer, told me. He composed an essay, praising each one of the dead, including the valorous Americans who had lost their lives "in a noble cause." Deng Yingchao was also grieved. She had cared for Ye's daughter for many months in Yenan and cherished the girl.

The villa the Zhous occupied in Nanjing was named New Plum Garden. There were fruit trees and a rhododendron hedge. There was the usual round of banquets and receptions to attend. Deng Yingchao again wore her best dresses. But, to signify his discontent with Marshall, Zhou left Nanjing in August for Shanghai. In Shanghai the sister of Gung Peng and Gung Pusheng, whose husband owned some real estate in the city, made a house available to Zhou, No. 107 Massenet Road, in the French Concession. Here, Zhou was not as subject to surveillance by the Dai Lee police, though plainclothesmen would follow him, rather clumsily. He sometimes stopped his car, walked up to theirs, and lectured them. He and Yingchao renewed old friendships and made new ones. Yingchao was busy, for there was a large women's section of the Party in Shanghai and many sympathizers. Zhou called on Shanghai capitalists, assuring them that they need have no fear of the Communists. He held press conferences, denouncing unilateral help to Chiang, condemning the presence in Chiang's headquarters of forty military advisers from the United States. He also reestablished his intelligence network. It was so efficient that Kang Daisha, in far-off Sichuan, was warned by a message from Zhou in Shanghai to run away, in time to escape being arrested. On September 3, Zhou wrote to Mao: "The people in Shanghai now understand us better. . . . I am deliberately avoiding Marshall and Leighton Stuart."

Then, on November 16: "The door has now been slammed by the single hand of the Guomindang authorities . . . while the bloody war waged against the liberated areas is going on with full vigor, and the policy of the U.S. government to assist Chiang in the civil war remains unchanged. A false peace, a false democracy, cannot but fail to deceive the people."

The full fury of the Communist press was now turned against the United States. Student demonstrations against U.S. intervention took place. In December 1946, Zhou told Marshall: "This is a farce . . . we cannot go on cheating the Chinese people." Marshall flew back to Washington, and Zhou and Yingchao returned to Yenan, where they were greeted at the airport by a cheerful Mao, who handed Zhou a lined overcoat to wear, a sign of caring.

To say that Zhou was happy would be untrue. Perhaps he felt that there was something that he might have done and had left undone. . . . Both he and Mao realized that only America could help China industrialize swiftly. Otherwise it would be a long, long haul out of misery into prosperity. "It takes a long rope to catch a whale," Mao said to Zhou. "And you, Enlai, shall weave that rope."

13

Through these years of tension and travail, with their many demands upon body and mind, Zhou Enlai and his wife worked closely together, even if today Yingchao insists that "we were always independent from each other." In Chongqing she had worked in the Southern Bureau, and contributed much to the success of that little-known "second front" which Zhou organized among the intelligentsia, the middle ground ignored by both Chiang Kaishek and the Yenan Politburo. It is revealing to discover how many members of Zhou's Southern Bureau were women—teachers, doctors, nurses, students. Many were certainly recruited by Deng Yingchao.

When, in 1943, the couple had returned to Yenan for the Rectification, Yingchao was also criticized, though not as virulently as her husband. Although other women, under the strain, divorced or became estranged from their spouses, the couple found solace, comfort, and happiness in each other's company. Dr. George Hatem, known by his Chinese name Ma Haide, who had come to Yenan in 1936, and stayed all the rest of his life in China, told me, "They used to walk together, holding hands. It made one feel cheerful to see the couple, as if the sun had burst through dark clouds."

There had been a small epidemic of divorce and remarriage among the higher cadres when younger, better-educated women came to Yenan from Shanghai and the coastal cities. Not only did Mao have his romantic affair with Blue Apple—named Limpid Stream—but Liu Shaoqi, and others as well, quietly changed partners. "Liu Shaoqi divorced and remarried five times, but it was perfectly legal every time," Dr. Hatem said, with a small twinkle. Gossip was prevalent, almost a nightly occupation, in the caves of the troglodytic city, but there was never a word about the Zhou couple. Except once. Before climbing into a plane at the airport, which was to take him to Nanjing for a conference with Chiang Kaishek and George Marshall, Zhou Enlai hugged Yingchao and kissed her on the cheek, in front of everyone. Yenan gasped. Kissing in public is never, never done in China! Piotr Vladimirov, the Tass agency man in Yenan at the time, who hated everyone there, could not find a bad opinion of Zhou and Yingchao anywhere. "His wife is also his best friend," he said.

In November 1946, back from Shanghai and the failed Marshall mission, the couple again lived in their two-cave dwelling. Zhou Enlai took off his natty Western suit and appeared in the gray cotton padded garb of Yenan. It was a hard winter; massive sandstorms pelted the city with tons of yellow sand. Every day Zhou was in conference with Mao, Zhu De, Liu Shaoqi, the commanders, the political commissars. The Communists had their backs to the wall. With the breakdown of the Marshall mission, all hope of a settlement was lost. Chiang was starting a major offensive; the words "Red bandit" reappeared. The last members of the Liaison Office were ordered out of Nanjing, and Communist newspapers closed down. The United States would continue to provide weapons and money to Chiang Kaishek, to use in the civil war against the Communists.

In March 1947, Zhou circulated two documents, entitled "Guidelines for Work and the Tactics for Struggle in Areas Controlled by Chiang Kaishek." "Chiang's tactics of suppression are still of an exploratory nature, but due to the financial and economic crisis which prevails in his territories, life is becoming impossible for the people. . . . The mass movement will therefore continue." Agitation must be maintained but with prudence, avoiding direct confrontation. "We must expand the scope of our propaganda, win over the middle elements . . . utilize legal means, strive to form a broad front. This is not conservatism; rather it is steering around submerged reefs." Student demonstrations, which had taken place in 1946, must be avoided. "The tactics must change, or there will be massacres. . . . Students should always go in and out of school in groups for mutual protection, never carry identification papers. . . . Covert and overt actions must be separated." Zhou reinforced his intelligence apparatus by sending abroad some of the staff he had trained. Gung Peng and her husband, Qiao

Guanhua, left for Hong Kong to take charge of the Xinhua News Agency, reopened when the British colony was regained after the war with Japan. It was the best listening post Zhou had.

The war preparations against Chiang had to appear as merely self-defense. The time had not yet come to call for Chiang's overthrow. "Only fight back if attacked. All operations must be well coordinated. It may take us ten years." The propaganda teams with the PLA must appeal to the ordinary Guomindang soldier. "Come over, come over. Chinese do not fight Chinese. . . . Bring your gun with you. . . . You will be paid silver dollars." Now that inflation was uncontrollable, and paper money worth almost nothing, a silver dollar was a small fortune.

The Communists in Yenan were united around Mao in a singleness of purpose, a clear perception that this was a turning point in the long-drawn-out struggle. Hope knitted them together, all grievances forgotten. In 1947 Manchuria was already half conquered, 300,000 square miles and half the population in Communist hands. "But to delude the enemy, to give him an inflated idea of his own worth, we must sometimes appear to *lose* battles." Mao and Zhou agreed on this. "Never push an encounter to extremes. Always spare your forces. Alternate concentration and dispersion," prescribed Zhou Enlai.

In the next two years, many of Mao's documents were drafted by Zhou, all of Zhou's statements were submitted to Mao for checking. There was total harmony, ocean and shore come together; Mao sketching his grand visions, and Zhou objectifying, calculating, bringing precision and clearness. Both must have been quoting Sun Tzu's *The Art of War* to each other; the campaigns were based on that Grand Master's precepts.

A feature of the "self-defense" period was the relinquishing of cities, not only to delude but also to get Chiang Kaishek—an astute politician, but a lamentable war strategist—to immobilize more of his armies, closeting them into these strongholds, lone islands floating on the great ocean of rural China. "I gave up two cities and gained 60,000 men," Liu Bocheng said to American journalist Anna Louise Strong, who was in Yenan at the time. A constant stream of victory bulletins came from Chiang's military headquarters in the first months of 1947. Mao planned to give him even greater joy. "We shall arrange a great triumph for him. . . . We shall let Chiang's brilliant General Hu Tsungnan capture

Yenan. The day Hu's crack troops enter the emptied city will be the day of his defeat." Hu Tsungnan had blockaded the Yenan base since 1938. His headquarters were at nearby Xian. Hu's armies glittered: splendid uniforms, brand-new American guns and tanks. Hu ran fourteen thought-reform camps for the youths who tried to reach Yenan and were caught by his secret police.

A high-cheeked, dark-skinned man named Xiung Xianghui, the son of a high court judge, became Hu Tsungnan's personal secretary and aide-de-camp. In 1937, Xiung had tried to reach Yenan, and, after some trouble, succeeded in getting known by Zhou's underground. Zhou convinced him to avoid Yenan and to stay and work with the Guomindang. Xiung had been a mole for ten years. "Hu Tsungnan was one of the very few Guomindang commanders to use ex-Communists," Xiung told me. "But if he suspected a double cross, he ordered instant execution. One day he suspected me, though I told him I was not a Communist. He was reassured by my father's position and my own lifestyle. Communists often betrayed themselves by being too good, not black-marketing or having women around." Xiung chuckled, but did not tell me which foibles he had to flaunt to reassure Hu Tsungnan.

Xiung did so well that he became a friend of Chiang Kaishek's second son, who paid for a gala reception for three hundred guests on the occasion of Xiung's wedding in Nanjing. Through him, Zhou knew three months ahead that Hu Tsungnan contemplated taking Yenan. Mao's proposal to let him do so, because that "will be the end of him and of his army," encountered serious disagreement from some of Mao's colleagues. Yenan was sacrosanct. It was the Mecca of the faithful. How would Party members, now 3 million of them, react when they heard that Yenan had been taken by the Guomindang? Mao and Zhou were able to persuade the reluctant Politburo. Yenan would be evacuated before Hu Tsungnan could reach it. Where would the leaders move? Mao suggested what sounded like a wildly fanciful scheme, though it was based on historic precedent. The Communist high command must divide. Mao, Zhou, and 20,000 troops would remain in Yenan to supervise the evacuation of the units, the hospitals and schools. Then they would march away, march deep into the yellow loess, into Northwest Shaanxi, making Hu Tsungnan pursue them. "We shall lead him by the nose, make him follow, make him run, tire him out trying to find us. Then we'll swoop on him and finish him off." A spare Central Committee and Politburo, with Liu Shaoqi and Zhu De at the head, would move eastward with the bulk of the cadres and the army, and establish headquarters at Xi Baibo, in Hebei province. Another working and liaison headquarters would be sited at Linfeng, in the successful base run by Nie Rongzhen. There were at the time six major theaters of war in operation. By pinning down Hu Tsungnan and his crack troops—some 300,000 men—forcing him to hunt for the elusive Mao and Zhou in that yellow land of cliffs and gullies which shifted as the wind blew, they were removing one of Chiang's main forces from other war theaters, where the real "peaches of victory" were to be plucked.

With 20,000 men, 150 bodyguards, one stretcher, portable radio equipment with plenty of spare batteries, field telephones, and Mao's wife, Limpid Stream, Mao and Zhou moved out from Yenan, Zhou remaining to supervise the evacuation until the last day. Deng Yingchao was sent to Linfeng, taking with her Mao's little daughter. Zhou at first argued that he and Mao should separate. "Let me, with some troops, act as a decoy, go off in one direction while you go in another. . . . You must first of all protect yourself," said Zhou, always the Grand Vizier, careful of the sovereign's well-being. But Mao did not agree. "This is the best terrain for regular troops to be buried in," Mao remarked as he and Zhou walked, walked the yellow earth, walked the perilous pathways between gully and cliff, an ambling course in and out of thirty-seven troglodytic villages. Mao called it "a small promenade," but Zhou, in later years, remarked, "There was a great deal of walking to do." Zhou developed a massive nosebleed, probably due to the harsh wind. He had to lie down on the stretcher for a day until it stopped. There were encounters, alarms, battles. One at Sheep and Horse River, on April 14; another on May 4 at Panlung, where they found a depot with arms, clothes, and ammunition. The two men took pseudonyms, because the villagers knew their names, though not their faces. Mao became Li Desheng, and Zhou was Hu Picheng. Hu Tsungnan sent troops in hot pursuit. They fell into ambush, were lured into gullies, trapped between cliffs, lost their way. . . . Battalions of the PLA, hidden in the yellow waste, blocked their rear, cut them to pieces.

During the one year and five days of this "promenade," the Mao-Zhou duo was never cut off from receiving information, either by radio or by liaison couriers trotting seventeen to twenty miles a day. Details of the campaigns fought in other theaters of war were reported to them. Nie Rongzhen asserts that major steps in the campaigns were directed by Mao and Zhou, from wherever they were in the yellow immensity of the loess. Zhou's information even covered personal matters. He was told of the death of Evans Carlson, the naval attaché whom he had helped to get away from Nanjing in 1937. Carlson had died in the United States in late May 1947; in August, Zhou sent his condolences to Carlson's family.

In September, they established headquarters at Yang Family Ditch, in the county of Mi, once renowned for its beautiful women. Hither came the commanders and political commissars from various fronts for a reappraisal of the war situation. Here also came the underground men, reporting on the growing collapse of the economy in Chiang's territories. On September 28, 1947, Zhou issued a landmark directive: LAUNCH A MASSIVE NATIONWIDE COUNTEROFFENSIVE TO OVERTHROW CHIANG KAISHEK.

"Self-defense" had ended. The Communists were going over to the attack. This needed unity of views and perfect coordination among the various commanders. It needed boldness and imagination, but the exaltation of near-victory was theirs. They now felt that five years at the most would see the end of Chiang, who was finding it exceedingly difficult to get his generals to work together or to take the least initiative. In some cities, the Guomindang battalions were fed by airdrops from U.S. planes manned by American pilots. They could not, or would not, venture out of the city walls for food.

Chiang made things worse for himself by arresting liberals, members of the Democratic League, anyone suspected of having ties with the Communists . . . and who, among the more eminent scholars, had not seen or spoken with Zhou at least once? In vain did Ambassador Leighton Stuart and General Albert Wedemeyer, in command of the U.S. forces in China, plead with him for political and economic reforms, tell him how badly his commanders and his officials behaved. "There are some splendid liberals," was Leighton Stuart's wistful remark, but what hope was there when they were being jailed? Inflation was so bad that "we walked about with a suitcase of bank notes to pay for a meal. We paid before eating, because the food went up in price during the time it took to swallow it," says one of my cousins, who was a university professor in those years.

"There is increasing demoralization, a fatalistic feeling that collapse is inevitable," warned Leighton Stuart. General Wedemeyer concurred, but proposed intensification of American aid to Chiang. Because of the Cold War, and for fear of being called "soft on Communism," Truman had to continue helping Chiang. Privately the President exploded. "There wasn't anything that could be done. I wasn't going to waste a single American life to save him." Three and a half billion dollars' worth of matériel and money had been funneled to Chiang Kaishek, and more would be forthcoming in the next eighteen months.

"The decision to overthrow Chiang Kaishek was made long ago," Zhou Enlai now stated. "We fought ten years of civil war with this in mind." The war against Japan had necessitated enrolling Chiang for a while, but "for some time after the Japanese surrender, we tried to overthrow him by peaceful means. . . . Now we fight."

Were all these feints and passes, those on-and-off negotiations, the Marshall mission, the appeal for coalition government, only accomplished deception? Only camouflage? The "we" used indicates a collective will. Zhou did, for a while, believe in a coalition government and he wanted the United States on his side. But Mao never believed in Chiang, and was proved right.

Yet once again, in December and January, Zhou broadcast that the CCP was ready for "peace negotiations." Which seems to contradict the order for a counteroffensive against Chiang. But it resulted from a rigorous assessment of the fact that within the Guomindang a rift was taking place. It was also because the Communists were encountering problems in their all-out drive for power. One of them was land reform. Another was Mao's decision to continue the war into South China, a decision that brought controversy, not only within the CCP but also with Moscow.

Wherever the PLA went, it carried out land reform. In 1946, Mao had drafted a mild program. The middle peasant must become an ally of the Communists, he must not suffer. Small landlords were not to be pilloried. However, Liu Shaoqi, heading the "spare" Central Committee in Hebei, had instituted harsh policies, somewhat resembling Wang Ming's bolshevization methods.

Zhou sent out his own men to investigate, and their reports

make grim reading. Landlords big and small were invariably liquidated or driven out of their holdings. Liu used the odious "class origin" rule even to throw out many Party members or subject them to gross ill-treatment. Mao asked Zhou to handle the matter, and Zhou did so. "It is impermissible to encroach on the land of the middle peasant. . . . We must unite with more than 90 percent of the masses. . . . Absolute egalitarianism is totally wrong."

Some cities were beginning to fall into the hands of the Communists, and these methods were provoking hostility and terror among the inhabitants. "The petty bourgeoisie, the merchants and traders, must be protected," said Zhou. In an inner-Party letter dated February 5, 1948, Zhou condemns the tendency "to suspend and sometimes exterminate comrades with contrary opinions." The "indiscriminate suspension from Party membership of tens of thousands of Party members of landlord and rich peasant status in the villages must stop immediately." "A good leader must unite with comrades whom he dislikes. . . . We must have faith in comrades with shortcomings. . . . This is Comrade Mao Dzedong's style of work." Someone had once remarked that Zhou always got his way: he invoked Mao, even when it was he who made the decisions. But in this case, it was by common agreement that the two men decided to stop Liu's "left" methods. By forced marches, they left Mi county in late February to reach Xi Baibo on March 23, to be met by Liu Shaoqi, Zhu De, and other Politburo members.

The major problem now facing the PLA in their drive to power concerned carrying the war into South China. The Yangtse River had formed a natural boundary for two millennia between north and south. Taking Nanjing, Chiang Kaishek's capital, and then Shanghai, pushing southward and westward to take over the whole mainland, would depend on the PLA's success in crossing the mighty stream.

Stalin viewed Mao's successes with apprehension. In the winter of 1947–48, worried because of Chiang's failure in Manchuria, the Russian had already offered to mediate. Mao ignored this offer, but it is perhaps the reason why Zhou, a consummate artist in double-dealing, called for "peace negotiations," knowing full well that the real situation, the down-to-earth territorial gains, were not in favor of Chiang Kaishek. But Stalin, whose deplorably inexact understanding of the Chinese situation seems curiously akin to the American one, sent a message to Mao suggesting that he content himself with North China and leave South China to Chiang Kaishek. The message warned that America might use the atom bomb in China should the Communists "challenge" the United States' commitment to Chiang Kaishek. Zhou replied that "Comrade Mao has rightly said that the atom bomb is a paper tiger." But Liu Shaoqi, Peng Dehuai, and other commanders seemed to have qualms about crossing the Yangtse. An ill-defined controversy broke out that April, and the very fact that in May collective leadership had to be reasserted at a major meeting reveals how serious the disagreement was. Mao Dzedong then suggested to Stalin a trip to Moscow, to explain to Stalin what the Chinese position was. A long silence followed.

Mao Dzedong and Zhou Enlai went to Linfeng, to be greeted with joy by Nie Rongzheng, and, for Zhou, to see his wife again. Mao, in good humor, teased her. "Little Chao, Enlai missed you very much."

It was in this interim period that Zhou became *the* statesman, building the future government of China. In Linfeng, with his old friend Nie, he prepared a draft regarding scientific education, "of the utmost importance for China's development," and began to fashion the political-economic structure which was to replace the crumbling Chiang regime.

He had to plan the formation of ministries, of an administration. There is no administration without civil servants, and where would he get them? "We need all the skills and talents available." This was his leitmotiv, his obsession, for the next decade and more. Wherever there was a Chinese writer, artist, engineer, or scientist abroad, he should be contacted. "Some of them may want to return." But first they must be reassured, and therefore all policies must be made clear. . . . "Support can only be won when new policies, changes in policies, decisions as to the correctness or incorrectness of any particular policy, all is promptly made known." In every city conquered, professionals of all kinds must be reassured and their needs seen to.

He concerned himself with the handling of industry, the banks, commerce. He envisaged three sectors of the economy under the "new democracy" formula promulgated by Mao. The public sector, which meant the nationalized industries, must, of course, be the main sector; but the private sector, "which we shall need for a long time," must encourage the capitalists to produce and to cooperate with the government. The cooperative sector, a mixture of both, was to be set up. "Political power, the law, prisons, taxation, rewards, loans, prohibitions, new approaches to accounting procedures . . . all these must be worked out." The major problem was the small number of able and skilled personnel at his disposal, even though he had done his best to train many young people. In that April 1948, he began to elaborate a Ministry of Foreign Affairs. China could not progress unless it had wide, extensive connections with all nations, not just with socialist states.

"One could always tell whether a man or a woman was trained by Zhou Enlai. To begin with, he or she is a workaholic. Secondly, never will that person be slipshod in anything. Whatever he or she does is a total commitment," the Indian diplomat, P. K. Bannerjee, said to me. To fashion an administration from scratch, everything had to be done. The CCP could not count on the ex-Guomindang bureaucracy. Still, Zhou directed that bank managers, accountants, cashiers, office workers in trading houses, postal and telecommunications workers, railway and engineering personnel, should not be labeled capitalists, suspended, or liquidated in bursts of misguided zealotry.

Zhou knew that many of the 3 million or more Party members would want jobs and very few of them were well educated. But he had to rely on them to carry out the needed control of the country. Many of them had never seen an electric lamp, or an indoor toilet, or an elevator. Technical apparatus in the scientific research institutes filled them with suspicion. They did not know that the earth was round, and Zhou, when he instituted academic research, found himself challenged by the flat-earthers in the Party. "We shall need everyone who has any talent. . . . We do not have enough educated people. . . . It is in the army itself that we shall have to find our cadres." The army, the PLA, had discipline. Its soldiers had been taught how to read . . . just barely. There was the non-Communist intelligentsia he had labored for many years to rally to the Party. Talent outside the Party, that second front which he had established, was essential. . . . But could it be entrusted with running the country?

In industrial plants and factories, Zhou suggested factory committees, with the main responsibility for production resting on the factory manager. This provided an escape route for the managers, and this is what Zhou wanted. Competence. Talent. "New democratic economic construction is *incompatible* with the economic policies of agrarian socialism or with extreme egalitarianism," Zhou Enlai reiterated.

In those months, Zhou Enlai would devise, with the participation of aquiline-nosed Chen Yun, with Nie Rongzhen, with his friends from the time they were together in France, Li Fuchun and Li Weihan, and with the help of non-Communist economists, a Common Program. It was devised to practice a mixed economy, although of course the aim was to "*gradually* achieve socialism." The Program was backed by Mao at the time.

In April, Yenan was retaken by a PLA army under the command of Ho Lung, the Winsome Dragon. Hu Tsungnan's troops were almost pulverized. Ragged bands remained, running back to their villages or rushing to join the victorious forces marching in. By the summer of 1948, 95 percent of North China was under the Communists. Only some cities, Beijing and Tianjin among them, remained to be captured. Chiang Kaishek declared, in a speech so devoid of reality that it produced general mirth, that the situation was getting better every day and that he would be generous to his adversaries if they sued for peace.

Zhou had already begun to woo, through intermediaries such as Pan Hannien, the military commander whom Chiang had charged with the defense of Beijing, Fu Tsoyi. Disenchanted with Chiang, Fu Tsoyi listened to Zhou's siren song, and after some simulacrum of resistance, handed over Beijing to the Communists at Christmas 1948. Zhou and Mao had ordered the PLA *not* to fire destructive artillery into the city, lest it damage palaces and temples. The professors and students of the universities formed welcome parties to greet the PLA, which marched into Beijing in excellent order, equipped with American guns, even with tanks, seized from the Guomindang. Another Mao-Zhou feat was performed. Beijing was liberated peacefully.

In January 1949, Chiang Kaishek prepared his withdrawal. He had appointed Li Tsungjen, ex-warlord of Guanxi province, to the position of vice-president of the Guomindang. Li was known to be anxious for peace. Chiang retired on January 21, and Li Tsungjen sent a delegation to Beijing to confer with Zhou Enlai.

Negotiations did take place. They gave the Communists more scope, yet another chance to rally still more of the noncommitted. At the time, the Americans pinned their hopes on what was described as a Third Force, represented by a few Western-educated intellectuals. Of course, this Third Force never exerted any influence. Meanwhile preparations for taking South China went on apace.

Stalin's envoy, Politburo member Anastas Mikoyan, arrived on January 31, 1949, to see Mao. The meeting took place at Xi Baibo. Mao deliberately, it seemed, made Mikoyan come to this small, out-of-the-way village-townlet. Zhou, Zhu De, and Liu Shaoqi were there. Mikoyan began by telling Mao that his request to see Stalin in Moscow had been considered but in view of the crucial developments Mao's presence was required in China. Besides, his health must be considered (there was nothing wrong with Mao's health). It was a thorough brush-off. But, Mikoyan said, "I have brought my two ears with me." He would listen to what the Chinese comrades had to say. He would report it all to Stalin. He would not comment on anything the Chinese comrades told him. What Mao said to Mikoyan the three times they met is wrapped in euphemism. Interpreter Shi Ji reticently records that Mao refused considering sparing Chiang Kaishek. "The revolution must be carried through to the end." This meant taking South China. Zhou held a fourth meeting alone with Mikoyan, save for interpreter Shi Ji. Shi Ji records that Zhou did not talk of politics, but of China's reconstruction after the war.

"He talked in detail, covering every aspect of China's economic needs." Mikoyan would report that Zhou would be an excellent Prime Minister. That he held Zhou in high regard, and transmitted his impression to Stalin, would be confirmed when, in the following year, Mao Dzedong went to Moscow and was unable to achieve anything before Zhou Enlai was sent for, to "extract a little meat out of the tiger's mouth," to get from Stalin some aid for China's urgent needs.

A Chinese People's Political Consultative Conference (CPPCC) —a continuation of the People's Political Council instituted in 1937—was to be created, starting with a Preparatory Committee, organized by Zhou Enlai. He called on the intelligentsia, university professors, scholars, minority party members, "eminent personages," such as Nankai University president Zhang Boling. It was extremely important, symbolically, that Soong Chingling become a member. In April 1949, Zhou and Mao sent her an urgent telegram addressed to her rue Molière house in Shanghai. But she did not reply. Nor did she reply to other telegrams or to the urgings of Pan Hannien, Zhou's all-weather man. Letters and telegrams sent through her secretary, Grace Liao, the sister of Liao the Sailor, also remained unanswered. Finally, in June, Zhou Enlai sent his wife to Shanghai. She succeeded. Soong Chingling came back to Beijing with Deng Yingchao. With her she brought non-Communist women of standing and influence, such as Shi Liang, later to become Minister of Justice in Zhou's government.

The Preparatory Committee of the CPPCC assembled in Beijing. There were 134 members, representing twenty-three organizations and eight democratic parties. They were lodged at the Peking Hotel and the Wagons-Lits Hotel. These were, at the time, deluxe establishments, reserved for Westerners and very wealthy Chinese. With his usual obsessive meticulousness, Zhou inspected the rooms, talked to the staff and the waiters, reassured them that their jobs were safe. "One day we shall build many, many hotels. . . . Many people will be coming to China . . . and you will be teaching young people to continue the good work you have been doing."

Zhou's first report to the committee was given on April 17. The conference took place in the Hall of Nurturing Benevolence in Zhongnanhai, the assemblage of pavilions and gardens around the large lakes in the heart of the Imperial City, which was to become the residence of the Communist leaders and remains their residence today.

The report was a very full one. It began with an account of the peace talks taking place at the time with a delegation from the Guomindang. Zhou spoke respectfully of Li Tsungjen, but during the meeting the PLA were taking Nanjing and sweeping southward. Zhou left an opening for a "revolutionary Guomindang" to join in rebuilding China, as one party among others. Of course, the CCP would be the leading party, though Zhou did not insist too much on its overwhelming strength, speaking of "democratic centralism" instead.

Chiang Kaishek had left for Guangzhou. In May, he reached Taiwan. Zhou offered Chiang's generals a share in China's future.

Fu Tsoyi, Tsai Tingkai, and some others chose to remain, largely because of Zhou's persuasion and their trust in him.

The work required to build a strong, modern, industrialized China was arduous, said Zhou. He hoped that military operations would soon cease. "We want to minimize damage to the nation, to conserve manpower and material resources for our reconstruction. . . . The Communist Party cannot provide all the qualified personnel needed. Public figures in all walks of life must participate. . . . I am afraid the Peking Hotel and the Wagons-Lits Hotel, where you are staying, will soon be empty," said Zhou, urging them to set to work immediately. He also delineated the principles on which foreign relations would be based. "We are willing to cooperate with *all* countries that treat us as equals. We don't discriminate against foreigners or engage in provocation. . . . We take a firm stand, but we must also be very careful, handle problems according to the principle 'On just grounds, to our advantage, and with restraint.' "

On May 7, he gave a major speech at the first National Youth Congress held in Beijing. This speech was not published until October 8, 1978, and for a good reason. Its title was: LEARN FROM MAO DZEDONG, but it was most frank in warning against any deification of Mao.

"You must not regard Mao as a chance leader, a born leader, a demigod. . . . If you do . . . it will be empty talk. Making Mao a deity apart . . . that's the kind of leader publicized in feudal and capitalist societies. Our leader is born of the Chinese people, born of China's revolution. . . . In learning from Mao Dzedong, we must learn in the light of his own historical development, not just looking at his great achievement today and neglecting the process of his growth. . . .

"Mao Dzedong was superstitious in childhood, but yesterday's superstitious child was able to become today's Chairman Mao. . . . His greatness lies in the fact that he dared to face up to the past."

Zhou made another point. Even if the new government must fight against feudalism, "we realize that if there is anything good in what Confucius says, we can quote him for our use. *And if our parents come and stay with us, we should take care of them.*"

The Soviet ambassador, Paniushkin, followed Chiang Kaishek in his peregrination to Guangzhou, and on to Taiwan, whereas the American ambassador, Leighton Stuart, stayed in Nanjing. Leighton Stuart tried to contact his former students, Huang Hua among them, tried to reach Zhou for a meeting. But Zhou could not see him at the time, since Washington had reacted with panic, anger, and more aid to Chiang. Through American scholar Edmund Glubb, Zhou tried to convey a message to Washington. China was prepared to establish relations with *all* countries, irrespective of their systems. Through an Australian journalist, Michael Kerr, Zhou repeated the message to Leighton Stuart. "We are not against the United States. There is no conflict of interest between our two countries. We want to do business with all countries, for mutual benefit."

Leighton Stuart could elicit no approval for a meeting from Washington. He asked whether he could see Zhou personally. Zhou sent Huang Hua. "Leighton Stuart can come to Beijing in a private capacity, as the guest of the present chancellor of Yenjing University." He could not be received as an ambassador, since there were no diplomatic relations, nor was Washington prepared to extend recognition to the new regime. Leighton Stuart remained for some months and was then recalled to the United States.

The Chinese People's Political Consultative Conference met on September 21 and sat for nine days. On September 30, 1949, in the evening, it proclaimed the legal foundation of the People's Republic of China. The Common Program, which Zhou had elaborated, was adopted.

On October 1, Mao stood on the gate of Tienanmen and proclaimed: "The Chinese people have stood up. No one will insult us again." Zhou turned to his "foreign affairs" staff. They must make sure that the message was widely broadcast, was translated. . . . "The whole world must hear us now."

Out of the shambles, the ruins of decades of war, a new land, a new order, must be created. "All we have inherited is a blanket full of holes," said Mao. China was in appalling condition. It was up to Zhou, the "housekeeper" as Mao called him, to patch up the blanket, repair it . . . and provide, one day, new blankets. He was fifty-one years old.

A Monument to the Heroes of the People stands in the great square facing Tienanmen Gate. The inscription, to the memory of those who died since the first Opium War of 1840 so that China might be freed from exploitation both internal and external, was devised by Mao Dzedong. But the calligraphy is Zhou Enlai's.

IV
1949–1966

Building the New China
The Korean War
The Hundred Flowers Movement
The Great Leap Forward
China explodes an atom bomb
and reenters the world stage

14

In 1949, China was a ruined land, a shambles created by continuous wars for over a century, by exploitation on a scale unknown anywhere else in the world. It had begun in 1842 with the Opium Wars, when Great Britain and later France tried to force opium on China in payment for silk, tea, and porcelain. It had continued with Japan's attempt to conquer China. Now, for the first time in more than a century, there was peace. The Communists had achieved their goal, with the overwhelming enthusiasm of the population, but the fruits of victory they reaped were, said Mao, "an old blanket full of holes." Their only asset was the fervent patriotism of the Chinese people, buoyed by immense hope that now China would be unified and that reconstruction of the beloved land could begin. My generation remembers how, by the million, the people gave the best of themselves to that exalting vision. "The Chinese people have stood up. No one will insult us again," Mao Dzedong had stated on October 1, 1949, standing on the main gate of what had once been the Forbidden City, and the crowds had roared their faith in the brave new world to come.

Zhou Enlai had successfully promoted the "second front": non-Communist, even anti-Communist, but patriotic intellectuals, scientists and scholars, brought together by ardent love of country and dedication to shaping its future. He now began to transform that inchoate assembly into a driving force for China's industrial revolution. He reassured the capitalists who remained in China; they too had a role to play in the restructuring of the economy. He expounded a common front program, in which all classes of society could contribute, irrespective of social background.

The most urgent priority was to reopen the coal mines of North China, flooded by the Japanese. Zhou delegated Li Fuchun and

Chen Yi to call in person upon engineers. My father was one of those who found Chen Yi on his doorstep one afternoon, asking him whether he could help. "Of course," he replied. He packed a small suitcase and went off to the Kailan coal mines in North China, without asking any pay for his work. So did many, many others. Within six weeks coal returned to the cities, in time for winter. Zhou Enlai organized the cleanup of Beijing's sewers, blocked by tons of filth. Thousands of volunteers, ordinary citizens, enrolled for the job and new pipes were laid, more between December 1949 and early 1952 than since the beginning of the century. Millions of beggars haunting the cities, most of them poor peasants, were rounded up, fed, and returned to their native villages. Most of the countryside was, at last, at peace, even though bandit gangs still roamed in the provinces. But the peasants had begun sowing and planting, helped by the soldiers of the PLA, who also repaired the roads and railways and worked in the fields. Thus food reached the hungry cities.

To stifle inflation, which in 1949, under Chiang Kaishek, had risen to 10 million percent per month, prices were pegged to an equivalent in grain. By December, inflation was curbed. The problem of opium was then tackled. Throughout China, the PLA destroyed opium poppies, as part of the mopping-up campaigns against Guomindang remnants, bandits, and gangsters. Addicts— at the time 90 million out of a population of 450 million—were gathered in group therapy sessions. Within the next four years the habit disappeared. Drug peddlers and drug merchants were summarily executed.

By November, Zhou had established his cabinet, the core of the government, later known as the State Council. Forty-seven percent of his ministers and vice-ministers were non-Communists, as were half the officials in the various commissions set up. "All those who can contribute to the rebuilding of China must do so. We welcome them irrespective of politics," said Zhou, whose indefatigable energy galvanized all those around him. "These were fabulous days. Life held glorious meaning for us. We truly believed," said a non-Communist scholar, talking nostalgically to me in 1988.

Zhou Enlai's work pattern, which had started during his early days in Shanghai and then in the Ruijin base, continued throughout the next twenty-four years. He seldom went to bed before 4:30 or 5 a.m., when dawn, known as "fish-belly silver light" in China, touched the roofs of Beijing. He slept till 10 or 10:30 a.m., unless there was a meeting to attend. He took a short after-lunch siesta in the early afternoon. One of his secretaries kept a diary of a day in the life of the Premier. "Premier gives directives against forest fires after a meeting with forest inspection teams at 11 a.m. He receives education experts at noon and pores over their reports while eating lunch at 12:30 p.m. His lunch is as usual, two dishes, one with meat, one vegetables only, and two rough millet buns. After lunch he exercises his right arm [by playing Ping-Pong] for fifteen minutes while we read out reports to him. He then lies down, but after thirty minutes gets up to read reports on the number of tons of grain and tons of coal needed for the next six months. He interrupts himself at 2 p.m. to ask us, 'What about flood control this summer? How can we be sure of the autumn harvest?' It is true that the dikes are ruined and have to be rebuilt. Premier orders teams to go and inspect the dikes, and mobilize the PLA and civilians to repair them. He determines the various army units to be drafted to help civilians in drought- or flood-affected areas. He looks over the plans for housing in the cities. The workers' slums must be razed. New four-story brick apartment houses built for them. 'But don't forget that pipes for running water must first be laid.' 4 p.m. He debates with engineers on the siting of factories. How can factories be established without coal, oil, electric power? China is most deficient in electric power, and in oil. . . . A meeting with economists, scientists, engineers, to study the pattern of industrialization throughout China takes place at 5 p.m. and goes on till 8 p.m. 'At the moment we cannot even produce a needle or a bicycle . . . yet we must learn to produce airplanes,' says Premier. He eats a bowl of gruel. His friend Guo Moro, president of the Academy of Sciences, shares it with him and reminds him that Premier started an aviation school in Yenan 'when no plane wing ever crossed the sand-filled air.' 'We learn by first preparing our minds,' replies Premier. It is night, many of us are tired. We take a quick run in the courtyard, rub our eyes, and return to work. Premier holds a conference on vaccination against smallpox and on cholera prevention with members of the newly established Public Health Ministry at 9 p.m. 'We must also teach good habits to our people to avoid cholera.' Two hundred million inoculations against smallpox will be given within the next two years.

"The transcripts of world broadcasts for the day are brought in and Premier scans them. He sends for the Minister of Trade. 'Japanese businessmen indicate they would like to make contacts. We must respond. This can be done through Hong Kong.' He glances at the Chinese press editorials. He frowns because one is, according to him, too provocative. He attends a meeting at 10 p.m. at the Military Affairs Commission—he is its vice-chairman—regarding the PLA's advance into Tibet. The PLA must only enter the region *after* agreement with the local Tibetan authorities. A Tibetan delegation is on its way to Beijing. Premier says they must be honored. He sends for the relevant expert on Tibet to come to see him. 'We must never exhibit great-Han chauvinism. We have many national minorities, and we must learn their customs and languages.' He renews directives to the army to respect monuments, statues, ancient buildings. Premier had already issued a catalogue of historical sites and temples to be respected in 1948. It was sent to all military commanders and political commissars, and now it is to be reissued, and to include temples and monasteries in Tibet. 'Ask our experts to draw a list. There must be no encampment of soldiers in temples or monasteries, no lighting of fires. . . . We are not the Guomindang.' At midnight he receives for two hours members of the Academy of Sciences to discuss establishments for fundamental research. 'China must invest in her own scientists.' At 2 a.m. he receives archaeologists and historians. 'An archaeology institute must be set up. China's culture must be preserved. It is our valuable inheritance. Not everything in the past is bad.' At 3:30 a.m. he receives documents to read, and reads till 4:30 a.m. He dictates answers to a few of them. Clutching the others in his hand, he goes to bed at 5 a.m."

This is a "normal" Zhou Enlai day. From the sublime to the trivial, from the important to the apparently irrelevant, he cared for everything, aware that a small detail was often a clue to the discovery of new structures of thought and performance. Reading a Hong Kong magazine, he found out that two valuable scrolls of the twelfth century were on sale in Hong Kong, and sent a cable to Gung Peng and her husband Qiao Guanhua, in charge of the Xinhua News Agency in the crown colony. "Buy them back. They are part of our national treasure." This made him remember—for that was the way his mind worked, one action becoming the impetus for another that Liang Secheng, the son of the reformist Liang Qichao, whose mellifluous prose had influenced his adolescent essays, was an architect, living in Beijing. Zhou sent for Liang Secheng.

"We have to replan our cities for the modern age. Your help will be most valuable." Beijing must have wide roads, city walls must come down, along with the cumbersome *pailus*, ornamental wooden gates which narrow many streets. Liang disagrees, because he loves the quaint, ornate *pailus*. Zhou talks of modernization. "We must be like Washington, like Paris." From architecture his mind bounces to opera. Zhou recalls that Mei Lanfang, the world-renowned female impersonator in Chinese opera, was his neighbor in Shanghai, and that Mei grew a beard during the Japanese occupation, so that he could not perform for the Japanese. Mei Lanfang must be given funds to revive Chinese opera, to train many youths. He writes a letter to Mao Dzedong insisting on extra subsidies for primary school teachers. "Education is our paramount need, and it starts in the primary schools." He assembles university presidents, the representatives of teachers colleges, and of higher middle schools, for a major seminar on education. How many scientists, engineers, doctors, researchers, does China have in 1950? Six thousand engineers, half the number available in India. Twelve thousand Western-trained doctors, more than half of whom have never practiced but turned to moneymaking careers. The infant mortality rate is over 200 per 1,000. There are no more than 50,000 teachers of all grades for nearly 500 million people. "We need new vocational schools . . . we need thousands of technicians of all grades, as well as high-level scientists and researchers." Zhou, with Mao's assent, introduces the idea of shortening courses to speed up training. Medical training takes eight to ten years, but China has a dearth of front-line medical workers for rural areas. "They can be trained in three to four years," Zhou says. This will enable the government to carry out preventive work, inoculations, basic health education in regions that have never seen a doctor or a nurse.

There were more weighty matters, among them the establishment of a national budget, the calculation of national revenue. No budget, not even an estimate of revenue, had been prepared in China for a decade. Nationalization of whatever industries there were—chiefly textiles—was easy, because they had already been concentrated in the hands of a few high officials of the Guomindang, known as "the four big families." With control over cotton and grain, textiles and food processing, Zhou could look forward to a modicum of economic planning.

Very soon "Premier Zhou" became a byword for frugality, meticulousness, parsimony toward self, relentless commitment to work, aversion to inefficiency. Because he did with so little sleep, he forgot that his staff did not have the same stamina. Wang Bingnan, who ran his office, received one day a stiff note from "Premier." "Why is there no one to answer the phone at three in the morning?" The young man in charge had fallen into deep slumber. "It won't do, one must always keep alert," said Zhou. A messenger on a bicycle mislaid some documents in going from one office to another. Zhou had the flustered culprit brought to him. Did he not love his country? If so, how could he indulge in any slackness? "Zhou never shouted, he did not call people names, but the colder his voice, the more he said—'It is my fault . . . I have not taught you properly'—the more we felt as if we were being sliced through by a steel blade," says Wang Bingnan.

A young woman, a clerk in the Finance Ministry, saw him only once, but "all my life through I would ask myself, 'How would Premier Zhou deal with this matter?' One could never forget him. I was an apprentice accountant, but I accompanied officials from the newly founded Bank of China to see the Premier, to decide on the new currency issued by the People's Republic. Premier Zhou scanned every design for the new bank notes, debated on the size, the printing, the price. He ordered that we collect samples of the sixty-odd provincial bank notes which existed before 1949, issued by various warlords. 'We must keep them in a museum . . . our posterity must know what China was like in the past.' "

Nor did Zhou forget China's women. One of the major documents issued in 1951 was the Marriage Law, a Bill of Women's Rights, the first of its kind in China. Deng Yingchao, Shi Liang, the non-Communist Minister of Justice, Tsai Chang, and several women educators framed the law. It forbade female infanticide, forced marriages, and child marriages. The right to marriage "based upon mutual love" was enshrined in the document, as was the right of widows to remarry. Zhou spoke at the meeting to launch this Bill of Women's Rights. "There are still a good many Party members with feudal ideas . . . who ill-treat women and children." The right to "love marriage" encountered enormous resistance. The last instance of putting a widow to death because she dared to remarry occurred in 1956, five years after the law was promulgated.

Zhou walked into city markets, into shops, checking on the efficiency of razor blades, the quality of shoes, the fabric of ready-made trousers. Unannounced, he appeared at public canteens, queuing up with bowl and chopsticks, to check on the quality of the food. If it was bad, Zhou lined up the cooks, the waiters, the manager, and delivered a lecture. "No one ever knew what he would do next, where he would turn up, and the people loved that. It made everyone take pride in doing their work right. Everyone did his best," says his secretary, Pu Shouchang. "A blade of grass is no less than the journey-work of the stars," poet Guo Moro had quoted to Zhou, from Walt Whitman. Zhou gave importance to every mouthful of rice, every yard of cloth. He refused to buy himself new shirts. "Just use some of the old shirttails to make me new collars," he said to Yingchao. He refused to have his residence repainted. He did not collect paintings and antiques. Every gift sent to him was promptly returned. And when he bought anything, he immediately paid for it—unlike some of his colleagues, who pretty soon got used to receiving precious heirlooms and *not* being charged for what they purchased.

Everything, in those early days, when all had to be done, came to Zhou Enlai. When he was called upon to decide on the face for a new statue of the Buddha to be erected in a temple, he stated, "Buddha was Indian, so don't make him look too Chinese."

The government leaders, the Politburo and Central Committee, were housed, and had their offices, in that immense stretch of pavilions, palaces, and gardens called Zhongnanhai, or Middle and South Sea, right in the heart of the Forbidden City, surrounded by purple walls, pierced by five main gates, with a large lake in its center. Zhou's offices and living quarters were among the smallest, and close to the Western Gate. He found it convenient to be on the periphery of the complex, a few minutes' walk away from the gate. His friends, and those who called on him, did not have to go far to reach him. His living room was bare of any adornment. A sofa, some chairs. When I went to visit him, I had occasion to use the single bathroom-toilet, and crossing the bedroom to reach it, found his used slippers neatly by the side of the bed. It could have been any modest employee's bedroom. Did he have no indulgence toward himself? He had two. One was drinking *mao-tai*, though he was seen drunk only twice in his life. He kept a bottle in his desk, and his friends remember how when one of them came to see him, he poured out one small thimbleful of the strong liquor for himself and one for the visitor. Another of his pleasures was dancing. "Premier Zhou really loved to dance. He went with friends, very often Ho Lung the Dragon and footballer Chen Yi and Nie Rongzhen, the engineer, scientist, and military commander, to the Saturday-night dances held at Zhongnanhai. When the musicians caught sight of Zhou they pepped up and played more lively tunes. He brought with him gaiety, lightheartedness," Zhu Qing, his interpreter during the Marshall mission, told me. She added, "All of us vied to dance with him. 'Dance with me, dance with me,' we would say to him, and he smiled, and danced with each of us in turn. He loved to waltz. One of his colleagues who did not like him remarked that Premier Zhou turned to the right when he danced the waltz . . . as if this was a political matter. . . . But it was because he could not use his right arm, which was bent at the elbow, to encircle his partner." Deng Yingchao told me, "I did not like dancing as much as Enlai did. I only went occasionally, but I thought it relaxed him . . . it was good for him." However, if Mao Dzedong happened to be present in the dance hall—and for Mao dancing meant walking stoically and unrhythmically about the dance floor—Zhou would vanish. He did not want to compete with the Chairman, even at a dance.

"A sound mind in a sound body" had been Nankai school's motto. Zhou resurrected it by inaugurating a Ministry of Sports, under Ho Lung, the commander who had set up football and volleyball fields in his guerrilla base. "China must have her own athletes. Modern technology requires physical fitness, endurance . . . to fly a plane, to drive a tank." He ordered all government offices, schools, factories, to allow a ten-minute break twice a day for gymnastics.

Thus Zhou founded not only an administration, a government, but a style of work, a way of life. And all those who worked with him, or like myself spent some hours, over the years, in talks with him, were somehow changed, enhanced, in our commitment to whatever we had the capacity to do.

The Soviet Union was not Mao's or Zhou's first choice as a source of aid and support for China's industrialization. They had wanted the United States to help China's economic transformation. But American hostility forced the new government to adopt what Mao called a "lean to one side" attitude. In December 1949, Mao set off for Moscow, having beforehand consulted—as a matter of courtesy, and possibly to give Stalin a more favorable opinion of himself—his old enemy Wang Ming, still a member of the Central Committee. This did not help. When he reached Moscow on December 17, his encounter with Stalin was no lovefest. Stalin asked Mao why he had delayed capturing Shanghai for a whole month after securing Nanjing. He could have taken the city within a week. "The food situation in Shanghai was extremely bad and we would have had to feed another six million," Mao candidly explained. "Now that's true peasant logic," Stalin commented aloud to his entourage.

Stalin made sure that the subsequent talks led nowhere. Mao was whisked away to a dacha some distance from Moscow. He was taken to museums, lectured on Russian art and history. When he mentioned territory the U.S.S.R. had recently taken from China, Stalin was furious. Chiang Kaishek had signed away mining rights in Xinjiang province to the U.S.S.R.; he had recognized Outer Mongolia as an independent state, with no proper delineation of its boundaries with China's Inner Mongolia province. The Dalien-Lushun port complex, virtually ceded by Roosevelt to the Russians at Yalta in January 1945, Mao now claimed back, as well as the Chinese railways in Manchuria, ceded under a joint control clause in the treaty of August 1945 between Moscow and Chiang. The new government, said Mao, denounced all unequal treaties, including those made with Chiang Kaishek. This enraged Stalin. "Will he also want back Lake Baikal?" he fumed, thinking of the million square kilometers of territory wrested by Czarist Russia from China in the nineteenth century. Tito had defied Stalin in 1948. Was Mao another Tito?

One afternoon, an angry Mao, staring at his bedroom ceiling, let out a blast of choice invective, hoping the microphones worked. The talks bogged down and tempers rose. Mao sent for Zhou Enlai. He arrived on January 20, bringing a team of economists and engineers, producing neat reports, facts and figures. At the negotiating table, Zhou outsat, outtalked, outdrank Mikoyan and Vishinsky. Molotov unbent to him. He did not grate on Stalin. "Comrade Stalin, we are the first *large* Asian country to join the socialist camp under your guidance," purred the consummate diplomat. Stalin was mollified. The talks moved forward. A treaty of friendship, alliance, and mutual help valid for thirty years was drawn up. Zhou obtained a credit of 300 million rubles spread over five years, far less than the 2 billion he had planned for. The mining concessions in Xinjiang were ratified as joint ventures, but the naval complex of Dalien-Lushun was to be returned to China by 1952, or at the conclusion of a peace treaty with Japan, whichever came earlier. The thirty-year lease on the Manchurian railways was cut down to two years. "The Communist Party is more patriotic than Chiang Kaishek," was the comment of non-Communist intellectuals who disliked the U.S.S.R. "At least, we have extracted a little meat out of the tiger's mouth," was Mao's remark.

In a flourish of speeches, praising Moscow's unselfish help, vowing eternal friendship and solidarity, Mao and Zhou prepared to leave. Stalin would shoot a last poisoned arrow at Mao Dzedong.

"Comrade Mao, some of your colleagues are very happy with our collaboration in Manchuria." He extolled Gao Gang, the Party secretary overlording the three provinces of Manchuria, who, Stalin said, was so grateful for Russian help that he had declared, "There should be no frontiers between us." "Now here we have a true internationalist," Stalin threw at Mao.

Gao Gang was the man who, with Liu Jidan, had founded the small base in Northwest China where, in 1935, the Long Marchers had found shelter at last. This base was to extend and become the world-famous Yenan. Gao Gang had supported Mao in the struggle against the group led by Wang Ming between 1942 and 1945, and after the Seventh Party Congress of 1945, which consecrated Mao's triumph, Gao became a member of the Politburo. In 1949 he was the only Party secretary who held both top civil and top military posts in Manchuria. In July 1949, Gao had gone to Moscow, five months before Mao, and there had initiated trade agreements, arranged to send Chinese students for training, and invited Russian experts, with only token consultations with the CCP leaders in Beijing. Was Gao, with Stalin's covert backing, setting up a semi-independent pro-Russian state in Manchuria? "We must step with caution as if walking on thin ice," Zhou warned Mao. On their return by train they stayed five days in Manchuria, and were greeted by Gao Gang in a brand-new Russian car, a gift from Stalin. Zhou was at his most affable, asking Gao Gang many questions, cocking his head sideways, as he did when he listened attentively. On his return to Beijing, he and Mao were convinced that control must be reinforced over far-flung provinces, such as those in Manchuria, lest they gravitate into the Russian orbit.

In that spring of 1950 all looked set for modest progress. A million and a half PLA soldiers were demobilized, enrolled in state farms. "All our efforts must go into production and rehabilitation," said Zhou, planning three years for rehabilitation, ten years for building an industrial infrastructure and an agricultural system "appropriate to China." No one in China expected conflict. Zhou had been reassured by a speech, delivered on January 12, 1950, by Dean Acheson, the American Secretary of State. Acheson had defined America's defense perimeter in the Pacific Ocean as running "from the Aleutian Islands off Alaska to Japan, Okinawa, and on to the Philippines." He had omitted Taiwan and the Korean peninsula. Zhou concluded that the United States harbored no warlike intent and that China could therefore proceed with her sorely needed internal restructuring. In mid-June, a confident Mao announced that the PLA was to be drastically reduced, as it consumed 30 percent of the state revenue.

A week later the Korean War began. In 1945, at the Yalta conference, North and South Korea had been arbitrarily split between the Soviet and American forces, the division running along the 38th parallel. This had led to two separate governments, one Communist in North Korea, the other anti-Communist in South Korea. On June 25, 1950, North Korean forces crossed the 38th parallel, alleging intrusion by South Korea's U.S.-backed army.

On June 27, the United States' delegate at the United Nations in New York called for an emergency session and a resolution was passed for collective action against the North Korean invasion. An expeditionary force, the bulk of it made up of American units, with token troops from several countries, was sent to South Korea. The U.S. Seventh Fleet sailed into the Taiwan Strait, between the island and China.

There was dismay, and anger, in Beijing. Zhou watched the war unfold, expand, with great anxiety. He had not expected it. He listened with puckered brow to the broadcast of a fighting speech by President Truman and remarked, "Truman has changed Dean Acheson's policy." He sent a barrage of telegrams to the United Nations protesting the Seventh Fleet's presence, which blockaded China's southern coastal ports. However, Beijing did not want the

North Korean armies to continue their onslaught into South Korea. Why had Kim Il Sung, North Korea's leader, chosen this time to act?

By July, the American people had been thoroughly media-washed into war hysteria. Communism was on the rampage, was out to overrun the whole world, beginning with South Korea. John Foster Dulles was thoroughly in favor of a war to the finish. Truman obtained an unlimited draft on American manpower for a crusade against "international Communism." General Douglas MacArthur, the hero of the Pacific war against Japan, was named Supreme Commander of the U.S.-UN forces sent to Korea.

Zhou listened to every radio dispatch, scanned the transcripts of all Western broadcasts. For weeks the lights burned through the night in his office. The Politburo, along with the Military Affairs Commission, held almost continuous meetings. The French government joined in the clamor against international Communism. French expeditionary forces which had reoccupied "French Indochina"—i.e., Vietnam, Laos, and Cambodia—announced themselves ready to participate in the "crusade." A jubilant Chiang Kaishek in Taiwan pledged 30,000 of his best-equipped troops.

Was a three-pronged offensive against China contemplated? Would the U.S.-UN forces cross the 38th parallel, then advance to the Yalu River, the boundary between North Korea and China? MacArthur's statements sounded bellicose. He was ready to take on not only Korea but much more. The Seventh Fleet might launch coastal attacks; from Taiwan, American planes might bomb Chinese cities. A combined French-American force based in Vietnam might be set up to invade China's southern provinces.

And what was the U.S.S.R. doing? Jacob Malik, Moscow's ambassador to the United Nations, issued strong protests, but always fell short of committing his country to any military defense of North Korea. Malik had been conveniently absent when the United States' resolution was passed that June, so that he did not veto it. Zhou sent a message to Moscow, asking to see Stalin. Stalin was not available. Did Zhou suspect that perhaps Stalin had encouraged the North Koreans in this enterprise?

In early September, the North Korean forces retreated toward the 38th parallel before a triumphant MacArthur. On September 20, a bleary-eyed Zhou, gaunt from lack of sleep, made a reference to the "military thinking of Chairman Mao." A campaign to resist America and help Korea was launched. Victory bonds were issued

to mop up spare money. Then Mao conceived the notion of sending Chinese "volunteers" to help North Korea. The PLA must not
confront the U.S.-UN backed forces, but "volunteers" could be
sent.

On September 30, MacArthur's forces crossed the 38th parallel.
That evening Zhou invited Indian ambassador K. M. Pannikar to
his home in Zhongnanhai. India's behavior at the UN had been
exemplary, reproving the sending of UN forces to Korea and
offering to negotiate. Through Pannikar, Zhou issued the first of
many warnings. "China cannot remain passive while our neighbor
is being invaded. . . . We need peace, we want peace, we do not
want war for a single day. War would slow down our reconstruction. But we cannot be bullied. We are not afraid to resist invasion.
This must be understood." Pannikar did his best to pass on Zhou's
warning. But the consensus at the Pentagon and the State Department was that China would not move. Air reconnaissance had
revealed no troop movements toward the Yalu River. From his
headquarters in Tokyo, MacArthur stated his conviction that
China would remain passive.

In October, Pyongyang, the capital of North Korea, fell to the
UN forces. MacArthur then prepared to carry the war to the Yalu
River boundary, despite cautionary restrictions issued by President
Truman at the time.

In Beijing, the Politburo held anxious debates. Gao Gang was
against sending volunteers. Why not simply fortify the Yalu River
border? Zhou reminded him of the border's great length, which
meant unbearable cost and the dispersal of many military units. It
made better military sense to launch swift, smashing attacks by
concentrating the volunteers to carry the war into North Korea.
"This is Chairman Mao's military thinking." Scarlet Virtue, Zhu
De, was worried. "Suppose the Americans drop an atom bomb
on us? Why not let the North Koreans get out of their own mess
themselves?" Mao and Zhou won in the voting, and the volunteers
scheme was adopted. Boring Through Rock, Peng Dehuai, who
loved a battle, any battle, happily agreed to lead them. Zhou tried
again to extract a commitment from Stalin. Would the U.S.S.R.
provide air cover for the Chinese volunteers? The answer was that
any such action by the U.S.S.R. would inevitably lead to universal
conflict and to atomic warfare. Moscow would gladly *sell* to China
any equipment needed for the volunteers.

In November, Zhou persuaded the UN General Assembly to

receive a Chinese delegation. Led by Wu Xiuquan, Otto Braun's interpreter during the Long March, now a diplomat under Zhou, the delegation traveled to New York. But on the day Wu Xiuquan was to speak, November 24, MacArthur launched a 100,000-man offensive to the Yalu River.

The volunteers were ready. Since November 10 they had infiltrated into North Korea in small groups, wearing white coveralls, invisible against the falling snow. On November 26, they attacked along the entire front and smashed MacArthur's combat lines. The retreat of the U.S.-UN forces began as a rout. Within the next ten days 200,000 Chinese volunteers had crossed into Korea, walking across the frozen Yalu River.

By December, the disarray of the U.S.-UN forces was total. The retreat to the 38th parallel began, costly in manpower because in the advance so much had been heedlessly destroyed and the population was utterly hostile. The 38th parallel was reached by year's end, and there seesaw battles took place for the next six months. The United States began massive bombing attacks in which the volunteers, and the North Korean armies, suffered heavy casualties before they learned to dig burrows as shelter from the bombing.

The Prime Minister of Great Britain, Clement Attlee, was alarmed by MacArthur's manic determination to push the war into China, and flew to Washington to confer with Harry Truman. The American President was also perturbed by the conduct of his commander, who had ignored Truman's restrictions on the prosecution of the war toward the Chinese frontier and who, of his own volition, went to see Chiang Kaishek in Taiwan, without first informing his commander in chief, the President of the United States. In April 1951, Truman fired his all too active commander, and by June cease-fire talks began at Kaesong, in Korea, almost exactly a year after the war had started.

But meanwhile China had been branded as an "aggressor" by the United Nations, and a United States embargo was placed on all goods to and from China, an embargo followed by all of Western Europe.

The outcome was to make China even more dependent upon the U.S.S.R., precisely what Mao and Zhou had tried to avoid.

As vice-chairman of the Military Affairs Commission, Zhou was in charge of the logistics for the Korean War: transport, the feeding of volunteers, medical care, the conveyance of war matériel. He was also pressured by the anti-American surge in China which arose because of the war. Several times, as I learned later from Qiao Guanhua and Zhang Hanfu, appointed by Zhou to conduct the cease-fire and later the armistice talks, the negotiations were bedeviled by incidents that aroused the inflexibility of some of his colleagues. The war slowed China's recovery, not only eroding the material means at China's disposal but also arousing hatred and extremist emotions. Zhou did accomplish something akin to a miracle, keeping China's railway system going, making sure there were no food shortages in the cities. But half of the budget prepared for reconstruction of China's shattered economy went into the war, including 40 percent of the Russian loan. The Russians demanded immediate payment for equipment supplied to the volunteers. "We paid with sacrifices, with the blood of our heroes. Nothing was given to us, we paid for every weapon," noted Zhou Enlai. The cease-fire in June was welcome, but military activities continued for another two years. Thirty-five thousand Americans died in the Korean War, and more than 150,000 Chinese volunteers.

But the fact that China had dared to confront the United States, and that within a year the volunteers had fought the U.S.-UN forces to a standstill, had a great impact upon the Asian and African countries emerging from colonial domination. Zhou is reported to have got drunk—the first report of any drunkenness—when the cease-fire was announced. Drunk with joy. There would be no war between China and the United States. Of that he was now certain. Patience, and diplomatic skill, would deal with the future.

The time had come for another trip to Moscow. In July 1952, Zhou took the road to the Kremlin. Before leaving he wrote to Mao Dzedong and to Liu Shaoqi suggesting that some of his responsibilities be given to second-echelon officials. "I should now concentrate on the First Five-Year Plan and on external affairs." The cease-fire talks could be handled by his subordinates. It was a Zhou empowered with new authority, with a country united and at peace, surviving and feeding its population, repaying the Korean War debts to the U.S.S.R., who arrived in Moscow in August, to be received with something like reverence.

Stalin had achieved his goal. A state of antagonism would prevail between China and the United States for the next two decades. He could now afford to be more generous.

But Zhou had acquired some clout. He *could* maneuver the

Korean negotiations to the benefit of the United States, and Moscow must be careful, since no state of war was imaginable now between China and America.

Agriculture was paramount in Zhou's program. To his dismay, Zhou found that the U.S.S.R. did not have fertilizer plants. He had to go to East Germany, to Czechoslovakia, where he attended the funeral of Party head Gottwald, to get know-how and help to build chemical fertilizer plants. He took a good hard look at machinery in both countries and also at oil refineries. China was heavily dependent on the U.S.S.R. for oil, but Zhou had already initiated an intensive search by Chinese geologists for oil sources in China itself.

China's First Five-Year Plan was Soviet-conceived, stressing heavy industry and swallowing enormous amounts of investment with very little immediate return. Yet China needed swift capital formation, and that meant light industry. Above all, China needed to increase agricultural production. The Soviet model was not structured to meet these demands. But nothing could be done. Fully 67 percent of China's resources went into the building of heavy industrial plants in the First Five-Year Plan, and less than 7 percent into agriculture. One hundred fifty-six major projects were undertaken by the U.S.S.R. in China, and 8,000 students were trained in the U.S.S.R. Nonferrous and rare metals and agricultural produce continued to pay the bill for this "unselfish, fraternal help." "We paid for everything, and it was not cheap. A ton of tomatoes for a small generator. The Russian inspectors would throw back at us any tomato they considered overripe or underripe. They behaved very arrogantly and we could not say anything." These are the words of a Chinese official in charge of consignments to the U.S.S.R. during those years.

The Korean War had other ill effects on China. It negated Zhou's common front program. It tightened the control of the Party. The plans in favor of the small capitalist sector were now rescinded. Decontrol in that area had led to a renewal of the profiteering, bribery, and corruption that had prevailed under Chiang Kaishek. Old customs die hard, and because some of China's capitalists once again began to profiteer, the Party clamped down on all of them. The U.S. embargo of May 1951 encouraged smuggling, shoddy work on state contracts, sabotage, black-marketing, hoarding of essential raw material resources. The private sector swiftly acquired a stranglehold on needed commodities, and Party cadres were easily bribed to cooperate.

This situation was harshly dealt with by two campaigns. One of them, called the *San Fan*, or three-anti movement, was directed against Party cadres who connived with private capitalists. The *Wu Fan*, or five-anti movement, targeted capitalists and private businessmen who committed sabotage of one kind or another. These purges were probably necessary, but as usual were conducted with excesses. They destroyed a good deal of that initial, starry-eyed fervor among non-Communists in China. A million Party cadres were expelled, and there were thousands of summary executions. Some of the Party members I saw and talked to in 1956 about these campaigns said that they cured Party corruption. But in 1952 Zhou wrote at length to Mao, pointing out that the movements had been harmful. "A little less zeal might have brought about better results." Nie Rongzhen was forthright in his memoirs. "Always, in every movement launched by the Party, there are excesses. . . . After each one, we have to overhaul, reassess who is really guilty." There were always innocent victims, unjustly accused.

The Korean War gave rise to spy mania, which also affected religious organizations. Zhou had reassured Christian leaders in 1949, "We do not want to start an antireligious movement." Provided all ties with imperialism were cut, the churches could go on. A patriotic Catholic Church, independent of the Vatican, was encouraged. It survives until today and has its own seminaries. But in the wake of the purges several prominent Christian leaders were imprisoned and some were executed as spies.

Perhaps the worst outcome of these purges was the ascendancy, within the Party, of ill-educated Party cadres. The Guomindang government had left behind some 2 million state functionaries, who continued to be employed, though shifted to more lowly positions, in post offices, banks, trade organizations. But their loyalty was forever suspect, and friction between Party men "in charge" and the staff who had to obey them worsened. Universities were under Party supervisors who might have been splendid guerrillas, adept at tearing up railway tracks, but who suspected professors doing research with delicate apparatus of sending "messages" to the enemy. Guo Moro, the writer-poet, told me the story of two cameramen, one of whose flashbulbs exploded while they were taking pictures at a public meeting. Both men were immediately arrested and accused of trying to assassinate the leaders present.

The "germ warfare" allegedly carried out by the United States in Korea had led to campaigns in China against rats, mosquitoes, and flies. It was useful to promote mass vaccination against small-pox, but it also led to the arrest of beekeepers and entomologists. An attempt, suggested by Zhou, to institute crash courses for Party cadres "who have had no opportunity of acquiring an education due to the prolonged war situation" was deeply resented. The Party rank and file protested against the implication that they were incompetent. "We won the war. What's so difficult about running a university?"

March 1953. Stalin died. Zhou went to Moscow for the funeral and was placed first among the delegates from socialist states and Communist parties. More economic agreements were drawn up. Because Stalin's successor, Malenkov, was insecure in his position, Zhou obtained better terms than in 1950. Zhou broached the subject of advanced technology transfer, notably in the field of nuclear research. He had brought Nie Rongzhen with him, and some promises were made, though no definite commitment. Still, the two returned to Beijing with solid gains, more money, an improved atmosphere of cooperation. Zhou could now wind up the Korean War, and in July 1953 an armistice resulted. The war had lasted three years, one month, and two days.

Zhou now turned to the matter of consolidating the central govern-ment, dealing with headstrong Party secretaries and commanders. China had been divided into six military regions in 1949, each with its regional area government. Gao Gang of Manchuria was among the most powerful area commanders, since he held top posts in both the army and the Party. By late 1953, many of the military commanders were brought to Beijing, removed from any temptation of establishing their own strongholds. The six military regions were divided into thirteen regional area governments. Zhou tightened control over finances by transferring the right of taxation from these regional area governments to the central gov-ernment in Beijing. Overall economic planning and control was vested in the State Planning Commission, directly under his State Council.

Gao Gang was directly affected by this change, which now compelled him to seek authority from the center before embarking on any project. In Shanghai, Gao's counterpart, a man named Rao Shushi, who also functioned semi-independently, was similarly reined in. Zhou proposed that the less prosperous areas in China's hinterland benefit from moneys gained by the enterprises in Manchuria and Shanghai. Gao was given the post of head of the State Planning Commission, but was solidly hedged in by other veteran leaders, notably Deng Xiaoping, appointed second-in-command to Gao. He was being encircled, and he knew it. He showed his discontent. "What center? What center?" he blurted when Zhou told him that all directives must first obtain the center's approval. The Party had never been anything but an amalgam of *two* parties, said Gao. There had been Mao's party of guerrillas, and Liu Shaoqi's party of urban-based Communists from North China. The time had come for new men, new ideas. Both Mao and Liu, Gao said, were passé and should "take a rest."

On January 10, 1954, Zhou gave a speech against "bourgeois individualism" to an assembly of Central Committee and Politburo leaders. Individualism led to jockeying for positions, to cliques and factions, said Zhou. Party discipline must be rigorously enforced. But, anxious to avoid a disruptive confrontation, Zhou added that "on the other hand . . . we must always listen to the other side. We must distinguish between words and actions injurious to the Party and beneficial ones, even if unpleasant to hear." Too well did Zhou know that Party struggles were ferocious, sanguinary, and he wanted to avoid another massive purge.

But Gao Gang had endangered Liu Shaoqi by his outspokenness, and Liu, with Deng Xiaoping, denounced him and Rao Shushi. Gao committed suicide in jail in the summer of 1954. His death, under murky circumstances, led even Mao to protest, but the anti-Gao Gang movement swept China in a relentless hunt for "hidden counterrevolutionaries in the Party," the *Sufan* movement. The *Sufan* purge lasted till the autumn of 1955.

Some of the institutions Zhou controlled, such as the Academy of Sciences, were able to put limits on the accusations launched against their members. "But it was not so in other units. Some of our best cadres were destroyed," Guo Moro said to me in 1956. One of the victims was Zhou Enlai's faithful subordinate Pan Hannien, the subtle underground man, who in 1937 had done so much to bring documents from Chiang Kaishek to Zhou when the latter was waiting, in Xian, for news of an alliance with Chiang Kaishek to fight Japan. Pan Hannien, with a wealthy wife, with wide connections, had become vice-mayor of Shanghai. He died in a labor camp and was posthumously rehabilitated only in 1980. Zhou tried several times to save him, "but Pan Hannien had too many connections. With secret societies. With the Guomindang. With Hong Kong. He was too difficult to define."

Years later, Mao Dzedong would state that "Stalin thought we were like Tito of Yugoslavia. Only when we fought in Korea did he know that we were not Tito." Zhou Enlai, however, worded it in a far more precise and condemnatory manner. "We fought in Korea so that the U.S.S.R. would not be involved in a war with the United States. And we paid for everything." Never again would China be used as a pawn by the U.S.S.R.

Had there been no Korean War, the ensuing intra-Party struggles, the purges, might not have taken place with such mercilessness. Zhou Enlai's attempt to create a competent administration and a civil service might have proceeded unhindered. This brings us back to the problem of Stalin's responsibility in—possibly—instigating the Korean conflict. It is a question that so far cannot be categorically answered. All that can be said is that China paid a gruesome price for help from the U.S.S.R., or, to repeat Mao's phrase, to extract a little meat out of the tiger's mouth.

15

On April 24, 1954, newsmen and photographers packed Geneva's
Cointrin Airport to watch a Russian Illyushin land. Down the steps
came a slightly built man in a black fedora hat and black overcoat.
The cameras clicked to capture Zhou Enlai's impassive face. "Stern
. . . unsmiling . . . grim," were the press comments. "We thought
it a solemn occasion and that we should look solemn," Wang
Bingnan, Zhou's chief aide, told me as he was writing his memoirs
of what would become known as the Geneva conference on Korea
and Indochina. Wang was in charge of the delegation's clothing
and had ordered black suits for everyone. "I thought this would
indicate our seriousness. But as we walked in the streets of Geneva, people took off their hats to us. They thought we were
clergymen." A woeful Wang confessed his mistake to Zhou, who
burst out laughing. Within a few days the delegation not only
appeared in light-colored attire, or in Western-style suits, but
smiled amiably into camera lenses.

In January 1954, John Foster Dulles, Molotov, Minister of Foreign Affairs of the U.S.S.R., Anthony Eden of Great Britain, and
Georges Bidault of France had met in Berlin. They discussed a
conference to settle the wars in Korea and in "French Indochina."
Without the presence of China, however, such a conference was
palpably an exercise in futility. Despite Dulles's persistent refusal,
China was invited through Molotov, who also secured the presence
of the Democratic Republic of Vietnam. Dulles expressed his
disapproval of the Chinese presence by laying down rigorous rules
of conduct for the American delegation. They were to ignore
totally both Chinese and North Vietnamese representatives. No
socialization, no handshaking. As a result, not only the Americans
but other delegates present at the Geneva conference spent much
time avoiding each other. "I've never known such a conference,"

drawled Anthony Eden. "Everyone appears to shun everyone else."

Zhou had taken a staff of 150, including Li Kenung, the smiling Buddha, as well as Wang Bingnan, Zhang Hanfu, and Huang Hua. Many of the younger men and women around him were trainees of his Foreign Affairs Ministry. He had the best interpreters available, including Harvard-trained Pu Shouchang. The Chinese rented the large Villa Montfleuri at Versoix, surrounded by a spacious garden and vineyards. Zhou had carpets and antiques brought out from China, and two of Beijing's best chefs for the parties he planned to give. One of his first guests was Charlie Chaplin, who had left the United States in 1953. Because of the prevailing McCarthyism, Chaplin was listed as a danger to the safety of America, and lived in Switzerland at Vevey. Chaplin gave Zhou two of his films, *City Lights* and *The Great Dictator.* "You must come to China, you are very popular there," said Zhou. The two men exchanged lighthearted talk, and Chaplin gave an impersonation of his famous little tramp. Another informal guest was Canadian ambassador Chester Ronning, who had been born in China and spoke fluent Chinese. Anthony Eden, undeterred by Dulles's frowns, came for lunch and dinner and quiet talks.

On April 28, Dulles made the keynote speech on the Korean issue. While he spoke, Zhou was seen scribbling notes onto his prepared address. Zhou often deviated from his written text, which made the work of his interpreters more demanding. "He had his own ideas about English words and their meaning. If I said 'soldiers,' and he wanted the word 'troops,' he would correct me right in front of everyone," said one of his interpreters, Chen Wei, reminiscing some years later. Chen Wei never quite forgave Zhou for this loss of face. But Pu Shouchang found Zhou "wonderful to work with." "One only had to pay attention to him, not to the printed words. He was always clear and precise, and he wanted clarity in formulating what he had said."

Zhou's speech was made to a packed hall. His presence had all the fascination of the unknown, the feared. The way Zhou bore himself, his aristocratic looks, compelled appreciation, even if resentful. "This is the first time," Zhou began, "that the Foreign Ministers of the U.S.S.R., the U.S.A., the U.K., the Republic of France, the People's Republic of China, and other countries . . . have met at the same table." He stressed that China wanted peace, and looked forward to "settling international disputes by the peaceful means of negotiations." The speech was described as "ranting" by part of the press, because it dwelt on the decolonization process, "which no force can stop." He made the point that Korea was in Asia and that the nations of Asia should take part in what concerned their continent. Consultation between Asian nations themselves was of great importance in solving problems. "All foreign military bases in Asia should be removed," said Zhou, and the word "all" was significant. Zhou deplored the absence of major Asian countries such as India and Indonesia from the conference. He thus established what would be a major feature of his foreign policy, and lead to the first Afro-Asian conference in the world, held the following year at Bandung, in Indonesia.

The conference on Korea was marked by tedious argumentation. It dragged wearily on, overlapping with the conference on Indochina. "It was a harsh time, and a tense meeting," writes an observer. Nevertheless, it consecrated the end of hostilities in Korea. On June 15, 1954, the sixteen signatories to the concluding agreement on Korea "reluctantly and regretfully" informed the world that no basis for an accord on Korean reunification had been found. Zhou Enlai, on June 5, emphasized that China proposed international supervision of free elections in Korea. He was by no means downcast, for the unexpected had happened.

"We had not thought that the Geneva conference would lead to direct talks between us and the United States, but this was the final outcome," Wang Bingnan wrote. Because John Foster Dulles (who remained only a week in Geneva) had issued strict rules of behavior for the American delegation, Zhou also made rules. "Do not *offer* to shake hands. But if anyone extends a hand, never refuse it." He sent back to China a young military attaché who had ignored the proffered hand of a Swedish diplomat. Despite the rules, relaxation did occur when Walter Bedell Smith took over as head of the delegation. Bedell Smith even appeared to agree to certain of Zhou's proposals, only to be contradicted the next day by his deputy, Walter Robertson. Zhou became angry, and berated Robertson. "Do you mean what you say? Do you say what you mean?" "He sounded like a mandarin of the Chinese Empire admonishing some uncouth barbarian," commented a Swiss correspondent. But Bedell Smith, who had already broken the nonsocializing edict by exchanging pleasant remarks with Pu Shouchang about Harvard, gripped Zhou's left arm, instead of shaking hands. "It's been an honor and a pleasure to meet you here," he told Zhou. The latter was deeply affected. His eyes lustrous with emotion, he replied, "The American and Chinese people will always keep a deep affection for each other."

It was through Anthony Eden that the breakthrough took place. In May, Eden had dinner with Zhou Enlai, and during the meal the two talked of the foot-dragging over Korea, especially over the question of the prisoners of war in Korean camps and of Americans detained in China. The British chargé d'affaires in Beijing dealt with these problems, and Zhou now suggested to Eden that since China and the United States both had delegations in Geneva, talks could be held directly between them on the prisoner issue. "This is, after all, a secondary problem." Eden relayed this suggestion to Bedell Smith, and the latter obtained President Eisenhower's assent, bypassing Dulles. The first round of direct talks between Chinese and American delegates took place shortly afterward. Wang Bingnan and Huan Xiang, conversant in English, German, and French, represented the Chinese side, and Ambassador Alexis Johnson the American one.

The Geneva conference thus fortuitously provided opportunities for meetings between China and the United States during the next fifteen years, "the first strands of the long rope," as Wang Bingnan recalled. They enabled the two countries to convey to each other landscapes of the mind, perceptions of problems. They continued in Warsaw, where Wang Bingnan became ambassador the following year. They were broken off in December 1957, resumed at the end of 1958. By December 1960 there had been a hundred meetings, testimony to the desire, on both sides, not to lose sight of each other. There was also substantive action. Nuclear physicist Qian Xuesen, "detained" in the United States, was sent back to China to help his country in the field of nuclear research. To reciprocate the gesture, some Americans were released in China. "This is why Premier Zhou was secretly happy, even if the conference on Korea was inconclusive," Wang Bingnan told me. When I asked him whether it was true that Zhou had extended a hand to Dulles, who had refused it, Wang categorically said, "It is not true. This never occurred."

The conference on French Indochina was more dramatic than the conference on Korea. Despite a flourish of promises at the

United Nations, the end of World War II witnessed recoloniza-
tion, with the British returning to Malaya and Singapore, the Dutch
to Indonesia, and the French to "French Indochina." The term
"Indochina" is a French creation. It consisted of three ethnically
separate states, Laos, Cambodia, and Vietnam. Cambodia, however, was a "protectorate" of France, but its king, Norodom Sihanouk, was now claiming total independence for his country.

China, traditionally, recognized three clearly defined states, and
the word "Indochina" smacked of French colonialism. In 1929,
when Ho Chi Minh had founded his Communist Party in Shanghai,
it was to represent only Vietnam, but in 1930, at the suggestion
of the Comintern, it became the "Indochina" party, comprising
also the Khmer Issarak, later to be known as the Khmer Rouge
of Cambodia, and the Pathet Lao Communist Party of Laos.

Underlying the Indochina conference, therefore, was an unspoken, subtle conflict between the Chinese and the Vietnamese view.
Pham Van Dong, head of the DRV (Democratic Republic of Vietnam) delegation, proposed that the Khmer Issarak and the Pathet
Lao be seated at the conference as "representatives." But there
were monarchic governments in Cambodia and in Laos, even if
admittedly under French "protection." China's foreign policy was
to support governments claiming *national independence*, whether
socialist or not. China could not approve of a "socialist Indochina"
(under Vietnamese hegemony) to replace "French Indochina."

The battle of Dienbienphu between the French colonial forces
and the DRV armies was being fought as the Geneva conference
opened on April 27. Zhou followed the situation closely. General
Wei Guoqing of Guangxi province collaborated with Vietnamese
general Vuo Yuan Giap in preparing the onslaught upon the be-
leaguered French. The French had made the same mistake as
Chiang Kaishek, said Zhou. Chiang had cloistered his men in cities,
the French had entrapped their forces in a hollow surrounded by
jungle. But Georges Bidault, the French representative at the
Geneva conference, appeared full of confidence. He claimed that
at any moment Ho Chi Minh would "sue for peace." French commanders in the field saw "light at the end of the tunnel." On May
8, a sad but dignified Bidault had to acknowledge the fall of Dienbienphu on the previous day, May 7.

Zhou had worried that the Americans might make an armed
commitment to the French, but he was soon reassured. Having

extricated the American armies from Korea, President Eisenhower was averse to another military venture. The Indochina war was increasingly unpopular with the French people, who found it hurtful to their civic sense of liberty. It also proved alarmingly costly. In 1953, France had spent double what she received from Marshall aid to fund the war, 1,600 million francs. But despite an unwillingness to become militarily involved, America could not accept the reunification of Vietnam under a Communist regime. At the Potsdam conference, in 1945, Stalin and Truman had agreed on a division of Vietnam, and both Molotov and Zhou realized that too militant a posture would raise the specter of "rampaging Communism" once again. Hardheadedly, Zhou set himself to achieve a peace agreement based upon the *temporary* acceptance of two Vietnams. The first step was the recognition of three distinct countries, Vietnam, Cambodia, and Laos. King Norodom Sihanouk of Cambodia was pledging himself to a neutral, independent Cambodia. This fit in well with Zhou's perspective. It was also acceptable to the United States.

But the overwhelming victory at Dienbienphu had encouraged Vietnamese hopes for immediate reunification. Carried by their own impetus, exalted by victory and the support of their own people, the Vietnamese guerrilla armies had already penetrated into the lowlands of South Vietnam, now under the rule of the French-supported "emperor," Bao Dai. In quiet talks with Pham Van Dong of the DRV, Zhou suggested "temporary restraint" and bilateral talks with the French. However, Bidault had haughtily refused to meet with Pham Van Dong. The impasse was broken when the French government fell after Dienbienphu, and Pierre Mendès-France, nominated because he had been vigorous in denouncing the colonial war, formed a new French government on June 18. He pledged to end the unpopular conflict by July 20 or resign. Between June 18 and June 23 discreet comings and goings took place at Villa Montfleuri, and on June 23, Zhou Enlai went secretly to Berne, to meet with Mendès-France.

There was immediate sympathy, rapport, between the two men. Mendès-France was charming, courteous, erudite. Zhou Enlai spoke in French, to show his friendliness. The quiet meeting lasted several hours. "Zhou is one of the most intelligent men I have ever met. He has the caliber of a world statesman, the sharpest, finest mind one could wish for," said Mendès-France. And Zhou was similarly pleased with Mendès-France. "He has an excellent grasp of politics. He will make a very sincere friend." Zhou told Mendès-France that France had a "certain responsibility" toward her ex-colonies, because France had a tradition of liberty, equality, fraternity, and must live up to it by setting an example of "enlightened diplomacy." The next day, June 24, Mendès-France and Pham Van Dong met. Zhou had succeeded in getting a dialogue going. "The bilateral talks must proceed with *no interference from anyone,*" declared the Chinese Premier, who, on that very day, to prove that he was not interfering, boarded a plane for India.

In his speeches in Geneva, Zhou had emphasized the role of Asian countries in settling Asian problems. "We do not claim a monopoly to speak for Asian nations, but the aspirations of the Asian peoples cannot be ignored when pressing problems facing Asia are discussed." He had particularly mentioned India, and a beaming Krishna Menon, Minister for External Affairs of India, made a special trip to Geneva to invite Zhou to New Delhi, for Nehru was mortified to have been kept out of the Geneva talks.

Zhou was made welcome in New Delhi, where he and Nehru discussed a proposal for a major conference in which all nations emergent from colonialism, in Asia and in Africa, would come together and assume their new world identity. In this approach to India, China began a separate, independent foreign policy, distancing itself from the U.S.S.R. Zhou clearly was placing the U.S.S.R. among Western nations, not among Asian ones. The joint communiqué with India embodied what came to be known as the five principles of peaceful coexistence to govern relations between *all* countries, irrespective of any ideology.

Nehru was exultant, and Zhou's profuse thanks for India's attitude on the Korean War contributed to a feeling that the two countries might create a solid relationship, to the greatest benefit of Asian solidarity. There were, however, latent problems. The boundaries between India and China had been arbitrarily drawn, in some areas, by the British, and there had been British encroachments when British troops twice invaded Tibet in the late nineteenth and early twentieth centuries. The Indian government appeared to have inherited from its erstwhile colonial masters certain attitudes of possessiveness toward Tibet which the Chinese greatly resented. However, Nehru and Zhou now avoided discussing these minor irritants. Zhou had already stated that they were problems "left over from colonialism."

On June 28, 1954, Zhou Enlai was in Rangoon to meet Burmese

leader U Nu and to sign a communiqué on the five principles of peaceful coexistence similar to the one signed in Delhi.

On June 30 he returned to Guangzhou, and from there proceeded to Liuzhou, a city in adjacent Guangxi province, to meet Ho Chi Minh, who maintained a villa in Liuzhou, in an area which, since the 1930s, had been a sanctuary for many Vietnamese revolutionaries. Until his death in 1969, Ho Chi Minh stayed several weeks a year here, attended by Chinese physicians, for he believed in herbal remedies.

In the luxuriant garden surrounding Ho Chi Minh's villa, he and Zhou spent the next three days discussing the problem of Vietnam's reunification. "Conditions are not ripe," said Zhou. It was more reasonable to accept temporary partition, but to insist on free elections for reunification in two years' time. Meanwhile the withdrawal of *all* foreign troops must also be a condition for acceptance of the Geneva agreement. "I can wait a few more years for the other half of my country, but reunification there must be," said Ho Chi Minh. "There will be. At that time China will be your most reliable friend," promised Zhou Enlai.

At the sixth plenum of his party in Hanoi, on July 15, Ho adopted Zhou's suggestion. "The Americans are seeking to prolong the war. We must make reciprocal reasonable concessions; otherwise we shall be isolated."

Zhou had flown from his meeting with Ho to Beijing, then back to Geneva, where he landed July 10 and immediately called upon Pham Van Dong. The latter reluctantly agreed to temporary partition, demanding that it be at the 13th parallel. The French proposed the 18th parallel, and finally the 17th was agreed upon. The DRV armies had to withdraw from some territory they had already overrun, and there was rancor, not only from Vietnamese military commanders but also from Pham Van Dong. Pham never quite forgave Zhou Enlai, whom he considered the architect of this arrangement. The grievance was brought up more than two decades later, in 1979, when relations between Vietnam and China deteriorated.

A flurry of activity took place, with meetings between Zhou, Molotov, Anthony Eden, Mendès-France, and the two Vietnamese delegations. "Everyone concerned wants peace and that means taking steps toward each other. Not everyone, however, can take the same number of steps," said Zhou to Mendès-France. "You have helped all of us to take a big step forward," replied the latter. Villa Montfleuri hosted the final meeting between Pham Van Dong and Mendès-France, and on July 21, the plenary session of the Geneva conference produced agreements on the cessation of hostilities. Free elections were to be held in 1956, under the supervision of an international commission. The American delegation issued a statement "taking note" of the agreements, and declared that it would "refrain from the threat or the use of force" to contravene the agreement. Zhou was perplexed. "What do they mean? How can a country both agree and yet remain so ambiguous?"

In September, the United States set up the Southeast Asia Treaty Organization, SEATO. A clause gave its partners the right to "defend" any state—and that included South Vietnam—which was "threatened." "We were cheated at Geneva," Zhou ruefully admitted. "This was a failure for me. The Americans cheated us, but in the end, they cheated themselves even more."

On the last day of the Geneva conference, Zhou invited the two Vietnamese delegations, and the delegations from Laos and Cambodia, to a banquet at Villa Montfleuri. "There were thirty of us, seated at round tables," recalled Ambassador Ha Van Lau, at the time a colonel on the staff of the North Vietnamese delegation. "The Chinese Premier came to toast each of us in turn, emptying his small cup of *mao-tai* each time. He did this thirty times. He really could drink."

Zhou chatted with Ngo Din Lyuen, the brother of Ngo Din Diem, who was to become, within two years, America's strongman in South Vietnam. Zhou invited Ngo Din Lyuen to come to Beijing. "Though we are ideologically closer to Mr. Pham Van Dong, you are also welcome. Both of you are Vietnamese. You should work together to reunify your country." The North Vietnamese Party men found this eclecticism distasteful. Obviously Zhou favored a coalition government in Vietnam less ideologically pure, but bringing faster progress than a long grim struggle to achieve socialism. There was another reason why Zhou did not encourage immediate socialism in Southeast Asia, and that was the presence of the Overseas Chinese communities, wealthy and unbendingly capitalistic, in all these countries. They sent money back to China; whole regions in the southern provinces, many villages, thousands of families, relied on these funds from abroad. Zhou Enlai envis-

aged drawing Overseas Chinese capitalists to contribute financially
to China's industrialization, and they could not do so if the countries they inhabited turned to socialism. There was another concern. China must never be drawn into a Korea-type situation again.
No cause must be given for an American military presence of
overwhelming size in any region close to China. Cambodia's formula of neutrality and independence, proclaimed by Norodom
Sihanouk, was most appropriate. One may suspect that Zhou
would have liked a similar "neutralist" stance for Vietnam, even
if he could not say so openly.

After the Geneva conference, the road to Beijing became a highway of diplomacy. Delegations and heads of state jostled for space
and time to see and talk with those legendary leaders, Mao Dzedong and Zhou Enlai. The visit of the U.S.S.R.'s new top man,
Nikita Khrushchev, in the autumn of 1954 was a triumph. It was
the People's Republic's fifth anniversary, and Khrushchev, flanked
by the durable Mikoyan and Bulganin, exhibited enthusiastic
friendliness. Mao was hailed as a great theoretician of Marxism-
Leninism. Never had the "alliance" appeared more solid.

Khrushchev's visit lasted from September 29 to October 12,
and during these days the seeds of future disagreement were sown.
Khrushchev was anxious to secure China's support, for he had
opponents within his own Central Committee. He was envisioning
détente with the United States, and this was not acceptable to the
hard-liners in the Party. On this point, he found Mao very reserved. The Chinese did not at the time formally oppose such
détente, but they reacted by taking care that nothing should be
done by Khrushchev *at their expense*. The Gao Gang affair, with
its subsequent grim purge, was vivid in their minds. It was in that
very July, while Zhou was away in Geneva, that Gao Gang had
died in jail. "We still did not clearly understand that what Khrushchev wanted was a two-power hegemony between the United
States and the U.S.S.R.," Wang Bingnan said to me as we talked
over these episodes some years later. Mao and Zhou took this
opportunity to assert China's independent role, even if within "the
socialist camp." An agreement was concluded with the stipulation
that relations between countries *must* be based "on equality of
rights, mutual advantage, mutual respect of national sovereignty,
and territorial integrity," a restatement of the five principles for

peaceful coexistence enunciated in New Delhi and in Rangoon. On *global issues*, there must be mutual consultation between China and the U.S.S.R. The bitter experience of the past in dealing with Stalin found expression in this assertive claim by China to *equality*.

A long-term credit of 520 million rubles, fifteen more large industrial projects, the return of the two joint ventures in Xinjiang province and transfer to China of two more, the return to China of the Dalien-Lushun complex, without any payment, came out of this meeting, but the talks were a warning to Khrushchev that China would not be a compliant satellite.

The plans for the projected Afro-Asian conference got underway that winter. The site was to be Bandung, a beautiful city on the island of Java in Indonesia, and the date would be April 1955.

An attempt to murder Zhou Enlai added drama to the project. Nehru had courteously placed an Air-India plane, the *Princess of Kashmir,* at the disposal of the Chinese delegation since China did not as yet have her own airline. The plane was to refuel at Kaitak Airport in Hong Kong. A time bomb was placed in it by Guomindang secret service men—so it is alleged—and the plane exploded over the ocean three hours later. There were no survivors. But Zhou was not on the *Princess of Kashmir.* He had been involved with problems among national minorities, including Tibet. He had successfully arranged amnesties for captured Guomindang commanders, whom he invited to dinner. "Tell our compatriots in Taiwan that we are ready to talk with them at any time," he said to one of them, General Wei Lihuang. In the midst of these activities he was struck down with what seemed to be acute appendicitis and spent a few days in the hospital. As a result, he was not on board the Indian plane. "Premier Zhou would not have been on board anyway," says Wang Bingnan. "It was too well known that an Indian plane was to convey our delegates." Zhou went to Rangoon, and from there a Dutch KLM plane was to fly him to Indonesia.

There was a short, unscheduled stop in Singapore. The brilliant and popular Malcolm MacDonald, son of Great Britain's first Labour Prime Minister, Ramsay MacDonald and British high commissioner in Malaya, wanted to meet "that illustrious man," Zhou Enlai. "I felt sorry that their airplane did not plan to land for refueling in Singapore." Somehow, this desire was conveyed to

Zhou in Rangoon. Malcolm received a message that the aircraft was suffering "from slight engine trouble" and would have to alight briefly in Singapore to check on the mechanical fault. "I was delighted," Malcolm told me.

Through the Indian consul in Singapore, MacDonald arranged a meeting in the VIP lounge. "The plane had been restored to excellent condition some time earlier. All members of the Chinese party were on board, except for Zhou Enlai, Marshal Chen Yi, and an interpreter. We conversed relaxedly about the forthcoming Bandung conference. . . . We strolled across the tarmac to the foot of the aircraft . . . and bade each other friendly farewells. . . . That was the start of one of the most fascinating friendships of my life."

Zhou landed in Djakarta on April 16, smiling, elegant in a lightweight summer tunic, to be greeted by a vast crowd. On to Bandung, where in the palatial mansion designed by President Sukarno twenty-nine government delegations had assembled in a fiesta atmosphere. The beauty of the land and the lavish hospitality contributed to the delight of all participants. Zhou strolled in shirt sleeves, and like a small boy turned up his trouser legs to wade in the clear stream which ran through the garden of his residence.

Not all the delegations at the Bandung Afro-Asian conference were friendly. The representatives of the Philippines, Japan, South Vietnam, Sri Lanka, and Pakistan denounced "Communist imperialism" with impressive forcefulness. Zhou had prepared himself and his staff. "Whatever the provocation, there must be no show of temper, no hot words. The United States tries to isolate us, but we are now breaking through. We shall go through all the curtains, iron curtain, bamboo curtain, smoke curtain. . . . I notice that some of you exhibit great-Han chauvinism. You find customs, manners, unusual, such as eating with fingers. You too must learn to eat with your fingers." He had often denounced great-Han chauvinism toward the national minorities in China, and continued the lesson. "How else do we practice the spirit of fraternal solidarity?" He drilled his staff on behavior toward the press. Correspondents who asked unpleasant questions or made discourteous remarks must be treated with uniform courtesy. "We believe in Communism but we don't need to proclaim it all the time. It is perfectly unnecessary that others should believe as we do. Beyond all ideologies are common interests, national interests, and goals."

Speech after speech denounced the lack of religious freedom in China, China's "subversive" activities abroad. Zhou, apparently unruffled, took notes, and when his turn came, announced that his prepared speech would be distributed but that he would now speak extempore. "The Chinese delegation has come for the purpose of seeking unity, not to pick quarrels. There is no need to trumpet one's ideology, or the differences that exist among us. We are here to seek a community of views, not to raise points of difference. . . . Most of the countries of Asia and Africa have suffered from colonialism. . . . We are economically backward. . . . If we seek common ground to remove the misery imposed upon us, it will be easy for us to understand each other, to respect each other, to help each other." Applause, at first hesitant, then enthusiastic. An ovation, as Nehru came up to embrace Zhou, who had transformed hostility into regard, admiration. His talk had touched that chord of nationalism and resentment of Western domination which existed in so many of those present. Fifteen years later in 1970, Carlos Romero, Minister of Foreign Affairs of the Philippines, said to me during my visit to Manila, "Please convey my regards to Premier Zhou. . . . I never forgot the speech he gave in Bandung."

For some enchanted days, it appeared that a new sense of brotherhood had been aroused. Suspicion, doubts, were lulled. Zhou's work continued, in personal meetings. He refuted with calm urbanity accusations against China by both Western and Asian correspondents. He invited the delegates "and anyone else" to come to China. "Come and see for yourselves. Anyone is welcome." Sensing the wind in his favor, he pushed on, offering to hold talks with the United States over Taiwan. "We do not want war with the United States. We are ready to sit down and negotiate, anywhere, at any time. The Chinese and American people nurture friendship for each other."

Daily Zhou sat for an hour or two in the garden, resting or talking with Zhang Hanfu and other Chinese diplomats about the prospects of the conference. He accompanied Sukarno to the dancing and music shows the latter was so fond of. Most of his staff found the heat distressing and kept ceiling fans on. Zhou discovered that Sukarno and his Foreign Minister, Subandrio, were afraid of drafts, and fans were turned off whenever they appeared.

To the suspicious Thai and Philippine delegates, Zhou, exuding charm—"We are neighbors"—stressed peaceful coexistence. To the Japanese, he talked trade. Three years previously he had already made approaches to Japan for commercial links, and now remarked that Dalien and Lushun were ideal ports for trade. "We have no aggressive thoughts against anyone." He dispatched Guo Moro to Japan. The latter had spent many years in that country and had married a Japanese. To U Nu of Burma, Zhou presented a tooth of the Buddha, a precious relic kept in China for many centuries. He praised Norodom Sihanouk's neutral, independent Cambodia. Afghanistan's Premier invited him to Kabul. Mohammed Ali of Pakistan assured him of Pakistan's friendship, even if Pakistan had joined SEATO. Pakistan expected aggression from India, not from China, and Zhou said he "understood." Pakistan had propounded a resolution at the conference to condemn "Communist imperialism." Zhou successfully changed the resolution's wording to "condemn all forms of colonialism."

Nasser of Egypt came to speak to Zhou regarding the Suez Canal, and Zhou promised moral support. Cairo became the most important center in the Middle East for Zhou's diplomats, and Arabic one of the main languages taught in China's foreign-language schools. Zhou invited Islamic imams to visit Chinese mosques. "We are not opposed to pilgrimages to Mecca." Was not the government allotting money to repaint and redecorate the mosques in China? The leaders of the Algerian independence movement, the FLN, hovered in the corridors and Zhou spoke with them. "Every nation . . . is capable of liberating itself through its own efforts," said the suave Premier. China would certainly supply the FLN with arms and equipment, but all the fighting must be done by the Algerians themselves.

"Our principle is . . . to seek common ground, while reserving differences." This was the leitmotiv of Zhou's numerous exchanges, and with an impish grin he said to a particularly vituperative delegate, "We disagree, but agreeing to disagree is already some kind of agreement." He also opposed condemning any country by name at the conference. "This is no place for private quarrels between Asian nations."

Bandung was a great personal triumph for Zhou Enlai and an international breakthrough for China. Back in Beijing, however, he found himself criticized by some of his colleagues. Scrutiny of his speeches had revealed that his version of coexistence was politically impure. He had used the words "let us live together in peace." Did that mean accepting peace with imperialism? He also had to explain the formula "all forms of colonialism." "By this I meant political, economic, military, and cultural colonialism," explained the harassed but quick-witted Zhou. With such friends and comrades, did Zhou sometimes find enemies more easy to contend with?

Zhou brought back from Bandung the problem of the Overseas Chinese. A campaign against them was starting in some of the Western and local newspapers. They were evidence of China's imperialist aims in Southeast Asia, went the story. One particular correspondent in Singapore published a book describing all Chinese abroad as potential fifth columnists for Beijing. Zhou explained that the presence of Overseas Chinese was due not to a deliberate policy of any Chinese government but to Western colonial powers, who had needed cheap labor for their mines and plantations and for road building. From China's millions had poured out hordes of poor peasants, to work in the tropical lands of Southeast Asia, to build railroads in Canada and the United States, to dig the Panama Canal. The survival capacity of the race, the genius for getting on, had allowed a good many to prosper, a few to achieve wealth.

But the Overseas Chinese formed close-knit communities, with much economic clout. They had their own schools, clubs, and welfare organizations. As the countries of Southeast Asia became independent, where did the loyalty of the Overseas Chinese lie? With their land of origin, China, or the land of their thriving? "My dear brother, what is the answer?" Sukarno said to Zhou as, away from prying newsmen, they talked of the problem. "You will forgive me, but we Indonesians are worried." Zhou Enlai nodded. "It is a problem." Throughout the decades, and also under Chiang Kaishek, the *jus sanguinis* principle had held sway. Every Chinese was unalterably Chinese by birth, even if he acquired a foreign passport. This meant automatic dual nationality. In 1950 the new government had organized an Overseas Chinese Bureau, under Liao Chengzhi (Liao the Sailor), himself from an "Overseas" family, to contact Overseas Chinese communities and rally them to the new regime.

On April 22, Zhou Enlai came to an agreement with Sukarno.

China would abandon the *jus sanguinis* principle. Overseas Chinese abroad could renounce their Chinese nationality and adopt the nationality of their country of domicile. "If they wish to return to the motherland, they will be welcome. Should they adopt the nationality of their country of domicile, they must be treated fairly and equitably, but can no longer claim to be Chinese. Should they want to keep their Chinese nationality but remain abroad, they must totally abstain from any political activity." This formula appeared to satisfy Sukarno. But it provoked much resentment among the Overseas Chinese, who felt emotionally betrayed. Even sixteen years later, in Manila, Philippine Chinese expressed to me their bitterness at being "deprived" of their Chinese birthright if they acquired a Philippine passport. Chiang Kaishek in Taiwan proclaimed that the Overseas Chinese could always count on his protection. He would not abandon the *jus sanguinis* principle. On several occasions in the next few years, Zhou Enlai had to explain to Overseas Chinese communities that they could not claim to be Chinese and then expect not to be discriminated against. In 1959, massive anti-Chinese riots occurred in Indonesia. Many Chinese were killed, and China sent ships to repatriate some 300,000 Overseas Chinese.

Old habits die hard. Even today, Chinese with American passports are described in Chinese newspapers as "American-nationality Chinese." In 1973, Zhou Enlai remarked, "They live within their own communities . . . and even if they live their whole lives abroad, they still make arrangements to be buried in China."

16

On a cold afternoon in January 1956, while an arctic wind flung showers of yellow sand against the purple walls of Zhongnanhai, members of the Central Committee, ministers, vice-premiers, Party secretaries from the provinces, and members of the eight non-Communist parties gathered in the Hall of Nurturing Benevolence to listen to Zhou Enlai speak on the problems of the knowledge-bearers, the intellectuals.

"Ordinary knowledge-bearers" meant anyone who had successfully finished high school. "Higher knowledge-bearers" were those with university degrees: professors, scientists, engineers. Seventy percent of the members of the CCP were semiliterate; only 11 percent were reckoned educated. Of these, only a handful were high knowledge-bearers.

Until 1949, the reality of China had been expressed in the old adage: "He who reads and writes will rule. He that does not, obeys and labors." It was Zhou who had mobilized the invisible second front, the intelligentsia, so effectively against Chiang Kaishek. It was he who had persuaded many knowledge-bearers, even those hostile to Communism, to remain in China. They had done so because he was "one of them," because he was convincing, because he looked like them and spoke their language. They stayed because they hoped to make the Common Program work; they thought they could devote their best, irrespective of personal political leanings, to the exalting task of putting China back on her feet, of bringing her into the modern age.

But in the various campaigns since 1951, they had been mistreated, humiliated, even punished. Most galling was to be "guided and supervised" by Party cadres with little or no education, who not only bore the traditional resentment against the literocrat-official but also had Party ideology on their side. The notion of "class" prevailed. Most of the intelligentsia were from bourgeois families, the only ones who could afford education for their children. They were not reckoned of the "correct" class background.

At first the intellectuals submitted, because they loved their country and wanted to serve it. Even while the purges were going on, they were paid higher salaries than the Party cadres who "supervised" them. But the Chinese intellectual was especially sensitive to loss of honor, self-respect. To face. And all that was now gone. One professor, reading a letter from a friend, had had the letter snatched from his hand by the Party secretary. "What are you reading? I must check what you read," huffed the official. The professor noted that the secretary was holding the letter upside down. Some, unable to endure the insults, had committed suicide.

Since 1953, Zhou had become increasingly anxious about the situation. He had met again and again with intellectuals, both Communist and non-Communist. He had consulted with Zhou Peiyuan, a renowned, American-educated physicist, with the famous writer Mao Dun, with Guo Moro, the poet, and with many others. All too clearly Zhou saw the intellectuals lapsing into resentful passivity, paralyzed by fear or anger, or both. He had gone to Mao time and again in the last two years, and had finally convinced him that the mishandling of the knowledge-bearers hampered China's progress into the future.

Now he was ready to act, and he did not mince his words.

There were, he said, no more than 5 million knowledge-bearers among China's 500 million people; of high-grade scientists, research workers, and university professors, a mere 100,000. They were China's only pool of knowledge and expertise. Yet only *with* them, and *through* them, could China progress and modernize. But the political purges—the last one had been the worst—had antagonized many. They had had to attend meetings lasting weeks, to compose self-criticisms which destroyed their self-respect. They were weary, overwrought, afraid. "Our intelligentsia are benumbed . . . they do not dare to speak the truth. . . . A chasm has been created between them and the Party. . . . This is not in line with Chairman Mao's thought.

"All our plans for development, our advance, depend upon the proper use of the knowledge-bearers. . . . Without scientists, without teachers, we shall not be able to lift ourselves out of backwardness. . . ." The *purpose* of the revolution was to liberate productive forces, to transform China from a medieval agricultural land into a modern industrial country, to raise the living and cultural standards of the people. "It is in research that we are weakest, and we cannot catch up unless we have a large number of trained scientists. We must trust them, support them. Some are not given the books or the apparatus they need. Our Party cadres say to them, 'Why should I do anything for you?'

"The new developments in science are bringing humanity to a new technological and industrial revolution. . . . We must conquer these new heights in science to reach advanced world standards."

To drive the lesson home, Zhou uttered a memorable phrase, which many, two decades later, would credit Deng Xiaoping with having invented.

"Mental labor and manual labor are both needed. Our intellectuals, by deploying mental labor, *are part of the working class.*"

In this single sentence, Zhou presented a formula which he hoped would defang the class struggle that was at the heart of the Party's abuse of the intelligentsia.

The Common Program drafted by Zhou in 1949 had stressed *democratic consultation*, which meant dialogue and discussion to reach consensus among the CCP and the eight non-Communist parties. It was on this understanding that the People's Republic of China had been founded by the Chinese People's Political Consultative Committee—the CPPCC—whose members were all intellectuals. "Before any meeting is convened, all parties should be informed of the agenda, and decisions made only on the basis of discussions at the meeting," ran the preamble of the document confirming the CPPCC. But by 1955 the Party merely handed down decisions already taken. "We have nothing to do but nod our heads in agreement, raise our hands in approval." Zhou told this story to his audience, then looked around at them. He knew that many Party members were mentally squirming while he spoke.

Intellectuals had valiantly striven to "remold their thinking," said Zhou. He cited examples of their willingness to change. Only 10 percent could be considered more or less hostile to the Party, and that was not their fault. "It is because of defects in our work. . . . We have not exerted ourselves to explain to them our policies, or to reassure them, or even to care for their needs."

Thus began Zhou's extraordinary attempt at something like *perestroika*, Chinese-style, to introduce some measure of democracy and free discussion within and without the Party. It was called the Hundred Flowers Movement, from a classic snatch of poetry, "Let a hundred flowers bloom / A hundred schools of thought contend." Guo Moro, the poet, in a discussion with Mao on various philosophies which flourished in China around 500 B.C., had lit upon this phrase. "Chairman Mao," he told me, "approved of the title."

In April 1956, Mao delivered a long, rambling discourse to a meeting similar to the one Zhou had addressed in January. In May, Lu Dingyi, the Minister for Propaganda, circulated this speech, somewhat abridged and edited, in all the universities.

That April, I returned to China for the first time since 1949. The internal document, entitled "Let a Hundred Flowers Bloom, A Hundred Schools of Thought Contend," was handed to me by my cousin, a professor at the university. Guo Moro, with whom I had a long talk three weeks later, confirmed its importance. "What we want is an intellectual renaissance, which means freedom of debate." Fei Xiaotung, a social scientist, had proclaimed the document a "major thaw," a "reliberation of the intelligentsia." But other knowledge-bearers, dismayed by the purges, were skeptical. "Those who do not open their mouths are still able to think," another cousin of mine, a scientist, told me. "Those who talk are deprived of the right to think. I am not going to talk."

On June 25, I met with Zhou Enlai and his wife, Deng Yingchao, at their private residence in Zhongnanhai. I had prepared many questions, under six headings. Three headings concerned the knowledge-bearers, freedom of speech, and political representation of other parties in the government.

I had seen Zhou Enlai in Chongqing in 1941 and fifteen years later he did not appear older. His eyes sparkled. He exuded cheerful confidence. I was to see him again about a dozen times and have long talks with him eleven times in the course of the next nineteen years. On only one other occasion did I see him as burstingly happy, almost glowing with joy, as in that June of 1956. And that second time was in 1972, after President Richard Nixon's visit to China.

The living room was starkly simple: a worn-out sofa covered in nondescript gray cloth, some chairs, with those lace antimacassars still favored in China. It could have been any minor university professor's living room. No antiques, no priceless porcelain, no paintings of value. Gung Peng, my friend, Zhou's press relations officer, made the introductions. Zhou congratulated me on my Chinese. "People who live abroad sometimes forget their native tongue." We drank tea, and then Zhou, wasting no time, although no limit had been set to the visit (it lasted two and a half hours), went straight into the matter.

"You have asked six major questions. I shall deal with three. I have asked some of my colleagues to answer the others when they talk with you. Your question on the efficacy and creativity of a controlled versus an uncontrolled intelligentsia, and whether control, for a set purpose, does not in the end stunt creativity and prove counterproductive."

There was no society without controls of one kind or another, he pointed out. In capitalist countries, organized research was controlled by the money expended in some areas and not in others, by the needs of the system, the perception of economic and national interests.

Obviously, Zhou was talking of science, not of art or culture. Throughout our talks, he spoke of science, not culture, and I later found out why. Although the Ministry of Culture was part of the government, which he administered, and Zhou had a large number of friends among artists, writers, film and opera stars—many came to lunch with him, dropping in informally—this was a sensitive sphere in the system, closely linked to ideology, and therefore far more a Party matter than was science. Zhou, and his friend Nie Rongzhen, vice-premier and director of the Science Commission, controlled the sphere of research, the education, training, and employment of scientists. But the writers were under other leaders.

"Our intelligentsia only began to learn science around half a century ago. Very little original scientific work has been done, and most of what has been accomplished has followed the Western pattern. We must now develop our own subjects of research, focus on what is necessary and appropriate for China, and in an independent way. What you call controls we might call orientation rather than controls.

"There are two approaches," said Zhou, raising two fingers. "Some people pay attention only to what yields practical results. They think all else is a waste of time. Others [here he probably meant himself] believe in another approach, believe in fundamental research. However, we are a poor country, with few financial resources. We have to plan carefully how to spend our money. Of paramount importance is to raise agricultural production, create our own industries, produce our own machines, not buy all machines from abroad, and look forward to independent, fundamental and theoretical research, to new creations. . . .

"You write of the need for free discussion. But we do discuss, we argue a great deal, on everything." Here Zhou suddenly stopped, possibly seeing polite incredulity cross my face. Suddenly I felt in him a passing wrack of grief. I had a glimpse of hastily repressed anguish.

"I understand that you are acquainted with our recent efforts in the direction of more debate," Zhou went on. "We must indeed widen and extend discussions for *all* intellectuals, both in and out of the Party, *in all spheres*. Without dialogue there is no communication, no understanding. But we also need unity of purpose. We cannot return to past exploitation. We must go toward socialism. We must explain to the intellectuals the problems we face, and listen to them . . . but we cannot abandon the goals of our revolution."

I argued. Many discoveries, creations of art and science, were accidental, inadvertent, fraught with human incongruity. Individualism was valuable, was to be cherished. Whether in science or in art. Moralistic, political judgments on works of art, on books, or on any other matter smothered that unpredictable essence called genius. Anything new, any discovery, was always met at first with incomprehension and rejection, but leeway, tolerance, gave a chance for later understanding and acceptance. This was the way of progress. To condemn a writer's works *in toto* because the writer had indulged in a love affair was to mix up two separate realms of action—and it was destructive. I wanted to add, "Even Marx had an illicit love affair," but refrained. I was mentioning a case which had recently been brought to my attention in China.

Zhou beamed. Dullness, acquiescence, irritated him. He loved an argument. He would often ask his staff, "Don't you have anything new to tell me?" When someone unctuously agreed with him, he became irritable. "Can't you find *something* to disagree with in what I've said?"

"We are certainly not against individualism. We want to encourage the expression of new ideas, new values, but *not* in the direction of selfishness, of greed, of 'me above all.' That is what capitalist society does. We think the finest individualism is when a person works selflessly for the benefit of others, when his ideal is to serve the people.

"We are still very feudal. We make many erroneous judgments, many mistakes, because of our deeply grounded feudalism." The "we" here meant himself, his colleagues, the Party. "I admit it. But what individualism was possible in old China, when so many starved? Look at our schools. Within a few years we shall have education for all. Look at our new maternity hospitals. We shall have healthy children. How many died, how many were stunted in mind and body for lack of food and care? Individualism . . . for the well-off few, but nothing, not even the next meal, for so many!"

I too hoped that the new order might abolish the old tyrannies. But was the price new tyrannies?

"Every revolution has taken its toll, committed many errors. . . . The French Revolution did. . . . It abolished religion for a while. We have not done so. It had the guillotine. They cut off the heads of their kind. We are reeducating our last emperor. . . . But in such an enormous change, there are many blood debts to be paid, and inevitably there are excesses. We do, however, reappraise ourselves, go over the errors committed, we try to repair injustices.

"You find thought reform repugnant." I nodded yes. "It is indeed a painful process, and I speak to you from personal experience. Each one of us constantly has to remold himself, in order to advance."

"Premier, *my* rate of advance is very slow," I interjected. Zhou roared with laughter. But it was quite obvious that he was not interested in freedom for its own sake. I can best describe him as an enlightened Confucian. Free discussion, yes, but *for the well-being of society*, the efficiency of the Establishment. For this was China, and China had never known democracy. Perhaps people like Zhou Enlai were taking the first steps toward some form of *tolerance*. One could not, at the time, ask for more. New China was only seven years old.

Zhou was now ticking off on his fingers the ministers, vice-ministers, and other officials in his government who did not belong to the Party. In the CPPCC and the NPC—the National People's Congress, supposed to be the highest authority in the land—the intelligentsia were represented in a proportion far in excess of their numbers within the population. "We cannot have proportional representation. Not one of them would ever get to become minister or vice-minister. The people don't know them. The workers and peasants have never heard of them." There was a scheme afoot to overweigh the seats allotted to the knowledge-bearers, so that one vote by an intellectual would count, say, as twelve normal votes, to make up for their numerical deficiency. There was indeed a gap between them and the Party. Most Party members needed further education. "Workers and peasants must attend adult literacy classes. . . . We must close the gap."

He agreed that the problem of legal institutions was a deeply vexing one. "The idea of a separation of powers between legislative and executive bodies cannot at the moment be entertained in China," he said flatly. (Later that week I would meet the Minister of Justice, non-Communist Madame Shi Liang, who talked at length on the difficulties of creating a judiciary, introducing legislation, and even the notion of "the rule of law.")

Some days later I was invited to listen to Zhou at a meeting of the CPPCC, held in the Hall of Nurturing Benevolence. With me was French correspondent Jacques Locquin of Agence France-Presse. Zhou's speech electrified Locquin, who sent a euphoric report on the prospects of democracy in China to Paris. In substance, Zhou delineated the largest freedom of debate. To ensure "the utmost confidence and enthusiasm of all," dogmatic thinking and bureaucratism must be eliminated. The non-Communist parties "must be brought into full play." The CCP "needs to hear the criticism of other parties. Commandism only hampers advance."

I looked for the speech in the newspaper the next day, and found a very attenuated version. The air was thick with hostility to what Zhou was advocating. I remained skeptical. I thought the Hundred Flowers would not work, and it saddened me. "It will take another twenty years before *you* understand the meaning of democracy," was my message to Zhou Enlai. By "you" I did not mean Zhou personally, but the Party as a whole. However, it was also clear that Zhou was not talking of democracy in the Western sense of the word.

On this Mao Dzedong and Zhou Enlai agreed. Neither of them saw the Hundred Flowers Movement as a sharing of power, as a multiparty system on the Western model, though Zhou admitted the dangers inherent in a single-party system. Because of the concrete problems she faced, China needed "an opposition which does not oppose the Party."

But Zhou and Mao differed in their interpretation of the meaning of the movement. Zhou meant the movement to free the intellectuals from Party dogmas and restraints so they could lead China's technological development. "Even as early as 1956," the physicist Zhou Peiyuan, president of the Academy of Sciences, told me, "the Premier worried about the insufficiency of laboratories. He understood the importance of theoretical and fundamental research. . . . But others did not. They did not want democratic consultation to be exercised."

Mao, on the other hand, seems to have seen the movement as only a part of a total social mobilization and remotivation of the people, and it is possible that he looked forward to a bit of bashing of his own Party. He did not like what was happening. Increasingly, power was falling from his hands into the hands of others. He was being passed by.

Until 1954, Mao had had the right to promulgate decrees, annul or revise governmental decisions, appoint the Premier and all important officials, and deal with questions of war and peace. He was now hedged about by committees, standing committees in the Politburo, in the Central Committee. He had no right of veto. In early 1954 he had expressed the wish to relinquish routine Party affairs and to concentrate on theoretical work, just as in Yenan he had retired to his cave to write a sinicized version of Marxism. Increasingly, it was Liu Shaoqi, the vice-chairman, who held the reins of Party control through committees at every echelon, where his men—urban cadres, hence better educated—could dominate the Party structure. Mao remained chairman of the Military Affairs Commission, but the division of China into thirteen instead of seven military regions worked against him, and the appointment of Peng Dehuai, Boring Through Rock, as Defense Minister further limited his power.

The Eighth Party Congress held in September 1956 would cut down Mao's power even further. Clearly, Khrushchev's speech earlier that year denouncing Stalin had had some impact. The new Party constitution contained no reference to Mao's thought, but a great deal of stress on "collective leadership," which Khrushchev had emphasized in his February speech. At the same time, Liu Shaoqi and Deng Xiaoping decried "personality cult" in their

speeches, just as Khrushchev had in his anti-Stalin outburst. There
was no reference to any needed change in the Party superstructure,
or to the Hundred Flowers. Class struggle, said the final resolution,
was basically resolved, and the main contradiction now was between the objectives of industrialization and agricultural backwardness.

Mao and Zhou both questioned the model of industrial development, even before the First Five-Year Plan, based on the Soviet
model, was completed. The plan was capital-intensive, not labor-
intensive, and labor was China's greatest resource. Heavy industry
swallowed 67 percent of China's scarce investment capability in
money and resources other than labor. The plan ignored light
industry, and almost all the investment required was derived from
agriculture—with very little returned to the farmers.

In the summer of 1955, the government speeded up agricultural
collectivization, with the aim of rationalizing agricultural output
and providing more capital for industrial development. There was
no other way to fund industrial development, unless China went
to the U.S.S.R. for more loans. In the end, the question was: What
is the model of development appropriate to China?

At the same time, Mao began to doubt the centralized Party
machine. It administered, it expanded. But it seemed neither to
produce anything nor to stimulate productivity. He felt that decentralization, an end to the rigidity of central planning, would
release local and regional initiatives. But could he decentralize
without producing disruption? By initiating discussions with the
intelligentsia, stimulating a joint search for the solution to problems, Zhou thought that perhaps swifter progress could be made.

Though Nikita Khrushchev had denounced Stalin shortly after
Zhou's Hundred Flowers speech (the text of Khrushchev's speech
reached Beijing in mid-February), it was pure coincidence that
China and the U.S.S.R. seemed to be moving along the same path.
Since Khrushchev had lauded Stalin only the previous December,
his *volte-face* was a surprise to the Chinese. They managed faint
praise for the Soviets' "courageous self-criticism," but they saw
Khrushchev's move as a blatant buttering-up of the United States,
not as something which could be to their advantage.

Already in 1955, remarking that "Stalin has killed too many
people," and that "heads are not cabbages, they do not grow again,"
Mao was engaged in elaborating a thesis to distinguish between

two types of conflictual situations, or "contradictions." One type was antagonistic, such as between socialism and imperialism. The other was "contradictions among the people," differences of standpoint or opinion, not to be regarded as enemy attacks on socialism or counterrevolutionary. The reason for elaborating this theory was, apparently, to justify theoretically the Hundred Flowers project. How otherwise would the Party tolerate the criticisms of non-Party intellectuals, or distinguish what was "constructive, correct" (merely contradictions among the people) and not counterrevolutionary attacks against the Party?

Mao and Zhou now collaborated on a seminal document known as "The Ten Great Relations and Contradictions," which summarized China's modernization dilemma. It is one of the least publicized of Mao's works. Zhou Enlai had submitted to Mao thirty-seven reports on the failures of the First Five-Year Plan to assist him in preparing this document. It defined the contradictions between agriculture and industry, between heavy and light industry, between urban and rural development, between coastal areas and the hinterland, between centralization of power and decentralization. It stated that there were contradictions "between the leadership and the led." It envisaged, possibly through the Hundred Flowers Movement, a correcting mechanism, to bring a solution to these contradictions.

Zhou Enlai's diary notes his visits to many factories and industrial plants, to expound the document, to urge better cooperation between technical staff and Party cadres. He decided that long-term, twelve-year programs in industry, education, research, would allow for better budgeting, improve allocation of funds, make it possible to overhaul and reappraise on a long-term basis, to verify and to check, and to change certain policies if needed. The State Council sent out directives to all relevant ministries.

Almost immediately after the Eighth Party Congress in Beijing had ended in September 1956, the Polish and Hungarian uprisings occurred. Zhou went to Moscow, to Warsaw, to Budapest. China had to have a "firsthand" understanding of what was really happening. After on-the-spot visits, Zhou qualified the Polish and Hungarian events as "contradictions among the people," and therefore not counterrevolutionary. When he arrived in Moscow, he had unpalatable things to say to Khrushchev. First, he expressed Mao's disapproval of the way the Stalin issue had been handled.

"Stalin committed many errors, but he was not *always* in error."
Second, he recalled the agreement on mutual consultations between the U.S.S.R. and China on matters affecting the common
interests of the socialist camp. China disapproved of sending Russian troops into Poland. The Poles were perfectly capable of handling their own crisis. Where Hungary was concerned, however,
Zhou had to reverse himself. Outside interference—inflammatory
broadcasts of Radio Free Europe, the Voice of America, and other
channels—was all too obvious. A Hungarian aristocrat who fled
Budapest when the Russian tanks drove in confirmed to me that
the radios had incessantly beamed encouragement to the demonstrators. It was not possible for China to approve an uprising
so openly encouraged by outside "imperialism."

But, Zhou told Khrushchev, both events had been triggered by
the "great-power chauvinism" practiced by the U.S.S.R.

From Moscow, Zhou flew to Hanoi, to meet an apprehensive
Ho Chi Minh. The scheduled elections in Vietnam were not going
to take place. Even the International Commission *in situ* was aware
that Ngo Din Diem, South Vietnam's President and the United
States' choice, had begun a major drive of killing "Communists."
But what was even more alarming was Khrushchev's proposal, that
autumn, for the simultaneous admission of North Vietnam and
South Vietnam, *as two separate states*, to the United Nations, totally
ignoring the Geneva agreements of 1954, which the U.S.S.R. had
signed. Zhou Enlai reassured Ho Chi Minh. "We shall never agree
to such a proposal. We shall not be a party to this betrayal."
Khrushchev was "selling out." He was intent on beginning a dialogue with the United States.

Ho Chi Minh had internal problems. Collectivization of agriculture, on the Chinese pattern, was not going well. Zhou advised
him to refrain from haste. "Such changes must come step by step."
He told Ho of the Hundred Flowers project. In Vietnam too, a
drive to rally intellectuals to the regime might be beneficial.

Zhou Enlai spent the month of December in a series of official
visits to India, Burma, Pakistan, but he was back to visit Warsaw,
Budapest, and Moscow in January. "I told Enlai to give Khrushchev
an earful," Mao said. Enlai did. A heated argument took place.
Zhou castigated "great-Russian chauvinism" and "big-power complex" to denounce the actions of the U.S.S.R., particularly the
treatment of Vietnam as a pawn in the game of "contention and

collusion" which the U.S.S.R. was engaging in with the United States. Khrushchev was outraged. "You cannot speak to me like that. After all, I come from the working class, while you are a bourgeois by birth." Zhou was silent for a while, then replied, "True, comrade, but we have something in common, you and I. Both of us are traitors to our class."

Seven months after the Hundred Flowers speech, nothing had happened. The intelligentsia were too insecure to act. The Party as a whole was obdurately against the project.

In February 1957, Mao addressed a gathering of the Politburo, the Central Committee, and regional and provincial officials. His speech lasted four hours, and was not printed until July. It was entitled "On the Correct Handling of Contradictions among the People." It endorsed the Hundred Flowers Movement.

The majority of Party officials present showed their hostility. "Some even got up and walked out during the meeting." Liu Shaoqi did not attend.

Mao had now gone further than he had the previous year in backing the project. The Hundred Flowers was not only an opening for discussion with intellectuals, it was to become a *rectification of the Party* and its "bureaucratism, which suppressed the people's legitimate demands." The very idea of a Party rectification being handled by non-Party intellectuals was so heretical, so unorthodox, that it is extraordinary it could even begin. On May 1, the Hundred Flowers was publicly proclaimed as a political movement, and Party cadres were ordered to solicit criticism of their behavior and actions from the intelligentsia they had hitherto supervised and guided.

Emboldened by Mao's backing, Zhou held seminars. "All the democratic parties in China have a representative value: They grew out of Chinese soil. . . . They cannot be equated with British or American political parties." Utterly daring, he stated, *"Socialism . . . does not mean only one party. . . . This is a dogmatic attitude."* Though he reasserted that the CCP must remain the leading party, and that the Western multiparty system was inappropriate, he added, *"But to think that with just one Communist Party all problems can be solved is simplistic."*

In front of stubbornly hostile colleagues he stated, "Some people in the Party think that all under heaven belongs to them. . . . They do not want to agree to supervision. . . . There are also certain people in the Party with *personal ambition*. . . . They are a danger."

But were Zhou and Mao naive enough to believe that Communists like Liu Shaoqi, for whom the Party machine was the revolution itself, would, as English historian Dick Wilson remarked, "stand quietly by and let themselves be criticized by bourgeois novelists, ivory tower professors, or philosophy lecturers?" "This is very dangerous. . . . It weakens socialism." "We fought for everything under heaven. Now the knowledge-bearers want to rule everything under heaven." These were the comments, even though the Party cadres, obediently, notebook in hand, came to the intellectuals. "Please criticize us," they said.

Suddenly a tornado of bitter recrimination, of denunciation, of wrathful condemnation, whirled through the land, with such virulence, such unbridled anger, that one can only wonder at the depths of frustration, pent-up resentment, which engendered those strange blossoms.

Leaders of the Democratic League and of other parties, major figures in educational and cultural institutions, scientists, members of the CPPCC, school heads, vied to heap sarcasm, criticism, vituperation, upon the CCP. "It is now the ignorant who rule the knowledgeable. We may be thrown into the fire, pushed into water, cast into hell or lifted into heaven all at the whim of the Party secretary. We are no longer able to endure the spiritual torture, the shame inflicted upon us."

The front page of the *People's Daily* and other Communist newspapers duly carried, sometimes with banner headlines, articles denouncing almost everything, from the way teaching was done to the cutting down of old trees. One headline ran: "Mao Dzedong, Zhou Enlai, it is time for you to step down."

There were also measured, reasonable demands. For an appropriate legal system, a civil code, a criminal code, adequate police regulations. None of these existed. But it was of course the more erratic and extravagant statements which stood out. "The masses may knock you down." . . . "Kill all the Communists." . . . "The machine guns will be turned one day against you." Posters reading "Down with Communism" were brandished in some universities. Mob violence and murders of Party cadres broke out in some regions.

On June 7, five weeks after the proclamation of the movement, an article in the *People's Daily* entitled "What is the meaning of all this?" signaled the end of this astonishing blooming and contending. The point had been reached where some naive non-Communist party leaders claimed that each party should rule in turn, with full powers. The movement became almost uncontrollable.

Mao and Zhou attempted to conduct the retreat from the movement in orderly fashion. There must be well-chosen arguments, countercriticism against extreme demands. But the Party machine had begun a move to crush all opposition, an unstoppable juggernaut.

Deng Xiaoping was in charge of what became the "antirightist" purge. Throughout the Party, unit by unit, each organization was to hold sessions to ferret out "rightists." Many of the criticisms had come from Party members, Party writers, Party journalists and editors. These were to be more severely dealt with. Ten percent in every organization . . . this was the quota. Had not Zhou himself said that "ten percent are more or less hostile to the Party"? The statement was now being used against him.

For over half a year Zhou refused to dismiss the non-Party ministers in his government, even though they had also been critical. Nie Rongzhen refused to have his teams of scientists decimated. In Peking University the search for rightists was low-key, but not so in other universities. The Writers Association became a forum for unpleasant accusations and counteraccusations. There were suicides.

"I am responsible . . . this is my fault. . . . But there are unfair and unrealistic practices being carried out. . . . We must continue to make readjustments," said Zhou, trying hard to save as many as he could among those accused. One of them was Qhiao Guanhua, the husband of Gung Peng. "When I was entrusted to form a government I drew up the composition of the State Council in accordance with the principles of the People's Democratic United Front as stipulated in the constitution," said Zhou, defending his ministers. But he was defeated. His propensity for having high-grade intellectuals, poets, artists, as his friends went against him. "Enlai has always been on the best of terms with the bourgeoisie," said one of his colleagues disparagingly. Fortunately, because most of the rightists' ideas fell within the category of "contradictions among the people," their lives were spared. Nevertheless, Zhou

Enlai had lost. Not only did his attempt to promote dialogue, discussion, and exchanges fail, but his plan to promote a larger role for the non-Communist intellectuals was aborted. Worst of all, his relationship with Mao was affected.

Mao had suffered a setback, a defeat. He had supported his Premier, and the result was a humiliating loss of face. In the autumn of 1957 the relations between the two men deteriorated almost to the point of no return.

17

"This is haste . . . adventurism . . . this is guerrilla tactics, quite incompatible with the running of complex modern industrial plants," Zhou Enlai said at the September 1957 Third Plenum of the Party when Mao formulated his new policies.

It was scarcely three months since the foundering of the Hundred Flowers and the onset of the antirightist drive. The universities and educational institutes lay under a thick pall of silent fear; relentless self-criticism sessions went on in their precincts. Party members crowed triumphantly. Liu and Deng had never been more popular with middling Party cadres, who now zestfully indulged in finding fault and purging any person who had dared to say a word against them. Gung Peng invited me to lunch. She and her husband, Qiao Guanhua, offered to explain to me the meaning of the campaign, but I refused politely. "I understand. You may remember that I did not believe the Hundred Flowers would succeed. Now I only want to say: Don't blow too hard on the cat's fur to find the cat's fleas."

"We were shoved in the icebox, there to remain frozen until we were again needed," laughed my relative, a member of the Democratic League, now become a "rightist." He was rehabilitated some years later, and today continues to represent the League. The fundamental problem, the one which underlay the Hundred Flowers attempt, had not been solved. What was China's development model? "There is no appropriate model we can take as an example. China's realities are very different from those of the U.S.S.R. or the West. We shall have to devise one for ourselves," economists Ma Hong and Lung Yungwei told me later.

The Second Five-Year Plan, framed by Zhou Enlai, corrected the ambitious growth expectations of the First. It revised factory management, substituting committee management, made up of Party cadres, technical staff, and workers—a concession to "democratic centralism." But no technical staff dared to contradict the Party men in the committee. And the workers knew very well that if they opened their mouths, their expectation of bonuses might vanish.

Mao Dzedong had now moved further in his vision of the revolution and China's role in the world. After his defeat at the Eighth Congress the previous year, he was more convinced than ever that the Party machine was a top-heavy, bloated, and parasitic bureaucracy impeding rather than stimulating production. He now turned to "the masses" and called for rejecting any model of central administrative planning. He encouraged instead spontaneously initiated mass economic activity, and released economic and political authority to local and regional bodies. He quoted: "In the beginning was Chaos, and out of Chaos came order."

Zhou Enlai's whole being refuted chaos. He was for order, administered with leniency, reserving a place for dissent. He was a born administrator, taking into account each one of the multiple problems he faced, devising ways to reach maximum effectiveness with minimum violence and waste.

He had his reservations about the Party machine and its increasingly rigid, vertical system of control. But Liu Shaoqi was not a stupid man. He agreed with Zhou about the importance of orderly administration. Zhou Enlai agreed with Mao that a horizontal coordinated web of activity must also be created, a sector of initiative and enterprise. Zhou's administrative structure had integrated as many non-Communists as possible. There was a State Planning Commission, a Statistics Bureau, an Economic Commission, a Science Commission, all under the State Council with himself as its head. Zhou thus hovered between Mao and Liu. Although against the rigidity of a Party machine controlling everything, he was also against total decentralization, spontaneity, with concomitant loss of control. But Mao was determined. And his resolve to carry out another model of advance, at high speed, entirely reliant on popular enthusiasm, was reinforced after his visit to Moscow in October 1957 for the fortieth anniversary of the Russian revolution. He returned to China convinced that Khrushchev would sacrifice anyone, any other "fraternal" country, to win his goal, détente with the United States. China must therefore prepare for "self-reliance," prepare to go it alone.

It was this concatenation of circumstances and perceptions which pushed Mao, and the Communist Party, into that enterprise known as the Great Leap Forward. In vain did Zhou and Chen Yun object. The Party machine might be cumbersome and inefficient, but it provided some sort of order. It assured salaries and bonuses to workers. It could not be randomly upset. . . . But their preliminary negative reports were not published. Liu Shaoqi, Deng Xiaoping, and many others, including Peng Dehuai, who later was to denounce the Leap, enthusiastically agreed to Mao's grandiose vision. Top publicity was given to Deng Xiaoping's report on the successes of the antirightist campaign. As a result, the repression grew. Anyone who did not share in the frenzied enthusiasm which now seized the Party was looked upon as a "rightist," and this included those who spoke of "haste" and "adventurism," and that was Zhou Enlai. They were out to "impede our advance," said some of Zhou's colleagues, looking askance at him. Party members deficient in the required enthusiasm were shifted, replaced by zealots. Liu Shaoqi organized work conferences, so named because they were attended by several echelons of Party cadres, including provincial officials. This made it possible to convey the center's directives swiftly to lower levels throughout the country. In January 1958, Mao Dzedong and Liu Shaoqi drew up "sixty points on methods of work," which became the charter of the Leap. Out of 11 million Party members, 1.5 million urban cadres were transferred to rural areas in that month.

Almost immediately, miraculous advances, record-breaking production in factories, and staggering agricultural gains were reported. At the work conference held in Chengdu, in March 1958, to promote the Great Leap Forward, Mao lashed out at Zhou Enlai. "You said this is adventurism . . . you called it haste, impatience. . . . But so was the Long March, so was our war of liberation. Did we not dare Chiang Kaishek and the imperialists when we crossed the Yangtse River? Our motto should be: Dare."

He was bitter because, even before the Leap had been formally conceived, Zhou had warned against "haste." Mao now muttered that Zhou's attitude was a "political problem"—a grievous accusation. Dutifully, members of the Central Committee—except for Chen Yun, Ho Lung, Li Fuchun, and Chen Yi—echoed Mao, castigating "those who want to hold us back." Chen Yun's health broke down under the strain and he retired to Hangzhou to nurse his ulcers.

Zhou continued to function. He went on a survey of the Yangtse River for a projected dam where the river hewed its way among a series of narrow gorges. "What will happen upstream?" he asked, for he worried that Sichuan province, the granary of China, might suffer, and decided to study the situation more deeply before coming to a decision. The Russian "experts" were now building a major dam on the Yellow River, and Zhou went to see it. It would later prove to be a catastrophe, for no study of the amount of silt which the Yellow River brought down—and the silt of the Yellow River is far more than that of any other river in the world—had been made.

In March 1958, I was back in China. I witnessed in Beijing the killing of sparrows, supposed to be harmful to crops.

It was impossible then to see Zhou Enlai. I did not know that precisely in March had occurred the Chengdu work conference. Would Zhou too go the way of Gao Gang? Would he be pilloried as anti-Party? Zhou seems to have suffered from a crisis of depression for several weeks. He sat for hours, staring into space. He still worked, but when he did not work, he just sat. "It is my thinking, I cannot get away from feudal, bourgeois thinking," he said about himself, bleakly, mechanically. None of his colleagues, neither Liu nor Deng, seemed to agree with him. In February he had handed over the Ministry of Foreign Affairs to Chen Yi. But the latter refused to go against Zhou. Whenever there was a problem, he galloped across the courtyards of Zhongnanhai to consult Zhou. Chen Yi's loyalty, his robust sense of humor, cheered the downcast Zhou, as did the visits of Ho Lung the Dragon, who never failed to extinguish his pipe before entering Zhou's rooms. Others supported him: Li Fuchun, Li Xiannian . . .

Nevertheless, he was now formally ordered to write his self-criticism. One of his secretaries, Fan Royu, tells in his memoirs the story of how Zhou Enlai did it. "I went to see Premier Zhou in his office, because I was to help him write his self-criticism. Premier said to me, 'I have committed errors. My thinking has not caught up with the thinking of Chairman Mao.' Premier Zhou, usually so quick, so precise, who wrote directives himself and seldom needed to correct a word, was now unable to put words together! He dictated a sentence, I wrote it down. He would remain silent for a while, then say another sentence. While we were together, he received a telephone call from Vice-Premier

Chen Yun in Hangzhou. Premier Zhou listened, listened, then put down the phone. He looked as if he was falling into a stupor. Then he started again to dictate, painfully, stopping three or four minutes between each sentence . . . by then it was very late, midnight." Fan Joyu suggested that he should leave, let Zhou rest, think things over. "Premier Zhou was torn with doubts. That is why he could not find the right words."

At 2 in the morning Fan Royu was awakened by Deng Yingchao. "Why have you left the Premier alone? He is sitting there, not moving at all, as if he had lost his spirits." "She was upset," says Royu. The two then decided that Royu should compose the self-criticism, using what Zhou had dictated, rearranging the paragraphs. "I wrote: 'Chairman Mao and I have been through wind and rain together, sailing the same craft, toiling toward the same goal, but my thinking is still very inferior to that of Chairman Mao.' When Premier Zhou read this he was upset. 'This is incorrect! It is only true after 1945. Before 1945 I was not always in agreement with Chairman Mao. This shows you don't know Party history.' He looked almost on the point of weeping."

Composing the self-criticism took ten days. It was sent to the Standing Committee of the Politburo and to the Secretariat. It came back with the word "self-examination" crossed out, and some of his self-accusatory sentences altered for the better. "This made his heart lighter, and also mine. Gradually Premier became himself again. But I noticed that during the fortnight we were together, white hairs had grown upon his head."

Zhou, though cheered by this support, continued to be picked on, as if he were the Party's errand boy. He had argued that it was normal that there should be wage and income differentials, but in the new mood of total egalitarianism which prevailed, this was heavily criticized. He had spoken repeatedly on the problems of national minorities. They had different languages, cultures, social patterns. They must have their own autonomy. They could not be compelled to carry out reforms for which they were not ready. He condemned "great-Han chauvinism," and promised Tibetans that social changes in Tibet would be delayed until 1962.

All this was swept away by overzealous cadres in the frenzy of setting up communes, of "liberating" the Tibetan serfs from the monasteries, the landlord-priests who owned 90 percent of Tibet.

Foreign relations were also affected. The talks between China and the United States in Warsaw were suspended in late 1957, not to be resumed until September 1958. Trade with Japan, which Zhou had worked hard to promote, also became a casualty of the Leap.

Through Zhou's exertions 30,000 Japanese prisoners of war, including 1,000 "war criminals," had been repatriated to Japan. Between 1953 and 1957, 12,000 Japanese visitors, many of them businessmen, had come to China. Now trade with Japan was arbitrarily suspended and all commercial exchanges and contracts held in abeyance.

Relations with the U.S.S.R. now worsened. In July 1958, a revolution took place in Iraq, and American marines landed in Lebanon. Khrushchev called for a summit meeting among the U.S.S.R., the United States, France, Great Britain, and India, ignoring China. The summit did not take place, and he then asked that the UN Security Council meet to debate appropriate measures. Zhou sent a stiff warning to Khrushchev, reminding him that a situation involving Arab states which had recognized China could not be placed before the UN Security Council so long as China's place was occupied by Chiang Kaishek's representative from Taiwan.

On July 31, Khrushchev arrived in Beijing. A stormy meeting took place. He railed against the Leap, the communes, Mao's "bellicosity." Then he suddenly altered his tone, and became wheedling, proposing, "for eternal friendship," a joint defense pact, involving patrolling of China's coastline by Soviet naval units, cooperation of military and air forces, and suggesting that Soviet scientists set up nuclear installations in China. Mao asked, "Whose finger will be on the nuclear button?" and turned down all these proposals, which would have made China a mere appendage of the U.S.S.R. However, some of China's military commanders, dazzled by Russia's might, considered the offer favorable, and among them was Peng Dehuai. "We shall never be dictated to, by anyone," Mao said. Zhou backed Mao. "Even if we have to go trouserless, we shall have our own nuclear power in our hands," Foreign Minister Chen Yi told me three years later when I met him in Geneva. He was echoing what Mao and Zhou had said at the meeting. Khrushchev had gibed: "The Chinese peasants do not even have trousers to wear."

Zhou spent the summer months on inspection tours of the new

communes, cocking his head when he heard exaggerated claims
of five tons of rice per mu (15 mus to a hectare of land). He kept
silent when he saw the hastily built factories with their thousands
of peasant recruits and the machines lying outside in the rain
because no one knew how to set them up. Had there not been
this planless haste, this credulous conviction that "the masses"
could solve any problem on their own, some of the concepts of
the Leap might have worked. Some did. One of them was irrigation
of arable land. This involved a massive mobilization of the peasant
millions to dig wells, construct dams and dikes, reservoirs and
canals. This had been done for many centuries, it was a pattern
the peasants understood, and it did provide water to around 40
percent of China's arable land.

The communes, designed to ensure agricultural rationalization,
laid the foundation for future mechanization and a self-supporting
infrastructure of schools, agricultural institutes, public health services, as well as small electric power projects and chemical fertilizer
plants. Unfortunately, the communes were created with the slogan
"Communism is near at hand." Millions of peasants translated this
as "Now the government will provide for everything we need."
They slaughtered their livestock to indulge in orgies of meat eating, for they truly believed that miraculously all would be provided
through "Communism."

At the same time 17 million peasants were drafted into the cities
to work in newly built factories. As a result, harvests rotted in the
fields. No one was available to reap and to thresh.

Perhaps the crowning aberration was the steel-making campaign.
Mao thought everyone in China should understand the need for
steel in industry. Everyone was to make steel, and primitive brick
furnaces were erected by the million. But this meant transporting
coal and iron. For this, carts and wheelbarrows and mules were
used, the peasants collecting the coal and iron slug to make steel.
But after the "steel" was made, it could not be carted away, because
the vehicles had to be used to transport whatever grain there was.
Of course, the steel made was of very poor quality, and was later
to be smelted back, in some areas, into cooking pots.

Small factories utilizing manpower to manufacture semifinished
consumer goods from agricultural produce were set up in the new
communes. But they competed for raw materials with the larger,
established factories in urban areas. Zhou Enlai went on a round

of universities to exhort the students to participate in manual labor. He was aware of the traditional aversion among the educated to manual toil, an aversion inherited by the newly educated elite, ashamed to confess that their parents were poor workers or peasants. "There is a falling away by the young who have not known want, hunger, or war," said Zhou. He inspected military units and found young recruits "without any experience of hardship. Our seasoned veterans are leaving. Some are sent to run communes. Others are old and have to be retired." He found officers' families enjoying special privileges and amenities in garrison cities and ordered them sent back to their original villages. He led 250 of his State Council vice-premiers, ministers, and staff to work for a week on a new reservoir eighty kilometers from Beijing. He toured coal mines, and when a major flood washed away a bridge on the Yellow River, Zhou arrived at night and did not leave till he had satisfied himself that the rescue work was efficient. He visited a barren North China village. It was winter, an icy, dusty wind blew. The assembled villagers faced the wind, while he was protected by a mat alcove, the wind at his back. He ordered that the villagers turn around, and the platform be displaced, so that he now faced the wind. During these explorations he came upon the gruesome conditions still prevailing in some areas when a woman gave birth. "They prop up the mother after birth, and will not let her sleep for forty-eight hours," he told me. He wrote to the Health Minister that the villages needed well-trained midwives, more acceptable than male doctors. "Health care must become available to all." The following year the Ministry of Health was divided into two sectors, and public health clinics were established in the communes. Education also split in two, the Ministry of Lower Education providing for the vast deprived sector of the population in rural areas.

In the work conference held from November 24 to December 10, 1958, in the city of Wuhan, the truth about the failures of the Leap began to seep out. Impassive, cold-voiced, Zhou Enlai reported that the agricultural situation "was somewhat disturbing . . . unrealistic figures are being quoted." Mao was shaken, but defiant. "The lies are squeezed out of the lower cadres by a higher level," he accused. Zhou went on talking of dislocation, of serious difficulty in transport capacity. Mao interrupted. Transport was Zhou's responsibility. Why hadn't he provided for transporting the steel? Impassively Zhou carried on. There should be monthly or quarterly tables of production from every county, not in percentages, but in exact figures, and inspection teams to check upon the figures.

The result of the work conference was another flood of directives, which fell upon the unfortunate lower cadres, and without any effect. For the Leap was a maelstrom feeding upon itself, and it would take another eighteen months to reverse its course.

In January 1959, Zhou went to Moscow to attend the Twenty-first Congress of the Soviet Party. "Comrade Zhou, where are all the steel engineers we trained for you?" gloated Khrushchev. "In the countryside, forging their proletarian consciousness," replied Zhou. "I could tell that Zhou thought the whole thing pretty stupid, but he could do nothing. The Leap was not his idea," Khrushchev observed.

That same month Liu Shaoqi was proclaimed Chairman of the People's Republic, replacing Mao, who retained Party chairmanship and chairmanship of the Military Affairs Commission. This ascension of Liu led Khrushchev to believe that Mao was perhaps being countered effectively. He agreed to thirty-one new projects and a new loan of 208 million rubles, making a total of 430 million rubles since Stalin's death.

In March a revolt erupted in Tibet. The Dalai Lama, with a suite of several hundred, fled Lhasa, to seek asylum in India. He had already, in 1954, been to India for a Buddhist celebration, and there asked Nehru for asylum. Zhou had arrived in India in that June, from Geneva, and been unpleasantly surprised to find the Dalai Lama on the same platform as he, sitting not far from him. Nehru had persuaded the Dalai Lama to return to Tibet. Now, five years later, India did give asylum to the Dalai Lama.

On June 20, Khrushchev canceled the agreement to provide nuclear technology to China, six weeks before his scheduled summit meeting with President Eisenhower at Camp David.

July 1959. Lushan. A cool mountain resort 1,426 meters above sea level, not far from Nanjing, Chiang Kaishek's erstwhile capital, his refuge from the sweltering Nanjing summer. His Communist successors held political sessions during the day and dances at night in the same villas and assembly halls that Chiang had used. An "enlarged" Politburo work conference was starting. Even before the conference had begun, there was tenseness, expectation of change. Mao now acknowledged that there had been excesses in the Leap. Zhou was talking of "readjustment and retrenchment," sending teams to inspect and gather material. Although the communes were extolled, they were clearly unwieldy, and accounting for production was returning to the village production team. Talk of "Communism" had stopped. It was whispered in the Party that Mao was going to make some kind of self-criticism.

Zhou Enlai, with Deng Yingchao, Li Fuchun and his wife, Tsai Chang, arrived together at Lushan on July 2. On the previous evening the four friends had dined together, eating "long life" noodles to celebrate the Party's thirty-eighth anniversary. Zhou as usual walked briskly about, inspecting the rooms that were to be used. He spoke to the cooks. "Remember the Chairman likes his food with red chili." It had become second nature to Zhou to care for Mao's bodily comforts, as he cared for his wife's, for his friends'. But he was also exhibiting his affection for the Chairman, possibly to make Mao feel he was revered and loved, for he sensed how mortified, how heartsick Mao must be, now that his grandiose scheme had broken down. Even Mao's ex-wife, Ho Dzejen, whom he had divorced to marry Jiang Qing, Limpid Stream, had sent an affectionate message.

They were all there. Tall, big-nosed Liu Shaoqi, as usual unable to smile or to crack a joke, but a figure commanding respect, and also awe, for was he not, clearly, Mao's successor? There was agile, short, square-headed Deng Xiaoping, who bluntly remarked, "Comrade Enlai was the first to mention unreliable reports . . . a practice which does not seem to have stopped." Many Party leaders came up to speak to Zhou Enlai. Had he not been the first to stand against the Leap? Zhou Enlai strove to establish a rational platform for discussions. "While struggling against those who hold different views on questions of principle, one should achieve the necessary compromises on questions of current policy or of a purely practical nature," he said, in his suavely mordant manner, and continued: "We have to learn many lessons . . . on how to handle the economy." But could the Leap be envisaged as merely a series of practical problems? Or was it going to be handled as a question of principle?

Li Rui, the minister in charge of hydroelectric power, has left a handwritten memoir of what happened at Lushan. He describes how, after some halting skirmishes, some lame remarks about "mistakes . . . unreliable reports," it was Minister of Defense Peng Dehuai who, on July 14, presented a 10,000-word "letter of opinion" addressed to Mao Dzedong. It was read by Mao on July 17. Meanwhile, it had been copied and circulated—exactly how is not known, or rather not said—to all those present at Lushan. The letter was a total denunciation of Mao, as well as of the Leap. "Petty bourgeois fanaticism . . . people who become dizzy with success . . . no longer able to understand the masses." Boring Through Rock waxed eloquent about "the mess. . . . My soldiers receive news from their homes which stuns them. . . . If the Chinese peasants were not as patient as they are, we would have another Hungary."

Peng appears to have worsened matters by referring to past disagreements with Mao. "You cursed me for ten days, now I'll curse you for twenty." Emboldened, other Party men began to speak in the same vein, and the meeting took on the aspect of an all-out ad hominem assault against Mao Dzedong. Every evening, after the day's infighting, there was dancing in the large hall or smaller ones, depending on the attendance. An evident majority was pleased with Peng's frankness. "There was a dance party on the twentieth and I sat with the Premier and asked him, 'What is your view of Peng's letter?' " writes Li Rui. " 'Why, it's quite normal, nothing to it,' replied Zhou Enlai."

This reply was not entirely frank. Zhou must have known how wounded Mao would be. Zhou himself was doing more to stop the Leap than many of those who now so eagerly denounced it. He had collected facts and figures from all the provincial Party secretaries, insisting on "actual figures, not percentages." In the memorandum he presented to the conference he wrote that the necessary balance between finances, resources, and production had been totally upset in 1958. The steel drive alone had cost the country over a billion and a half yuan. But Zhou knew it was important to save Mao's face.

"I have taken sleeping pills. I haven't slept well for three days," said Mao, as he began in his usual rambling manner his answer to the criticisms leveled against him.

Mao had come to Lushan with the intention of making a self-criticism. Now he had changed his mind. He saw Peng's initiative as part of a plot against him. Boring Through Rock had led, that spring, a military delegation to the Warsaw Pact meeting. He had met with Khrushchev at least once, and the two had exchanged views and opinions. In June, as Peng returned to China, Khrushchev had canceled the agreement on nuclear technology, but Peng had written to plead for "better understanding" with the U.S.S.R. Whether by coincidence or as a deliberate insult, Peng, in his letter of opinion, and in the remarks he made, used the same terms that Khrushchev had used the year before: "petty bourgeois fanaticism . . . dizzy . . ." The Russian press reproduced some of these terms, though without ascribing them to an attack against Mao.

Mao continued: "In the past, the responsibility [for mistakes] was upon others, such as Enlai. . . . This time, it seems I am to blame. . . . Enlai was criticized, but now he is standing firm. Enlai has a lot of energy. He is quite untiring. Strange that those people who criticized Enlai at that time now find themselves in his shoes. . . ."

Thus Mao made an apology to Zhou Enlai, who had not joined in the attack against him. And now the Lushan meeting, which had assembled to criticize "left extremism," became, amazingly, a meeting to condemn "right opportunism."

Boring Through Rock was abandoned by all his friends, including those who had urged him on. One by one the marshals and the commanders rose and pledged their loyalty to Mao Dzedong. Lin Biao, the thin, sallow-faced commander, violently attacked Peng Dehuai as ambition-ridden, a plotter, a counterrevolutionary. Peng had not deserved this.

The question remains: Who encouraged Peng, provoked him to write this "letter of opinion"? For no Chinese ever embarks on such a serious gesture without at least consulting a friend or two. Who were the people who then abandoned Peng to his fate? Liu Shaoqi attempted a very weak defense. "What is really left, what is really right?" Zhou Enlai sat quiet as a stone. He knew the dimensions of the conflict taking place. It was not merely a critique of the Leap, of Mao's populist vision. It was also a bid for power. "During those days in Lushan," Li Rui hints in his memoirs, "even a chance meeting between Party leaders, stray words, a remark, might lead to rumors, to suspicion." In the tense, miasmic atmosphere, an increasing number of people were now suspected of "right opportunism." Abandoned by his friends, Peng was ordered to write his self-criticism.

Zhou Enlai got drunk. He drank in his room until he was stuporous. Deng Yingchao could not do anything. "He got drunk with happiness when the Korean War came to an end. Now he got drunk with grief. Because his brain told him that what was happening was an ominous event. He had envisioned Mao making a mild self-criticism, and then again unity in the Party, and the pursuit of progress."

On August 26, without a word of blame against anyone, Zhou addressed the Standing Committee of the National People's Congress on needed "readjustment" and proclaimed a campaign of savings and austerity. In the name of savings and austerity, he was able to take back from local authorities the funds that had been so lavishly disbursed. Once again the statistics bureau, which had been paralyzed, sprang into activity.

Boring Through Rock was demoted, assigned a residence in Sichuan province. This followed the pattern of imperial China, which sent out-of-favor officials to distant provinces. He remained unmolested, even if in a lower position, until the Cultural Revolution of 1966.

As the drama at Lushan wound toward its climax, Ho Chi Minh appeared. A photograph shows him, arms linked happily with Tsai Chang and Deng Yingchao, laughing uproariously as they stroll on a mountain pathway. But he was worried. What did the projected Khrushchev-Eisenhower summit presage for Vietnam? Ho had come from Hanoi to tell Zhou that the South Vietnamese Communists were forming a Liberation Front, that Le Duan, their leader, was in Hanoi, and that the time had come for military action to enforce reunification. Would Zhou now fulfill his promise to help?

Yes, said Zhou.

He assured Ho that by year's end China would give some $500 million worth of weaponry, equipment, and funds to Vietnam's projected war of liberation. (This was only the beginning. Altogether, from 1960 to 1978, according to Vietnamese figures, China gave Vietnam aid worth $20 billion. This aid was given; no repayment was ever asked.)

In September, Chinese and Indian forces clashed at Longju, a garrison point on the contested border between China and India, called the McMahon Line.

The year 1959 was a calamitous one for China. Nevertheless, it was also the tenth year of the People's Republic of China, and a huge celebration was scheduled for October. Ten large buildings had been erected in Beijing, among them the monumental Great Hall of the People, a Chinese-style Parthenon. Among the countless other details to which he attended, Zhou selected appropriate paintings to hang inside the new hall. "He did this as he did everything—punctiliously. He stood on stairs to gauge the effect, walked up to scrutinize the work," painter Wu Tsojen (now Dzoren) told me. No hint of criticism, however veiled, must appear in the paintings, and the Chinese are remarkably adept at finding political allusions in a shadow, the crooked limb of a tree, a despondent cloud.

Very few of the heads of state, members of delegations, and Communist Party representatives gathered in Beijing for the October celebration knew of the drama that had taken place that summer at Lushan, and nobody could predict that it would lead, a few years later, to that extraordinary decade called the Cultural Revolution.

But Peng Dehuai was missed. Anna Louise Strong, the stalwart American writer, who now resided in Beijing, asked me, "What has happened to him?"

"I don't know."

"My guess is that he has been sent to direct the war in Vietnam," said Anna Louise. She was reasoning by analogy, thinking of General Wei Guoqing, who had also disappeared from view while helping the Vietnamese in the battle of Dienbienphu in 1954.

Bouncing down the steps of his plane, Khrushchev, in an exuberantly joyful mood, arrived in Beijing for the October festivities. Fresh from the Camp David summit with President Eisenhower, he extolled the American President, and was even prepared to be somewhat generous to the intransigent Chinese. For had he not succeeded in his aim of an entente with the United States?

Five days of acrimonious debate behind closed doors followed, but the two countries decided to paper over their differences for the time being. A large meeting of all the Communist parties of the world would be held the following December, to debate the issues.

When Khrushchev had gone, Mao and Zhou discussed the problem of nuclear research with Nie Rongzhen. "We shall have to do it on our own. We must do it on our own. We can do it on our own," Nie said.

Zhou Enlai with his wife, Deng Yingchao, on an inspection tour in China (c. 1959)

Playing Ping-Pong (c. 1960)

Zhou Enlai with Prime Minister of France Pierre Mendès-France in Geneva in 1954. The man standing behind Zhou is Wang Bingnan

With Nehru in 1954. On the right is Ho Lung

Zhou Enlai, in late 1959, with released generals and other military personnel of the Guomindang who were captured in the civil war. He enjoined them to work for the reunification of Taiwan and China

With Ho Chi Minh and Pham Van Dong in Hanoi (1952)

Receiving Field Marshal
Montgomery on his visit to China
(1962)

Talking to women in a peasant
village in Liaoning province
(June 15, 1962)

With musicians, actors, and Chinese opera artists (c. 1960)

On a visit to Burma with Marshal Chen Yi (1964)

Zhou Enlai in September 1965. Photo taken by author

Zhou greeted by Mao on his return from Moscow on November 1964. Standing behind Zhou is Marshal Zhu De. Liu Shaoqi is at far right

The campaign against "rightist opportunism" proceeded. Not only Peng Dehuai but other commanders and Party leaders who sided with him were also demoted. Twenty years later, Deng Xiaoping, asked about the Lushan drama, would be truthful. "We all bear responsibility for what happened. Mao was hotheaded, but what about all of us? We did not oppose him. We went along with him."

A moment's faltering changes the course of history. The Lushan meeting will remain a controversial, hotly debated event for some decades. Peng Dehuai's rash courage is to be admired, and the timorousness of the friends who abandoned him should not be soft-pedaled.

But what would have happened had Mao lost? The dispute with Moscow would have been patched up. Moscow would have been greatly strengthened vis-à-vis the United States. Moscow's terms would have been accepted by a compliant China, and history would be very different from what it is today.

Zhou Enlai himself remained totally mute, refusing to condemn anyone at the Lushan meeting. But one can assume, I think, that he saw clearly the tremendous power shift in favor of the Soviet Union which Mao's downfall—or even his mere diminishment in stature and influence—would have brought about. And though he would stem the ocean's fury, shore up the disasters, he went along with Mao, knowing that in the end China must remain independent from the U.S.S.R. He and his team, including the rehabilitated economist Chen Yun, began the needed "readjustment and retrenchment." All the commissions were now reactivated. And he immediately set out to contact the Japanese through Prince Kinkazu Saionji, a Japanese aristocrat who lived in Beijing. He proclaimed an amnesty for the remaining eleven Guomindang generals still held in China and gave a banquet for them. Among the eleven was Du Yuming, whose son-in-law is famed Nobel Prize winner Yang Chen Ning. Zhou Enlai talked at length with General Du of patriotism, of reunification between Taiwan and China. He praised Chiang Kaishek for refusing the American-Russian concept of two Chinas. "Tell our compatriots abroad when you return to Taiwan that our hearts meet across the Straits. That we are one family."

Neither did Zhou forget the Young Marshal, Learning Excellence, still a prisoner of Chiang Kaishek in Taiwan. On Christmas Day 1957, he had asked the relatives of the Young Marshal to his house, to commemorate the courage and the patriotism of the unfortunate man. He now arranged for the Young Marshal's beloved mistress to go to Taiwan "in order to comfort him and to look after him." He released the last emperor of China, Pu Yi, who, after spending years in a Russian jail, had been since 1949 undergoing reeducation in a factory in China. "Ten years is quite enough for reeducation," Zhou said, and invited Pu Yi and his brother, their families and relatives, to dinner. I saw Pu Yi in that October at another banquet. He was unable to carry on a proper conversation, bowed to everyone, including me. I shook his hand. "I won't shake hands with that bastard," said Edgar Snow, who was with me, and had a very lively sense of right and wrong. He did not agree that Pu Yi was a victim, not a performer, of history's misdeeds.

Zhou arranged a decent house for Pu Yi, doubled his monthly allowance, made his brother, Pu Shou, a member of the CPPCC representing the Manchu national minority—some 3 million people. Deng Yingchao set out to find him a wife, a personable nurse. "We need descendants from families like yours," said Zhou to Pu Yi, disregarding the doctrine which predicated the elimination of exploiting classes. Pu Yi became a botanist, lived seven more serene years, and died of cancer in 1967.

Now Zhou became the man around whom hope crystallized. As he had swept up the glass debris on his friend's floor in Japan, he reassembled the disordered fragments of the economic structure to get the country back in order. Once again honored, respected, listened to, Zhou arranged, with Mao's assent, the rehabilitation of some 40,000 "rightist" intellectuals. Many more were rehabilitated by 1962. Liu Shaoqi thoroughly agreed to this measure, but rehabilitations were not popular with a good many Party members. Strict orders from the State Council went out. The rehabilitated must be well treated and be given back their jobs.

Readjustment and retrenchment. Zhou spent hours checking the figures for the production of grain, cotton, soybeans, meat. He lay in bed, surrounded by stacks of reports, checking every province, every one of China's 2,000-odd counties. "Premier, someone else can do this for you," an anxious secretary suggested. "Someone else? Then how shall I know what is really happening?" said Zhou.

Zhou Enlai never went back to his native town, Huai An. Even when he went to visit his ancestral clan in Shaoxing in 1939. There he had duly swept the ancestors' graves, faultlessly performed all the required ceremonies.

But now, in 1959, when all was in disarray, he suddenly ordered that the Zhou family graveyard in Huai An, where his grandfather Panlong and his own mother and adoptive mother were buried, be made public property, turned over to the communes.

The tombstones had to be removed, and the coffins were buried deeper, "so that the land, which is good arable land, may be used for tilling . . . we have far too little land for our farmers and far too many graveyards."

This, by Confucian standards, was an abominable crime. Cemeteries, ancestral graves, hold the spirit of the family, and hence are more valuable than houses for the living. And this is felt even today among China's intellectuals, however "Westernized" some of them seem to be.

Why did he do it? "Because he had a sense of responsibility, he was a true intellectual, a true Chinese knowledge-bearer." "Because had he returned to Huai An to visit his relatives, they would have received favors and privileges from the local officials." "Because he wanted to set an example of integrity." I have discussed the matter with many of Zhou Enlai's trainees, and also with some of his relatives, whom I met in 1988. "Uncle Zhou was imbued with a sense of responsibility toward the people, toward China. Hunger stalked the land, and he razed the family graveyard because he wanted to give an example. It was the greatest sacrifice of all."

But nostalgia also inhabited his spirit. In one of the courtyards of the house in Huai An, I saw in March 1988 a splendid wintersweet covered in pale gold buds. It had been planted by Zhou Enlai when he was seven, in 1905. In 1960, he remembered the tree, and asked a relative from Huai An who came to see him, "Is the wintersweet still there, and does the old well still give water?"

18

The hectoring mood of the Leap still prevailed in Beijing in late October 1959, as frost whitened the muffled streets and the first consignments of winter cabbage reached the dusty lanes. I found it disconcerting to attempt any conversation; everyone seemed abrupt, umbrageous. There were food shortages, and by November a lack of soap, household goods, clothing, shoes, needles. Food rationing had been introduced in 1955 and now the amounts were drastically reduced. They would be further reduced in the following two years.

I felt less than welcome. I was lodged in a dismal hotel and visited by one of Gung Peng's subalterns—even she was apparently shunning me. "We are not interested in television," this person loftily declared when I offered my copy of a television program, *Small World*, as an example of discussions between myself and a well-known American newsman. "In that case, there is no need to have a press relations office, radio, the Xinhua News Agency, or even newspapers to make China known abroad," I retorted somewhat testily. Within three days all had changed. I was moved to a good room. I traveled, visiting communes and factories. On November 10, I was summoned to see Premier Zhou Enlai.

Zhou received me in one of the ornate state rooms of the Great Hall of the People. He was imposingly flanked by officials. The news that I had spoken favorably of China at a major conference held on China (in Canada, at Couchiching) had at last reached him. Zhou looked gaunt and tired. His happy, confident manner of 1956 was replaced by a steely determination, quite perceptible because it changed the set of his face. He gave me that wrapping-up look of his, taking everything in, from hair to shoes, as if he was putting me through a scanner. I did not know, at the time, what had happened at Lushan, nor did I know much of the dispute with Khrushchev. Somehow I had been classified "hostile" and received the "cold" treatment. But had not Zhou himself said, "We must listen to people, even if they say unpleasant things"? I had unpleasant things to say.

After the usual inquiries about my health, Zhou apologized. "We were wrong to deny you a visa this summer. Gung Peng was absent, the matter was dealt with by someone else."

Ritually, I replied, "It is my fault. I was too hasty. . . ."

"You defended China at a conference in Canada. We only learned about it a few days ago. I have also seen your television tape." He stopped a while, swallowed, as if his throat were dry. "Last time you asked many questions. What questions do you now wish to ask?"

"I have a question. About Tibet. Why did you let the Dalai Lama go, with a suite of many people? It took him three weeks to get to India. You could have stopped him at any time. . . ." The Chinese army had the day, the hour, and the spot at which the Dalai Lama and his slow-moving retinue crossed the border with India. A hundred Western newsmen, ill informed, had waited at a different entry point until notified by the Chinese of the exact spot.

Zhou almost smiled with relief. Some of the old fire came back. "We could have stopped him, but this would have meant the use of force, and the Dalai Lama might have been hurt, which would have greatly affected the Tibetan people. At first we thought he had gone unwillingly. He had written letters to us, saying he would come to us, but then he left. We thought he could have been kidnapped by the monks around him. We have kept open his position and rank in our central government and in the Tibetan autonomous government. The door is open for his return at any time."

I said I did not believe the Dalai Lama would return, or that matters would be easily settled. Zhou went into a long, precise, meticulous account of the history of Tibet. It had been part of China since the Mongol Yuan dynasty (1271–1368 A.D.). Even the British had recognized that Tibet was part of China when they invaded it in the early 20th century. "After liberation we urged the monasteries to make reforms. We cannot, in a socialist country, have a region where serfs work for priest-landowners. Then we decided we could not press reforms, and we agreed to wait. But history does not walk backwards. When reforms swept over China, Tibet was also affected." This euphemistic account meant that Zhou's promises to delay reforms were wiped out by the Leap.

But, said Zhou, the flight of the Dalai Lama was also due to outside interference. This was proven by the Khamba revolts in southern Tibet, supplied with weapons through India by the CIA. "It is no secret, they have even published their own accounts of their help to the Khambas. Tibet must move forward, it cannot become a museum for an antique social system, or a preserve, like the Red Indians of America. It must share in the development of the Motherland. Not one hospital in Tibet, no schools, except religious schools . . . all this must change," he said.

The British, after their occupation of Lhasa, had installed a trading agency there. In 1911, a British official, Arthur McMahon, "using a thick red pencil on a small map," had drawn a line incorporating a large part of Tibet into British India. No Chinese government had ever recognized the McMahon Line as a boundary. The border clash in September with India had been along the McMahon Line, as had a previous engagement in 1958. "Nehru," Zhou said to me, "is very British. He behaves as heir to British colonial expansionism." When in October 1950 the PLA had entered Tibet, with the consent of the Tibetan authorities, the Indian government had called the move "regrettable." The British trading agency was closed, but the question of boundaries had not been tackled.

I knew that Nehru's advisers had been divided on the matter. Some had warned Nehru that China's denunciation of all unequal treaties included arbitrary demarcations. "The McMahon Line is our boundary, map or no map," Nehru had snapped.

Since then Zhou and Nehru had been haggling over the question of the border, but without any resolution. Zhou showed me a copy of Nehru's autobiography, printed in London in 1956, in which a map appeared that placed the boundaries where the Chinese said they were, not where the Indians now claimed they should be. "Can it be," asked Zhou, "that Nehru has not checked the map in his own book?"

I pointed out that the border clashes, sensationally reported by the Western press, the clamor of "invasion" set up in India, and the Dalai Lama's flight in March all had combined to damage the image China tried so hard to project of a reasonable, conciliatory country, yearning for peaceful coexistence with its neighbors. Zhou nodded. He, the public relations man par excellence, understood the harm done. I added that vituperative articles in the Chinese press attacking Nehru personally "serve no useful purpose."

"Certain of our younger cadres do give vent to ill-thought-out feelings," Zhou replied, throwing a look around his entourage, as if to say, "Listen carefully. We should indeed be more careful." (I learned later that he had written to Nehru in conciliatory fashion.) "But Mr. Nehru contradicts himself. We do not understand what he really means. We have read his speeches, and he says one thing, then another thing the next day."

Zhou continued: "We know too little about each other, we Asians."

Suddenly, he abandoned the subject of India.

"Imperialism wants to provoke bad feelings between Asian nations. *Some people* do not see the issues clearly. . . . Imperialism has not changed, but *some people* put their hopes in meetings and in summits. They even talk of a new spirit which will save the world. At the present time these are illusions bound to deceive."

Who were *some people*? Then I remembered the Camp David summit between Eisenhower and Khrushchev.

"I too believe that the Camp David meeting is good for the world, Premier," I said.

Thunderous silence. The secretary who took notes remained gaping, pen in the air. Zhou looked tired, a creeping of small wrinkles began around his eyes.

"We do not think so," he said. Peace was concrete, not an abstraction. There would be no disarmament for a long time. On the contrary, there was an arms race on. "Reasonable compromise . . . cannot mean selling out *other* countries. We must decide now whether the peoples of the world have a right to their own national liberation, their own independence, or whether they will remain slaves for a thousand years. On this point we can never compromise. We believe in national independence. We approve of Cambodia's neutrality and independence. As for Vietnam, the agreements of the 1954 Geneva conference have not been kept. . . . There is bound to be resistance from the people, who want reunification."

This was what the West called "Chinese intransigence."

He was tight-strung. He saw me out, unsmiling, after some two hours. I decided to fly to New Delhi. After a talk with Nehru, I wrote to Zhou, concluding that the boundary dispute would not be easily settled. It was not in Nehru's interest to settle it.

A play much favored in Chinese opera is called *The Tale of the Empty City*. Its hero is Chuke Liang, China's Merlin, Grand Vizier to the Han emperor. One day Chuke Liang found himself in a city without an army, his troops engaged in battle many leagues away. Standing on the watchtower, he saw an enemy commander with a large number of soldiers advancing toward his citadel. "Quick, we must close the gates," shouted his captains. "On the contrary, open them, send men to sweep the entrance road, let the people carry on as usual," said Chuke Liang. He seated himself on the terrace atop the main gate and ordered his musicians to play gentle melodies, while he strummed a zither. The enemy general halted and Chuke Liang amiably invited him in. "This is a trap," said his adversary to those around him. "But I detect a slight quiver in Chuke's zither notes," whispered his adviser. The commander did not believe him, and withdrew.

Zhou Enlai now performed in the tradition of *The Empty City*. China was battered, in dire economic straits, but no one would have guessed it from Zhou's unfaltering calm, his public pronouncements, his air of confidence in the future. He refused to criticize Mao or to condemn the Leap, even while he was dismantling the Leap's policies, restoring orthodox methods, returning millions of peasants to their villages. He spoke in measured terms. "The simultaneous development of large, medium, and small industrial enterprises, the use of both modern and indigenous methods, or walking on two legs, certainly have their advantages. This is an experiment unparalleled in Chinese history." This was in praise of the Leap's bold concept of mass mobilization. And of the deplorable steelmaking adventure: "A truly magnificent spectacle. Part of the people's understanding how to transform China from a poor and blank country into an industrial state."

Refusing to condemn, to accuse, he inspired those around him, the men and women he had nurtured and trained, the "Zhou people." They followed his example. Not a word of complaint, of grievance. "He told us that spirit was our main, our major resource.

That without spirit there could be no way out of difficulties. We did not lament, despair. I think that, at the time, if Premier had asked me to die, so that China might live and things become better, I would have said, 'Yes, Premier, gladly.' "

So speak, even today, those he trained, now ambassadors and eminent ministers, such as Huang Hua and Qian Jiadung and many others.

In order to cope with acute food shortages, Zhou studied the number of calories required per worker, per teacher, per sedentary employee. The intelligentsia received more oil, more sugar, more meat. The workers received more grain, carbohydrates, and heavy industry workers—coal miners, steel plant workers—got extra rations. In light industry factories employing women, work was cut to one day in two. Schoolchildren went to school one day in two, to save their strength. People were enjoined to sleep a lot, to lie down. Everyone lost weight, including Zhou and his wife. They too were on ration cards, and Zhou refused to buy any of the extras available in special shops for foreign residents and for high cadres. Cheerful Chen Yi lost fifteen kilograms and mislaid his ration cards. He had to cadge meals from his friends until they were replaced. Zhou served hot water instead of tea, since tea was very scarce. In late autumn Yingchao swept up fallen tree leaves in her garden in Zhongnanhai and boiled them for decoctions. She told the security guards standing outside to come into the house, to rest and conserve their strength.

"Due to . . . inadequate allocation of labor power . . . which led to rather hurried reaping and threshing . . . due to lack of experience in assessing harvests under bumper conditions . . . temporary difficulties are being experienced," Zhou said. "Did you believe him?" Wu Quanheng, Zhu Qing, Kang Daisha, all of them my friends, laugh when I ask them. "It is not a question of belief. It was *necessary* for us to keep courage, morale, and Zhou put it in the best way. We survived *because* we adopted this attitude." There were droughts in North China and floods in South China. No meat, no eggs, no bean curd, no milk. . . . Ways to produce food were devised. Schools, factories, administrative offices, universities, bureaus, organized their own transport corps to outlying communes to get food for their employees and families. Gardens, parks, courtyards, became vegetable plots. City balconies sheltered hen coops; hens could be seen walking up and down the stairs of apartment houses. Each window sprouted pots growing cucumbers, potatoes, tomatoes. . . . Zhou refused to have his rooms heated during the harsh winters. He worked in an overcoat with a muffler around his neck. Deng Yingchao wore earmuffs and padded cloth boots. Office heating was cut to two hours per day. No coal.

I traveled. Noted the industrial collapse. Smokeless factories. The new steel plant in Wuhan had stopped functioning. "Repairs," the bland-faced director told me. No cooking pans, no scissors, no thread, no matches, no paper, the cotton ration per person down to one meter a year. (Newborn babies, however, received fifteen meters.)

Zhou appeared on BBC television in an interview with the English correspondent Felix Greene at the end of 1960. He repeated China's view on relations with the United States, her stand on Taiwan. "There is no conflict of interests between us and America. We are ready to negotiate. . . . Taiwan is Chinese territory and our own internal affair." He spoke as a man in full control, both of the internal situation and of external affairs. After the interview he said to Greene, "Why are you so worried? All your questions are worried questions. Look at me, I'm much older than you, and I'm not worried . . . why should you be?"

Not worried, said he. But he did not attempt to gloss over the situation when I talked with him that winter in his home. The room was very cold. I kept my fur coat on, my boots, my cap. Zhou wore two sweaters, but no overcoat. He was thinner, his collar was too large for his neck. He projected a disembodied, palpable intensity. The room seemed to vibrate with it. We both sipped hot water. He spoke steadily without looking at me, almost as if he were talking aloud to himself, as if he *needed* to relieve himself of a burden of words.

"You have traveled . . . seen some of our problems. But we have also had results, results that people don't know about. *Some people* would like to bring us to our knees, but we shall not give in. *Some people* think that all wisdom is theirs, that only they can interpret Marxism. I expect by now you have read a few of our documents."

I had. Millions of words were pouring out of Moscow against China, out of Beijing against "revisionism," in the theoretical dispute which went on and on.

"I now understand what it's all about," I told Zhou. He smiled. "Your rate of advance is increasing." He had not forgotten what I had said in 1956. "It is better to be slow and sure, *not hasty*," he said, in English. A film was being shown on Lenin, on the Russian famine of the early 1920s. "Lenin did not give in. . . . He never lost hope."

The subject of the Indian border came up again. Zhou had already settled or was in the process of settling similar undefined border problems with Burma, with Nepal and Pakistan. India was now being lauded—and courted—by both the United States and the U.S.S.R., and was receiving generous aid from both. Nehru had no reason to settle the Chinese border problem. "I tried everything I could, but I could not move Nehru at all," Zhou said.

He went into a lengthy discourse on economics. Shortages. Shortcomings. Achievements. He had asked me to tell him exactly what I saw during my travels. "We do not always get the truth from below. . . . We have to hear from all sides." By the way, did I know the difference between long-fiber and short-fiber cotton? I did not and had no rest until I learned. He spoke of pigs. Swept by the notion that Communism would supply all their needs, the peasants had slaughtered their pigs and gorged themselves with meat. "We have to breed larger pigs, to do crossbreeding. We must import those big white pigs they have in the West. We have to improve our sheep. We must pay more attention to cattle. We have many areas which could be used for cattle breeding, but our people are not herders, they do not understand cattle, only the national minorities do." There was a promising short-stemmed rice that did not break in strong winds, very useful in the typhoon-swept provinces of South China. The first institutes in biogenetics were being set up. "We have so much to learn. We cannot take an economic model from any other country and transplant it in China. The basic relationship of land to people is very different. We have very little arable land. To find our own model will take time. . . ."

He spoke of the liberation of the peoples of Asia, Africa, and Latin America. "The main contradiction in the world is *not* between the U.S.S.R. and the United States, but between imperialism and the peoples of these regions who struggle for liberation . . . and by liberation I also mean *economic liberation*."

It was in that winter of despond that I too became one of the "Zhou people"—in spirit, since I never joined any government or party. A workaholic. Committed not to Communism, but to China and her people's welfare. And for many years this was represented by Zhou. He was, for me, for so many, both the old China that we had known and the striving toward that unknown China to come.

China's situation was aggravated by the withdrawal, in July 1960, of 1,300 Soviet experts and the cancellation of all agreements under which the U.S.S.R. promised to supply scientific and technical assistance, supplies and equipment. Khrushchev's revenge. "The return of some Soviet experts is quite natural. . . . Surely, they cannot stay here all their lives," a calm Zhou told a puzzled Edgar Snow.

That fall, John F. Kennedy was elected President of the United States, and entered office in 1961.

"Readjustment, consolidation, filling out and raising standards," proclaimed Zhou in January 1961. With Chen Yun and other economists, and with the full backing of Liu Shaoqi and Deng Xiaoping, Zhou set out to put China back on her feet. "Agriculture as the foundation, industry as the leading factor. The scale of industrial development should correspond to the volume of marketable grain and the raw materials made available by agriculture." Proportionate growth among agriculture, light industry, and heavy industry. Retrenchment of the 60,000 small industrial workshops at the county level born during the Leap and the 200,000 at the commune level. This marked the abandonment of Mao's social mobilization, and was a blow to the initiative and enterprise of the common man, but there was no other way to manage the foundering economy.

Perhaps Zhou was right to say that "spirit" was essential to China's survival. Swifter than expected, there was improvement. A major triumph was the opening of the Da Qing oil field in Manchuria, which dramatically relieved China's dependence on the U.S.S.R. for oil. A jubilant Zhou spent five days at the oil field talking with the 5,000-odd demobilized soldiers who had accomplished the opening. Another cause for quiet rejoicing was Nie Rongzhen's cautious prediction: "Possibly, Enlai, within two years, we shall have solved the problem of nuclear energy."

But China had to reorient her trade away from the U.S.S.R. and toward the West. Could it be done? The United States had imposed a trade embargo in 1951, and all NATO countries had abided by it. Nevertheless, West German and British businessmen had begun quiet import/export dealings with China. In 1961, Zhou hoped that the new American President would initiate a fresh look at U.S.-China relations. He sometimes seemed obsessed with Kennedy. Theodore White, Zhou's old friend from Chongqing days, waxed dithyrambic about Kennedy. "Why?" asked Zhou.

On May 10, 1961, Kennedy assented to a Pentagon demand for an immediate deployment of American forces in South Vietnam. Most of Kennedy's entourage—save for Under Secretary of State George Ball—was loudly in favor of sending American forces to Vietnam. Kennedy had suffered a psychological setback with the disastrous Bay of Pigs expedition, and was meeting Khrushchev in Vienna on June 3. He had to appear tough, a man of guts. Zhou understood this, and chiefly blamed Dean Rusk, Robert McNamara, and the Pentagon hawks. The anti-China chorus from the President's men was so persuasive that even levelheaded individuals were affected. Averell Harriman described China as "more dangerous to the world than the Soviet Union," and the historian John Fairbank, who should have known better, argued that military containment of China, "on the Korean border, in the Formosa Straits, *and in Vietnam*, cannot soon be abandoned." "They say China is the *enemy*," Zhou said to me. "They don't know any history."

Yet Zhou was doing all he could on his side to "contain" the slowly growing Vietnam War. China could certainly not oppose the Vietnamese goal of reunification. Since the Geneva agreements had been sabotaged by South Vietnam's U.S.-backed regime, the decision to reunify by military means was taken in December 1960 at a meeting of the Party congress of the DRV together with the South Vietnam Liberation Front. "The liberation of the south is as important a task as the construction of socialism in the north." The war of liberation had begun. Zhou had promised help, but he was cautious. No Chinese volunteers would be sent. "The Vietnamese are perfectly capable of liberating their country by their own efforts, through a people's war, through protracted war," he said. This meant low-key guerrilla operations, slow attrition. No spectacular, professional military campaigns. Did Zhou hope that Kennedy had noticed and understood China's cautionary advice to Vietnam? If anything could further bedevil China's nonrelations with the United States, it was hostilities in Vietnam and the attribution to China of Vietnamese militancy. "Kennedy is more warlike than Eisenhower," remarked Zhou. "He is engaging in what he believes will be a small, containable war."

Zhou's last confrontation with Khrushchev took place in October 1961, at the Twenty-second Congress of the Soviet Communist Party. In the vast hall of the Kremlin, under the immense crystal candelabra, the world's Communist Party representatives had assembled. Zhou led the Chinese delegation. Few came to shake hands with him. Albania, China's staunch supporter in the quarrel with "revisionism," had refused to attend. Maurice Thorez, the head of the French party, made unpleasant remarks about China. Khrushchev ascended the rostrum, and in his speech directly attacked Albanian "dogmatists." In the political jargon of these assemblies, "Albanian dogmatists" meant China, just as in Chinese speeches "Yugoslav revisionists" meant the U.S.S.R. Hammering each word, pounding his fist, Khrushchev said that the U.S.S.R. would not give in on questions of principle to the Albanians "or to anyone else." All eyes were upon Zhou, who sat, phlegmatic, arm flung over the back of his chair. Three days later Zhou counterattacked. "We believe in unity. There should be absolutely not one word or deed to harm this unity. Any public, one-sided censure does not help. To lay bare a dispute, openly, in the face of the enemy . . . can only grieve those near and dear to us and gladden our foes."

The next day, after laying wreaths on the tombs of Lenin and Stalin, Zhou left Moscow.

"We need ships, we must buy ships, lease ships . . . one day we shall build our own ships." Japanese ships were bought and chartered. A new port, Xingang, was built, facilities of others were enlarged. Zhou met every Japanese delegation or group that came to Beijing, including Ping-Pong teams and chess players. He again invited to dinner ex-emperor Pu Yi and his brother Pu Jie; the latter's wife, Lady Hori, was Japanese, daughter of the Marquess of Saga. He reinforced appeals to the Overseas Chinese, calling in person, with Soong Chingling, on prominent Overseas Chinese who lived in China. Though most Chinese were on short rations, Zhou decreed that extra rations of meat and oil be given to the Overseas Chinese. A special savings bank was set up to process

overseas contributions in foreign exchange. Hong Kong's importance to China grew with this decision to turn seaward and westward. Hong Kong's water shortage was solved by a new canal dug
for the purpose, bringing water from the Pearl River. "Hong Kong
must stay capitalist," said Zhou Enlai. In a speech on the economy
in 1962, Zhou boasted that most of China's debt to Moscow was
repaid. "Now," he said, "we must expand our trade exchanges
with capitalist countries."

In the summer of 1962, I learned from Indian friends that a projected push from India would occur and that it had Moscow's
blessing. "Oh yes," said Zhou. "We know that the Indian military
have made plans. But we have made our own plans. . . . We do
not want war, but we shall not be bullied."

Border clashes between Soviet and Chinese patrols in Xinjiang
province occurred in July 1962, and 40,000 of the Uigur minority
in Xinjiang, at Moscow's urging, fled to the U.S.S.R. At the same
time, Moscow was encouraging India's so-called forward policy of
inching step by step into Chinese territory.

In September, Nehru made a speech in Madras, in which he
used the phrase "throw the Chinese out." On October 10, he
called for military action.

Indian troop movements, in both the eastern and the western
sectors of the border, had begun in May. Now prestigious General
Kaul, one of Nehru's favorites—a Brahmin from Kashmir, as
Nehru was—went on the offensive with 30,000 troops. Zhou
solemnly warned Nehru three times, imploring him to "withdraw
from the brink of the precipice," but to no effect.

On October 21, the well-prepared Chinese divisions returned
the Indian attack, and within a fortnight had routed the ill-
prepared, ill-equipped Indian forces. The Indian army had performed pathetically, and hysteria followed in India.

On November 18, Zhou announced that the Chinese would
withdraw unilaterally to ten kilometers *behind* the McMahon Line
in the eastern sector. The Chinese returned all captured weapons
and ammunition and buried the Indian dead with full military
honors. Three thousand prisoners of war, including eleven officers,
were returned to India with their weapons intact.

This extraordinary magnanimity dumbfounded the world. It
provoked a split in the Indian military. General Kaul was retired,

with Nehru's regrets. Defense Minister Krishna Menon resigned. And Nehru never recovered from his miscalculations. His self-respect was shattered.

The unilateral withdrawal was immediately identified by all Chinese in China and abroad as a replay of the classic contest led by the same Chuke Liang of *The Empty City*. Every child in China knows by heart the classic *Three Kingdoms*, in which Chuke Liang appears. In that time (220–280 A.D.) a prowling Burmese chieftain, Mon On, invaded China's territory. Seven times he was captured, and seven times released by Chuke Liang. "His heart was touched, and at last he swore eternal friendship," goes the tale. Zhou's action was in this grand tradition. But I doubt whether Nehru appreciated being likened to a Burmese marauder.

Nor were some Chinese commanders happy with Zhou's imaginative way of dealing with the situation. They muttered that the territory they had conquered—rich land, with fine weather, like eternal spring—had been China's before the British put it in India and that they should have been allowed to hold on to it. But Mao, a classicist like Zhou, was pleased. China's prestige in Asia was immensely enhanced. Six countries—Sri Lanka, Cambodia, Ghana, Pakistan, Indonesia, and the United Arab Republic—joined in December to urge negotiations. Nehru refused.

India benefited at the time from the presence in Beijing of its ambassador, P. K. Bannerjee. Bannerjee has written his memoirs of those years, and they afford a remarkable picture of Zhou as a human being. Bannerjee saw Zhou many times, in unrecorded 2 a.m. meetings. In January 1963, Zhou sent Nehru a verbal message through Bannerjee. "War has never really solved any problem. The need is to search for peace and for understanding. . . . I do understand Mr. Nehru's difficulties, but he must also try to understand my difficulties."

There was no answer.

In April 1963, I went to New Delhi to see Nehru again. "Premier Zhou holds you in high esteem," I said. "Thank you," replied Nehru. The rest of our meeting consisted of trivialities, Nehru painfully articulating an occasional "I see" or "Yes, India is progressing very well."

"I think Nehru is ill. . . . He is imprecise in speech," I said to Zhou Enlai when I went again to Beijing. Zhou was scathing. "He has been saying imprecise things for a long time." Neither Ambassador Bannerjee nor I ever told Zhou that, on receiving Zhou's friendly message, Nehru's reaction was: "I've had enough of Zhou's friendship."

When, in July 1963, Khrushchev scored a major political victory through the signature of the nuclear test ban treaty, Zhou vented his anger. "This is to keep a monopoly of atomic might between the two superpowers. There will be no disarmament, both will continue to stockpile nuclear weapons, but they are trying to stop everyone else from having nuclear know-how. It is like the bandit who sets fire to a house but does not allow an honest man to light a candle."

From then on, Zhou seems to have abandoned hope for a quick solution in Vietnam. It would be "a long-term, protracted effort." On August 1, 1960, he had proposed a peace pact between China, the United States, and other Pacific nations, and a nuclear-free zone in Asia and the Pacific. There had been no response. "Only the total interdiction and total destruction of nuclear weapons will do. But now, it seems only those who have nuclear weapons will be listened to."

By that July of 1963 the Ngo Din Diem regime in South Vietnam was politically bankrupt. Buddhist monks were burning themselves alive, and in the villages Ngo's officials were being killed at the rate of around twenty-five a day. In October, Ngo Din Diem and his brother were both killed—in a coup which was not opposed, and was perhaps instigated, by certain United States agencies and individuals. What would the United States do now? Once again, Zhou felt the stirring of faint hope. . . . But John Kennedy was assassinated in Dallas three weeks after the demise of the Ngo brothers in Saigon.

Right up to 1963, Zhou entertained the belief that if he could understand Kennedy, his character, perhaps a dialogue could begin, and trade, lifeblood for China, could improve. China was ready to open her markets to America, said Zhou. American businessmen on the West Coast wanted to do business with China and resented being cut out. He was right, as I found out.

During his friend Malcolm MacDonald's visit to Beijing at the end of 1962, Zhou had spoken to him at length of Kennedy. "There is no conflict of interests between America and China, *not like with some other countries.* . . . Is the U.S. President aware of this?" asked Zhou.

"He appears to hold some rancor against Kennedy. At times he sounded a bit bitter," Malcolm MacDonald told me. "I think he expected some sort of signal, some relaxation of the embargo. Now he seems to think Kennedy is too inclined to listen to the Russians, to ignore China. He may have a point there."

As late as July 17, 1963, Zhou, still baffled by the Kennedy phenomenon, had asked Ambassador Bannerjee, "What is so special about Kennedy?"

"He has charisma, he is youthful . . ."

"You talk like a stooge," Zhou snapped, then was immediately contrite. "I am sorry. I did not mean this. But everyone says the same thing. Nothing concrete. I want to know more." And then Kennedy was murdered. "I am sad and shocked," said Zhou. "Now we shall have to wait and see what Lyndon Johnson is going to do. . . . But there is opacity. It is like looking through a window thick with dust." American perception of reality, Zhou felt, was dangerously wrong. Could they not see that the heedless Vietnam War was turning into a hopeless quagmire?

It was in those years, 1962, 1963, that Zhou sent out of China a good many Overseas Chinese. "You can do more for the Motherland abroad. Our diplomats are confined to the embassies. . . . They know little about the people. We need persons who understand other countries," he remarked to one Overseas Chinese. "Tell the people you meet that we want trade, we want good relations, not war." When he learned that I was going to lecture in the United States in 1964 and for the next four years, he gave me a long lecture, going right back to the Dixie mission in 1944. "Please tell the Americans that we have never been against a United States presence in the Pacific. That is a fact we have to live with. But Taiwan is part of China, it cannot become an occupied protectorate under the United States. Nor can there be two Chinas. Chiang Kaishek and we are in total agreement on this point.

"Some say we have a closed-door policy, that we isolate ourselves. It is not true. We want to open doors. But both superpowers try to isolate us. We are doing all we can to approach other countries, but we are kept out. We want to trade with *all* countries, even if diplomatic relations have not been established."

19

China's economy was recovering. Zhou had competent, hard-working men in charge in various ministries and departments. But, like scrupulous housekeepers making sure all is in order, he and Deng Yingchao went to the nuclear research center in China's Xinjiang province. Nie Rongzhen was with them, and Zhou was satisfied that Nie had all he needed. On no account must this project be taken over by anyone else, least of all by the Ministry of Defense. He also discussed with Nie the newly installed missile-making sites in the hinterland. "Without him, nothing could have been done," Nie Rongzhen told me in 1988. "Comrade Enlai told me, 'If we don't make a loud bang, we won't be heard.'" This was Zhou's prettification of Mao's remark that a loud fart draws more attention than a lecture.

In December 1963, Zhou began a seventy-five-day tour of Asian and African countries. Flying in a leased KLM plane incongruously named *The Baltic Sea*, Zhou set out with Foreign Minister Chen Yi to Rangoon. Rangoon was balmy in December. Zhou wore a Burmese shirt and *lungi*, went to the seashore to bathe (he could not swim, because of his arm). He visited Rangoon's magnificent gilded pagodas, offered Burma a $50 million interest-free loan. The Chinese ambassadors from Cambodia, Indonesia, and Sri Lanka came to meet him in Rangoon. Zhou detailed China's foreign policy strategy to them. The U.S.S.R. and the United States had signed the test ban treaty in July. Both now employed dissimilar, but equally disabling maneuvers to isolate China. Both must be countered. There was a need to refashion the image of China; the brief conflict with India in 1962 had aroused doubt in certain countries, which must be dispelled. Zhou was intent on organizing another Afro-Asian conference, similar to that held in Bandung in 1955. To counter the global hegemony of the two superpowers, it was necessary to arouse that "intermediate zone," emergent from colonial domination, later to be known as the Third World. This time, Latin America must also be included. . . . China needed to know all these countries better, to expand relations and develop trade. Zhou had prepared an eight-point program of aid to these countries. Though poor, China was capable of helping others, and would do so. "We must break down the walls the two superpowers are trying to build around us. We must go out, be seen, be heard."

From Rangoon, Zhou and Chen Yi flew to Cairo. The Chinese ambassador there, Chen Jiakang, was discomfited, for he had to warn Zhou that Nasser was not there to greet him. The Soviet ambassador in Cairo had threatened to cut off a major loan should Nasser show too much friendliness to the Chinese. Nasser had suddenly had urgent business, but turned up with profuse apologies some twenty-four hours later. Zhou appeared totally unflustered by the lapse. He tried to persuade Nasser to sponsor a second Afro-Asian conference. Nasser remarked that the U.S.S.R. should be invited . . . it backed so many Afro-Asian organizations. (The Afro-Asian writers' meeting in 1962, in Cairo, had been the scene of fairly violent polemics between pro-Chinese and pro-Russian writers.) "The U.S.S.R. is a European, not an Asian country," said Zhou Enlai. "This is embarrassing," Nasser replied. There were also the matters of India, of Yugoslavia. Both Nehru and Tito were Nasser's good friends. The three had been prime movers in the Nonaligned Movement. But China was condemning Tito as revisionist, and there had been a clash with India. "I was chagrined when I heard of the conflict between brother nations," Nasser said. This was not a propitious beginning. "It is good that we should know clearly how our friends feel. Criticism should always be welcome," Zhou replied, and proceeded to explain at length the India border problem. . . . Nasser's attention wandered. Didn't Zhou understand that the matter had to do with the Russian loan, with Nasser's own problems? Zhou was taken to see the Aswan Dam, built by the U.S.S.R.—surely not a tactful gesture. He had a heavy nosebleed on the way up to the hydroelectric plant atop the dam. He stayed for an hour, bleeding fairly profusely, then was taken back. He managed to obtain a vague commitment to a second conference from Nasser, who said that "in principle" only African and Asian nations should participate, but left open the question of the U.S.S.R.'s Asian origin.

Zhou left Cairo for Algeria. In Algiers a great welcome awaited him. Ahmed Ben Bella embraced him vigorously, called China "Algeria's best friend." China had been the first country to recognize the Algerian provisional government and to extend aid to the liberation forces. The site for the intended conference was selected: Algiers. After signing the usual communiqué, Zhou went on to Morocco, to a courteous, if rather stiffly formal welcome, then flew to Albania for a rest over the New Year.

Zhou spent ten days in Tiranë. Albania survived because of aid from China. A powerful radio transmitter was set up in Albania to relay Chinese broadcasts to Europe. Zhou explained to Enver Hoxha his concept of a broad "united front" against both the U.S.S.R. and the United States, both now "imperialist." "Even kings, princes, aristocrats, are patriotic," said Zhou. It was on the basis of patriotism, national liberation, that the intermediate zone—the Third World—would achieve independence and progress. De Gaulle was more farsighted and patriotic in some respects than French Communist Party head Thorez. Zhou insisted that each country was free to choose its own regime, but it must not be used as a pawn in the contention and collusion between the two superpowers. There could be legitimate and good relations between capitalist and socialist countries, based on the principles of peaceful coexistence. Hoxha was shocked, and later would describe Zhou as a man "always ready to compromise." Zhou met some Romanian diplomats in Tirana and harped on the "great-power chauvinism" of the U.S.S.R., which had led to the tragedy of Hungary in 1956. Romania had also adopted an attitude of quasi-independence from Moscow.

From Albania to Tunisia, where Bourguiba was brutally frank. China's vehement diatribes discouraged potential friends. "You want us to be an enemy of the West. You have a conflict with India. You condemn Tito and also Khrushchev. Others won't tell you, but I will. You won't get far in Africa with this kind of talk." Bourguiba regarded the test ban treaty as "hope for humanity." Zhou thanked him. "This is true friendship indeed, to speak your mind so openly. You have helped me to understand the situation." He then set forth China's analysis of the existing conjuncture. Bourguiba was a good listener, and though he did not agree with Zhou, diplomatic relations were established the following day.

On to Ghana, where, at the airport, Zhou learned that a coup was in progress. Kwame Nkrumah was hidden in his well-guarded mansion, afraid of being murdered. Zhou improvised. "No need for the President to come out to meet us. In time of danger, we must show our support." The Chinese delegation drove straight to the presidential palace. It was in Ghana that Zhou made public the eight-point program for Chinese economic and technical aid to developing countries. Because of the attempted coup, a number of newsmen were present, and Zhou received more coverage than he expected.

On to Mali, Guinea, and the Sudan, taking in Africa's immensity, the diversity of its landscapes and peoples. Zhou was amazed, appalled, at the extent of the Sahara Desert. "I had not realized it was so large. We in China must take care. We have deserts too. We must learn to control them." Forthwith a letter went back. The Chinese Desert Institute must study thoroughly causes of desertification, must send out experts to Africa to learn about desert formation, must increase tree planting in Northwest China to stem the invading sands. . . . An open motorcade through Khartoum, the capital of the Sudan, had been arranged, and Zhou, brushing off his security men, said, "We must abide by our hosts' arrangements," and with Chen Yi he rode bareheaded in an open car.

In Khartoum he spoke against colonialism, recalling the British military man Gordon of Khartoum. "He was known also as Chinese Gordon, because he killed so many Chinese. We must thank you for ending his life before he could do more harm."

There was still trouble in Kenya, turmoil in Uganda and Tanzania. Zhou went on to Ethiopia, to Somalia, stressing that Africa had "excellent prospects for revolution. . . . We share the same pulsation. . . . Our common objectives are national independence and development."

But this was 1964, not 1955. There was revolution fatigue in Africa. There were power struggles between military cliques, afraid of being toppled by other cliques. Even if the African heads of state spoke with hatred against white colonialism, they did not want local uprisings against their own rule. Zhou was told of his faux pas some months later by gentle, unassuming Julius Nyerere of Tanzania. "I did speak of revolution, but I did not say *when* it would take place," amended Zhou Enlai.

On February 2, 1964, he was back to spend the Chinese New

Year—called in China the Spring Festival—in Chengdu, Sichuan province. Deng Yingchao was there to greet him. Chengdu is lovely in the winter, with almond and magnolia in blossom and a clear, cool sun. The harvests had been good, and promised to be even better that year. Zhou had many friends in Sichuan, having spent so many years in Chongqing before liberation in 1949.

On February 14, he and Deng Yingchao went on to Rangoon, and from there Zhou sent another message to Nehru, again suggesting a meeting, but obtained only a polite refusal.

Protest notes, a paper war, had hurtled back and forth between India and China and would continue until Nehru's death later in 1964. In a sudden 2 a.m. colloquy, Zhou had said to his friend P. K. Bannerjee, "I have received seventeen protest notes from your Ministry of Foreign Affairs today." Bannerjee replied, "Your Excellency, today happens to be my birthday, and I was gratified to receive twenty-three notes from your ministry." "Zhou laughed like a child, he could not stop laughing," Bannerjee told me. "On another day, Zhou picked up a protest note from India and showed it to me with an Indian map of the border and a Chinese map. 'Your ministry has alleged violation of territory at a certain place which does not exist. Neither on our maps nor on yours can we find such a place.' It was hard to explain to Zhou that Indians thrive on vagueness and inaccuracy."

Nehru was a master politician, for whom words were tools to discard, twist, reshape facts. Words were not to assert, but to blur inconvenient reality. He deliberately cultivated nebulousness, was often deliberately vague, because it served his purposes. Whereas Zhou painstakingly lined up facts, ticked off topics, working toward a conclusion, Nehru ignored details, mantled facts in high-sounding abstractions, and probably never looked closely at any maps. Zhou strove for precision, accuracy, order. He sometimes interrupted himself, rose from his seat to walk across a room and put a tablecloth straight or shift a vase. It is a tragedy that these two brilliant men never really understood each other.

From Rangoon, Zhou and Deng Yingchao flew to Pakistan, where Ayub Khan entertained Zhou most royally and put a Pakistan Airlines plane at his disposal. "Let me talk to Nasser. . . . I'll bring him around," said Ayub, offering unstinting support for a second Bandung conference. The friendship and alliance between China and Pakistan was reinforced. Previously, Zhou had refused any commitment on the problem of Kashmir. The state of Kashmir, at the partition of India and Pakistan, was supposed to exercise the right of self-determination, to join either India or Pakistan. But Nehru, although at first agreeing to this, now refused. Zhou switched from neutrality on the issue to support for "self-determination."

To Zhou's chagrin, the Vietnam War escalated. The Tonkin Gulf incident, in which American vessels were allegedly attacked in the night of August 2–3, 1964, by North Vietnamese boats, gave President Lyndon Johnson a pretext to obtain congressional approval for committing more American troops to the war. The bombing of North Vietnam—"bombing them back to the Stone Age" was the way some hawks described it—the use of napalm on villages, of defoliating chemicals over rural areas, began at this time.

September 10, 1964, and a lovely autumn afternoon. Zhou and I sat in his living room, the windows open and a blackbird thrashing in the trees outside. "Should the United States invade North Vietnam, *then* we shall be *forced* to consider this a threat to ourselves," said Zhou Enlai. "We are of course helping Vietnam with what she needs for her just war of liberation. We are confident that the Vietnamese can liberate their own land entirely through their own efforts. . . . But the entry of American troops into North Vietnam we shall consider to be a hostile act against China. . . . We have made full preparation for this as well."

There was the constant danger of a loss of "clear thinking" in Washington, said Zhou. What would Lyndon Johnson do next? "The Americans cannot win this war. The logistics are against them. The people are against them, and soon the people in America will realize this."

Two unrelated, but major events shook the world in October 1964. One was the fall from power of Nikita Khrushchev on October 15. The second was China's first nuclear explosion, on the following day. China's bomb immediately changed her status in the eyes of the world's nations. "*Enfin*," said de Gaulle. France had recognized China in early 1964. Only the Algerian War—concluded by 1963—had held up diplomatic relations. Georges

Pompidou wrote: "Immediately China's situation in the world was changed. Now there is only talk of her being seated at the United Nations, for her participation at such and such a conference. . . . The moment approaches when the United States will have to recognize the People's Republic of China."

Zhou announced the news on October 16, to the Standing Committee of the National People's Congress. On her own, counting only on self-reliance, and with the "correct policies of Chairman Mao," and the heroic work of China's scientists, she had achieved this breakthrough. On October 17 he cabled all the heads of state in the world, calling for a world conference "for the total interdiction, total destruction . . . eradication, of *all nuclear weapons*, including our own." There was no gloating, no parade of triumph, but obvious prideful joy. Despite the embargo, despite the total lack of aid, despite the "sabotage" by Khrushchev, China had reached atomic club status.

With Khrushchev out, would relations with the U.S.S.R. improve? Zhou flew to Moscow on November 5 to meet Khrushchev's successors, Brezhnev and Kosygin.

The meeting was at first cordial. Moscow proposed to resume aid to China—in that year China had repaid all of the Russian aid received—to normalize relations, on condition the verbose flow of invective stop. It became obvious that there was no change in the U.S.S.R.'s policy of sharing global hegemony with the United States.

There was also a Russian angle to the Vietnam War. Before his downfall, Khrushchev had queried the Tonkin Gulf incident, almost adopting the American version of the event. This had greatly angered Hanoi. Kosygin flew to Hanoi in February 1965, anxious to reestablish good relations. However, he told Pham Van Dong that Hanoi should not "provoke" the United States, and hinted at negotiations. The Vietnamese was indignant. Was over 100,000 U.S. troops in Vietnam not provocation? And the hail of American bombs which fell on Hanoi the day Kosygin arrived, what was that but provocation?

On his way back to Moscow, Kosygin stopped in Beijing (February 6–9) and saw Mao and Zhou. He proposed that polemics should stop, and suggested "united action" to aid Vietnam. This meant transit rights through China for Russian war matériel, an air corridor for Soviet planes, the use of Chinese airfields and the admission of 500 Russian technicians, passage for 5,000 military advisers to North Vietnam. Mao refused point-blank to stop the polemics and rejected "united action." "This is another hoax," Zhou said. China would convey Russian war matériel, but *no* Russian technicians would be allowed in China.

Due to different railway gauges, the equipment had to be unloaded from Russian trains, placed on Chinese trains for the journey across China, then transferred again to narrower-gauge Vietnamese trains. This proved to be a considerable strain on China's rail system, but it was preferable to having Russian "interference" in China.

Ho Chi Minh came to see Zhou, quietly and privately. The problems facing Vietnam were indeed grievous. Zhou reassured him. China would not let Vietnam down. In Wuhan a banquet was prepared for Ho. The two men spoke nostalgically of their youthful days in France, and again in Wuhan, in 1927. Ho Chi Minh had, after a few months at the Whangpu Military Academy, been assigned as secretary to Comintern agent Borodin. And where was Borodin now? Dead, purged by Stalin. Zhou talked of the Comintern, of the errors which had proven so costly to the Chinese revolution. Did the Vietnamese really need 5,000 Russian advisers who knew nothing about the country or the terrain?

At the end of the meal Ho Chi Minh looked around for a toothpick. There were no toothpicks on the table, nor in the hotel. With a small flourish, Zhou opened the flap covering the top pocket of his jacket, and produced a toothpick, wrapped in paper, for Ho Chi Minh.

"You really never forget anything. You remembered that I use toothpicks. You are really a great man," said Ho. "I am only the first among China's waiters," replied Zhou Enlai.

Whether he convinced Ho that the U.S.S.R. plan for "united action" was only a trick "to use this war for their own purposes," we do not know. But Zhou had carefully set the terms, the conditions, for China's help to the Vietnamese. It could *only be won* if it was played the way China had outlined. Mao's strategy of a people's war. Anything else was foolish, and dangerous, not only for Vietnam but also for China.

A major meeting of all Communist parties had been planned for June 1965 by Khrushchev. The intention was to rally the parties to expel China from the "socialist camp." Zhou demanded that all the splinter, pro-China groups in various Communist parties in Europe and elsewhere should be acknowledged, and also that China attend the conference. The talks broke off. They were the last that a major Chinese leader would hold with Soviet leaders for the next twenty-four years, until the visit of Gorbachev to Beijing in May 1989.

On landing at the Beijing airport, Zhou was greeted by a happy Mao Dzedong, with a large bouquet of convolvuli, which he handed to his Premier. Zhou, at least, was not "pro-revisionist," not like some other colleagues of Mao in the top leadership.

China's new clout brought a flood of delegations, many of them Japanese. The latter always performed the ceremony of apologizing for Japan's behavior in China during the war. "Please do not apologize. The war hastened the crumbling of our old system, increased our patriotism. We should thank you."

No longer were the Russians welcome in China. Stories of their inefficiency, high-handedness, and greed circulated. The wives of technicians had bought literally kilometers of cloth in the special "friendship" stores. The dam constructed with the help of Russian engineers on the Yellow River in 1959 was almost totally silted up. Zhou went to the spot to inspect the damage and make a decision. "If there's really no way to evacuate the silt, we'll have to blow the dam. No one dares to say this, because it has cost us so much. But let's think of the worst." Somehow, an ingenious way to remove part of the silt was devised by the Chinese engineers with him, and Zhou seized the occasion once again to laud China's scientists, to emphasize the value of the intellectuals. "There is no way of achieving a strong socialist economy without scientific progress. . . . We need a strong army of scientists to do this."

Zhou went to Djakarta in April 1965, on the tenth anniversary of the Bandung conference, to confer with Sukarno. All seemed set for a renewed attempt to launch a second Bandung. In June 1965, Zhou flew to Tanzania, to meet Julius Nyerere. Nyerere had visited China and admired Zhou a great deal. A Catholic, he found in Zhou the same commitment to humanity's welfare as in himself. "Zhou does not seek power. That is his most admirable quality, but it is also, possibly, his greatest weakness," said Nyerere. Zhou proposed to Nyerere, within the eight-point aid program, the building of the Tanzania–Zambia railway, which would free Zambia of reliance for transport on the Republic of South Africa. Other countries, including the U.S.S.R., had refused to build it. It took six years to complete.

Leaving Tanzania on June 8, Zhou flew back to China, to watch the launching of China's first missile in the Taklamakan Desert. On the nineteenth, indefatigable though now sixty-seven years old, he was again in Cairo. Misfortune struck. On that very day a coup took place in Algeria, and Ahmed Ben Bella was deposed. Zhou still wanted to hold the Afro-Asian conference, arguing that the coup was "an internal affair," but Nasser refused. Despite Ayub Khan and Sukarno, nothing could be done, and the project was abandoned.

More trouble was to come. In October, a right-wing military coup took place in Indonesia. Close to a million people were massacred and the Indonesian Communist Party was annihilated.

Here the usually careful, prudent Zhou was either badly informed by his diplomats in Djakarta or overly optimistic. The Indonesia Communist Party had 3 million adherents. It looked very strong, but it was very loosely organized, as my own contacts with Indonesians, including D. N. Aidit, the head of the Party, had convinced me. On the other hand, the Indonesian army was disciplined, well organized, and very well equipped. I had seen the tanks roll on the streets . . .

The army won, and Sukarno was retired. Relations between China and Indonesia became very tense, and broke down completely in 1967. Only twenty years later did attempts at normalization of relations begin again.

In the autumn, I spoke again with Zhou Enlai about relations with the United States and about the Vietnam War. I was going to the United States in January 1966 to attend a seminar at the University of Chicago on U.S.-China relations. The economic situation in China had improved remarkably. Food was now more abundant. Though 16 million tons of wheat had been purchased —from France and from Australia—China was selling rice to offset wheat purchases.

Zhou was back to his usual weight, and he appeared far more confident on the Vietnam issue. He repeated that even with "half a million U.S. soldiers in Vietnam, or more, this war cannot be won.

"I have said again and again that we want to be friends with

America, that there is no conflict of interests whatsoever between America and China. But we cannot sell out our friends, nor can we compromise on the subject of Taiwan."

He spoke of Vietnamese tenacity, of their long and fierce desire for independence, going back to the third century A.D., when two women, the Truong sisters, had led a war against the Chinese. On a visit to Hanoi, Zhou had insisted on paying his respects and bowing to their memory in the temple erected to them. "The Americans must understand that this is a people's war. All the people are with the Liberation Front. The Americans set up one 'strongman,' one warlord, after another, not one of them even up to Chiang Kaishek's standard. Americans can trust no one in Vietnam, certainly not their so-called friends. They will put in more men, more big guns, but one day they will have to go away." Some British experts had suggested surrounding all the villages in South Vietnam with barbed wire, as had been done in Malaya during the emergency. "But this won't work in Vietnam. In Malaya the Chinese were barbed-wired in their villages, guarded by Malay police, but in Vietnam they are one people." There was logistics too. American mobility was confined to drivable roads, while the Vietnamese could move anywhere, everywhere. And there was the psychological element. "The American people are not geared to long-drawn-out conflicts with indecisive ends. They want quick results. Pretty soon American families will ask for their sons to return. And this time, no other country sympathizes. There is no moral support for this war."

Zhou's grand tour had met with mixed success. He failed in his attempt to hold another Bandung, and could China really carry out her eight-point program and all it promised? But he had projected an image of China as independent and daring, which, with the decisive break with Moscow and the explosion of China's own atomic bomb, had made her a leader in the Third World. By sheer willpower, it seemed, he had pulled China from the brink of economic disaster and widespread famine, and set her among the nations of the world as a force to be reckoned with. "It was the song of the empty city, and he *became* Chuke Liang," those who knew him would later say of his performance during those years.

Nevertheless, at the end of 1965 Liu Shaoqi criticized both Zhou and Chen Yi for their conduct of foreign affairs, for the failure of the Afro-Asian conference and the handling of the situation in Indonesia. But this criticism was part of the power struggle between Liu and Mao which had been brewing in the Party since 1959 and which would culminate the next year in the Cultural Revolution.

V
1966–1978

The Cultural Revolution
The treachery, flight, and death of Lin Biao
The Nixon opening
The Gang of Four
Zhou's death
Epilogue

20

Mao Dzedong had seemed to accept with good grace the winding down of the Leap carried out by his Premier and by his Vice-Chairman, Liu Shaoqi. He even mentioned, in a conversation with General Montgomery, that he knew very little about economics. Reassertion of Party control had strengthened Liu's position. It was partly Mao's own fault, since in 1955 he had handed over routine Party affairs to Liu. That Mao felt he was being increasingly bypassed and ignored is obvious from his own remarks. "They acted as if I were already dead."

But the restoration of control carried within itself the seed of further turmoil. "The Party structure at the time came into sharp contradiction with the requirements of developing productive forces, and the democratization of the state . . . and thus led directly to preparing the ground for the Cultural Revolution," write some scholars of the Academy of Social Sciences.

There was little alternative for Zhou. He collaborated closely with Liu and Deng in reinforcing central control, even if he was against Party arbitrariness. He was caught between two evils, the reestablishment of order and the threat of further disequilibrium such as the Leap had caused. He tried to incorporate some elements of the Leap's mass motivation and initiative into readjustment to democratize the process of government, but without success. Decision making, on all major and even minor issues, now rested with committees at every echelon, run by Party secretaries. The Premier, who had wanted to release discussion and initiative, found himself having to decide on all matters great and small, many of which could have been decided at a lower level. "You must learn to make decisions yourselves. Not everything should be referred to the top for approval," he said, but after the zigzags of the Leap and its aftermath, very few in the Party's middle and lower echelons wanted to be held responsible for judgments that might prove controversial. Even the law courts, never anything but timorous, were now subject directly to local Party committees. Liu's selected cadres were gradually filling all major posts in the provinces and the major cities. Whoever came into office could oust the cadres below him, replacing them with his own supporters. "Good comrades are being replaced. . . . One group removes great numbers of other cadres, and brings in new ones. It becomes an *unprincipled* struggle as to who is to be in power," accused Zhou Enlai. But the ideological phantasms of the Leap produced a backlash of skepticism and self-seeking among a good many middle-rankers. Still, small doses of democracy crept in. In the factories, enthusiasm among workers was replaced by material incentives. Piecework became one of the main stimuli to increase industrial productivity. In agriculture there was liberalization of control. Accounting returned to the village level, and private plots were guaranteed, their income belonging entirely to the peasants. Though the communes remained, their role was weakened. They proved useful in maintaining schools and public health services, and in mobilizing peasant labor during the slack season to repair roads, reservoirs, dikes, and to dig wells.

Mao was not happy with the trend toward strengthened Party control which automatically led to a rigid bureaucracy endowed with a prodigious capacity for self-multiplication. He might have put up with an administration that functioned adequately, had not what he thought was an offensive against him, intended to remove him from power, begun at the time.

In January 1961, the mayor of Beijing, Peng Zhen, initiated a review of responsibility for the Leap. His subordinates, following his orders, gathered evidence, and the conclusion was that "the lower levels should not be blamed for the mess." The main cause of the mistakes made was the loss of touch with the masses, said the report. It was "a mistake in line." This was a serious accusation. Mistakes in line brought down many a top leader in the Party's history. During the Cultural Revolution, Peng Zhen was accused of deliberately trying to place the responsibility for the Leap's failure upon Mao. After the Cultural Revolution, in the major review undertaken, Peng Zhen was exonerated of any such attempt.

Zhou's opinion in this survey of responsibility does not appear to have been solicited. He was known to object to head-on ad hominem attacks within the Party, for such struggles had been both savage and occasionally sanguinary in the past. His emphasis on discipline, on the need for competence, made him an objective ally of Liu Shaoqi, but he did not try to improve this rapport with Liu at Mao's expense. Some streak of traditional loyalty, an integrity of the heart, did not allow him to join in any attack against Mao.

In January 1962, a major reassessment of the Great Leap took place. An enlarged work conference of 7,000 Party cadres from central, regional, provincial, district, and county echelons, together with Party secretaries and managers of several large industrial plants, assembled in Beijing to hear Liu criticize the Leap. "The situation is disastrous . . . the economy on the brink of collapse. . . ." The Leap was 70 percent man-made disaster and 30 percent natural calamities. Liu defended Peng Dehuai for his criticisms of the Leap. "It is not an offense to speak one's mind, to state known facts at Party meetings."

The conference lasted from January 11 to February 7. Zhou praised "those who speak the truth, energetically take action, and carry out correct decisions." "There has been a bad tendency in the Party for the past three years. There is not enough democracy. Our aim is to liberate thought, to abolish superstition, to dare to speak, to think, to act. But now people don't dare to speak or to act, though of course they still think. If there is freedom of criticism, mistakes can be rectified. . . . We cannot have only one voice in authority. . . .

"Comrade Mao asks us to seek truth from facts, but in recent years there have been a lot of lies. People first look at the color of the leaders' faces before opening their mouths. The fault lies with us, the leaders. We bear down too hard upon you [he was addressing provincial delegates from Fujian province]. We must speak the truth, encourage democracy, strengthen it in the Party. *This is the thought of Mao Dzedong for Party building.* In our economic construction, successes are important, the defects secondary, as Comrade Liu Shaoqi himself points out." Thus quoting Mao Thought to Mao, quoting Liu back at Liu, Zhou Enlai circumvented both, then gave everyone a public lesson on how to behave as a good Party member by starting an exemplary self-criticism of his own work in the State Council. "I must bear total responsibility for the mistakes made there," he said.

But Liu Shaoqi seems to have been more on the offensive. He

exhorted intellectuals to "air your views . . . vent your feelings."
Satirical pieces, articles, and essays against "would-be emperors"
appeared in increasing number. To believe they were spontaneous
expressions from free intellectuals is somewhat naive, though undoubtedly there was an element of release in such effusions. But
they would never have been published in the official press without
political backing. There was now a division in the Party press.
Some newspapers and magazines, *Red Flag, Liberation Daily*, were
run by Mao supporters. Others, such as *Frontline, People's Daily*,
were under Liu's men in the Ministry of Propaganda or Beijing's
municipal officials.

Liu Shaoqi was not only a very efficient Party man, a seasoned
veteran of trade union organizations and of committees; he was
also reckoned a Marxist theoretician. In Yenan his works had
helped to establish Mao's supremacy and Mao Thought. Now,
close on the heels of reprints of Mao's works came Liu's works.
In one of his essays occurred the following sentence: "No member
of our Party has any right to demand that the rank and file should
support him or keep him as leader." This had been written in the
1940s to counter Wang Ming. It was being repeated now. A favorite innuendo—heard several times from several quarters—
caught the ear. "Chairman Mao, Chairman Mao . . . surely he
wasn't born with the word Chairman tacked on to him?"

Was Liu Shaoqi pro-"revisionist"? Mao certainly thought so. In
December 1960, a conference of eighty-one Communist parties
had been held in Moscow. It was part of that great theoretical
battle between Mao and Khrushchev. Liu had led the Chinese
delegation, and in six speeches had only mentioned Mao once.
The conference had ended in a compromise statement of inor-
dinate verbosity and vagueness. Zhou Enlai gave me a copy for
"study and comment." All I could say was that it appeared self-
contradictory. I would never know whether this remark was apt
or not, since Zhou never mentioned the document again. Certainly
Mao felt that Liu had given way to "revisionist" Khrushchev.

Zhou avoided being snared in the growing confrontation. He
was far more of a technocrat, in the modern sense, than Mao or
Liu. He understood that a new technological revolution was trans-
forming the world, that computers, space exploration, biogenetics,
were bringing about far-reaching social changes. With unswerving
tenacity, in those few years between two volcanic eruptions— the

Leap and the Cultural Revolution—Zhou once again put together the "front" of the intelligentsia. Liu Shaoqi was also keen on rehabilitating "rightists."

On March 2, 1962, Zhou had addressed a large assembly of several thousand scientists and rehabilitated "rightists." He extolled "the criticism *with good intent* which you have formulated in the past," thus implicitly condemning the campaign against the rightists. He went on to criticize the "left tendency" which had smashed the concept of the Hundred Flowers. But now this concept must be revived, there must be a Hundred Flowers again— and on a permanent basis. "Intellectuals have endured many hardships . . . they must have the right to free discussion." He addressed himself to the non-Communist parties. "Remember that you have the right to assemble, to recruit members, according to the constitution." Some of his speeches at the National People's Congress bear quoting even now. "Our *main task* is . . . within a reasonable historical period, to build up our country with modern agriculture, modern industry, modern defense, modern technology." A decade later, in one of his last speeches before his death, Zhou repeated this call for the *four modernizations* of China.

"We cannot afford to lag behind. We must use advanced technology to build up our country. *This is the true meaning of the words 'leap forward.'* It is in the process of economic construction that we can unfold mass movements. . . . Of course, the performance of tasks should be discussed by the masses."

A sop thrown to Mao. But how, through what organizations or structures, could the masses "discuss"?

Mao's counterattack had come in September 1962, at the Tenth Plenum. "What will you do if revisionism appears in the Chinese Party?" The main problem, he said, was the danger of "capitalism" within the Party itself. The Party was becoming an elitist bureaucracy, divorced from the people, an elitist apparatus. Liu and Mao openly clashed. Zhou, attempting to mediate, found an enraged Mao turning against him. "It is people like you, middle-of-the-roaders, who are a threat to the Party's revolutionary spirit." Zhou showed no resentment, made no rejoinder. "Accept disgrace willingly; then you can be trusted to care for all things," says the master of Tao.

Mao had won, and had resumed an active executive role in policy making. He had launched the Socialist Education Movement

(SEM) with the idea of once again shaking up the Party *from below*. There was to be planned interchange of Party cadres. Those at a higher echelon should "go down to lower levels" to do manual labor, experience real contact with working people, and accept criticism from the lower-level cadres and from the people. The downward transfer was accompanied by the setting up of peasant committees at the base, and giving these committees the right to criticize the upper cadres, to air their grievances and discontent.

The SEM became an extremely complex affair. Liu and Deng mastered the process by apparent compliance. Actually, they deflected the whole experiment; they organized "work teams" of higher cadres, who went down in a body to lower levels, not to listen and labor, but to "lead" movements to "correct errors," which then became systematic purges against low-level cadres. The campaign soon degenerated into a crudely simplistic way of punishing, replacing, transferring men at the base, while the higher officials went quite untouched. Zhou had been on record for protesting against the way the SEM was carried out. "Many good cadres are simply punished or got rid of. . . . One batch of people is replaced by another one." All this had done nothing but precipitate even more bewilderment and resentment at lower levels. "The leaders put a lid on. Mao, during the Cultural Revolution, took the lid off," a friend of mine, Xin Jiang, also drafted into these campaigns, told me.

It was impossible for Liu Shaoqi and Deng Xiaoping to accept any real challenge or criticism of the Party apparatus. "Whoever is against the Party is a counterrevolutionary," Liu flatly declared. If the masses rose against the Party, then it was a counterrevolutionary plot. For him, the Party was the revolution. Not for Mao. If a party went rotten, became corrupt, no longer represented the people, then the people had the right, nay the duty, to rise against it. And it was one of Mao's last injunctions, before his death, to say that he called on the Chinese people "to rise against the Party" should the latter degenerate.

Zhou Enlai had had very little to do with the SEM. His absence on travels, his multifarious activities, had not allowed him to participate. But he had given a great deal of attention and time to the educational institutions. These were training the heirs and successors of the revolution, and Zhou was finding out, with dismay, that the sons and daughters of high Party cadres exhibited a total lack of social conscience. He had lectured them severely. Among the educated young there was abhorrence of any work that looked manual, a throwback to the old traditional contempt for toil. Young students in universities were ashamed to acknowledge that they came from humble peasant or worker origins. Zhou favored including manual labor in the school curriculum. He ordered batches of young people transplanted from their cocooned lives in the large coastal cities to the hinterland where new cities, hospitals, industries, universities, were growing. "We are breeding a generation of would-be bureaucrats. Every one of them dreams only of having his backside screwed to a safe chair until his death and wearing a fountain pen in his jacket pocket," Chen Yi said to me with brutal frankness. "The intelligentsia must be respected, but they must earn this respect by working for the people," said Zhou. There were now millions of middle school graduates coming on the labor market. How, where, could they be employed if they all wanted to become office pen-pushers?

The SEM had gotten nowhere. Mao had been outplayed. He turned to the army.

Under Defense Minister Lin Biao, who had succeeded Peng Dehuai, the smart uniforms, the gold braid, copied from the Soviet Union, all had gone. Officers and men again wore—approximately—the same garb, distinguishable, however, by the quality of the cloth and also by the leather shoes, highly polished, worn by officers.

Into all administrative and Party offices now came small groups of soldiers, led by demobilized veterans. Every plant, factory, bank, post office, unit, enterprise, institute, university, ministry, even the foreign-language press, had its modest, eager, smiling young soldiers, coming to "learn" but also to teach the virtues of the PLA. Self-sacrificing army heroes became models for the young. "Learn from the army" was the new slogan.

This investing of Party apparatus by army groups was merely a preparatory step for the vast campaign Mao had in mind.

Zhou Enlai seems to have become alarmed. He went to see Mao Dzedong. Although the SEM had been managed "in an unprincipled way, merely a struggle over who is in power," yet it was also incorrect to *overestimate* the danger of "capitalism" in the Party. "It is not unavoidable." But Mao Dzedong had made up his mind that he was going to get rid of Liu Shaoqi, and of all Liu's men as well. . . .

In the winter of 1964 Edgar Snow had been in China. He had asked Zhou whether he could have a talk with Liu. "Now why should you want to see him?" Zhou had asked. Snow had reminded Zhou that it was through Liu's cadres of the Northern Bureau that he had reached Yenan in 1936. Zhou had arranged for Snow to be present at a banquet with Mao and his wife, Limpid Stream, Liu and his wife, Luminous Beauty, and Zhou with Deng Yingchao. Everyone had been there, all very friendly and talking amiably with each other. "Now you've seen them *all*, haven't you?" Zhou said to Snow at the end of the party. Snow had inferred that Zhou had not particularly wanted him to meet and talk with Liu Shaoqi. The American had never realized that this would have been a deep insult to Mao Dzedong, who considered Snow his own friend.

Why could not Liu Shaoqi, with all the support he had in the Party, with Deng Xiaoping on his side, do to Mao what had been done to Khrushchev in a Party caucus in Moscow? Liu also had his supporters on the Military Affairs Commission, even if Mao was its chairman. Why did he not "displace" Mao? Did he try?

Liu's attempts seem to have been forever halfhearted, even if tenacious. He and Deng did bypass and ignore Mao, and often issued directives without consulting him. But they never really came to grips with engineering a total overthrow of Mao. Perhaps they underestimated the man and his visions.

Chief of staff Lo Ruiqing, tall, handsome, and bold, from Sichuan province, was one of the vice-chairmen of the Military Affairs Commission. He now challenged Mao. He produced in May 1965 an article that praised the Soviet Union for having won the war against German fascism. He indicated that the next threat of war came from the United States, and every other issue was secondary. He argued for Chinese involvement in the Vietnam War. This article went against both Mao's and Zhou's views. Only a few days before Lo's article was published, on April 29, Zhou had again stated: "If the U.S. imperialists do not invade North Vietnam, if there is no invasion above the 17th parallel, China will not provide troops. . . ."

In September 1965, Mao had begun in earnest his attack against his opponents. For some time, Mao had been speaking of the need for a "Cultural Revolution." Chinese books and plays, he said, were infested with all that was perniciously capitalist or feudal. There must be a change in thinking, in behavior, in attitude. Zhou Enlai had talked to me for some two hours about the idea of this Cultural Revolution. "Our need is for a total change in outlook. . . . The aim of revolution is to change man himself," said Zhou. He talked of it as if it were a spiritual exercise, something to be achieved by conscious effort of will, an educated discipline of the mind.

Mao chose to begin by targeting a play shown in Beijing. It was written by Beijing's vice-mayor, Wu Han. The hero was Hai Rui, an official of the Ming dynasty, who had boldly upbraided the emperor for his misdeeds. All too clearly, the allusion was to Peng Dehuai, or so Mao chose to see it. He demanded that the matter be investigated. A five-man team, with Peng Zhen heading it, was to carry out a major inquiry in the domain of culture, beginning with this play. In November 1965, a young polemicist from Shanghai named Yao Wenyuan, who had become a favorite "pen" for Madame Mao's literary campaigns, wrote an article attacking the play. It was published in Shanghai, but Peng Zhen refused to publish it in Beijing. Zhou went to see Mao in Shanghai, where the Chairman now spent a good deal of time, avoiding Beijing, which had become Liu's stronghold. He received Zhou affably in the new mansion surrounded by acres of park constructed for him. Yes, he told his Premier, the article should be published "to begin a discussion on art and literature." Zhou returned to advise Peng Zhen, and an introduction to the article, which, some say, Zhou agreed to, made the point that this was in order to start a debate and to distinguish good from bad literary works. The five-man Cultural Revolution group dragged its examination of the play through the winter. Mao called a Central Committee meeting in December, and denounced Lo Ruiqing. Lo's article was "revisionist." It was Zhou who was entrusted with the very unpleasant task of interrogating Lo and "reeducating" him. Lo was a friend of several of Zhou's inner circle of friends, such as Chen Yi. Zhou had many talks with Lo, since Zhou was vice-chairman of the Military Affairs Commission and Lo the chief of staff. Lo appeared to be in favor of "unity of action" with the U.S.S.R. over Vietnam, against the resolution taken by the Central Committee that there would not be unity of action. Lo maintained steadfastly that he did not oppose Mao Dzedong. His real testing time would come

in March 1966, when he was questioned by other army commanders and tried to kill himself (March 18) by jumping from the
upper story of the building where he was detained. He survived,
though a badly shattered leg had to be amputated.

In February 1966, Liu Shaoqi chaired a meeting of the Politburo's Standing Committee, to hear Mayor Peng Zhen and the
five-man Cultural Revolution group read their Outline Report
concerning the play about Hai Rui and its creator, Vice-Mayor
Wu Han. Four of the five exonerated Wu Han of any willful attack
against Mao or socialism. "We must not behave like scholarly
tyrants, always arbitrarily attacking others," courageously stated
Peng Zhen.

Zhou attended the meeting. He had been busy throughout December and January with conferences on cotton output, on transport, on afforestation. He had toured drought-ravaged areas in
North China. He was studying plans for another big dam on the
Yangtse River, not at the site originally contemplated. There were
plans for bringing Yangtse River water to the water-deficient rivers
of the north.

Peng Zhen personally took his Outline Report to Mao, then
wintering in the city of Hangzhou. He returned to say that Mao
was satisfied with the report. But it was not so. On March 28,
Mao called a meeting, at a time when Liu Shaoqi and his wife were
away on a state visit to Pakistan and Afghanistan.

The only man on the five-man team who had dissented from
the conclusion was Kang Sheng, the chain-smoking, sinister security head, who once again would come into the limelight. On
April 16, Peng Zhen was suspended, as were the Minister of
Propaganda and the Minister of Culture, the editors of various
national newspapers under Liu's wing. . . . Liu was present. Had
he then defended Peng Zhen with the same courage which Peng
Zhen showed in defending his vice-mayor, had he rallied his
supporters, perhaps Mao could have been stopped. But Liu was
no strategist. He hesitated, gave in, did not defend Peng Zhen,
perhaps feeling Mao's anger would be content with the mayor's
overthrow.

On May 4, 1966, Mao called a meeting in Beijing. Zhou was
away in Manchuria with an Albanian delegation from April 26 to
May 11. Little is known of what went on at the meeting, apart
from the fact that Mao had brought in a large majority of his own

supporters from Shanghai in order to outnumber regular Party
men. But when Zhou returned, it was very clear to him that he
was once again caught in the middle of a major power struggle,
this time between the President of China, Liu Shaoqi, and Party
Chairman Mao. The Cultural Revolution had begun.

For Mao, contradiction was a permanent state of things, equilibrium between contradictory forces temporary, disequilibrium the
normal condition of the universe. He was convinced that the Party
machine under Liu and Deng no longer represented the people.
It had become an elite caste of bureaucrats. The army—until taken
in hand in 1964—was changing; not a people's army, but a "club"
of privileged officers. Renewal, Party rejuvenation, could be
achieved only by a surge "of the masses, and from below." The
Cultural Revolution was a fire in which all that was impure in the
Party would be burned, and Party members should welcome going
through the crucible to renew their revolutionary ardor. "Many
of us did believe that we had erred, that we had indeed become
complacent bourgeois. I cannot explain why we thus believed, but
there was something so tantalizing in what Mao said . . . perhaps,
for us, it became a collective hypnosis," I was told by Yen Wenjing,
an official of the Writers Association, whom I have known for
some three decades.

Zhou Enlai and the other leaders of the Party were confronted
with a situation that left them baffled, helpless. They had paced
history's cunning and contrived corridors, had endured and survived the traps and pitfalls of many an intra-Party struggle. They
had fought for years in the wilderness, and known triumph and
disaster. But somehow, there had always been certain safeguards,
a certain community spirit with Party rules, Party discipline. Now,
however, all of this was wrenched away. How could they have
guessed that their own Party chairman, Mao, would engineer the
ruin and the downfall of his own Party's top-ranking echelons, and
call upon the raw, untried youth of China to help him in this
phantasmagoric assault?

Liu Shaoqi, second after Mao in the Party, looked upon as Mao's
heir and successor, must have become uneasily aware in that summer of 1966 that he had somehow sacrificed Beijing mayor Peng
Zhen in vain. He appears to have continued to believe that Mao
would not push to extremes, that the Party apparatus was strong

enough to withstand Mao in the end. "It was Liu's personality, his own personal honesty, which failed him," Yang Xianyi, one of China's well-known intellectuals, said to me. "He had no adroitness, no imagination. He had a big nose, the nose of a stubborn man, but he had no sense of humor. Zhou had all of that. Zhou could talk, and shone with integrity and conviction. Liu could only speechify, or harangue. He could not persuade. Zhou could laugh, be debonair. Liu found it difficult to laugh, and his only reaction to a joke was a strangled hm-hm.

"But Wang Guangmei, his wife, was beautiful," Yang continued. "Luminous Beauty, his fifth wife. She dressed well, and she began to act as 'first lady,' for was she not the wife of the President of China? In a country where jealousy, envy, what we call the 'red-eyed disease,' is so prevalent and powerful, she outshone other wives, especially Mao's wife, Jiang Qing."

In a country where the first virtue is self-abasement, Luminous Beauty was carelessly joyous, intelligent, good-looking. On trips abroad, she would smooth over conversations with heads of state when her husband's stiff inability to communicate made things awkward. And this made it even more difficult for Liu Shaoqi in the end.

Did Zhou Enlai try to warn Liu Shaoqi about Mao? Liu obviously underestimated Mao Dzedong. He did not realize what Zhou had grasped, that Mao was almost an elemental force of nature, disregarding "all laws of heaven and earth," comparing himself to the Monkey King, who produced "a great uproar in paradise, upsetting all the bureaucrats in heaven." Since the Tsunyi meeting in 1935, Zhou Enlai had been Mao's friend and opponent, implacable shore curbing the unpredictable ocean. But he too appears to have been hypnotized, for a few months at least, by the grandiose vision of a revolution within the revolution, a renewal. For he knew that the Party was both aging and becoming corrupt, increasingly a rigid bureaucracy, and that the Socialist Education Movement of 1963–65 had failed to bring young blood into its caucuses.

In that summer of 1966, all was poised in dangerous suspense. In July, an Afro-Asian Writers' Emergency Conference was held in Beijing, and there I saw Zhou Enlai, looking dapper. "What are *you* doing here?" he asked me, in the direct way he had with people he felt he could trust. "I'm an observer," I grinned. For, as a "bourgeois writer," I could not be allowed in the majestic cogitations of the dedicated participants. Zhou looked away, and I could tell that he was reassured. What was wrong with the meeting? I wondered. Yet he was there, and to the sessions and the banquets came Liu Shaoqi, and Soong Chingling, and also Chen Yi.

During that July, a curious, loaded charade was taking place in the universities, directly linked with the conflict between Liu Shaoqi and Mao Dzedong. With Mao's ambiguous approval Liu Shaoqi had sent "work teams"—i.e., Party cadres of proven worth—to the universities, to carry out the Cultural Revolution and to dig out the revisionists and the bourgeois among Party academics and administrators. But just as the work teams during the Socialist Education Movement had protected the Party cadres of the Liu-Deng machine, so it became clear that the teams were sent to divert attention from the real targets, and of course to heap contumely and condemnation upon the unfortunate professors, lecturers, those who had no "backing" and could thus become easy victims. Pretty soon the methods of the work teams stirred a good many students against their professors. My niece tells me, "In our school we were told to beat our teacher. We did, and he died."

It soon became clear to me that, amid the Afro-Asian writers, many were not writers at all, but foreign students from the universities, recruited to attend the conference, and not witness what was happening to their professors and fellow students.

It also became obvious that this conference was contrived. Contrived in that, at the meetings, certain of the participants tried to push, along with the Vietnamese delegation present, for "united action" in Vietnam. The Japanese delegation also urged united action. This was the line taken by the U.S.S.R., which Mao furiously repudiated. Was Liu trying to mobilize some support for himself through this conference? What was the game being played here? A few days later, Liu made a speech in which he pledged support to Vietnam, including "military help if needed." This went directly against Mao's determination—clearly enunciated by Zhou—that China would *not* be involved in a second Russian-engineered war against the United States, another "Korean" conflict.

Wading in a bog of confusion and ambiguities, the "writers" and myself were taken to Wuhan, where I would be among those who saw—some were told, because they were too far away—Mao swimming in the Yangtse River, while our boats sailed its majestic waters. It was July 16. Mao was back in Beijing on July 18, to denounce Liu's work teams and what he called the "fifty days of terror" imposed by them upon the universities.

From August 1 to August 12, a session of the Central Committee of the Party was held. But it was an "enlarged" session, which meant that it also comprised people Mao co-opted to attend, among them his supporters in the Group in Charge of the Cultural Revolution, or GCCR, which had been organized in a reunion of the Politburo—also at an enlarged meeting—on May 18. Also there were teams of revolutionary students recruited by Mao's secretary, Chen Boda, now head of the GCCR, and Mao's own wife. The bona fide members of the Central Committee were outnumbered and overborne. It was at this meeting that a sixteen-point program for the Cultural Revolution, first discussed in the May meetings, now acquired definite form.

Zhou Enlai fought, fought over many of the sixteen points or clauses. At least ten of them were altered due to his intervention. Together with him fought Tao Zhu, former Party secretary of Guangdong province, considered at the time a staunch Mao sup-porter and suddenly elevated to the Politburo and to the GCCR. Zhou crossed through the sentence in a clause which asserted that there had been, continuously, "a black line in the Party for the past seventeen years," operated by "a black gang." These words, said Zhou, were totally inappropriate. There had not been a black line or a black gang opposing Mao in the Party since 1949. But he was overruled by Lin Biao and the members of the GCCR. With Mao's approval, he would add a limiting formula:

"Meticulously distinguish between the two kinds of contradic-tions, antagonistic and contradictions among the people." This reference to Mao's major article of 1956 was important. It would exonerate the overwhelming majority of Party cadres and also cast some doubt on the accusations against Liu Shaoqi himself. Were the latter's crimes really "enemy" contradictions, or merely inac-curate, faulty understanding? Zhou also underlined: "The majority of the cadres are good or relatively good, and we must unite with at least 95 percent of them." This had to be kept in mind. The "black gang" was only a small minority. Tenaciously, he added, and was successful in getting it included, a clause to protect sci-entific and technical personnel "who had made contributions." He hoped to wrap a mantle of safety around his scientists, those engaged in atomic research, those in the biogenetic laboratories, the physicists in the universities and technical institutes. Nie Rongzhen and Tao Zhu strongly supported him in this, and Mao was persuaded as well. A major clause was one which, with Zhou fighting to get it included, would be penned in by Mao, in his own hand. *"Struggle must be conducted by reason, not by force."* This meant that no violence should be used, and it was to be the most disregarded clause in the program. As Nie remarked later, in his memoirs: "Every political movement in the Party has been accompanied by exaggeration and distortion . . . so that many individuals suffered instead of a few. This was not Mao's intent." But one of the features of Chinese Communist Party statements, directives, programs, is their vagueness. The "spirit" of the document must be seized, but that spirit can be interpreted in many ways, according to the understanding of the Party official in charge. Even today, each Party secretary, each official in charge, echelon by echelon, can interpret a directive in his own way, twisting it to fit into his own preconceptions.

Zhou renewed the objection he had already made in May to the term "capitalist-roader in the Party." "Within our Party the struggle has been between a right and a left line. . . . There has never been a capitalist road within the Party," he said. If such a phrase was used, then many resolutions, policies, adopted by the Politburo and the Central Committee since 1949 would be tainted with ambiguity. "Capitalist" might mean anything. "Do you mean to say that if a peasant sells a few eggs privately, he is a capitalist?" But Mao would not change the term.

Zhou, in the months to come, and in his many speeches during that first, violent period of the Cultural Revolution, would find a way to get around this mind-boggling phrase. Capitalist-roadism "has never been the dominant Party line," he announced. It was only practiced "by a small handful." He boldly continued to say that "it is a question of lack of understanding . . . therefore it is a contradiction among the people." This was heroic of him, because it made of Liu Shaoqi's errors merely lacunae, which could be corrected, but did not necessitate the utmost penalty.

Yet Zhou had no particular liking for Liu Shaoqi. In fact, Liu had tried to bypass him in handling external affairs. Zhou was not battling for Liu alone. It was the whole of the Party that he was concerned about.

As the meetings continued, the members of the GCCR hurled accusations at Liu. During one of these abusive sessions Zhou Enlai would acidly comment that, surely, there must have been something wrong with the Rectification Movement of 1942–45 in Yenan if, suddenly, so many "traitors and renegades" were discovered in the Party. Zhou's sarcasm cannot have been lost on Kang Sheng, now adviser to the GCCR, and so very useful for the next round of the Party's internecine struggle because of his control of the files. Kang Sheng had been one of Liu's supporters during the Yenan Rectification Movement, when Liu's Northern Bureau cadres had been spared and attacks centered on the Wang Ming group and on other bureaus, including Zhou Enlai's. Kang Sheng was now the most thorough prosecutor against Liu Shaoqi's "capitalist-roadism."

Liu admitted that he had made mistakes during the fifty days that the work teams operated. He made a self-criticism, but rejected the notion that he had acted as a capitalist-roader since 1949, since his previous actions had received the approval of the Central Committee.

He went on to argue that "the masses cannot rise against the Party without becoming counterrevolutionary." This view was diametrically opposed to that of Mao, who believed that the masses, the people, were entitled to rise against a party, even a Communist party, if the latter became corrupt, or "capitalist."

Spinning a strand of nuanced reasonableness, Zhou Enlai argued that the masses "are only correcting the errors of a few Party members, not the Party itself." The notion of the Party itself being overthrown he too could not accept. This sentence upheld the ultimate authority of the Party, just as he insisted that the Party, "with the help of criticism from non-Party elements," must correct itself by accepting criticism—an idea which went back to the Hundred Flowers Movement in 1956. But Mao would not deviate from his decision that the Party could only be rejuvenated by launching a populist, mass movement, against the Liu-Deng nomenklatura.

To protect the scientists, his main concern, Zhou had to let go of the Ministry of Culture, which with the Ministry of Propaganda, the press media, once strongholds of Liu and Deng, now passed under the GCCR. In Education, Zhou lost control as well, though he tried, through Foreign Minister Chen Yi, to keep the Foreign

Language Institute and various schools for the training of future diplomatic personnel.

He kept, for a while—until their personnel were sent away for reeducation—the State Planning Commission, the Economic Institute and its departments. He also kept the Foreign Ministry under Chen Yi until mid-1967. He tried to protect individual artists, opera singers, actors, and writers. So many of them were his friends. So many came to his home to share his frugal "two courses, one soup" meals. But here too he was unsuccessful. Except in the case of his good friend the writer Guo Moro. Guo Moro had been well warned beforehand, and he had made a resounding self-criticism in April at the Afro-Asian Writers' Emergency Conference, declaring that all he had written should be burned. He therefore survived unmolested through the following years, but not all writers showed the same alertness.

On August 18 the first half million Red Guards paraded in Tienanmen Square. There would be seven more parades in the next four months, altogether 15 million of China's youth. They came by rail from all over China and free of charge. They had to be lodged and fed. Inevitably, caring for those millions became the responsibility of Zhou Enlai, the man who could always be relied upon to see that everything was done, and done well.

Extensive democracy. Great criticism. Wall posters everywhere. Absolute freedom to travel. Freedom to form revolutionary exchanges. These were the rights and freedoms given to the Red Guards, and no wonder it went to their heads and very soon became total license. In that August the simmering Cultural Revolution exploded in a maelstrom of violence.

"None of us had imagined what fury would be unleashed. We were totally unprepared," Nie Rongzhen told me in October 1988 when we talked of these years. Seasoned in Party conflicts, the veterans were left gaping and demoralized by the volcanic eruption launched by Mao. "You call it chaos, perhaps it is right to call it so. I was as unprepared as you were," Mao candidly said to the other Long Marchers a year later. He had envisioned upheaval, "great disorder under heaven," to last for a few months, a year. He had not reckoned that he would lose control of the havoc he had launched.

From November 1966 until the end of his life, Zhou was on

cardiac medicines four times a day, suffering from arrhythmia, shortness of breath, and fainting spells. But after each spell, lasting a few minutes, half an hour, he would stand up, brushing aside his doctors, and though his hands shook and he was unsteady with fatigue, he would say, "Now let us go on."

21

"It is unimaginable. . . . Cold gooseflesh in summer," Zhou Enlai, in a rare outburst, said of the Cultural Revolution while he lay in bed, felled by a heart attack after twenty-two hours of being surrounded and shouted at by hordes of Red Guards. He had not faltered, had tried as usual to talk with them, to talk until his voice had failed him, and also his body. It was November 1966.

Why did the Red Guards become so violent, when so many of them were *educated* youths? It was precisely some of the better-educated ones who became savagely cruel. I have met many ex-Red Guards who today ask themselves about the infective ferocity that afflicted them. They were subject to massive propaganda, they heard inflammatory speeches from Lin Biao, from the members of the GCCR, but what they devised as ways of punishment were totally *feudal* methods, and this explosion of feudalism, its psychological implications, remains unexplored. Perhaps the Cultural Revolution provided them with a brutal catharsis; impulses buried deep under Confucian-Communist authoritarianism were released. Perhaps the brutalities against designated Party members liberated them from ages-old submission to the domination of elders, as well as the regimentation of the regime.

It seems that Zhou still nurtured hope that the marching, the shouting, the sloganeering, might exhaust itself swiftly, for at a Politburo Standing Committee meeting in September, he promoted a resolution that "the problems of production must be attended to," a ploy to limit the actions of the Red Guards. On September 27, Zhou told the State Council that the Party must maintain control; authority was not to pass into the hands of the mobs. Until October 1, Zhou appeared to believe that the Party might be strong enough to channel and control the Red Guards. "Surely, the Premier will now readjust the situation?" one anxious university president hopefully asked Chen Yi, who simply made a little head movement, neither yes nor no.

On that October 1, Zhou's hopes were shattered by Lin Biao's speech. Lin Biao was now the sole vice-chairman of the Party, and everywhere Mao was, there was Lin: thin, sallow-faced, a cap firmly screwed upon his bald head, trotting behind the ever more portly Mao.

"We shall strike down those in authority who are taking the capitalist road. . . . We shall strike down strike down strike down all the old culture old customs old habits. . . ." Lin said each phrase three times for more effect. In a voice reedy with exhaustion, Zhou would follow with his speech, praising the Red Guards but reminding them that they should struggle "by reason, not by force."

Deliberately, Lin Biao, and also Jiang Qing, as well as the more extremist of the GCCR group, called the Wang-Guan-Qi trio, pushed the young into violence. They ransacked houses, beat Party members and officials, hauled them off to kangaroo courts, grillings which sometimes lasted days or weeks, without allowing them any sleep, working in relays to keep their victims awake.

Within each institute, organization, unit, and also in the ministries, "revolutionary rebels"—i.e., cadres or employees of lower rank—assaulted their superiors in the name of smashing "capitalist-roaders." This made Zhou's running of the government extremely difficult. One after another his ministers and department heads were attacked, or hauled away to be "struggled against," which might mean anything from hours of grilling to being physically mauled, and dying.

Zhou's telephone rang day and night with appeals for help. One of his secretaries suggested that the number be changed. "What? Then how will they be able to find me?" said an indignant Zhou Enlai. Hundreds of letters a day reached his office, imploring him to intercede, to save. . . .

For he remained the pivot, a man who could intervene, and did. He ran the State Council, and the government, while increasingly his staff diminished, his ministers disappeared, until he was reduced to writing his own correspondence by hand himself. At one point, his staff had dwindled from several thousand under his jurisdiction to a mere couple of hundred clerks.

He endured. The GCCR openly denounced Liu and Deng as

capitalist-roaders. Zhou had to take over and run the Party Secretariat when Deng Xiaoping was ousted.

"Destroy the four olds; erect the four new," was a slogan meant to encourage people to do away with old ideas, behavior, customs, and attitudes. But the Red Guards took it to mean such things as antiques and books, which they confiscated and destroyed in their house searches. Zhou tried to stop this. What was taken from the houses of individuals, whether bourgeois or Party cadres, must be turned in, must be stored in museums if valuable. And he directed the museums to be closed, in order to keep their contents safe. Zhou made lists. Of monuments and temples to be respected as national treasures. The Tunhuang grottoes, along the Silk Road, and many other old temples were thus saved, but in Tibet, in Yunnan, in Sichuan, the orders were ignored by local and provincial Red Guards. Zhou could not single-handedly roll back that brave new world which the young thought they were building by trampling upon their ancient heritage. He intervened to save people . . . but was too late to save all.

As the weeks passed, and the violence increased, life for Zhou was a waking nightmare. But he waved the Little Red Book, climbed in jeeps along with Kang Sheng and Jiang Qing, and shouted slogans as they did.

"Zhou Enlai said many things, did many things, which were against what he truly believed and felt . . . but he was keeping in mind the larger interest of the nation," Deng Xiaoping said of Zhou in later years.

"Comrade Zhou Enlai was caught between two alternatives, both of which required a total sacrifice of himself," Pu Shouchang, Zhou's secretary for many years, told me. If he repudiated the Cultural Revolution and denounced it, he would have become an anti-Party renegade, a traitor, a "monster." "And no one would have followed him." Then what would have happened to the Chinese people, to the economy, to the state? His disappearance would mean the triumph of the extremists in the GCCR—Lin Biao, Jiang Qing, Kang Sheng—and the collapse of the Party. With Liu and Deng ousted, no one could maintain Party authority, no one had the stature and influence, bar Mao, that Zhou Enlai had.

"Mao also needed Zhou Enlai," says another one of Zhou's aides, Zhang Wenjing, as we talked of "the beloved Premier." "Though Mao used the GCCR to create turmoil, he was too canny not to keep Zhou Enlai as a brake when the process of the Cultural Revolution would have run its course." "How shall we govern China without the Premier? It is quite impossible. He is the *house-keeper*," Mao repeated to all those who came to him with accusations against Zhou Enlai.

"Zhou kept in mind a long-term vision. He did not make a bid for power. He did not challenge Mao's preeminence. One day, when the turmoil was over, he would be there, putting everything back in shape," says Huang Hua.

"I think Zhou remembered the hero of his childhood, Han Hsin, the man who had crawled between the bully's legs," says another former ambassador. "Did not Zhou say in 1928, 'For the sake of the revolution, we must even become like a prostitute'?" He sacrificed himself, his honor and his repute. It was an agony he endured, unrelenting, through the months and the years. But he saved countless men and women. "Without him the situation would have been far more catastrophic," says economist Chen Yun.

"He shared with the people their sorrows and their misfortunes. He made the most difficult decisions, and he made them alone. The young today have no idea what it was like for him. Only those of us who were with him at the time know that he walked through the ninefold hell, and led us out of it in the end."

The ninefold hell. . . . To these survivors, there is nothing good in the Cultural Revolution. Yet, one day, Mao's wave of populism against the Communist bureaucratic machine might be appraised differently, as the Paris Commune has been.

But in 1966, 1967, it was indeed hell for many of the Party veterans. And all pinned their hopes on Zhou. "If I do not enter the tiger's lair, who will seize the tiger cubs? If I do not enter the mouth of hell, who will save the souls in hell?" said Zhou.

And so he pretended to be one of them, those who now crowded around Mao, and egged on the young Red Guards against the Party cadres.

From 1937 onward and throughout the years of his government, Zhou had believed in working with non-Communists. His first preoccupation was to save them from the violence deliberately aroused by the GCCR. He felt deeply responsible, for it was he who had brought many of these non-Communist intellectuals to side with the Party. He had seen them shamed, mangled, in the

1957–58 antirightist movement. Now, when in September 1966 the house of a well-known scholar was ransacked, Zhou wrote to Mao, who wrote back, "Let the Premier deal with this matter." Zhou took action. He not only had all the scholar's belongings restored and the house protected but also drew up lists of other "persons to be protected," using Mao's letter as authority. The list comprised Pu Yi, ex-emperor of China, his wife, dependents, and relatives, all the members of the National People's Congress Standing Committee, all the heads of the non-Communist parties, the judges of the Supreme Court, the chairman and vice-chairman of the PPC, as well as former Guomindang generals such as Tsai Tingkai and Fu Tsoyi. For those more seriously in danger, there was another device. Zhou sent them to the safety of Hospital No. 301, reserved for high cadres. The medical staff there fully understood the situation, and in collusion with Zhou discovered in their patients diseases which would not permit their leaving the hospital grounds. Years later many of these "patients" would emerge unscathed. On Zhou's list, in fact heading it, was the respected widow of Sun Yatsen, Soong Chingling. She was a ready target for the Red Guards, since she lived in a palatial mansion. The Red Guards had broken in, and wanted to cut off her long hair. Reached by phone, Zhou stopped them in time. He sternly lectured them on the lady's great contributions to China. To reinforce the lesson, he presided over a major rally of 20,000 in honor of Sun Yatsen's birthday in November 1966, and made sure that Sun's bronze statue and his mausoleum in Nanjing were protected.

A list of sixty-one Party members who had at one time or other been jailed by the Guomindang and then released was circulated. All of them were Liu Shaoqi's men, or so reckoned. They were now dubbed "renegades," for how otherwise could they come out alive from Chiang Kaishek's jails? They were to become targets for the Red Guards. Mao is said to have personally "dotted" their names. Zhou warned one of the men on the list, Bo Yibo, beforehand. The latter tried to flee, but was discovered and brought back to Beijing. He might have died had not Zhou managed to put him in Hospital 301. He is still alive today. But there were others among the sixty-one who were victimized. Finally Zhou Enlai went to Mao and confronted him directly. "The center *must* acknowledge past decisions of the Party; otherwise the center's authority will become insecure." The sixty-one had been released in an exchange, arranged with the Guomindang, approved by the Central Committee at the time. It seems that Mao Dzedong gave way on this point, and Zhou extended protection to cover many of these "renegades."

Zhou varied his tactics, using many devices to save a colleague. "He would sometimes severely denounce the person targeted, in order to get himself included among those who would pronounce a verdict. Then he would find extenuating circumstances." This tactic of "appear to blame, in reality exonerate" he had used in the past to save Liao the Sailor during the Long March. He now did it again for Liao, whom Jiang Qing particularly disliked because in 1937, Liao, then agent for the Party in Hong Kong, had, at the order of the Politburo, investigated her past. Blue Apple, now Limpid Stream, Jiang Qing, was going to make Liao pay for that report. He was accused of debauchery, assaulted by Red Guards, and would have died had not Zhou called him for "an urgent meeting of the Overseas Chinese Commission," and then installed him in his own house. For several weeks he refused to hand over Liao, warning that the Overseas Chinese would be very much alarmed. Liao went to Hospital 301. "Do you wish him to die?" asked Zhou of Madame Mao and her Wang-Guan-Qi trio when they demanded that Liao be handed over to them. "The Overseas Chinese will turn against the Cultural Revolution if he dies. Chairman Mao's directive on the Overseas Chinese must be respected."

Using the same trick, he tried to save Rung Guotuan, Vice-Minister of Sports. "Comrade Enlai called my wife 'Big Joy of Heaven' and my son 'Little Joy,' " Rung told me in 1987. "I always went to see Zhou in his office after lunch. This was the only time he had for a chat. Then we played Ping-Pong to exercise his arm. We all went dancing together, Zhou and Ho Lung and Chen Yi and myself. The three of them were all good dancers and good drinkers. Zhou liked people who were cheerful, not stiff, he liked to laugh."

Rung Guotuan was hauled off for trial in front of 6,000 Red Guards, to answer for his crimes in sport. To his astonishment, Zhou ranted publicly against him. "He read out a catalogue of my crimes. I was extremely upset." But after those imprecations, Zhou addressed the Red Guards. "This is the way we can help people in error. By attacking their souls, not their skins." Rung was saved from being possibly beaten to death, but he would spend the next ten years in jail. "For the first four years I sang opera to myself, recited poetry. I remained silent for the next six. When I came out I had forgotten how to speak." Rung still criticizes Zhou a little. "I think he became too fascinated by Mao."

Another man Zhou could not save was Li Lisan, who had been with him in Paris and headed the Party from 1928 to 1931, until displaced by Wang Ming and the Twenty-eight Bolsheviks. Li Lisan died in jail in 1967.

Ho Lung, handsome and debonair, with his English pipe, his beautiful suits, his flashing smile, was Minister of Sports. He very often came to Zhou's office, to sit quietly, watching Zhou work, comforting him by his presence, and occasionally poured him a cup of *mao-tai*. Zhou, now bereft of much of his staff, was like the captain of a ship in a typhoon, his crew washed away, trying single-handedly to pilot the ship, batten the hatches. "But he never had a word of self-pity. He simply did not speak even to me of these things," Deng Yingchao told me. Ho Lung asked no questions. He always put his pipe in his pocket when he went to see Zhou, knowing how Zhou hated the smell of tobacco.

Between Ho Lung and Lin Biao an old quarrel festered. It dated back to those fateful Rectification days in Yenan, 1942–1945. Ho Lung's wife was employed in the Party's security department, and was ordered to investigate Ye Chun, soon to become Lin Biao's wife. Ye Chun had worked for the Guomindang, and was suspected of being an infiltrator. Although she was cleared as Blue Apple had been cleared, Ye Chun still felt insecure. Suppose Ho Lung's wife talked? Or garrulous Ho Lung, making some joke about the past? A case against Ho Lung was built up.

Confessions about Ho Lung's misdeeds were extorted from his staff. There were mysterious rumors about his past. Puzzled and angry, Ho Lung complained to Mao, who laughed. "There's never been any problem about you." Never had the debonair Dragon been ambitious or involved in any power struggles. Ho Lung thought himself safe, but relays of Red Guards invaded his house, ransacked his belongings, and began to "struggle" against him and his wife. Zhou Enlai stepped in. "Marshal Ho is not well. He cannot be struggled against. If you want to discuss any problems concerning Marshal Ho, come to me." He sheltered the couple in his own house in Zhongnanhai. There was respite for some weeks, even though Zhou's other ministers were being hounded, disturbed in their sleep at night, paraded with dunce caps in the streets. Between bouts of ill-treatment at the hands of the young, these courageous men around Zhou Enlai would wash their faces, comb their hair, straighten their jacket suits, and return to their duties.

The spring of 1967 brought a campaign of vilification against Zhou Enlai. He now realized there was a deliberate plan to single out his friends for ill-treatment. Because he had praised Fang Yi, who was his special adviser on Vietnam and chairman of the Economic Council for Foreign Trade, Fang was repeatedly beaten about the head just before he was to meet a foreign trade group. Fang had a birthmark on his face and this was hit to make it bleed. Zhou sent him to Hospital 301. It was in that spring that the Wang-Guan-Qi trio of the GCCR set up a special group of Red Guards, called the May 16 Group, with the purpose of collecting incriminating material against Zhou. In April, they found out that Ho Lung was hiding in Zhou's house. Zhou sent Ho Lung and his wife to a hideout in the western hills outside Beijing. There the couple was safe for a while, but the hiding place was discovered. Ho Lung was incarcerated. A diabetic, and given no medical care, he died in 1969. He was seventy years old. Zhou grieved a great deal for Ho Lung, a congenial and devoted friend. Ho Lung was rehabilitated, his honor restored, in 1975.

The most harrowing event, and the least publicized, was the arrest and death of Zhou Enlai and Deng Yingchao's adopted daughter, Sun Weishi. Her mother had been an actress in Shanghai and had known Blue Apple, Jiang Qing. Sun Weishi had returned from the Stanislavsky School, where Zhou and Yingchao had placed her in 1940, and since her Russian was excellent she was an occasional interpreter for both Mao and Zhou, and at times for Chen Yi. In 1967 she was asked to produce evidence against Foreign Minister Chen Yi. She refused, and she and her husband were jailed in December. Weishi died in jail eight months later. Neither Zhou nor his wife could find out where she had been imprisoned. Told of her death, Zhou asked for an inquest. The reply was: "Dealt with as counterrevolutionary. Cremated. Ashes not kept." This cruelty is ascribed to Jiang Qing, who feared anyone who might have known of her past in Shanghai.

From the important to the trivial, Zhou Enlai was involved, was everywhere, did everything. He personally drafted editorials for the *People's Daily*, enjoining abstention from violence—to no effect. When the waiters of the Peking Hotel decided they would no longer clean the shoes or answer the ring of foreign guests, capitalists, or Overseas Chinese, the distraught manager appealed to Zhou, accompanied by a surly delegation of the "rebel" waiters. He had been talking to three Red Guard groups since ten o'clock the previous night, and it was now six in the morning. "Very well," said Zhou, looking at his watch. "I still have two hours before going to the airport to welcome a head of state. I shall now proceed to your hotel and clean the guests' shoes."

The delegation shuffled guiltily. Zhou lectured them. "You are hurting your country and the revolutionary cause by refusing to serve our guests."

Zhou is reckoned to have had, during 1966 and 1967, a hundred meetings with Red Guards. His speeches seem to toe the line, but always there is a nuance, a twist. He was an accepted spokesman for Mao, but in this role he had fierce contenders, Lin Biao, Madame Mao herself, and the Wang-Guan-Qi trio, dedicated to his downfall. His artfulness weaves right through every one of his speeches. He does not disagree with or contradict his colleagues, but he edulcorates, modifies, chips away at what they say.

He lavishes praise on Jiang Qing, and undermines every one of her diatribes. He praises the Red Guards, calling them "little generals." "You have been brought up under the Red Flag of Chairman Mao's Thought . . . Chairman Mao's Thought must guide your every action." He then expounds Mao Thought in the Zhou way.

Through his verbal marathons run three main topics. First, that everything the Red Guards do must be done with logic and reasoning, and not violence. Second, that revolution is for production, and not "the antithesis of production." And third, that class struggle did not mean defining a person by his class origin, going back three generations. "Many people who come from a bad class background can reform themselves . . . this is Chairman Mao's view." He gives himself as an example. "Born into a corrupt feudal family, but saved by following Mao Thought."

He ran China—whatever could still be run of it—and surprisingly he managed to keep it afloat. He also ran transport of war matériel to Vietnam. The war there was escalating, as President Johnson poured American troops into the country, until their number rose to half a million by 1968–69. Zhou Enlai linked up "aid to Vietnam" with a determined attempt to regain control of all transport in China, despite the dislocation caused by the Red Guards and their travels throughout the country without paying any railway fares. Dislocation was also caused by the rebels of the railway administration. The slogan "To Rebel is Justified" was one which allowed anything to be done, and never did Zhou have more trouble than trying to prove that "rebellion means increased production." He kept, however, his Minister of External Trade, Li Chiang, safe from the Red Guards by ordering him to inspect personally the Ho Chi Minh Trail. "And if you don't get there, don't come back." Of course, Minister Li got there, and stayed away a long time. Only in late 1967 did Zhou regain control over communications, road and railway transport.

In October 1966, Zhou prevented the Red Guards from burning down the Canton Fair. The fair, held once a year in Guangzhou —previously known as Canton—was open to foreign companies. It was an important component of external trade. It sold porcelain figures of classical heroes, copies of antiques, rugs and silks and embroideries, and machinery. Zhou harangued the various Red Guard groups of the city for days. The fair must not be touched. It provided foreign exchange "to help our heroic Vietnamese brothers against U.S. imperialism. We have to sell these old things abroad to help them, otherwise we shall fail in our internationalist duty." The next year, and the next, he made sure, by going personally, that all was well with the fair.

Rapier-thin, frail-looking, but formidable, the sixty-nine-year-old man fought on. Debilitating battles, week after week, month after month.

"Zhou Enlai led us out of hell. He fought the demons, one by one," say those who were there, who endured with him, who, as he did, lied to save others. Some voices are raised today among those who do not know their own history. "Why did he not stand up to Mao? The Party would have followed Zhou."

No, the Party would not have followed Zhou. Zhou was an intellectual, immensely liked, popular, but he was not a peasant, not a worker. Mao's charisma was enormous with the rank and file, who came from the peasantry. Liu Shaoqi and Deng Xiaoping might have controlled a strong bureaucratic machine, and how strong it was would be tested by the Cultural Revolution. But they could not win against Mao. Zhou had no chance to win, except by doing what he did, biding his time, and getting rid of the demons, one by one

22

Despite his multiple efforts to contain the turmoil of the Cultural Revolution within the cities, and in the cities to confine it to the universities and middle schools, Zhou Enlai found to his dismay that disorder spread widely to the factories and to the peasant communes. This imperiled the nation's economy. The situation was worsened by the steady flow of sulfurous speeches from Lin Biao and Jiang Qing. Lin Biao stated that *everyone*—except Mao and himself—could become the target of *extensive democracy*, the name given to the activities of the Red Guards. This meant that the State Council, the government, and Zhou Enlai himself were not to be spared.

Reckoning that, of the demons he had to contend with, Jiang Qing was probably the one he could handle best, Zhou attached himself to her for a while, fawned upon the lady, blunted her appeals to violence by fulsome praise, and in the process of lauding her speeches managed to give them an entirely different meaning. It was a virtuoso performance, and he repeated it many times. He would remind his audience that *of course* "to make revolution is *for* production." He waved the Little Red Book, shouting, "Let us learn from Comrade Jiang Qing." To puzzled Japanese visitors who asked his views on the events he said, with a bleak half smile, "An individual's personal opinions should advance or retreat according to the will of the majority."

Zhou also made a temporary alliance with Chen Boda, the nominal head of the GCCR, Mao's erstwhile secretary and editor of *Red Flag*. He was not gifted in cunning, and Zhou courted him with ingratiating deference. A delegation of Red Guards returning from a visit to Albania was to be greeted at the airport by Zhou and Chen Boda. But the chief of protocol, Li Lienqing, in charge of the arrangements, failed to notify Chen Boda that the plane had been diverted to another airport, though Zhou was notified. "Where is Comrade Boda?" asked Zhou when he reached the airport. Li said he had forgotten to tell Chen Boda of the change. "Premier Zhou's face became quite grim. He shook his head. 'Comrade, comrade, you don't know what injury you've done to me.' I was so unhappy," says Li Lienqing, who told me this story in September 1987, twenty years later. "Of course this lapse would be used against Premier Zhou. The GCCR was trying to find fault with him, all the time. He would be accused of deliberate sabotage. He would have to go through hours, days, of self-criticism . . . and I had done this to him!"

But the ever resourceful Premier's face cleared. "He had thought of a way out, for himself and for me. 'From now on, Comrade Lienqing, to save the valuable time of the leaders, only departing delegations will receive official send-offs. Returning delegations, such as this one, will be greeted on a more minor scale. Please announce this to Comrade Boda." Thus the faux pas was turned into consummate flattery.

By January 1967, 40 million workers were involved in the mounting anarchy. Forming their own "rebel" groups, they crowded the trains, demanding to be carried to Beijing to parade before Mao as the Red Guards had done. Zhou issued orders to curb the workers' travels. Only one worker from each small factory and two or three from large factories were allowed to come as delegates, the total number to be received at any time not to exceed three hundred. "It will not be possible to deal with thousands. This is harmful to production. It impedes transport and communication." Zhou addressed one hundred fifty or more industrial organizations and factories in December and January. He lectured several thousands of workers for nine hours on one occasion on the theme: "Make revolution by *promoting* production, not by lessening it." He dealt with the difficult problem of wages. Millions of temporary workers were being laid off. They turned themselves into "rebels," to promote "seizure of power" in factories, turn out the real workers—and get paid or pay themselves.

In that same January, a young worker in Shanghai named Wang Hungwen had organized his factory workers and overthrown the municipal government. The powerful Party committee of Shanghai had been eliminated, its members jailed. This feat attracted the attention of Jiang Qing and her closest associates, Zhang Chunqiao (Spring Bridge) and Yao Wenyuan (Preeminent Learning). Both of them were from Shanghai. Worker Wang Hungwen might prove a valuable addition to the GCCR, and they went to see him.

Mao intended to proclaim Shanghai a commune, on the model of the Paris Commune, which fascinated him because it was an example of seizure of power by the people, the masses, *without* a Party and without an army. It corresponded to his populist vision of what democracy should be, of what the people could achieve. But he changed his mind a few days later. Zhou Enlai, armed with facts and figures, and Chen Yun, the economist, bluntly told Mao that the fall in production was bringing China to ruin. Disorder had to be checked. On January 14, 1967, Mao decided to call on the army, the PLA, to restore order.

The PLA was enjoined to support the "left" or "revolutionary rebel" groups, and to take power from the Party machine at every echelon. But the Party was proving very strong, still solidly entrenched in the provinces. It was not easy to dismantle it. With great skill, provincial Party secretaries gave large bonuses to the workers, who then vouched for them as "genuinely left." They organized their own Red Guard groups, who fought against the Mao-inspired Red Guards.

This propensity for infighting among the Red Guards is not surprising. The same penchant for puerile violence is observable in many countries, including America and Europe today. Small groups form, and unless a charismatic leader emerges, they fall upon each other in internecine conflicts. The situation in China was worsened by the fact that some groups were deliberately used. The encouragement to violence came from the GCCR group in an almost unending flow of vitriolic condemnation, which seemed to justify the Red Guards in their brutality toward their elders.

The PLA enjoined students to return to their schools, peasants to stay in their communes, and workers to confine their revolutionary ardor to their machines and to production. Zhou's many links with army commanders, spanning the years, helped him to get their cooperation to protect transport and trade networks. The PLA guarded strategic points such as radio stations, warehouses, bridges, railroad stations, airports, arsenals, granaries, and prisons.

The army was not altogether enthusiastic about the Cultural Revolution. It had been ordered to "support the left," but where and who was the left when everyone claimed to be left and to be pro-Mao? The PLA floundered, began to favor some groups and to disband others. The members of the GCCR clustered around Lin Biao and Madame Mao found their favorite Red Guard groups pushed out. Posters appeared, denouncing "power holders in the army who are taking the capitalist road." Zhou Enlai, aware of the danger of antagonizing the army, warned that *no* power seizure could be carried out against "the Central Committee, the State Council, the GCCR, or the PLA."

Zhou suffered a setback when his ally, Tao Zhu, lost his position in the Politburo and the GCCR that winter and was jailed as "counterrevolutionary." The three most active and radical members of the GCCR, the Wang-Guan-Qi trio, had scrutinized Tao Zhu's speeches and found one dated four years back in which he had stated that "even the sun has spots." Was not this an insult to Mao, "the red sun in our hearts"? It was April 1969 before Zhou Enlai could rescue Tao Zhu from jail and send him to Hospital 301.

The "seizure of power" game went on throughout 1967. There were hundreds of local conflicts between groups of Red Guards, between rebels from every organization, all claiming they were Mao's chosen. The PLA, ordered *never to fire* on the people, often had to intervene . . . and soldiers were wounded and killed. Because of its preponderant role, the PLA had to be included in any future Party reorganization. Mao's idea was to create revolutionary committees at every echelon, consisting of a "three in one" combination—i.e., those Party cadres absolved from any capitalist-roading, the military, and representatives of the people. At least 30 percent of the members of each committee should come from the masses, said Mao, in order to democratize the Party apparatus. On January 31 the first provincial revolutionary committee was set up in Heilongjiang province, Manchuria, and was hailed as a model for other provinces . . . until its military commander, Pan Fushen, was demoted three years later. Walking the thin edge of dissent, Zhou began to say that "the reputations of those unjustly accused should be revived, they should be cleared, and set free." This was very bold, for he was a minority of one. It meant releasing many Party cadres. "The economy cannot be allowed to deteriorate further, for then the very foundation for promoting revolution is being destroyed." There is Machiavellian cunning in his speeches.

"The capitalist-roaders, by resisting the 'left,' imperil production," he announced. Which meant that those who endangered the economy were not truly left, but capitalist-roaders at heart. It turned upside down what Lin Biao and Jiang Qing and the Wang-Guan-Qi trio were saying: "The more disorder, the better."

The need for competent cadres led to the meetings of February, where old party veterans were to hold discussions with the members of the GCCR. Zhou, who certainly stage-managed the affair, presided, but never said a word either for or against any side during the hectic exchanges that took place.

The meeting place was the Hall of Nurturing Benevolence, where in 1949 the CPPCC had proclaimed the People's Republic of China. Here gathered Ye Jianying (Heroic Sword), Li Fuchun, Li Xiannian, Nie Rongzhen, Chen Yi, Gu Mu, Tan Zhenlin . . . the Long Marchers. Facing them were the members of the GCCR, Chen Boda, Zhang Chunqiao (Spring Bridge), Yao Wenyuan, and also Ye Chun, Lin Biao's wife. The meetings lasted two days, February 13 and 14, and were full of invective and fury.

Pallid, thin Zhang Chunqiao, with a disdainful air, accused the veterans of trying to overturn "the just verdicts" of the Cultural Revolution and therefore of being anti-Mao. Ye Jianying lost his temper. "Are all of us old cadres to be thrown away on the garbage heap, treated as renegades and counterrevolutionaries?" He struck the table so hard that he fractured a small bone in his hand. Tan Zhenlin, from Hunan province, and hot-tempered, called Madame Mao "more perverse than the Empress Wu" and even wrote this in a letter to Lin Biao. Zhou expostulated with some veterans who started to leave the meetings. "No, you cannot leave, we have to talk this through." But he took no part in the discussions.

Mao Dzedong was told by Lin Biao, and by his wife, that the meetings were questioning the arraignment of Liu Shaoqi, who, in the preceding January, had had his theoretical books burned publicly on Tienanmen Square. Zhou explained that there was no intention of reversing the verdict on Liu, but Mao brushed aside his explanation. Mao's wrath centered on Tan Zhenlin. Tan had organized his own Red Guards, his own Mao Thought propaganda teams, and resisted all attempts to take over his office as Director of Agriculture and Forestry.

Zhou attempted to plead for Tan, but he had to protect the others, all of them his working companions and friends. He too, despite his prudence, was now implicated. Had he not suggested "restoring reputations"? "True, but only those unjustly besmirched. I did not ask to restore the reputations of the capitalist-roaders," said Zhou, sidestepping the issue. He nevertheless had to make two self-criticisms: admit his lack of understanding and his propensity to compromise. The February meetings were dubbed "counterrevolutionary . . . an adverse wind." Ye Jianying lost the vice-chairmanship of the Military Affairs Commission, and Zhou was more seriously weakened than ever. But he could not be directly overthrown. Not yet.

The May 16 Group, organized by his enemies in the GCCR to gather material against him, now escalated their campaign. There had been fitful posters against Zhou, but now a systematic poster war against him began, with the cooperation of the Red Guards of the Foreign Trade and Economy Institute, which was under the State Council. Huge banners were erected: "Burn Zhou Enlai's right-wing opportunism at the stake." "Ten questions to address to Zhou." "Twenty-three whys to Zhou." "Why does Zhou prevent Li Xiannian from being struggled against?" "Which class does Zhou represent?" "Bury Zhou Enlai alive," was the message which greeted his eyes one day as he came out of the Western Gate of Zhongnanhai.

On the subject of class origin, Zhou and his wife had unwaveringly stuck to the view that not birth, but personal attitude and action was what counted in a revolutionary. But the Cultural Revolution was "class struggle," and the Red Guards spread a wave of class demarcation through China. Nine classes were defined as "against the revolution," among them bourgeois intellectuals, which Limpid Stream, boasting of her proletarian origin, called "the stinking ninth."

Zhou had to abandon Tan Zhenlin, but did not do so before June 15. "He fought four months for Tan. Then I heard his voice on the loudspeaker: 'Down with Tan Zhenlin.' It made me wonder. What kind of a man was Zhou? How could he do this?" This testimony, given me verbatim by a member of the research group studying the life and works of Zhou Enlai, illustrates once again the way Zhou proceeded. Even while shouting against Tan, he refused to allow the latter to be dragged to a mass criticism rally, a fearful experience, where Tan might have been kicked, pummeled, mauled. He allowed only a medium-sized meeting. Tan spent two years in jail and was, of course, sent to Hospital 301 in 1970 . . . by Zhou Enlai.

The May 16 Group obtained from the files the notorious fabrication by the Guomindang concerning the abjuration of Wu Hao—Zhou's pseudonym—and 240 Communists. Exultantly, the Wang-Guan-Qi trio sent evidence of this alleged renegacy to Mao. Mao ignored the first letter, but to their second replied, "This matter was cleared up long ago. It was a fabrication by the Guomindang." The woefully harassed Zhou, in the middle of trying to run a China shredded by anarchy, had to delve into his own files and send them to Mao. "I have been busy with problems in Sichuan province, in Inner Mongolia. Only today do I have the time to go over the material which appeared in the Shanghai newspapers," he wrote to Mao, enclosing whatever clippings he had kept of the affair.

His enemies did not relent.

The ebullient Foreign Minister, Chen Yi the footballer, was an appropriate target. If he could be ousted from the Ministry of Foreign Affairs, this would destroy Zhou Enlai, already in a minority of one due to the downfall of Tao Zhu, of Ye Jianying, and of Li Xiannian. Chen Yi had already been subjected to verbal sniping since early in September 1966. His most vociferous opponents were from the Foreign Language Institute, which trained future diplomats, and which outshone other places of higher learning for the viciousness of some—not all—of its students. Zhou refused to let them get their hands on Chen Yi. The Red Guards set up loudspeakers outside the Western Gate of Zhongnanhai and shouted, "Drag out Chen Yi." Since Zhou's office and home were nearest the Western Gate, the cacophony deprived him of any sleep. Less circumspect, less patient than Zhou, Chen Yi called the youths "*wahwah*," meaning babies, and said they were "still in their slit pants," the equivalent of diapers. "If you want to make revolution, why don't you go and fight in Vietnam?" he said to the young when they crowded around to shout at him. At one of the rallies against him which he was forced to attend, later that year, he held up the Little Red Book solemnly. "Turn to page 127." Every one present did. There was no page 127. Chen Yi, pretending to read, intoned, "Chairman Mao has said: Chen Yi is a good comrade." Then lifting his eyes to his tormentors: "How can you think that everything Chairman Mao has ever said or written is all in this small book?" Chen poured sarcasm upon Lin Biao. "What a great man Vice-Chairman Lin must be. . . . Just fancy, he's the only one who has never contradicted Chairman Mao," Chen Yi knew full well that during the Long March Lin Biao was called to order when he refused to obey Mao. Chen Yi made a self-criticism in February 1967 which pleased Mao, who mentioned it as "a good piece," upon which Zhou forthwith ordered this "model" to be printed in the newspapers. "Comrade Chen Yi *never* engaged in any double-crossing," wrote the editor. Zhou thus diverted the attack upon Chen Yi. But not for long.

While coping with the cruel puerility of the Red Guards, Zhou not only ran the government but conducted day-to-day Party affairs, replacing Deng Xiaoping. His nosebleeds increased. His heart troubled him, and at times he gasped for air. All those who served him were worried. His cook, his bodyguards and chauffeurs, his secretaries and the personnel of his cabinet, got together and wrote a "big poster," which they affixed to his office door, "criticizing beloved Premier Zhou for taking too little care of himself and sleeping too little." Ye Jianying and Li Fuchun, Nie Rongzhen and Li Xiannian, other callers, all signed. "We agree with this criticism of Comrade Enlai." Deng Yingchao pasted up a supplementary "small poster." "I heartily endorse the criticism." She begged her husband "for the sake of the revolution, of the Party, and for the long term . . . to take more rest and care more for his health." "I accept the sincere criticism. We shall see whether I am able to put it into practice," replied Zhou Enlai. This small jest, parodying the vicious posters which flayed him daily, alleviated for a while the inhuman pressures upon him. But despair was a word Zhou did not allow in his mind or in the minds of those around him. "We are being tested," he said.

In the summer more attacks were mounted against Chen Yi. Reluctantly, Zhou had to allow criticism meetings of his Foreign Minister, but he warned, "All must be well prepared beforehand. Minister Chen is very busy, his time cannot be wasted." But the GCCR left extremists had decided to take control of the Foreign Affairs Ministry, and the Wang-Guan-Qi trio directed a team of Red Guards to search the ministry rooms where confidential documents were stored. "What is so confidential? Why all these secrets?" cried the ignorant young as they tossed the files about. Zhou, incensed, called the Red Guards and the ministry employees who, as "rebels," had abetted their intrusion, and talked with them for four hours, insisting on the return of the files. "This is totally incorrect. I said that Chen Yi could be personally criticized, but the work of the ministry cannot be interfered with. The Foreign Minister cannot be overthrown." At the end of June, nevertheless, another raid took place. Zhou complained to Mao, and got the files and documents back.

In July came the climax of the war upon the Foreign Affairs Ministry. A diplomat named Yao Dengshan, interim chargé d'affaires in Djakarta, had been expelled from Indonesia in late April. He was received as a hero in Beijing, photographed arm in arm with Mao and Jiang Qing. Yao was groomed by the GCCR to capture the ministry. He accused Chen Yi of having stopped patriotic Overseas Chinese from denouncing the governments of the countries where they lived, dampening their righteous anger. "It was Chairman Mao and myself who decided the policy concerning the Overseas Chinese many years ago," Zhou snapped back. The last thing Zhou wanted was pogroms, general massacres throughout Southeast Asia, of the vulnerable Overseas Chinese communities, already resented because, overachievers, they had become economically a power in every land they inhabited.

On August 7, Yao Dengshan led three hundred Red Guards to occupy the Ministry of Foreign Affairs and to overthrow Chen Yi. He became, for sixteen days, Foreign Minister de facto. This was done while Zhou was away in a province, settling a major row.

During the sixteen days that Yao acted as Foreign Minister, Zhou, who could not remove him, asserted his right, as Premier, to oversee the work of his unwanted colleague. Yao sent telegrams and instructions to all the Chinese embassies abroad. Zhou called him to task. "Who gave you permission? No one understood your telegrams . . . they were all sent back."

On August 22, mobs of Red Guards, inflamed by reports of so-called atrocities perpetrated in Hong Kong by the British, invaded the British embassy. Previously the youths had stopped at the gates, shouting slogans and waving banners, while two Scots pipers in kilts walked up and down the embassy's front courtyard, playing bagpipes in an exhibition of cool courage. But now the gates were broken, petrol cans were thrown at the buildings and set them afire. The diplomats were rescued by the PLA and police sent by Zhou Enlai. The following year Zhou not only personally extended apologies, but had the British embassy buildings reconstructed at China's expense.

On August 26, a meeting of 10,000 Red Guards was convened against Chen Yi at the Great Hall of the People. Zhou, who had spent the previous twenty hours on his feet, had a fainting spell, but recovered, and insisted on facing the mob. "If you try to take Chen Yi away, I'll stand at the entrance of the hall, you'll walk over my body to do so." Zhou took Chen Yi home with him.

At the end of the summer, Mao Dzedong, back from an inspection tour, and appalled—possibly—by what had been unleashed in his name, ordered the Cultural Revolution wound up.

Zhou sprang into action. In the name of the Central Committee, the State Council, the Military Affairs Commission, and the GCCR, everything was now reversed.

With great temerity, he lectured the Red Guards on the insufficiency of class background as sole criterion for revolutionary fitness.

The young were forbidden to roam about as they had done since the summer of 1966. No seizure of weapons or equipment from the PLA would be tolerated. For the first time, the PLA was given permission to return fire if attacked. Assaults on foreign embassies were totally forbidden. Struggle by violence would not be tolerated.

Zhou regained the Foreign Affairs Ministry. Yao Dengshan vanished and, by year's end, had been jailed as counterrevolutionary—no convenient hospital for him.

It would take a few more weeks for Zhou to get rid of the Wang-Guan-Qi trio. All three were arrested for having incited violence, against Mao's dictum that the Cultural Revolution should be carried out by reason and not force—the clause which had been inserted in the program which was to guide the Cultural Revolution.

Zhou Enlai was winning, winning against the demons of chaos and confusion. But he did not pose as a victor. All this, of course, was in conformity with the Chairman's thinking. In a fit of frankness—which, of course, was a quality best kept under wraps—ninety-one ambassadors and members of the Foreign Affairs Ministry jointly signed a plea in defense of Chen Yi on February 13, 1968. "This is interference from the right. The poster is mistaken in principle," said Zhou Enlai, now a blameless exponent of "the true left." "He was a virtuoso," says Pu Shouchang, his secretary, "A master of the art of turning situations around." Zhou acquired the nickname of Bu Dao Wong, the man nothing can overthrow, whose oscillations, back and forth, right and left, only confirm an unshakable steadiness.

Zhou also waged his lonely battles in the provinces. Quelling disturbances, arbitrating, laying down directives. In Sichuan, Long Marcher Li Jingquan, Party secretary for the province, faced hundreds of thousands of Red Guards, many from outside the province and all fighting each other. The deaths took on the dimension of a small hecatomb. There were scores of Red Guard groups, dozens of industrial workers' combat corps. In that rambunctious and fertile region, China's granary, industrial plants producing tanks and fighter aircraft were occupied by Red Guards who turned them into armed camps, all in the name of "extensive democracy." "The youths stole weapons from the army, then they machine-gunned each other," my cousins, who worked in the province as engineers, told me, and this was confirmed by ex-Red Guards I interviewed later. Li Jingquan had tried to arrest the ringleaders, but had got nowhere. "Jailing will not solve the problem," said Zhou, appointing another PLA commander, Zhang Guohua, to deal with the problem. But he found out that "though Comrade Zhang Guohua is able, he mutters and mumbles. He cannot explain things to the young." So off went Zhou to explain, braving bands armed with guns. He insisted on dialogue. "Only in the last resort shall we use other means." He quoted to his pessimistic colleagues the old ditty: "Long before China is in chaos, Sichuan is chaotic. When China restores order, Sichuan continues in chaos."

He dealt with Henan, Anhui, Yunnan, Inner Mongolia—provinces rocked by the violence of the young. In Hong Kong some local "Red Guards" manufactured homemade bombs which killed several people. Panic spread in the British colony during the summer of 1967, abetted by the secret societies. Hong Kong was enormously sensitive to whatever happened in China. The rumor had spread that the Red Guards were marching against Hong Kong to seize it. "There will be no change in the status of Hong Kong," said Zhou, calling to Beijing the newsmen of the Xinhua News Agency stationed there. Hong Kong *must* remain capitalistic; it earned half of China's foreign exchange for the mainland. Under Zhou's skillful guidance the newsmen, among them Fei Yiming, who ran the *Ta Kung Pao* newspaper, played out a comedy in keeping with the times, chanting from the Little Red Book but rigorously abstaining from inciting violence. Hong Kong calmed down.

In July, two members of the GCCR had flown to Wuhan. They had come to disband a Red Guard organization called the "one million bold warriors." The GCCR said it was not "true left." They were promptly kidnapped by the regional commander, General Chen Caitao, who backed the "bold warriors." This had been the first manifest challenge by a PLA commander against the GCCR.

Was this the start of an army mutiny? The army was sore pressed, and very disgruntled by the continuing havoc. An airborne division was sent against Chen Caitao, and five gunboats were readied to sail upriver from Shanghai to Wuhan. Would there be clashes between various military commands?

Hospital-neat in a pale gray summer suit, Zhou Enlai flew to Wuhan. Rumor had had it that some twenty-five truckloads of troops were waiting for him at the airport in order to kidnap him. He landed at another airport. Resourceful as ever, he had found an officer who had been one of his students at the Huangpu Military Academy. Calm, persuasive, using a mixture of dignity, cajolery, and appeal to principles, he managed to get Chen not only to agree to the release of the two GCCR members but also to surrender and accompany him to Beijing.

The GCCR clamored for Chen Caitao's blood, but of course neither Mao nor Zhou would touch a commander of the sacrosanct PLA when it was teetering on the verge of discontent. The PLA would not tolerate one of its officers being punished. Chen was treated with great leniency, wrote an amiable self-criticism, and promised to study Mao Thought a little harder. Zhou had won another round. The GCCR's appeals to "drag out the handful of capitalist-roaders in the army" were extinguished by a Zhou braced by Mao. "There are *no* capitalist-roaders in the army," said Zhou Enlai. This episode marked Zhou's slow return to control. It was at first impalpable, for a good general "walks invisibly, like a ghost in starlight." It would take more months to regain a total grasp of the situation. But Zhou knew how to make one event serve another, and link an irrelevant happening to make it serve a set purpose. In late June he had made time to go with Nie Rongzhen to watch the explosion of China's first hydrogen bomb. He would never allow Lin Biao any control of nuclear research, its laboratories, its scientists and workers. He reported to Mao on this success, and implied that many more scientists and young researchers would be needed . . . prelude to the release of many intellectuals, the restoration of scientific research, and the reopening of the universities.

He flew to Guangzhou, where Red Guards were cheerfully shooting at each other, and spent hours talking with them. Apparently here he made a mistake, backing the wrong group as "true left," a group which turned out, in the turgid jargon of those days, to be "waving the red flag to beat down the red flag." But for Zhou the important thing was that the trade fair should not be interfered with. Many Western businessmen arrived in Guangzhou thoughtfully provided with Mao badges and Little Red Books, and Zhou must have grinned appreciatively.

Now that Yao Dengshan had been disposed of, Zhou turned back to foreign affairs. Apologies to Norodom Sihanouk of Cambodia, to Ne Win of Burma. Stern warnings to the Overseas Chinese "Red Guards." In December, he held talks with delegates from the South Vietnam Liberation Front: weapons destined for Vietnam had been pillaged by Red Guards. Zhou ordered army commander Wei Guoqing, in charge in the province of Guangxi, which bordered on Vietnam and was the site of the arsenals supplying war matériel to the Vietnamese, to go ahead with suppression of the Red Guards. Wei mortared the small bunkers which the Red Guards had erected, took many prisoners, and sent them to labor camps. The Vietnamese got the supplies they needed.

In July 1968, Mao assembled a dozen of the most prominent leaders of the Red Guards and told them, "You have let me down. . . . You have disappointed the workers, peasants, and soldiers of China." The program of transferring hundreds of thousands of youths to army-run farms, to communes, to far-flung provinces, was confirmed. Zhou delivered his last warning to the now downcast youths. "You do not listen, you go on causing turmoil." Those who refused to disarm, to go back to school, would find themselves punished. There were summary executions of "murderers, rapists, looters, and counterrevolutionaries." But now the word "counterrevolutionary" meant the exact opposite of what it had meant in 1966 and 1967. "Down with the ultra-left," read the wall posters. Teams of workers backed by soldiers entered the universities to stop the young from killing each other. Order was restored in most regions.

By sending the Red Guards out of the cities, it became possible to restore many Party cadres to their original work posts without their being harassed again. Zhou hoped that the end of the Cultural Revolution was near. "The handful of capitalist-roaders in the Party have been smashed," he announced. On the occasion of a major speech on the topic, he invited Jiang Qing to be present and to speak as well. Angry and unhappy, because she was being deprived of her favorite audience, the Red Guards, Limpid Stream spoke with asperity. "I only knew this morning that I would have to give a talk." She asked the assembly not to forget the revolutionary youth or how much they had achieved. The power relationship between her and Zhou had now changed. Zhou was beginning to hold the upper hand. When an enraged Jiang Qing asked him, "Why are you still sheltering so many people? Why do you refuse to let them be struggled against?" Zhou replied, "Big struggle, little struggle, civilized struggle, violent struggle, I'll allow *no* struggle against them." Acerbic, showing how deeply he had been scarred by what had happened: "What has taken place is worse than anything that Wang Ming and the Twenty-eight Bolsheviks ever did. If any of these people die, will you take the responsibility?" Mao's wife withdrew for a few months to one of her residences in the south. "Resting from her arduous labors," was the suave way Zhou described her temporary retirement from the scene.

23

In late 1966, as the Cultural Revolution roared forward and Liu Shaoqi was being targeted—though not yet by name—as "capitalist-roader," Zhou had warned him and his wife: "Do not leave the safety of Zhongnanhai." But Wang Guangmei, Liu's wife, was inveigled out of the protected compound. A telephone call told her that her daughter had suffered an accident. She rushed to her daughter's university campus, and there was surrounded by jeering Red Guards. She was forced to stand for several hours on a platform, with a necklace of Ping-Pong balls around her neck. She was rescued when Zhou Enlai, hearing of the incident, sent his personal secretary to bring her back. Jiang Qing had inspired this exhibition, for she considered Luminous Beauty a rival. Wang Guangmei had worn a pearl necklace when on a state visit with her husband to Indonesia, as well as a silk dress and high heels. "She threw away the face of China," said Mao's wife.

In January 1967, Liu's books on Marxist theory were burned in a bonfire on Tienanmen Square. They were declared to be poisonous weeds, yet they had been a mainstay of the theoretical construct which in Yenan in 1945–47 had brought Mao to power. Did no one remember Liu's contribution to the rise of Mao and of Mao Thought?

Liu made one self-criticism after another. To no avail. In 1967 he was openly denounced by name—until then it had all been hints—as "the biggest capitalist-roader in the Party" and "China's Khrushchev." Zhou Enlai, however, remained punctilious over Party rules. Though certainly not fond of Liu, even with Liu's name plastered all over the walls of the city in huge posters, he still treated Liu Shaoqi as President of China. When Liu refused to attend a major rally on Tienanmen Square, Zhou came to see him. "You are the President of China. You have been denounced in wall posters, but the Party has not yet declared itself. Your place is with us." He personally saw to it that Liu was in his proper place, with Vice-Presidents Dung Biwu and Soong Chingling on either side of him.

Zhou fought for Liu's and his wife's physical inviolability. In the summer of 1967, the Red Guards of the Architectural Institute set up loudspeakers outside the Western Gate of Zhongnanhai, as was done in the assault against Chen Yi. But this was far worse. In relays, they mobilized some 100,000 youths from every other college and university in China to keep up a noise war, singing and shouting slogans, demanding that Liu be delivered to them. The howling went on day and night, and drove many of the high-ranking inhabitants of Zhongnanhai to seek shelter elsewhere. Zhou remained, working despite the noise, working though unable to rest at night. The Red Guards tried to rush the Western Gate, then turned to the four other gates leading to the vast enclosure. Every time, the gatekeepers telephoned to Zhou. He would appear, stopping forcible entry by his presence. "You are not allowed in here. I am speaking for the center, for Chairman Mao. Liu Shaoqi is the President, the vice-chairman of the Party. He cannot be dragged out."

But Zhou Enlai could not stop the brutality of Liu's own body-guards, who had been told by the GCCR to have no compassion for him. They would not bring him hot water to wash; nor would they clean his clothes. He was not properly fed or allowed a barber. Had they shown any kindness to their charge, the bodyguards might have been accused of aiding and abetting a counterrevo-lutionary. His wife, Wang Guangmei, was taken to the prison for high cadres near the capital, and was there for the next ten years. Liu was alone, and posters against him were plastered all over the walls of Beijing, as well as the walls of the bedroom to which he was confined. A voluminous pile of incriminating documents was now collected against him.

From October 13 to 31, 1968, the Twelfth Plenum of the Eighth Party Congress was held in Beijing. The material collected against Liu was studied by the rump Central Committee. Zhou Enlai was assigned to preside over the special investigation committee and to chair the meetings that were to judge Liu Shaoqi.

When the voting was called for, Zhou Enlai cast his vote against

Liu Shaoqi, as did all those present, except for one courageous woman, whose name is not recorded. In 1977, nine years later, I asked Deng Yingchao, "I have also written certain things against Liu Shaoqi. He is now being rehabilitated. I was misinformed. Should I now apologize publicly to his wife, Wang Guangmei?"

"Why should you? You did nothing against him. You believed us. It was Enlai who signed the document that expelled Liu Shaoqi from the Party . . . can we apologize for this?" said Deng Yingchao. "It was painful, so painful for Enlai, but he had to do it . . . he kept the larger view in mind."

Zhou Enlai's relations with Liu had not been harmonious. And in the dispute with the U.S.S.R., Zhou stood solidly on Mao's side, knowing full well that Liu's views would have brought about a satellitization of China. But in the matter of handling economic reforms, Zhou had been in agreement with Liu, now condemned as traitor, renegade, scab, and to be "forever expelled" from the Party.

Could Zhou have refused to vote? What would have happened to him had he voted against the verdict?

Mao Dzedong, seeing China's role as an independent great power, was determined to get Liu out of the Party. And Liu had indeed tried to weaken Mao, had, in Mao's view, double-crossed him. Liu had encouraged Peng Dehuai, that innocent and well-meaning man, to challenge Mao in 1959. He had tried to oust Mao from supreme power since early 1962. Mao was convinced —and perhaps he was right—that power in Liu's hands would ultimately make of China a compliant follower of the Soviet Union. Had not Liu, even in the summer of 1966, asked for "unity of action" with the U.S.S.R., suggested sending Chinese armies into Vietnam to help the Vietnamese against the United States?

Everyone agrees, and by everyone I mean the highest leaders, including his own wife, Deng Yingchao, that Zhou Enlai "did things against his own heart." The condemnation of Liu Shaoqi was one of these things. Had he opposed it, he would have been ousted within a day. And this would have meant the total success of the GCCR group, and of Lin Biao. "The whole chessboard would have been in the hands of Lin Biao and the gang around Mao's wife," Qian Jiadung, one of Zhou's aides at the time, later ambassador to the United Nations in Geneva, told me. It was repeated to me by Huang Hua, by so many others who worked with Zhou Enlai. "In 1968 the Premier was coming back into power. He was already whittling away at the left extremists. He had even got some of them suspended or arrested. He *had* to condemn Liu Shaoqi." That the decision he made was agonizing for him is clear. He unburdened himself to Edgar Snow one evening in October 1970.

"I have almost no one, no one of my old comrades left around me," he said. He dwelt at length upon the dangerous flood of history, the scalding emotions, the suffering which every tidal wave of political struggle brought. And in the course of it he mentioned "Comrade Liu Shaoqi."

"Comrade. Now Liu was no longer a comrade, since he had been expelled two years before," Edgar Snow told me. "It was astonishing to me that Zhou called him Comrade, and at first I did not understand the implication." Yet this was Zhou's confession that he did not agree with the verdict against Liu. "He was bone-tired that night, with grief, perhaps also with guilt. He knew I would not write down everything he said to me. I would not betray his trust." Edgar Snow said this to me, and I too did not betray the trust during the lifetime of Zhou Enlai.

The seventy-year-old Liu Shaoqi was moved to Kaifeng City in Henan province in October 1969 and died in November. He was cremated and his ashes thrown in a common grave, and under another name.

With smooth precision and ruthless skill Zhou got rid of the Wang-Guan-Qi trio in the GCCR, thus weakening the faction of Madame Mao. They were now dubbed "counterrevolutionaries" and disappeared from the scene. But there remained a formidable enemy, Lin Biao.

By ordering the army to deal with the anarchy which the Red Guards had created, Mao had increased Lin Biao's influence, but also that of Lin's rivals in the PLA. And Zhou Enlai, the man who had, in 1927, begun to form the army, was popular with the latter. Unsurprisingly, therefore, Lin Biao, watching Zhou's reemergence, would try to weaken him by attacking some of his supporters. Zhou now spoke as representative of "our great leader Chairman Mao and Vice-Chairman Lin, the Central Committee, the State Council, the Military Affairs Commission, and the Group in Charge of the Cultural Revolution." For he too had become a member of the GCCR. His outward deference to Lin Biao made it difficult for the latter to fault him. However, in the spring of

1968, three senior staff officers linked to Zhou, and also to Nie Rongzhen, were suddenly accused of various crimes and arrested. At the same time, Liu appointed his own protégé, Huang Yungsheng, as chief of staff. An indirect blow to Zhou, who of course appeared totally unruffled. These shifts were in preparation for the Ninth Congress of the Party, to take place in 1969, when Lin Biao was to be consecrated as Mao's appointed successor.

By September 1968 there were revolutionary committees in all twenty-nine provinces, autonomous regions, and municipalities. More than 60 percent of the provincial posts were in the hands of military leaders. Only 6 percent of the former Party secretaries remained in office. Zhou Enlai would have minimal support at the congress.

The invasion of Czechoslovakia by Russian forces in August 1968 gave Lin Biao another opportunity to stress the danger to China of an invasion. Brezhnev was invoking the recently hammered-out "Collective Security Pact," which gave Moscow the right to intervene whenever the socialist camp was threatened.

Lin Biao warned the Politburo and the Military Affairs Commission that China would be attacked by the Soviet Union; preparations for defense could not be delayed. In October, he issued the famous Directive No. One, setting China on a war footing. Air-raid shelters were dug in every city. A labyrinth of tunnels to connect them honeycombed the ground below the streets in the capital. Youths were drilled for defense, and Lin Biao could now send to faraway "battle stations" those commanders he wanted out from the center, Beijing.

Zhou, of course, did not think war would come. There would be no full-scale war, and no nuclear war, said Zhou. Russian "saber rattling" was an exercise in psychological terror.

Paradoxically, the situation allowed Zhou some leverage. In September 1968, he declared that "the great victory of the proletarian Cultural Revolution" was now *completed*. The enemy *might* retaliate, both within and outside China. Therefore unity was needed. The revolutionary committees *must* therefore comprise Party cadres as well as army men, and representatives of the masses, to forge unity. (This was Mao's triangle of one third each of PLA, CCP, and the people.) And youth must "go to the lowest echelons . . . turn to production, go into the villages, the factories, mines . . . to labor."

In March 1969, Lin Biao's predictions of imminent war seemed confirmed when an armed clash occurred over an island named Chenbao in Chinese, Damansky in Russian, in the Ussuri River. Soviet diplomats in Washington, London, Paris, and Bonn denounced China as "most bellicose" and the greatest danger to peace. A report states that the Russian ambassador in Washington asked for "cooperation" in restraining China, even suggesting attacks on her nuclear sites. But American policy was changing, had changed, as the new President, Richard Nixon, was already initiating a series of "signals" in China's direction.

The Ninth Congress took place from April 1 to 24, 1969. Fifteen hundred delegates, 44 percent of them military, appeared to seal the triumph of Lin Biao. Lin was officially proclaimed the successor to Mao Dzedong. In his speech Lin claimed that the Party was now renovated, rejuvenated, its "dark aspects" had been exposed. Since hundreds of thousands of youths had been transferred from the cities to rural areas, the congress could not be challenged by rebellious adolescents.

Zhou had his own army adherents, whom he recommended as delegates to the Ninth Congress, which hints at his preparations to erode Lin Biao's dominance. His Minister of the Petroleum Industry was a delegate, and his people controlled a few alternate seats in the Central Committee. In addition, Chen Yi, Chen Yun the economist, and, of course, Nie Rongzhen were there, as well as Xu Xiangqian, Going Forward, the man who had gone over to Mao's side during the Long March. Zhou was nonetheless in a small minority. Still, he was back. Even if working with one fifth of his usual staff. He proclaimed the reopening of science courses in the universities, and reasserted the importance of fundamental science and research. "The professors are needed to teach our worker-peasant-soldier youth," said Zhou virtuously. He also insisted on reopening foreign language schools. "How otherwise can we communicate with our friends abroad and make the victories of the great proletarian Cultural Revolution known to the whole world?"

He went in person to the Foreign Language Institute to lecture to the students. "Short courses in a foreign language are inadequate. Foreign languages must be practiced every day. An hour a day is not enough, nor is it enough to learn set phrases. History, geography, the culture of foreign countries, all these must be learned. Translation is not an easy task. It demands all-round knowledge."

He scoffed at the textbooks devised for minimal courses. "They only contain political phraseology. How ridiculous." He read out a sentence in an English textbook used in Peking University. " 'Are you of working-class family?' Is no other class origin possible?" asked Zhou Enlai.

Picking up the shards, the broken fragments of the edifice he had built at so much cost, with so much pain and sacrifice, Zhou went on to defend "democratic parties and personages." He presided over the funeral ceremony for Li Tsungjen, who with his wife, both brimful of hope, had returned to China in 1965 . . . only to encounter the Cultural Revolution. The eight small non-Communist parties had been declared abolished in 1966, but Zhou resurrected them in 1969. He placed their members under the protection of Wang Dongxin, once Mao's bodyguard, now commander of the elite 8341 Guard Regiment, the praetorians whose duty it was to watch over the leaders. The People's Political Consultative Conference, Zhou's cherished creation, begun at the time of the common united front with Chiang Kaishek, was now reborn.

"Non-Communists should not be expected to have the same standards as Party members," said Zhou. The "united front" to which he had given so much of his life had been destroyed, but Zhou would try to keep the notion alive. He could not have done this had not Mao, at the time, begun to doubt Lin Biao, and therefore to rely more on Zhou, who was forever careful to consult Mao before every move, and to refer to Mao Thought, presenting all he did as its implementation. There is, in 1969, a detectable, renewed mastery and crispness in Zhou's speeches. He sloughs off the lamentable phraseology which he had had to use in order to keep himself, and so many of his colleagues, alive. But he had to be very careful. He must not be accused of trying to restore "capitalist-roadism," even if he was getting back into their jobs as many Party cadres as possible. And therefore, during the next few years, he would be, more than ever, subtle, devious, subservient in appearance. In the name of Mao, he would undo what Mao had attempted to do.

Chen Yi, the ebullient Foreign Minister, was stricken with cancer of the bowel. Zhou had reassumed total control of the Foreign Affairs Ministry, and just in time to receive the signals from President Nixon. In June 1969, a world congress of Communist parties in Moscow had rejected a proposal to expel China from the world

Communist movement, with Romania and Yugoslavia leading the opposition to Moscow's suggestion. All this consolidated Zhou's position, and made the clash with Lin Biao inevitable.

The Party was back. In the Central Committee, less than 7 percent were "the masses." The Party cadres and the army prevailed, the bases of their strength intact. A sharing of the golden peaches of power between Party and army was the next move. And this move would not be good for Lin Biao. He did not command the loyalty of all Party commanders, which belonged in a fluid, esoteric manner to Mao. The "saber rattling," as Zhou had called it, of the U.S.S.R. had misfired. In the Politburo, Zhou had reintroduced, with Mao's approval, the formidable Ye Jianying, Heroic Sword. And now the possibility of talks with Washington reinforced Zhou's position; it made Mao dependent on his Premier, who handled foreigners so superbly. Consistently, Mao had clung to the vision of an understanding with America, and he would give Zhou his full support. Lin Biao thus felt threatened, by a renascent Party, an increasing portion of the army *not* impressed by his preeminent position, and Zhou Enlai's return as Mao's indispensable man of all work.

Lin Biao's biographers have not delved into his personality, his psychological makeup. He was certainly schizoid, with fits of depression followed by manic exaltation. He is said to have been a drug addict, taking morphine and opium frequently, though where he acquired the habit is not known. He was afraid of cold, wind, drafts, heat, and insects. A hypochondriac, he traveled with a suitcase of pills. "He talked very little. He was always worried about his health," says Nie Rongzhen. Nie had been Lin's political commissar in 1937, at the famous battle of Ping Xing Pass.

Had he wanted to commit suicide, Lin Biao could not have thought up a better way than to proceed as he did. A mysterious directive, untraceable, but confirmed to me by newsmen employed by Hong Kong's Communist newspapers, was issued, ordering that there should be no contact whatsoever with any Americans. This was in autumn 1969. Surely, a foolish move, and one calculated to irritate Mao, who was keen to enlarge the American connection.

Lin Biao had inserted into the Politburo and the Military Affairs Commission his "four golden stalwarts," devotees of his in the army: Huang Yungsheng, Wu Faxian, Li Dzopeng, and Qiu Huidzo. Also his wife, Ye Chun. But he still felt insecure. When Liu Shaoqi died in 1969, and the post of President of the Republic became vacant, Lin Biao somehow decided that the post should be his. Yet Mao, at a session of the National People's Congress in March, had wanted the post abolished, and unitary control, merger between Party and state offices, instituted. But Lin Biao, at a Politburo meeting on April 11, introduced a motion to retain the post. "We do not need a President, your resolution is inappropriate," Mao told his appointed successor. Foolishly, Lin Biao persisted.

In July, the usual roundup meeting of the Central Committee, Politburo, and Military Affairs Commission took place at Lushan. Perhaps the ghosts of previous meetings, the shades of previous encounters, roamed in the spacious halls and badly disturbed Lin Biao's brain, for he now obstinately proceeded to destroy himself. Chen Boda, on Lin's advice, extolled Mao as a genius at the Lushan meeting. "Genius makes history. Geniuses change the world. They are above the norm of ordinary men." Zhou was the first to protest. "Chairman Mao believes in the masses, in the people," said Zhou. Chen Boda angrily refuted Zhou. Did he not recognize Mao's genius? Was he casting doubt on Mao's supreme wisdom?

But Mao Dzedong himself objected to the notion of genius. On August 25, he notified the assembly that the speeches on his "genius" should be expunged from all records. None of them was allowed to be broadcast, or discussed, either by word of mouth or in writing. What Chen Boda had said was "un-Marxist."

It was Zhou Enlai who was entrusted with "reprimanding and investigating" Chen Boda and the other men who had made speeches extolling Mao's genius. "It was all over in two days," the archivists of the Central Committee tell me. "Mao wrote: 'Is it geniuses who make history, or slaves who make history? It is the slaves.' Mao then compared the whole episode to an attempt 'to flatten Mount Lushan, and stop the earth turning.' " He had used the same words eleven years previously, in his speech against Peng Dehuai.

This was a warning to Lin Biao, whom Mao spared, concentrating, in the usual Chinese manner, on Lin Biao's supporters, notably Chen Boda. Mao compounded the assault against Lin Biao by inquiring about Deng Xiaoping. "And how is Comrade Xiao-

ping?" asked Mao aloud of Zhou Enlai. The latter assured Mao
that Deng was making great progress in remolding his thinking.
He had made sure that Deng had a comfortable two-story house
and worked only half a day in a factory; the other half he spent
gardening or reading. Zhou's face betrayed nothing of what must
have been for him a moment of exhilaration. Another Great Demon, Lin Biao, was in danger of being expunged from the political
landscape through his own foolishness.

But Mao needed help to sap the structures Lin had put in place.

It was now very clear that Lin Biao had assiduously built up a
power base. In 1965, Wu Faxian, one of his four golden stalwarts,
had become commander of the air force. Lin Biao's son, Lin Liguo,
and one of his daughters had also entered the air force. The navy
had followed, with Li Dzopeng installed in 1967. And Huang
Yungsheng was army chief of staff. In major cities, the garrison
commanders were Lin Biao's men, since Directive No. One had
enabled him to shift those commanders not of his liking to distant
provinces.

How would Mao remove his heir without a major army upheaval? The ever resourceful Zhou found a formula. "Chairman,
why not reinstate the system of rotating commands, as was done
in the past to avoid mountaintopism?" So that a commander might
not get too powerful locally, so that he could not build his own
"mountain to sit upon," he was moved around. Zhou's advice
would enable Mao to remove Lin Biao's supporters, without apparently attacking his successor.

With Mao and Lin now maneuvering against each other, Zhou was
free to start some major restructuring. He instituted surveys of
cotton and coal production, overhauled banking and finance, drew
up itemized lists of needed machinery in China's limping factories,
initiated trade contacts with Japan and with Western Europe. His
teams reached into every corner of the country. With the prospect
of a breakthrough in relations with the United States, the Housekeeper was setting the house in order with his usual formidable
efficiency. The public health personnel of an area that had experienced earthquake tremors were reprimanded for not hastening
to the spot to care for the wounded and the homeless. Geologists
and seismologists were called, and told to review their work. Delicate instruments had been destroyed by the "revolutionary reb-

els." "How can revolution mean tragically neglecting the lives of thousands in an earthquake? And don't waste time studying their class background back three generations," shouted Zhou.

"In a socialist state, everyone who suffers is entitled to help." He defended scientist Hua Logeng, whose research papers had been confiscated by Red Guards. "This is stealing. We must establish and reinforce appropriate conditions for scientific work." Wresting every second from unforgiving time, yet never looking at his watch, Zhou was everywhere, pouncing upon counties and upon bureaucrats, inspecting machines, going down coal mines . . . he even made time to listen to the doleful story of a dung carrier. The man had had the bad luck to be picked by the unfortunate Liu Shaoqi as a hero of labor. When Liu became a traitor, a scab, etc., the man was immediately called a "counterrevolutionary." "How can an ordinary dung carrier be the target of the Cultural Revolution? Is he a capitalist?" Zhou Enlai asked, and restored the dung carrier to his occupation and his family.

Chen Yun and other economists were all back at their jobs. It was in 1970 that the program later to be called the Four Modernizations was first discussed. Again Zhou had to cope with the centralization-decentralization dilemma, one which still plagues China's economic structure. Central planning had disintegrated, and provincial structures had benefited. Around 70 percent of the income from industry and agriculture was retained by the provinces. But this left the center without enough resources for investment in major projects. Zhou restored centralization and central planning, though not to the extent that it had operated in the 1950s.

More rice and wheat had to be produced. This meant an increase in chemical fertilizers, and not only from commune-based small fertilizer plants. Fertilizers, plastics, artificial fiber, received priority in planning. Flood control, reservoirs, dikes, were overhauled. Zhou ordered teams of agriculturists to study Japanese methods of rice planting, after several hours spent questioning a Japanese agricultural delegation. He ordered a major overhaul of all road, rail, and air transport. "How can we modernize without transport, without energy sources?" And he ordered the construction of the major Gezouba Dam.

On October 23, 1970, China's first underground atomic explosion took place, and a second hydrogen bomb was exploded in the Taklamakan Desert. China also sent up her first space satellite. "All this is due to Zhou's crusade for high technology," said Nie Rongzhen. "The nuclear scientists who were safeguarded by Zhou Enlai worked on these projects throughout the Cultural Revolution."

Zhou called an all-China conference of publishers, printing presses, and editors. He lashed out at the scarcity of books. Of course, the works of Mao, Marx, and Lenin must come first, but "there must also be books for children, for the young, there must be scientific and technical books, history, geography, international knowledge. . . . None of these can be ignored." The memory of man is fallible; one generation's experiences are ignored by the following one. On his sixtieth birthday he had urged his colleagues to write their memoirs "while the episodes are still fresh in your minds." Now he returned to the topic. "The young *must* be taught history. I am told there are places where old books stored for many years were burned. I think we shall be very sorry that this has been done." The works of Lu Xun, the revolutionary writer, had been forbidden in a university, and Zhou stormed, "This is nonsense, absolute nonsense." But, of course, his main preoccupation was to restore scientific studies. "This matter cannot be delayed any longer. We cannot neglect fundamental science or we shall never be able to catch up on the latest technology. . . . So much to do, so little time left."

While Mao and his heir, Lin Biao, maneuvered and feinted, circling around each other in an unsuspected killing game, Zhou put the country back on its feet. He also helped get rid of Lin Biao. But so deftly, in such gossamer fashion, that no trace of it is left. In his mind a thousand stratagems, but his face serene, he waited for one of his chief enemies to fall.

With the help of the three venerable old marshals on the Military Affairs Commission and the astute, formidable Ye Jianying, Mao had successfully reinstituted rotation of commanders. This kept Lin Biao under psychological stress. Mao had also perused the self-criticism of the "four golden stalwarts" and of Lin's wife, Ye Chun. This had been required of them after the "genius" controversy at the Lushan meeting. Mao wrote sarcastic comments on each of them. On Ye Chun's he wrote: "It was not enough for you to be a Politburo member. You now wish to ascend heaven itself."

"They live, we die." With these words, Lin Biao, his wife, and their supporters began to tighten the bonds of self-interest among themselves. They seem to have been singularly inept as conspirators, telephoning each other, sending each other messages, swearing oaths of loyalty to each other. . . . They adopted pseudonyms "for secrecy," and called Mao B.52 (because of his size or because they were impressed with the bombing potential of American planes?). Several schemes were proposed, and rejected. One of the more harebrained was the extermination of the Politburo, including Mao and Zhou. Another was the kidnapping of Mao. Yet another was setting up another Party center in Guangzhou and calling for a nationwide uprising against Mao. All this sounds unreal, the stuff of a badly written thriller. The plotters met and talked, talked and met.

In April 1971, Chen Boda was expelled from the GCCR and from the Politburo. He was not condemned by name, but the press warned, on July 1, about "individuals like Khrushchev . . . nestling by our side," the same words Mao had used to warn against Liu Shaoqi in 1966.

The summer came, a sweltering summer, and Lin Biao with his wife went to Beidaihe, the seaside resort near Beijing. The Party would soon hold another plenum. The National Assembly would hold a session and "power distribution will change," said Lin Liguo, the twenty-nine-year-old ambitious son of Lin Biao.

Mao went on a trip south, to Wuhan, to Changsha, to Hangzhou, everywhere meeting the military commanders of the provinces, and speaking to them, exposing Lin Biao's ambition. "I do not believe the army will rise to make a coup . . . not a revolutionary army." Meeting some of Lin Biao's supporters—for Mao was extremely well informed—he taunted: "And what new plans have you devised recently?" Shielded by a loyal guard, he traveled by train—planes were too risky. The train was meticulously inspected every six hours. Lin Liguo suggested killing Mao by bombing the railway carriage in which he was due to return to Beijing. This scheme also failed. On September 12, Mao's train reached Fengtai, a station some twenty kilometers from Beijing. He was met by the Beijing municipality officials and spoke to them about Lin Biao.

Two different ends are given to the tale. One is that Lin Biao was invited to dinner by Mao, and that Zhou arranged for him, his wife, and his confederates to be mown down by the 8341 praetorian guard. The bodies were then placed in a Trident plane which took off and crashed in Outer Mongolia.

But this version is denied by everyone in China. It is totally unconfirmed.

The other version is that, on hearing of Mao's return, Lin Biao and his son decided to flee. A Trident plane had been put at their disposal, and waited at Shanhaiguan, not far from Beidaihe. Till the last moment Lin was undecided. To fly to Guangzhou or to fly to the U.S.S.R. and there set up an opposition to Mao? Lin had spent many years in the U.S.S.R. and did not doubt that he would be welcome.

In any case, Lin Biao's daughter, who was terrified of the comings and goings and the agitation around her, spoke of her father's "leaving" to her fiancé, and he reported the matter to the 8341 elite guard officer in charge. It was then ten o'clock at night on September 12, 1971. A phone call from the officer found Zhou in his office at ten-thirty. Zhou ordered all planes in the whole of China grounded, and telephoned Wu Faxian, the air force commander. "What is an air force Trident doing in Shanhaiguan?" Wu Faxian pretended ignorance, and warned Lin Biao. Lin panicked. Around midnight, he, his wife, his son, and some confederates left hastily for Shanhaiguan, reaching the Trident before a jeepful of 8341 guards sent to confiscate the plane. The pilot had no time to fill the tank, and the plane took off.

Zhou sat up all night. The radars monitored the flight. Zhou attempted to speak to the pilot and to the passengers, but in vain. Asked if the plane should be shot down, Zhou demurred. "No, Lin Biao is still vice-chairman of the Party."

The frontier with Outer Mongolia was crossed by 1:50 a.m. on September 13 and Zhou telephoned the news to Mao, who was asleep. "The sky must rain, a woman must wed. Let Lin Biao go," Mao said, and went back to sleep. Zhou stayed on. The radar lost track of the Trident. Zhou personally reiterated the orders, himself ringing every major commander. Nowhere in China must any plane fly. No army movements of any kind must take place. All troops must stay where they were. No navy ships may sail from any port. Zhou telephoned the twenty-nine provincial Party heads and all the cities. "He had no rest at all until late afternoon. He was up thirty-six hours at a stretch, without any sleep."

By midday on the thirteenth Lin Biao's supporters were being arrested throughout China.

The Trident attempted to land on a flat pebbly plain in Outer Mongolia. It caught fire as it skidded on uneven ground. All the occupants died. They were identified a few days later by the Chinese ambassador to Outer Mongolia, called to the spot by the Mongolian authorities.

Lin Biao's disappearance left Zhou in a dominant position. Precisely as this tragedy was being played out to its end, the major breakthrough took place. It was in that summer of 1971 that Henry Kissinger, President Richard Nixon's adviser, went on his first visit to China, and it was on July 15 that President Nixon announced his intention to visit Beijing. The United States and China, after twenty-two years of hostility, were coming toward each other. Zhou's unflagging efforts to bring about reconciliation had been successful. No one was happier than the French ambassador, Etienne Mana'ch, who, with me, toasted this breakthrough one night in Beijing. "The hour of Zhou Enlai has come," he said. And millions in China thought the same, and toasted, silently, the resilient and formidable Premier. It is reported—but this may be just gossip, and China is prolific in imaginative rumor—that when Lin Biao had heard the news, he had said, "If Zhou Enlai can invite Nixon, then I can invite Brezhnev."

Lin Biao's death was kept a close secret for many months. Although the news circulated in confidential documents within the Party a few days after the plane crash, no one would "know" about it until it was publicly announced, a year later.

24

On the evening of March 31, 1968, President Johnson had stated in a televised address that the bombing of North Vietnam would be restricted to below the 20th parallel, and offered talks to end the war. He also announced that he would not stand as a candidate for the next presidential term. America was awash with a tidal wave of opposition to the Vietnam War. The next President would have to promise, and deliver, disengagement and the return of the 525,000 American soldiers in Vietnam (30,000 of them had died by the end of 1968).

Unyielding, astute, continuing to fight while negotiating, the North Vietnamese agreed in May to meet the Americans in Paris. They proved masters at *tata tantan*, talking and fighting at the same time, making the discussions drag endlessly while their military offensives continued, and enlarged. The peace talks lasted five years, and fighting did not stop for a day.

Zhou told Pham Van Dong, the Vietnamese Premier, that the American offer was a trick "but of course the decision is in your hands." His suspicion was based on the fact that Moscow had welcomed the offer. Zhou saw this as a Soviet plot to strengthen their hold on Vietnam and weaken China's influence. In fact, because of the Cultural Revolution, China's delivery of weapons to Vietnam had been erratic. Chinese aid to Vietnam was now stepped up, reaching its highest point in 1971.

Yet Zhou knew that there was fresh thinking in Washington about China. Dean Acheson, former Secretary of State and one of Washington's most balanced men, had bluntly told Johnson that the administration had to find a way out of a thoroughly unpopular and profitless war. Writing in October 1967 in *Foreign Affairs Quarterly*, Richard Nixon, the Republican candidate for the presidency, had envisaged China being brought into the world community of nations and not left "in angry isolation." Nixon's views were influenced by General de Gaulle, a man Nixon greatly admired. In 1963 and in 1968, the two had met and talked about China, and de Gaulle had recommended that normal relations be established, for the benefit of the West.

Zhou had indeed detected "some change in the climate in Washington," as he remarked to his staff. He increased the number of employees in charge of collecting material about the United States. He floated another offer to resume the talks in Warsaw between China and the United States, interrupted after their 134th meeting in early 1968. The talks had got nowhere, "but the purpose is not to get anywhere, it is to indicate that we are there," Qiao Guanhua remarked to me. "It takes a long rope to catch a whale."

Nixon was not yet President, and everything was stalled. Moscow remained a problem. Since 1964, when Zhou had precipitated the rupture with the U.S.S.R., and despite the ravages of the Cultural Revolution, Moscow had been unable to drum China out of the socialist camp. In July 1968, Brezhnev enunciated the doctrine of "limited sovereignty," arrogating to the U.S.S.R. the right to intervene in any socialist state when socialism was reckoned "in danger." In August, Russian armies had marched into Czechoslovakia.

Zhou made full use of this event, attending a reception at the Romanian embassy on August 23, where he denounced "the abominable crimes of the U.S.S.R. against the Czech people . . . with the tacit accord of American imperialism." The last words were part of the standard phraseology used throughout the years.

While the United States was showing signs of a change of heart toward "Red China," Soviet Russia was increasing her pressure. In March 1969, when a clash occurred on the Ussuri River between Russian and Chinese troops, Soviet ambassadors in Washington, London, Paris, and Bonn told Western governments that China was a great danger for everyone, even suggesting "concerted action," including a strike on China's nuclear sites. It was Nixon, now President of the United States, who had made it very clear to the Russians that the United States would not move against China.

On March 21, Kosygin, more alert to the changing situation than Brezhnev, tried to telephone Zhou Enlai. He was unable to reach him, because the young telephone operator in Beijing, full of Cultural Revolution spirit, told Kosygin, "We do not speak to revisionists," and refused to put him through. Zhou was only told forty-eight hours later.

Throughout these alarums and excursions, and despite Lin Biao's calls for war preparedness, Zhou had persistently maintained that it was all "thunder and lightning with no rain."

Meanwhile, things were moving on the American side. In February 1969, Richard Nixon was again in Paris, conferring with de Gaulle. "Of course, de Gaulle had to wait until Nixon became President," Etienne Mana'ch told me in one of our talks. "No action could be taken until an understanding was reached between the general and the President of the United States." The President and his adviser, Henry Kissinger, had a different perspective on China from that of many State Department experts, who never questioned their assumption that the Vietnam War was a product of Chinese belligerence. They saw China as *the* main enemy. The whole process of change would need an infinite amount of delicate diplomacy.

On April 22, 1969, Mana'ch was personally briefed by de Gaulle. "Washington will now try to open a real dialogue with China. The United States is disposed to recognize China, and her admittance to the United Nations."

Diplomatic etiquette made it difficult for Mana'ch to reach Zhou Enlai. Yet the latter had often in the past brushed away protocol. He had summoned Indian ambassador P. K. Bannerjee to long colloquies at night. But the Cultural Revolution lingered on; Lin Biao had just been promoted successor and heir to Mao. The patiently waiting Mana'ch was shunted to an audience with Vice-Chairman Dung Biwu on May 22. Dung Biwu was a gentle soul, but very old. His entourage of cadres either did not understand the importance of the message or thought it best to relay it with no insistence on what Mana'ch really had meant. It was September before the knot was untied, as Zhou put it.

The American-Vietnamese talks in Paris and the military successes on the ground by the armies of the DRV also posed a problem. The American delegation in Paris found itself balked and harried as it tried to come to grips with the North Vietnamese delegation, superbly competent, with the Liberation Front of South Vietnam, and with their own "allies," the representatives of the government in Saigon, perhaps in the end the most troublesome of all.

Nixon adopted a careful, step-by-step approach. He hinted in his speeches at another assessment of relations with China. In the summer of 1969, he allowed certain relaxations of the embargo —Americans could now purchase a hundred dollars' worth of Chinese goods per person. These advances were noted, but Zhou had to be extremely careful. The irascible Vietnamese were only too prone to suspect China of double-dealing. He did not want to destroy the equilibrium achieved between China and the U.S.S.R. in their delicately poised relationship with Vietnam. Zhou did not want a predominantly Russian influence in Vietnam, which, with a hostile India, would mean a total land encirclement of China.

Nixon was losing patience with the Vietnamese. He threatened to resume the bombing should the Paris talks go on being mere waffle. But Ho Chi Minh's last act of supreme defiance was his reply, late that August of 1969, that there would be no compromise in Vietnam's aim of reunification. Ho Chi Minh died on September 2, and Zhou, in a moving talk, acclaimed Ho. "He was my friend, my teacher. . . . I knew him since 1922 when we were together in Paris." He flew to Hanoi for the obsequies, and during his stay reassured Pham Van Dong that China would continue to provide the required weaponry. But the clashes of that spring between its two main supporters had greatly worried Hanoi, and its press issued articles and editorials proclaiming the necessity of "unity" and "one Communist world." Kosygin and Zhou, who had avoided each other in Hanoi, met on September 12, in a four-hour talk, at the Beijing airport.

The talk ranged over many contentious and prickly issues. "We have never asked for the return of territories annexed by Czarist Russia through unequal treaties," Zhou stated. But China wanted no further encroachments. There must be a clear delineation of the frontiers. Meanwhile, a total cease-fire, and careful troop supervision at the borders, would prevent further clashes. On October 20, negotiations on frontier delineation began in Beijing.

Having thus defused the situation with the U.S.S.R. and reassured Vietnam, Zhou could now attend to Mana'ch's message, which he did on September 27. It was the celebration of Afghanistan's National Day. Zhou as usual walked to each table, toasting the guests. "But then he came straight back to me, and also saluted my wife. 'Madame,' he said, bowing to her. Zhou always noticed women, did not treat them as mere adjuncts. He grinned charmingly at my wife. He again raised his glass to mine. This was the signal. Two days later, I received a call to see him. I told him what General de Gaulle had said to me. 'It's almost unbelievable. . . . I cannot quite believe it,' said Zhou. 'Is this also your own conviction?' I assured him that I thought Nixon really meant what he had said to de Gaulle. 'Nixon wants to end the Dulles policy. I am not pleading for the United States, Your Excellency, they are big enough to speak for themselves.' Here Zhou laughed, throwing his head back, a happy man, still a little amazed that suddenly all he had hoped for might be within reach. 'I am convinced that the United States does want normalization with your country. It is in their best interests.' Zhou Enlai nodded. This is what he had said for twenty-five years, since he had seen the members of the Dixie mission in Yenan, in 1944. 'There are no conflicts of interest between China and the United States,' Zhou Enlai repeated. He cogitated for a while, then, in an easy way, added: 'But the United States does not recognize their defeat in Vietnam. Their announced withdrawal is fictitious. They want to leave a puppet government in place in South Vietnam.' "

"But they want their head out of the tiger's mouth, Your Excellency," Mana'ch replied, and this made Zhou laugh again.

It was on October 2, four days later, that I received a suggestion from Gung Peng that I might "unofficially" invite General de Gaulle to visit China. My attempts to pierce the wall of the Quai d'Orsay bureaucracy proved fruitless. Finally a message did reach the general through his good friend Jacques Rueff. But de Gaulle was unwell, and though he finally received the invitation, he was physically unable to accept. He died in the fall of 1970.

An intricate, delicately stylized play, full of coy feints and staged pursuits, took place between Zhou, Nixon, and Henry Kissinger. The new U.S. President, with singular courage, responded positively to Mana'ch's account of his conversation with Zhou. Zhou's suggestion to resume the Warsaw talks was promoted with much vigor, so that the American ambassador to Poland literally ran after a fleet-footed Chinese ambassador down the corridors at an official reception, to inform the latter that Washington wanted to talk. A fortnight of ponderous silence from Beijing followed. Zhou received secret messages from President Yahya Khan of Pakistan, from Ceausescu of Romania. Both of them had been approached by President Nixon in July 1969, on his return from Guam, where in a major speech he had swept away many of the cobwebs enmeshing the minds of China experts, and raised the problem of global relationships in a new perspective.

The talks in Warsaw between China and the United States resumed in February 1970. Further relaxation of the embargo took place in March 1970. But in March a coup took place in Cambodia, ousting Norodom Sihanouk, replacing him with a pro-Western government headed by General Lon Nol, erstwhile Premier of the Cambodian state.

The reasons for this coup are not entirely clear. The CIA is blamed, and also Henry Kissinger. The provocation was the existence of thirteen North Vietnamese bases on Cambodian territory. Despite his suspicions—based on historical precedent—that North Vietnam "tends to consider that the whole of erstwhile French Indochina should be under their hegemony," Norodom Sihanouk had allowed these sanctuaries "out of solidarity for the Vietnamese war of liberation." This, of course, went against Cambodia's stance of neutrality. But through the port of Sihanoukville in Cambodia, war matériel was being transported to the thirteen bases and on to the Liberation Front of South Vietnam. This matériel was not only Russian but also Chinese. It was the Chinese who paid for the conveying of goods, and the man who was being paid was . . . Lon Nol, through his wife's transport company. In 1969, during an official visit to Beijing as Premier of Cambodia, Lon Nol had asked for more money. "He made quite irrational demands," Zhang Wenjing told me.

Then why the coup? Perhaps Lon Nol would get more money from the Americans, who now and for the next three years were to extend largesse to him, hoping that a Cambodian army could be trained to participate in the Vietnam War. Nixon wanted the war de-Americanized. Evidence, therefore, points to an American-mounted plan, despite Kissinger's denials. In the previous eighteen months, American planes had made more than 3,600 sorties in massive bombardments against the thirteen sanctuaries identified.

Norodom Sihanouk was away on a state visit to Moscow when the coup against him took place. He arrived in Beijing on March 18, the very day that Lon Nol took over the government in Cambodia. Sihanouk, however, was received with all the honor and ceremony befitting a head of state, and Zhou Enlai was there to welcome him at the airport. The two rode together in the car taking Sihanouk and his wife to the State Guesthouse. Sihanouk himself told me the story when we met in August 1988 to recapitulate the whole episode. "Zhou Enlai asked me, 'Are you going to withdraw now that you have been deposed, or are you going to fight? The decision is yours.' 'I am going to fight, this is totally illegal.' Zhou Enlai then gripped my hand in both of his. 'Then we shall be with you, right until the end,' he said to me."

Because of this American-supported coup in Cambodia, the Sino-U.S. talks in Warsaw, scheduled for that May, were postponed as being "inappropriate at this time." On July 10, 1970, in a reciprocity of signals, an American bishop arrested in 1958 in China was released from jail and in return Washington granted further commercial concessions.

Edgar Snow, who had not been issued a visa to China during the years 1968–69—due to the overwhelming influence of Madame Mao—had been invited back by Zhou in that summer of 1970. On October 1, Zhou brought him and his wife to stand next to Mao Dzedong atop the main gate overlooking the crowds gathered in Tienanmen Square to celebrate the anniversary. This was a major signal to Washington, flaunting Mao's favorable consideration of American overtures, and was ignored by most of America's China experts. But Nixon and Kissinger did not miss the gesture, and Nixon told *Time* magazine on October 5 that he hoped to go to China in his lifetime. To Pakistan President Yahya Khan, he confirmed his decision to normalize relations with China.

By November 1970, less than a month later, the Vietnamese had mounted a large-scale military offensive, which proved successful. Zhou allayed Vietnamese fears of a letdown, and even undertook unofficial negotiations with Lon Nol to let matériel through Cambodia, for the Ho Chi Minh Trail, though enlarged, was insufficient. Lon Nol's anti-Communist troops were animated by a great instinct for self-preservation. They regularly disappeared before the whiff of any battle could reach them. Reassured that he would not be negotiating from weakness, Zhou Enlai sent a message through Ambassador Hilaly of Pakistan. The message was orally delivered to Kissinger. Zhou specified that "an emissary from Washington" was welcome "to discuss the problem of Taiwan." He carefully avoided any reference to Vietnam.

The American answer, typed on xerox paper without letterhead or watermark, and unsigned, stated that the discussion would not be limited to the Taiwan question, but would also encompass other

Mao, Zhou, and Red
Guards in Beijing
(October 1964)

Zhou Enlai laughing
during an interview with
the journalist K. S.
Karol (1965). Photo by
Marc Riboud

Mao and others swim the
Yangtze River before
flying to Beijing to begin
the Cultural Revolution.
Photo taken by author on
July 16, 1966

Zhou paying a visit to Ho Chi Minh, who was at the
time receiving medical treatment in Liuzhou (early 1969)

Author and her husband, Colonel of Indian Army Vincent
Ruthnaswamy, being received by Zhou Enlai in September 1970
to mark the beginning of the restoration of relations between
India and China. Xiung Xianghui (second from right) was at the
time chargé d'affaires to Great Britain. Everyone but Zhou is
wearing a Mao badge

The handshake that shook
the world. President Richard
Nixon and his wife arrive in
Beijing (February 1972)

Receiving Japanese premier
Kakuei Tanaka
(September 25, 1972)

Kim Il Sung of North Korea visits Zhou in hospital. At far right is
Zhou's already chosen heir, Deng Xiaoping (1975)

Zhou, gravely ill with cancer, announcing China's opening to the world and the "four modernizations" (January 1975)

Author with Zhou Enlai's nephews and nieces at the commemoration of his ninetieth "birthday-anniversary" in March 1988

steps designed to "improve relations and reduce tensions." The most important sentence was: "The policy of the United States government is to reduce its military presence in the region of East Asia and the Pacific as tensions in this region diminish." "Our bureaucracy was not informed," Kissinger writes gleefully, reveling in the secrecy of the whole affair. Zhou pondered the message, which was an appeal for help—or so he would interpret it—with the intractable problem of Vietnam. It was an exalting message, a compliment to the newly perceived importance of China. But Zhou could not appear to give in to America on Vietnam, now the cherished cause of every liberal in the world, and of millions of ordinary people who admired the courage of that small nation, and saw on TV the horrors of the war. Mao was more impatient. On December 18, he gave a long interview to Edgar Snow, in which he clearly mentioned that the President of the United States would be welcome in China, in whatever capacity he came.

To Snow's intense surprise, a prestigious American newspaper turned the interview down. It was published in *Life* magazine on April 27, 1971. Mao could not wait. Another message had gone to Washington through the Romanian ambassador, Corneliu Bogdan, on January 11, 1971.

"President Richard Nixon . . . as a visitor, tourist, or as President of the United States," was invited. Zhou added to this document: "Since President Nixon has already visited Bucharest and Belgrade, we would like to state that he shall be warmly welcome."

Even before the two sides had met, their reasoning ran along broadly parallel courses. Both were aware of the changing equilibrium of power which dictated new alliances. It is to the enduring credit of Nixon and Kissinger that with imagination and intelligence they began to structure a new course of thought and action to sweep away decades of hostility.

In April 1971, an American Ping-Pong team competing in Nagoya, Japan, was invited to China. The phrase "Ping-Pong diplomacy" was coined, and seemed to awaken the experts from their lethargy. The next move was Kissinger's secret visit to Beijing in July, confirmed by a two-page aide-mémoire from Zhou Enlai, sent through the Chinese embassy in Paris.

During these months, Lin Biao had been engaged in that strange and deadly duel with Mao. Zhou, thinking ahead, multiplied his efforts to get China back in working condition, and especially its scientific sphere, to prepare it for the impact of America. He saw this impact as an opening to new technology. "Only America can help China to modernize," Zhou repeated. There were Chinese-American scientists of great expertise, and messages went out to them. "We need every patriotic Chinese," he had told Guomindang general Du Yuming, whose son-in-law was the well-known Nobel Prize-winning physicist Yang Chen Ning. "We have many intellectuals in America. We must enlist their cooperation." The first computer units were set up in the universities with the help of the physicist Zhou Peiyuan in 1971. Plans for needs in energy, transport, and communication, the expansion of the electricity grid, were now given priority. Zhou ordered large amounts of books to be purchased from the West "on anything that will help us to understand high technology. . . . We have been deprived of good books for too long." I was asked to supply books, and sent through Wang Bingnan a good many, including David Halberstam's *The Best and the Brightest*. A team of biogeneticists was called to meet Zhou Enlai, who wanted to know everything about genetic manipulation. "He grasped what we said, though he was untrained. 'This way lies the future for us,' he told us." He asked of every scientist he saw, "What do you need most at present?"

On July 9, 1971, in total secrecy, Henry Kissinger boarded an aircraft in Pakistan, and arrived the same day in Beijing, to see Zhou Enlai at 4:30 p.m. Present at the talks were a galaxy of Zhou trainees. Huang Hua, Han Xu, Zhang Wenjing, Zhi Chaozhu, the brother of scientist Zhi Chaoting. None of them needed an interpreter, their English being perfect, but of course interpreters had to be there, *pour la forme*. "Premier Zhou had reviewed all the previous data, the correspondence, briefed himself on everything that had happened in the United States in the past several weeks," Zhang Wenjing told me. "Then he wrote down some of the main points on a small piece of paper, and that was all the material he brought to the meeting." Kissinger was captivated, and his fascination increased as the meetings multiplied. "Zhou moved gracefully and with dignity . . . filling a room . . . by his air of controlled tension." At the first meeting Zhou gave Kissinger a half smile—an acknowledgment, cordial but not off-guard—and the meeting was on.

"At first we were rather puzzled by Mr. Kissinger. We thought, quite frankly, that he was being arrogant . . . but then we were not used to his style. He talked much of philosophy, and general principles, but it seemed to us inappropriate, a little like a moral lecture. However, Premier Zhou set the tone and pace, and got to the matters to be discussed; Kissinger changed immediately." Courtesy and humor alleviated the ponderousness of these important exchanges lasting many hours. Perhaps Kissinger had at first used an overconfident, slightly aggressive vocabulary, but "being a man of great intelligence, I think he admired Zhou for cutting through the thickets of verbiage," says Zhang Wenjing, who grew to admire Kissinger very much, especially when Zhang became ambassador in Washington.

Kissinger writes of Zhou's moral ambivalence and inner serenity. Zhou could indeed endure immense battering of spirit with apparent stoic placidity and emerge unscathed. But how much private agony it cost him we will never know, for "he swallowed it all, swallowed the grief, as a child swallows saliva. It would disappear in him." "Moral ambivalence" is an inapposite term, indicating Kissinger's ignorance of Taoism, that fundamental duality of spirit which made Zhou accept that good and evil are inseparable Siamese twins. The Judaic notion of guilt and expiation did not haunt him. What mattered was the notion of righteousness, and especially responsibility and honor in friendship.

What was accomplished at this first meeting was remarkable. A wide, broad exchange, and once this was achieved, everything else became subsidiary, problems which time, skillful handling, mutual understanding, and generosity of spirit would solve. The two implicitly recognized that they would be natural partners in a strategy which, for the Pacific region, would define the twenty-first century.

"We are on the threshold of a technical revolution which will alter all views and concepts. We must ready ourselves for it," Zhou told his staff after Kissinger's visit. Kissinger suggested that Paris should become the main channel of communication, since he was frequently there, engaged in parleys with the Vietnamese. Zhou accepted, but insisted that Pakistan, which had rendered such exquisitely discreet service in this most difficult of all diplomatic affairs, also be used. "One does not break a bridge after crossing it," Zhou reminded the American.

Even if Taiwan was, for the Chinese, the most substantive issue, the stubborn, unyielding problem, in this and other meetings, was Vietnam. Zhou lectured Kissinger on Vietnam. How could America, gifted with so much strength, so many intelligent people, commit such a mistake? It was neither morally nor politically possible for China to give up her commitment to Vietnam. The United States should withdraw swiftly, to avoid more losses. "Vietnamization, Laoization, Cambodiazation of the war, you will find that none of these schemes will work," said Zhou Enlai.

"We have decades of mutual ignorance between us, many bridges to cross," Zhou said to his guest. Fundamentals, rather than specifics, must be the substance of the first talks. Kissinger remained haunted by the many bridges, big and small, marble, straight, or camelback, zigzag devil-stopping bridges, which dotted the State Residence. "We sought to convey that we could still turn back, that we had not crossed our Rubicon. Yet all the time we knew that the Rubicon was behind us . . . we had nowhere to go but forward."

Both men established an extraordinary rapport, perceptive, appreciative, stimulating. Kissinger praised Zhou's "luminous personality and extraordinary perception." Zhou thoroughly enjoyed the wit and thrust of Kissinger's conversation. "Come again, just for the pleasure of talking," he said to Henry. During those lonely years of the Cultural Revolution, Zhou had been starved of intelligent talk. During those weeks and months through the valleys of grief, he had had to dim his own intelligence, as one turns down a lamp. He had to prate and chant slogans, to flatter and prevaricate. . . .

Before Kissinger departed, Huang Hua gave him the draft of a joint communiqué which would be read at the same hour in both countries on July 15. "There was only one word to change," writes Kissinger, not telling us what the word was.

On July 15, President Richard Nixon read out the announcement in Washington at the same time that it was read in Beijing. Kissinger's secret trip was now revealed to the world. The message read:

"Premier Zhou Enlai and Dr. Henry Kissinger, President Nixon's Assistant for National Security Affairs, held talks in Beijing from July 9 to 11, 1971. Knowing of President Nixon's express desire to visit the People's Republic of China, Premier Zhou Enlai, on behalf of the government of the People's Republic of China, has extended an invitation to President Nixon to visit China at an appropriate date before May 1972. President Nixon has accepted the invitation with pleasure. The meeting between the leaders of China and the United States is to seek the normalization of relations between the two countries and also to exchange views on questions of concern to the two sides."

World reactions were of stupefaction, joy, or dismay.

In the Kremlin, the words "before May 1972" evoked disquiet. A summit with the President, in May 1972, had been tentatively fixed. With Machiavellian cunning, Zhou had succeeded in getting *his* summit before Moscow's. Moscow asked if it would be possible for President Nixon to come to Moscow before going to Beijing. Nixon replied in the negative.

The Japanese had not expected such a swift outcome. When I had lectured in Japan in 1970, I hinted that American foreign policy might swiftly change. "It will take another ten years," said a confident member of the Japanese Foreign Ministry. I was grateful to receive later a charming note acknowledging that I had been right. The Japanese now hurried to make up for not having been told—which chagrined them—what was going on in the sinuous alleyways of American diplomacy.

It was in that summer of 1971 that Mao Dzedong went on an extended tour of China, to rally the military commanders and to rail at Lin Biao. And in that September, Lin Biao and his wife and son died in the plane crash in Outer Mongolia.

Kissinger's next trip to China took place three months later, in November 1971. It was a well-publicized excursion to finalize the program for the reception of President Nixon in February 1972. Once again Vietnam was discussed. There would be no sellout of Vietnam, said Zhou. Nor must the Chinese overture be played against Moscow. "We have our own problems with the U.S.S.R., but the United States must not stand on China's shoulders to reach Moscow . . . nor must Washington come to any secret agreement with Moscow as regards China."

Vietnam. Vietnam. Zhou was adamant. "You will not be able to stay . . . you will fail." Kissinger showed his notorious temper. "One day, *you'll* have to cope with the Vietnamese . . . and then you'll know what SOBs they are," he is supposed to have said to Zhou Enlai.

With the impassioned hatred of those who love passionately, the United States had assiduously blocked China's admission to the United Nations year after year. In 1971, Kissinger told Zhou that his country would continue to block China's seating at the UN. The wily Henry proposed two formulas. One was dual representation of China and Taiwan. The other was continued United States support for Taiwan regardless of what happened at the UN . . . a support undermined by his presence in Beijing. Zhou said support for Taiwan was preferable to dual representation. "If the motion fails, we can wait a little longer . . . we have already waited twenty-two years," said Zhou.

The second visit was extremely cordial. Kissinger had come with a large staff and Zhou had studied the life story of each member. He took the time to speak to each of them and made a gracious, informal speech. "A new chapter is about to open in the history of relations between China and the United States. The credit for this should go to Chairman Mao and to President Nixon. It was Dr. Kissinger who courageously made a secret visit to China, the so-called land of mystery," said Zhou, eliciting reminiscent grins from Kissinger, who had indeed called China a land of mystery in his first talk with Zhou. Zhou had matter-of-factly replied, "It won't be mysterious when you become familiar with it."

One of Zhou's talents was his ability to pick up a conversation precisely where he had left it days, weeks, months, even years previously, and carry on as if neither time nor absence had interrupted the flow of talk. Anyone who talked with Zhou noticed this. "You say that . . . ," he would begin, as if one had just said it, when it might have been a year, or two, or five previously. This was somehow overpowering. He remembered that at my first encounter with him I had said, "My rate of progress is very slow," meaning that I was not ready to become an instant Marxist. Ten years later, with a twinkle in his eye, Zhou asked me, "What is the rate of your progress now?" It took me at least half a minute to remember. "Just as slow as before, Premier." With Kissinger, Zhou never let go of a remark, a word. Whether it was the word "mystery," or "bridges," or "philosophy," which Kissinger was fond of employing.

The Shanghai communiqué, a statement which Nixon would sign when he reached China some months later, was worked out at this second meeting, as were the details of Nixon's trip. Twenty-five hours were devoted to this exercise. But the pair also again covered the world situation. "I met no leader—with the exception of de Gaulle—with an equal grasp of world events," writes Kissinger. It was Zhou's understanding of the interrelationship of countries which Kissinger admired. The American draft of the communiqué had followed the conventional style, "highlighting fuzzy areas of agreement and obscuring differences with platitudinous generalizations." It inserted more areas of agreement than Zhou was willing to concede.

On March 5, 1987, Winston Lord, ambassador to China, who had been with Kissinger on his visits in 1971, recalled some of the drama of the drafting. The U.S. draft was "papering over differences . . . strained for common approaches and mutual agreements." He recalls that Zhou made, at the time, a "scorching" one-hour speech against the American concoction. Chairman Mao, said Zhou, viewed the draft as unacceptable. The wording was untruthful. The communiqué used hackneyed formulas. "Our two countries have fought, been hostile and isolated for over two decades from each other. We hold profoundly different views on how to shape our societies and engage the world. Who will then believe that we have suddenly closed these gaps and discovered broad affinities?"

The American draft was "consigned to the dust heap of history," to use Winston Lord's words, and in the evening, after the usual Peking duck banquet, Zhou presented the Chinese version, unprecedented in that it allowed for two utterly different views of every problem. It left blank pages after each Chinese statement of a point for the Americans to insert their own position. Kissinger, at first taken aback, realized that such a communiqué, which was also a statement of differences, gave the United States much leeway in stating its own views. "It is a novel type of communiqué," said Zhou. "Each side clearly sets forth its own position, then we sketch in those principles and areas where we can agree and forge cooperation." For the next forty-eight hours, there was frantic writing and rewriting, minute poring over every word. What to say about Taiwan proved most difficult and it was Kissinger who found the acceptable formula. "The United States acknowledges that all Chinese on either side of the Taiwan Strait maintain there is but one China. The United States government does not challenge that position." Zhou read the sentence and a wide grin spread over his face. "I do not think anything I did or said impressed Zhou as much as this ambiguous formula with which both sides were able to live," writes Kissinger.

On February 21, 1972, Richard Nixon arrived in China. He came down the steps of the plane with his hand extended toward the gaunt, thin man who waited bareheaded for him. "Your handshake came over the vastest ocean in the world, twenty-five years of noncommunication," said Zhou to Nixon.

Within two hours Nixon met Mao, who had a cold. He seemed fit enough, and conducted the conversation skillfully, the tone set being crucial to the climate of trust and frankness so carefully built. Mao and Zhou acted completely in unison, and Zhou's position was now considered so secure that rumor addicts began to speak of him as Mao's "successor," a word which Zhou shunned. Mao's evident approval made it impossible for anyone to utilize "the American connection" against Zhou Enlai.

Conversations continued between Nixon and Zhou. The fine points of the Shanghai communiqué were given meticulous and careful polishing. Nixon opted for a "weasel-worded" statement, covering up the problems, but Zhou was against it. "If we were to act like this we would not only be deceiving the people, we would be deceiving ourselves."

Once again, Vietnam. The negotiations in Paris dragged on, with Le Duc Tho of North Vietnam suggesting that Kissinger get rid of Thieu, the head of the Saigon government, "to facilitate agreement." This, of course, was unthinkable. Though Kissinger found all Vietnamese, including Thieu, impossibly irritating, Thieu could not be replaced by someone secretly compliant toward Hanoi. In one of his meetings with the stubborn Vietnamese, Zhou suggested that Hanoi work out an accommodation with Thieu. The Vietnamese, with atavistic suspicion, considered this a Chinese ploy to keep Vietnam divided. Zhou told Kissinger that in no way would China exert any pressure on Vietnam. He urged Nixon to withdraw swiftly. "This is a most pressing question. The American Democratic Party makes things more difficult for you by saying that you came to China to settle the Vietnam problem. Of course this is not possible." With some emotion, he repeated: "The later you withdraw, the more difficult it will be. Now the whole world is watching what is being done in Vietnam. The Vietnamese are fighting for their country, and as long as they continue fighting, we must continue to support them."

Among the more agreeable moments were those in which the former enemies could speak with humor and detachment of their previous pronouncements. Nothing is more relaxing than to admit before an enemy whom one now considers a friend the phantasms one's mind has created about him. Zhou was full of stories, one being about Walter Bedell Smith in Geneva, ordered by Dulles not to shake hands and therefore holding a cup of coffee in his right hand. "But he used his left hand to shake my arm." Zhou mused about the term "monolithic." "Now we know that there is no monolithism, neither in Western nor in socialist countries." When Nixon asked a question about Mao, the Great Helmsman, Zhou stated with fetching blandness, "But the helmsman must know how to ride with the waves, or he will be submerged by the tide."

Nixon returned to Washington to be confronted with the disturbing fact that Hanoi was mounting another major offensive, involving 200,000 men on four different fronts. The situation prompted Nixon to resume bombing one hundred kilometers above the 17th parallel, which elicited strong protests from China and the U.S.S.R. But Moscow did not postpone its planned May summit, which took place when the bombing was at its heaviest. And when pressed by the Americans to speak to Hanoi, Moscow remained bleakly reticent.

On January 27, 1973, an agreement was solemnly signed in Paris by all four parties attending the Vietnam conference. "It's all over," wrote *Stars and Stripes*. The relief was immense. But of course it was not over. The war continued.

Zhou, however, did feel some relief. The end was near. The Americans would be beaten. Zhou, pragmatically, looked forward to a diminution in the amount of aid to Vietnam. Twenty billion dollars' worth of matériel and equipment, never to be repaid, had gone from China to help fraternal socialist Vietnam.

In the summer of 1972, Zhou Enlai passed some blood in his urine. He was examined, tests were carried out, and cancer of the bladder was diagnosed.

I saw Zhou Enlai that summer. I was at the airport, together with Rewi Alley. He had been invited to welcome some dignitary, and then Zhou Enlai appeared. He launched himself out of the small Polish-made car which he had used for years. No secretary was with him, and he was as sprightly and cheerful as ever, carrying his own briefcase. "Don't you think that Zhou Enlai is getting quite transparent?" Rewi Alley asked me. Rewi knew the verdict of the medical examinations, but of course he did not tell me. He merely gave me a hint. But Zhou looked so well, so cheerful . . .

The health of China's Premier was to remain a closely guarded secret. However, it was no secret among the top leaders, and of course his enemies knew. Jiang Qing and her cohort of supporters were elated. They had been sidestepped, overshadowed, outplayed. Zhou Enlai had brought off that extraordinary feat: The U.S. President had come to Beijing. He had landed the great and beautiful whale, at last.

But if he was ill, then there was hope for them. They would now begin a renewed bid for power.

In that summer of 1972, Zhou Enlai was seventy-four years old.

25

Wu Huanxin—also known as George Wu—and I had been medical students in Belgium in 1935. A cancer specialist, Dr. Wu returned to China in 1936 to set up China's first cancer hospital in Shanghai. An Overseas Chinese from a wealthy family in Mauritius, Wu was ardently patriotic and chose to serve his own people "through hard times or good times." Under him cancer work in China had greatly progressed. He had created an all-China network of early cancer detection. During the Cultural Revolution he was downgraded, his house was ransacked twice by Red Guards, and he was abused by the "rebels" among his own staff as a "bourgeois tyrant." But Zhou Enlai saw to it that the Cancer Hospital's Revolutionary Committee was headed by Li Bing, a nurse, the daughter of Zhou's old friend Smiling Buddha Li Kenung. Discreetly, Li Bing allowed George to work as he had always done, even when the "rebels" removed the files of the patients, "state secrets" which George was accused of passing on to foreign doctors.

After President Nixon's visit in February 1972, Beijing was perpetually garlanded. Droves of heads of state now found the road to China, to Zhou Enlai. In June, Zhou entered the hospital for a thorough examination, where a team of cancer specialists had to decide on the Premier's health. George Wu was one of the team, but when he walked to the door of Zhou's hospital suite he was stopped by the security guard.

George was a bourgeois, not a Party member. "How can we trust the Premier's life to an unreliable bourgeois?" Madame Mao had exclaimed. Yet she herself had had George dance attendance upon her many times. "She took me away from my work. I had to wait a week in her own residence before the capricious woman was available," he told me.

A Prime Minister's illness is a state affair. A special committee was formed to supervise the medical care given to Zhou Enlai. It comprised two supporters of Jiang Qing, Zhang Chunqiao (Spring Bridge) and the young worker Wang Hungwen.

How could Wang Hungwen be suddenly "helicoptered" to such high rank? Thirty-eight years old, a worker in textile factory No. 17 in Shanghai, a field messenger during the Korean War, he had been picked up by the GCCR. Many of his supporters were nominated delegates at the Ninth Party Congress in 1969. He became a Central Committee member, and in 1972 was co-opted to the Politburo. Some records seem to indicate that it was because he helped in the downfall of Lin Biao. The Shanghai clique, also to be known as the Gang of Four, a name which Mao gave to the four around him in 1973, thus came into being.

"Because of Jiang Qing and Wang Hungwen," George Wu told me, "Zhou Enlai did not have an early operation. My advice to operate early was turned down. The Premier had cardiac problems. It was considered unsafe." Years after Zhou Enlai's death, George Wu wept when he talked to me of Zhou's last years.

To those who did not know that Zhou had cancer, 1972 was his year of triumph. The year when he appeared in total control. And when coldly, detachedly, he began to prepare the future, knowing that he had little time left to live.

Did Zhou Enlai, lying in bed after his usual strenuous day, doing with less sleep than ever, review in his mind his life and the beliefs that had inspired him? The adolescent Zhou had clung to faith in the human spirit. To him revolution could never be merely a mechanistic, social-material process. "The heart of man must also change," he had written at nineteen, and in 1938 he had talked about his faith in the "new man" to Bishop Roots in Wuhan. Buddhism also influenced him in his conviction that the spirit must strive for human perfection. He had perhaps been captivated by Mao's grand vision, the Cultural Revolution, with its appeal to the masses. Disillusion followed. The Cultural Revolution, like all human upheavals, had been a passionate excuse for many crimes, had engendered its monsters of greed, ambition, and carnage. Now both he and Mao were old. But man must live and eat, must be educated, a country must progress. . . . On the edge of departure from life, Zhou turned to establishing a stable and orderly base for the living. To him this meant reassuming Party control, restoring the Party machine to working order. Populism was all very well; the masses might, one day, grow to be eminently wise. But it was necessary to ensure an administration, to elaborate policies, to fulfill the grand vision of a China "modern and prosperous." It could not be done unless the Party reassumed control.

He now deftly promoted policies opposite to those promoted by the "left," and in some cases contrary to those Mao had enunciated. But Mao had reversed himself on several occasions. He was prone to making contradictory remarks, but each remark had the force of an edict. The Four would eagerly snatch at some phrase of his which they could use as a new "supreme directive." So did Zhou Enlai. Zhou went regularly to report to Mao, and returned with Mao's acquiescence to what Zhou had already decided. The Four would surround the aging Mao, coax words out of him to their benefit. Zhou would quote Mao against Mao.

Zhou had always been quick and light on his feet. In the autumn of 1972, I had watched him run, run out of his car, followed by a panting secretary. Was this a man with cancer already gouging his body? A man in a hurry, but on his face no shadow of distress. A man buoyed by urgency, the urgency of beckoning death. He smiled a wonderful smile as we met that September at the airport and he asked my husband, "How was your trip to Singapore?" It was impish of him, for my husband had been denied a visa to Singapore.

When Zhou had left Japan in 1919, he had been penniless, confused, a failure as a student, his future unclear and unpromising. On the train to Tokyo in 1918, he had spoken with Professor Shoto Motogi, who remembered the encounter with great fondness, and had given the professor his card. Now, fifty-four years later, on September 29, 1972, Motogi's grandson, a member of a Japanese delegation to Beijing, brought back the card with greetings from Shoto Motogi, then eighty-eight years old. Zhou was deeply moved.

On the card, Zhou had inscribed his *hao*, Xiang Yu, Soaring in Space. The *hao* had proved prophetic.

A noticeable acceleration in Party and government reconstruction began in the summer of 1972. The eighteen functioning ministries and commissions of 1969 were increased to thirty-one by the end of 1973. The Planning Commission was restored in July 1972. The number of military representatives in the provincial governments was lowered from 57 to 40 percent. Party secretaries returned and reassumed their jobs. The format of these restorations is depicted in one of Zhou's letters: "I have seen Chairman Mao. . . . The Chairman has said that Tan Zhenlin has committed errors but is still a good comrade . . . he should return. . . . It now appears that the Hall of Nurturing Benevolence events were misrepresented by Lin Biao to overthrow old comrades. . . .

"Comrade Deng Xiaoping has asked several times to be allowed to do some work. . . . The Chairman has also mentioned this several times." Armed with Mao's approval, Zhou Enlai began the work of Party resurgence. He got them all back. Tan Zhenlin, Li Jingquan, Deng Xiaoping.

It was at Chen Yi's funeral that Zhou first initiated the return of Deng Xiaoping. Chen, retired from the Ministry of Foreign Affairs, had died of bowel cancer in the autumn of 1972. Zhou Enlai sent a message to Mao, and Mao, who had always liked bluff Chen Yi, came to the funeral in his pajamas, a coat thrown over his shoulders. He fingered the large wreath provided by Zhou in his name. "Enlai, you think of everything." He said to Chen Yi's widow, "Chen Yi was a good comrade," and added, as an afterthought, "So is Deng Xiaoping a good comrade. . . ."

And Zhou, who watched every gesture, every word, took heed. He gently led the grieving Mao to his car. Later he sent, indirectly, a message to Deng Xiaoping, who was in a southern province, with his family around him. It indicated that soon all would be well. . . .

Deng was back in Beijing in April 1973, at a banquet given for Norodom Sihanouk, to be noticed, to signal his reentry into the leadership. I knew Deng by sight, and spotted him before being told that he was there. He was still accompanied by a public security man, and when the banquet ended, he went out of the hall by the back door. But he would enter and leave by the front door at the next banquet. Zhou, it seems, had chosen his successor.

On the faces of the Gang of Four wrath and disapproval at Deng's presence were writ large. But Zhou no longer maneuvered as a ghost in the silver light of the moon. His time on earth was short, and each day shortened it.

In December 1971, Zhou had begun a Party rectification, a purge of Lin Biao's adherents. Deng Xiaoping had solid support in the army, and now he and Zhou proceeded to clean it up, with replacements, demotions, shifts at various echelons to isolate Lin's partisans and render them ineffectual.

He met in 1973 with several scientists from abroad, including the Nobel Prize-winning physicist Yang Chen Ning. Again he pushed for the study of fundamental science and theoretical research. "All obstacles in the way of these studies must be removed," he wrote in a letter to members of the Academy of Sciences. "Strengthening fundamental science and research can no longer be delayed. It is absolutely essential to our progress. It should become one of the chief aims of the Academy."

In January 1973, a peace agreement had been signed in Paris between the North Vietnam and U.S. governments. This made it possible for a U.S. liaison office to be set up in Beijing, and a Chinese one in Washington, preliminary to full normalization of relations and the opening of embassies. In February, Kissinger was back in Beijing to talk with Zhou Enlai. Zhou enjoyed two days with Kissinger. This was the last time he would talk freely to the man he valued, whose conversation delighted and refreshed his spirit.

"Coal production is deficient, and so is electric power . . . how can overall production increase if these problems are not taken in hand?" At a meeting of the Planning Commission, Zhou urged that criticism of Lin Biao and "ultra-leftist" errors be pushed more vigorously, "otherwise some people still believe that they do not need to work." The perennial problem of equilibrium between centralization and decentralization came up. Capital construction, said Zhou, was being pushed haphazardly. "This has to stop." Local, decentralized small factories and centrally organized industries competed for coal, iron, machinery, producing disarray and disorganization of material allotments. Zhou went to war against extreme egalitarianism. "Remuneration must be according to work done . . . this is socialism. Egalitarianism does not stimulate initiative and efficiency."

Zhou's most revealing speech was the one he delivered, extempore, on March 8, 1973, Women's Day, before the "foreign experts," the European, American, African, and other employees of the Foreign Language Press. He started by denouncing Lin Biao and Chen Boda. "They have caused losses *more serious than has Liu Shaoqi*." He apologized to those among the foreigners who had suffered duress and ill-treatment. He mentioned an American by name, Rittenberg, who was, he said, a "negative element." The latter had been a breakfast companion of Jiang Qing for a short while, and is alleged to have inflicted some persecution on his own colleagues. But the main thrust was the relations between Chinese and foreigners. "Two years ago no one dared to speak with foreigners. This is quite wrong. It is said that Chinese girls do not want to marry foreigners. How can we contribute more to humanity unless there is intermarriage? How can we practice internationalism?" Xenophobia existed among the Chinese, "due to their long resistance to imperialist oppression. Even the Overseas Chinese have this attitude. They live in their own quarters, eat Chinese food, and when they die they want their coffins sent back to their homeland. We must now cultivate a new spirit. . . ." He paid a glowing tribute to Tsai Chang, the wife of Li Fuchun, his old friends from their days together in France. "Tsai Chang, president of the Women's Federation, has always and with courage kept contact with foreigners. We must learn from her."

Zhou's endorsement of intermarriage was repeated on several occasions, notably when he spoke with some French visitors. He praised France, "where I have seen people of all races and where marriage between the races occurs." His talk shocked many cadres, and was never circulated or officially printed.

With unrelenting intensity, the Gang of Four strove against Zhou. Outwardly, he was in command, but he was being undermined. The undermining could only be done by finding theoretical errors in his speeches.

The "Wu Hao renegacy" case had been brought up again in 1972. Since the decision not to operate had been taken, Zhou had been treated with Chinese medicines and cauterization of his bladder papillomas. Back from the hospital, Zhou was again forced to defend himself against the alleged renegacy. He settled the matter—temporarily—by sending all documents to the Central Committee Archives, "so that, in the future, *certain people with ulterior motives could not once again resort to fabrication.*" He knew, of course, who these "certain people" were.

The Gang of Four now emerged with a new theoretical attack. While Zhou, in his speeches, linked Lin Biao with "ultra-leftism," they quoted a new "thought" from Mao. "Lin Biao's mistakes were not 'left' mistakes. They were essentially of the 'right,' though left in appearance," Mao had said. Yao Wenyuan (Preeminent Learning) and Zhang Chunqiao (Spring Bridge) seized upon this cursory remark. To negate the "left," as Zhou was doing, was to negate the correctness of the Cultural Revolution.

Mao was deteriorating. He had had a stroke in the winter of 1971, following the death of Lin Biao. The latter's betrayal, his intense hatred of Mao, had deeply grieved the old man. His eyesight was failing. He had atherosclerosis of the brain's blood vessels and his hours of clear-mindedness alternated with periods of futile reminiscing about the past. But he was still formidable, and at times piercingly shrewd. What he had said about Lin Biao was not necessarily designed against Zhou; it was a political judgment. But was it not also a warning to Zhou Enlai? The restoration of a Party machine, the return of an establishment Mao had sought to change, was all too evident. In that perpetual shield-and-spear, ocean-and-shore relationship between Mao and Zhou, the probability cannot be ignored that Mao was deliberately trying to curb his Premier.

The criticism of Lin Biao's mistakes as "ultra-leftism" was indeed intended to bring the Gang of Four's own deeds under scrutiny. Now the Four fought back. Lin Biao was *not* a leftist, but a rightist. Mao *had said so*: "There should be no hurry in criticizing Lin Biao till the theoretical background is clear. Lin Biao's crimes were left in appearance, but right-wing-inspired," said Zhang Spring Bridge. Lin Biao was "just like Chiang Kaishek, like the Guomindang . . . he worshipped Confucius. . . ." A major ideological struggle, whose target was Zhou Enlai, now began.

Zhou had to extricate himself from the accusation of instigating an attack against the Cultural Revolution under cover of criticizing Lin Biao. Apparently unfazed, Zhou explained: "My speech of August 1 concerning this matter was addressed to the staff of the Foreign Affairs Ministry. . . . It was *leftist behavior and excesses* which I condemned. . . . I did not go into the matter of Lin Biao's actual theoretical stand. . . . *Lin Biao has deceived a great many people*," Zhou continued, carefully avoiding a glance toward Madame Mao. But the Gang of Four would press on, taking advantage of Zhou's lapse, and also of Mao's liking for the young Wang Hungwen. On December 28, 1972, at another upper-level meeting, Ye Jianying had had to announce that "Chairman Mao has been preoccupied with the problem of successors. . . . Now here is Comrade Wang Hungwen . . . from a poor peasant family, and a worker, still in his thirties. . . ."

Mao's choice. Jiang Qing gleamed with triumph. Zhou, with his usual calm, would add: "Chairman Mao is considering Wang Hungwen as vice-chairman of the Military Affairs Commission and also vice-chairman of the Party."

Zhou had lost a major battle in the merciless war against the Gang of Four. Wang Hungwen was now regarded as Mao's potential heir, superseding everyone, including Zhou Enlai. The media knew that they must write articles lauding Wang Hungwen, citing him whenever possible, "informing" the public of a bright new star in China's firmament. The movement to "criticize the extreme left, criticize Lin Biao" became *pi lin pi kung*—"criticize Lin Biao, criticize Confucius."

Why Confucius?

Only someone acquainted with the tortuous way in which the Chinese intellectual-political mind works would understand that Confucius, the sage who had died 2,500 years ago, had to be resurrected to epitomize all that the "right" stood for: Tradition, Education, Conservatism. Had not Mao on several occasions condemned the Sage, and spoken in favor of the Ch'in emperor, who had burned the books of Confucius and buried Confucian scholars alive?

Confucianism extolled rule by the "upright and superior person," a sovereign who governed with morality, a link between heaven and mankind. The hacks writing for the Gang of Four took to their pens. They excoriated Lin Biao for his Confucianist ideas. They extracted from China's massive past the 2,500-year-old history of *legalism*, which was anti-Confucianist. To the astonishment of many Westerners, the press warned daily against Confucius, who sought to "reverse" the course of history. Kissinger was also puzzled. Irreverently he remarked to Zhou that Confucianism was still prevalent in China, in its traditions, and even in the Party. Zhou hastily cut him off.

The Tenth Congress of the Party was held in August 1973. Zhou Enlai made a speech, and so did Wang Hungwen. The two speeches differ markedly from each other in thrust and meaning. Zhou's speech was a denunciation of Lin Biao, followed by a brief outline of the manner of his demise. But, said Zhou, the struggle between two lines in the Party "has not stopped with Lin Biao." It would erupt again, "perhaps ten or twenty times."

Wang Hungwen's speech was very different. It covered a revision of the Party constitution, which was designed to favor the ascendancy of Party cadres chosen from among poor peasants and workers. There was no sign of disunity, the participants made strenuous efforts to appear amiable and friendly toward each other, and Deng Xiaoping was confirmed as one of the vice-premiers.

In December, at a Politburo meeting, Mao made some remorseful remarks. He had erred in listening to Lin Biao, said he. Ho Lung, Lo Ruiqing, Yang Shangkun, were all "good comrades." The always attentive Zhou leapt into action, taking in hand the return of those who were still alive. Ho Lung's posthumous rehabilitation was decided. More important, the Military Affairs Commission was to be reorganized, and Deng Xiaoping became its chief of staff; Ye Jianying had already been reinstalled. Thus the second round of the battle was won by Zhou Enlai. But the "criticize Lin, criticize Confucius" campaign took on added venom and emphasis.

Zhou was hospitalized for a total of seventy-two days in 1973. In between, he continued to work at his usual frantic pace, an average of sixteen to eighteen hours a day. In the autumn, he welcomed some Japanese delegations. Premier Tanaka paid a solemn visit. Zhou had wooed Japan since the 1950s. Japan needed China, but China needed Japan for her technological revolution. Zhou confirmed that China would not seek any war indemnities from Japan. "The Japanese people have also suffered because of the war. . . . We must now turn a new page in history." In December, Kissinger came again to see him, with woeful countenance. Things were not going well, neither in Vietnam nor with President Nixon, now involved in the Watergate scandal.

The House of Representatives had in June voted a cutoff of all military aid to Thieu's South Vietnamese government in Saigon, leaving Thieu without any support, depriving the U.S. presence in Vietnam of any credibility or leverage. There was now no holding back Hanoi's victory. The Paris peace accords were ignored, and North Vietnam pressed on to total conquest. In June, Pham Van Dong and Le Duan had come to Beijing, and since it was obvious that victory was inevitable, and China wanted to preserve Vietnamese goodwill, Zhou had ordered increased aid to Hanoi. The U.S.S.R. zealously supported Vietnam's undisguised claim to the Indochinese peninsula. Kissinger was plainly told by Le Duc Tho, the North Vietnamese emissary to the Paris talks, that Vietnam "rejected neutrality for both Cambodia and Laos" and "emphasized that it was his people's destiny not merely to take over South Vietnam but to dominate the whole of Indochina." This was not acceptable to China. Ever since the Geneva conference of 1954, the hidden contention between Vietnam and China had been precisely on this issue. The regard and honor given to Norodom Sihanouk, Zhou's staunch support of him, were evidence that China did not want Vietnamese hegemony over Cambodia.

Zhou tried to assure Sihanouk's return in a "neutral, independent, peaceful Cambodia," for it was certain that Lon Nol's days of power in Cambodia were numbered. His American-backed regime was crumbling, as was Thieu's American-backed regime in South Vietnam.

In April, Zhou had spoken to Ambassador Mana'ch, insisting that France should take a hand in the restoration of Cambodia under Norodom Sihanouk. France had, he said, a "moral obligation" toward its former colonies of Indochina. "The problem for the Chinese," Kissinger pertinently wrote, "is to stop Hanoi, or Moscow, from laying their hands on Cambodia." In my talks with Zhou regarding the history of Southeast Asia and the wars between the kingdoms of Indochina, Zhou had always pointed out that Cambodia's independence was "nonnegotiable." When Minister Jacques Chaban-Delmas had arrived from Paris in June, Zhou spent an hour with him talking about Cambodia. Mana'ch in his memoirs points out that Norodom Sihanouk failed to ingratiate himself with the French, despite his French upbringing. "But de Gaulle would have understood," said Zhou Enlai. Zhou admired de Gaulle, and expressed much regret that de Gaulle had been unable to visit China.

Zhou Enlai was also concerned about the dominance of the Khmer Rouge, who were winning against Lon Nol's American-equipped army. The Khmer Issarak (Khmer Rouge) and the Vietnamese guerrillas had at one time been allies, members of an Indochina Communist Party. Zhou insisted that Cambodia "must be *neutral*, peaceful, and independent." In fact, Zhou was against socialism in any of the Southeast Asian countries—whether Singapore, Malaysia, Indonesia, or Cambodia. "The time is not ripe."

When President Georges Pompidou came to Beijing on September 14, 1973, Zhou spent a great deal of time with him, accompanying him to the Datung Buddhist caves, to Hangzhou, to

Shanghai. In his welcoming speech he said of de Gaulle, "We are sorry we could not have the opportunity to receive him . . . this inflexible warrior against fascist aggression and for the safeguard of France's independence." In conversations with Pompidou, Zhou pressed the case of Norodom Sihanouk. "The French value independence, patriotism. Norodom Sihanouk is a patriot." He tried to persuade Pompidou to recognize Sihanouk's party and mediate a solution in Cambodia. But the French did not wish to perceive, or could not accept, the Chinese view of an independent Cambodia under Sihanouk at the time.

The simmering anti-Lin Biao, anti-Confucius campaign was given a boost, with a fanfare of editorials, in January 1974. It was now obvious to any educated Chinese, trained in the art of indirection, that the campaign was aimed at some *current* leader, since Lin Biao was as dead as Confucius. The Gang of Four's propagandists achieved miracles of contorted prose to prove that constant vigilance must be exercised against people *like* Lin Biao and Confucius. In the usual Aesopian manner of writing about historical personages long since dead to refer to living ones, an article appeared against a Prime Minister of the Ch'in dynasty (200 B.C.) who had tried to "reverse" the existing regime. This was followed by an article on the Han dynasty, which had instituted the public examination system for civil service recruitment. "What were good cadres? They were slavish, submissive." The Prime Minister of those days was "a cunning old bureaucrat, very good at arranging connections, never getting himself into trouble." Even the most obtuse Party cadre got the point when to the slogan "criticize Lin, criticize Confucius," *pi Lin pi Kung*, was appended *pi Zhou Gung*—"criticize Lord Zhou." Who was "Lord Zhou"?

A mass meeting took place at the workers' stadium. Zhou was forced to listen to the speeches against Confucius "and all those who are his disciples." At the meeting Madame Mao's supporters condemned "those cadres who return by using the back door." Obviously, Deng Xiaoping.

Zhou was losing a great deal of blood in his urine. He had to have blood transfusions fairly frequently, at first every three weeks or so, later more often. But he sat still as a stone, apparently relaxed, not giving a hint that he was aware of being the Confucianist. "Who is that Lord Zhou being condemned?" a newsman asked of Madame Mao, in Zhou's presence. "Of course a historical personage," she replied, flustered, and walked away.

Everyone knew that Zhou Enlai was "the great Confucianist," daily denigrated in the press. And indeed, he *was* a great Confucianist. His life was a fulfillment of the Sage's ideals of integrity, self-sacrifice, dedication to the welfare of the people. In him the Chinese found their ideal "ruler." He was a revolutionary, but in practice the theories of revolution went into the Confucian mold of the "man of total integrity, the father and mother of his people."

In March 1974, Limpid Stream added another dimension to the attack. Right after Kissinger's first visit in 1971, Zhou had begun to refurbish hotels, in view of an anticipated influx of delegations, businessmen, tourists, from the world over. The China Travel Service, dormant for years, sent cadres to Switzerland for training. Swiss hoteliers went to Beijing, to Tianjin, to Shanghai, to Guangzhou. Chinese painters were commissioned by Zhou to produce works to decorate the dining halls, lobbies, reception rooms, and guest rooms of hotels and assembly halls.

But when Zhou entered the hospital in March, Jiang Qing collected a good many of these paintings and organized an exhibition of "black"—i.e., politically unsound—works of art. About 40,000 people were marshaled to "indignantly condemn" these "black" creations.

In May 1974, Zhou underwent a major operation. In July, he left his pavilion in Zhongnanhai. A suite in the hospital became his office and home and he continued to work from it. Deng Yingchao stayed with him.

The press wrote ignoble articles against him, allegedly excerpts from a life of Confucius. "A man of advanced age, very ill and confined to his bed . . . but still trying with all his might to plot. . . . A deceitful and treacherous political cheat. . . . When the sovereign calls, he rushes even before the chariot is prepared."

"Confucius had a broken arm"—this was for anyone who had not yet made the link between Confucius and Zhou Enlai. The most disgusting attacks were those in which his conduct toward Mao was ridiculed. Zhou did exhibit, toward Mao, a singularly filial protectiveness. "The Confucian Grand Vizier" had indeed, in 1945, tasted Mao's wine in Chongqing to make sure that there was no poison in the cup.

Zhou had reestablished in 1971 the system of examinations in schools and universities. But the students of "worker-peasant-soldier" origin were also of inferior education. University professors were forced to give special tutoring to around 80 percent of the new entrants. A student from Zhou's former Tung Guan school in Shenyang, Manchuria, was selected to become a new type of hero when he turned in a blank sheet at his examination.

"Quite right," the wall posters of the Gang of Four praised the youth. Teachers were "ignoramuses" and "tyrants" who followed "the capitalist road."

Deng Xiaoping took over the day-to-day work from Zhou. He opposed the Gang of Four with grit, and unlike the suave Zhou, he was rude. "If you cannot shit, you should not occupy the toilet," he said to some of the Gang's incompetent appointees. Every day, with Li Xiannian, Ye Jianying, he went to see Zhou Enlai. Perhaps what caused Zhou much sorrow—grief unspoken, swallowed down, invisible—was the fact that his good friend Guo Moro, president of the Academy of Sciences, wrote a poem in praise of the *pi Lin pi Kung* movement which "awakened the earth like spring thunder. . . ." How could he do this? Cowardice? Fear? Guo Moro was over eighty, and decrepit, almost senile. Zhou wrote a letter saying that Guo Moro "should have someone with him twenty-four hours a day" and "his rooms should be carpeted, so that he does not slip when he walks." Everything to solace his old friend's last days.

In July 1974, Mao, in a sudden fit, stormed at the Gang of Four. "Do not make a gang. You are making a gang." And of his wife he said, "She wants to become head of the Party, make Wang Hungwen head of the National Assembly, Zhang Chunqiao Premier, and Yao Wenyuan the Party General Secretary."

Mao had learned that his wife, without the permission of the Central Committee, had managed to persuade an American sinologist to write a book about her. In 1972, Ms. Roxane Witke had come to write about women in China, and asked to see Madame Mao. Zhou advised Limpid Stream to see her "for an hour or so . . . that will be sufficient." Instead, Limpid Stream spent weeks securing the attention of the American. She had long felt that her life should be written up. She wanted her own "Edgar Snow," as the two officials delegated to look after Ms. Witke told me.

Zhou asked Huang Hua, then ambassador to the United Nations, to persuade Ms. Witke not to publish the book. But the latter refused. "I think Madame Mao is going to be a very important woman in China," she said to me in New York.

Limpid Stream had been estranged from Mao since 1972. She did not live with him, but at No. 17 Diaoyutai, the Imperial Fisherman's Terrace. A grand campaign for Madame Mao's self-aggrandizement began. Female historical personages were refurbished and beautified. Empress Wu had not been a tyrant, nor Empress Lu a monster. No, no, they had all been good and wise women rulers. The Gang of Four hoped Witke's book would become part of a campaign for a new personality cult centering on Blue Apple–Limpid Stream: Jiang Qing.

Zhou, from his hospital room, with Deng Xiaoping, Li Xiannian, Ye Jianying, Chen Yun, drew up major plans for the modernization of China, the foundation for China's future.

The last time Zhou saw Kissinger was in late November 1974. Kissinger arrived prepared to negotiate further improvement in Sino-American relations. But he was unprepared for the tortuous attacks against Zhou and for Zhou's ill health. Zhou could only spare him half an hour.

Another convoluted, reptilian onslaught against Zhou took place. He had given authorization to Michelangelo Antonioni to make a documentary film on China. Madame Mao denounced this film as shameful, a distortion. Then came the Beethoven affair. Beethoven's music was reactionary, utterly bourgeois, extolling princes and monarchs. . . . Zhou Enlai and Zhu De (Scarlet Virtue), in their young days in Berlin, had enjoyed Beethoven concerts. Zhou still had some old phonograph records which he played occasionally.

Julius Nyerere came to Beijing to see Zhou Enlai. He was deeply affected by the way Zhou looked when he visited him in the hospital. "He was so thin, so thin. But he jested with me. It was nothing. Merely overwork. We spoke affably for an hour or more, he was still vibrant with energy."

On the evening of September 30, 1974, the usual banquet was held for the celebration of National Day, October 1. The vast hall was crowded. I was seated at a table with my good friend Wang Bingnan, former ambassador to Warsaw. All around us were the resurrected, the returned from disgrace or from jail. But at each round table seating ten guests, were two watchers, Madame Mao's "artists," from her model operas. Next to me was a famous pianist who had "recanted" Beethoven and was now creating new music to fit into the new operas.

Suddenly a stir, the national anthem. The leaders filed in, and at their head Zhou Enlai.

"He is back, he is back," one could *hear* the thought from every brain, though not a word was said.

"There have been rumors that he was very ill, but his gait is as agile as ever. The whole Politburo follows, and the guests of that year. Zhou stands up to speak. We all stand up and clap and clap, we cannot stop. We just go on and on, an ovation of love, and shared grief, and gratitude. Without him so many, so many of those here today would not have been present. Many weep openly, including myself. When at last we stop, Zhou Enlai speaks, and his voice is extraordinarily strong, resonant. He pours the last of his strength into a short address. China has undergone many tests, and come out victorious. China's people will go forward, in friendship with all the nations of the world. But the essential thing is Unity. 'Unity,' he cries, 'Unity.' I look at the head table. The Gang of Four is there. And also Deng Xiaoping. . . . Unity?"

26

On January 13, 1975, thin and gaunt, his skin the color of ash, but standing straight, in a gray suit too large for him, Zhou Enlai delivered his last speech at the Fourth National People's Congress. It was a long speech, an exhausting task, but he never faltered. At the end his hands shook with exhaustion but he walked away erect as ever. That night, his urine was almost pure blood.

The speech announced the Four Modernizations, Zhou's comprehensive plan for China's progress, China's open-door policy to the world. "To accomplish the comprehensive modernization of agriculture, industry, national defense, and science and technology, before the end of the century, so that our national economy will be advancing in the front ranks of the world." His testament, his legacy.

To get Mao's assent to his speech, Zhou Enlai had had to go to Changsha, where Mao stayed, in December 1974. Emaciated, his hands trembling, he painfully climbed onto the plane, helped by a secretary.

The airplane crew had worried about his health, to which Zhou had replied, "One must fight on. . . . I haven't flown for a year, and I've spent eight months lying in bed, but I'm much better now." He was so weak that he had difficulty unwrapping the sweet which the stewardess gave him.

He arrived in Changsha on December 24, saw Mao on December 26, Mao's birthday. The young Wang Hungwen had gone to Changsha earlier in November, to reveal to Mao a "plot" by Zhou Enlai. Zhou was visited by so many old cadres—"there was surely scheming going on." He was only pretending to be ill. But Mao dismissed the young man with the terse remark: "The Premier does not plot."

Zhou did not live long enough to see his "Grand Design"—as

it is called today—realized. But he bequeathed it to those who would inherit, from him and from Mao, the beloved ancestral land.

March 29, 1975.

"Chairman, during the past four years, some blood was noticed in my stools, but since my digestive system functioned well, no examination of stomach and bowel was performed. In the last two years, because of the bladder cancer, there is blood in my urine. . . . Medical care has centered on curing the bladder cancer. I have had two main operations, and electro-cautery three times. This year, after the meeting, blood was found in my stools every day. There was also obstruction in the large bowel, near the liver; a tumor the size of a peach was found. Passage of food is slow since the bowel is narrowed. The site of the tumor is precisely where, forty years ago, at the meeting in Sandy Burrow, my liver abscess extruded into the large bowel, and I was cured. This was when you, Chairman, led us northward across the grasslands, so that we have lived until this day. . . ."

This letter from Zhou Enlai to Mao Dzedong makes painful reading. It is a pathetic plea for a gesture, for the recognition of a long partnership. Zhou goes on to say that he will now undergo a third major operation to extract the growth, "whether benign or malignant," in the large bowel. The letter ends: "Because I realize how concerned Chairman is about my illness, my having to report this new mishap makes me sorrowful, for I am adding to your concern. Please do not worry. After my two operations last year, I had asked Wang Hairong and Tang Wensheng to report to Chairman. . . . I think I can withstand another surgical intervention and I am preparing myself for it."

Could not Zhou speak to Mao directly? When the two men had in the past been so close, why did he need intermediaries? Zhou's recall of that episode of the Long March was a way of telling Mao: "Of all your companions and comrades-in-arms in the long and dolorous journey of the Chinese revolution, I have been the one irrevocably loyal, even when I opposed your ideas. All the others are gone: Liu Shaoqi, who elevated your thought to irrefutable doctrine; Lin Biao, who proclaimed you a genius the better to shove you aside. All failed you, but I propped you up, saved you even from yourself. . . ."

Precisely because Mao was so indebted, he was resentful. It is hard to acknowledge gratitude. There is something dramatically gripping about the relationship between these two old men at the end of their lives. Zhou had sacrificed himself, his dignity, sometimes his conscience, to stem the upheaval inflicted by Mao's tornado visions upon China. What did he receive in this last extremity, in the last year of his life? Only silence. Mao was not totally incapacitated, even if he shuffled, at times unsteadily. He still held audiences with heads of state until mid-1976.

I asked Deng Yingchao: "Did Chairman Mao visit the Premier at any time during his illness?" She replied, in a totally colorless voice: "Chairman did not visit Enlai."

Too much had happened, which, like dangerous nuclear waste, must be wrapped in leaden silence. The drama remains entire, marriage of lawless ocean and steadfast shore, paradigm of shield and spear. It was too simple to believe that the two could meet at last as untrammeled human beings.

Li Bing, daughter of Smiling Buddha Li Kenung, was present at every operation performed on Zhou Enlai. She told me that as he was being wheeled into the operating theater once again he said, "Comrade Li Bing, do you know that in the mines of Yunnan the incidence of lung cancer among the miners is on the increase?"

"Premier, our cancer hospital has discussed the problem."

"That's not enough. The problem must be tackled. The cause for this increase must be found."

"That was Zhou Enlai," said Li Bing. "He had read up on cancer while lying in bed." The next day, Li Bing, together with my friend George Wu, left for Yunnan province. The cancer teams of the hospital had already done studies on the incidence of nose cancer, liver cancer in South China, and esophageal cancer in the Taihang mountain area. "A month later the Premier called me again. Lung cancer, he said, was on the increase in Manchuria. He wanted a preliminary report. 'We must do something about it now.'"

Zhou recovered from the operation and the procession of heads of state to the small reception room next to his bedroom began again. Malta and Mozambique, Guyana and Tunisia. Kim Il Sung of North Korea came in June. Zhou's legs were badly swollen. His leather shoes did not fit, and he wore cloth shoes. But since no one is more conscious of status and etiquette than a proletarian Communist leader, the head of protocol had to reassure Kim Il Sung that no offense was intended if the Premier received him in cloth slippers.

Tindemans of Belgium and Razak of Malaysia found Zhou as well informed as ever. His meeting with the Thai Premier, the talented Kukrit Pramoj, delighted him. He pressed Kukrit to stay longer, spoke about the Thai minority in Yunnan province, recalled his meeting, twenty years previously, with a Thai prince at Bandung: "It is still clear to me, as vivid and clear as if it were but yesterday."

Gabon and Denmark, Zaire's Mobutu, Ferdinand and Imelda Marcos of the Philippines, came to the small room with its stiff leather sofas and lace antimacassars. None appeared to realize how ill he was. Zhou, who was kept going with blood transfusions, would smile urbanely and say, "I am improving slowly," while he knew he was dying a little more every day.

A few days before his operation in March, Zhou had dragged himself to a Central Committee meeting, where he obtained the release and the restoration of political rights of 203 wartime collaborators with Japan. This was to establish the right climate for Deng Xiaoping's talks with a major Japanese delegation, from which Zhou hoped to obtain an import of technology, including a steel plant. Deng Xiaoping was ebullient, but lacked Zhou's charisma, his compelling dexterity at handling people. Still, Zhou wanted to establish Deng's position vis-à-vis other contestants, and in May attended a Politburo meeting to support Deng as first Vice-Premier, in opposition to the Shanghai clique. A flamboyant article had been penned against Deng Xiaoping. "The greatest danger at present is empiricism." Deng's bluntness, his scratchy overreaction to anything said or written against him, did not help. Zhou remained suave, his silken voice wrapping a steel blade of irony, but Deng exploded quickly into invective. Fortunately, Mao had recently remarked aloud that his wife had a "power-hungry heart," and this compelled Jiang Qing to pretend that she was not fighting the Premier or his appointee . . . for a while.

In June, accompanied by Deng Yingchao and Tsai Chang, the wife of the late Li Fuchun—Li had died the previous year—Zhou left the hospital to attend the official ceremony for the rehabilitation of Ho Lung. He was driven to Eight Talisman Hill, Babaoshan, the cemetery for revolutionary heroes and high Party cadres. He was erect, his step unfaltering, as he came out of the car and climbed the steps to the funeral pavilion. All the old warriors were there, including ninety-year-old Zhu De (Scarlet

Virtue). Above the high table on which stood the urn containing Ho Lung's ashes was hung his portrait, young-looking, showing the fine teeth, the sensual mouth with its well-groomed small mustache. Zhou stood staring, staring at the portrait of his friend. To Ho Lung's widow Zhou said, "I failed him, I failed him, I failed to protect him well enough." Ho Lung's son, who stood next to his mother, said, "Uncle Zhou, you *must* take care of your own health." Zhou shook his head. "My own time is running out," he replied.

This was the first time that Zhou acknowledged in public that he was a dying man.

He delivered the funeral eulogy, though at the end he could hardly stand, and had to be assisted to a chair. He penned his name upon the long scroll of those who had attended the ceremony. "Send the list to Comrade Xiaoping. He is away, but he must sign it," said Zhou, thus publicly conferring his approval upon Deng Xiaoping.

In July, Nie Rongzhen returned from a visit to the atomic research centers in West China to report to Zhou. He showed Zhou the film of the launching of China's third satellite. "It was all due to Zhou Enlai that China engaged in atomic and missile technology," Nie told me in October 1988. "Enlai knew very well that we must catch up, catch up not only on one industrial revolution, but on two. . . ."

Government ministers came to the hospital daily, for Zhou insisted that he must be kept informed. A new coalfield had been discovered in a hinterland province. "This matter cannot be left only to the provincial authorities. It is a national resource, and the center must fund it." Coal, oil, sources of energy, preoccupied him, but he remained undecided about building the large Yangtse hydroelectric dam, for which plans had been drawn in the late 1950s. Money must not be wasted on nonessentials, he kept saying, lying gaunt and out of breath on his hospital bed. His mind was clear but at times he had to stop talking and inhale oxygen. He was very quickly out of breath.

In August, Norodom Sihanouk came to say goodbye. The regime of Lon Nol in Cambodia had collapsed. The debacle of the American-supported Saigon regime was completed when in April Hanoi's tanks rolled into the city, while from the roof of the American embassy the last helicopters took off. On April 17 the Khmer Rouge, at the time allies of the North Vietnamese, as well as members of the Alliance under Norodom Sihanouk, had entered Phnom Penh. The Khmer Rouge had had no success while Sihanouk ruled, but had prospered because Lon Nol's corrupt regime alienated the people. They were now in control of the country. Zhou had received the Khmer Rouge representatives Khieu Samphan and Ieng Sary five days before Sihanouk's visit. He had told them: "Norodom Sihanouk *must* be protected. He is the head of state. He *must* remain your common rallying point. You must unite, bring together all those you can, to build up a *neutral, independent* Cambodia." Zhou was still fighting to maintain Cambodia as a neutral nonsocialist country, a bulwark against Vietnamese hegemony. "Socialism is not an easy road to walk," he warned the radical Khmer Rouge leaders. "China is now walking along that road, and it is a very long road, with many obstacles." But he was talking to men who thought in terms of instant Communism and who would disregard his advice.

With Sihanouk, Zhou spent an agreeable hour, and at the end wished him and his beautiful wife, Princess Monique, a happy return to his own country. "We shall always firmly support *you*," he told the Prince. As long as Zhou was alive, Sihanouk was fairly well treated by the Khmer Rouge.

In early September, Illie Verdet, Party secretary of the Romanian Communist Party, came to see Zhou. Zhou found walking difficult, but insisted on meeting Verdet in the hospital lobby and conducting him to his reception room. On Verdet's solicitous inquiries regarding his health, he said wryly, "I have received my formal invitation from Marx, and it is impossible not to accept it. This is something beyond man's control . . . how swiftly time goes; only ten years ago, in March 1965, I was in Bucharest. It was cold, but I did not wear an overcoat, and I walked some four hours. Now I cannot walk even four minutes." This was how Zhou announced his impending death. He went on to talk about China. "We have overcome many difficulties, and now the Party has seasoned leaders, tempered in trials. The Vice-Premier has assumed overall charge." Deng Xiaoping was sitting beside Verdet, and one of Zhou's secretaries indicated him. This was the last time Zhou would receive guests from abroad.

On September 20, as he was being readied for another surgical exploration, he was told that the Wu Hao affair of 1931 had again been brought up. Would he verify and sign all the documents and tapes submitted on this matter? Past anger, past disgust, Zhou signed, writing the date and the hour on every item presented. This unrelenting cruelty to the dying man arose from a clash five days earlier between Deng Xiaoping and Madame Mao. They had met at the model brigade of Dazhai, promoted since 1964 as an example of agricultural self-reliance. Unable to camouflage his feelings, Deng had been his usual impatient, tactless self, and Limpid Stream unleashed a flow of invective, both against Deng and against portly Hua Guofeng, the head of the Public Security Bureau and also a Vice-Premier. Hua Guofeng was not yet a threat to her, but he might become one, for he had been personally selected by Mao to assume these posts at the January Congress. He was, therefore, another impediment placed by her husband on her way to power. Suppose he and Deng became allies, a threat to her own clique? All this the dying man knew, and having signed, he solemnly shook hands with all present—Ye Jianying, Li Xiannian, Wang Hungwen, and Zhang Chunqiao—and with Deng Xiaoping last, saying, "You have done well, continue, be steadfast," in the loudest voice he could muster.

October, and still Zhou did not die. Another attack was devised. While rereading *The Water Margin*, Mao, who was fond of analyzing old tales in the light of new revolutionary principles, asserted that one of the folk heroes of this tale, Song Jiang, was a renegade, and not an exemplary figure as had been assumed for several centuries. Leader of a rebel band, he had risen against the tyranny of the imperial bureaucracy, but finally had given in to imperial "grace and favor." With tortuous illogic, Song Jiang was now to be pictured as a "revisionist." Immediately the Gang of Four seized upon this latest crumb of Mao wisdom. Song Jiang was a revisionist, and had not Zhou Enlai, and Deng Xiaoping, also rubbed shoulders with warlords and capitalists, with Western-educated scholars? Were not kings and tycoons and imperialists now flocking to China and praising Zhou Enlai? The newspapers were filled with articles, a maze of references to long-dead figures, examples of treachery. Uncanny threats hovered in the air around Deng Xiaoping. His orders were ignored or rescinded.

September 30, the eve of National Day. The usual banquet was held at the Great Hall of the People. But Zhou Enlai was not there. Instead, Deng Xiaoping as first Vice-Premier led the members of the government into the hall. Jiang Qing was much in evidence, and so was her faction. "Did you see them, glowering at each other like porcelain dogs?" Soong Chingling said to me when I went back with her to her home for a chat and coffee after the reception.

Though Zhou was absent, no fewer than forty-nine veteran cadres who had been in disgrace made their reappearance that night, among them tall Lo Ruiqing, sitting in a wheelchair. Deng Yingchao rushed to him and shook his hand in both of hers, and the guests clapped—except for the Gang of Four and their supporters. Lo Ruiqing's presence confirmed Zhou's victory. The Party was back. The Party had not been destroyed by the Cultural Revolution. Other battles loomed, battles that Deng would have to fight alone when Zhou died. But he was vulnerable, too vulnerable, and to withstand the Four, Zhou must be kept alive, must be kept living as long as possible. "We kept him alive . . . it was torture," Dr. George Wu told me. "Because he wanted to keep his mind clear, he refused to take painkillers . . . just clenched his teeth and endured. Sometimes he would sigh a little and grope for his wife's hand."

His brain gave him no peace. "I can still hear. I can still think." He wanted to leave everything in order, neat. He raked his memory. Was there any one thing left undone that he could now do? Had he forgotten anyone or anything? Suddenly he remembered the scholar Yen Fu, one of China's first reformists, born in 1854, who had died in 1921. Yen Fu's brilliant translations of Thomas Huxley, Montesquieu, and John Stuart Mill had stirred the minds of Zhou's generation, had made possible access to non-Confucian thinking, fueled that long revolution begun in Zhou's youth and not yet ended, even today. Zhou dictated letters to the curator of the National Museum to make sure that Yen Fu's documents were safely stored. He remembered another man, Yang Du, who had died in 1931. An archconservative in his youth, Yang had become a Communist in 1927, and one of Zhou's moles, communicating with Zhou through the film director Xia Yan. Yang Du had been a friend of Big-Eared Du Yuesheng, godfather of Shanghai's Green Gang, and it was also through Yang that protection for the CCP in Shanghai had been available. Safe houses, escape from the British, French, and other police patrolling the concessions. . . . Zhou wanted Yang Du to be recognized as a good Communist, and fretted that Pan Hannien, who had served him so faithfully, had still not been rehabilitated. He would be, posthumously, in 1980.

The Four could not resist coming to watch the dying man, gauging how many days he had left in him. Wang Hungwen stalked in, and when Deng Yingchao begged him to let her husband rest, he said, "But I have state business to discuss with the Premier . . . it cannot wait." Jiang Qing telephoned, saying she had important matters to discuss. Zhou once interrupted a blood transfusion to reach the telephone and speak with her.

The Gang of Four added a useful man to their outfit in the person of Mao Yuanxin, Mao's nephew, who was now appointed his uncle's liaison officer. Every visitor, every document, had to be seen by him before reaching Mao Dzedong. Though Mao mumbled against his wife, "She wants to be Party chairman . . . her heart is rotten with ambition," his nephew blocked other contacts. It looked as if, at Zhou's death, Mao would have no other option but to nominate Zhang Chunqiao (Spring Bridge) as Premier.

By the end of November 1975, Zhou had had six major surgical interventions, eight bladder cauteries, and one hundred blood transfusions. Between June 1974, when he entered the hospital, and December 1975, he had received sixty-three heads of state or foreign delegations, held one hundred sixty-one meetings, and managed to get out of the hospital twenty times. Not only for major events like the Politburo meeting, or his speech on the Four Modernizations at the National People's Congress, but on two occasions to go to the Peking Hotel, once to look around, checking that all ran smoothly, and once to have a haircut.

Zhu Dianhua had been Zhou's barber for many years. The last time Zhou visited the hotel he said to Zhu, "Let us take a photograph together." It was late September, and no photographer was available. "Perhaps next time, Premier," said Zhu Dianhua. Zhou smiled at him and left. But this was the last time that Zhou was able to sit in a barber chair. In November, Zhu would inquire, "Does Premier need a haircut?" "Don't let him come, he would be heartbroken to see me as I look now," said Zhou Enlai.

He was worried that, at his death, his relatives, nephews and nieces, or one of their numerous "children by affection," the orphans they had cared for, would leave their jobs to come to his funeral. "No one must abandon his post, even for a day." He had always been uncompromising toward his relatives, refusing them any privilege. One niece, sent to an Inner Mongolian sheep farm, had not been allowed by him to return to Beijing. Not one of Zhou's relatives would become a "golden youth," as so many of the children of high-ranking officials would become. Toward his own wife Zhou would be as unbendingly incorruptible. He persistently refused to permit her to hold high office, for that way lay nepotism, the return of government by relatives and family ties. He and Deng Yingchao must be an example to all China. Deng Yingchao, whose ability and talent for organization had been fully deployed before 1949, was given no credit for the work she did and held no important official position. How can this unrelenting harshness toward the wife he so obviously loved be reconciled with his general respect and regard for women? Zhou had supported very strongly the Marriage Law, the charter for women's equality, drawn up by his wife. He had daringly approved of interracial marriage. He employed a number of women in his ministries.

But he knew his countrymen well, their ingrained feudalism. He had seen Liu Shaoqi's case made worse because of glamorous, intelligent Wang Guangmei, brought into the limelight by her doting husband. He had seen Lin Biao catapult his wife into the Politburo, and she had helped his mad schemes. Here was Madame Mao (Blue Apple–Limpid Stream), whom Mao had loved so much at the time of the caves in Yenan. Now she was hated and feared, called a white-boned demon.

Deng Yingchao, Zhou resolved, would not be snared into the webs of feudal power. And with sublime abnegation, Little Chao agreed to remain in the shadow of her husband. Only in December 1975 did Mao submit to the Central Committee a resolution making Deng Yingchao vice-chairman of the National People's Congress. This would ensure for her a better status and income when Zhou passed away, and bypassed Zhou's injunction that his wife "should not enjoy special privileges, only what is befitting to her own rank in the Party."

George Wu, oncologist Wu Jieping, and six other medical experts were present when Zhou was operated on for the seventh and last time in November 1975. "We found cancer cells everywhere," George Wu said. "We managed to make another intestinal bypass so that he could live a little longer."

"Tell me exactly how long I have. There is still much work to do," said Zhou to his doctors.

"We hedged. . . . He knew, and said, 'Then there is nothing more for you to do here. You had better attend to other patients, who need you more.' "

New Year's Eve came.

In 1965, Mao Dzedong had written two poems, "Return to Jingang Mountains" and "Dialogue Between Birds," both with political allusions against revisionism. They derided those who put material progress foremost. Zhou, it is said, "laughed gently" when the poems were brought to him by his wife. Legend has embellished this, saying he clasped them to his heart. But his wife remains silent on this point. He whispered to her, "Little Chao, there are so many things, so many things that I have not told you, and now it is too late."

"I too, Enlai, have kept many things to myself," replied Deng Yingchao.

Zhou Enlai died on January 8, at 9:25 in the morning.

Mao Dzedong was told. He said nothing. Nothing at all. But that night, while he was watching television, his nurse and companion noticed that tears were running down his face.

Dry-eyed, all tears spent, Deng Yingchao told the committee set up to organize her husband's funeral rites of his wish that his ashes be strewn over the mountains and rivers of his country; that no monument, grave, stela, or statue, not even an urn in the Eight Talisman cemetery, should commemorate him. Gossip, street prattle, always luxuriant in China, reported that Zhou had said, "I don't want to lie next to Kang Sheng." Kang Sheng, of sinister memory, had died on December 16 of lung cancer. Zhou thus broke with tradition, both Confucian and Communist, and returned to that imperishable Taoist source of Chinese culture, where the body's elements weld in the Oneness of the universe.

On January 10, his body lay in state, to be shown to a select crowd of forty thousand. By order, no mourners were allowed to come to Beijing from any other city. Wreaths, black armbands, white flowers, in China the signs of mourning, were forbidden. On January 11, in a totally unadorned minibus, the body of Zhou Enlai was taken out of the city to be cremated. Though there had been no announcement, two million people turned out to line the twenty-mile road in absolute silence.

The small box containing his ashes was turned over to his widow during a three-day ceremony at the Workers' Culture Palace. Streams of mourners flowed past the altar with the box and his portrait. At the end, Deng Yingchao, holding the box in her hand, faced the audience. "In my hands are the ashes of Comrade Enlai. Thank you all for your presence here."

China continued to mourn the beloved. "I was then a young soldier in the army," Tang, my driver, says to me as he drives me home in 1988. "We were forbidden to wear mourning, but my battalion went and bought armbands and white flowers with their own money. Within three days, the whole of the army was wearing mourning. The orders had to be rescinded."

A plane scattered Zhou's ashes over the land. And in death, he would prove stronger than in the last years of his life.

Now that Zhou was dead, the Gang of Four tried to bring down Deng Xiaoping.

The campaign against the restoration of standard school examinations was reinforced. Strikes against "production for capitalism" took place in factories. "Better late trains or no trains for socialism than trains on time for capitalism," was one of the more absurd mottoes of the campaign. Deng was helpless. Sabotage at all levels rendered him ineffective.

But the army, though apparently passive, backed Deng. "Without guns, we shall remain sitting targets," Zhang Chunqiao had said. He was quite right. That was why he had supported Wang Hungwen, who in 1967 began to organize a workers' militia. By 1976 Wang was at the head of a sizable force of 200,000 men, with two factories turning out military equipment.

The disquiet of the Shanghai clique changed to outright fear when, on February 3, Mao Dzedong issued his own Directive No. One, designating portly Hua Guofeng as acting Premier in place of Zhou Enlai, bypassing both Deng Xiaoping and his wife's protégés.

In March, posters suddenly appeared in Chongqing and several other cities: "Down with the ambition-mad plotters, down with Jiang Qing." A twelve-page pamphlet denouncing the Four circulated in Guangzhou. On March 5, Zhou Enlai's birthday, the *Wenhwei* newspaper canceled a commemorative article on Zhou, and issued instead a scurrilous piece on the renegacy of "Wu Hao." This brought out the irate students of Nanjing University with a collective letter of protest. On March 19, the children of a primary school marched to Tienanmen Square in Beijing to deposit wreaths in honor of the heroes of the revolution at the foot of the monument. "Beloved Uncle Zhou, you live in our hearts forever," read the words on the wreaths. Other schools and institutes followed, a swelling number. Soldiers came in trucks, armed with bouquets. By April 1, the crowds numbered in the thousands, especially at night after work. Banners to Zhou hung from the lampposts. In university dormitories students sat up at night making white paper flowers. On April 2, the police began to remove the wreaths and to scrape off the wall posters, but factory workers arrived in trucks with rolls of wire to secure the wreaths to the fences around the monument. On April 3, there were 50,000 people on the square during the day, and more than 100,000 that night.

April 4, Sunday, was Bright and Clear Day, *Tsing Ming*, the day when ancestors' graves are tidied and the names of the beloved dead called out. On that day 300,000 people gathered at Tienanmen Square to mourn Zhou Enlai. Young men and women stood to recite poems, sonnets, impassioned verses of love for him and of hatred and defiance against Jiang Qing and her supporters.

On the afternoon of April 5, the arrests began. Police armed with sticks hauled off orators, and this continued through the night. Some workers burned a building in a side street and there was violence, with twenty dead.

On April 7 the incident was declared "counterrevolutionary," a word whose vagueness encompasses theft, rape, destruction of state property, seditious harangue, and political malfeasance of both vast and nebulous range. Deng was once again deprived of all his posts, but "permitted to retain his Party membership so one may see how he behaves in the future." This leniency was "at the suggestion of our great leader Chairman Mao." Thus, once again, Mao spared an adversary of his wife.

At the end of July, a massive earthquake destroyed the city of Tangshan in North China, killing some 400,000. "The earth opened under us, everything fell into it," my niece, a nurse at the Tangshan Hospital, told me. The reaction of the Gang was outrageous. "Develop and deepen the criticism of Deng Xiaoping," proclaimed the newspapers; not one of the Gang of Four visited the stricken city. In Beijing, seismic shock waves brought down 30,000 houses and killed 1,000 people.

In that summer, Mao deteriorated swiftly. He was reported to have pressed a piece of paper into Hua Guofeng's hand. Scribbled on it: "With you in charge, I am at ease." Spurious or not, this conferred the succession upon Hua. "Prepare for a showdown," announced Spring Bridge to Madame Mao. Nephew Mao Yuanxin was sent back to Manchuria to ready such army contingents as would be favorable to the Four.

Ye Jianying, Nie Rongzhen, and Li Xiannian got together. They sent a secret message to Deng Xiaoping, who had taken refuge in the south: "We cannot let these scoundrels take over." The plan took shape. Ye talked discreetly with Wang Dongxin, the commander of the 8341 Guard Regiment.

Mao died on September 8.

On October 6, Wang Dongxin sent a message to Zhang Chunqiao, to Yao Wenyuan, to Wang Hungwen. An emergency session of the Politburo was to take place in the Great Hall of the People that evening. Their presence was required. Since Wang Dongxin had been their ally, they did not suspect him, and drove to the brightly lit hall, which from the outside gave the appearance of being host to a full session—official cars were in place. As they passed through the swinging doors into the entrance lobby, they were apprehended and led off in handcuffs. A special 8341 unit then went to Madame Mao's residence at No. 17 Fisherman's Terrace and arrested her. That night Mao Yuanxin was arrested in Manchuria, and the propagandists of the Gang of Four in Peking University and in newspaper offices were taken into custody. All was done with quiet and superb efficiency. In Shanghai, the Gang's supporters received a message to come to Beijing "for a meeting." They came and were arrested. Thus, without shedding a drop of blood, the plans of the Gang of Four to wield supreme power were ended.

Epilogue

"Beloved Premier Zhou lives forever in our hearts." Heartfelt outpourings of grief, love, and respect continue to flow in books, songs, and poems from China's millions, years after Zhou Enlai's death. To the Chinese, Zhou remains an outstanding example of virtue, in the grand tradition of the "superior man," a being of flawless integrity, immune to corruption, unsparing of himself, dedicated to the people's welfare. He is an avatar of the ethical and moral standards which molded China's culture through the millennia. He was, however, far more than that. He was modern, in the sense of being aware, more than many of his colleagues, that China needed to accomplish *two* revolutions at once: first the industrial revolution, which had taken place in Europe three centuries ago; then the technological revolution, which had started at the end of World War II.

Throughout his life, advances in science and technology were a paramount preoccupation of his. And for him this also meant political enlargement, freedom of discussion, encouraging fundamental research. Hence his repeated efforts to obtain the participation of non-Communist intellectuals; to involve representatives of other political parties in the decisions of the government; to enlarge the right to criticize, to hold divergent opinions.

But Zhou was not a democrat in the American sense of the word. He was not for a "pluralism" that would wreak havoc in a China just emerging from decades of civil war and misery and attempting to break free of millennia of autocracy. He believed in a "common front" representing all tendencies, achieving consensus. He believed that the Chinese Communist Party needed to hear "unpleasant truths . . . accept criticism."

During the mid-1980s, an attempt by some young academics to disparage all of China's revolutionary heroes included some attacks against Zhou Enlai. They criticized his conduct during the Cultural Revolution. He should have organized a rebellion in the Party against Mao, some averred. Only spurious scholarship and shallow knowledge of the historical circumstances of those years could lead to such an inane conclusion. Zhou Enlai did exactly what had to be done in the historical context. And thus he saved hundreds, thousands of lives.

Zhou Enlai was honored, respected, popular among many statesmen in the West for his outspokenness, his grasp of issues. He was even liked by his enemies, and government leaders mourned him in Taiwan. He was not only a statesman of world magnitude, a consummate diplomat, a skillful administrator, but also a human, witty, endearing person. Despite all this, there are few books about him, and that is because his activities were so numerous, his talent for adaptation, for changing and surviving, so manifest, that he is at times unseizable. One cannot slot him into a recognizable category. He was indeed a man for all seasons, weathering every storm and vagary in those tumultuous decades of the revolution. He bridged the gap between the past and the transient present, and showed the way to the future. He had no ego, not in the usual narrow sense of the word. He was possessed by something far larger, a sense of total responsibility toward his people and his country. All this makes it difficult to write about him without sounding hagiographic.

Since Zhou's death in 1976 and under Deng Xiaoping—Zhou's chosen successor—economic reforms, the opening up of the country, implicit in Zhou's last speech on the Four Modernizations delivered in January 1975, have brought about great changes in China. But the very success of the reform policies fostered manifold problems. The erosion of the moral authority of the Communist Party, an avalanche of news and ideas from the West, have awakened new aspirations and desires. The disappearance of traditional ethical and moral standards has created a vacuum of values. Notions of self-sacrifice are ridiculed by a certain portion of the elitist youth in the universities. Greed and self-serving, impatient puerility have surfaced. These are only too easily disguised under the word "democracy," which is still ill understood in China, where its connotation is too often the idea that it means freedom to do anything one pleases. Role models are no longer revolutionary heroes, but rock singers and pop stars and successful carpetbagger millionaires from the new, thriving private sector which is growing fast. However, this is not the full picture. Cynicism, unscrupulousness, may be manifest in the cities, and certainly among the privileged young—who too often are the ones courted by Western observers, and who all too easily get scholarships for trips abroad. But there is also, among the many millions of the young—and 65 percent of China is under thirty-five years old—a genuine hunger for truth, for freedom of discussion, for more participation in decision making.

This is what, way back in the 1950s, Zhou Enlai had sensed, had tried to establish, through the ill-fated Hundred Flowers experiment.

Everywhere in China today, one hears people say openly, loudly, and repeatedly, "Had Premier Zhou Enlai been alive, there would not have been . . . such bad handling of the youth demonstrations." This refers to the tragic events of Tienanmen Square in June 1989. "Premier Zhou would have gone personally to meet the students. He would have been there every day, talking with them, also listening . . . he would have spent hours with them, as he did with the young Red Guards during the Cultural Revolution." "Zhou Enlai would have said to them, 'It is my fault, my fault, that things are not clear to you.' He would have won them over, he would have given them a sense of purpose, of dedication."

The collapse of the Soviet Union, the reemergence of the nations once comprising Central Asia—and all of them belonging to the Muslim religion—was duly noted in China. It did not produce any panic. "On the contrary, we can now cut down on the border armies which for so many years had to patrol the frontier between China and the U.S.S.R.," was the way one ex-ambassador put it to me. Since then, the evident chaos in the former Soviet Union has effectively reinforced China's view that the line adopted—i.e., of making economic reforms first before attempting any political liberalization—was the correct choice. This assured a basic stability, and the student movement of the last few years, though certainly expressing urban discontent, did not touch the 80 percent of China's people who live in rural areas, and who are far better off at present than at any time in the previous decades.

In fact, the present disorder—the economic chaos, the rise of ethnic and religious turmoil, and, quite possibly, the reemergence of old-fashioned right-wing dictatorial regimes—has had a contrary effect on the Chinese people, persuading them against a desire to emulate what Gorbachev tried to do.

But economic reforms will inevitably also bring about political reforms. At this juncture, the ideas of Zhou Enlai, the consensus he tried to establish between the Communist Party and the non-Communist parties in China, assume a new importance. "We certainly do not want to see chaos, the mess that Russia is in today," is what most intellectuals in China today say. "This would set China back at least a century." "China will find her own way, and Zhou remains an inspiration for all of us. He was defeated in his lifetime, but he may now succeed, beyond death. For men such as he live in our minds forever."

Notes

Material for this book comes from my numerous personal visits to China since 1956 (around sixty in all), from my eleven meetings with Premier Zhou Enlai (nine full interviews, one lunch conversation, and a casual meeting), and from many Chinese sources, including records and memoirs published in Huai An, the town where Zhou was born, in Shaoxing, where his family issued from, and in other places in China. I have also drawn on records of conversations with many of the men and women who worked with Zhou Enlai through the decades and whom I know personally, and on interviews with some of Zhou's relatives. Articles, essays, and documents which were submitted by scholars and researchers at the Zhou Enlai seminar held at Nankai University, Tianjin, in October 1988, were made available to me and are in my files. The scholars attending the seminar, and also other researchers, were consulted to check or verify details. I am grateful to the curator and research scholars of the Zhou Research Study Team of the Central Committee Archives Press, the director and members of the Sichuan Publishing House, and other individuals who have given much time to many talks with me. I have also used such works as *The Selected Letters of Zhou Enlai, The Diary of Great Events in the Life of Zhou Enlai, The Youth of Zhou Enlai,* and *The Selected Works of Zhou Enlai,* in Chinese and (the latter; i.e., *Selected Works*) in English, published by the Sichuan Publishing House.

In the following notes, I refer often to the five volumes of my autobiography, all of which were published in London by Jonathan Cape, Ltd. The dates of first publication are:

The Crippled Tree, 1965
A Mortal Flower, 1966
Birdless Summer, 1968
My House Has Two Doors, 1980
Phoenix Harvest, 1980

Numbers at the beginning of each note refer to pages in the text.

CHAPTER 1

PAGE

13. During the latter part of the nineteenth century China was bankrupted by Western countries' substituting opium for silver in payment for exports. This led the rulers of China to extort what they could from the peasants, and this in turn led to immense peasant revolts. For more information, see:

The Taiping Rebellion (in Chinese: *Zhung Guo Shihxuehui Zhubien Shenzhou Guoguang Shih*), 8 volumes, the author's archives.

Central Committee Archives: Documents on the rebellions of the nineteenth century (in Chinese).

English scholars such as Victor Purcell and C. P. Fitzgerald are also valuable sources of information on this period of Chinese history.

20. Regarding the "Boxer Rebellion," as it was called, there are extensive records in Western countries. In France, *Les Grands Dossiers de l'Illustration: La Chine, Histoire d'une Siècle*, Sefar and Illustration, 1987, is one of the best and most extensive records on the depredations then committed by the Western powers. *The Boxer Uprising*, by Victor Purcell, Cambridge, Cambridge University Press, 1963, is also worth studying.

22. For the life of Dr. Sun Yatsen, see James Cantlie, *Sun Yatsen and the Awakening of China*, London, Jerrold and Sons, 1912. I had a long conversation in July 1943 with Robert Cantlie, a physician and a friend of Sun Yatsen, who described how his father had been instrumental in freeing Sun Yatsen from a British jail. Sun had been kidnapped by the British Secret Service to be handed over by the latter to the Manchu imperial police.

23. This essay is reproduced, along with other articles and essays by Zhou Enlai, in *The Youth of Zhou Enlai*, Sichuan Publishing House.

CHAPTER 2

Much of the material in this chapter and the next comes from the archives kept in Tianjin at the Nankai University Zhou Enlai Museum.

27. There are fifty-six ethnic groups in China, known as national minorities. The Hui, or Chinese Muslims, were descendants of Arab or Persian settlers. The Muslim religion was brought to China via two routes, over the Northern Silk Road and by sea to South China. Communities of Muslim traders, merchants, and craftsmen were established in major cities. Zhou Enlai's physique, and the fact that he grew a heavy beard, rare in a Chinese, may point to some admixture of Hui blood among his ancestors.

NOTES

27. Quotations and testimonies found in the material stored in the Nankai University Zhou Enlai Museum. These testimonies have been abridged and condensed.

28. Although the capital, Peking, is now spelled Beijing, the old spelling has been retained for Peking University.

29. Speech of October 3, 1916, by Zhou Enlai, in *Early Writings of Zhou Enlai*, Sichuan Publishing House, and also in archives at the Nankai Museum.

35. Nankai Middle School became Nankai University in September 1918. In July 1937, it was bombed by the Japanese. Nankai's professors and students emigrated to the hinterland, trekking thousands of miles with books and equipment upon their backs. They returned to Tianjin at the end of World War II in 1945. It is one of China's most successful and prestigious institutes of learning today.

37–38. Some Chinese historians aver that the decision taken by the Chinese Communist Party and government not to exact any war indemnity from Japan was due to Zhou Enlai and his deep feeling for the Japanese people. Discussed by the author with aforesaid historians in October 1988.

CHAPTER 3

39. See Michael Summerskill, *China on the Western Front*, London, published by Michael Summerskill, 1982. More than 200,000 Chinese laborers were sent to France in 1917 to work in factories and also on the war front. Around 150,000 were sent to Great Britain.

42. The militarist in question was Tsao Julin, well known at the time for his pro-Japanese stance.

43. For the rules governing the Awareness Society, see *Youth* and *Diary*, Sichuan Publishing House. Also writings of Zhou Enlai in his youth, Central Committee Archives, Beijing, in the author's collection.

47. Concerning Li Yuju: In 1955 Zhou Enlai and his wife, Deng Yingchao, paid a visit to her and to her husband, Pan Shilun, a classmate of Zhou Enlai at Nankai. A photograph was taken, and published in a magazine (*Zhou Enlai's Youth*, No. 5). Copy of photo in the author's files.

47. Liu Chungyu, lawyer (1877–1941). Zhou Enlai exchanged many letters with him, but only one letter in *Selected Letters* is available (pp. 12–13).

CHAPTER 4

51–52. Letters dated January 25 and February 8, 1921, from *Selected Letters*.
The author's conversations with the curator of the Central Committee Archives Press, 1987, and with the Zhou Research Study Team, 1987 and 1988.

50–52. Material quoted from *Selected Letters* and from other publications mentioned.

52–53. Controversy over the exact date Zhou became a Communist Party member has gone on for some years. Because of a long history of clandestinity, Party members did not carry cards and often only knew their two sponsors. It was difficult to verify Party membership because of infiltration tactics by the Guomindang. Zhou himself wrote "autumn 1922" instead of May 1921 as the date of his admission as a Party member at a verification carried out before the Party's Seventh Congress in 1945. "I was a member of the Socialist Youth League," he explained. But it is now agreed that the French branch of the Chinese Communist Party began with the Youth League, and Zhou was therefore a bona fide Party member starting May 1921. Why then did he write "autumn 1922" as the date of his membership? Possibly because claiming Party membership as of May 1921 would give him "seniority" over many other Party leaders, including Mao. The Seventh Congress was the one that consecrated the supremacy of Mao Dzedong and made him the Party founder. Hence, possibly, Zhou's tactful change of date.

57. Funds were obtained from the Communist International. The author's conversation with two French Communists: Régis Bergeron and Annie Kriegel, 1987. Funds distributed by French Party members are mentioned in the biography of Kang Sheng. See *Kang Sheng et les Services Secrets Chinois*, by Roger Faligot and Remi Kauffer, Paris, Robert Laffont, 1987.

Also see *Dictionnaire Biographique du Mouvement Ouvrier International*, in which the names of Chinese students known to French Party members are mentioned—i.e., Tsai Hosen, Li Lisan, Chao Shiyan (Zhao Shiyen), Li Weihan, Chou Enlai (Zhou Enlai).

59. The files of the minutes of the First Party Congress have been lost. This was confirmed by the curator of the Central Committee Archives Press.

60. Soong Chingling (1893–1982). Wife of Sun Yatsen. The importance of the Soong family in Chinese history cannot be underestimated. See *The Soong Dynasty*, by Sterling Seagrave, New York, Harper & Row, 1985.

62. John Knight, the "English" version of Zhou Enlai's name, is mentioned in Zhou Enlai's own letters.

CHAPTER 5

68. Liao Zhungkai, his son Liao Chengzhi, his daughter Liao Mengxin (Grace Liao), and his wife, the famous painter He Xiangning, were a highly educated Overseas Chinese family which played a major role in many events of the Chinese revolution. See biographical notes.

68–69. The Hakkas, or "guest people," emigrated from North China and settled, during the centuries, in various parts of Central and South China. Hardy and adventurous, the Hakka are well known for their fighting spirit and never followed the custom of foot binding prevalent elsewhere. See Han Suyin, *The Crippled Tree*, for more details on the Hakkas and their customs.

69. Du Yuesheng, one of the best-known leaders of the secret society known as the Green Gang in Shanghai. Chen Lifu, Chen Guofu, closely connected to Chiang Kaishek, and Chiang Kaishek himself were all members of the Green Gang.

69. The Blueshirts were closely knit with loyalty oaths to each other and to the "Supreme Leader," Chiang Kaishek. They studied *Mein Kampf*, required in their training curriculum. The author's first husband, Tang Baohuang, was recruited into the Blueshirts in 1939. See *Birdless Summer*.

71. The East Expedition documented by researchers at the Zhou Enlai seminar, October 1988. See also letter of April 15, 1925, in *Selected Letters*.

72. In a talk with correspondent James Bertram, in Yenan, Mao gave credit to Zhou Enlai for this early demonstration of military acumen.

73. Peasant Training Institute in Guangzhou. Visited by the author several times. See Han Suyin, *The Morning Deluge*.

75. Ho Chi Minh, also known as Nguan Ai Guoc. See Philippe Franchini, *Les Guerres d'Indochine*, Paris, Pygmalion, 1988. Also Ho Chi Minh biography by Jean Lacouture.

76. Documents supplied by Professor Liu Xi and other researchers at Nankai University seminar by the curator of the Central Committee Archives.

76. See *La Question Chinoise dans l'Internationale Communiste* (1926–27), Paris, EDI, 1965.

79. Interviews with Deng Yingchao in 1987 and 1988. Altogether the author had six major interviews with Deng Yingchao.

CHAPTER 6

80. The appalling conditions of workers in China in the Western-owned factories of Shanghai have been described in many books. See Rewi Alley, *At 90: Memoirs of My China Years*, Beijing, Foreign Language Press, 1986. Rewi Alley was a factory inspector in Shanghai during the late 1920s.

85. Biography of Zhou Enlai, Beijing, Central Committee Archives Press (in Chinese).

Also interviews with the curator and researchers at the Central Committee Archives. Notes of interview concerning Zhou's arrest in the author's files.

89. See *La Question Chinoise dans l'Internationale Communiste* (cited above) and Stalin's speech. This speech was kept secret for many years.

88–89. Discussion with Zhou Research Study Team, Central Committee Archives. Zhou's work in creating the Chinese Communist Party secret service and a Party underground has hitherto been shrouded in secrecy.

88–89. Feng Yuxiang (Fong Yuhsiang). See biographical note. There is a photograph of the author, aged five, with Feng Yuxiang. Also Han Suyin, *The Crippled Tree*.

89. Interview with Anna Louise Strong concerning the train episode.

89. Interview with John McCook Roots, son of Bishop Roots, in New York, 1972 and 1973. Also conversations with Ms. Hadden, sister of J. M. Roots. The author is indebted to the Rootses for material on Zhou Enlai. See *Chou* (previous spelling of Zhou) by John McCook Roots, New York, Doubleday, 1968.

89. See the late Percy Chen's book, *China Called Me*, Boston, Little, Brown, 1979. Percy Chen, son of Eugene Chen, Sun Yatsen's Foreign Minister, drove Borodin and Anna Louise Strong across China to the U.S.S.R. in 1927.

89. Gelao (Kelao), or Elder Brother Society, also known as Brothers of the Robe, one of the most powerful secret societies in West and Northwest China. While Shanghai was mainly in the hands of the Green and Red gangs, five inland provinces were the Kelao domain.

90. Guo Moro (Kuo Mojo) (1892–1977). Guo joined Sun Yatsen's government in 1923 in Guangzhou and met Zhou Enlai in 1924. Guo's own biography was published in French by Gallimard, Paris, 1970. Interviews of the author with Guo Moro in 1956, 1960, 1965, and 1969.

90. Interview with Deng Yingchao, in the author's archives.

90. Anna Louise Strong (1885–1974). American left-wing writer and journalist. Author of many books. The author saw Ms. Strong, who lived in Beijing, over a fifteen-year period almost every year and had long talks with her. See biographical note.

90. Chu Chiubai (Qu Qiubai) (1899–1935). See biographical note. Zhang Guotao (Chang Kuotao) (1897–1974). See biographical note.

91. Interviews by the author with Nie Rongzhen, 1990. Also memoirs of Nie Rongzhen, Beijing, People's Liberation Army Publishing Press, 1986.

93–94. Peng Bai. See biographical note.

CHAPTER 7

95. Sun Tzu's *The Art of War*, said to date back to the sixth century B.C. The best translation in English is by Samuel Griffith, Oxford, Oxford University Press, 1963.

96. Interview of the author with Marshal Ye Jianying, October 1977. Also information from Zhou Research Study Team. See also *Wind in My Sleeve*, by

Han Suyin, London, Jonathan Cape, 1992, pp. 16, 17, 18, for interview with Ye.

97. For more details, see Zhou Enlai, *Selected Works*, Vol. I (in English), Beijing, Foreign Language Press, 1981. "On the Sixth Congress of the Party," lecture by Zhou Enlai.

101. *Selected Works*, Vol. I. Letter to Ho Lung dated March 17, 1929.

103. *Selected Works*, Vol. I. Letter of September 28, 1929.

104–5. Rewi Alley, *At 90: Memoirs of My China Years* (cited above). The author is a personal friend of the aforesaid businessman, living in Brussels.

105. Reminiscence of Xia Yan (Hsia Yen), who was present at those "flying demonstrations" and vividly described them to the author in 1981. See biographical note.

106. Shaoshan Report (September 24, 1930). See C. Brandt, *A Documentary History of Chinese Communism*, London, Jerrold and Sons, 1952.

107. Wang Ming's real name was Chen Shaoyu. The real name of Po Ku (Bo Gu) was Qin Bangxian (Chin Panghsian). See biographical notes.

108. Oyuwan base. One of the main bases besides that established by Mao Dzedong. Its commander was Hsu Hsiangchian (Xu Xiangqian) (Going Forward). See biographical note.

109. The author's conversation with Zhou Research Study Team. There was always family responsibility, dating back to imperial times, for all "crimes" committed by any individual. No Chinese really acts outside a "network" of family or friends.
    Regarding the letter by Gu Shunchang, the author asked the curator of the Central Committee Archives whether it was still extant and could be consulted. The reply was negative.

CHAPTER 8

111. Tsai Tingkai (Cai Tingkai). See biographical note.

112. There was controversy within the Party at the time regarding the purge. Details in Han Suyin, *The Morning Deluge* (cited above). New information released at the Zhou Enlai seminar of 1988 reveals that it was a severe and unwarranted purge.

112. Xiang Ying (Hsiang Ying). See biographical note. He was left behind with Chen Yi when the Ruijin base was evacuated in 1934.

114. Deng Xiaoping (Teng Hsiaoping). See biographical note. He appears to have married three times. His second wife and he were divorced in Ruijin in 1933. He married again in 1940.

114–15. Zhou Enlai's intelligence apparatus relied on some Americans and Europeans in Shanghai. Rewi Alley was one of the most important men in the radio information network. Conversations of the author with Rewi Alley.

115–16. Seminar on Zhou Enlai, 1988. Researchers contributed information in talks with the author.

116. Nelson Fu (Fu Lienchang). See biographical note.

117. Ningdu meeting. As above. Also see Zhou biography, Central Committee Archives Press (in Chinese), pp. 255 ff.

119. The policy of control of salt and iron was practiced for two thousand years by the imperial dynasties to curb peasant rebellions. It was employed by Chiang Kaishek in his campaigns against the Communists.

119–20. Base of Ho Lung. Established in Hunan province near Lake Hung. Ho Lung had been successful, almost achieving liaison with the Oyuwan base. He maintained fighting strength till 1935, when he was attacked by superior numbers and forced onto a short "Long March" of his own, to join Mao and Zhou in the Northwest base at the end of 1936. See biographical note.

CHAPTER 9

126. Wu Xiuquan (Wu Hsiu-ch'uan). (1908–). Joined the revolution as a student, spent 1926–1931 in the U.S.S.R. and Germany. Returned to join the base at Ruijin, acted as interpreter to Comintern agent Otto Braun (alias Li De). Well known to the author personally. Led first delegation to the UN in November 1950 at the time of the Korean War. Heads the "common front" organizations in China.

127–29. Resolutions of the Tsunyi meeting. Published in *China Quarterly*, No. 40, October–December 1969. Translated by Jerome Chen. A report by Chen Yun, bringing more clarification and corrections to the above report, was published in *Xinhua News*, March 4, 1984, Beijing. Divergences as to the numbers attending are due to the fact that the meeting went on for some days and sometimes all participants could not be there. For instance, on the third day Peng Dehuai had to leave the meeting because of a military alert.

136. Hu Tsungnan. See biographical note.

139–41. For some details, see Percy Jucheng Fang, *Zhou Enlai: A Profile*, Beijing, Foreign Language Press, 1986. Also conversation of the author with Liao Chengzhi, 1978.

CHAPTER 10

145. Agnes Smedley. See biographical note. "Charlie," whose real name was Liu Ding, was one of Zhou's underground men in the entourage of the Guo-

mindang commanders in the northwest. He was adept at providing means to fund the Communists. Provincial bank notes were issued by every warlord in authority in the provinces, and the central government would redeem such bank notes at par. This was a way of "controlling" the militarists and winning their support, but it was also utilized by the Communists through such agents as Liu Ding. Rewi Alley told the author how he traveled back and forth to "redeem" such provincial bank notes at the central government banks in Chiang's capital city of Nanjing.

146. Regarding the infiltration of the Gelao, see *Zhou Enlai on the United Front* (in Chinese), Vol. I, pp. 24–25. Zhou Research Study Team, 1988.

146. The massive student demonstrations throughout China began in Beijing, December 9, 1935. They were led by students of Yenjing and Peking universities. One of them was Huang Hua (see biographical note), a student at Yenjing and a longtime friend of the author.

146. General Yang Hucheng (Tiger City). See biographical note. He and his wife came to Europe with one of her sons in 1937–38. Met by the author in Brussels in early 1938.

146. Zhang Xueliang (Chang Hsuehliang). See biographical note.

147. Wang Bingnan (Wang Pingnan). See biographical note. Much of the material in this chapter is derived from numerous conversations between the author and Ambassador Wang Bingnan, who became one of China's most prestigious diplomats. Also from memoirs written by Wang Bingnan, in the author's possession.

151. Although Mao is reported to have said this, he was far too astute a politician not to realize that Chiang Kaishek must not be brought to trial. But it does seem that Zhou persuaded him to contain his anger against Chiang.

151. "Tim" is Timothy Lee, old classmate and friend of the author, now living in Hong Kong. He told this story to the author.

151. General Gung Chengzhou (Kung Chengchou), father of two famous women, Kung (Gung) Peng and Kung (Gung) Pusheng. See biographical notes. The two Kung (Gung) sisters, both friends of the author, contributed material to this book. Also see Han Suyin, *My House Has Two Doors*.

155–56. The agreement (provisional) was: cessation of hostilities; withdrawal of the advancing Guomindang armies; reform of the Nanjing government; expulsion of its pro-Japan clique; release of all political prisoners; guarantee of democratic rights; cessation of anti-Communist campaigns; unity with the Red Army against Japan; recognition of the Chinese Communist Party and of its base; a general assembly of all parties, all groups, to be called as soon as possible for the salvation of China; the organization of a government of national defense; cooperation with countries who sympathized with resistance to Japan.

CHAPTER 11

158. Mao: Declaration of August 1936, repeated in August 1937. See letter by Mao of September 25, 1937, to Zhou Enlai, Liu Shaoqi, and Yang Shangkun, at the time of the Tsinan campaign.

159. Statement by Zhou published July 15 in Yenan. Original date of writing July 4, 1937. Published September 22 in Nanjing.

159. See Agnes Smedley, *Battle Hymn of China*, London, Victor Gollancz Ltd., 1944.

160. See Madame Li Jifang, *A Memoir*, Beijing, Foreign Language Press, 1979. This is an account of Deng Yingchao's stay in the sanatorium. The account by Edgar Snow of his helping her to safety is somewhat different.

161. People's Political Council (PPC). See *Glorious History of the Chinese People's Political Consultative Conference (CPPCC)*, Hong Kong, Motherland Press, 1985. The PPC would become the CPPCC. It functions even today and has shown signs of becoming more vigorous and influential lately.

161. Kang Daisha. Friend of the author, daughter of a prestigious family allied to the author's family in China. See *Birdless Summer* and *My House Has Two Doors*.

164. File of correspondence and interviews with son and daughter of Bishop Roots, in the author's possession.
   Joris Ivens and Marcelline Loridan, friends of the author. Direct interviews and conversations with Joris Ivens. Also see *Joris Ivens and China*, Beijing, New World Press, 1983. The cable from Soong Meiling mentioned is in the Ivens archives, but there is a copy along with letters from Joris Ivens in the author's files.

166. Regarding Zhou Enlai signing the proclamation, the author has consulted the curator of the Central Committee Archives. Zhou was not in Wuhan when the proclamation was published. Apparently Wang Ming would sign for the other members of the Party who were not there, and even signed in the name of Mao. Zhou insisted that he had never signed the proclamation. It was not something he would do without consulting Mao. Hence, it was not mentioned among the "errors" he was accused of during the Rectification Movement in Yenan.

166. The author was part of this exodus. Travel by river up to Chongqing (Chungking) was most hazardous at the time, as the Japanese bombed the boats. A Xinhua News Agency staff boat going upstream was bombed with great loss of life. Hence a circuitous way, via Changsha, down to Hengyang, then to Guilin, and up via Guizhou province to Chongqing, was the route undertaken not only by the Guomindang but also by many Communist groups.
   See Han Suyin, *Destination Chungking*, London, Jonathan Cape, 1943. Also Little, Brown, Boston, 1942, and *Birdless Summer*.

168. Zhou did not visit Huai An, his native town, on this occasion, perhaps because it was unsafe, but also because he did not want the members of his family to receive any special privileges because of his eminence. He did not visit Huai An even when he became Prime Minister later, for the same reason.

168. The arrival of Zhou's father was facilitated by units of the New Fourth Army, which had its agents in Huai An at the time.

169. For more details, see *History of the Xinhua News Agency* (in Chinese). In the author's files.

170. Long lines of manacled peasants being taken from the fields to become soldiers in the Guomindang army were personally seen by the author at the time.

170. See Ross Terrill, *The White-Boned Demon*, New York, William Morrow, 1984. Also Roxane Witke, *Comrade Chiang Ching*, Boston, Little, Brown, 1977. This book is not entirely reliable, for it gives too much credence to Madame Mao (Jiang Qing). One incident—i.e., her swallowing her Party card—is fable, for there were never any Party cards issued to Party members at the time. This was pointed out by the author to Witke. In the author's files.

170. George Hatem, known by his Chinese name of Ma Haide. See biographical note.

Even then, Limpid Stream, Jiang Qing, appears to have been hated by a good many people. The Chinese habit of imaginative gossip, completely devoid of fact, attributed Zhou's accident to her. Likewise, only recently (1992) the author was told by a Chinese woman writer that she was approached by a British publisher to write a "true story" claiming that Limpid Stream was a lesbian. Such are today's pitfalls of research into the facts concerning personages in China!

171. Shi Ji, *Memoir of Zhou's Trip to Moscow* (in Chinese), 1939–40. In the author's files.

172. Guo Moro returned from Japan to China in 1937. He was employed in the propaganda department of the Guomindang. Letter from Zhou to Guo Moro regarding orphans, dated January 29, 1938. Zhou, *Selected Letters*.

173. *Memoirs of Nie Rongzhen*.

174. The name of the deputy who delivered the ultimatum was Bai Chongxi, a warlord from the province of Guangxi.

174. This story is also told by Theodore White. It is not entirely validated by the author's research. Unless Zhou was drunk at the time—and he had a very good head for wine—one cannot see him accusing Chiang Kaishek of being "undemocratic." Zhou was always careful not to insult Chiang Kaishek.

175. "A lonely leaf" refers to the character for Ye in Ye Ting, which means "leaf."

175. David Barrett. Friend of the author. U.S. military attaché to China at the time.

175. See *Birdless Summer* for Zhou Enlai's speech. The author was present.

176. See *Birdless Summer*. The author was in Chongqing at the time and witnessed the elation of those around Chiang Kaishek, including her own husband. "At last the fat boys will be on our side," was one comment. Chiang sang the Ave Maria that day. It was his favorite song.

CHAPTER 12

178. Much of the material on the Rectification in Yenan comes from the usual sources, but also from Chinese witnesses, people who endured the event, historians at the Central Committee Archives, and scholars at the Zhou seminar of 1988.

178. For the sinicization of Marxism, see Mao's own works. Also Han Suyin, *The Morning Deluge* (cited above). Mao's writing in the years preceding the Rectification were probably his most creative. See also Han Suyin, *The Acculturation of Revolution*, 1975. Filed in the Boston University special collections.

179–80. Liu Shaoqi's speech against Zhou. A record exists in the Central Committee Archives. Only extracts were made available to the author, but it was mentioned by two friends of the author who were in Yenan at the time. "It was really a most condemnatory speech, we heard it all." Apparently a tape exists, not available, in the Central Committee Archives. Data regarding Zhou's replies from the Zhou Research Study Team, also in *Selected Works* (English translation), Vol. I.

180. See previous chapter, where Wang Ming's signing a proclamation in the name of Zhou is mentioned.

181. The woman writer was Ge Cuilin, now vice-president of the Bingxin Fund for children's literature, Beijing, and a friend of the author.

181. Mao's apologies. Told to the author by Ge Cuilin and two other writers present at the time.

181. The poet in question is Ai Qing, highly regarded and translated into French.

184–85. "Ultimate weapon." This seemed to be the thinking before discovery of the atomic bomb. See letter from Zhou Enlai to Wang Bingnan in *Selected Letters*.

185. See David D. Barrett, *Dixie Mission: The United States Army Observer Group in Yenan, 1944*, Center for Chinese Studies, University of California, Berkeley, 1970.

185. Conversation with Edgar Snow, October 1970.

186. David Barrett. Personal conversation with the author, 1952.

187–90. See *China White Paper: U.S. Relations with China*, Stanford, Stanford University Press, originally issued as *U.S. Relations with China*, Department of

State Publication 3573. Much of this material checked with Chinese sources, also conversations with Wang Bingnan.

190–91. Zhu Qing, wife of Ambassador Tian Jin. See biographical note.

190–91. Yang Tiger City (Yang Hucheng) and his family were slaughtered when Chiang left Chongqing, 1945.

194. The sister of Gung Peng and Gung Pusheng lives in California. The author had a long telephone conversation with her concerning the rental of Zhou's house in Shanghai.

196. Material from Zhou Enlai seminar of 1988. Also *Selected Letters*.

CHAPTER 13

196. See *Selected Works*. Also *Zhou Enlai on the United Front* (in Chinese) (cited above).

198. Hsiung Hsianghui (Xiung Xianghui). See biographical note. One of Zhou's capable trainees, a mole for many years, he became a member of the Ministry of Foreign Affairs and chargé d'affaires in Great Britain.

199. Li Desheng means Li Winning Victory. Hu Picheng means Hu Certain to Win.

199–204. Material from biography of Zhou Enlai, Beijing, Central Committee Archives Press (in Chinese), pp. 704 ff. Also from *Diary* and from author's personal interviews.

200–1. For details on the inflation in China much documentation is available. Inflation was 10,000 percent per week in the last months of Chiang Kaishek's reign.

204. Quotation from a manuscript by Indian ambassador P. K. Bannerjee, who had many contacts with Zhou and his staff. Copy of the manuscript in the author's possession.

207. Grace Liao (Liao Mengxin), sister of Liao Chengzhi. Secretary to Soong Chingling for many years, member of the CPPCC.

209. Edmund Glubb. Well-known American sinologist, whose books contributed greatly to an understanding of China. Victim of McCarthyism in the 1950s.

CHAPTER 14

Quotations, as previously, from letters, speeches, *Diary* of Zhou Enlai. Also private conversations with individuals who had worked with Zhou, such as Zhou Peiyuan, president of the Academy of Sciences. Author personally saw Mr. Liang

Secheng, grandson of Liang Qichao (Liang Chichao), whose style Zhou had admired and strove to emulate in his youth.

213. Gung Peng and her husband, Qiao Guanhua, were sent by Zhou to Hong Kong to handle the Xinhua News Agency there, which has always functioned as a nonofficial "embassy" for China in the British colony. The author met them again in 1949 when in Hong Kong. They returned to Beijing the year after and were closely associated with Zhou for many years, until Peng's death in 1970. See Han Suyin, *My House Has Two Doors* and *Phoenix Harvest*.

214–20. Pu Shouchang, secretary to Zhou and chief translator for many years. Educated at Harvard. See biographical note. Interviewed by the author in Beijing.

222. Gao Gang (Kao Kang). See biographical note.

223. Accounts of the Korean War abound in the United States. See General Matthew B. Ridgway, *The Korean War*, New York, Doubleday, 1967, for the best and most succinct account.

226. See John Spanner, *The Truman-MacArthur Controversy on the Korean War*, New York, W. W. Norton, 1965.

228. The drafting of a policy for economic control by the central government over the provinces was done by economist Chen Yun and Li Fuchun, husband of Tsai Chang and Zhou's friend from their student days in France. See also Carl Riskin, *China's Political Economy*, New York, Oxford University Press, 1987.

CHAPTER 15

The bulk of information concerning the Geneva conference comes from Chinese sources, such as the recollections of Ambassador Wang Bingnan and of Pu Shouchang. The unedited original manuscript in English from Wang Bingnan is in the author's possession. Regarding the Bandung conference, there are Zhou's *Selected Letters*, his *Diary*, and other Chinese as well as non-Chinese sources. A valuable Western source has been *The 1954 Geneva Conference, Indochina and Korea*, New York, Greenwood Press, 1968, with an introduction by Kenneth T. Young, president of the Asia Society.

233. Nineteen countries were present at the Geneva conference. The United States, the U.S.S.R., China, Great Britain, France, North Korea, South Korea, Australia, New Zealand, Belgium, Canada, Colombia, Ethiopia, Greece, Holland, the Philippines, Thailand, Luxembourg, and Turkey.

236. According to sinologist Harish Kapur, CNRR, Geneva, it was a suggestion from India (through Krishna Menon) which triggered the event by advising that an exchange of prisoners of war might open the dialogue. India was a member of the committee in charge of prisoners of war in Korea. Private interview with author.

239. The five principles of peaceful coexistence were first announced by Zhou in Beijing during the course of talks with an Indian delegation in 1953. They are: mutual respect for sovereignty and territorial integrity; nonaggression; non-interference in internal affairs; friendship and equality; striving for peaceful negotiations in any dispute that may arise. These still form the basic principles of China's relations with other countries today.

240. At the Potsdam conference in 1945, Truman, Stalin, and Churchill, who met there following the meeting at Yalta between the late Roosevelt and Stalin which partitioned the world (or attempted to), had chosen the 16th parallel as the "temporary" demarcation line between the United States-backed South Vietnam territory and its government and the North Vietnam territory. This was done without any reference at all either to France (then the colonial power in Vietnam) or to China (supposedly an important ally in the war against fascist Germany and Japan).

241. SEATO, the Southeast Asia Treaty Organization, consisted of the United States, France, Great Britain, Australia, New Zealand, Pakistan, the Philippines, and Thailand. It was a pact elaborated by Dulles, purporting to resist any "Communist aggression." But Pakistan's Premier, Ali Bogra, had already hastened to assure Zhou Enlai that Pakistan had only joined SEATO in order to assure its own security against India. Manifestly, SEATO was designed to prevent "Chinese Communist expansionism" in Southeast Asia.

241. Zhou's statement. Told by Wang Bingnan to the author. Also said in conversation between Zhou Enlai and Felix Greene, British journalist, and the author. See biographical note on Felix Greene.

241. Ha Van Lau was a member of the North Vietnamese delegation at the Geneva conference and later ambassador to France. In conversations with the author in Hanoi, and in Paris, September–October 1988.

242. In a conversation with the author in 1964, Zhou Enlai made it clear that he did not wish any of the Southeast Asian countries to become "socialist." This also applied to Hong Kong, which China still wishes to remain capitalist.

243–44. Conversation between the author and Malcolm MacDonald, but also mentioned in Malcolm MacDonald, *A Constant Surprise*, pp. 393–96 (unpublished). Seen by the author.

244. With surprising and somewhat less than honest disregard of history, renowned "sinologists" confected books purporting to see in the Chinese of Southeast Asia a deliberately planted fifth column operating for the Communist regime. The author was in Malaya and Singapore then and witnessed the suspicion and persecution of any youths who studied Chinese. See *My House Has Two Doors* by the author.

247–48. See Zhou Enlai speech on the problems of the Overseas Chinese, in *Diary* and *Selected Works*. For more background, see Victor Purcell, *The Chinese in Southeast Asia*, London, Oxford University Press, 1965.

CHAPTER 16

250. The story of the letter was told to the author by Guo Moro (Kuo Mojo).

250–51. Zhou's speech was printed in the *People's Daily*, January 30, 1956. It was an edited and shortened version of the original.

251. List of the non-Communist parties:

Guomindang Revolutionary Committee, organized in January 1948 by former members of the Guomindang opposed to Chiang Kaishek.

China Democratic League. Minister of Timber Industry Lo Lungzhi and Minister of Justice Shi Liang, both in Zhou's first cabinet, belonged to it.

China Democratic National Construction Association, mainly comprised of industrialists, businessmen, persons in industry and commerce. Two ministers in Zhou's cabinet belonged to it.

China Association for Promotion of Democracy. Two of Zhou Enlai's vice-ministers in education belonged to this party.

Chinese Peasants' and Workers' Democratic Party. Zhang Pochun, Zhou's Minister of Communications, was a member of this party.

Chikun Tang Party, with many Overseas Chinese members.

Chiusan Society, comprising intellectuals in scientific and technical fields. Its vice-chairman was Vice-Minister of Forestry under Zhou.

Taiwan Democratic League.

258. Today (1992) this emphasis on the main problem in China being the contradiction between the objective of modern industrialization (progress) and residual backwardness has continued to be the basis for policies pursued by Deng Xiaoping.

259. For the "Ten Great Relations," see Han Suyin, *Wind in the Tower*, London, Jonathan Cape, 1976. The full text of Mao's article would not be available until 1968.

262. This comment made by Dick Wilson in his excellent book *Chou: The Story of Chou Enlai, 1898–1976*, London, Hutchinson, 1984.

262. This headline was shown to the author by her father in Beijing in 1957.

CHAPTER 17

265. Zhou is on record as condemning "haste" and "extremism" before the Leap was officially announced, when in the countryside a "tide" of communization (the first steps to set up communes) began. He was the sole leader who warned of the dangers of such policies.

265. Relative of the author. This refers to Zhao Yiming, head of the Democratic League in the province of Sichuan. He and his wife (my cousin) were both condemned as "rightists" for many years.

266. Economists Ma Hong and Lung Yungkwei. Both interviewed by the author.

268. This trip of Zhou was to study what is now called the Three Gorges dam project, approved for construction in 1992. It appears that Zhou had misgivings about the project, misgivings which continue even today. See Han Suyin, *Wind in My Sleeve*, London, Jonathan Cape, 1992.

268. The author had written a short story, "The Sparrow Shall Fall," published in *The New Yorker*, which greatly displeased the Chinese authorities.

268. Fan Royu (Joyu)'s memoirs. The quotation is in the author's files.

269. Tibet was governed by a theocracy of monks, the majority of the population being serfs employed in the huge monastery domains. Attempts to change this were made, and produced the agitation led by the monks in 1959. Zhou knew this and attempted to mitigate the problem by halting reforms. But reforms could not be stopped, once begun. The root cause of the unsettled condition in Tibet is the attempt to extirpate the old theocratic order, to build schools and hospitals, to bring Tibet into the modern age.

270. Conversation of the author with Foreign Minister Chen Yi in Geneva in the spring of 1961.

274. Memoir by Li Jui (Li Rui). Handwritten. Copy in the author's files.

277. Zhou's drinking. Seminar, October, 1988. This was recorded because Zhou was very seldom drunk. Talk with Professor Liu Xi confirms this.

277. Longju. See Neville Maxwell, *India's China War*, London, Jonathan Cape, 1970. This episode was a prelude to the border conflict which took place in October 1962.

278. Painter Wu Tsojen and painter Kuan Shanyue, both friends of the author, contributed these details.

279. Prince Kinkazu Saionji was a Japanese aristocrat who resided in Beijing for many years.

279. An example of Deng's blunt truthfulness.

CHAPTER 18

282. Television interview by Edward R. Murrow on *Small World*. The author was with Joseph Alsop and E. Boothby. The subject was China, the Leap, and the communes. Summer 1959.

282–83. The author was invited to speak at the Couchiching conference in Canada, which was an attempt by Canada to open up relations with China but which encountered strong opposition from the American delegation present. See reports on the Couchiching conference, Canada, summer 1959. At the time it was not fashionable to say anything more or less balanced about "Red" China.

283. There are voluminous documents on Tibet, in Chinese and also by English authors of the nineteenth and early twentieth centuries. The Chinese documents

include copies of letters from the Dalai Lama to the Chinese garrison commander just before his flight, in which he complains of being coerced by his fellow monks. The British invasion of Tibet is also well documented. See also Neville Maxwell, *India's China War* (cited above).

284. "A thick red pencil." Also quoted by Rajiv Gandhi, late Prime Minister of India (murdered in 1990), on his state visit to China in December 1989.

288. Felix Greene, author and correspondent. See biographical note.

291–92. Mao favored a "people's war" in Vietnam rather than massive classic military offensives. Zhou referred to "the military thinking of Chairman Mao" in a private talk with me. A book, *The Military Thinking of Mao Dzedong*, was published in English in Hong Kong (1992).

293. Information about India's plans was given to the author by the late S. Sharma (died 1968), photographer, journalist, a friend of Nehru. Sharma came to Singapore to tell the author that the Indians were preparing a military onslaught and had the full backing of the U.S.S.R. The author mentioned this to Foreign Affairs Minister Chen Yi, who blandly replied, "We know all about it and have made full preparation."

294. Chinese commanders' displeasure. Talk with a relative of the author employed in the armed forces of China.

294–95. Memoirs of Ambassador P. K. Bannerjee. In the author's archives.

CHAPTER 19

I am indebted for details in this chapter to Dick Wilson's book *Chou* (cited above). Also the usual Chinese sources, interviews with Chinese personalities close to Zhou, including Ambassador Chen Jiakang.

298. The author attended the conference held in Cairo, but only as an observer. She was not allowed to speak, being a "bourgeois writer," unless she toed the Soviet line. See Han Suyin, *My House Has Two Doors*.

300. Concerning General Gordon and his activities in China, see *The Taiping Wars (Shen Zhou Guoguang Shih)* (in Chinese), Beijing, 1960–62.

304. The toothpick anecdote was told to me in June 1985 by the man who ran the hotel and arranged the dinner for Zhou Enlai and Ho Chi Minh that night. This dinner took place in 1965.

305–6. The author was in Indonesia at the time and met Sukarno, Subandrio, his Foreign Minister, and also Aidit and members of the Indonesian Communist Party. She felt the latter were "cloud-walking," apparently unaware of the strength of the Indonesia army. "Aidit does not seem to notice the tanks on the street," the author wrote to Gung Peng. Note in the author's files. Also see *My House Has Two Doors*.

CHAPTER 20

311. Conversations with General Montgomery have been recorded in numerous books on Mao Dzedong.

311. See *Social Sciences in China* (in English, Vol. IV, 1987), a quarterly issued by the Chinese Academy of Social Sciences, Beijing. "The Party and State Leadership Structure" by PaN Song and HaN Gang.

312. Zhou's accusation. Verified with scholars of the Zhou Research Study Team of the Central Committee Archives.

312. The Peng Zhen affair (known during the Cultural Revolution as the Zhang-Guan-Lou affair) was given much prominence during the Cultural Revolution, when Peng Zhen was accused of plotting to discredit Mao. This interpretation of his action is now denied, and indeed, even if some "material" was gathered which seemed to show Mao in a bad light, it does not appear to have had any effect at the time.

315–17. The Socialist Education Movement (SEM). See Richard Baum and Frederic Teiwes, *Su Ch'ing: The Socialist Education Movement of 1962–66,* China Research Monographs, Center for Chinese Studies, University of California, Berkeley.

318. Personal talks with Edgar Snow in Beijing and Switzerland, where Snow lived for some years until his death in February 1972.

319. Private talks with Zhou Enlai, September 1965, before the Cultural Revolution was launched.

319–20. The introduction or preamble was not penned by Zhou but had his approval.

321. The Taoist concept of duality in all things permeates all of Mao's Marxist writings. It is fundamental to dialectics, whether in present-day physics or in Marxism, but Mao gave to Marxism a "Chinese" color. Hence today China claims to follow "socialism with Chinese characteristics"—which means with heavy infusions of capitalist practices (1992).

322. Yang Xianyi, longtime editor of Chinese literature in Beijing, friend of the author. Many conversations over the last thirty years. See biographical note.

322. Mao described himself to Edgar Snow in December 1970 as *"wufa wutian,"* which implies total disregard for the laws of heaven or of mankind. This had already been said about him by some hostile colleagues, such as Zhang Guotao, but Mao seemed to revel in the fact that nothing could trammel him. He also used the symbol of the Great Monkey, a tale known to every Chinese child. See Arthur Waley, *Monkey,* 1942, or translations of the famous *Western Pilgrimage.* Books available both in French and in English. See also Edgar Snow, *The Long Revolution*, New York, Random House, 1970.

323. The story told to the author is that Liu Shaoqi went to see Mao and suggested sending work teams to investigate "revisionism" in academic circles. "Do as you see fit," Mao had replied. Liu had already used work teams during the Socialist Education Movement to stem challenges from below against the Party. By repeating this procedure, he devised a trap for himself which brought about his downfall.

324. An "enlarged" meeting means that it was packed with other than the usual members entitled to attend. This one was filled with Mao's adherents, including university student representatives. Lin Biao's army units were stationed in Beijing at the time, surrounding major buildings, thus exercising psychological pressure on members of the meeting who might have been against the proceedings now undertaken.

324. The sixteen-point declaration can be found in Chinese records of the time; also published in the *People's Daily* and other newspapers in August 1966.

324. In 1966 the members of the GCCR were: Chen Boda, former secretary to Mao, chief editor of the magazine *Red Flag*, and nominal head of the group; Jiang Qing, Mao's wife, first deputy head; Zhang Chunqiao (see biographical note), editor of the Shanghai newspaper *Liberation Daily*; Kang Sheng, adviser to the GCCR; *Tao Zhu; Wang Renzhung; Li Jiqian;* Yao Wenyuan; *Zhang Pinghua; Mu Xin*; and the three "extremists," whose main job seems to have been to gather material against Zhou Enlai—i.e., *Wang Li, Guan Feng,* and *Qi Penyu* (see biographical note). By 1968, only five of the above remained members of the GCCR. The names *in italics* were those who disappeared, denounced as "left extremists."

327. See *Memoirs of Nie Rongzhen*. Confirmed in conversation with members of the Central Committee Archives Zhou Research Study Team.

CHAPTER 21

329. The brutality of the Red Guards, a good many of them educated, continues to be a source of speculation in China today. "Why did our children suddenly exhibit such cruelty?" ask a good many writers and social scientists known to author.

330. The Wang-Guan-Qi trio. See previous chapter and biographical note (under Wang-Guan-Qi).

331. Zhang Wenjing (1920–1989), ambassador to the United States, president of the Association for Friendship with Foreign Countries. His wife, Zhang Ying, is a friend of the author and accompanied her on many trips. Conversations with the couple date back to the late 1960s.

333. To save their lives, Liu Shaoqi permitted Party members to deny belonging to the Party. This was done in the U.S.S.R. to save the lives of Party members in Hitler's Germany and was adopted in China. The measure was approved by

the Politburo then, but during the Cultural Revolution it was brought up as evidence against Liu.

333. Bo Yibo. See biographical note. Born 1907, was in 1966–67 a vice-premier working on the State Planning Commission.

334. Interview with Rung Guotuan (Jung Kuotuan), March 1987. The Rung family lived next door to the Zhous in Chongqing during the war. Rung's little son was a favorite of Zhou.

336. Jiang Qing's vindictiveness was notorious. The cruelty toward Sun Weishi, adopted daughter of Zhou Enlai and Deng Yingchao, was motivated by her jealousy of Sun's mother, in the 1920s more famous than she was in the film world of Shanghai. "This was settling old scores," Szeto Huimin, a film director of that time, told me in 1987.

338. Li Chiang, Zhou's Minister of External Trade. One of Zhou's main problems was making sure that war matériel reached the Vietnamese. Zhou switched shipments of rice from land convoys to flotillas of small junks and sampans in the Bay of Along. The United States bombed the flotillas, or they blew up after striking floating mines, but much more rice got through than if sent by land. Zhou studied the tides of the bay, and ordered the rice bags wrapped in four layers of plastic and dropped at high tide to float toward the coast. Interview by the author of army personnel then in charge.

CHAPTER 22

339–40. Li Lienqing, later ambassador to India. The author had several meetings and interviews with him. Author of a biography of Indira Gandhi.

340. Zhou's orders and speeches. Directives of November 28, 1966, December 9, 1966, and January 15, 1967. See Zhou, *Selected Works*, Vol. II. Speeches of December 9, 1966, and January 15, 1967. Other speeches made during the Cultural Revolution are recorded in the Central Committee Archives.

340–41. Wang Hungwen. See biographical note. Later adopted into the entourage of Jiang Qing and became part of the Gang of Four—composed of Wang, Jiang Qing, Zhang Chunqiao, and Yao Wenyuan. Mao coined the name Gang of Four against them in 1974, though they banded together in 1972.

342. Pan Fushen. The author went to Heilongjiang province to interview him in 1969. Pan later disappeared at about the same time as Lin Biao.

343. Striking the table. This incident was told to the author by Marshal Ye Jianying in an exclusive interview in October 1968. See Han Suyin, *Wind in My Sleeve* (cited above).

343. Empress Wu of the Tang dynasty reigned in place of her husband, whom she deposed (652 A.D.). In the male-dominated Confucian feudal society of China, she represented the epitome of cruelty and lasciviousness.

350. The Little Red Book. A manual for the use of the army, said to have been compiled by Lin Biao in 1965. Was at one time in everyone's hand, including Western traders attending the Canton Fair. It denoted "loyalty" to Chairman Mao.

350. Fei Yiming. Editor of *Takungpao* in Hong Kong. 1908–1988. See biographical note. In constant liaison with Zhou, he stopped the Red Guards from Guangzhou from marching and "liberating" Hong Kong. The troubles in Hong Kong were due partly to Red Guard agitation but also partly to the secret societies prevalent there.

351. Wei Guoqing was the commander who helped the Vietnamese in the famous battle of Dienbienphu in 1954, which broke the French domination over Vietnam. See biographical note. In 1989, General Giap of Vietnam came to China to pay his respects to the late Wei Guoqing.

352. Speeches by Zhou Enlai and Jiang Qing. Central Committee Archives. Also in several reports published abroad by the press at the time, heavily slanted in favor of the Red Guards.

CHAPTER 23

353. This incident concerning Wang Guangmei, wife of Liu Shaoqi, has been related many times and need not be elaborated.

354. The way in which material against Liu Shaoqi was collected or concocted, even forced from one of his former wives and one of his children, is reported by scholar Yen Jiaqi in his book *Ten Years of the Cultural Revolution* (in Chinese). Liu was not liked by some of the older intellectuals because of his role in Yenan in 1944–45, when some of them suffered because they did not belong to his Northern Bureau.

The author has not changed her view that Liu Shaoqi, had he been in power, would have been a close ally of the U.S.S.R., unlike Mao. History might then have been very different from what it is today.

356. Part of the conversation between Edgar Snow and Zhou Enlai is found in Edgar Snow, *The Long Revolution* (cited above). Snow spoke to the author about Zhou's acute anguish. "For a man who had always been so unflappable, he really exposed his soul . . . yet the next day he appeared as impassive as ever." Talk with Snow, October 1971.

356. The origin of the Communist army is dated to August 1, 1927, when Zhou Enlai led an armed onslaught against the city of Nanchang.

357. The invasion of Czechoslovakia. See François Fetjo, *Chine-URSS: De l'Alliance au Conflit*, Paris, Editions Seuil, 1973, pp. 389 ff. China strongly denounced the invasion. Zhou's speech on the occasion was delivered at the Romanian embassy on August 23, 1968.

361. The Politburo Standing Committee members at the time were: Mao Dze-dong, Zhou Enlai, Chen Boda, Lin Biao, Kang Sheng. Other members: Jiang Qing, Yao Wenyuan, Zhang Chunqiao, Ye Chun (Lin Biao's wife), Wang Dongxin, head of the 8341 Guard Regiment (elite troops whose responsibility was to assure security for all leaders), and three old marshals, Zhu De, Liu Bocheng, Ye Jianying, who had retained their Politburo membership. Lin Biao had nominated Huang Yungsheng, chief of staff, and Chen Xilian, in control of Manchuria. Yet Mao was still able to get Chen Boda downgraded. This was the beginning of Lin Biao's downfall.

362. The author's interview with Jiang Qing, Kang Sheng, and others, in October 1969. At the meeting the author pleaded that Edgar Snow should be allowed to visit China. The importance of this plea was noted by Hsiung Hsianghui (see biographical note), who was also present at the interview. "This was just what was needed at the time." A "hint" had been dropped the previous day to the author by Hsiung; of course, Zhou had suggested it. The author was also to make a plea for Harrison Salisbury. The author was in Hong Kong at end of 1969. Harrison Salisbury was trying to contact Chinese newsmen there, but was constantly rebuffed. The author was told by some friends in the Xinhua News Agency that, "by order," no one was allowed to speak to any American. See Han Suyin, *Phoenix Harvest*.

364. The author's interview with Zhou Peiyuan, president of the Academy of Sciences, concerning the restoration of fundamental scientific research. Meeting suggested by Zhou Enlai, October 1969.

364. Edgar Snow quotes Mao as saying to him in December 1970, "The four greats . . . great this and great that . . . what a nuisance." This was an expression of his growing dissatisfaction with the fulsome praise lavished upon him. He was beginning to suspect Lin Biao and Chen Boda.

365–66. The first version of Lin Biao's end is a product of certain "experts" in Taiwan and some sinologists.

366. See *Diary*. Also the author's interview with the Zhou Research Study Team. The author visited the house inhabited by Lin Biao in Beijing, where his belongings are kept.

367. Etienne Mana'ch (d. 1992), French ambassador in Beijing. A brilliant diplomat, and friend of General de Gaulle.

CHAPTER 24

369. Talks with Gung Peng and her husband, Qiao Guanhua, then acting Minister for Foreign Affairs, 1969.

370. Zhou's view that there would be no war with the U.S.S.R. was repeated to the author when she brought him Harrison Salisbury's book on the subject

of a possible conflict: *The Coming War between Russia and China*, London, Secker & Warburg, 1969.

370. Etienne Mana'ch, *Mémoires d'Extrême Orient*, Paris, Fayard, 1977, 1980. Also *Une Terre Traversée de Puissances Invisibles*, Paris, Fayard, 1983. An invaluable record of the Cultural Revolution years and the negotiations between France, the United States, and China, containing many insights into the positions of France and China vis-à-vis Vietnam and Cambodia, erstwhile French colonies.

372. Jacques Rueff, brilliant French economist, a friend of de Gaulle, also well known to the author, who saw him many times in Paris in the years 1967–74.

373–74. Nine interviews with His Royal Highness Norodom Sihanouk, covering the period from 1970 to November 1988, took place in China, in North Korea, and also in France. Also see William Shawcross, *Sideshow*, New York, Simon and Schuster, 1979.

376–77. Talks with Zhang Wenjing, later ambassador to the United States, regarding the alleged "arms traffic" with Lon Nol. Also in September–October 1988 conversations of the author with Minister of Foreign Affairs Nguen Co Thach of Vietnam in Hanoi, concerning alleged Chinese double-dealing. In author's files. Also speech by Zhou Enlai, April 30, 1970, and letter dated May 5, 1970, recognizing GRUNC (Gouvernement Royal d'Union Nationale du Cambodge) under Norodom Sihanouk.

376–77. Zhi Chaozhu and his brother Zhi Chaoting. Zhi Chaoting was an economist, author of *Key Economic Areas in Chinese History*, London, Allen & Unwin, 1936. Zhi Chaozhu is a distinguished diplomat at the UN.

377–78. Henry Kissinger, *The White House Years*, London, Weidenfeld, 1979. See pp. 701 ff.

379. The voting at the United Nations in late 1971 was 76 in favor of seating the People's Republic of China and unseating Taiwan, 25 against, and 17 abstentions.

382. For an excellent account of the Vietnam wars, see Philippe Franchini, *Les Guerres d'Indochine*, Paris, Pygmalion, 1983.

CHAPTER 25

386. The Gang of Four. See previous reference to this appellation, coined by Mao himself in July 1974. According to other data, Mao had already used it, scornfully, a year previously to castigate the ambition of his wife and her adherents. However, he still seems to have backed Wang Hungwen, one of the Gang.

388. Events in the hall. This refers to the meeting of February 1967 at which Ye Jianying broke a small bone in his hand. Referred to in conversation with Ye. See also Han Suyin, *Wind in My Sleeve* (cited above).

390–91. Zhang Chunqiao and Yao Wenyuan organized writing teams in all the newspapers and also in the universities. The most active were at Peking University, under the pseudonym of Liang Xiao, and in Shanghai, under the pseudonym of Luo Seding. Some of these writers were still employed on the editorial staffs of certain newspapers in 1992!

392. Speech of Zhou Enlai at Tenth Congress, August 31, 1973. At this congress the Gang of Four became members of the Politburo and Wang Hungwen was later nominated vice-chairman of the Party and vice-chairman of the Military Affairs Commission.

393. Yang Shangkun (1907–). Although one of the Twenty-eight Bolsheviks, he became a military commander of distinction and President of China. Retired in 1993.

394. Jacques Chaban-Delmas. French Minister of State, Prime Minister, (ex) President of the National Assembly, mayor of Bordeaux.

394. Conversations of the author with Norodom Sihanouk and Ambassador Etienne Mana'ch.

394–95. Zhou Enlai was always sensitive to the vulnerable position of Overseas Chinese communities in Southeast Asia. He repeatedly made it clear that they could not indulge in adopting a pro-China stance in politics. Overseas Chinese have always been a source of funds for their families in China and are now a source of investments in China. It was, therefore, though never openly mentioned, Zhou's idea that, like Hong Kong, these communities must remain capitalist "for a long time to come." Conversations with the author in 1961–62.

The Chinese economic minority in South Vietnam was a victim of Hanoi's victory, since they were the wealthier capitalists of the region. Many of the boat people are of Chinese ethnic origin. A purge was extended to all people of "Hua," or Chinese, origin after 1968 by the Vietnamese government.

398. The author talked to the women cadres ordered by Jiang Qing to look after Ms. Witke. In the summer of 1973, Ms. Witke came to see the author in New York. Witke earnestly believed that Jiang Qing would become "very important" in China. The author told her that "the people of China do not like her, so do be careful."

398–99. Extract from Han Suyin, *Phoenix Harvest*.

CHAPTER 26

401. Liver abscess. This refers to the episode in September 1935 when the Politburo had met over the Zhang Guotao affair. Zhou was then seriously ill with a liver abscess, which seems to have spontaneously resorbed. See also *Selected Letters*.

401. Wang Hairong (Wang Haijong). Mao's niece, promoted to Vice-Minister of Foreign Affairs during the Cultural Revolution. Tang Wensheng. American-

educated, a most able interpreter, employed in the Foreign Affairs Ministry. Both took part in the negotiations between Zhou Enlai, Henry Kissinger, and President Nixon.

403. Conversation of the author with His Excellency Kukrit Pramoj in Bangkok, 1981.

406. This article against Deng Xiaoping (and of course Zhou Enlai) was penned by Zhang Chunqiao, Jiang Qing's collaborator, member of the Gang of Four.

407. Madame Soong Chingling was frequently visited by the author, whom she entertained informally at tea, or dinner, and at films.

408. "Children by affection" were the orphans that Zhou and his wife cared for. Among them is today's Premier, Li Peng. There are reckoned to be around forty of such protégés.

Note on Romanization of Chinese Names

Anyone writing about China must face the irritating and baffling problem of new (pinyin) versus conventional romanization. It is almost impossible to be consistent, for certain names in current use—such as Peking, Canton, Hong Kong—have been transformed beyond utterance or recognition. The author is also faced by the problem that in Taiwan, in Hong Kong, and among the Overseas Chinese in many countries (altogether around 55 million people), the conventional romanization is still in use. Thus Chiang Kaishek is so well known as it is spelled that to transform it into pinyin would make the person unrecognizable. The author has tried her best in the following biographical notes to give both the pinyin and the conventional forms. In certain cases, she has stuck to the old spelling, because the new spelling made the names uncomfortably difficult for the average reader. Thus she has retained Tsai Hosen (old) instead of Cai Hosen (new) and also Tsai Chang and Tsai Tingkai. Likewise Ho Lung instead of He Lung because Western readers would pronounce it *he* instead of *ho*. Had all the names in the book been in the new spelling, then Hong Kong would have become Xiang Gang—identified by no one—and Chiang Kaishek would become Ziang Jieshi. Similarly, Yenan has been retained.

The author infinitely prefers the old romanization and finds the use of *x* and *q*, so abundant in pinyin, detracts from the practical recognition of a name. Thus my friend Xu Xiangqian (Hsu Hsiangchian) is identified as Xu Going Forward (the English translation of his personal name) to escape from the unwieldy pinyin.

It is necessary once again to state that in Chinese the family name *always* comes first, followed by the personal name. The biographical notes appended cover only the more important personages in the book.

Biographical Notes

Alley, Rewi (1897–1987). Born in New Zealand, enlisted in the New Zealand Expeditionary Force in World War I. Left for China in 1926 and arrived in Shanghai in early 1927. Worked for the International Famine Relief Commission and on flood relief. Became factory inspector in Shanghai. Engaged in clandestine activities for the Communists with Agnes Smedley. In 1938 initiated, with Edgar Snow and his wife, the Gung Ho Movement for industrial cooperatives in China. Traveled the length and breadth of China and knew more about the country, its culture, and its people than any other man alive. Joined the Bailie School projects and set up a school in Shandan, Northwest China. After the Communist victory of 1949 lived in Beijing, traveled widely, and also wrote extensively.

Bo Gu (Po Ku, a.k.a. Qin Bangxian or Chin Panghsian) (1907–46). Involved in student politics in middle school, became Communist Party member in 1925. Sent to Moscow in 1926. Went to the Ruijin base and clashed with Mao on policies. Took part in the Long March at Tsunyi. Mao—with the backing of the army generals and of Zhou Enlai—took over conduct of the march (see text) and Bo Gu was ousted from the leadership.

Bo Yibo (Po I Po or Po Yi Po) (1908–). Joined the Chinese Communist Party in 1926 at the age of eighteen, and was sent to jail in 1932. Released in 1936, and worked openly as a Communist, maintaining a close connection with Liu Shaoqi's Northern Bureau. Became Minister of Finance, October 1949 to September 1953. Was involved in the Economics and State Planning commissions. Is still today at eighty-four (in 1992) a person whose advice in economic matters counts.

Cai Chang. See Tsai Chang.

Cai Hosen. See Tsai Hosen.

Cai Timgkai. See Tsai Tingkai.

Chen Boda (Chen Pota) (1904–89). Educated in Shanghai, joined the Chinese Communist Party in 1924, was arrested and spent some years in jail. On release he went to Moscow, 1927. He returned to do underground work in North China, then went to Yenan. He became secretary to Mao Dzedong. He proved a prolific writer for many years on political subjects. Became member of the Central Committee and occupied a variety of posts. During the Cultural Revolution he sided with Lin Biao and the Gang of Four. Later fell into disfavor with Mao and was under house arrest after Lin Biao's conspiracy.

Chen Duxiu (Chen Tuhsiu) (1879–1942). One of the prime movers of the May 4, 1919, Movement. From a scholar-official family, Chen studied naval architecture and French, then went to Japan. Returned in 1902, and went to France, 1907 to 1910. He wrote many political tracts and at thirty-seven launched *Youth* magazine, renamed *New Youth* in 1916. Chen was attracted to Marxism and the May 1919 events confirmed his doubts about Western democratic liberalism. In 1920 he met Comintern agent Voitinsky, and together with eleven other participants he founded the Chinese Communist Party. Chen became involved in the common front organized between the Guomindang and the Chinese Communist Party to eradicate the warlords. In 1927, Chiang Kaishek, commander in chief of the United Front armies, turned against the Communists and massacres began throughout China. Chen, who adhered to the line of compromise with Chiang laid down by the Comintern, was repudiated and expelled from the Chinese Communist Party in November 1929. He now identified himself with the Trotskyites. In 1932 he was arrested by the French police in Shanghai's French Concession and turned over to the Guomindang government. He was imprisoned till 1937 and released when the United Front against Japan was formed in that year.

Chen Yi (Chen I) (1901–72). Born in Sichuan province, Chen Yi, from a family of scholars, wanted to be both a poet and a painter, and left for France in 1919. He studied for a while in art schools. In 1921 he was involved in the Lyons incident and was deported. Returned to Sichuan in 1922 and became a Party member in 1923. In 1926 joined up with Zhou Enlai in Guangzhou, took part in the Nanchang uprising of August 1, 1927. Chen Yi was a lifelong friend of Zhou Enlai, and became Foreign Minister when Zhou relinquished the post in 1957. One of China's ten marshals, he was a target of the Red Guards during the Cultural Revolution, and died in 1972 of cancer.

Chen Yun (1905–). Born near Shanghai, one of the few real "workers" (a typesetter) among the Chinese Communist Party leaders, joined the Chinese Communist Party in 1924. He helped Zhou Enlai in the February–March 1927 strikes designed to gain control of Shanghai in advance of the expeditionary forces. He was in Ruijin, and on the Long March, and later in charge of labor affairs in the Guomindang-controlled areas. He did not go to the Soviet Union, unlike other Chinese leaders, before he set out on the Long March. When he went to Moscow in July 1935, he was not entirely welcome by the Comintern, though he remained for about two years. In 1937 he was in Xinjiang province. Reached Yenan by the end of 1937. Disagreed with Mao on the policies of the Great Leap Forward and again later on the reorganization of the economy. Continued, under Zhou Enlai (Chen Yun was Vice-Premier), to have a role in economics. His later dominance in the field of economics, particularly in the period of 1949 to 1952, and again after the Leap, can scarcely be exaggerated. He is rated today as a "conservative," opposed to economic reform. This, of course, is not correct. He is opposed to hasty, ill-planned "modernization" procedures which have ruined so many other Third World countries. Chen Yun's "step-by-step" moderate program may not entirely fit the exigencies of today, however, but he is still worth consulting.

Chiao Kuanhua. See Qiao Guanhua.

Chu Chiubai. See Qu Qiubai.

Deng Xiaoping (Teng Hsiaoping) (1904–   ). Born in Sichuan province, real name Kan Tsekao. His present prominence and the importance of his ideas in the development of China's modernization make him the continuator of Zhou Enlai in many ways. A brief biographical note would not do him justice. See biography of Deng Xiaoping by Uli Franz, New York, Harcourt Brace Jovanovich, 1987, 1988. Political biography of Deng Xiaoping by Chi Hsin, Hong Kong, Cosmos Books, 1988.

Deng Yingchao (Teng Yingchao) (1904–92). Wife of Zhou Enlai, one of the most popular and revered figures in China today. Her mother encouraged her, when young, to participate in student activities. Met Zhou Enlai in 1919, when she was almost fifteen years old, and joined his Awareness Society. Stayed in China to continue the work of the society and became a teacher at the Tajen girls' school founded by Ma Qianli. Married Zhou Enlai in 1925. Became Party member probably in 1924. Became afflicted with pulmonary tuberculosis, but was on the Long March, though often had to be carried on a stretcher. Her life activities inseparable from those of her husband. Nevertheless, when Zhou Enlai became Prime Minister of China, her role was confined mainly to leadership in women's causes, though she also exercised great influence by her constant dedication to the cause of women's liberation and the welfare of children.

Fei Xiaotung (Fei Hsiaotung) (1910–   ). Attended Yenjing University and London University. Was in Southwest China during the anti-Japanese war (1937–45), at Southwest China University. Received many honors and posts in the government after 1949. Conducted many investigations into the condition of the peasantry. Was dubbed "rightist" in 1957 because he disagreed with Chinese Communist Party plans for higher education, but rehabilitated in 1959. Has since been a representative of the non-Communist Democratic League, and has made many trips abroad.

Fei Yiming (1908–88). Born in Shanghai, educated at the Catholic University, was a brilliant linguist, versed in French, English, and German. Chiefly known for having run the highly respected newspaper *Takungpao* (first in Shanghai, then in Hong Kong). He was successful not only in surviving the Cultural Revolution but also in checking some of its effects in Hong Kong. He was a close friend of Zhou Enlai.

Feng Yuxiang (Fong Yuhsiang) (1882–1948). One of the most colorful of China's thousands of warlords, Feng came from a poor peasant family, and rose to power through organizing his own armed forces among the peasantry. Unlike other warlords and militarists, he never lost touch with his own soldiers. He was open to new ideas, one of them being Christianity, which he adopted in a most colorful way, baptizing his soldiers with a fire hose. He married Christian-educated Li Techuan (Li Dequan), later Minister of Public Health in China, who bore him five children between 1925 and 1930. After an exciting career as a warlord, Feng supported the Communist government, though never a Communist himself.

Fu Lienchang (Nelson Fu) (1898 or 1895–1969). Was the first physician in the Communist Red Army. His father was a Christian, and Nelson Fu was reared by an English Protestant mission and became a doctor in the medical school run by the mission in Fujian province, where he was born. He saw the Communist forces retreating after the failed August 1, 1927, uprising and was greatly moved. He joined the Chinese Communist Party in 1928, made his way to Mao's base in the Jingang Mountains, and moved with the army to Ruijin. He founded hospitals, a Red Army school for nurses, and was on the Long March. He appears to have suffered from tuberculosis, hence his assertion to Zhou Enlai that he knew "how to deal with it" and that he would cure Zhou's wife, Deng Yingchao, similarly afflicted. He was dedicated to his work, and was greatly honored by Mao and the other leaders. He was tortured during the Cultural Revolution, and died under ill treatment by the Red Guards in 1969.

Fu Tsoyi (Fu Zoyi) (1895–1974). A graduate of Baoding Military Academy, joined the Guomindang. Distinguished himself by fighting against the Japanese in 1936 in North China when very few of Chiang's troops did so. Was entrusted, as was Tsai Tingkai, with "liquidating" the Communists (see text). Continued after World War II to fight the Communists, but had a change of heart in 1948 and when in command in Beijing went over to the Communists. He has since had a satisfactory career, becoming Minister of Electric Power and Water Conservancy. Protected during the Cultural Revolution by Zhou Enlai.

Gao Gang (Kao Kang) (1891–1955). Joined the Chinese Communist Party with Liu Jidan and in 1927 began peasant insurrections. In the 1930s, together with Liu Shaoqi, established the first guerrilla base near Bao An. His ability earned him Mao's regard, and in 1945 he went to Manchuria with Lin Biao, Chen Yun, and Li Fuchun to establish a base against the Guomindang in the civil war. Was highly successful and set up the Northeast Military Region in May 1949. Gao established links with the U.S.S.R. government, often without referring to his superiors, and was transferred to Beijing in 1953. Accused of "conspiracy," he committed suicide in prison.

Geng Biao (Keng Piao) (1909–). Born in Hunan, participated when still a teenager in Communist Party underground activities, and by 1929 had joined Mao in Ruijin. His personal courage, especially during the Long March (see text and interview by author), and a certain feistiness made him a popular figure wherever he was. He served under Nie Rongzhen in the important base created by the latter. After 1949 he spent a good deal of time abroad, and was China's first envoy to several countries.

Greene, Felix (1909–85). British journalist, of the same family as the author Graham Greene. Worked for the BBC, then as a free-lancer. Produced the first TV interview of Zhou Enlai (1960). Made full-length documentaries on China, on Tibet, on Vietnam, and also wrote many books, including A Curtain of Ignorance, pointing out the deliberate spread of misinformation about China in the United States.

Gung Peng (Kung Peng) (1915–70). Educated at Yenjing University, was an early student activist. Went to Yenan and later served under Zhou Enlai. Became very popular as Zhou's secretary in charge of press affairs. Married Qiao Guanhua and with him was in charge of the Xinhua News Agency in Hong Kong (1946–49). Later headed the Information Office under Zhou Enlai and accompanied Zhou on numerous visits abroad. Became Assistant Minister for Foreign Affairs. Died of a cerebral hemorrhage in 1970.

Gung Pusheng (Kung Pusheng) (1917–). Sister of Gung Peng. Graduated from Yenjing University, went to the United States, where she became a friend of Eleanor Roosevelt. Has had a prestigious career in the Ministry of Foreign Affairs and was ambassador for some years. Is still very active in international relations. Married Zhang Hanfu, a very close friend of Zhou Enlai and a well-known diplomat (deceased).

Guo Lungzhen (Kuo Lungchen, a.k.a. Guo Liyin) (1893–1930). A girl student of the Hui (Muslim) nationality, she engaged early on in revolutionary activities, and became a member of the Awareness Society founded by Zhou Enlai. She became a Communist in 1922, and went to France (1922–25). She returned to China and was captured and executed after being tortured in 1930.

Guo Moro (Kuo Mojo) (1892–1977). One of the major figures of Chinese revolutionary literature, he was also a translator and an archaeologist. His interest in science was as extensive as in literature. He translated Walt Whitman, much French poetry, and introduced "new wave" blank verse in China. Met Zhou Enlai in 1924. Throughout his life he was a major influence in bringing the problems of intellectuals to the attention of the Communist leaders, although this role has been ignored.

Hatem, George (Ma Haide) (1910–88). Born of Lebanese parents in Buffalo, New York, studied medicine in the United States, then in Beirut and Geneva. In 1933 went to Shanghai and started research in venereal diseases and dermatology. In 1936 went with Edgar Snow to the North China base where the Communists had established themselves at the end of the Long March. Did medical work in the guerrilla bases till 1949, became medical adviser to the Red Army. In 1949, at liberation, helped to organize the Ministry of Public Health and took a leading part in the nationwide campaigns against VD. After the eradication of VD (by 1958–59), shifted to the control of leprosy and its eradication. Took Chinese passport and changed his name from George Hatem to Ma Haide. Became a member of the CPPCC (Chinese People's Political Consultative Conference). Received many awards, including the Lasky Prize in the United States. He is one of the most honored and respected figures in China. He died of cancer in 1988.

He Xiangning (Madame Liao Zhungkai, a.k.a. Ho Hsiangning) (1876–1972). A painter and patriot, never a Communist, she founded the Guomindang Revolutionary Committee, one of China's eight democratic parties, in 1948. She became honorary chairman of the Overseas Chinese Affairs Commission, though it was her son, Liao Chengzhi, who ran the commission. Her paintings are highly valued by connoisseurs.

Ho Lung (He Lung) (1896–1969). A dashing, debonair figure, Ho Lung received no formal education. Born a cowherd, he became famous for his courage. At fourteen, he killed a corrupt local magistrate, which made him a very popular outlaw. Joined in the Nanchang expedition of August 1, 1927, and became a Communist under Zhou's influence. Although allegedly semiliterate, he was a remarkable leader of men, and a close friend of Zhou Enlai. Was on the Long March, and became one of China's ten marshals in 1958. During the Cultural Revolution, Ho Lung became a target of the Red Guards. Despite Zhou's efforts to save him, he died of deprivation of medicine (he was a diabetic).

Hsiung Hsianghui. See Xiung Xianghui.

Hsu Hsiangchian. See Xu Xiangqian.

Hsu Teli. See Xu Teli.

Hua Guofeng (Hua Kuofong) (1920 or 1921–). Born into a peasant family, joined the Red Army in 1936 after the Long March. Became Party secretary in Hunan province and worked in rural areas. He was known for his thoroughness and honesty. In 1959 he met Mao, who seems to have been impressed by him. Survived the Cultural Revolution and was sent to restore order in Guangzhou in 1972. Became member of Politburo in 1973. In charge of Public Security in 1975. Became acting Premier on February 7, 1976, four weeks after the death of Zhou Enlai, and successor to Mao at the latter's death in October 1976. With the return of Deng Xiaoping, lost his dominant position, but remained member of the Central Committee. Hua is respected for his dignified behavior at all times.

Hu Tsungnan (1896–1962). One of Chiang Kaishek's ablest generals, graduate of the Huangpu Military Academy, where he met Zhou Enlai. Entrusted by Chiang with some of the latter's best troops. During the Sino-Japanese war his headquarters were in Xian, from where he operated detention centers for Communist suspects and young students who wanted to leave Chiang-controlled China for the Communist bases. He was for a while highly regarded because of the fall of Yenan (see text), but suffered overwhelming defeat. Went to Taiwan with Chiang Kaishek, 1948.

Huang Hua (1914–   ). Huang Hua (real name Wang Rumei) was educated at Yenjing University, joined the Chinese Communist Party underground when scarcely twenty. He was one of the organizers of the massive student anti-Japanese demonstrations in December 1935. Went to Yenan in 1936, and was an interpreter for Mao with Edgar Snow. He was also involved in the truce talks of 1953 at the cessation of the Korean War, and was at Bandung with Zhou Enlai. He was the first ambassador sent to the United Nations in New York in 1972. He and his charming and able wife, Ho Li Lian, continue to work for broadening international exchanges.

Joris Ivens (1898–1989). Born in Holland, early interested in photography, worked as an apprentice in the factories of Ica and Ernemann and then Zeiss (1924–25). Associated with student movements and in 1930 went to the U.S.S.R. Participated in the Spanish Civil War in 1937, where he met Ernest Hemingway, John Dos Passos, Lillian Hellman. Filmed *Spanish Earth*, the first full-length documentary on the Spanish Civil War. Went to China in 1938 and met Zhou Enlai in Wuhan that year. Never got to Yenan as planned (see text), but at Zhou Enlai's suggestion gave his camera and several thousand feet of film for filmmakers in Yenan. American foundations invited him to make films. Later filmed in Indonesia. Returned several times to China (1958, 1961) and later filmed in Vietnam. In 1972–75 made a twelve-part documentary in China. Continued filming until his death in 1989.

Jiang Qing (Chiang Ching) (1914–91). Born into an impoverished family, went to Tianjin with widowed mother in 1927. By 1931 became a member of left-wing theater groups. Joined the Chinese Communist Party in 1933 and went to Shanghai. Briefly jailed by the Guomindang, 1934–35. Under the name of Lan Ping (Blue Apple) became film actress and in 1937 went to Yenan. Met Mao and started living with him in 1938. Married Mao in 1939. Until 1965 did not play any major role, though was associated with the condemnation of works of art and films. Was treated for cancer in Moscow for some years. From 1962 onward began to attack the "bourgeois" trends in literature and art and to sponsor new Chinese operas. Became prominent in the Cultural Revolution and became a member of the Politburo. Organized a team of supporters. In 1973 was denounced as "too ambitious" by her husband. In 1975 led attacks against Zhou Enlai and Deng Xiaoping. Was arrested in October 1976, a month after the death of Mao. Condemned at a public trial and remained under house arrest until her death.

Kang Keqing (Kang Keching) (1912–91). Born into a very poor family. A servant at the age of six, she did not go to school until she joined the Communist Youth League in her province at the age of twelve, and was active in ten villages at the age of fifteen, when she was already organizing guerrilla bands. Married Zhu De when she went to Mao's base in 1928 and became a Party member. Chief of detachment of women army volunteers by 1932, fought at the front against Chiang Kaishek's "annihilation" campaigns. Joined the Long March, where she carried the equipment of weaker men or wounded soldiers. Was involved throughout her life in work for women and children. A splendid woman, unrecognized in the West, she agreed during an anticorruption sweep in the 1980s that one of her grandchildren, who had committed rape, should be shot as the law required, sacrificing family connection to principle.

Kang Sheng (1899–1975). Studied in Shanghai, became a Communist Party member in 1924, a labor organizer in Shanghai in 1925, and also director of the organization department of the Chinese Communist Party (the Party intelligence organ). Joined the faction of the Twenty-eight Bolsheviks at the Party's plenum in January 1931 and continued as head of the OGPU (intelligence department), known in Chinese as the Te Ke. Stayed in Shanghai underground until 1933 and then went to Moscow, where he studied Soviet security and intelligence techniques. Was Chinese Communist Party representative on the Comintern Committee, became friendly with Wang Ming, head of the Twenty-eight Bolsheviks. The two were published together in Soviet magazines. In 1937 accompanied Wang Ming back to Yenan (see text). Returned to his special field of intelligence and security work until 1946, when replaced by Li Kenung. In Yenan was responsible for much of the "terror" unleashed during the Rectification Movement (see text). Became prominent at the Seventh Party Congress in April–June 1945 and by 1954 was a Politburo member. Became a major figure in liaison with outside Communist parties, and sided with Mao in the Sino-Soviet dispute (1960). Sided with Madame Mao in the Cultural Revolution. See *Kang Sheng et les Services Secrets Chinois*, by Roger Faligot and Remi Kauffer, Paris, Robert Laffont, 1987.

Kung Peng. See Gung Peng.

Kung Pusheng. See Gung Pusheng.

Li Dazhao (Li Ta Chao) (1888–1927). Chinese Communism owes its inception largely to Chen Duxiu and Li Dazhao. Born into a peasant family, Li enrolled in 1905 in a school of "new learning," spent six years studying political economy, then studied in Japan at Waseda University in Tokyo (1913–16), and worked with revolutionary groups in Japan. In 1916 he returned to China and became an editor of Chen Duxiu's *Youth* and *New Youth*. He was also librarian of Peking University (1918) and professor of history and political science (1920). Li was one of the most prominent and revered leaders of China's revolutionary intelligentsia. He became attracted to Marxism and founded the Society for the Study of Socialism at Peking University. He met Comintern agent Voitinsky, and participated in a conference preliminary to the inauguration of the Chinese Communist Party in Shanghai (May 1921) but did not attend the First Congress (July 1921). In 1926 he was forced to take refuge in the Soviet embassy in Peking (Beijing), but was captured and executed by strangling in April 1927 along with nineteen other Communists.

Li Fuchun (1900–75). Went to France with Tsai Hosen in 1919, and in 1921 was one of the founders of the French branch of the Chinese Communist Party. Did underground work for a considerable time, was on the Long March. An excellent organizer, entrusted with the handling of economic and other Party affairs, he worked closely with Zhou Enlai.

Li Kenung (Li K'onung) (1898–1962). Was a student activist in the May 4, 1919, Movement, and a Party member by 1922. He worked underground from 1925 onward, although records show that he was trained in intelligence in 1928 by Zhou Enlai. From then on his role in the intelligence network seems to have been prominent. He is credited with having penetrated even the Guomindang intelligence apparatus. When he and others were betrayed by Gu Shungchang (see text), he went to Mao's base. He remained in the intelligence field, and was one of the Long Marchers. He was present, along with Ye Jianying, at Zhou Enlai's talks with Chiang Kaishek in 1936–37 (see text). Became a major figure in liaison between Guomindang and Communists in the United Front. In 1954 accompanied Zhou Enlai to the Geneva conference. He became ill and died of cancer in 1962.

Li Lisan (Li Li San) (1899–1967). Was in contact with but did not join the group around Mao Dzedong and his New People's Study Society. Left for France in 1919, where he worked with Tsai Hosen and Zhou Enlai. Was expelled, along with Tsai and others, after the Lyons incident (1921). Swiftly rose in prominence as a Party and labor leader. Attended, with Zhou Enlai, the Sixth Party Congress, held in Moscow. Zhou seems to have defended him against the Comintern and the Twenty-eight Bolsheviks. He never attained prominence again after 1930. Died of ill-treatment during the Cultural Revolution.

Li Tsungjen (1892–1968). Native of Guangxi province, was one of the more successful militarists (warlords). Alternatively fought against and joined Chiang Kaishek. In 1948, when Chiang left for Taiwan, Li Tsungjen became President in his stead and sent a peace mission for talks with the Chinese Communist Party. These were unsuccessful and Li retired to the United States, but returned to China in 1965, on the eve of the Cultural Revolution. Though protected throughout the first years of the Red Guard rampage, his health broke down and he died in 1968.

Li Xiannian (Li Hsien Nien) (1905–92). Born a carpenter's son, he joined the Northern Expeditionary Army in 1926, and like many others, when the split came with Chiang Kaishek, remained with the Communists and entered the army. Went to Yenan in 1937 and organized guerrilla forces. Joined the New

Fourth Army and managed a breakthrough. After 1949 became mayor of Wuhan and then Vice-Premier and Minister of Finance in 1954. Became President of People's Republic of China but retired due to ill health. Highly respected as a man of total integrity.

Liang Szecheng (Liang Su Cheng) (1901–72). Son of the famous scholar and reformist Liang Qichao (Liang Chi Chao), whose mellifluous prose influenced Zhou Enlai. Graduated from Tsinghua University and received MA in architecture from the University of Pennsylvania. Fought for the preservation of historical sites and buildings and was regarded as a "bourgeois." Joined the Chinese Communist Party in 1958. Led a delegation to attend the Eighth International Architecture Conference in Paris in June 1965, but when the Cultural Revolution came, was ill-treated by the Red Guards. The author, on the advice of Premier Zhou Enlai, went to see him in 1969. This was meant to have some influence in subduing the attacks against him, and also consoling a sick man.

Liao Chengzhi (Liao Chengchih) (1908–83). The only way to describe this man is to say he was "bonny, full of adventurous spirit, and full of humor." The son of Liao Zhungkai, he became a revolutionary at sixteen in 1924 and a Chinese Communist Party member in 1927. He sailed as a seaman for Europe in 1928, attempted to foment strikes (there were many Chinese among the sailors). He was arrested in Holland, then in Germany, and returned to China in 1932. Ran a Communist underground in Shanghai. His career was eminently variegated. He was fond of Pekinese dogs and also of Dutch herring. He was persecuted during the Cultural Revolution but survived.

Liao Mengxin (Liao Menghsin, a.k.a. Grace Liao) (1909–88). Sister of Liao Chengzhi. Secretary to Soong Chingling for many years, she was also prominent in United Front organizations and the Overseas Chinese organizations in China.

Liao Zhungkai (Liao Chungkai) (1877–1925). An important and prosperous descendant of an Overseas Chinese family, Liao early associated with Sun Yatsen, and supplied both money and influence in support of Sun's cause. The Overseas Chinese communities had a great deal to do with the Chinese revolutionary process in the early twentieth century, and Liao sacrificed his personal wealth to promote his country's advance. He had many connections in Japan, where Sun Yatsen established a solid base for his United League, precursor of the Nationalist Party, or Guomindang. Liao was multilingual, having received part of his education in the United States. He became Sun Yatsen's most helpful and loyal minister, but was constantly outmaneuvered by more ambitious personalities. Regarded by the Guomindang "right wing" as an obstacle, was murdered in 1925.

Lin Biao (Lin Piao) (1907–71). Lin does not seem to have been an early student activist, but in 1925 gained admission to the Huangpu Military Academy. His ability was never in doubt, but identifying him as China's main military strategist (as some Western sinologists have done) will not bear scrutiny if we compare him with other military figures of the Chinese Communist Party. He was not yet twenty when the Nanchang uprising occurred, in which he joined. He was under the command of Zhu De and Chen Yi in the subsequent retreat to reach the base established by Mao. Lin Biao seems to have attracted Mao's attention, and Mao wrote letters to him. Lin rapidly rose in the army, joined the Long March. Even then, he appears to have been prey to illness, and this is mentioned in accounts of the Long March. He became president of Kangta, a university set up in Yenan. He was listed third, after Zhu De and Peng Dehuai, as one of the ten marshals of the army in 1955. He appears to have been "ill" for several crucial years, notably during the Korean War, which he spent in Moscow as a patient. Plotted against Mao although proclaimed Mao's heir, and died in dramatic circumstances (see text).

Lin Boju (Lin Pochu) (1886–1960). Lin adhered early to Sun Yatsen's United League. When the Guomindang broke with the Communists, Lin went over to the Communist side and took part in the Nanchang uprising of August 1, 1927. He went to Moscow via Japan, arriving in 1928, and returned to China in 1932, joined Mao Dzedong's base in Ruijin, where he sided with Mao and Deng Xiaoping against the Wang Ming clique, and was demoted as they were. He joined the Long March in charge of logistics, and became an assistant to Zhou Enlai in his negotiations with Chiang Kaishek in 1936–37. Lin was one of the first Communist leaders to reach Beijing in 1949 in a peaceful victory. He continued promoting, under Zhou, a legal research society, a political science society. He had always been interested in the reform of the Chinese language and this was one of his many activities. He died of heart failure in 1960.

Liu Bocheng (Liu Pocheng) (1892–86). One of the most able of Red Army veterans, early became an officer and lost one eye in battle (hence nicknamed the One-Eyed Dragon). Like Zhu De and other minor warlords, Liu joined the Nationalists (Guomindang). When a split occurred, he chose the Communist side, and went to Nanchang, where he assisted Ho Lung in the August 1, 1927, uprising. At the end of 1927 he went to Moscow, where he spent three years at the Red Army Military Academy. He returned to the base established by Mao and was on the Long March. Known as one of the best tacticians of the Red Army, he became one of China's ten marshals in 1955. He was not only an excellent military commander but also a prolific writer of books on guerrilla warfare and tactics. Wrote a lengthy account of the Long March, published in Hong Kong in 1960.

Liu Jidan (Liu Chitan) (1902–36). Born in Shensi province, became a student at the Huangpu Military Academy. Served under Feng Yuxiang (see biographical note) for a short while. When Feng chose Chiang Kaishek instead of "the left," organized an uprising against him but was defeated. This uprising is still regarded as an important beginning of Communist resistance in the northwest. Founded the northern guerrilla base sited around Bao An (see text), which became the final destination of the Long Marchers. Fell afoul of the bolshevization campaign launched by Wang Ming, and was liberated from jail when Mao and Zhou arrived at the base in October 1935. Accompanied Mao in a later expedition into Shansi province, was wounded and died of his wounds.

Liu Shaoqi (Liu Shaochi) (1898–1969). Born in Hunan province, as was Mao, joined Mao's New People's Study Society. In Shanghai, 1920, as labor organizer, went to Moscow in 1921. Joined Communist Party in Moscow. Returned to China in 1922 and was active in labor unions in his own province. After the Shanghai massacres, shifted to North China, where he organized a workers' movement and also recruited intellectuals by setting up nuclei of Communist Party members in the universities. Became chairman of the All-China Federation of Labor in 1932. Tried to increase the industrial possibilities of Mao's Ruijin base, where he went in 1932. Did not go on the Long March (only part of it according to some records), but went into underground work connected with the party's Northern Bureau. Liu's rise was due to the fact that he was a re-markable organizer, and also had considerable leverage among the intellectuals in North China's universities. Became a Party theoretician in the early 1940s and made major speeches on Party organization, leadership, and discipline, wrote key documents in the conduct of the Chinese Communist Party in 1941–45. Was responsible for coining the phrase "Mao Thought." It was in the late 1950s, because of divergent views on the economy, and also on the Soviet Union, that Mao began a major offensive against him (see text). This would culminate in the Cultural Revolution, which was designed to destroy Liu.

Lo Ruiqing (Lo Juiching) (1906–78). Born in Sichuan province, enrolled in the Huangpu Military Academy (1926). Took part in the Northern Expedition and joined the Chinese Communist Party. Was at the Nanchang uprising with Zhou Enlai on August 1, 1927. Joined Mao's base and went on to Ruijin, where he was wounded in the fighting against Chiang's annihilation campaigns (1932). Made the Long March, in the First Front Army. Worked closely with Peng Dehuai, in subsequent anti-Japanese campaigns, then under Ye Jianying and Nie Rongzhen. Was given top appointments after liberation in 1949, including the running of Public Security. In 1959 Lo became a member of the powerful Military Affairs Commission. Disagreed with Mao around 1963–64 and an article of his was deemed "pro-Soviet" by Mao. Became one of the targets of the Cultural Revolution. Was seen by author when he reemerged at a banquet in 1973.

Lo Yinung (Lo Inung) (1901–28). Joined the May 4, 1919, Movement as a student in Shanghai, becoming a Chinese Communist Party member in 1921. Sent to Moscow that year and spent four years at the University of Toilers of the East. Returned in 1925 and organized labor strikes, including the famous Hong Kong–Canton railway strike. Collaborated with Zhou Enlai in the events of 1926–27 in Shanghai. Was captured and executed in April 1928.

Ma Haide, a.k.a. George Hatem.

Ma Jun (1900–27) A friend and classmate of Zhou Enlai in Nankai and a Hui Muslim, Ma Jun probably became a Party member (or a sympathizer) in 1922 or 1923. He was a member of the Awareness Society, and perished in the massacres of 1927–29.

Ma Qianli (Ma Tsianli) (1894–1927). A senior schoolmate of Zhou Enlai in Nankai Middle School, Ma "Thousand Mile Horse" was an impetuous, bold personality. He held a minor position in Nankai Middle School, and helped Zhou financially. According to the reminiscences of another classmate, Liao Yungwu, it was to Ma that Zhou sent a full manuscript, based on his prison diary, for publication in 1921. The manuscript was completed by Zhou aboard the *Porthos*, the ship that Zhou sailed on to France. Ma lost his post in Nankai Middle School (now become a university) and became editor of a news magazine. He set up the Tajen girls' school in Peking (Beijing). It was at this school that Deng Yingchao, later Zhou Enlai's wife, became a teacher, as did Xu Guangping (Hsu Kuangping), who became the wife of the revolutionary writer Lu Xun (Lu Hsun). Ma Qsianli was captured and executed in the anti-Communist massacres launched by Chiang Kaishek in 1927–29.

Mao Dzedong (Mao Tsetong) (1893–1976). There are many biographies of Mao available, and he is too great a figure for a footnote. His relationship with Zhou Enlai during the decades continues to evoke speculation among Chinese historians.

Nie Rongzhen (Nie Jongchen) (1899–1991). Nie Rongzhen is one of China's greatest military and scientific personalities. He played a major role in many landmark events of Chinese Communist history. He left for France in 1919, one of 1,600 Chinese students that year, spent a few months there, and then over two years in Charleroi, at the Université de Travail, sponsored by the Belgian Socialist Party. He joined the Socialist Youth League in 1922 and the Chinese Communist Party in 1923. Zhou Enlai visited Nie at least twice in Charleroi. Nie spoke German, French, and English. In 1924 he went to Moscow and acquired a knowledge of Russian. He returned to China in 1925. Was at the Nanchang uprising of August 1, 1927. Was on the Long March. Nie was involved in promoting scientific knowledge and building up the army, and collaborated with Zhou Enlai throughout his life. He was in charge of the science teams which independently produced the nuclear and missile capability of China. For vigor, farsightedness, and intelligence undeterred by the political quirks which often plagued his colleagues in their decision making, Nie remains an outstanding figure in the Chinese revolutionary pantheon.

Pan Dzenien (1895–1969). Pan Dzenien, brother of Pan Hannien, was prominent in intellectual circles, professor of history and literature when in his thirties, editor of the *Xinhua Daily News* and later its director. Collaborated with Zhou Enlai, who seems to have had great trust and regard for him. He continued in academic circles throughout his life.

Pan Hannien (Pan Han Nien) (1905–70). Joined the Communist Party early, and was a member of the Central Committee in 1933. His work was mainly as an intermediary in many underground negotiations and work with the Guomindang, and also with secret societies. His wife appears to have been a wealthy woman from Hong Kong. He took an active part in 1936–37 in the formation of a united anti-Japanese front following Chiang Kaishek's detention in Xian (see text). He became vice-mayor of Shanghai in 1952, but was arrested as a "counterrevolutionary" in 1955 and was in prison until his death. He was posthumously rehabilitated in 1980.

Peng Bai (Peng Pai) (1896–1929). Born into a "landlord" family, became ardently revolutionary and went to Japan in 1918. Studied at Waseda University, where he came in contact with Western and socialist ideologies. Returned to China in 1921, and in his own district of Haifeng began peasant associations, forcing landlords to reduce rents. Peng Bai recommended the establishment of the Peasant Movement Training Institute, in Guangzhou, where Mao Dzedong was to lecture. Killed in the massacres of Communists launched by Chiang Kaishek (1927–29).

Peng Dehuai (Peng Te Huai) (1902–68). Peng Dehuai was in some ways a folk hero in China. He had no formal schooling but herded cattle, worked in a mine, and became a platoon commander in the army at the age of eighteen. He joined the Guomindang and then the Chinese Communist Party in 1927, and was at Mao's mountain base, where his exploits earned him high praise from Mao. He was regarded as Mao's staunchest supporter and distinguished himself during the Long March. Supported Mao at the Tsunyi meeting (see text). But in Yenan he and Mao diverged on military strategy and policies, and this degenerated into a festering quarrel. Nevertheless, Peng continued to be an outstanding figure, particularly in the Korean War, in which he led the Chinese volunteers. Became one of the ten marshals of the PLA in September 1955. His main quarrel with Mao centered on the Great Leap Forward, but there were other points of controversy, unmentioned publicly, notably on relations with the Soviet Union. Demoted as Minister of Defense in 1959, he lived in obscurity until the Cultural Revolution, when he suffered a raid by the Red Guards, which led to ill-treatment and death in 1968.

Peng Zhen (Peng Chen) (1899–   ). Born in Shansi province, early influenced by left-wing teachers, devoted himself to student agitation. He became a Communist Party member in 1926. Led many guerrilla activities behind Japanese lines. Became mayor of Beijing in 1951. Made several trips abroad. Sided with Liu Shaoqi against Mao and was a target of the Cultural Revolution but survived. Is still influential though reckoned a "conservative."

Po I Po. See Bo Yibo.

Po Ku. See Bo Gu.

Pu Shouchang (1922–   ). Educated at St. John's College in Shanghai, and then at the University of Michigan and at Harvard, Pu Shouchang was one of Zhou

Enlai's closest collaborators from 1954 to 1965. He became Vice-Minister of Foreign Affairs, 1979–82, and is adviser to the Chinese Academy of Social Sciences.

Qian Jiadung (1924–   ). Born in Shanghai, attended Shanghai University of Telecommunications. In Shanghai became head of the Asia Department of Foreign Affairs. Was ambassador and representative to the United Nations in Geneva, 1985–89. Currently head of the Chinese Center for International Studies.

Qiao Guanhua (Chiao Kuanhua) (1908–83). Educated at Tsinghua University, went to Germany to study, returned to China in 1937. Married Gung Peng, aide to Zhou Enlai, in Chongqing. Accompanied Zhou Enlai on many trips abroad. Became Minister of Foreign Affairs in 1964. Remarried after the death of Gung Peng, but his health deteriorated and he died of lung cancer. In later years his renown was somewhat dimmed, as he appears to have briefly sided with the Gang of Four against Deng Xiaoping in 1975.

Qu Qiubai (Chu Chiubai) (1899–1935). Educated at Peking University, greatly influenced by Li Dazhao (Li Ta Chao). Attended in 1917 the tuition-free Russian Language Institute and actively engaged in the May 4, 1919, Movement. Became special correspondent in Moscow for one of Peking's leading dailies, the *Shen Bao*. Used the Russian name Strakhov for many of his articles. Translated Lenin's "Theses on National and Colonial Questions." Joined the Chinese Communist Party in 1922 and returned to China in 1923. Became editor of several Communist publications and played an active role in the Shanghai uprising of 1927. This placed him in an outstanding position in the (then) disintegrating Communist Party. He was made a scapegoat by the Comintern (see text) in June–July 1928 at the Sixth Congress, and downgraded when Stalin backed the Twenty-eight Bolsheviks. His subsequent career shows his ineffectiveness as a political figure. Left behind when the Long March began (October 1934), he was captured and executed in 1935.

Shi Liang (Shih Liang) (1900–85). A brilliant woman lawyer, was one of seven scholars who founded the Federation for National Salvation to resist Japan in 1931. Was arrested by the Chiang Kaishek government in 1935. This created such indignation that she and the six other founders were released in 1937. Shi Liang cooperated with Soong Chingling during the Sino-Japanese war, and after 1949 was prominent in shaping legal codes for the new regime. She was Minister of Justice from December 1954 to April 1959. Interviewed by the author concerning the application of law in China in June 1956.

Smedley, Agnes (1892–1950). A fiery personality, her father American-Indian, her mother Irish, born in Missouri into a poor family, Agnes Smedley was mostly self-educated. She started writing early, traveled in 1919 as ship stewardess to Germany, married an Indian Communist and went to the U.S.S.R. Returned to Berlin and opened a birth control clinic. Was a friend of Margaret Sanger, pioneer of birth control. Wrote *Daughter of Earth*, serialized in the *Frankfurter Zeitung* in 1928. Went to Manchuria as special correspondent for the *Frankfurter Zeitung*. Became a friend of Soong Chingling. From 1934 to 1936 was in Shanghai, living in the house of Lu Xun, the revolutionary writer, and reporting on China. Was at Xian when Xian incident took place, December 1936 (see text). Between 1940 and 1945 traveled in China, but poor health forced frequent stays in Hong Kong. Returned to the United States in 1945. In 1949 was accused by Mc-Carthyites of "espionage." Planned to return to China but fell ill and died in London. Wrote *Battle Hymn of China, Scarlet Virtue* (the life of Zhu De), *The Great Road* (published after her death), and other books.

Snow, Edgar (1905–72). Born in Kansas City, Missouri. Worked as a reporter while attending classes at Columbia University in New York. In 1928 took a job in Shanghai on the *China Weekly Review*, traveled throughout China, writing for American papers. In 1936 went to Bao An and was able to interview Mao Dzedong and other Communist leaders. In 1937 published *Red Star over China*, the enduring classic, which first told the world about the Communists in China. Met with Franklin Roosevelt in 1941 and again not long before the latter's death in 1945 (as told to the author by Edgar Snow). Returned to China several times in the late 1950s and also again in 1970. Died of cancer in 1972.

Soong Chingling (1893–1981). Born in Shanghai. At sixteen was sent to Wellesley College for Women. Returned to China in 1913. Married Sun Yatsen, then in exile, in 1915. Supported her husband's revolutionary activities until his death in 1925. Her sisters, Ailing and Meiling, joined the group around Chiang Kaishek, as did her brother, Soong Tsewen (T. V. Soong). Meiling married Chiang Kaishek in 1928, but Chingling remained staunch in her ideals and continued to denounce her brother-in-law's massacres. Left for Moscow and Berlin, but in 1931 returned to Shanghai, where she lived in the French Concession (rue Molière). Became the center of a group opposing the Japanese invasion of China, and one of the organizers of the Federation for National Salvation. Helped to save political prisoners from death at the hands of her brother-in-law. Continued to exert her influence in Chongqing during the Japanese war. Did not join the Communist Party, although she helped to send medicines (and weapons) to Yenan during the war years. Was persuaded by Deng Yingchao, the wife of Zhou Enlai, to come to Beijing in August 1949, and served as a member of the Standing Committee of the CPPCC, which, at its inaugural session in September, established the People's Republic of China. She continued to personify the long process of the revolution from Sun Yatsen's 1911 democratic revolution to the Communist revolution of 1949. Never compliant, she criticized Communist leaders with the same outspokenness as she had criticized Chiang Kaishek.

Strong, Anna Louise (1885–1974). Born in Nebraska, graduated from Oberlin. Her father was a congregational minister. Went to the U.S.S.R. as Russian correspondent for Hearst International News in 1920, and to China in 1925, where she worked as a correspondent for many American papers. Returned to Moscow in 1929 and organized *Moscow News*. Went to Chongqing in 1940, then returned to the United States. Went to Yenan to interview Mao Dzedong in 1946. Was arrested in a Stalin purge, and deported to the United States, where she remained from 1950 to 1958, returning to China in that year. Published *Letters from China*. Died at eighty-four in 1970. Wrote *China's Millions* and *The Chinese Conquer China*, among other books.

Tao Zhu (Tao Chu) (1906–70). Went into the army early and participated in the Northern Expedition. Joined the Chinese Communist Party and carried on guerrilla warfare. Directed army political departments for many years. In charge of Guangdong province in the early 1950s, vice-premier of the State Council in January 1965.

Tsai Chang (Cai Chang) (1900–92). Sister of Tsai Hosen. Studied in the progressive Chounan Girls' School and there began to study politics. With her sister-in-law, Xiang Jingyu, joined Mao Dzedong's New People's Study Society. Went with her mother to France on the work-and-study program in 1919. There met Zhou Enlai, Deng Yingchao, Li Lisan, and others, and joined the Chinese Communist Party. Married Li Fuchun in France, 1923. She was one of the few women who made the Long March. She occupied many posts, especially as an organizer of labor unions for women. Was one of the leaders of the All-China Democratic Women's Federation. With Deng Yingchao drafted the Marriage Law in 1950 giving women the right to refuse arranged marriages, prohibiting female infanticide, etc. Was for many years on the Standing Committee of the National People's Congress.

Tsai Hosen (Cai Hosen) (1890–1931). Tsai Hosen was a schoolmate of Mao Dzedong at the Hunan First Normal School and became his close friend in 1915. His mother was a very well-educated, politically conscious woman, and Mao held discussion groups at their home. Tsai and Mao were the leaders of the New People's Study Society founded in 1918. Many of its adherents, including Tsai, his sister, and his wife, left on the work-and-study program for France in 1919. Tsai helped establish, in 1921, the Socialist Youth League, which led in 1922 to the formation of a Chinese Communist Party branch in France. He was deported from France in 1921 (see text, the Lyons incident), and became a member of the faculty of Shanghai University, where he was involved in intense political activity. He attended the Sixth Congress in Moscow, together with Zhou Enlai. In 1931 he went to Hong Kong to direct Party work but was arrested and executed that autumn.

Tsai Tingkai (Cai Tingkai) (1891 or 1892–1968). Born in Guangdong province, joined the army at seventeen and later the Guomindang. Was at the Nanchang uprising in 1927 but against the Communists (see text). In 1932, led his Nineteenth Route Army to resist the Japanese invasion in Shanghai. Was transferred to Fujian province to oppose the Communists, but began secret talks with Zhou Enlai (see text). When these failed, left for Hong Kong and traveled in Europe and the United States, returning in 1937. Again joined the Guomindang, but in

1948 joined with the Communists and was protected by Zhou Enlai during the Cultural Revolution.

Wang Bingnan (Wang Pingnan) (1906–87). Born in Shaanxi province, Wang Bingnan, one of the ablest and best-known diplomats of China, worked closely with Zhou Enlai since the mid-1930s. His father was an intimate friend (some say a relative by marriage) of General Yang Hucheng (Tiger City). He joined the Chinese Communist Party in 1925, went to Germany in 1931, where he was active as a leader of the Chinese students and married a German, Anna von Kleist. He was called back to China in early 1936 by Zhou Enlai. There he made use of his former connection with Yang Hucheng (see text). He remained top assistant to Zhou for many years, participated in 1954 in the Geneva conference, and was appointed ambassador to Poland. He was ambassador at Warsaw for nine years, the longest continuous tour of any Chinese ambassador to one country. He became president of the Association for Friendship with Foreign Countries in the 1960s, a position he held until incapacitated by illness in the early 1980s.

Wang Hungwen (1930–92). Born in Shanghai, a worker, distinguished himself by seizing, in the name of the working class, the factory where he was employed during the Cultural Revolution (1967). Was selected by Madame Mao and her colleagues, and rose rapidly in the Party hierarchy to become vice-chairman of the Party in 1975. Arrested with the other members of the Gang of Four. Died of cancer of the liver in 1992.

Wang Li, Guan Feng (Kuan Feng), Qi Penyu (Chi Penyu). Usually referred to as the Wang-Guan-Qi trio. Qi Penyu was chief editor of the newspaper *Red Flag* and in 1966 joined the Group in Charge of the Cultural Revolution. Wang Li was connected with *Red Flag* and violently attacked Beijing mayor Peng Zhen in 1966. Guan Feng was also a journalist. The three operated together, denouncing many Party cadres, and inciting the Red Guards to violence by their articles. They fell into obscurity in 1968–69.

Wang Ming (a.k.a. Chen Shaoyu) (1904–74). Educated in Shanghai, became Communist Party member in 1925. Sent to Moscow in 1925 with some fifty Chinese students. Distinguished himself by his fluency in Russian and became leader of the so-called Twenty-eight Bolsheviks, assuming the name of Wang Ming. Acted as interpreter to Comintern agents in China but was for the most part in the U.S.S.R. during the 1920s. Engaged in the struggle against Li Lisan and supported by the Comintern, his group took over Party leadership (see text). Returned to the U.S.S.R. in 1956 and opposed Mao in many articles until his death in 1974.

Wei Guoqing (Wei Kuoching) (1908–89) (some say born in 1914). Wei was from the Zhwang (Chuang) minority nationality, living in Guangxi province. Was an early peasant revolutionary influenced by a relative (Wei Pachun, who founded a peasant training institute). Joined the early guerrilla armies of the Communists.

Entrusted with missions during the unstable truce between the Guomindang and the Communists which followed World War II. Proved a very able military commander. Held posts in Fujian province until the mid-1950s, a sensitive area because of its proximity to Taiwan. Became key official in his own province. During the Cultural Revolution played a major role in stemming the rampages of the Red Guards. He is also credited with being the man who took charge of aid to Vietnam during the war against French colonialism and with aiding Vietnamese general Giap to achieve the victory at Dienbienphu (1954).

Wu Han (1909–69). Born near Shanghai into a poor family, supported himself by working as well as studying and became prominent as a historian. Joined the China Democratic League in 1944, helped many Communists and underground workers and students. Became vice-mayor of Beijing under Peng Zhen. Filled prestigious posts in the educational field, but became a target when he wrote a play regarded as a defense of the disgraced former Minister of Defense Peng Dehuai (see text). Was a target of the Cultural Revolution and died in obscure circumstances.

Wu Huanxin (George Wu) (1912–86). Born of an Overseas Chinese family in Mauritius, George Wu attended Aurore University in Shanghai, then went to Brussels to specialize in cancer research. He returned to China to found the first cancer clinic with radium from Belgium, and continued through the decades his work in cancer research and treatment. He founded the country's first studies in tumors, and laid down the basis for nationwide studies, notably in cancer of the cervix and of the esophagus. Awarded the French Order of Merit in 1985. George Wu died of advanced leukemia in 1986.

Wu Quanheng (1920–). Attended school in Shanghai. Took part in anti-Japanese demonstrations in 1935. Went to Yenan to join the Communist guerrillas in 1938. Worked in Chongqing in Zhou Enlai's office as reporter and interpreter. Attended many international conferences and became Chinese representative for UNICEF. Is the wife of Hu Sheng, president of the Academy of Social Sciences.

Wu Xiuquan (Wu Hsiuchuan) (1909–). Was active in early youth in student movements, studied in Moscow 1927–30. Joined Mao's base at Ruijin and acted as official interpreter to Comintern agents (see text). Active in the military field and later in foreign affairs. Accompanied Zhou Enlai to Moscow in 1950. Wu became very prominent in the Ministry of Foreign Affairs and was a major figure in delegations to many countries.

Xi Jungxun (Hsi Chunghsun) (1910 or 1912–). Born in Shaanxi province, Xi was one of the ablest commanders in the PLA. He joined the Communist Youth Corps at fourteen. The story related in the text was told personally to the author in October 1988, when he claimed to be eighty, but probably, like many Chinese, added a year or two to his age. Xi was then vice-president of the National Assembly.

Xia Yan (Hsia Yen) (1900–   ). Eminent playwright and film director. Joined the Party in 1924 or 1925, and had a major role in the League of Left-Wing Writers in Shanghai. Has written his reminiscences.

Xiang Jingyu (Hsiang Ching Yu) (1895–1928). Wife of Tsai Hosen. Was one of the earliest and most active of China's revolutionary women of the early twentieth century. Graduated in 1915 from a progressive girls' school, and founded her own coeducational primary school. With her schoolmate Tsai Chang, Tsai Hosen's sister, organized women to go to France. Left for France in November 1919. Married Tsai Hosen in 1921. Was deported from France along with her husband and became active among women textile workers in Shanghai. Went to Russia with her husband in late 1925 and studied at the Communist University of Toilers of the East for a year. Returned to China and became labor organizer for women workers in Wuhan. Was captured in the spring of 1928 and executed.

Xiang Zhungfa (Hsiang Chungfa) (1888–1931). Xiang was a worker, educated through the Chinese Communist Party literacy night classes. Became an organizer for strikes in coal mines, rose to the post of general secretary of a labor union. Was sent to Moscow as a representative of the Chinese working class in 1925. Returned to China in 1927, where, due to the policy of exalting the "working class," he was elevated to a leadership position. Betrayed the Party in 1931. Apparently he made a full confession, but this did not save his life. Executed in 1931 by Chiang Kaishek's government.

Xiang Ying (Hsiang Ying) (1898–1941). Received only a primary education. In 1921 joined the Communist Party. Became involved in labor unions, organized the Peking–Hankow railway trade union, went into hiding after the 1923 suppression of the railway workers. He seems to have been briefly in Moscow in 1928–29, joined Mao's base in Ruijin in 1931. Fought against Chiang Kaishek's annihilation campaigns. Was left behind, together with Chen Yi, when the Long March began (see text). Appears to have differed from Mao on several occasions. When in 1938 the New Fourth Army was created, Xiang Ying was appointed to it. According to some reports, he did not get along with Ye Ting (see text), hence his work with the New Fourth Army is difficult to assess, but Mao appears to have blamed him for the tragedy that took place (see text). Was killed in January 1941 in the New Fourth Army incident.

Xiung Xianghui (Hsiung Hsianghui) (1917–   ). Son of an eminent jurist, Hsiung volunteered through patriotism when the Japanese invasion took place, and was chosen to be a "mole" by Zhou Enlai. He became a section chief in the Foreign Affairs Ministry in 1960 and was chargé d'affaires in Great Britain for many years.

Xu Teli (Hsu Teli) (1877–1968). A teacher of Mao Dzedong, and of many Hunan students, he influenced them into "new thinking," and therefore revolution. Toward the end of 1919, he arrived in France, despite his age, as a "student."

Went back to China in 1924. Became a Marxist at the ripe age of forty-nine. Participated in the Nanchang uprising of August 1, 1927. Left for the Soviet Union in 1928. Successfully accomplished the Long March though he was then fifty-seven years old. This stoical, extraordinarily youthful man—mentally youthful—deserves to be remembered.

Xu Xiangqian (Hsu Hsiangchian, a.k.a. Xu Going Forward) (1901–92). Went to Guangdong as a youth to attend the Huangpu Military Academy, joined the Guomindang in 1924, but became pro-Communist and joined the Chinese Communist Party after the split between the Guomindang and the Communists. Participated in the ill-fated Canton (Guangzhou) uprising of December 1927, escaped to Shanghai, later joined Zhang Guotao at the base established in 1929 (see text). Helped Zhang establish a base in North Sichuan when the first one was overrun. Joined Mao Dzedong on the Long March at Maoerkai (see text). Was involved in the struggle between Zhang Guotao and Mao but in the end joined Mao. Had a distinguished army career and became one of China's ten marshals in September 1955.

Yang Hucheng (1893–1949). Born into a poor peasant family, Yang Hucheng (a.k.a. Tiger City) early became an officer in that tangle of civil war which afflicted China during the period 1911–29. He then joined the Guomindang forces and was in the northwest when Chiang Kaishek turned against the Communists. Yang, though not a Communist, was troubled by the wholesale slaughter, and withdrew to Japan in April 1928. He returned in November to head his former troops and to fight Feng Yuxiang, one of the few remaining warlords challenging the rule of Chiang Kaishek. Yang was stationed in his own province of Shaanxi and was ordered to "liquidate" the "Red bandits." This offended his patriotic feelings, and he and Zhang Xueliang (the Young Marshal) actively collaborated in the detention of Chiang Kaishek at Xian in December 1936. In June 1937 Yang went to Europe, together with his wife and second son. When he returned, he was imprisoned by Chiang, as was his family. They were transferred to many prisons during the following years, and murdered in September 1949 by the head of Chiang's secret police, Dai Lee. See *The Life of General Yang Hucheng*, Hong Kong, Joint Publishing Co., 1981.

Yang Xianyi (1914–   ). Very well known to the Western community in Beijing, Yang Xianyi comes from a scholarly family. Was educated in England, where he married his English wife, Gladys Yang. Both were dedicated to establishing the Foreign Language Press in Beijing and both became major figures in literary circles. Endured great hardships during the Cultural Revolution but continued to work in their chosen field. Biography to be published in England in 1993.

Yao Wenyuan (1926–   ). Polemicist, journalist, rose to prominence when selected by Madame Mao to attack the vice-mayor of Beijing, Wu Han, in an article published in the Shanghai *Wen Wei* newspaper. Directed writing teams for the Gang of Four and was generally regarded as Madame Mao's "pen." Arrested at the same time as Madame Mao and condemned to life imprisonment.

Ye Jianying (Yeh Chienying) (1898–1986). Ye Jianying's contribution to the Chinese revolution cannot be overestimated. Born in Meixian (Meihsien), a district inhabited by the Hakka people (for information on the Hakka, see Han Suyin, *The Crippled Tree*, London, Jonathan Cape, 1965), he inherited the Hakka tradition of resistance. Participated in the Long March, and became one of the ten marshals of the PLA. Is famous for having, in a bloodless coup in 1976, arrested Madame Mao and her acolytes.

Ye Junjian (1914–). A scholar and translator, Ye studied in England, and returned to China to found the foreign-language section of the magazine *Chinese Literature*. One of the best-known writers in the 1950s for his books on the changes in rural areas. He has also published several books in English in England.

Ye Ting (1897–1946). Born in Guangdong province, Ye Ting distinguished himself by entering, in his sixteenth year, a military school and later the famed Baoding (Paoting) Military Academy. Opted to support Sun Yatsen, met Zhou Enlai probably at one of the Huangpu Military Academy gatherings. He formed an independent regiment—the Ironsides. His participation in the Nanchang uprising of August 1, 1927, determined his subsequent career. He is mentioned as one of the four main actors (with Ho Lung, Zhu De, and Zhou Enlai) in this essential uprising, which marked the birth of the Communist Red Army. Died in an airplane crash in 1946.

Yen Fangsun (Yen Hsiu, a.k.a. Yen Xiu) (1860–1929). A great scholar, trained in the old classical style, but also an ardent reformist. Yen was around twenty years old when the Dowager Empress put an end to the first attempts at reform. This made him a rebel against the Manchu Empire. He devoted himself to promoting "new learning" and dedicated his fortune to setting up Nankai Middle School, later to become Nankai University. He helped Zhou Enlai financially, as he helped many other students.

Zhang Boling (Chang Poling) (1876–1951). Born in Tianjin, into a scholarly family, devoted his talents to the field of modern education. At first taught in the school set up by Yen Fangsun and at other schools advocating reforms in education. With the help of Yen Fangsun founded Nankai Middle School in 1906. Was a Christian, interested in the work of the YMCA in China. When in 1937 Nankai (become in 1918 a university) was bombed by Japan, Zhang Boling led the school exodus from Japan-occupied North China to Sichuan province. He received many honorary degrees from American universities after the war, as a person of unwavering devotion to the education of Chinese youth.

Zhang Chunqiao (Chang Chun Chiao) (1917–). Born in Shandong province, Zhang was well known as a polemicist in his youth. His influence among the Communist media and the press was discernible by the early 1960s. He got in touch with Madame Mao and in fact is often thought to have been the real brain of her clique, known as the Gang of Four. Arrested in October 1976 and condemned in 1983.

Zhang Guotao (Chang Kuotao) (1897–1974). The personality of Zhang Guotao remains ambiguous. He was a zealot, very able and certainly a revolutionary, but lacked what distinguished Zhou—i.e., personal abnegation. He was among the first twelve founding members of the Chinese Communist Party gathered in Shanghai in July 1921. Left China in late 1921 for Moscow, selected by the Comintern, with which he maintained close connections for many years. His variegated career is available from his own recollections, published in *Ming Bao*, Hong Kong, Vol. I, no. 3–12 (1966). He defected from the Chinese Communist Party and lived in Canada and the United States until his death.

Zhang Wenjing (Chang Wenjing) (1920–1989). Born in Beijing, attended Tsinghua University, and was a member of Zhou Enlai's staff in Chongqing and of the delegation to the Geneva conference in April 1954. Acted as secretary to Zhou Enlai for many years, as did his wife, Zhang Ying (Chang Ying). Of undoubted ability, he was promoted very quickly and became ambassador to Pakistan, to Canada, and to the United States in the late 1970s. Became president of the Association for Friendship with Foreign Countries in the 1980s. Died suddenly of a heart attack.

Zhang Wentian (Chang Wen Tian) (1900–76). Born into a scholarly family, went to the United States in 1921, apparently paying his own expenses, and returned to teach. Began to translate under the influence of Mao Dun, a great literary figure, under the name of Lo Fu; became a Communist Party member in 1925 when he went to Moscow and was then influenced to join the Twenty-eight Bolsheviks. However, he appears to have been averse to the extreme measures of some of his colleagues. Took part in the Long March and formed a triumvirate with Zhou Enlai and Mao for a while. Collaborated with Zhou and became Vice-Minister for Foreign Affairs. He lapsed into obscurity after he was suspected of having sided with Peng Dehuai (see text) at the 1959 Lushan meeting.

Zhang Xueliang (Chang Hsuehliang) (1898–   ). Known as the Young Marshal, the son of famed warlord Chang Tsolin, he inherited control of Manchuria when his father was killed by a bomb placed by Japanese agents on his train (1928). Regarded as ineffectual and a drug addict, he proved, on the contrary, patriotic, and together with Yang Hucheng engineered the capture of Chiang Kaishek in order to force him to fight Japan (1936). When Chiang was released, the Young Marshal accompanied him to Nanjing (see text) in a quixotic demonstration of loyalty. He was tried by a military court and sentenced to ten years in prison. He was taken to Taiwan by Chiang, where he remained under supervision for the last four decades. It is only recently that he was released and has been traveling abroad.

Zhao Shiyen (Chao Shiyen) (1901–27). Early manifested a talent for writing; in 1917 learned French in Beijing, preparing to go to France on the work-and-study program. Became acquainted with Zhou Enlai in France and collaborated with him. Became secretary of the French branch of the Chinese Communist Party in 1922. Went to Moscow in 1923, returned to China in 1924. Was in

Shanghai with Zhou during the uprising of the workers in early 1927. Was captured and executed in July 1927 in the massacres launched by Chiang Kaishek.

Zhou Peiyuan (Chou Peiyuan) (1902–). One of China's best physicists, studied in the United States in 1925, returned in 1929 to teach at Tsinghua University. Was involved in many scientific planning commissions. Upheld the importance of fundamental science and research. Author had long talks with him on the subject during the Cultural Revolution, in 1969.

Zhu De (Chu Te) (1886–1976). One of the most colorful among that assembly of extraordinary men gathered around Mao Dzedong and Zhou Enlai. Was with Zhou at the Nanchang uprising, August 1, 1927. Was one of the main military leaders through the Long March. (See *The Great Road: The Life and Times of Chu Teh*, by Agnes Smedley, for a somewhat romanticized account, London, John Calder, 1958.) Zhu De became in September 1955 the first of the ten marshals of China's People's Liberation Army. He occupied a number of posts and remained popular throughout his life due to his integrity and the fact that he never engaged in struggles for power. Was attacked by posters during the Cultural Revolution, but otherwise remained unharmed.

Zhu Qing (1924–). Educated in Shanghai and Beijing, joined early student activities, went to Yenan, recruited by Zhou Enlai for his office as a translator and reporter. Wife of the former ambassador of the People's Republic of China in Switzerland (Tian Jin). Both are now active in international organizations.

Index

KODANSHA GLOBE

International in scope, this series offers distinguished books that explore the lives, customs, and mindsets of peoples and cultures around the world.

INVISIBLE MEN
*Life in Baseball's
    Negro Leagues*
Donn Rogosin
Introduction by
    Monte Irvin
1-56836-085-1

BLACKBERRY WINTER
My Earlier Years
Margaret Mead
New Introduction by
    Nancy Lutkehaus
1-56836-069-X

ELDEST SON
*Zhou Enlai and the
    Making of Modern
    China, 1898–1976*
Han Suyin
1-56836-084-3

THE AWAKENED SELF
Encounters with Zen
Lucien Stryk
New Introduction by
    the Author
1-56836-046-0

ALONE
Adm. Richard E. Byrd
Original Illustrations by
    Richard Harrison
Facsimile of the 1938 Edition
Introduction by David Campbell
1-56836-068-1

OF DREAMS AND DEMONS
*A Memoir of Modern
    India*
Patwant Singh
New Introduction by
    the Author
1-56836-086-X

**PASSING STRANGE AND
    WONDERFUL**
*Aesthetics, Nature, and
    Culture*
Yi-Fu Tuan
1-56836-067-3

**THE DESERT ROAD TO
    TURKESTAN**
Owen Lattimore
New Introduction by
    David Lattimore
1-56836-070-3

OPTIMISM
The Biology of Hope
Lionel Tiger
Reintroduction by the
    Author
New Introduction by
    Frederick Turner
1-56836-072-X

THE MOUNTAIN OF NAMES
*A History of the
    Human Family*
Alex Shoumatoff
New Preface by the Author
New Introduction by
    Robin Fox
1-56836-071-1

EMPIRES OF TIME
*Calendars, Clocks, and
    Cultures*
Anthony Aveni
1-56836-073-8

ESSENTIAL SUBSTANCES
*A Cultural History of
    Intoxicants in Society*
Richard Rudgley
1-56836-075-4

To order, contact your local bookseller or call 1-800-788-6262 (mention code G1). For a complete listing of titles, please contact the Kodansha Editorial Department at Kodansha America, Inc., 114 Fifth Avenue, New York, NY 10011.

8332